VUI

VULNERABLE PEOPLE AND THE CRIMINAL JUSTICE SYSTEM

A Guide to Law and Practice

Edited by

PROFESSOR PENNY COOPER
Barrister
Senior Research Fellow
Institute for Criminal Policy Research
Birkbeck, University of London

and

HHJ HEATHER NORTON
Resident Judge, Canterbury Crown Court

OXFORD
UNIVERSITY PRESS

OXFORD
UNIVERSITY PRESS

Great Clarendon Street, Oxford, OX2 6DP,
United Kingdom

Oxford University Press is a department of the University of Oxford.
It furthers the University's objective of excellence in research, scholarship,
and education by publishing worldwide. Oxford is a registered trade mark of
Oxford University Press in the UK and in certain other countries

Published in the United States of America by Oxford University Press
198 Madison Avenue, New York, NY 10016, United States of America

British Library Cataloguing in Publication Data
Data available

Library of Congress Control Number: 201794261

ISBN 978-0-19-880111-5

Printed and bound by
CPI Group (UK) Ltd, Croydon, CR0 4YY

FOREWORD

When HHJ Pigot QC's advisory group on video-recorded evidence was established in 1988, its primary task was to consider the use of video recordings as a means of taking evidence of vulnerable witnesses in criminal trials. The *Pigot Report* signalled the need for change.

Progress has been slow. Almost three decades later, *Pigot's* proposal to pre-record the whole of the evidence of child witnesses has not yet been fully implemented, despite the wholehearted support of many experts and the judiciary. There is, however, a growing recognition amongst those who work in the criminal justice system that the way in which cases involving the vulnerable are investigated, charged, and tried needs to change. *Speaking up for Justice* from 1998, building on the *Pigot Report,* recommended the 'special measures' for vulnerable and intimidated witnesses introduced by the Youth Justice and Criminal Evidence Act 1999 and with which we are all now very familiar. Excellent advice and training is available for judges and advocates on how cases involving vulnerable witnesses and defendants should be handled. Successive judgments of the Court of Appeal have re-enforced the message that advocates and judges have a duty to ensure vulnerable witnesses and defendants are treated fairly and allowed to participate effectively in the process.

The challenge is to spread the message to all those involved in the system, to educate and inform them on how best to enable the participation of vulnerable defendants and witnesses, whatever the reason for their vulnerability and whatever the type of case.

This is not a straightforward task. The law, procedures, and practices designed to enable the effective participation of vulnerable witnesses and defendants have developed significantly over the last fifteen years. Taken together, the provisions are now complex. Those with the task of investigating, preparing, and presenting cases involving vulnerable people must be aware of these provisions and how to bring them into effect. This book provides a comprehensive guide on how to respond to vulnerability at each stage of the criminal process.

The editors of this book have brought together an exceptional team of contributors and the result is an extremely helpful, practical, and accessible volume. Each chapter is backed by authoritative research. The aim is that the book will equip those who practise, in whatever capacity, in the criminal justice system to deal with cases involving vulnerable people with calmness, authority, and confidence.

Whilst the justice system has undoubtedly moved on in the last thirty years, no doubt there be further changes in the years to come. I believe this book will be of great assistance to us all in adapting to them. I commend it to everyone who is committed to supporting and delivering a fair criminal justice system.

The Rt Hon. Lady Justice Hallett

ACKNOWLEDGEMENTS

In September 2013, Ruth Marchant—registered intermediary and co-director of Triangle in Hove—invited a small group of academics and judges to Triangle to discuss improvements in the way in which evidence could be obtained from vulnerable people and presented to the court in criminal cases.

Present at that meeting with Ruth Marchant were District Judge Emma Arbuthnot, Professor Penny Cooper, and HHJ Heather Norton.

As a result of our discussions that evening, a number of issues became apparent: first, that despite undoubted improvements in the ways in which the criminal justice system facilitates the participation of vulnerable people, there is still much more that could be done; second, that there have been widespread misunderstandings about best practice and how to apply it; and, third, that there is no single resource available which deals, in a clear, practical, and accessible way, with how to manage cases in which a vulnerable person is a party—whether as a complainant, a witness, or a defendant—from the moment that a complaint is made until the conclusion of any case that follows.

It was from those discussions that the idea for this book was born.

Turning an idea into reality, however, has only been possible thanks to the enthusiastic response of nearly everyone we approached to take part in this project. Each of the chapter authors is an acknowledged expert in their field, whether as an academic, senior practitioner, or member of the judiciary; and as editors we wish to acknowledge our appreciation for the enormous amount of work each one of them undertook on top of their already demanding professional commitments.

Many others have also contributed to this book, directly or indirectly: whether through carrying out research on behalf of the authors, proofreading, reviewing, and commenting on various chapters, or by supporting and enabling the authors to have the time and space to write.

In particular, we gratefully acknowledge the assistance given by: Martin Vaughan and Leslie Cuthbert ('Vulnerable Suspects'); David Ormerod QC ('Unfitness to Plead'); Emma Scott and William Cholerton ('Disclosure'); Dr Clare Allely ('Defences'); and Mark Ashford and Howard Riddle ('Youth Courts and Young Defendants').

We are grateful to Riel Karmy-Jones QC and Peter Carter QC for a great deal of additional work that was carried out behind the scenes.

We are indebted to Fiona Sinclair, Peter Daniell, and their colleagues at Oxford University Press for their support, encouragement, and seemingly inexhaustible patience as deadlines came . . . and went.

As all practitioners in this field know, Lady Justice Heather Hallett has been central to developments in the case law to improve access to justice for vulnerable people; we are therefore delighted and very grateful that she has written the Foreword to this book.

And finally, the editors wish to record in print their thanks to their families— Bob, Christopher, and Bobby; Nick, Barnaby, and Thea—for each of whom the summer of 2016 will forever be remembered as the summer of 'the book'.

Professor Penny Cooper
HHJ Heather Norton

CONTENTS

TABLE OF CASES

EU CASES: EUROPEAN COURT OF HUMAN RIGHTS

OTHER NATIONAL CASES: AUSTRALIA

TABLE OF STATUES

n = footnote. *f* = figure/diagram.

TABLE OF STATUTORY INSTRUMENTS

TABLE OF PROTOCOLS

TABLE OF EUROPEAN LEGISLATION

Treaties and Conventions

Directives

TABLE OF INTERNATIONAL TREATIES AND CONVENTIONS

LIST OF ABBREVIATIONS

AA	appropriate adult
ABE	Achieving Best Evidence
ACPO	Association of Chief Police Officers
ADHD	Attention Deficit Hyperactivity Disorder
AIDS	Acquired Immune Deficiency Syndrome
APP(DC)	Authorised Professional Practice, Detention and Custody
APP(MH)	Authorised Professional Practice, 'Mental Health'
ASD	autism spectrum disorder
CAA 1968	Criminal Appeal Act 1968
CAC	Child Advocacy Centre
CDA 1998	Crime and Disorder Act 1998
CJ	Chief Justice
CJA 2003	Criminal Justice Act 2003
CJIA 2008	Criminal Justice and Immigration Act 2008
CJJI	Criminal Justice Joint Inspection
CPIA 1996	Criminal Procedure and Investigations Act 1996
CP(I)A 1964	Criminal Procedure (Insanity) Act 1964
CP(IUP)A 1991	Criminal Procedure (Insanity and Unfitness to Plead) Act 1991
CPS	Crown Prosecution Service
Crim PD	Criminal Practice Directions
Crim PR	Criminal Procedure Rules
CSA	childhood sexual abuse
CYPA 1933	Children and Young Persons Act 1933
DoJ	Department of Justice
DTO	Detention and Training Order
ECHR	European Convention on Human Rights
ESMD	Early Special Measures Discussion
GRH	ground rules hearing
HHJ	His/Her Honour Judge
HMCPSi	Her Majesty's Crown Prosecution Service Inspectorate
HMCTS	Her Majesty's Court & Tribunals Service
HMIC	Her Majesty's Inspectorate of Constabulary
HMSO	Her Majesty's Stationery Office
IDPC	initial details of the prosecution case
IDVA	Independent Domestic Violence Adviser
IPCC	Independent Police Complaints Commission
IPP	imprisonment for public protection
ISS	intensive supervision and surveillance
ISSP	intensive surveillance and support package
ISVA	Independent Sexual Violence Adviser

J	Mr/Mrs/Ms Justice
LASPO 2012	Legal Aid, Sentencing and Punishment of Offenders Act 2012
LCJ	Lord Chief Justice
LJ	Lord Justice
MARAC	Multi Agency Risk Assessment Conference
MHA 1983	Mental Health Act 1983
MoJ	Ministry of Justice
MOPAC	Mayor's Office for Policing and Crime
NAAN	National Appropriate Adults Network
NCA	National Crime Agency
NFG	Notes for Guidance
NHS	National Health Service
NOMS	National Offender Management Service
NSPCC	National Society for the Prevention of Cruelty to Children
PACE	Police and Criminal Evidence Act 1984
PCA 1953	Prevention of Crime Act 1953
PCC(S)A 2000	Powers of Criminal Courts (Sentencing) Act 2000
PII	public interest immunity
PTPH	plea and trial preparation hearing
PTV	pre-trial visit
QC	Queen's Counsel
RI	registered intermediary
ROVI	Record of Video Interview
SARC	Sexual Assault Referral Centre
SI	Statutory Instrument
UNCRC	UN Convention on the Rights of the Child
UNCRPD	UN Convention on the Rights of Persons with Disabilities
VPS	Victim Personal Statement
VRI	Video Recorded Interview
WAVES	Witness and Victim Experience Survey
YCC	youth conditional caution
YJB	Youth Justice Board
YJCEA 1999	Youth Justice and Criminal Evidence Act 1999
YOS	Youth Offending Services
YOT	Youth Offending Team
YRO	Youth Rehabilitation Order

LIST OF CONTRIBUTORS

Editors

Penny Cooper (co-author Chapters 6, 12, and 16)
Professor Penny Cooper was called to the Bar in 1990 and is a Door Tenant at 39 Essex Chambers. She has also been a legal academic since 2002. She became a professor in 2009, was an Associate Dean of City Law School for many years and now holds two visiting professorships at London Law Schools. She is a Senior Research Fellow at the Institute of Criminal Policy Research and leads the *Vulnerability in the Courts* research project. She is the Co-founder and Chair of *The Advocate's Gateway* and author/co-author of numerous books, toolkits, and peer-reviewed articles on vulnerable witnesses and parties. Penny designed the English witness intermediary model, created the 'ground rules approach' and co-authors witness intermediary procedural guidance in three jurisdictions. She regularly lectures in the United Kingdom and overseas.

Heather Norton (Chapters 13, 14, 15; co-author Chapter 16)
Heather Norton practised at the criminal Bar for twenty-four years from 23 Essex Street and QEB Hollis Whiteman, specializing in serious crime and regulatory and disciplinary law. She was appointed a Recorder in 2007, and a Circuit Judge in 2012. She has contributed to a number of publications including several of The Advocate's Gateway Toolkits, and is the co-author of a number of books on the Police and Criminal Evidence Act. She is a tutor judge for the Judicial College and is currently the Resident Judge at Canterbury Crown Court.

Authors

Emma Arbuthnot (co-author Chapter 7)
Emma Arbuthnot prosecuted and defended in numerous rape trials in practice as a barrister before becoming a full-time district judge (magistrates' courts) in 2005. She sits as a Recorder in crime and family cases and is authorized to hear serious sexual offences in the youth court and the Crown Court. In 2012, she became the Deputy to the Chief Magistrate of England and Wales (the Deputy Senior District Judge) and in October 2016 became only the second woman Chief Magistrate. She was the youth court judicial lead for the Young Witness Protocol and has an interest in young and vulnerable witnesses and defendants in the criminal justice system.

Tracy Ayling QC (co-author Chapter 8)

Tracy Ayling QC defends and prosecutes in serious sex cases. Her particular expertise is in the ever-developing areas of child sex offending, grooming, and human trafficking. Tracy was leading defence counsel in Operations Bullfinch and Sabaton (very high profile, widely reported cases concerning gangs of Asian men grooming and abusing very young girls over a period of many years in Oxford). Bullfinch was the second case of its type. As an advocacy trainer for the Inner Temple, she teaches a unique course on how to cross-examine very young and vulnerable witnesses. A leading specialist in matters of Public Interest Immunity and disclosure, Tracy was appointed in 2010 as a Special Advocate for the Attorney General, and was a Special Advocate in the terrorism case— Operation Lanosity.

Miranda Bevan (Chapters 4 and 5)

Called to the Bar in 2000, Miranda Bevan practised as a criminal barrister at the Chambers of Jonathan Laidlaw QC, 2 Hare Court, maintaining a special interest in vulnerable defendants and witnesses. In 2012, she left the Bar to complete a MSc in Criminal Justice Policy at the London School of Economics. She then spent two years at the Law Commission, as the lawyer with responsibility for drafting the Law Commission's Issues Paper and Report on Unfitness to Plead (Law Com No. 364). She is currently conducting doctoral research at the London School of Economics. Her research focuses on the experience of children and young people detained as suspects in the police station.

Rosina Cottage QC (co-author Chapter 9)

Rosina Cottage QC has been instructed in many high profile cases—for example, *R v W and M* (2010), *R v Max Clifford* (2014), and *R v Balakrishnan* (2015). She has prosecuted and defended in cases involving very young defendants and child witnesses and those vulnerable through physical or cognitive disability and mental illness. Rosina is a member of the Sentencing Council and was appointed a criminal Recorder in 2012. She is a lead facilitator for the Inns of Court College of Advocacy vulnerable witness training course.

Laura Farrugia (co-author Chapter 12)

Laura Farrugia has worked in the field of mental health for approximately ten years and is Registered Intermediary accredited with the Ministry of Justice in the United Kingdom. She works with vulnerable witnesses and defendants (in particular those with learning disabilities, autism, and various mental health conditions), from the initial stages of the investigation, including the police interview, through to the court proceedings. Laura is completing a PhD at Goldsmiths, University of London. Her unique research focuses on exploring police officers' perceptions of working with mentally disordered suspects, as well as investigating current interview practice and whether such practices are appropriate for this vulnerable group.

Felicity Gerry QC (co-author Chapter 6)
Felicity Gerry QC is a barrister admitted in England and Wales and Australia, and has had ad hoc admission in Hong Kong and Gibraltar. She has specialized in serious and complex cases involving children and vulnerable adults throughout her career and has a particular expertise in special arrangements for vulnerable suspects, particularly those with cognitive impairment and mental health issues. Felicity is an Adjunct Fellow at Western Sydney University and a Senior Lecturer at Charles Darwin University. She is also on the Management Committee of The Advocate's Gateway and was the expert on an MDAC project in 2016/17 to train lawyers across all EU Member States on the rights of children with mental disabilities (which included training on communication skills). She is co-author of *The Sexual Offences Handbook* (Wildy, 2015) and a contributing author to *Human Trafficking: Emerging Legal Issues and Applications* (Lawyers & Judges Publishing Co., Inc., 2017). Her chapter on vulnerable witnesses and parties in civil proceedings in *Addressing Vulnerability in Justice Systems* (Wildy, 2016, edited by Cooper and Hunting) was described as 'such a broadly comprehensive chapter on the subject of vulnerability within the legal system that it could stand as a practitioners' potted guide in itself'.

Linda Harlow (co-author Chapter 3)
Linda Harlow retired after thirty years of working in the staffing and recruitment industry. After volunteering as a witness supporter in both magistrates' and Crown Courts, she was asked to 'help out' temporarily with managing the Witness Service at the Central Criminal Court. Four weeks became five years at the 'Old Bailey', where Linda now manages a team of thirty highly trained and experienced volunteers who provide emotional and practical support to families bereaved by homicide, and to vulnerable and intimidated witnesses in the most serious cases. The team is passionate about supporting the vulnerable at court.

Jessica Jacobson (introduction and co-author Chapter 3)
Dr Jessica Jacobson is Director of the Institute for Criminal Policy Research at Birkbeck, University of London, and was formerly a researcher in the Home Office. She undertakes research and publishes widely on many different aspects of the criminal justice system, including prisons, sentencing, and the work of the criminal courts more widely. Her recent publications include *Inside Crown Court: Personal experiences and questions of legitimacy* (Policy Press, 2015, with Gillian Hunter and Amy Kirby) and *Imprisonment Worldwide: The Current Situation and an Alternative Future* (Policy Press, 2016, with Andrew Coyle, Helen Fair, and Roy Walmsley).

Ruth Marchant (Chapter 10 and co-author Chapter 11)
Ruth Marchant co-directs Triangle, an independent organization enabling the evidence of children and young people in criminal and family proceedings. Ruth's

background is in psychology; she has completed a range of specialist training in interviewing and is currently studying for a PhD by publication on children's evidence, with the University of Portsmouth. Ruth is an experienced forensic interviewer, having interviewed or facilitated interviews with more than 1,000 children, and is also a registered intermediary with the Ministry of Justice, providing communication support to very young children and children with complex needs in their involvement with the police and the courts. Ruth also teaches and writes on these issues and at Triangle leads multidisciplinary teams providing expert opinion to the family courts.

Michelle Mattison (co-author Chapter 16)
Dr Michelle Mattison is a lecturer in psychology at the University of Chester, where she teaches cognitive psychology, forensic psychology, and research methods and statistics. Her primary research interests are in applied cognitive and developmental psychology within forensic settings. Michelle's PhD explored the use of drawing to support children and young people during investigative interviews, and had a particular focus upon children with autism spectrum condition. Michelle also works as an intermediary for the Ministry of Justice and Triangle. She regularly trains police, advocates, and judges about effective communication with vulnerable people, and has published widely on these issues.

Rebecca Milne (co-author Chapter 2)
Rebecca Milne is a Professor of Forensic Psychology at the Institute of Criminal Justice Studies at the University of Portsmouth. She is Director of the Centre of Forensic Interviewing and works closely with the police and other criminal justice organizations, both in the United Kingdom and abroad. Rebecca is a member of the National Police Chiefs' Council National Investigative Interviewing Strategic Steering Group and was part of the writing team which developed the 2007 revision of 'Achieving Best Evidence in Criminal Proceedings'. In 2009, Rebecca received the Tom Williamson Award from the Association of Chief Police Officers for her outstanding achievements in the field of investigative interviewing.

Joshua Normanton (co-author Chapter 9)
Joshua Normanton is a barrister at 5 Paper Buildings. He has a particular interest in the developing law and practice surrounding vulnerable witnesses and has written extensively on the topic. He appears on the training video which will be part of the new national advocacy course for all advocates in England and Wales and designed some of the course materials.

Angela Rafferty QC (co-author Chapter 9)
Angela Rafferty QC is a barrister at Red Lion Chambers and prosecutes and defends in high profile, sensitive, and complex cases. She is the Course Director for HHJ Rook's 'Advocacy and the Vulnerable' group. She is one of two course designers for an advocacy course on the cross-examination of vulnerable witnesses

for all advocates in England and Wales. She is involved in the training of registered intermediaries at City, University of London, and regularly lectures on the
role of counsel and the function of cross-examination. She also sits as a Recorder
at the Old Bailey.

Naomi Redhouse (co-author Chapter 7)
Naomi Redhouse is a district judge (magistrates' courts) based in Sheffield. Prior
to full-time appointment, she was a solicitor specializing in the youth court and
trial advocacy. She is the co-author, with Mark Ashford, of Blackstone's *Youth
Court Handbook* (Oxford University Press, 2013) and *Defending Young People in
the Criminal Justice System* (3rd edn, LAG, 2006). She has extensive experience
of training solicitors, barristers, and judges on the law relating to the youth justice system. Naomi is authorized to deal with serious sexual offences in the youth
court and is a member of the Judicial Youth Justice Committee.

Karen Robinson (co-author Chapter 8)
Karen Robinson is a barrister at QEB Hollis Whiteman. She prosecutes and
defends in all areas of criminal law, both as a leading junior and junior alone, and
has significant experience in cases involving serious sexual allegations (including historic allegations) and cases involving vulnerable witnesses and/or defendants. Karen has extensive experience of dealing with complex disclosure exercises,
including those connected with third parties, Public Interest Immunity, and
Regulation of Investigatory Powers Act material.

Kevin Smith (co-author Chapter 2)
Dr Kevin Smith is the National Vulnerable Witness Adviser for the National
Crime Agency. He spends most of his time travelling to police investigations to
assist in the development of victim and witness interview strategies and plans in
complex cases. He has been involved in interviews with vulnerable victims and
witnesses since 1989. He is a member of the National Police Chiefs' Council
National Investigative Interviewing Strategic Steering Group and was part of the
writing team for the 2007, 2011, and 2017 revisions of 'Achieving Best Evidence
in Criminal Proceedings'. He holds a PhD in psychology and is a chartered
psychologist.

Simon Taylor (co-author Chapter 9)
Simon Taylor is a barrister at 6 Pump Court. He specializes exclusively in criminal law and is regularly instructed to act as junior or leading counsel in cases of
homicide and in cases involving allegations of serious sexual misconduct. He has
provided training to the CPS, police, local authorities, and advocates on issues
relating to vulnerable witnesses.

David Wurtzel (co-author Chapter 11)
David Wurtzel practised at the Bar for twenty-seven years before joining City,
University of London in 2003. There he helped Professor Penny Cooper to devise

and deliver the training for registered intermediaries on behalf of the Ministry of Justice and in Northern Ireland. He has written about intermediaries and vulnerable witnesses, co-authored (with Penny and the Ministry of Justice) the 2015 *Registered Intermediary Procedural Guidance Manual*, and lectured to the Bar and the judiciary. For six years, he was consultant editor of *Counsel*, the magazine of the Bar. He is now Fellow Emeritus of City, University of London, a Bencher of Middle Temple, and an Honorary Door Tenant of Red Lion Chambers.

1

INTRODUCTION

Jessica Jacobson

A. Scope and Purposes of the Book

(a) Background

Those who come into contact with the criminal justice system, whether having **1.01** been suspected of committing a crime or as a victim or witness of an alleged crime, often experience the system as slow-moving, convoluted, and, in many respects, bewildering. This applies all the more to defendants and witnesses who are vulnerable—whether the vulnerability is a reflection of youth or immaturity, communication difficulties, learning disability, mental health needs, physical impairment, fear or distress relating to the criminal case, or any combination of these or other factors. Vulnerable individuals face multiple barriers to understanding and, more broadly, to engaging with the justice process, and particularly where a case proceeds to a contested trial.

1.02 Ultimately, the vulnerability of individuals caught up in the criminal justice system can undermine their exercise of the right to a fair trial and access to justice. Further, there are aspects of the experience of the judicial process which potentially threaten the well-being of vulnerable defendants and witnesses and can thereby further entrench pre-existing needs and difficulties.

1.03 In 1989, the Home Office published the 'Pigot Report' on the use of video-recorded evidence in criminal trials.[1] The report, noting that children found appearing in court to be a 'harmful, oppressive and often traumatic experience',[2] recommended that pre-recorded evidence-in-chief and cross-examination of child witnesses should be admissible in court. The situation of vulnerable victims and witnesses was thereafter highlighted by the Home Office report 'Speaking Up for Justice' in 1998.[3] This gave rise to the Youth Justice and Criminal Evidence Act (YJCEA) 1999, Part II of which provided for a series of 'special measures' to assist vulnerable and intimidated witnesses to give evidence in court proceedings. It can be argued, as by Marchant in Chapter 10 of this volume, that the effect of the YJCEA was essentially to formalize, rather than to introduce, measures that had already evolved through the practice of the courts.

1.04 The YJCEA special measures include provision for pre-recorded evidence-in-chief (s. 27) and for pre-recorded cross-examination (s. 28) for children and vulnerable adults. The latter has not yet, however, been fully implemented. Only in 2014—a full twenty-five years after the original 'Pigot Report' recommendations—did the first pilots of pre-recorded cross-examination begin in three court centres across the country. At the time of writing (March 2017), a phased expansion of use of s. 28 to other courts and other groups of witnesses is planned.

1.05 Thus, in some respects the law in relation to vulnerable witnesses has moved very slowly indeed over the past quarter century. Legal reform with regard to vulnerable defendants has progressed even more slowly, and in a largely piecemeal fashion. Statutory provision for vulnerable defendants is to date much more limited than that for vulnerable witnesses—with, most notably, defendants having been explicitly excluded from most of the special measures introduced by the YJCEA.

---

[1] Home Office, 'Report of the Advisory Group on Video Evidence' (Chairman HHJ Thomas Pigot QC) (1989).
[2] ibid. para. 2.10.
[3] Home Office, 'Speaking Up for Justice: Report of the Interdepartmental Working Group on the Treatment of Vulnerable or Intimidated Witnesses in the Criminal Justice System' (1998).

On the other hand, the past twenty-five years have also seen growing recognition   **1.06**
among practitioners and policy-makers of the significance and implications of
vulnerability within the criminal justice system; and an ever stronger commitment to finding and implementing ways of addressing the problem. One recent
manifestation of this commitment is the introduction of some specialist training
for practitioners: for example, training on vulnerable witnesses for the judiciary
was instigated in the summer of 2014, albeit only in relation to sexual offences
and for sex-ticketed judges; and pilot training programmes for advocates dealing
with vulnerable witnesses commenced in 2015.[4] (Calls are still being made for
mandated training for advocates working with young defendants.[5]) While the
competency of practitioners varies, there is no doubt that there have been significant changes in practice which seem likely to be sustained.

(b) The picture today and the contribution of this book

Reflecting the developments referred to above, the picture today with regard   **1.07**
to vulnerable individuals in the criminal justice system can be described as a
mixed and complicated one. There is some statutory provision; a growing body of
case law; a multiplicity of procedural rules and guidance for the judiciary, advocates, and other practitioners; some evolving specialist training; and a substantial
amount of will on the part of many stakeholders to see further improvements to
the ways in which vulnerable witnesses and defendants are dealt with throughout
the criminal justice process.

This book aims to bring clarity to this confusing picture. It is intended to be an   **1.08**
authoritative, detailed guide to the existing provision for supporting and facilitating the participation of vulnerable defendants and witnesses in the criminal
justice process, whatever the reasons for their vulnerability. As such, the book
seeks to equip practitioners of all kinds with the information they need to deal
effectively, fairly, and confidently with cases involving vulnerable individuals.
The book also highlights gaps and shortcomings in current policy and practice;
and it is hoped that this will inform the continuing debate about what reforms
are still needed and how these should be put into place if we are to see the emergence of a criminal justice system that is truly accessible to all.

For the purposes of this volume, the 'criminal justice process' is understood as   **1.09**
the process that begins with the police investigation of a reported crime and
ends, in cases in which there is a conviction, with the court's sentencing of the
offender(s). It is a process which encompasses the adult magistrates' court, the

---

[4] HHJ Peter Rook QC, 'Sea-Change in Advocacy', *Counsel Magazine* (February 2015); see
also <http://www.advocacytrainingcouncil.org/advocacy-training/31-home/av-programme/av-
training#> accessed 8 March 2017.
[5] Oliver Hanmer, 'Youth Advocacy, Standards and Specialism', *Counsel Magazine* (February
2016).

Crown Court, and the Youth Court, and a multitude of associated practitioners and services, including, for example, the police, judiciary, lawyers, court staff, the Crown Prosecution Service, the Witness Service, and intermediaries. This book is concerned with those who experience the criminal justice process as suspects, defendants, prosecution witnesses (including complainants[6]), and defence witnesses alike—and with both the commonalities and the differences in needs, expectations, and entitlements across differing court user groups.

1.10 The remainder of this introductory chapter will look at the meaning of vulnerability in the context of the criminal justice system; consider why vulnerability matters; outline some of the most important ways in which the needs of vulnerable witnesses and defendants are currently addressed (and which are described in detail in the chapters that follow); and describe the overall structure of the volume. This chapter concludes with a list of the main sources of information and guidance on vulnerability in the criminal justice system that are currently available to practitioners.

B. Understanding Vulnerability

1.11 'Vulnerability' is a broad term which can be understood in a variety of ways, depending on context and the specific group of court users to which it applies. Reflecting the gradual and piecemeal way in which much of the formal provision for vulnerability in the criminal justice process has developed, a range of definitions and associated terminology appear in existing policy and guidance.

(a) Questions of capacity and competence

1.12 Some of the most vulnerable individuals who are potential defendants or witnesses may ultimately be deemed unable to engage meaningfully with the criminal justice process on the grounds that they lack the necessary capacity or competence to do so. In other words, the term 'vulnerable' when applied to a defendant or witness generally denotes an individual who faces difficulties in participating in criminal proceedings, but whose difficulties are not so severe as to rule out that participation altogether.

1.13 The point at which an individual's needs have the effect of taking him or her out of the usual justice process, as opposed to making him or her a vulnerable participant, of course, depends not simply on the severity of the needs, but also on

---

[6] Over the course of this volume, the terms 'complainant' and 'victim' are both used to refer to those who are or are alleged to be the victims of the offence being prosecuted. The specific term used depends on the context; for example, much of the policy documentation on court users' entitlements refers to 'victims'.

the availability and effectiveness of measures to ameliorate or make allowances for them if the criminal case proceeds. It is clear, for example, that the development of the range of special measures for vulnerable witnesses has permitted large numbers of individuals, including very young children, to give evidence in criminal trials who previously might never have been considered competent to act as witnesses.

As discussed in detail by Bevan in Chapter 5, a defendant may be deemed 'unfit   **1.14** to plead' if he or she is considered unable to do one or more of the following:

- understand the charge(s);
- decide whether or not to plead guilty;
- exercise his or her right to challenge jurors;
- instruct solicitors and/or counsel;
- follow the course of the proceedings; and
- give evidence in his or her own defence.

Under s. 4 of the Criminal Procedure (Insanity) Act 1964, a defendant who has   **1.15** been deemed unfit to plead (on the grounds that he or she is, in the terminology of the Act, 'under a disability') may then be subject to what is commonly known as a 'trial of the facts'.[7] If the jury decides at this trial that the defendant 'did the act or made the omission' that relates to the allegation, the judge has the option of imposing a hospital order, a supervision order, or an absolute discharge. However, the courts have generally applied a high threshold for a finding of unfitness to plead, and hence the numbers of formally 'unfit'—relative to vulnerable but 'fit'—defendants remain extremely low.

If there is a question over a potential witness's competence to give evidence at   **1.16** trial, this would generally be addressed by the advocate at the pre-trial stage (see Chapter 9 by Rafferty, Cottage, Normanton, and Taylor in this volume). Witness competence is dealt with by s. 53 of the YJCEA, which states that the essential test is that the witness (of any age) should be able to:

- understand questions put to him as a witness; and
- give answers to them which can be understood.

(b) Vulnerable and intimidated witnesses, as defined by the YJCEA

Arguably the most explicit and specific definition of a vulnerable participant   **1.17** in the criminal justice process is contained in the Youth Justice and Criminal Evidence Act 1999, and applies to witnesses (both prosecution and defence). As detailed by Marchant in Chapter 10, the special measures provided for by Part II

---

[7] This statutory unfitness to plead provision applies to cases being heard in the Crown Court only; the existing (non-statutory) provisions with regard to defendants with participation difficulties in the adult magistrates' courts and youth courts are described, respectively, in Chapters 5 and 7.

of the YJCEA are available to witnesses deemed 'vulnerable' on the grounds that they are aged under 18 or, if they are adults, 'the quality of evidence ... is likely to be diminished' because they:

- are suffering from a mental disorder (within the meaning of the Mental Health Act 1983);
- have a significant impairment of intelligence and social functioning; or
- have a physical disability or are suffering from a physical disorder.[8]

1.18 While it is more specific than many other definitions of vulnerability in the sphere of criminal justice, the core concepts contained in the above definition—that is, mental disorder,[9] impairment of intelligence and social functioning, and physical disability or disorder—remain broad. A theme that cross-cuts many of the chapters in this volume is the inherent difficulty of identifying the presence of any such disorder, disability, or impairment, especially where it is hidden or masked by other needs, or in circumstances where the individual is experiencing considerable stress. Further, the critical question which pertains to an individual witness's vulnerability is whether the identified need or difficulty is of such a kind or degree that it is likely to impact that witness's evidence and, if so, whether one of the available special measures will assist. This decision, which must ultimately be made by the court, is necessarily a matter of judgment—and, often, a fine one.

1.19 Section 17 of the YJCEA sets out another category of witnesses who are eligible for most (although not all) special measures: namely, those whose quality of evidence is likely to be 'diminished by reason of fear or distress on the part of the witness in connection with testifying in the proceedings'. Factors relevant to a consideration of a witness's 'intimidated' status include: the nature and circumstances of the alleged offence; the witness's age; and any behaviour towards the witness on the part of the accused. Complainants in sexual offence cases, and witnesses to certain gun- and knife-related offences, are automatically eligible for special measures on grounds of intimidation, unless they wish to opt out of the provisions. As with vulnerable witnesses under the YJCEA, the court must make the decision whether or not to grant special measures to a witness on grounds of fear or distress.[10]

---

[8] YJCEA s. 16.

[9] Itself defined by s. 1(2) of the Mental Health Act 1983 as 'any disorder or disability of the mind'.

[10] Ministry of Justice guidance on *Achieving Best Evidence* defines as an additional special category of witnesses those who are 'significant', on the grounds that they have witnessed an indictable offence and/or have a particular relevance to the victim or a central position in the investigation. Significant witnesses are not entitled to special measures (unless they are also vulnerable), but special consideration is likely to be given to their evidence and, for example, their interviews with the police will usually be video-recorded. See Ministry of Justice, *Achieving Best Evidence in Criminal Proceedings: Guidance on Interviewing Victims and Witnesses, and Guidance on Using Special Measures* (MoJ, 2011).

(c) Young witnesses and defendants

While there is a subjective element to many of the attributes which are associated **1.20** with defendant or witness vulnerability (as noted above, for example, with regard to the YJCEA definition of what makes a witness vulnerable for the purpose of receiving special measures), an individual's young age is largely treated as an objective and unambiguous marker of vulnerability—at least in formal policy, if not always in practice. All witnesses aged under 18 at the time of the hearing are automatically eligible for special measures under the YJCEA.

Young suspects, defendants, and convicted offenders—that is, those aged **1.21** between 10, which is the age of criminal responsibility, and 18, the age at which an individual becomes an adult in the eyes of the law—are largely treated as a distinct sub-group within the wider population of suspects, defendants, and offenders. (For detailed discussion of the Youth Court and surrounding provisions for children and young people who offend or are accused of having offended, see Arbuthnot and Redhouse's Chapter 7 in this volume.) The 'principal aim' of the youth justice system as a whole, as set out in the Crime and Disorder Act 1998 s. 37(1), is the prevention of offending by children and young people. The other guiding principle for the system is the statutory obligation on all courts, under the Children and Young Persons Act 1933 s. 44(1), to 'have regard to the welfare' of every child or young person who comes before them 'either as an offender or otherwise'.

While there is a close association of 'youth' with 'vulnerability', as manifest in the **1.22** wide range of formal provisions for young people in the justice system and in the welfare principle set out in the Children and Young Persons Act, this association is not always entirely straightforward. Children and young people in the justice system, whether they are defendants or witnesses, frequently have multiple and complex needs, many but by no means all of which are likely to be related to their chronological age.

Another factor complicating the relationship between youth and vulnerability is **1.23** that the ages at which individuals are considered 'young' have varied over time and by provision. At the time the YJCEA was enacted, the cut-off age for automatic eligibility for special measures was 17; this was raised to 18 by the Coroners and Justice Act 2009 s. 98. Likewise, in October 2013, Code C of the Police and Criminal Evidence Act 1984 (PACE)[11] was amended such that police detainees who 'appear to be' aged 17 became automatically entitled to certain safeguards which had previously been automatically available only to those appearing to be the age of 16 and under (see Chapter 4 by Bevan). The very terminology of 'youth'

---

[11] Revised Code of Practice for the Detention, Treatment and Questioning of Persons by Police Officers, Police and Criminal Evidence Act 1984 (PACE)—Code C. Presented to Parliament pursuant to PACE s. 67(7B), May 2014.

may imply differing levels of concern with vulnerability; as noted by Bevan, there has been a move away from the term 'juvenile' within policing policy, although it still appears in PACE. In most policy documentation today, the preferred terminology is 'children and young people'.

(d) Vulnerable adult suspects and defendants

1.24 Under PACE, vulnerable adult suspects, like suspects aged under 18, are entitled to additional safeguards while in police custody. For this purpose, vulnerable adults are defined in Code C of PACE as those who are 'mentally disordered or otherwise mentally vulnerable'; with 'mental disorder' understood in the terms of the Mental Health Act 1983, and 'mentally vulnerable' said to apply 'to any detainee who, because of their mental state or capacity, may not understand the significance of what is said, of questions or of their replies' (Code C guidance note 1G). (See Bevan's Chapter 4 for more detail.)

1.25 As noted above, vulnerable defendants are not encompassed by most of the special measures provisions of the YJCEA; and hence the Act, as originally formulated, did not include a definition of vulnerability with regard to defendants. However, the legislation has since been amended so as to extend two of the measures to defendants. Section 47 of the Police and Justice Act 2006 allows a 'vulnerable accused' to give evidence to the court by a live link under certain circumstances, while s. 104 of the Coroners and Justice Act 2009 (which is not yet implemented) provides for vulnerable defendants to have the assistance of an intermediary when giving evidence. Vulnerability of defendants is defined in these YJCEA amendments[12] in the same terms as for witnesses: that is, with reference to 'mental disorder' or another 'significant impairment of intelligence and social functioning'. It is, further, stipulated that a defendant's mental disorder or impairment merits a special measures direction by the court only where it renders the defendant 'unable to participate effectively as a witness giving oral evidence in court', and where the direction would help to ensure a fair trial or facilitate more effective participation by the defendant. (These provisions are further discussed by Marchant in Chapter 10.)

(e) Vulnerability in the Criminal Procedure Rules and Criminal Practice Directions

1.26 As is made clear in the chapters on case management and trial management in this volume (Chapter 9 by Rafferty, Cottage, Normanton, and Taylor, and Chapter 13 by Norton, respectively), vulnerability is a prominent theme in the current Criminal Procedure Rules and Practice Directions.[13] The importance

---

[12] The new provisions were inserted as ss 33A (live link) and 33BA (intermediary assistance) of the YJCEA.

[13] October 2015, amended April 2016.

of facilitating witness and defendant participation, including by helping both groups of court users 'to give their best evidence', and ensuring that defendants 'can comprehend the proceedings and engage fully with his or her defence', is highlighted in the specific Practice Direction on 'Vulnerable people in the Courts'. This section cites the YJCEA definition of a vulnerable witness for the purpose of eligibility for special measures. However, it is also noted that this definition is by no means an exhaustive account of what amounts to vulnerability or need in the context of the criminal courts: it is stated that '*many other people giving evidence in a criminal case, whether as a witness or defendant, may require assistance*' (emphasis added).[14] This broader conception of vulnerability is not defined, and the Directions do not offer a specific set of criteria by which a witness's or defendant's need for assistance should be assessed.

C. Why Does Vulnerability in the Criminal Justice System Matter?

The importance of addressing defendant and witness vulnerability over the course **1.27** of the criminal justice process can be conceived in terms of three main—closely interlinked—imperatives which have shaped public policy in this field. The first imperative, from a legal perspective, is to ensure that vulnerable individuals have *access to justice and can exercise their right to a fair trial*. Second, there is the broader social and political imperative to seek *equality and social inclusion*. Third, implicit or explicit in many of the policy developments is the recognition of the state's legal and moral obligations to *protect the welfare* of vulnerable people in the criminal justice system.

(a) Access to justice and the right to a fair trial

The principle that defendants must be able to 'participate effectively' in the crim- **1.28** inal proceedings which concern them is reflected in the right to a fair trial— enshrined in Article 6 of the European Convention of Human Rights[15]—and the surrounding case law. It is reflected also in the criteria by which a defendant's 'fitness to plead' are determined. Accordingly, vulnerability is a fundamental problem because it inhibits a defendant's capacity for effective participation— whether, for example, this is a matter of lack of comprehension of proceedings, limited ability to make and articulate decisions, or speech or communication problems which impede the giving of evidence. The capacity of non-defendant

---

[14] Criminal Practice Directions I: General matters: 3D: Vulnerable people in the Courts, 3D.1–3D.2.
[15] Convention for the Protection of Human Rights and Fundamental Freedoms, Rome, 4 November 2011.

witnesses, too, to give evidence can be seen as essential to a fair trial; and 'the trial process is perfected when those giving evidence do so to the best of their ability and in the most accurate and comprehensive way possible and this is so quite irrespective of which side of the trial divide they are on'.[16]

1.29 Alongside the right to a fair trial, the implications of vulnerability for access to justice are a vital policy consideration. Access to justice is a more amorphous concept, but can be broadly understood in terms of entitlement to legal protections and legal redress for harms suffered. In 2011, a report published by the Advocacy Training Council, *Raising the Bar*, looked at how the courts, and particularly advocates, should best address the vulnerabilities of all groups of court users. The context of this publication was described as the situation in which vulnerable people were encountering 'almost insurmountable barriers to justice, from the first stages of making their complaint or giving an account, to their experience in the courtroom', while a gradual shift in social attitudes was producing a 'a growing concern that those most at risk of marginalisation by virtue of age, learning disabilities or a mental health diagnosis should have, and be able to exercise, equal access to justice'.[17]

(b) Equality and social inclusion

1.30 Where individuals, because of their vulnerability, lack access to justice and are unable to exercise the right to a fair trial, the implications of these extend beyond the legal sphere, as it is likely to be a manifestation of more general social exclusion and inequality. Conversely, the development and implementation of measures to address vulnerability within the criminal justice system can be seen as part of a wider public policy agenda to promote inclusion and equality.

1.31 Hence, for example, the Equality Act 2010 has a significant bearing on the treatment of people with disabilities (defined by s. 6(1) as physical or mental impairments which significantly impact individuals' 'ability to carry out normal day-to-day activities') within the criminal justice system. Under s. 20 of the Act, service providers and public authorities should make 'reasonable adjustments' to avoid putting disabled individuals at a substantial disadvantage; while s. 149 imposes the 'Public Sector Equality Duty' on all public bodies, requiring such bodies to seek to eliminate discrimination and advance equality of opportunity when conducting their activities.

[16] The Hon Mr Justice Green, 'Introduction: Vulnerable Witnesses in Courts—Why?' in P. Cooper and L. Hunting (eds), *Addressing Vulnerability in Justice Systems* (Wildy, Simmonds & Hill, 2016).

[17] The Advocacy Training Council, *Raising the Bar: The Handling for Vulnerable Witnesses, Victims and Defendants in Court* (2011) 2.1–2.2.

10

From a social inclusion perspective, the participation of vulnerable individuals in **1.32** the criminal justice system is a measure of their wider participation in a society in which they have the same rights and obligations as anyone else. This applies whether they are defendants who are expected to comply with the law and to be held to account to the extent that they do not do so; or witnesses or complainants whose reported experiences are listened to and acted upon, as appropriate, by the authorities.

(c) Welfare

It is noted above that the courts have a statutory duty to 'have regard to the wel- **1.33** fare' of all children who appear before them, in any capacity. Safeguarding duties apply not only to children, but to all vulnerable people in the criminal justice system, and have become an increasingly prominent feature of public policy in recent years. As observed by Jacobson and Harlow in Chapter 3, all organizations are legally obliged to safeguard any children and vulnerable adults with whom they work. Thus, the courts and other criminal justice agencies must protect such individuals from abuse and neglect, and seek to promote their welfare.

Welfare considerations bring clearly into focus not only the needs of those who **1.34** are vulnerable by virtue of age, impairment, or similar factor, but also the needs of individuals whose distress or anxiety may be the primary barriers to their full and effective participation in the criminal justice process—such as witnesses defined as 'intimidated' under the YJCEA. The *Equal Treatment Bench Book* points to the potential for the court experience to be 'devastating' and a source of 'secondary abuse' for some individuals where they are poorly treated, and notes the importance of the judicial role in safeguarding children and vulnerable adults at court.[18] In any given case, it is possible that there will be a direct conflict between safeguarding considerations and the demands of the investigative and prosecution process. In such a scenario, as Smith and Milne observe in Chapter 2 in this volume, a safeguarding policy will always prioritize a witness's safety and welfare over the investigation. In Chapter 4, Bevan notes the inherent challenges faced by police custody officers who must simultaneously seek to ensure the welfare of a suspect and the integrity of the investigation in the highly pressured environment of the custody suite.

(d) Distinguishing vulnerable from non-vulnerable defendants and witnesses?

Consideration of the rationales for provision for vulnerability necessarily raises the **1.35** question of whether those who are *not* deemed vulnerable stand to be disadvantaged by this provision. From the discussion of definitions of vulnerability in the

---

[18] Courts and Tribunals Judiciary, *Equal Treatment Bench Book* (2013) paras 43, 45–9.

previous section, it is evident that the groups identified as vulnerable are potentially very large indeed, to the extent that the 'non-vulnerable' might be seen as a minority of court users. With the caseload of the courts changing over time—for example, far fewer young people are entering the youth justice system than was the case a decade ago, but those who are doing so tend to have more complex and entrenched needs (see Chapter 7), and more than one-third of contested cases now being heard at the Crown Court involve allegations of sex offences[19]—it can be argued that dealing with vulnerability is now routine, core business for all criminal justice practitioners. Moreover, it should be borne in mind that there are aspects of criminal justice proceedings, and particularly the contested trial, that can in themselves exacerbate or even be a cause of vulnerability.

1.36 In this context, the drawing of distinctions between the vulnerable and non-vulnerable would be an almost entirely arbitrary process, and addressing vulnerability should not be regarded as an obligation on practitioners that is separate to the others that they must meet on a day-to-day basis. Rather, sensitivity and responsiveness to vulnerability should be seen as an integral part of the work of the criminal justice system, and of the pursuit of the wider objectives of access to justice, social inclusion, and the promotion of individuals' welfare.

D. Addressing Vulnerability: Key Provisions

1.37 The law and procedural directions and guidance which shape the treatment of vulnerable defendants and witnesses are complex and multi-faceted. The details and nuances are discussed in detail in the substantive chapters of this volume; to set the scene for these detailed accounts, a brief overview is offered, below, of some of the most important provisions.

(a) Protections for suspects and witnesses during the investigation stage

1.38 The treatment of all suspects in police custody is governed by PACE and its accompanying Codes of Practice—of which Code C, in particular, is concerned with detainees' legal rights, conditions of detention, and questioning. As noted above (and discussed in detail in Chapter 4 of this volume), child and vulnerable adult suspects have additional safeguards beyond the entitlement of all suspects to be treated in a fair, respectful, and non-discriminatory manner.

1.39 Under Code C, all suspects must be determined fit for interview before they can be questioned, and the assessment should include consideration of any risks to

---

[19] HHJ Peter Rook QC, 'Sea-Change in Advocacy'.

physical or mental health which might follow an interview, and any safeguards required for an interview. The presence of an 'appropriate adult' is required when a child or vulnerable adult is interviewed, who has the role of providing support, advice, and assistance to the suspect, including help with communication. The appropriate adult role is most frequently played by a family member or carer of the suspect, but there are also statutory, private, and voluntary sector providers of appropriate adults.

Effective support for and protection of vulnerable witnesses at the investigation **1.40** stage often depends on the development by the police of an explicit 'interview strategy', as described in Chapter 2. The strategy should include: specification of how and when to make initial contact with the witness; any pre-interview processes to be followed, such as assessment of needs and capacity, and the obtaining of consent to an interview; the conduct of the interview itself; and post-interview processes, such as evaluation of the information obtained and post-interview witness management and support. Details on preparation for and conduct of police interviews with witnesses, including children and vulnerable adults, are provided in the Ministry of Justice's *Achieving Best Evidence* guidance.

A key decision to be made as part of a vulnerable witness's preparation for inter- **1.41** view is whether the interview is to be video-recorded, in which case the recorded interview can be admitted to the court as evidence-in-chief; another consideration is whether a witness intermediary should be present to assist with communication during the interview (see below).

(b) Special measures and other adjustments to the court process

The YJCEA sets out eight special measures to assist vulnerable and intimidated **1.42** witnesses, whether they are appearing for the prosecution or for the defence, with giving evidence (see Chapter 10 for more details):

- *Use of screens* (s. 23): a witness may give evidence in the courtroom from behind a screen, in order to avoid seeing and being seen by the defendant.
- *Live link* (s. 24): this permits a witness to give evidence over a live video link from outside the courtroom—usually from a specific room in the court building, although it is also possible for the link to be set up in a remote location.
- *Evidence given in public* (s. 25): while a witness is giving evidence, the court can direct that the courtroom be cleared of all people other than the defendant, legal representatives, anyone appointed to assist the witness, and a nominated member of the press if there is one. This provision only applies in cases involving sexual offences or where it appears that the witness has been intimidated (by someone other than the accused).
- *Removal of wigs and gowns* (s. 26): in the Crown Court, the judge's and barristers' wigs and gowns may be removed while a witness is giving evidence.

- *Video-recorded evidence-in-chief* (s. 27): there is a general presumption that the police interview with a witness aged under 18 will be recorded and admitted to the court as evidence-in-chief; however, a young witness can opt out of this if he or she so chooses, with the court's agreement. Adult vulnerable or intimidated witnesses are also eligible for video-recorded evidence-in-chief, and eligibility is automatic, upon application, for those who are complainants in Crown Court sexual offences trials.
- *Video-recorded cross-examination* (s. 28): under this section, where a video recording of the witness interview has been admitted as evidence-in-chief, the court may also direct that the cross-examination and any re-examination of the witness be recorded in advance of the trial and admitted to the court. At the time of writing, roll-out of this provision is under way.
- *Witness examination through an intermediary* (s. 29): a vulnerable (not intimidated) witness may be assisted by an intermediary in giving evidence. Intermediaries are communication specialists, with responsibility for ensuring that questions and answers can be fully understood by both the witness and advocate. (The intermediary role is the subject of Chapter 11 of this volume, by David Wurtzel and Ruth Marchant.)
- *Communication aids* (s. 30): the court can direct that a vulnerable (not intimidated) witness be provided with such means, including an interpreter or a specific device, as are needed to enable questions and answers to be clearly communicated.

1.43 As noted above, the live link provision was extended to vulnerable defendants in certain circumstances by the Police and Justice Act 2006, and the intermediary provision by the Coroners and Justice Act 2009, although the latter has not yet been implemented. However, the courts can use their inherent powers to appoint an individual with the necessary skills to act as an intermediary for a defendant, either to assist throughout the trial or solely with giving evidence.[20]

1.44 Beyond the statutory provisions for special measures, the criminal courts have the flexibility—and indeed the obligation—to make other adjustments in response to any defendant's or witness's specific needs. Since 2013, the courts have been required by the Criminal Procedure Rules to 'take every reasonable step … to facilitate the participation of any person, including the defendant' (para. 3.9(3)); this supports the courts' and wider justice system's Equality Act duty to make 'reasonable adjustments' to avoid disadvantaging those with disabilities. The courts have the freedom to determine precisely what constitutes a 'reasonable step', which might include, for example, adaptation to the lay-out of the court or scheduling of evidence, or directions on styles of communication with participants.

---

[20] Criminal Practice Directions I: General matters: 3F: Intermediaries, 3F.11–18.

Putting the appropriate measures or adjustments in place demands early identifi- **1.45** cation of needs, the relevant parties' active engagement with the issues throughout trial preparation, and close and careful management of the process by the judge (as is made clear in Chapter 13 on trial management). Another consideration for the judge is the need to include in the directions to the jury an explanation of the purpose of any measures or adaptations (see Chapter 14 on jury directions).

(c) Ground rules and new approaches to cross-examination

The Court of Appeal has stated, in *R v Lubemba*, that in all cases involving a **1.46** vulnerable witness, other than 'in very exceptional circumstances', a ground rules hearing should be held in advance of the trial.[21] The purpose of a ground rules hearing—as set out in detail in Chapter 12, by Cooper and Farrugia—is for the judge to set the parameters for the fair treatment (including cross-examination) of a vulnerable witness or defendant over the course of the trial. The amended Criminal Procedure Rules which came into force in April 2015 included provisions on ground rules hearings which specify that the court may make directions about relieving a party of putting their case, the manner of questioning witnesses or defendants, the duration of questioning, any specific questions which may or may not be covered, allocation of questions between defendants if there is more than one, and the use of models, plans, body maps, or other communication aids (para. 3.9(7)).

There is a clear expectation, under the Criminal Procedure Rules, that ground **1.47** rules should be set in any case in which an intermediary is appointed, and that the intermediary should be present at the ground rules hearing, along with the trial judge and counsel. The intermediary is, further, expected to provide the court with a report on his or her assessment of the vulnerable party, containing recommendations for ground rules.

The scope and content of cross-examination of the vulnerable witness or defend- **1.48** ant is necessarily a core concern in any ground rules hearing. There is growing recognition that traditional approaches to cross-examination can not only be bruising or distressing for vulnerable individuals, but can also fail to elicit the desired information if the questions are overly complex or otherwise inappropriately formulated. The Criminal Practice Directions note that the 'form and extent of appropriate cross-examination will vary from case to case', and that helping vulnerable witnesses and defendants to give their best evidence may be a matter of 'departing radically from traditional cross-examination' (para. 3E.4). Accordingly, judges are increasingly imposing restrictions on advocates' questioning, which sometimes—although not necessarily—includes a prohibition on the advocate 'putting his case' to a vulnerable witness (see Chapter 13 on trial

---

[21] [2014] EWCA Crim 2064 at [42].

management). This can be seen as one important facet of broader change to the trial process whereby advocates are now expected to 'adapt to the witness, not the other way round'.[22]

(d) Information and support for witnesses

1.49 The available safeguards and measures to ease vulnerable witnesses' experience of giving evidence make up one important part of wider provision for witnesses. As described in Chapter 3 of this volume, what can be broadly termed 'witness support' comprises a patchwork of provision targeting various overlapping groups by various means, most of which has evolved over the course of the past three decades. The emergence of witness support was in part a response to concerns that witnesses and victims of crime (the latter including complainants and those who do not necessarily give evidence, such as bereaved family members of homicide victims) were being marginalized by a justice system that appeared to focus primarily on defendants and defendants' rights.

1.50 Beyond the introduction of special measures and other adjustments to the court process, other significant developments include the development of the Witness Service. This now operates in all magistrates' and Crown courts in England and Wales and provides assistance to witnesses at court, whether they are deemed vulnerable or not, including through the hosting of pre-trial visits. These visits can play a particularly important part in helping vulnerable or intimidated witnesses to become familiar with the court environment and to consider the suitability of any proposed special measures. In the most serious cases involving witnesses with multiple and complex needs, it is common practice for the range of services engaged in providing support to the witnesses to hold a case conference as part of the trial preparation process, at which safeguarding and security arrangements, along with other matters, can be agreed.

1.51 The statutory Victims' Code, initially produced in 2005 and revised in 2015,[23] sets out the services that must be provided to victims by all criminal justice agencies. Provisions, to which victims are entitled under the code, include: an enhanced service if they have suffered serious crime or have been persistently targeted, or are vulnerable or intimidated; and a needs assessment and referral to support services. The code places a strong emphasis on keeping victims informed about the progress of their case, as is also a theme in the (non-statutory) Witness Charter, the most recent version of which was issued in 2013.[24] This specifies the standards of service that can be expected by all witnesses, including in relation

---

[22] *R v Lubemba; R v JP* [2014] EWCA Crim 2064 at [45].
[23] Ministry of Justice, *Code of Practice for Victims of Crime* (MoJ, 2015).
[24] MoJ, *The Witness Charter: Standards of Care for Witnesses in the Criminal Justice System* (MoJ, 2013).

to assessments of need and applications for any help required—such as special measures—to enable anyone who is vulnerable or intimidated to give evidence.

(e) Specific provisions for young defendants

The youth justice system—described in Chapter 7—is in many ways a distinct **1.52** part of the wider criminal justice system. If a child or young person (that is, aged between 10 and 17, inclusive) is arrested by the police, he or she is automatically entitled to certain safeguards, including the support of an appropriate adult. There is a presumption that children and young people who have engaged in minor offending and have little or no criminal history should be diverted away from the court process, whether through informal responses by the police or through the issuing of a 'youth caution' as a formal pre-court disposal.[25] Where a case proceeds to court, decisions on bail or remand are governed by a more complex set of procedures than applies to adult defendants, with greater restrictions on the use of custodial remands.

The large majority of cases involving young defendants are dealt with by the **1.53** Youth Court, a specialist type of magistrates' court, the structure and environment of which are specifically devised to be less formal and intimidating than the adult courts. For example, defendants are addressed by their first name and can sit with their advocate and/or supporters rather than in the dock; and judges and magistrates are expected to use clear and simple language geared to young defendants' level of understanding, to explain each stage of the proceedings, and to build up a rapport with the defendants. It is a closed court, meaning that members of the public cannot attend without permission and, under the Children and Young Persons Act 1933,[26] there is an automatic prohibition on publication of any information that could lead to the identification of any child or young person involved in the proceedings. In the small minority of cases in which a defendant aged under 18 appears in the Crown Court (either because of the seriousness of the offence, or because there are adult co-defendants), any of the various adaptations to the court process that might be applied to an adult vulnerable defendant can be applied to the young defendant. While young people in Crown Court proceedings do not have automatic anonymity, the court can make a direction to this end.[27]

There is a largely separate sentencing framework for young offenders, comprising its own distinct penalties. There is a general expectation, as stated in the **1.54**

---

[25] The youth caution is dealt with by ss 66ZA and 66ZB of the Crime and Disorder Act 1998, inserted by s. 135(2) of the Legal Aid Sentencing and Punishment of Offenders Act 2012.

[26] Section 49, as amended by the YJCEA, Sch. 2, para. 3.

[27] Under s. 45 of the YJCEA, an order can be imposed to restrict reporting on any victim, witness, or defendant aged under 18 who is concerned in proceedings in a magistrates' court or the Crown Court.

definitive guideline on *Sentencing Children and Young People* (which was published in March 2017 and is effective from June 2017), that 'the approach to sentencing should be individualistic and focused on the child or young person, as opposed to offence focused' and that, where possible, 'the sentence should focus on rehabilitation'.[28] The guideline also emphasizes that, in assessing a young offender's culpability, the court should recognize that '[c]hildren and young people are inherently more vulnerable than adults due to their age', and consider any mental health problems, learning disabilities, and the individual's emotional and developmental age.[29]

E. Outline of the Volume

1.55 The criminal justice process comprises a vast number of interconnected parts, and the topic of vulnerability has a bearing on many or even most of them. To ensure that this topic is addressed in a comprehensive manner over the course of this volume, the chapters that follow are structured partly by component or stage of the justice process, and partly thematically. Inevitably, there is a certain amount of overlap between some of the chapters; however, the authors have sought to minimize this by cross-referencing between the chapters wherever appropriate.

1.56 Following this introduction, Chapter 2, by Kevin Smith and Becky Milne, focuses on *vulnerable witnesses at the investigation stage* of the prosecution process—detailing the safeguards and supports that are most relevant to initial contact and police interviews with individuals who are or should be identified as vulnerable. Witnesses are also the focus of Chapter 3, by Jessica Jacobson and Linda Harlow: this chapter describes the main forms of *witness support* made available to all prosecution and defence witnesses, and particularly those who are vulnerable, throughout the 'witness journey' from the investigation stage through to trial, sentencing, and beyond. In Chapter 4, by Miranda Bevan, attention turns from vulnerable witnesses to *vulnerable suspects*, and the protections which should be applied to the latter group—including both adults and children—when they are in police custody.

1.57 The broad and complex topic of *unfitness to plead* is addressed in Chapter 5 by Miranda Bevan, who looks at the criteria and processes by which fitness is assessed, and the alternative procedures for testing an allegation which are followed when a defendant is deemed unfit. Chapter 6, by Penny Cooper and Felicity Gerry, is concerned with cases involving a 'fit to plead' but evidently vulnerable defendant,

---

[28] Sentencing Council, *Sentencing Children and Young People: Overarching Principles and Offence Specific Guidelines for Sexual Offences and Robbery*, para. 1.2.
[29] ibid. para. 4.5.

where the vulnerability is potentially relevant to specific *defences*. The chapter includes consideration of the circumstances in which a vulnerability falling short of insanity has a bearing on whether or not the accused had the requisite *mens rea* to be guilty of the alleged offence. The various components of the *youth justice system*, and particularly the remit and structures of the Youth Court, are outlined in Chapter 7, by Emma Arbuthnot and Naomi Redhouse.

Chapter 8, by Tracy Ayling and Karen Robinson, is concerned with the statu-   **1.58** tory *disclosure* regime which applies in all Crown Court proceedings, and the practical implications of a participant's vulnerability for disclosure. Such implications include, for example, the need to address questions of consent to the disclosure of medical records which might go towards the credibility of a vulnerable witness's account. Disclosure is just one of a great many issues that must be dealt with through the *case management* process, as discussed by Angela Rafferty, Rosina Cottage, Joshua Normanton, and Simon Taylor in Chapter 9. This chapter outlines the essential components of effective management of cases involving vulnerable participants so as to avoid unnecessary delay and distress.

The eight statutory *special measures* for vulnerable witnesses, as provided for by   **1.59** the YJCEA, are described by Ruth Marchant in Chapter 10, along with courts' wider scope for making adjustments to facilitate the participation of vulnerable witnesses and defendants. One of the specific and most innovative special measures, namely the provision for witness examination through *intermediaries*, is the subject of Chapter 11 by David Wurtzel and Ruth Marchant. The chapter includes description of the functions, principles, and practice of witness intermediaries, as well as discussion of the use of intermediaries for defendants. Intermediaries have a key role to play in *ground rules hearings*, which set the parameters for the fair treatment and questioning of vulnerable witnesses and defendants at trial, and are discussed by Penny Cooper and Laura Farrugia in Chapter 12. Heather Norton, in Chapter 13, then looks at *trial management*— describing the judge's powers and responsibilities to ensure that the trial can best be managed in accordance with the overriding objective of achieving justice when any party to it is vulnerable.

In the context of wider and substantial change to the ways in which *jury directions*   **1.60** can be given, in Chapter 14, Heather Norton considers to what extent and how directions should reflect any adjustments for vulnerability that have been made to the trial process, so as to avoid the risk of jurors making 'unwarranted assumptions' in their approach to the evidence. *Sentencing* is the subject of Chapter 15, in which Heather Norton looks at the circumstances in which vulnerability may be a factor in sentencing, how the courts should approach the sentencing of vulnerable offenders, and the available sentences and disposals under the Mental Health Act 1983. Finally, Chapter 16, by Penny Cooper, Michelle Mattison, and Heather Norton, concludes the volume by looking at *proposed changes to* *legislation and procedure*, and includes discussion of the commitment to pilot the 'Barnahus' model for gathering evidence from vulnerable witnesses.

Further Reading

Below are the main current sources of information and guidance for practitioners relating to the treatment of vulnerable people in the criminal justice system.

- Achieving Best Evidence in Criminal Proceedings: Guidance on Interviewing Victims and Witnesses, and Guidance on Using Special Measures (Ministry of Justice, 2011);
- PACE Codes of Practice, especially Code C: Revised Code of Practice for the Detention, Treatment and Questioning of Persons by Police Officers (2014);
- Code of Practice for Victims of Crime (Ministry of Justice, 2015);
- Criminal Procedure Rules and Criminal Practice Directions, October 2015 edition, amended April 2016, especially:
  - Criminal Procedure Rules, 3.9: Case preparation and progression; 3.11: Conduct of a trial or an appeal;
  - Criminal Practice Directions I: General matters—3D: Vulnerable People in the Courts; 3E: Ground rules hearings to plan the questioning of a vulnerable witness or defendant; 3F: Intermediaries; 3G: Vulnerable defendants;
- Crown Court Compendium—Part I: Jury and Trial Management and Summing Up; Part II: Sentencing (Judicial College, 2016);
- Equal Treatment Bench Book (Courts and Tribunals Judiciary, 2013);
- Overarching Principles—Sentencing Youths: Definitive Guideline (Sentencing Guidelines Council, 2009);
- Plea and Trial Preparation Hearings: Introduction and Guidance (Lord Chief Justice, 2015);
- A protocol between the Association of Chief Police Offices, the Crown Prosecution Service and Her Majesty's Courts & Tribunals Service to Expedite Cases Involving Witnesses under 10 Years (2015);
- Provision of Therapy for Child Witnesses Prior to a Criminal Trial: Practice Guidance (Crown Prosecution Service);
- Raising the Bar: The Handling for Vulnerable Witnesses, Victims and Defendants in Court (Advocacy Training Council, 2011);
- Registered Intermediary Procedural Guidance Manual (Ministry of Justice, 2015);
- Safeguarding Children as Victims and Witnesses (Crown Prosecution Service, 2012);
- Speaking to Witnesses at Court: CPS Guidance (Crown Prosecution Service, 2016);

- The Advocate's Gateway toolkits on preparing for trial in cases involving a witness or a defendant with communication needs:
  - 1. Ground rules hearings and the fair treatment of vulnerable people in court;
  - 1a. Case management when a witness or defendant is vulnerable;
  - 1b. Case management in young and other vulnerable witness cases—summary;
  - 2. General principles from research, policy and guidance: planning to question a vulnerable person or someone with communication needs;
  - 3. Planning to question someone with an autism spectrum disorder including Asperger syndrome;
  - 4. Planning to question someone with a learning disability;
  - 5. Planning to question someone with 'hidden' disabilities: specific language impairment, dyslexia, dyslexia, dyspraxia, dyscalculia and AD(H)D;
  - 6. Planning to question a child or young person;
  - 7. Additional factors concerning children under 7 (or functioning at a very young age);
  - 8. Effective participation of young defendants;
  - 9. Planning to question someone using a remote link;
  - 10. Identifying vulnerability in witnesses and defendants;
  - 11. Planning to question someone who is deaf;
  - 12. General principles when questioning witnesses and defendants with mental disorder;
  - [13. Vulnerable witnesses and parties in the family courts];
  - 14. Using communication aids in the criminal justice system;
  - 15. Witnesses and defendants with autism: memory and sensory issues;
  - 16. Intermediaries step by step;
  - [17. Vulnerable witnesses and parties in the civil courts].
- The Witness Charter: Standards of Care for Witnesses in the Criminal Justice System (Ministry of Justice, 2013).

2

VULNERABLE WITNESSES
The Investigation Stage

Kevin Smith and Rebecca Milne

A. Introduction

Investigative interviews with vulnerable witnesses often take place in the broad **2.01** context of an interview strategy. In complex cases involving multiple witnesses with challenging communication issues such as large-scale investigations into allegations of child sexual exploitation, the witness interview strategy should complement and be complemented by a victim care strategy that is intended to provide emotional, therapeutic, and safeguarding support to all the potential victims and witnesses identified by the investigation,[1] irrespective of the extent of their cooperation. In these circumstances, witness interview strategies and victim care strategies are usually set against the backdrop of a safeguarding policy that emphasizes the primacy of the safety and welfare of potential victims and witnesses over the investigative process where there is a conflict between the demands of the two.

2.02 This chapter describes the matters that should be considered when an interview strategy for vulnerable witnesses is developed.

B. Interview Strategies for Vulnerable Witnesses

2.03 Interview strategies should always be developed with an investigative mindset where investigators should 'keep an open mind and be receptive to alternative views of explanations'[2] when examining the source of material obtained during an investigation and considering its reliability. This is because one of the main threats to objective information processing in crime investigation is the tendency to focus on only one particular interpretation or to seek only confirmatory information to support any pre-existing hypotheses. With this in mind, the development of a vulnerable witness interview strategy should consist of the following four phases:

- initial contact, including pre-contact assessment;
- pre-interview processes;
- interview; and
- post-interview processes.

2.04 This chapter describes each of these phases and the considerations within them in turn.

C. Initial Contact

2.05 The extent to which initial contact needs to be planned depends on the circumstances. In some cases, the witness will have approached the police of their own

---

[1] While there was no specific guidance at the time of writing, a victim care strategy should describe the practical arrangements for taking action in the event that a witness's safety is at risk and the mechanisms that have been put in place for their therapeutic support. Such a strategy should take account of the guidance on investigating child abuse and child sexual exploitation on the College of Policing website at <https://www.app.college.police.uk/app-content/major-investigation-and-public-protection/> accessed 9 March 2017; and *Guidance on Safeguarding and Investigating the Abuse of Vulnerable Adults* (Association of Chief Police Officers, 2012).

[2] Association of Chief Police Officers, *Practice Advice on Core Investigative Doctrine* (2nd edn, National Policing Improvement Agency, 2012) 89, section 5.4.

volition, perhaps to report a crime. In other instances, the police will have instigated the approach as part of a proactive search for witnesses to a crime that has already been reported or to follow up a matter with a witness who was seen by the police in an earlier investigation that might have taken place many years ago. This section sets out a series of considerations that should be taken into account when preparing for initial contact with a potential witness. These considerations should not be thought of as a checklist of points to be exhaustively covered in every instance. Every investigation is unique; what is covered and the manner in which it is dealt with very much depends on the circumstances. Thus, a tool-belt approach should be adopted.

The considerations relevant to initial contact with vulnerable people who might **2.06** be witnesses are as follows:

- pre-contact assessment;
- deciding whether to contact a potential witness;
- welfare considerations;
- preliminary witness categorization and prioritization;
- when to contact the potential witness;
- location for initial contact;
- corporate message about the nature of the investigation;
- what to ask the potential witness;
- description of the potential witness;
- contingencies;
- message about potential collusion; and
- message to carers (if applicable).

(a) Pre-contact assessment

Pre-contact assessment involves trying to find out as much as possible about a **2.07** potential witness from any records that are readily accessible before they are contacted. Issues that may have an impact on their mental or physical health, learning disability, communication skills, safety, and welfare are likely to be very important and need to be considered. How much can be found out prior to making contact with any given potential witness obviously depends on their circumstances and the nature of the matter under investigation. In this sense, a comprehensive pre-contact assessment is something to be aspired to rather than something that must always be comprehensively achieved. The fact that a pre-contact assessment may not always be fully achieved should not diminish its importance; what is established about the potential witness can exert a profound influence on whether and how they are approached.

(b) Deciding whether to contact a potential witness

The potential witness's safety and welfare will always take primacy over the **2.08** demands of the investigation in any safeguarding policy. Thus, if pre-contact assessment suggests that the risk factors involved in approaching a vulnerable person who might be a witness are so severe that they cannot be satisfactorily mitigated, it may be that a decision will be made not to contact them. In these circumstances, professionals such as mental health clinicians are likely to already be working with the vulnerable person and any decision for the investigation team not to make contact with them is likely to be a provisional one taken in consultation with the clinician. The decision not to make contact with a potential witness should be kept under review since their circumstances might change to the point that any risks associated with contact from the investigation team can be satisfactorily mitigated. While the possibility that it might not be appropriate to contact a potential witness must always be acknowledged, such cases are likely to be rare and most if not all of the potential witnesses identified by an investigation will be contacted where it is practical and proportionate to do so.

(c) Welfare considerations

2.09 A witness interview strategy should always take account of the welfare of a potential witness, irrespective of whether or not they choose to cooperate. The events being investigated might have had a lasting impact on their emotional well-being and they could be suffering from trauma. In these circumstances, any contact from the authorities informing them that an investigation has commenced might open their emotional wounds and exacerbate the trauma. Steps should, therefore, be taken to help potential witnesses to manage trauma by facilitating their access to support and, if necessary, therapy as required by the statutory Code of Practice for Victims of Crime[3] and in accordance with the arrangements set out in the victim care strategy for the investigation. Potential witnesses who might be in need of support, particularly those who might be experiencing trauma, should be told how they can access support and therapy regardless of whether or not they choose to cooperate with the investigation.

2.10 Where pre-contact assessment suggests that it might be necessary, arrangements should be made for the transport of potential witnesses and any other children or vulnerable adults who might be at risk following initial contact (e.g. members of the witness's family) to a place of safety.

(d) Preliminary witness categorization and prioritization

2.11 Witnesses should be categorized and prioritized on the basis of the pre-contact assessment. Such categorization and prioritization should be viewed as

---

[3] Ministry of Justice (MoJ), 'Code of Practice for Victims of Crime' (MoJ, 2015) 41, para. 1.4 and 73, para. 1.3, available at <https://www.gov.uk/government/uploads/system/uploads/attachment_data/file/476900/code-of-practice-for-victims-of-crime.PDF> accessed 9 March 2017.

preliminary because pre-contact assessment is rarely going to be comprehensive and because witness assessment should be viewed as an ongoing process since their circumstances might change (e.g. their mental health).

Witness categorization operates in two ways: **2.12**

1. categorization as a vulnerable, intimidated, significant, or 'other' witness for the purposes of the interview product; and
2. categorization for the purposes of determining the order in which the potential witnesses are to be approached.

(i) Categorization for the interview product

Vulnerable and intimidated witnesses are defined in ss 16 and 17 of the Youth **2.13** Justice and Criminal Evidence Act (YJCEA) 1999 respectively. Vulnerable and intimidated witnesses are eligible for video-recorded evidence-in-chief if it is likely to maximize the quality of their evidence. Sections 21 and 22A of the YJCEA (as amended by the Coroners and Justice Act 2009 ss 100 and 101) have established rebuttable presumptions to the effect that video-recorded evidence-in-chief is likely to maximize the quality of the evidence of child witnesses (under 18) and complainants to sexual offences where the case is tried in a Crown Court. For any other vulnerable or intimidated witness, the court needs to be satisfied on a case-by-case basis that video-recorded evidence-in-chief is likely to maximize the quality of their evidence.

Significant witnesses are beyond the scope of this chapter; suffice to say that they **2.14** are sometimes interviewed on video to ensure that the interview is recorded in the most accurate and transparent way possible. There are no provisions in the statute law of England and Wales for playing interviews with significant witnesses as evidence-in-chief. The evidence from the recording must be transferred into a format that is acceptable to the courts (usually a full written Criminal Justice Act 1967 s. 9 statement). For more information about significant witnesses, see paragraphs 1.26 to 1.29 and 2.144 to 2.150 of the 2017 edition of *Achieving Best Evidence*.[4]

(ii) Categorization to determine the order of approach

Given that in most large-scale investigations the investigation team are unlikely **2.15** to have the resources to approach all the potential witnesses simultaneously, there should be a rationale for determining who should be approached first. The order in which potential witnesses are approached and interviewed should not be entirely random.

---

[4] MoJ, *Achieving Best Evidence: Guidance on Interviewing Victims and Witnesses, and Guidance on using Special Measures* (MoJ, anticipated 2017).

2.16 Categorization to determine the order of approach is case-specific, but it should always take into account the need to protect potential witnesses from any harm or further harm. It might also, for example, be based on a distinction between witnesses who have already come forward and those who have been identified but are yet to come forward. It could be based on the gravity of the alleged offence(s) about which the witness has complained or it could involve drawing a distinction between those still in contact with the suspected offenders and those who are not. Decision-making should also take potential witness contamination into account. The important point here is that there is some basis for determining the order in which the potential witnesses are approached.

(e) When to contact

2.17 Investigators should consider the availability of support in the days immediately following the proposed date of contact. Other than where there are immediate concerns for somebody's safety and well-being, it is unlikely to be appropriate to contact potential witnesses at the end of the working week (e.g. on a Friday) because support and investigative resources are likely to be limited over the weekend.

(f) Location for initial contact

2.18 A decision will need to be made as to the most appropriate location for initial contact to take place. While the potential witness's home address will often be entirely appropriate, it should not be viewed as a default position. Thus, investigators need to give the matter consideration and ask the question: 'Where is the best location?' The most suitable location for initial contact depends on the circumstances but, in addition to the potential witness's home address, it could include their foster placement, school or work place, while they are en route between their home address, foster placement, school or work place, and any other place that they frequent. A risk assessment taking into account all the available information should be conducted at any place identified as likely to be appropriate for initial contact (i.e. a safe place free from distractions).

(g) Corporate message about the nature of the investigation

2.19 It is important to develop a single corporate message about the investigation that is to be given to potential witnesses in order to avoid the confusion that can arise from different members of the investigation team, and those working on their behalf, giving different messages. Such a corporate message should be balanced between providing the potential witness with enough information to make an informed choice about their cooperation without providing them with so much information as to contaminate any account that they might provide.

The wording of the corporate message should be based on the search for poten-   **2.20**
tial witnesses. Where the wording of a corporate message is aimed at the identification of potential victims rather than witnesses, it is likely to be regarded as
'trawling' unless the people to be approached have previously identified themselves as victims on a statement, have been named as such in a statement made
by others, or there is clear intelligence to suggest that they might be a potential victim. The practice of 'trawling' has been heavily criticized in the courts
because it suggests that the investigation has not been approached with an open
mind, but contacting potential victims on a 'firm intelligence or evidence-led
basis' is permissible.[5]

CPS *Guidelines on Prosecuting Cases of Child Sexual Abuse* make it clear that   **2.21**
potential victims can be told that the suspected offender is the subject of complaints by others *after* they have participated in a video-recorded interview or
provided a written statement and if doing so is necessary to 'strengthen their
resolve to continue their engagement with the criminal justice process' (paragraph 43). In 'exceptional' circumstances and with the authorization of a police
officer not below the rank of superintendent, potential victims can be told
before they have participated in a video-recorded interview or provided a written statement (paragraph 44), for example, if it is necessary to do so in order to
encourage them to engage with the investigation. Where it is considered necessary to tell someone beforehand, there should be evidence or intelligence to
suggest that they are a potential victim. Where a potential victim is told, they
should only be informed in very general terms about the complaints against
a suspected offender, the details of the complaints should not be divulged to
them, and a record should be made of what they were told (paragraphs 43
and 45).

(h) What to ask the potential witness at the initial contact

(i) *No previous account*

What to ask the potential witness at this stage very much depends on the   **2.22**
circumstances. Where they have not provided a previous account it may be
appropriate to attempt to obtain a *brief* account from them to inform the
initial investigation plan. The account should only be probed as far as necessary to take any immediate action required (e.g. to prevent intimidation or to
secure forensic evidence that might otherwise be lost). The interviewer should
remember to make use of good questioning skills at this point as advised in

---

[5] Crown Prosecution Service (CPS), *Guidelines on Prosecuting Cases of Child Sexual Abuse*,
para. 47, available at <http://www.cps.gov.uk/legal/a_to_c/child_sexual_abuse/> accessed 9
March 2017.

paragraphs 3.49 to 3.69 of *Achieving Best Evidence*[6] and paragraphs 2.79 to 2.84 of this chapter. A more detailed account should not be pursued at this point, but should be left until the formal interview takes place. A comprehensive note should be made of the discussion,[7] taking care to record the timing, setting, and people present, as well as what was said by the witness and anybody else present (including the questions asked of the witness) (*Achieving Best Evidence*, paragraph 2.8).

(ii) Previous account to carer or professional

2.23 Where an account has previously been provided to a carer or a professional working with the potential witness, the decision about what to ask them should take account of how recently the previous account was taken and its adequacy. Any concerns about the integrity of a previous account that arise from the possibility of coaching or leading questions should not usually be pursued at this point, but should be left until the formal interview stage.

2.24 If a previous account provided to a carer or a professional working with the potential witness was recent, the account is relatively clear, and questions do not need to be asked to determine initial action, there is likely to be little value in simply asking a vulnerable person to repeat it. Indeed, asking a vulnerable person to repeat a recent and reasonably clear account prior to an interview is unlikely to take the investigation further forward, particularly since it is entirely possible that a vulnerable person might not be inclined to repeat their account to somebody who is a stranger to them. It is also unwise to encourage more recall than is necessary at this stage, since the memory of an event changes each time it is recalled, thus offering 'an opportunity for distortion and error to be assimilated to a memory and, possibly, incorporated into it on a longer-term basis'.[8] In these circumstances, it might be best to simply acknowledge the previous account and to inform the potential witness of the intention to talk about it in an interview. On the other hand, if a recent account is ambiguous and/or further questions do need to be asked to determine initial action, a further dialogue about what was said is likely to be necessary.

---

[6] The references to specified paragraphs from *Achieving Best Evidence* in this chapter refer to the previously mentioned 2017 edition of the guidance. It should be noted that it is anticipated that this revision of the guidance will be published by the end of 2017.

[7] The *National Policing Position Statement: Using Body Worn Video to Record Initial Contact with Victims, Witnesses and Suspects* (published by the National Police Chiefs' Council in 2015) discourages the use of body worn video to visually record initial accounts from vulnerable witnesses because they are unlikely to be in a position to give informed consent for the recording at the time and since they should be given a choice about how the formal interview is to be recorded later on (paragraph 4.2.1 of the position statement refers).

[8] British Psychological Society, *Memory and the Law: Recommendations from the Scientific Study of Human Memory* (British Psychological Society, 2010) 16, section 3v.

If a previous account provided to a carer or a professional working with the **2.25** potential witness is not recent, but adequate, it might be appropriate to refer to something having previously been said, without including the potentially significant contents of what is claimed to have been said, and ask for another account in order to determine further action. The risk of memory contamination needs to be kept in mind when asking questions.

(iii) Previous account to an earlier investigation

Where the witness has already provided an account during a video-recorded **2.26** interview or in a written statement for a previous investigation, what to ask a vulnerable witness very much depends on the nature and quality of the previous account. For example, if the previous account is entirely adequate, it might simply be a matter of asking them if they have recalled anything else and if they have had any contact with the suspect(s) or other victims/witnesses since. Alternatively, if the previous account is not entirely adequate, it might be a matter of conducting a further interview to clarify and develop certain aspects of the previous account; or, if it is completely inadequate, conducting a further interview with a view to covering the entire account again. Consideration as to how the previous account features in this process very much depends on what is known or believed about its accuracy and integrity and on the course of action proposed in respect of any further interview.

(i) Description of the potential witness

In some investigations, it may help if the witness's description is recorded so that **2.27** they can be identified in the accounts given by other witnesses if they are only referred to using part of a name (i.e. just by one of their forenames or just by their surname), by a nickname, or by description.

(j) Contingencies

(i) Intimidation

The strategy should also take into account the possibility that some witnesses **2.28** might discourage or even intimidate others from cooperating with the investigation. It is important that investigators understand that any instances of this nature should be brought to the attention of the officer in charge of the investigation at the earliest opportunity. The officer in charge of the investigation has a range of options open to him or her in these circumstances, including advising witnesses what to do if they are discouraged or intimidated by other witnesses, advising witnesses who discourage or intimidate other witnesses about their future conduct, taking safeguarding measures in accordance with the victim care strategy, or, if the circumstances make it necessary to do so, interviewing witnesses who intimidate others under caution (either at the commencement of a voluntary interview as a suspect or following arrest).

(ii) Reluctance

2.29 Unless it is impractical to do so, an attempt should be made to establish the source of any reluctance on the part of a potential witness. Witnesses can be reluctant for a variety of reasons, including distrust of the police, trauma, embarrassment, fear of or loyalty to the suspected offender, intimidation, concerns about how they will be treated in court, not wanting to upset those close to them, or simply wanting to move on with their lives. It is only by identifying the source of a potential witness's reluctance that there can be any hope of addressing it.

(k) Message about potential collusion

2.30 Witnesses should be asked not to discuss the case with others, either personally or via social media, so as to minimize the chances of memory contamination and to limit the possibility of a later claim that the allegations arose as a result of collusion.

(l) Message to carers (if applicable)

2.31 Carers should be given the corporate message and asked not to do anything intended to solicit an account or any explanation from the witness, but to listen to any unsolicited comments that they might make, acknowledge what has been said, make a record of what was said and the context in which it was said, and inform the investigation team as soon as possible.

The next stage in the process is the pre-interview phase, to which we now turn.

D. Pre-Interview Processes

2.32 The pre-interview processes relevant to vulnerable witnesses are as follows:

- needs assessment;
- consent and capacity;
- pre-interview rapport building; and
- witness preparation.

(a) Needs assessment

2.33 The idea of assessing witnesses before an interview to inform the interview planning process is nothing new. It has been around for at least twenty-three years, since the publication of the *Memorandum of Good Practice*,[9] and has been

---

[9] Home Office, *Memorandum of Good Practice on Video Recorded Interviews with Child Witnesses for Criminal Proceedings* (HMSO, 1992).

included in the *Achieving Best Evidence* guidance since it was first published in 2002.[10] Unfortunately, it appears that such assessments rarely take place; indeed, following a review of seventy-one interviews from six police forces in 2014, Her Majesty's Crown Prosecution Service Inspectorate (HMCPSi) and Her Majesty's Inspectorate of Constabulary (HMIC) concluded that 'the absence of an assessment was compounded by poor planning. There was a paucity of plans and record keeping was generally poor. The absence of effective planning was the root of the many failings observed'.[11]

The statutory Code of Practice for Victims of Crime makes it clear that 'all victims of a criminal offence are entitled to an assessment by the police to identify any needs or support required, including whether and to what extent they may benefit from special measures' (paragraph 1.4 on page 13). When an investigative interview is contemplated, the police are required to ensure that it is conducted by a 'suitably trained professional … in a way that considers the needs and views of the victim' and that it 'should be planned in advance', taking account of factors that include any disabilities or special needs of the victim, the need for a registered intermediary, and the need for an interview supporter (paragraph 1.5 on page 41 for adults, cross-referenced with paragraph 1.5 on page 73 for children). When considering the Code of Practice for Victims of Crime, it is important to remember that it should be regarded as secondary legislation, in that it is provided for by the Domestic Violence, Crime and Victims Act 2004 s. 32 and that a failure to comply with it may be taken into account by a court when deciding upon an issue during proceedings (s. 34(2)). The Witness Charter[12] also obliges the police to conduct a needs assessment to identify any assistance that witnesses may need when giving evidence to an investigation or in court, including any special measures that might be required where the witness is vulnerable or intimidated (see charter standards 4 and 8 on pages 2, 5, 9, and 11). While the Witness Charter is not underpinned by legislation, it does set down the minimum standards of care that witnesses should expect from professionals who work in the criminal justice system. **2.34**

Practical issues such as the witness's preferred mode of address should be explored during the assessment, where it is not already apparent as a result of earlier contact with them. However, the principal purpose of the assessment should be to determine how best to go about the interview and to identify which, if any, special **2.35**

---

[10] For a history of the guidance set out in the *Memorandum of Good Practice* and *Achieving Best Evidence,* see G. Davies, R. Bull, and R. Milne, 'Analyzing and Improving the Testimony of Vulnerable Witnesses Interviewed under the "Achieving Best Evidence" Protocol' in P. Radcliffe, G. Gudjonsson, A. Heaton-Armstrong, and D. Wolchover (eds), *Witness Testimony in Sexual Cases: Evidential, Investigative and Scientific Perspectives* (Oxford University Press, 2006).

[11] HMCPSi and HMIC, *Achieving Best Evidence in Child Sexual Abuse Cases: A Joint Inspection* (HMCPSi, 2014), 4 paragraph 1.4.

[12] MoJ, *Witness Charter* (MoJ, 2013).

measures the witness may be eligible for if they give evidence in court. It is not possible to list all the various issues that might be considered because the extent and nature of an assessment obviously depends on the extent and nature of the witness's vulnerability. Depending on the circumstances, however, the following might be included:

- the nature of the witness's vulnerability (e.g. age, disability, or both);
- the witness's first language or means of communication if they do not use spoken or sign language;
- the nature of the witness's routine, any aspects of the routine that are inflexible, and what needs to be done to prepare them for a change of routine (particularly where the witness is on the autistic spectrum);
- the extent to which the prospective interviewer is able to establish a rapport with the witness;
- the concentration span of the witness. Where a vulnerable witness can only participate in an interview for a very limited period of time, the maximum length of any interview session and the minimum duration of any break between interview sessions;
- the potential impact of trauma (e.g. any obvious signs of dissociation) and any potential ways of managing it (e.g. measures that might be taken to focus or ground the witness in the interview room);
- the extent of the witness's literacy skills where the witness does not use spoken language and is unable to sign proficiently, or their use of spoken language is limited in some way (e.g. a witness with selective mutism);
- any limitations on the witness's vocabulary, particularly where they use a communication board or only have limited sign language (e.g. the absence of any icons on a communication board for parts of the body where the incident is alleged to involve some form of contact);
- the witness's understanding of concepts that might be important to the investigation, such as
  - sequential concepts like before, during, after, first, last, and before;
  - spatial concepts like in, on, on top of, under, above, behind, in front, and in between;
  - temporal concepts like yesterday, tomorrow, last week, and last month;
  - frequency concepts like how many, how often, and how much;
- the ability to recount a narrative in the context of a neutral event;
- the witness's drawing skills where it is thought that drawing might assist in the interview; and
- practising the ground rules for the interview (see paragraphs 2.73 and 2.74).

2.36 An indication of these various issues can often be established by engaging the witness informally in conversation (e.g. by asking the witness what they did yesterday or how often they have been to a specified location such as a wildlife park) and by asking their carers and/or any professionals who are involved with them (e.g. questions about the witness's first language, their vocabulary, and their routine). The possibility that the witness might need a supporter to be present during the assessment should always be considered, particularly where they are a young child, have a learning disability or mental health issues, or are on the autistic spectrum.

In addition to special measures, the assessment should give a *preliminary* indication of any issues that might affect the competence of the witness. 'Competence' is defined for these purposes by YJCEA s. 53 with reference to the witness's ability to understand what is said to them and respond in a way that can be understood. The implications of this definition are considered in *R v B*.[13] The purpose of this assessment is to identify broadly what the witness can do and how they might be helped with what they cannot do without leading them. While interviewers should be aware of what witnesses cannot do, their focus should always be on how communication with the witness can be maximized by focusing on what they can do. **2.37**

Where the needs assessment raises the possibility that the witness's communication might be maximized by the assistance of an intermediary, the Specialist Operations Centre of the National Crime Agency (NCA) should be contacted.[14] The NCA will endeavour to identify a registered[15] intermediary (RI) with the appropriate skills to assist the witness. **2.38**

Where the NCA is unable to find a RI who can assist the witness within the timescales set by the investigation, a decision will need to be made as to whether an interview should go ahead without the assistance of a RI or whether it can be delayed until a RI with the necessary skills is available. Reasons for going ahead without the assistance of a RI could include potential degradation or contamination of memory, potential worsening of mental health as a result of an increase in the witness's anxiety due to the delay, and safety issues. **2.39**

Where a decision is made to go ahead with an interview without a RI, some consideration could be given to finding a professional with similar training and experience as a RI who is not registered with the Ministry of Justice and briefing them about their role in the interview. Alternatively, a decision could be made to go ahead with the interview without the assistance of an intermediary. In these circumstances, it is important that the interviewers properly prepare themselves for the interview by reviewing any guidance that is readily available on communicating with witnesses from the appropriate vulnerable **2.40**

---

[13] [2010] EWCA Crim 4.

[14] The relevant contact phone number as of August 2016 was: 0845 000 5463.

[15] Registered intermediaries are professional people with training and experience in communicating with vulnerable people (e.g. speech and language therapists). They are trained to use their skills in the criminal justice system and registered by the Ministry of Justice.

group (e.g. The Advocate's Gateway toolkits at <http://www.theadvocatesgateway.org/toolkits>) and that they only go as far in the interview as is possible without leading the witness. It is better to leave a point that is difficult to clarify until a further interview can take place with a RI than to risk leading the witness. A more detailed account of the role of an intermediary can be found in Chapter 11 of this volume, 'Intermediaries', and in O'Mahony et al. (2011).[16]

(b) Consent and capacity

(i) Consent

2.41 Consent and capacity are considerations when the investigation proceeds towards an investigative interview. In these circumstances, consent refers to the witness making an informed decision about the interview product in the form of a video-recorded interview or written statement. Consent is not required for the purposes of a brief account at the point of initial contact because the necessity for an investigation, the requirement for initial action, and/or the steps to be taken in respect of potential witnesses are usually unclear at that stage (*Achieving Best Evidence*, paragraph 2.42). To say that consent must be 'informed' with reference to the interview product means that the witness should be in a position to understand what it is that the product may be used for and who might view it. An explanation of the purposes for which a video-recorded interview could be used should include the following:

- the potential that the recording will be played in court as evidence-in-chief as a means of reducing the stress on the witness by limiting how often they will be asked to repeat their account;[17]
- who else might see the recording; notably, that if the case goes to court the defence team will be served with a copy and that the defendant will see it (as would be the case with a written statement); and
- if applicable, its potential use in care proceedings and/or disciplinary proceedings.

2.42 Such an explanation often gives rise to the need for further explanations. For example, it is usually necessary to point out using appropriate language the distinction between evidence-in-chief and cross-examination[18] so as to avoid giving

---

[16] B. M. O'Mahony, K. Smith, and R. Milne, 'The Early Identification of Vulnerable Witnesses prior to an Investigative Interview' (2011) *British Journal of Forensic Practice*, 13(2), 114–23.

[17] Home Office, *Report of the Advisory Group on Video Evidence* (Home Office, 1989).

[18] Video-recorded cross-examination had been piloted at the time of writing and is still available in the pilot courts at Liverpool, Leeds, and Kingston upon Thames for child witnesses under the age of 16 and vulnerable adult witnesses (but not for children aged 16 and 17 or intimidated witnesses). A phased expansion of the scheme nationally is planned for 2017/18 following an evaluation of these pilots.

the witness the impression that they will not have to attend court. For some vulnerable witnesses, an explanation of what a court is might also be needed.

(ii) Capacity

Capacity becomes an issue when the potential witness cannot understand the **2.43** implications of what they are being asked to consent to, regardless of how well the explanation is adapted to their communication needs. The following paragraphs describe the options available where children or vulnerable adults do not have the capacity to consent to an interview.

(iii) Child witnesses and consent

All children under the age of 18 should be given the opportunity to have their **2.44** interview video-recorded so that the court can consider playing it as evidence-in-chief in accordance with the rebuttable presumption established by YJCEA s. 21, as described above. If the child does not wish to participate in a video-recorded interview, a written statement should be considered.

Children can only consent to an interview in their own right if they can under- **2.45** stand the implications of doing so (i.e. if they have capacity). If they cannot understand the purpose of a video-recorded interview as described above or that a written statement is intended to make the various parties to the proceedings aware of what they are likely to say when giving live evidence in court (usually via live television link or from behind screens in accordance with the presumptions set out in YJCEA s. 21), the consent of somebody with parental responsibility is required unless an appropriate order has been made by the Family Court or the Family Division of the High Court. As a general principle, the child's birth mother always has parental responsibility, as does his or her birth father if his name is on their birth certificate. In addition, if the child is the subject of a court order which has the effect that the local authority shares parental responsibility, then the local authority may be able to give consent. In practice, this would mean liaising with the allocated social worker (who is likely to seek legal advice) before proceeding with an interview on the basis of local authority consent to interview the child. Even where a child has the capacity to consent, parents and carers should be informed in advance of the interview other than in exceptional circumstances (e.g. where the child's parents are the suspected offenders).

(iv) Vulnerable adult witnesses and consent

Some vulnerable adult witnesses might also not have the capacity to consent, **2.46** although a lack of capacity should not be assumed and should not be confused with a communication need. The Mental Capacity Act 2005 and the Code of Practice that accompanies it establishes the principle that everybody should be assumed to have the capacity unless the contrary is established. 'Capacity' refers to the ability to make a decision at the material time. In the context of an investigative interview, it refers to a witness's ability to give informed consent to the interview product (video-recording or written statement). The idea of a lack of capacity to consent to an interview can arise in respect of *some* witnesses with learning disabilities. It is not an issue for all witnesses with learning disabilities. It could also apply to *some* witnesses with mental health issues, although consent is irrelevant if they are not fit to be interviewed in the first place.

2.47 Where a witness cannot understand the implications of consenting to an interview regardless of how well the information is presented to them, consideration should be given to taking action in their 'best interests'. Acting in a person's 'best interests' is fully described in the Mental Capacity Act 2005 s. 4, but, in essence, it means:

- taking account of the witness's views as far as they have been expressed;
- consulting anyone named by the witness as someone to be asked about their participation in an interview; and
- as far as is practical in the circumstances, consulting anyone with an interest in the witness's welfare, including family members who are still in contact with them, carers, social workers, and other professionals, as well as anyone with lasting power of attorney granted by the witness or a court-appointed deputy.

(c) Pre-interview rapport building

2.48 It is important to have a clear understanding of what rapport is when considering the process of rapport building. Tickle-Degnen and Rosenthal's theoretical framework of rapport[19] states that rapport constitutes the following three inter-related elements which are demonstrated through a range of verbal and non-verbal behaviours:

1. mutual attentiveness, which refers to a cohesiveness of shared interest and focus;
2. positivity reflecting feelings of mutual friendliness and caring; and
3. coordination, which concerns the balance and harmony between the participants.

2.49 Thus, rapport development starts at the first point of contact and rapport maintenance continues throughout the relationship, i.e. across the complete interaction with the witness. Thus, the needs assessment should also give some indication about the extent of the pre-interview rapport development phase that is needed. With some witnesses, pre-interview rapport will be fairly brief and might, for example, be confined to a brief discussion over a hot drink immediately prior to the interview. For some vulnerable witnesses, however, rapport building might

---

[19] L. Tickle-Degnen and R. Rosenthal, 'The Nature of Rapport and its Nonverbal Correlates' (1990) *Psychological Inquiry*, 1(4), 285–93.

be a rather longer process. Young children, witnesses with learning disabilities, and witnesses with autism could find being asked to communicate with someone who they do not know a particular challenge and the impact of trauma (e.g. dissociation) could be exacerbated by an increase in the witness's anxiety levels as a consequence of being expected to talk to a stranger about intimate and disturbing things. In addition, the lifestyles of some potential victims of and witnesses to child sexual exploitation are such that they may need extensive rapport building before they develop enough trust and confidence in the investigation team to participate in an investigative interview.

At this stage of the pre-interview process, consideration should be given to getting the witness used to the long responses that will be needed following open-ended questions, since the use of such questions for this purpose is not common in everyday communication. A practice interview around a neutral topic may assist some witnesses.   **2.50**

It is important to document the reason for extensive pre-interview rapport building, as well as every contact or attempted contact with the witness. Care should also be taken to avoid any suggestion of coaching or the offer of an inducement. While it may be entirely reasonable in some situations for interviewers to purchase a meal or a snack for a witness, pay their travel expenses or accommodation costs, or supply them with a mobile telephone to replace one taken from them for forensic analysis, it is essential that the decision-making process for any such expenditure is properly documented. Records relating to extensive pre-interview contact with witnesses should be regularly supervised.[20]   **2.51**

(d) Witness preparation

The guidance set out in *Achieving Best Evidence* has always said that witnesses should be prepared for the interview by explaining when and where it will take place, how long it is likely to take, and the role of the interviewers and anyone else who will be present (e.g. interpreters, intermediaries, and supporters), and by briefly describing the general structure of the interview (see paragraphs 2.234 to 2.248). The ground rules for the interview (as described below) should also be explained so that the witness only needs to be briefly reminded of them during the interview. If it is necessary to cover truth and lies (see later), it may also help if the witness is told that it is a procedural requirement in advance of the interview and that it is not intended to undermine their integrity in any way, particularly in the case of older children. Some vulnerable witnesses should also be warned in advance that they might find some of the questions that they are asked to be intrusive, notably where the witness is a victim of a sexual offence and   **2.52**

---

[20] See further R. Marchant and P. Cooper, 'Re E 2016 EWCA Civ 473: ABE Interviews and the Importance of Recording What Happens Off Camera' (2016) *Family Law* 46 (Aug), 971–5.

particularly where the interviewer has spent some time in building a relationship during extensive pre-interview rapport with a victim or survivor of child sexual exploitation.[21]

E. The Interview: Planning and Conduct

(a) Planning

2.53 As with needs assessment, the idea of planning is nothing new; it has also been around since the publication of the *Memorandum of Good Practice* in 1992 and has been included in the *Achieving Best Evidence* guidance since 2002. Regrettably, planning rarely takes place,[22] even though the statutory Code of Practice for Victims of Crime[23] states that the police must consider *Achieving Best Evidence* if they need to interview a victim and that they should plan their interviews in advance (see paragraph 1.5 on page 41 for adults, cross-referenced with paragraph 1.5 on page 73 for children in the 2015 edition of the Code).

2.54 The interview planning process[24] consists of taking account of what is known about the following:

- the witness;
- the incident or events under investigation; and
- any wider investigative material that the witness might be able to provide.

2.55 What is known about the witness refers to what has been established by the needs assessment described above. It is difficult to see how an effective interview plan can be developed in the absence of a needs assessment.

2.56 The incident or the events under investigation should usually be defined by setting realistic time parameters for them (*Achieving Best Evidence*, paragraph 2.169). For example, it is unlikely to be appropriate to start an interview at the point at which a witness got out of bed where an unknown offender is said to be responsible for an incident that did not occur until the evening on the day in question. Defining the incident or events under investigation by setting realistic time parameters for

---

[21] H. Beckett and C. Warrington, *Making Justice Work: Experiences of Criminal Justice for Children and Young People affected by Sexual Exploitation as Victims and Witnesses* (University of Bedfordshire, 2015).

[22] HMCPSi and HMIC, *Joint Inspection Report on the Experience of Young Victims and Witnesses in the Criminal Justice System* (HMCPSi, 2012); and HMCPSi and HMIC, *Achieving Best Evidence*.

[23] The requirement to plan interviews has been in the statutory Code of Practice for Victims of Crime since 2013.

[24] For a detailed account of the interview planning process, see K. Smith and R. Milne, 'Planning the Interview' in M. E. Lamb, D. J. La Rooy, L. C. Malloy, and C. Katz (eds), *Children's Testimony: A Handbook of Psychological Research and Forensic Practice* (2nd edn, Wiley-Blackwell, 2011).

them is likely to make sense to most vulnerable witnesses who have a clear idea of what it is they are going to be asked to talk about in the interview. It is also likely to make sense to the courts in as much as most of the evidence is likely to relate to the incident or the events under investigation. It should be noted that interviewers do not necessarily need to know a great deal about the detail of the incidents or events under investigation to set realistic time parameters for them. Interviewers obviously need to have some general information about the matters under investigation, but how much they need to know about the specific detail is something that varies according to the circumstances. As a general principle, the more detail interviewers know of these matters, the greater the risk of confirmation bias, particularly by poor interviewers.[25]

2.57   Wider investigative material refers to matters that might advance the investigation in some way that fall outside the time parameters that define the incident or events under investigation. Such wider investigative material could include matters such as the background to relationships that might give the investigation team a broader view of the context in which the incident or events under investigation took place. It might also include access to vehicles and premises frequented by the alleged offender, any electronic devices used by the witness or the alleged offender, anything said about the alleged offences by the witness to other people, or any lifestyle information that is likely to be relevant.

2.58   Knowledge of the witness, the incident, or the events under investigation and any wider investigative material that could be relevant should then be used to set the objectives for the interview, determine the resources needed (personnel, facilities, and equipment), and the interview structure and the techniques to be used (truth and lies if applicable, method/supplementary methods of initiating the account, any special considerations for supporting and probing the account).

(i) Objectives

2.59   It is important that objectives are set that cover the topic areas to be dealt with to give the interview a clear focus, without constraining the response of interviewers to those rare occasions on which the witness reveals something wholly unexpected during the interview.

2.60   The objectives should be relevant to the matter under investigation, as it is understood at the time, and divided into those that cover the incident or events under investigation and those that cover the wider investigative material because the distinction between incident and investigation-based topic areas should be reflected in the interview structure. Setting out the objectives in a way that clearly distinguishes the incident-related topics from the wider

---

[25] M. B. Powell, C. H. Hughes-Scholes, and S. J. Sharman, 'Skill in Interviewing Reduces Confirmation Bias' (2012) *Journal of Investigative Psychology and Offender Profiling*, 9(2), 126–34.

investigative material reflects the dual purpose of the interview: to play the recording as evidence-in-chief and to advance the investigation. These purposes are seldom entirely consistent with each other; background information that is regarded as wider investigative material can prove absolutely crucial to solving a crime or corroborating an account, or in locating an offender, but it is not usually the stuff of evidence. In addition, reporting wider investigative material often relies on a different type of memory from that used to recall an incident; reporting wider investigative material such as background or life-style information relies on semantic memory, whereas the recall of an incident utilizes episodic memory.[26] Thus, it is essential that the differences between the different kinds of objectives are taken into account during the planning phase for two reasons:

1. memory recall might become increasingly difficult for a witness if they are frequently asked to switch between episodic and semantic memory; and
2. the courts may be reluctant to permit the playing of a lengthy recording when they consider that much of the material in it is irrelevant to the proceedings (i.e. not evidence) if it cannot be edited as a result of the interview being poorly structured and the topics being muddled up.

(ii) Sequencing topic material

2.61 Consideration should always be given to the sequencing of topic material during the interview, particularly in complex cases that involve multiple suspected offenders, multiple locations, and/or multiple incidents over an extended period of time. Some thought should be given to the sequence within which the alleged offences are to be covered (e.g. chronologically or thematically based on suspected offender or location) as a means of avoiding confusion during the interview and in order to make it easier to edit the recording should the need subsequently arise. While interviewers will obviously not know exactly what the witness is going to say before the interview, they usually have some idea from an initial account that has been provided. Where the initial account is only very limited and circumstances are such that it seems likely that the free-narrative account in the interview will be complex and protracted, it may be helpful if there is an extended break between the witness's free-narrative account and the questioning phase (see paragraph 2.70 onwards) so that the topics can be defined and appropriately sequenced.

2.62 Considerations around the sequencing of topic material should also take account of the likely number of sessions and the need for breaks.

---

[26] Episodic memory refers to a witness's autobiographic memory of specific events, whereas semantic memory refers to more general factual knowledge that can be used independently of where and when it was originally acquired. See E. Tulving, *Elements of Episodic Memory* (Oxford University Press, 1983).

(iii) Resources

Personnel   As noted above, the statutory Code of Practice for Victims of Crime   **2.63**
obliges the police to ensure that investigative interviews are conducted by a 'suitably trained professional' (paragraph 1.5 on page 41 for adults, cross-referenced
with paragraph 1.5 on page 73 for children). In practice, this means that the
interviewer should be competent to interview the vulnerable witness in front of
them. In joint investigative interviews between police officers (or police staff) and
social workers from either children's or adults' social care departments, decisions
about who should lead the interview should take account of the rapport that has
been established with the witness during the pre-interview stage (*Achieving Best
Evidence*, paragraph 2.35).

An interview monitor/second interviewer may also be required, as well as a cam-   **2.64**
era operator, if the interview is going to be recorded in an interview suite. There
is no hard and fast rule about the presence of a second interviewer. It very much
depends on the witness and their circumstances, although as a general principle
it is better to have as few people in the interview room as possible.

Video-recorded interviews should always have a camera operator and, as far as   **2.65**
technically feasible, the camera should be set up in such a way as to show the
witness's head, face, and upper body clearly, because 'a good, clear picture of the
witness's face may help the court to determine what is being said and to assess
the emotional state of the witness' (*Achieving Best Evidence*, Appendix M, paragraph M.3.3). Unfortunately, concerns have been expressed for some time about
the way in which cameras are set up for video-recorded interviews[27] and it seems
likely that the reasons for this include a lack of understanding about what is
required on the part of camera operators or the absence of a camera operator contrary to the guidance set out in *Achieving Best Evidence* (see paragraph 2.194 and
Appendix M, paragraphs M.1.3 and M.2.1). Where there is no camera operator,
the interviewer is in the position of having to set up the camera themselves prior
to the interview and to switch the recording off afterwards. Needless to say, this
is not good practice, because any technical problems with the recording equipment will not be discovered until afterwards and since interviewers who are in
this position often set the camera up so that it does not focus as closely on the
witness as is recommended by *Achieving Best Evidence* in order to compensate for
the possibility that the witness might move wholly or partially off-camera during
the interview.

Consideration should also be given to the potential need for an interview sup-   **2.66**
porter in accordance with the Code of Practice for Victims of Crime (paragraph
1.5 on page 41 for adults, cross-referenced with paragraph 1.5 on page 73 for

---

[27] HMCPSi and HMIC, *Joint Inspection Report*; and HMCPSi and HMIC, *Achieving Best
Evidence*.

children). The role of an interview supporter should not be confused with the role of an appropriate adult or with the role of an intermediary. Appropriate adults have not been required for *witness* interviews since the publication of the 2003 iteration of Code C of the Codes of Practice to the Police and Criminal Evidence Act 1984 (*Achieving Best Evidence*, paragraph 2.213). Interview supporters should not also be witnesses in the case (including witnesses to first complaint) and 'must be clearly told that their role is limited to providing emotional support and that they must not prompt or speak for the witness, especially on any matters relevant to the investigation' (*Achieving Best Evidence*, paragraph 2.215). The use of parents or carers as supporters in the interview is generally discouraged because their presence in the interview can be an additional source of stress for the witness.[28]

2.67 A registered intermediary should be considered where the Witness Needs Assessment suggests it is appropriate (see this volume, Chapter 11, 'Intermediaries').

2.68 There may be occasions on which a witness will ask that their solicitor or legal adviser is present during the interview (e.g. in the event of parallel civil proceedings against a police force or a local authority). Such a request is entirely within the scope of Article 20 of the European Union Directive 2012/29 on the Rights, Support and Protection of Victims of Crime and should be recognized and accommodated as such. There is, however, currently no national guidance in respect of the role of legal advisers in interviews with witnesses. It is, therefore, necessary to come to an agreement with solicitors as to their role on a case-by-case basis in advance of the interview. In addition to which, funding for the presence of a legal adviser during a witness interview may be an issue because it is unlikely to be forthcoming from the police service and certainly cannot be guaranteed from the Legal Aid Agency.

2.69 **Facilities and equipment** The statutory Code of Practice for Victims of Crime obliges the police to 'conduct the interview, where necessary, in premises designed or adapted for that purpose' (paragraph 1.6 on page 42 for adults, cross-referenced with paragraph 1.5 on page 73 for children). *Achieving Best Evidence* makes it clear that 'preference should always be given to the use of a fixed interview suite over the use of portable equipment' (Appendix M, paragraph M1.1) as a means of minimising auditory and visual distractions, particularly where the intention is to apply to play the recording as evidence-in-chief. The interview room should be set up in a manner that is appropriate for the witness who is to be interviewed (e.g. if the witness is a child, it should be set up in a child-friendly way that is appropriate to their age group). Where portable recording equipment is to be used, the environment in which it is to be used should be assessed before the interview to ensure that any potential auditory and visual distractions can be

---

[28] Smith and Milne, 'Planning the Interview'.

minimized. Every effort should be made to ensure that any portable equipment is in working order prior to its use.

(b) Interview structure

The guidance set out in chapter 3 of *Achieving Best Evidence* recommends that   **2.70** interviews with vulnerable witnesses should proceed through the following four phases:

1. maintaining rapport and ground rules;
2. free-narrative account;
3. questioning; and
4. closing the interview.

(i) *Maintaining rapport*

Rapport at this stage in the process is about rekindling the relationship that   **2.71** should have been established during the pre-interview phase and maintaining it throughout the interview. If it is necessary to settle the witness down by talking about neutral topics, it is important to keep it as brief as possible. A lengthy discussion about irrelevant matters risks tiring the witness, particularly young children and adults with learning disabilities, and distracting the court when it is viewed. *Achieving Best Evidence* has specified since 2011 that a discussion of neutral topics at this stage should only take place *if* necessary and that, if it is necessary, any such discussion should be very *brief* (*Achieving Best Evidence*, paragraphs 3.11 and 3.13 and figure 3.1). If the pre-interview assessment suggests that more extensive rapport building is needed, it should take place before the interview, as described earlier in this chapter (*Achieving Best Evidence*, paragraph 3.12). Lengthy coverage of neutral topics during the interview risks tiring vulnerable witnesses to the point at which they may not in any event 'achieve their best evidence' by the time the interviewer gets around to asking them about the incident or events under investigation.

Preliminaries   The preliminaries consist of a statement pointing out the day,   **2.72** date, time, and place, personal introductions, and pointing out the cameras and microphones so that the viewer is clear that the witness knew the interview was being recorded. It is permissible for the interviewer to introduce the witness. Interviewers should not insist on a witness stating their full name and, as is often the case, their date of birth, particularly if they are likely to struggle to do so. Similarly, there is no need for the witness to be encouraged to state the date and time of the interview in an attempt to demonstrate their ability. It is often more expeditious for the interviewer to simply state the day, date, time, and place. It is perfectly permissible for this to be done before the witness is in the interview room if appropriate (e.g. where the witness is a very young child or a vulnerable adult with a limited concentration span). When the introductions have been completed, the interviewer should briefly state the reason for the interview 'in a way that does not refer directly to an alleged offence' (*Achieving Best Evidence*, paragraph 3.9). For example, one way of doing this could be to refer to the circumstances[29] during which the witness previously said something about the events under investigation (*Memorandum of Good Practice*, paragraph 3.7).

2.73 **Ground rules**   Paragraphs 3.14 to 3.16 of *Achieving Best Evidence* recommend that witnesses be told about the following ground rules for the interview:

- that supplying as much detail as possible is important. It may help some vulnerable witnesses, particularly young children, if the interviewer also points out that they, the interviewer, do not know what happened because they were not present at the incident or events under investigation;
- that if the interviewer asks a question that they do not understand or asks a question to which they do not know the answer, they should say so;[30]
- that if the interviewer misunderstands what they have said or incorrectly summarizes what has been said, they should point this out; and
- that the witness can ask for a break at any time.

2.74 These ground rules are important because some vulnerable witnesses may assume that the interviewer already knows what happened, but, if the interviewer has already discussed them, practised them, and emphasized their importance when preparing the witness for the interview (as recommended above), it should be possible to cover them expeditiously at this point in the interview.

2.75 The guidance in *Achieving Best Evidence* also recommends that an understanding of the concepts of truth and lies be explored with some vulnerable witnesses, notably children (under 18 years of age) and vulnerable adults 'where there is likely to be an issue as to whether they understand the value and importance of telling the truth in court'[31] (paragraph 3.24). Given that truth and lies is a procedural requirement, it is important that it is covered with appropriate witnesses during the ground rules stage, not least because a failure to do so has led to some cases being challenged in court.[32] It should, however, be remembered that coverage of truth and lies is arguably something of an anachronism, in that its origins rest in the days before the implementation of the Criminal Justice Act 1991,

---

[29] While it is permissible to refer to the *circumstances* of a previous conversation, it is *not* appropriate to refer to its *contents*, since to do so is likely to be regarded as leading.

[30] Some vulnerable witnesses will need to practise the ground rules before the interview, particularly young children and adult witnesses with a learning disability. This is especially important in respect of saying that they do not know the answer to a question and telling the interviewer that they do not understand a question.

[31] The prospect of there being an issue as to whether a witness understands the value and importance of telling the truth in court is commonly taken to refer to *some* people with learning disabilities.

[32] HMCPSi and HMIC, *Achieving Best Evidence*.

when an understanding of the truth was part of the competency requirement for certain witnesses, including children.[33] It has not been a legal requirement since the implementation of the 1991 Act (*Achieving Best Evidence*, paragraph 3.20) and is no longer a consideration when establishing competency (see YJCEA s. 53 and dicta in *R v B*.[34] Where truth and lies are covered in the interview, it is important that they are covered as expeditiously as possible, since some vulnerable witnesses have a limited attention span and lengthy coverage of truth and lies has been reported as a source of concern to the judiciary and prosecutors.[35] One way in which the coverage of truth and lies could be expedited might be to make use of the video produced by Triangle at <http://www.triangle.org.uk/resource-categories/media> (as reported in Marchant et al., 2013, and Collins and Marchant, 2014[36]). Where a vulnerable witness's communication skills are such that truth and lies cannot be covered within a reasonable period of time during the interview, consideration can be given to commissioning an expert witness to conduct an assessment afterwards if necessary (*Achieving Best Evidence*, paragraphs 3.22 and 3.26).

(ii) Free-narrative account

When planning the interview, interviewers should always consider how a free-narrative account might best be prompted. In some instances, a simple 'tell me why you're here today' will probably suffice, but interviewers who do not plan a supplementary means of prompting a free-narrative account in the event of such a prompt failing run the risk of having to hastily improvise and this could result in them unintentionally leading the witness. Alternative methods of initiating a free-narrative account include the following:

2.76

- Attempting to mentally reinstate the context of the incident or events under investigation as used in the cognitive interview.[37] It should be noted that while

---

[33] Home Office, *Memorandum of Good Practice on Video Recorded Interviews with Child Witnesses for Criminal Proceedings* (HMSO, 1992).

[34] [2010] EWCA Crim 4.

[35] HMCPSi and HMIC, *Joint Inspection Report*.

[36] R. Marchant, J. Prior, and K. Collins, 'Truth, Lies and Muddles: New Ways to Explore Children's Understanding of Truth and Lies', paper presented at the 6th Annual Conference of the Investigative Interviewing Research Group, Maastricht, the Netherlands (2013); and K. Collins and R. Marchant, 'Truth, Lies and Muddles: Best Practice for the Introductory Phase of ABE Interviews', paper presented at the Special Measures Seminar, the National Crime Agency, Ryton, England (2014).

[37] Research suggests that people sometimes find it easier to recall information if they are in the same place or context in which the memory was formed. In a practical sense, however, it is not always possible or advisable to take a witness back to the scene of a crime. As a result, one of the techniques recommended in a method of interviewing known as the 'cognitive interview' is to ask the witness to mentally reconstruct the physical and personal context of an event at the time that they witnessed it before they are asked to recall it. See R. Milne, *The Enhanced Cognitive Interview: A Step-by-Step Guide*, unpublished manuscript (2004).

this technique may be useful with witnesses with mild learning disabilities,[38] research suggests that it may not be useful for witnesses on the autistic spectrum,[39] unless an autism-friendly version is used.[40] In the first author's experience, it might also be limited where a witness is clinically depressed and finds it difficult to mentally focus on one event at a time. Sketching (e.g. a sketch plan) has also been found to help attain full recall.[41]

- Reminding the witness of the *circumstances* of a previous conversation during which they are reported to have said something about the events under investigation (particularly where reference was made to a such a conversation as a means of explaining the reason for the interview, as suggested in paragraph 2.72 above) and inviting them to comment on it. If this method is used, it is important to remember that the interviewer should not refer to the content of what is previously reported as having been said, since to do so is likely to be regarded as leading. Witnesses should also not be asked to simply repeat what was previously said, since it is hearsay that will not necessarily be admissible under the provisions of the Criminal Justice Act 2003 s. 120 (*Achieving Best Evidence*, paragraph F.3.2.4). If a witness does repeat what was said in a previous conversation in these circumstances, a follow-up question should ask them to focus on what happened rather than on what they said about it—for the same reason. It should be noted that some elderly witnesses may not be able to generate the retrieval cues needed to respond to a very open-ended prompt;[42] in these circumstances it may be necessary to refer to the wider context in which something was previously said without referring to the content.

- Asking the witness to describe their routine at the time of the incident or events under investigation (e.g. bath time, bed time).

- Asking the witness to talk about a particular place (e.g. a care setting). It may be necessary to cue the recall of some particularly vulnerable witnesses by showing them a photograph of the outside of the building and asking 'do you know that place?' followed by 'tell me about that place' if they respond to the first question affirmatively.

---

[38] R. Milne and R. Bull, 'Interviewing Children with Mild Learning Disability with the Cognitive Interview' in N. Clark and G. Stephenson (eds), *Investigative and Forensic Decision Making: Issues in Criminological Psychology* (British Psychological Society, 1996).

[39] K. L. Maras and D. M. Bowler, 'The Cognitive Interview for Eyewitnesses with Autism Spectrum Disorder' (2010) *Journal of Autism and Developmental Disorders*, 40(11), 1350–60.

[40] J. Richards and R. Milne, 'The Cognitive Interview and Its Use for People with Autism Spectrum Disorder: Can We Create an ASD Friendly Version?' in *The Wiley Handbook of Autobiographical Memory: Autism Spectrum Disorders and the Law* (John Wiley & Sons, in press).

[41] See M. L. Mattison, C. J. Dando, and T. C. Ormerod, 'Sketching to Remember: Episodic Free Recall Task Support for Child Witnesses and Victims with Autism Spectrum Disorder' (2015) *Journal of Autism and Developmental Disorders*, 45(6), 1751–65; and J. Richards, R. Milne, and C. Dando (in submission).

[42] e.g. F. I. Craik, 'Age Differences in Human Memory' in J. Birren and K. Shaie (eds), *Handbook of the Psychology of Aging* (Van Nostrand Reinhold, 1977).

- Asking the witness to talk about a particular activity (e.g. an after-school club, their access to and use of a computer).
- Asking the witness to talk about the various people in their household or in their family (it should be remembered that younger children may not have a concept of 'family').

Where a particularly vulnerable witness only provides a very limited account, **2.77** the interviewer should promote further free recall, perhaps by using some of the techniques outlined above. This is because free recall produces the most accurate information, especially from vulnerable groups, as opposed to more specific questions. Other than where the witness's communication skills are so limited that it is unavoidable, interviewers should not rush prematurely into the questioning phase of the interview and probe a very limited account, particularly with a rapid sequence of specific-closed 'where', 'what', 'when', and 'how' questions. The development of an account should be supported by means of active listening (*Achieving Best Evidence,* paragraph 3.32); drawing [43] and scaffolding[44] may also be used.

(iii) Questioning

The questioning phase consists of the following two elements: **2.78**

1. questions intended to develop and, if necessary, to clarify the witness's free-narrative account; and
2. questions about any wider investigative material that might assist the investigation.

Other than in the most simple and straightforward of cases, consideration should always be given to having a break between these two elements and then asking questions about the wider investigative material on a separate recording. Mixing the questions about the incident or events under investigation with the questions about wider investigative material runs the risk of distracting the witness. It also needlessly extends the duration of the recording that is intended to be played back at court.

Questions should be kept as short and simple as possible. They should be phrased **2.79** in the past tense, not in the present tense 'because doing so risks confusing the witness and mentally reinstating any trauma that they have experienced' (*Achieving Best Evidence,* paragraph 3.42). The use of questions containing double-negatives, negative phrasing (e.g. 'you can't remember any more, can you?'), jargon, and technical terminology should also be avoided (*Achieving Best Evidence,* paragraphs 3.56 to 3.58).

---

[43] e.g. Mattison et al., 'Sketching to Remember'.
[44] R. Marchant, 'How Young is Too Young? The Evidence of Children under Five in the English Criminal Justice System' (2013) *Child Abuse Review*, 22(6), 432–45.

2.80 Questions can be categorized in a number of different ways, depending on the purpose for which the categories are to be used. In chapter 3 of *Achieving Best Evidence*, the categories are as follows:

- open-ended questions;[45]
- specific-closed questions;
- forced-choice;
- multiple; and
- leading.

2.81 Whether a question is open-ended or specific-closed can depend on the context. In a general sense, however, open-ended questions are those often exemplified as TED questions because they begin with 'Tell me ...', 'please Explain ...' or 'Describe ...' (*Achieving Best Evidence*, paragraph 3.51). *Achieving Best Evidence* recommends that open-ended questions should be used predominantly throughout the interview because they invite the witness to give an unrestricted answer, as they minimize the 'risk that the interviewer will impose their view of what happened on the witness' (paragraph 3.50), and they produce the most accurate recall. Unfortunately, open-ended questions are often not used as frequently as they should be.[46] This is because we do not use open-ended questions very often in everyday life and thus they need to be trained and then practised.

2.82 Specific-closed questions are exemplified in paragraph 3.54 of *Achieving Best Evidence* as questions beginning with 'what', 'where', 'when', 'how', and 'why' (often referred to as '5WH questions'). Of these questions, 'who', 'what', and 'where' are usually the most easily understood.[47] Specific-closed questions can give interviewers an opportunity to control the interview by focusing the witness on specified detail and minimising irrelevant information in their responses. However, the propensity that specific-closed questions have for narrowing down the witness's response is a disadvantage when an unrestricted account is sought. Specific-closed questions should only be used to ask for information that has not been provided during the free-narrative account or elicited by means of open-ended questions, since they result in more limited and, potentially, less accurate

---

[45] Powell and Snow (2007) draw a distinction between open-ended breadth and open-ended depth questions. Open-ended breadth questions are intended to ask the witness to expand on broad activities (e.g. 'what happened next?'), whereas open-ended depth questions are used to encourage more elaborate detail on a particular point (e.g. 'please describe that tattoo in detail for me'). For a detailed account, see M. B. Powell and P. C. Snow, 'Guide to Questioning Children During the Free Narrative Phase of an Investigative Interview' (2007) *Australian Psychologist*, 42(1), 57–65.

[46] HMCPSi and HMIC, *Achieving Best Evidence*.

[47] The Advocate's Gateway, *General Principles from Research, Policy and Guidance: Planning to Question a Vulnerable Person or Someone with Communication Needs* (Advocacy Training Council, 2015).

information due to the influence of the interviewer when compared to open-ended questions.

Forced-choice and leading questions should only be used as a last resort. Where   **2.83**
it is necessary to use forced-choice questions (e.g. with a witness who can only
respond by using yes/no in some way), as was the case in *R v Watts*,[48] it is important to structure the interview in such a way as to mitigate the potential effects of
leading the witness by means of this type of question. Where a leading question
is to be used, it should be carefully framed in the least leading way possible and
followed up with an open-ended prompt or question if the witness responds to it
(*Achieving Best Evidence*, paragraph 3.67).

Multiple questions should be avoided because they can put the witness in a   **2.84**
dilemma about which part of the question to respond to and can cause the interviewer to misunderstand what part of the question the answer refers to (*Achieving
Best Evidence*, paragraph 3.64).

While the type of questions that are asked are clearly important, it is also pivotal   **2.85**
that the subject matter of the questions is both relevant and necessary. While it
is fair to say that interviewers rarely know everything that is going to be relevant
prior to the interview, interviewers should not simply ask questions about, for
example, the descriptions of premises or people, or the colour of furnishings,
simply because that is what they always do. The relevance of the question to
the incident or events under investigation should be clearly understood by the
interviewer as the witness's account unfolds. Interviewers should only clarify a
witness's account as far as it is necessary to do so. To go through a clear account
in great detail simply because that is what the interviewer always does is likely to
create confusion and repetition and to create long-winded interviews, rather than
clarifying ambiguities.[49]

Interviewers should not summarize what the witness has said in relation to every   **2.86**
topic as a matter of routine. Summaries should only be used where what the
witness has said might be thought of as ambiguous in some way (*Achieving Best
Evidence*, paragraph 3.70). The inappropriate use of summaries risks inadvertently leading the witness if they are inaccurate. They also needlessly extend the
duration of the interview and risk tiring the witness out and irritating the court.
Where summaries are used, they should make use of the words and phrases used
by the witness wherever possible (*Achieving Best Evidence*, paragraph 3.71).

Some excellent advice on the issues involved in communicating with various vul-   **2.87**
nerable groups of witnesses and the use of communication aids can be found

---

[48] [2010] EWCA Crim 1824.
[49] HMCPSi and HMIC, *Joint Inspection Report*.

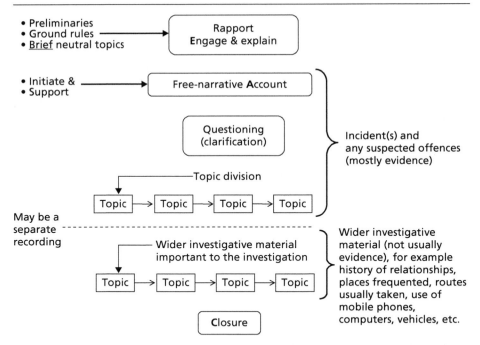

Figure 2.1 Typical interview structure (as recommended by 'Achieving Best Evidence')

in The Advocate's Gateway toolkits at: <http://www.theadvocatesgateway.org/toolkits>.

(iv) Closing the interview

2.88 *Achieving Best Evidence* recommends that interviewers should always try to make sure that the witness leaves the interview in a positive frame of mind. They should not be too distressed and should not feel that they have disappointed the interviewer, even if they have given little or no information. They should not, however, be praised or congratulated for providing information because it can be perceived as a judgmental practice in a situation in which the interviewer is supposed to have an open mind. They should be thanked for their time and effort and any questions that they may have should be addressed (paragraphs 3.88 to 3.91). Unfortunately, the closure stage of many interviews is all too brief. Interviewers do not always ensure that the witness is not distressed and it is rare for witnesses to be thanked for their contribution. Inappropriate praise and congratulations are, however, sometimes communicated to the witness.[50]

2.89 Overall, the structure of the interview should be as shown in Figure 2.1.

---

[50] HMCPSi and HMIC, *Achieving Best Evidence*.

F. Post-Interview Processes

(a) Evaluation

There are two aspects to evaluation: evaluation of the information and evaluation **2.90**
of the interviewer's performance. Evaluation of the information consists of identifying any immediate action that may be required and then considering what
the information contributes to the investigation. Evaluating the interviewer's performance with a view to improving and developing their competence has been
recommended by *Achieving Best Evidence* since it was first published in 2002,
even though feedback on performance rarely takes place in practice.[51]

(b) Interview product

Where the witness is under the age of 18 or is an adult complainant to a sexual **2.91**
offence, YJCEA ss. 21 and 22A presuppose that the best way forward is to play a
video-recorded interview as evidence-in-chief unless doing so is contrary to the
interests of justice (YJCEA s. 27(2)). In the case of other vulnerable or intimidated witnesses, the court will need to be satisfied that admitting the interview
recordings as video-recorded evidence-in-chief is likely to maximize the quality
of the witness's evidence.

The 2017 revision of *Achieving Best Evidence* recommends that video-recorded **2.92**
interviews should be supervised where it is intended to play them as evidence-
in-chief at a trial (paragraph 3.112). Specific guidance is yet to be developed to
support the supervision of interviews, but, given that its focus will be on what is
established about the matter under investigation in the context of *Achieving Best
Evidence*, it seems reasonable to suggest that it should include the following:

- the procedural elements of the process (e.g. coverage of truth and lies where
  appropriate);
- the structure of the interview (particularly coverage of incident-related topics before any wider investigative material and coverage of only one topic at a
  time); and
- adherence to the guidance in terms of questioning (notably in respect of leading questions).

Preliminary consideration could also be given to the potential relevance of the
topics that were covered in the interview by taking account of the charging decision made by the CPS and what is known about the likely defence from the
interview with the suspected offender. This could be of assistance when an early
special measures discussion takes place (as mentioned in paragraph 2.93 below).

---

[51] HMCPSi and HMIC, *Achieving Best Evidence*.

It is important to remember that some topics which were covered in good faith at the time of the interview might not be relevant by the time of the trial (e.g. where some of the suspected offenders identified in the witness's account are not charged, or where a detailed description is taken of a suspected offender who is later identified and acknowledges their involvement in the incident, but claims that the victim consented).

2.93 The supervisor reviewing the recording should have responsibility for the investigation or, in the case of a major enquiry, should be the supervisor or the interview adviser with responsibility for that part of the investigation. This supervisory review should take place prior to an early special measures discussion[52] between the investigation team and the CPS. The supervision of video-recorded interviews followed by an early special measures discussion is particularly important in complex cases such as child sexual exploitation because the accounts provided by witnesses can be lengthy and may contain some material that was gathered in good faith, but is no longer relevant by the time the case gets to trial.

2.94 An early special measures discussion that has been arranged in these circumstances should consider whether the video-recorded interviews are the best way of presenting the witness's evidence. If playing the video(s) as evidence-in-chief is considered the best way forward, consideration should then be given as to whether editing is appropriate so that the CPS can engage in a dialogue with the defence and directions can be sought from the court (ideally, at the Plea and Trial Preparation Hearing). If playing the video(s) as evidence-in-chief is not considered the best way forward, consideration should then be given as to how the witness's evidence should be presented to the court. The two options are as follows:

1. prepare a written statement after reviewing the recording and ask the witness to sign it, followed by live evidence-in-chief (via a live TV link, from behind screens, or in court without special measures); or
2. conduct a summary interview along the lines recommended in paragraph 250 of *Review of Efficiency in Criminal Proceedings* (Leveson, 2015).[53]

2.95 A Record of Video Interview (ROVI) providing an index to the interview should also be submitted with the case papers, as specified in *Achieving Best Evidence* (Appendix P).

---

[52] The practice guidance on early special measures discussions can be found in Office for Criminal Justice Reform, *Early Special Measures Discussions between the Police and the Crown Prosecution Service* (Office for Criminal Justice Reform, 2009).

[53] B. Leveson, *Review of Efficiency in Criminal Proceedings* (Judiciary of England and Wales, 2015).

(c) Post-interview witness management

Witnesses should always be aware of how they can contact the investigation team **2.96** if they need to do so and steps should be taken to keep them safe and to minimize the risk of intimidation where it is a concern. Witnesses who are victims should be updated on the progress of the investigation, including when suspected offenders are arrested, charged, or bailed as required by the Code of Practice for Victims of Crime. Consideration should also be given to briefing victims and their families before any media release and when the investigation is aware in advance of a media broadcast/publication relating to the investigation.

The nature and the amount of contact between the investigation team and the **2.97** witness depends on the circumstances. Care should always be taken to avoid any suggestion of coaching witnesses or offering them any inducements. All contact with witnesses and any unsuccessful attempts to contact them should be properly recorded. Where the investigation team is engaged in extensive contact with a witness, it is important that they are regularly debriefed and that an exit strategy is in place.

G. Summary

A vulnerable witness interview strategy consists of the following broad elements: **2.98**

- initial contact;
- pre-interview processes;
- the interview; and
- post-interview processes.

While circumstances may be such that some aspects of initial contact might not **2.99** be necessary, particularly where a witness has come forward and made themselves known to the investigation, pre-interview processes, interview planning, and post-interview processes should always be considered.

Further Reading

The Advocate's Gateway, 'Toolkits', available at <http://www.theadvocatesgateway.org/toolkits> accessed 13 March 2017.

CPS, *Guidelines on Prosecuting Cases of Child Sexual Abuse*, available at <http://www.cps.gov.uk/legal/a_to_c/child_sexual_abuse/> accessed 13 March 2017.

Ministry of Justice, *Achieving Best Evidence in Criminal Proceedings: Guidance on Interviewing Victims and Witnesses, and Guidance on using Special Measures* (MoJ, 2017).

Ministry of Justice, 'Code of Practice for Victims of Crime' (MoJ, 2015), available at <https://www.gov.uk/government/uploads/system/uploads/attachment_data/file/476900/code-of-practice-for-victims-of-crime.PDF> accessed 13 March 2017.

3

WITNESS SUPPORT

Jessica Jacobson and Linda Harlow

A. Introduction

The past three decades have seen a great expansion in the statutory and non-statutory support made available to witnesses over the course of the prosecution process. There are a number of dimensions to this support: **3.01**

- Provision for all witnesses that is primarily aimed at ensuring they are kept informed about the criminal investigation and court proceedings, and that they attend court to give evidence if and when required. Some measures only apply to prosecution rather than defence witnesses, while others apply equally to both groups.

- Specific provision for those witnesses—both prosecution and defence—deemed 'vulnerable' or 'intimidated'. The impetus for such support is the need to prevent cases being stalled or halted by witnesses' inability to give evidence; to protect the welfare of those giving evidence; and to ensure that the vulnerable and intimidated have access to justice as does everyone else.
- Provision for 'victims', including complainants and those who are not necessarily witnesses, but are, for example, bereaved family members of homicide victims. Provision for victims extends beyond the prosecution process, and has emerged in the context of a broad movement for 'victims' rights' which, since the mid twentieth century, has made the case for a greater focus on victims' needs and welfare across the criminal justice system.

3.02 What can be broadly described as 'support for witnesses' therefore comprises a complicated patchwork of provision targeting a variety of overlapping groups by a variety of means. The aim of this chapter is to provide an overview of this wide-ranging and diverse provision with reference to, first, its policy framework; second,

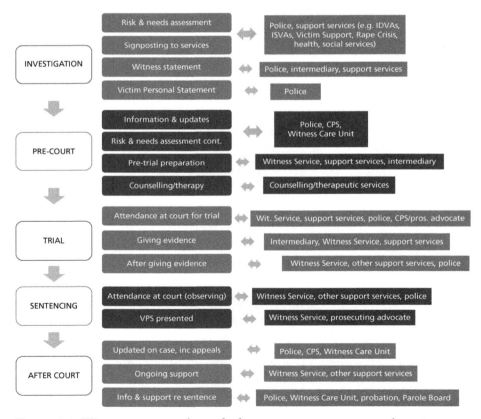

Figure 3.1 Witness journey through the prosecution process and services engaged in witness liaison and support

the services which deliver it; and, third, the key stages of the 'witness journey' at which it comes into play. The final part of the chapter will be a reflection on the adequacy of current witness provision, to include consideration of difficulties and shortcomings in the implementation of the standards set out in policy. This section will also include a short series of case studies illustrating some of the good practice and challenges associated with the provision of witness support.

As the starting point of this discussion, Figure 3.1 depicts the 'witness journey' in **3.03** a simplified form, from the perspective of a prosecution witness. The figure shows the range of services that potentially liaise with the witness as the case proceeds from investigation to trial through to sentencing. In cases with other outcomes— where, for example, sentencing follows a guilty plea, or the defendant is acquitted at trial, or charges are withdrawn prior to trial—certain but not all of these elements of the 'journey' will be relevant in differing combinations.

While Figure 3.1 shows provision for prosecution witnesses, this chapter will **3.04** include—in the detailed discussion of the witness journey, below—specific consideration of provision for defence witnesses.

B. The Policy Framework

The policy framework for witness provision has been established through **3.05** national legislation and various forms of non-statutory guidance; some elements of international law are also relevant. Key components of the policy framework are outlined below.

(a) United Nations Convention on the Rights of the Child

The United Nations Convention on the Rights of the Child[1] is a human rights **3.06** treaty setting out the civil, political, economic, social, health, and cultural rights of children. The Convention defines a child as any human being under the age of 18, unless the age of majority is attained earlier under a state's own domestic legislation. It emphasizes the need for adults and organizations, when making decisions that affect children, to consider the best interests and views of the child.

Articles of the UNCRC which have a specific bearing on the justice system **3.07** include Article 3.1, which states: 'In all actions concerning children, whether undertaken by public or private social welfare institutions, courts of law, administrative authorities or legislative bodies, the best interests of the child shall be the primary consideration.' Under Article 12.2, a child has the right 'to be heard',

---

[1] UN Convention on the Rights of the Child (adopted 20 November 1989, entered into force 2 September 1990).

directly or through an appropriate representative, 'in any judicial and administrative proceedings affecting the child'.

(b) Directive on victims of crime

3.08 The European Union Directive on crime victims establishes minimum standards with regard to rights, support, and protection of victims.[2] This is intended to ensure that individuals who have fallen victim to crime are recognized, treated with respect, and receive proper protection, support, and access to justice. It places an emphasis on the rights of victims and their family members to information, support, and protection, and on victims' procedural rights in criminal proceedings.

3.09 EU Member States were required to incorporate the provisions of the Directive within their national laws by 16 November 2015. In England and Wales, the Code of Practice for Victims of Crime (commonly known as the Victims' Code) is the primary means by which the Directive is implemented (see below). The Code was expanded in October 2015 to comply with the Directive.[3]

(c) Youth Justice and Criminal Evidence Act 1999

3.10 In England and Wales, the most significant legislative development aimed at supporting witnesses at court was the passing of the Youth Justice and Criminal Evidence Act 1999. Sections 19 to 30 of the Act introduced 'special measures' for *vulnerable* and *intimidated* (prosecution and defence) witnesses to improve the quality of the evidence they are able to provide, in terms of its completeness, coherence, and accuracy, and to relieve some of the stresses associated with giving evidence. Vulnerable witnesses are defined in the Act as all those under the age of 18 and those whose quality of evidence is likely to be impacted by a mental disorder, physical disability, or 'significant impairment of intelligence and social function'. Intimidated witnesses are those whose quality of evidence is likely to be impacted by fear or distress—including fear relating to potential intimidation by the accused.

3.11 'Special measures' allow for a number of adaptations to the normal court process (see further Chapter 10, 'Special Measures'). In summary, the main provisions are for:

- the giving of evidence from behind a screen in the courtroom or from outside the courtroom via live video link;

---

[2] Establishing Minimum Standards on the Rights, Support and Protection of Victims of Crime, Directive 2012/29/EU of the European Parliament and of the Council of Europe.

[3] Ministry of Justice, 'Code of Practice for Victims of Crime' (MoJ, 2015) (hereafter Victims' Code).

- the giving of evidence in private;
- admission of a video-recorded statement as evidence-in-chief and of pre-recorded cross-examination;
- removal of wigs and gowns;
- assistance of an intermediary; and
- communication aids.

(d) Safeguarding provisions

Under a range of legislative provisions—particularly those contained in the **3.12** Children Acts of 1989 and 2004 and the Care Act 2014—all organizations have legal obligations with regard to the safeguarding of children and vulnerable adults with whom they work. Safeguarding encompasses protection from abuse, neglect, and other maltreatment, and promotion of welfare. The criminal courts, like other agencies and service providers, have safeguarding responsibilities towards children and vulnerable adults who appear before them as witnesses or in other capacities.

(e) Code of Practice for Victims of Crime (Victims' Code)

The statutory Code of Practice for Victims of Crime was initially produced by **3.13** the Secretary of State for Justice in 2005, under s. 32 of the Domestic Violence, Crime and Victims Act 2004. A revised and expanded version was issued in October 2015.

The Victims' Code applies to all criminal justice agencies, including the police, **3.14** the Crown Prosecution Service (CPS), courts, and probation, and sets out the services that must be provided to victims by these agencies. For the purposes of the Code, 'victims' are defined as those who have suffered harm caused by a criminal offence, and the close relatives of people who have died as a result of a criminal offence.

A full and detailed list of victims' entitlements under the Code can be found in **3.15** its first three chapters. Key entitlements include:

- written acknowledgement that a crime has been reported;
- an enhanced service if the victim has suffered a serious crime, has been persistently targeted, or is vulnerable or intimidated;
- a needs assessment and referral to support services;
- the opportunity to make a Victim Personal Statement (VPS) to explain the impact of the crime, and to read the VPS aloud or to have it read, subject to the views of the court, if a defendant is found guilty;
- information about the police investigation, including whether a suspect has been arrested and charged and any bail conditions imposed;

- a review of the police's or CPS's decision not to prosecute a suspect in accordance with the police[4] and CPS Victims' Right to Review[5] schemes;
- information on the time, date, and location of any court hearings;
- if the victim is required to give evidence, prompt information about this and what to expect, a full needs assessment by the Witness Care Unit/police officer, and a pre-trial visit prior to giving evidence; and
- information on case outcomes, including any sentence passed, and any appeal.

(f) The Prosecutors' Pledge and 'Speaking to Witnesses at Court'

3.16 A ten-point Prosecutors' Pledge was introduced by the Attorney General in 2005.[6] This describes the level of service that victims and victims' family members can expect from the CPS and advocates instructed by the CPS. The pledge includes, for example, a commitment (where practical) to seek the victim's or family's view when considering a plea; to 'protect victims from unwarranted or unnecessary attacks on their character' during cross-examination; and to apply for appropriate compensation, restitution, or protection of the victim following a conviction. The prosecutor is obliged to introduce him or herself to the victim at court and answer any questions.

3.17 A more recent development has been the production of CPS guidance on 'Speaking to Witnesses at Court'.[7] This sets out the role that prosecutors should play before and at court to help witnesses to give their best evidence. It states that prosecutors should meet witnesses in advance or on the day of their court appearance, and that this is particularly important for those who are vulnerable and/or intimidated, for all of whom a 'pre-trial special measures meeting' should be considered. Following a pilot carried out by teams of CPS paralegal staff in a small number of Crown Courts in 2016, this guidance has now been rolled out nationally.

(g) Witness Charter

3.18 Another significant policy development was the publication of the Witness Charter in 2007; it was thereafter revised in 2013.[8] This sets out the standards of care and levels of service that all witnesses can expect to receive over the course of the criminal justice process from the police, the CPS, Her Majesty's Court

---

[4] Association of Chief Police Officers, *National Policing Guidelines on Police Victim Right to Review* (ACPO, 2015).

[5] CPS, 'Victims' Right to Review Scheme', available at <http://www.cps.gov.uk/victims_witnesses/victims_right_to_review/> accessed 13 March 2017.

[6] CPS, 'The Prosecutors' Pledge', available at <https://www.cps.gov.uk/publications/prosecution/prosecutor_pledge.html> accessed 19 July 2016.

[7] CPS, *Speaking to Witnesses at Court: CPS Guidance* (CPS, 2016).

[8] Ministry of Justice, *The Witness Charter: Standards of Care for Witnesses in the Criminal Justice System* (MoJ, 2013).

& Tribunals Service (HMCTS), the Witness Service, and defence lawyers. The Charter applies to both prosecution and defence witnesses, specified in its Introduction as 'all witnesses of a crime and ... character witnesses but not expert witnesses'.

Unlike the Victims' Code, the Witness Charter does not impose legal require- **3.19** ments on agencies to meet the specified standards; however, all agencies covered by the Charter are expected to comply wherever possible. The Witness Charter makes it clear that if a witness is also a victim of crime, the victim has legal entitlements under the Victims' Code.

The Witness Charter sets out the standards of service that can be expected by all **3.20** witnesses, including, for example: treatment with dignity and respect by service providers; provision of a main point of contact who will provide information on case progression; information on the court and court process in advance of giving evidence; the opportunity to view one's police statement prior to giving evidence; and the opportunity to claim expenses for travel to court and compensation for loss of earnings.

The Witness Charter also includes standards relating to assessment of a wit- **3.21** ness's needs, and the identification of and application for any help required—including special measures—to enable a vulnerable or intimidated witness to give evidence.

C. Services for Witnesses

Figure 3.1 demonstrates that a wide range of services potentially liaise with and **3.22** provide support to witnesses (or particular sub-groups of witnesses) as a case progresses through the criminal justice process. These services encompass the main statutory criminal justice agencies such as the police, the CPS, courts, and probation; prosecution and defence lawyers; statutory and non-statutory providers of specialist witness services; and non-criminal justice agencies and services such as health providers and social services.

The roles and remit of services with a dedicated or substantial focus on witnesses **3.23** are briefly described below.

(a) Witness Care Units

Witness Care Units were established in 2005 in the wake of the government's **3.24** 'No Witness, No Justice' initiative, which sought to improve care for victims and witnesses and improve levels of witness attendance at court. The units liaise between the police, the CPS, and victims and witnesses. Dedicated witness care officers (or named police witness liaison officers) guide witnesses through the witness journey, carry out needs assessments for witnesses with particular support needs, inform victims and witnesses of case progression and outcomes, and coordinate support and refer witnesses to other support services. While originally staffed jointly by the police and the CPS, most are currently staffed only by police personnel.

(b) The Witness Service

3.25 The Witness Service operates in all magistrates' and Crown Courts in England and Wales. It is the main provider of support to witnesses attending court to give evidence, and assists both prosecution and defence witnesses through a network of volunteers. The assistance includes the hosting of pre-trial visits, which enable witnesses to see a courtroom prior to the trial; the provision of quiet places for witnesses to wait before giving evidence; and accompaniment to the courtroom.

3.26 In April 2015, Citizens Advice took over responsibility for running the national Witness Service from Victim Support. Citizens Advice established a centralized system for handling referrals, assessments, and the booking of pre-trial visits in May 2016. Under the new system, vulnerable or intimidated witnesses may choose to opt into an enhanced 'outreach' service, to include pre-trial and post-trial support at home.

3.27 The Witness Service staff and volunteers should work with their respective court's 'witness liaison officer'—a named member of court staff with responsibility for ensuring witnesses receive consistent and appropriate care, including help to prepare for the trial.

(c) Intermediaries

3.28 Intermediaries work in the criminal justice system to facilitate vulnerable witnesses' communication with the police and courts, and thereby to help them to give evidence. Intermediaries must have specialist knowledge of language and communication needs. Their role and work in supporting vulnerable witnesses at court is discussed fully in Chapter 11, 'Intermediaries'.

(d) 'Witness supporters'

3.29 'Witness supporter' is a generic term, and can be used to refer to anyone who provides emotional support to a witness at court, including family and friends, as well as volunteers and professionals. The court has the discretion to decide whether a particular individual can sit with a witness for the purpose of providing support while he or she is giving evidence. Witness supporters may also assist witnesses prior to court by, for example, liaising with relevant services and communicating preferences on special measures.

(e) Specialist victim services

Many different statutory and non-statutory bodies provide specialist services to **3.30** victims. These include the CPS and probation; voluntary organizations such as Victim Support; and independent advisers working in statutory or voluntary settings with victims of sexual or domestic violence. While these services tend to engage with victims generally rather than specifically with those who are acting as witnesses, most do at least some work with victim-witnesses.

(i) CPS Victim Liaison Units

Victim Liaison Units were set up by the CPS in 2013–14, to improve compli- **3.31** ance with the Victims' Code and as a dedicated point of contact for victims after a case has been finalized. Victim Liaison Units are responsible for informing victims about a CPS decision to stop or significantly alter the charges faced by a suspect. If the decision is made at court and the victim is present, the prosecutor is expected to explain the outcome; otherwise, the decision should be communicated by the Victim Liaison Unit in writing.

(ii) National Probation Service Victim Contact Scheme

Also known as the Victim Liaison Service, the Victim Contact Scheme run by **3.32** the National Probation Service supports victims of specified violent or sexual offences where the offender has been sentenced to at least 12 months' custody. Victims who opt into the scheme are provided with information by an assigned Victim Liaison Officer about the offender's prison sentence, release, and any Parole Board hearings, and advice on making a statement at parole hearings.

(iii) Victim Support

Victim Support is an independent charity which aims to help people recover from **3.33** the effects of crime. It offers practical and emotional support to victims, whether or not they have reported the crime to the police, and provides information on the criminal justice process for victims who are attending court as witnesses. Victim Support runs a national Homicide Service supporting those who have been bereaved by murder and manslaughter.

(iv) Independent Sexual Violence Advisers (ISVAs) and Child ISVAs

An ISVA is a trained specialist who provides support and advice to survivors of **3.34** rape, sexual abuse, and sexual assault and, for those who choose to report the offence, helps to engage with the criminal justice system. ISVAs can provide support at police interviews and may attend court with the witness.

Child ISVAs provide advice and support to both girls and boys, under the age **3.35** of 18, who are or have been victims of sexual abuse or child sexual exploitation. Child ISVAs can liaise with school or college to ensure support is available and with other agencies to obtain counselling. They may also help parents/carers to support the child. Like other ISVAs, child ISVAs can attend police interviews and court hearings.

(v) Independent Domestic Violence Advisers (IDVAs)

3.36 IDVAs specialize in providing support and advocacy for those affected by domestic abuse. Their main role is to address the safety of victims at high risk of harm and their children—for example, by conducting risk assessments and safety planning, and providing information and assistance in relation to available sanctions and remedies through the criminal and civil courts. IDVAs may attend police stations and court with domestic abuse victims who are giving evidence against perpetrators.

(vi) Victims' Information Service

3.37 The Victims' Information Service was set up by the government as part of a broader set of commitments to support victims of crime. Its website[9] provides information on the criminal justice process and links to local support teams, and it also runs a telephone helpline.

D. The Witness Journey

3.38 This discussion of the witness journey will follow the structure depicted in Figure 3.1, which shows a case proceeding from investigation to trial to sentencing. Provision for prosecution witnesses at each stage of the process is described below; specific provision for defence witnesses is also discussed.

(a) Investigation

3.39 The police have a general duty to investigate reports of criminal behaviour.[10] An investigation may lead to the arrest of an individual who is suspected of having committed the offence, and the taking of statements from any witnesses. Assessment of risks and needs in relation to any witnesses should be undertaken from the initial stages of any investigation, along with signposting or referral to relevant services.

---

[9] See <https://www.victimsinformationservice.org.uk> accessed 13 March 2017.

[10] As to the police owing no general duty under the common law of negligence to individual members of the public, see: *Brooks v Commissioner of Police for the Metropolis and Others* [2005] UKHL 24; *Hertfordshire Police v Van Colle* [2008] UKHL 50; and *Michael v Chief Constable of South Wales* [2015] UKSC 2. However, in relation to a police duty where the allegation amounts to a violation of Article 2 (right to life) or Article 3 (right to be free from torture or inhuman or degrading treatment or punishment), see *Michael v Chief Constable of South Wales* and also *The Commissioner of Police of the Metropolis v DSD and NBV and Others* [2015] EWCA Civ 646.

(i) Risk and needs assessment

Responsibility for conducting risk and needs assessments Responsibility for **3.40** assessing risks and needs lies with the range of statutory and non-statutory agencies—within and outside the criminal justice system—over the course of their dealings with a witness. Such agencies might include, for example, the police, the Witness Care Unit, health and social services, the Witness Service, and an IDVA or ISVA.

For the police, a process of assessment should begin when the crime is notified **3.41** to them, and continue throughout the investigation.[11] Other agencies involved in providing direct support to the vulnerable or intimidated will usually undertake an assessment at the point of referral to the service and/or before making home visits; the purpose of such an assessment is to safeguard the supporter, as well as to identify risks to the witness and his or her needs.

The primary objective of a risk assessment is to determine if an individual may **3.42** be in danger or at risk of harm from another individual or at risk of harm to themselves; and, if so, to develop a safeguarding plan to address the identified risks. The police and specialists working in domestic abuse have a standard risk assessment checklist aimed at identifying degrees of risk so that the most serious cases can be referred to a local Multi Agency Risk Assessment Conference (MARAC), which aims to safeguard domestic abuse victims and their children.

Assessment of a witness's needs by the police and other agencies should identify **3.43** any language and communication needs, mental health problems, learning disabilities, and any other factors that may impact on the witness's welfare at each stage of the witness journey, and upon his or her ability to give evidence. If a witness has been identified as vulnerable and is expected to give evidence, the police and/or Witness Care Unit should ask the CPS to submit a special measures application.

Safeguarding Safeguarding entails taking measures to protect and promote the **3.44** health, well-being, and human rights of children and vulnerable adults in order that they can live free from abuse, harm, and neglect.[12]

The main responsibility for the welfare of children and vulnerable adults usu- **3.45** ally lies with agencies such as social, health, and educational services. However, all service providers and voluntary organizations must take responsibility for

---

[11] See, e.g., the College of Policing Authorised Professional Practice on 'Working with Victims and Witnesses', available at <https://www.app.college.police.uk/app-content/investigations/victims-and-witnesses/#significant-witness> accessed 13 March 2017.
[12] See, e.g., HM Government's statutory guidance, *Working Together to Safeguard Children: A Guide to Inter-Agency Working to Safeguard and Promote the Welfare of Children* (HM Government, 2015).

safeguarding children and vulnerable adults in the course of their contact with witnesses. Safeguarding concerns may arise in the course of initial risk and needs assessment, or also as a result of something seen or heard when supporting a witness before, during, or after the trial.

3.46 Care must be taken to ensure that personal and confidential information, pursuant to obligations under the Data Protection Act 1988, is only shared with appropriate agencies where consent has been provided for this. However, in cases of imminent risk of serious harm, information may be shared without consent in order to protect the safety and welfare of the vulnerable child or adult.[13] Safeguarding should be the primary concern and information should be shared with relevant parties in order to develop a plan to safeguard a witness through the witness journey.

(ii) Signposting to support services

3.47 Following an initial assessment of risks and needs, the police should provide a witness with information on how to access, or should make referrals to, relevant local support services—including, for example, specialists in domestic or sexual abuse.

3.48 If the witness is required to attend court, the police and/or Witness Care Unit should explain how support from the Witness Service can be accessed. The witness should also be directed towards the Witness Charter and, if he or she is a victim of the crime under investigation, the Victims' Code.

(iii) Witness statement

3.49 A witness statement is the witness's direct account to the police of what he or she saw or experienced. The statement, which can be in written or video-recorded form, may be used as evidence in court if the case goes to trial.

3.50 Provisions and relevant procedures in relation to the taking of statements from vulnerable witnesses are covered in detail in Chapter 2, 'Vulnerable Witnesses: The Investigation Stage'. In brief: where a witness has communication needs, the police may request that an intermediary attend the interview to facilitate the taking of the statement. The video-recorded statement of a witness who is vulnerable or intimidated (known as the ABE interview) can be shown in court as the witness's evidence-in-chief to reduce any stress or trauma associated with court attendance; however, the making of a video statement does not preclude the witness choosing to give live evidence at court, subject, where necessary, to the court's agreement or direction.

---

[13] See, e.g., HM Government's guidance, *Information Sharing Advice for Practitioners Providing Safeguarding Services to Children, Young People, Parents and Carers* (HM Government, 2015).

(iv)   Victim Personal Statement

Victim Personal Statements (VPSs) were introduced in England and Wales in **3.51**
2001, following the introduction of Victim Impact Statements in the 1970s and
1980s in a number of other common law jurisdictions such as the United States,
Canada, and New Zealand.

Any victim who has reported a crime to the police, and a bereaved relative of a **3.52**
person who has died through a criminal act, can make a VPS. It provides a means
by which victims can express how they have been impacted (physically, emotionally, or in any other way) by the offence. The content of a statement cannot be
cited as evidence in a trial, but it can be read aloud by the victim (or on behalf of
the victim) or referred to by the judge at the sentencing hearing. (See below for
further discussion of the VPS at sentencing.)

All victims should be given the opportunity to make a VPS when making their **3.53**
witness statement to the police, and should also be permitted to make a statement
or add to their original statement at a later stage in the prosecution process if they
wish. While the police almost always take the VPS, other agencies can do so if
they are appropriately trained.

Parents or carers of children, and of those unable to make their own VPS due **3.54**
to mental impairment or learning difficulties, may make a VPS on behalf of the
vulnerable victim.

(v)   Support for defence witnesses at the investigation stage

At the investigation stage of a prosecution, potential defence witnesses may be **3.55**
asked to make a statement to the defence lawyer and, in certain circumstances,
the police may also ask for a statement. If this is necessary to help a vulnerable
defence witness make a statement, the defence lawyer may seek to arrange for the
attendance of an intermediary when the witness is interviewed.

Throughout the prosecution process, defence witnesses should be kept informed **3.56**
of the progression of the case by the defence lawyer. Under the Witness Charter,
defence witnesses have the same rights to information and services—including,
where appropriate, to special measures—as prosecution witnesses.

(b)   Pre-court

If the police investigation into a reported crime results in a criminal charge, the **3.57**
case will proceed to court. Where the defendant pleads guilty, any witnesses
should be provided with help to prepare for giving evidence over the period—
which may be weeks, months, or even years—leading up to the trial. In cases
in which there is a guilty plea, witnesses are entitled to information about any
hearings that are scheduled, including for sentence; and those who are vulnerable
and/or the victims of the crime may require continuing support.

(i) Information and updates

3.58 The police and/or Witness Care Unit should provide witnesses with information and updates about the progression of the case on an ongoing basis, including the timetabling of any trial and the date on which they are required to attend court to give evidence as soon as this has been arranged (see further Chapter 9, 'Case Management').

3.59 Under the CPS Right to Review Scheme, the CPS Victim Liaison Unit should notify any victim where the criminal charges have been stopped or significantly amended, and the victim can request further information and a review of this prosecution decision.

3.60 Under the Victims' Code, victims are entitled to receive updates and information from the police about hearing dates and outcomes within five working days. For victims defined as vulnerable, information must be shared within one working day of the police's receipt of the information from the court.

(ii) Continuing risk and needs assessment

3.61 Throughout the pre-court period, risk and needs assessments should be updated where necessary by relevant service providers if there are any changes to the circumstances of a witness. Safeguarding plans should be reviewed accordingly, and consideration given to a request for special measures if this was not already dealt with.

3.62 If a witness is identified as vulnerable or intimidated or as having particular support needs, the Witness Care Unit should, at the pre-court stage, conduct a full needs assessment and make referrals to the Witness Service or other specialist support organizations.

3.63 The Witness Service and other services should liaise on an ongoing basis in relation to evolving witness needs—including, for example, in relation to medical conditions and any potential need to access post-trial trauma support.

(iii) Pre-trial preparation

3.64 There are various aspects to a witness's preparation for trial. These may include a pre-trial case conference, pre-trial visit, and identification of a witness supporter. The process of pre-trial preparation may include a ground rules hearing (see further Chapter 12, 'Ground Rules Hearings'), at which the judge sets the parameters for fair treatment of and communication with a vulnerable witness in the trial. Witnesses themselves do not attend the ground rules hearings.

3.65 **Pre-trial case conference** Some serious cases, such as where there are allegations of child sexual exploitation and grooming, historical sexual assault, and human trafficking, often involve highly vulnerable witnesses who may present with multiple and complex needs. Additionally, some of these cases generate high levels of media interest. They are likely to require a particular and individualized approach.

In such cases, a multi-agency case conference may be arranged as part of pre-   **3.66**
trial preparation. The meeting—which does not touch on the evidence to be heard at trial—is usually held at the court, and may be as much as six months in advance of the trial date, depending on availability of participants and the level of witnesses' needs. Attendees may include representatives of the police, the CPS, the Witness Service, and court staff (including the court witness liaison officer, the case progression officer/list officer, the press officer, and court security).

The primary objective of a case conference is to share relevant information with   **3.67**
all parties to effect a smooth trial and to ensure the safeguarding of witnesses. Specific topics covered may include agreement of safety and security arrangements (including witnesses' use of a special entrance to the court), management of the public gallery and press seats, timeliness of special measures applications, scheduling of pre-trial visits for witnesses, and HMCTS's obligations to support court users with disabilities or impairments.

In cases involving a homicide, the Independent Police Complaints Commission   **3.68**
(IPCC) may join the case conference, as well as agencies working closely with bereaved families—for example, Inquest,[14] Victim Support's Homicide Service, and the family solicitor.

Pre-trial visit   Any witness who wants one can request a pre-trial visit (PTV).   **3.69**
PTVs are arranged and hosted by the Witness Service in all courts. They should provide an opportunity for:

- the witness to meet and establish a bond with a supporter from the Witness Service;
- the witness to see the court layout and/or the video-link room, and to be informed about the court process and personnel;
- the witness to practise using the live-link room, ideally with assistance from the clerk or usher who is likely to be present at the trial;
- agreement with any intermediary who has been appointed (who should attend the visit, where possible) about methods of communication with the witness;
- updating of the risk and needs assessment;
- an application for the witness's use of a special entrance to the court; and
- agreement on how the witness will be supported at trial, and by whom, especially if there are a number of different agencies engaged with the witness.

Some vulnerable witnesses, including children or those with learning disabili-   **3.70**
ties, may be offered more than one PTV to reduce the risk that they will feel

---

[14] Inquest is a charity that offers support to families bereaved by a death in custody.

overwhelmed on the day of trial. Where possible, they should be shown the courtroom in which the trial will take place (particularly if they have a preference for giving evidence in the court rather than from a link room). It may also be beneficial and much more informative for a witness to view part of a trial in action during a PTV, and not just an empty courtroom. The Criminal Practice Direction emphasizes the necessity for a witness to see screens in place and 'practise speaking using a live link' in order to express 'an informed view'.[15]

3.71 During a PTV, it is possible that a need for a particular special measure is identified for the first time, in which case the CPS should be informed of this in order that an application can be made.[16] Moreover, a PTV may help a vulnerable witness to think about whether a proposed special measure is the right one for them. For example, there is often an assumption that children, young people, or complainants in sexual offence cases prefer to be cross-examined in the live-link room, but some of these witnesses opt instead to give evidence from behind a screen once they have visited the courtroom.[17] The very fact of being party to the decision about how to give evidence can help witnesses to gain some sense of control over a situation that they may otherwise feel is entirely out of their control. (See further Chapter 10, 'Special Measures'.)

3.72 Where a case is transferred from one court to another at a late stage (which could be for any of a number of reasons), consideration should be given to the potential impact on a vulnerable witness who is anxious about the court appearance. If a PTV was held at the original court, and arrangements relating to safety and security have been agreed, the implications of the change in venue should be carefully reviewed.

3.73 **Identifying an appropriate 'witness supporter'**   Where a vulnerable or intimidated witness is deemed to require a supporter, the views of the witness him- or herself should be taken into account in the decision as to who should play this role and the court must have regard to the witness's wishes.[18] If multiple agencies are involved, they should work together to avoid duplication or inconsistencies in support provided, to ensure clarity over roles and responsibilities over the course of the trial, and to ensure the integrity of the evidence. The Criminal Practice Directions state:

---

[15] Crim PD (2015) V18B.4.

[16] In line with the procedure set out at Crim PR 18.

[17] If the witness is a child, the 'primary rule' set out at YJCEA 1999 s. 21(3) requires the court to make a special measures direction providing for any ABE recording to be admitted as evidence-in-chief and for any other evidence given by the child to be given by means of a live link. This rule can only be disapplied if the child requests that the rule should not apply and to the extent that the court is satisfied—taking account of the witness's age, maturity, understanding, and the circumstances of the offence—that not applying the primary rule would not diminish the quality of the witness's evidence.

[18] Crim PD V18B.1.

It is preferable for the direction to be made well before the trial begins and to ensure that the designated person is available on the day of the witness's testimony so as to provide certainty for the witness.[19]

In identifying the appropriate supporter(s), consideration should be given to: **3.74**

- the witness's preference as to the supporter's gender, especially in cases involving sexual offences or domestic abuse;
- availability and continuity of support, where the witness is expected to give evidence over several days—in which case there may be a need to assign two supporters to one witness;
- ensuring the integrity of evidence in complex cases with multiple witnesses—in such a scenario, no supporter should give one-to-one help to more than one witness;
- the potential for an ISVA or IDVA, who may already be working with the witness, to provide support during as well as after the trial; and
- the need for clarity on roles and responsibilities of different service providers during each stage of the witness journey.

Where a family member or friend is available to act as a supporter, the court has the discretion to decide whether this is appropriate and would serve the witness's best interests.

(iv)   Counselling/therapy

Counselling or therapy may assist a vulnerable witness to cope better with the   **3.75** trial process. The Victims' Code states that vulnerable victims (including those who are adults, and children and young people) should be informed by the police or other service provider 'that pre-trial therapy is available if needed, and, if requested, will be facilitated'.[20]

Joint guidance produced by the CPS, the Department of Health, and the Home   **3.76** Office deals specifically with the provision of therapy for child witnesses in advance of a trial.[21] The Foreword to the guidance stresses that 'the best interests of the child are paramount when deciding whether, and in what form, therapeutic help is given'. Key considerations set out in the guidance include:

- It should be understood that those involved in the prosecution of an alleged abuser have no authority to prevent a child from receiving therapy.
- The police and the CPS should be made aware that therapy is proposed, is being undertaken, or has been undertaken.

---

[19] ibid.
[20] Victims' Code, 41, 73.
[21] CPS, 'Provision of Therapy for Child Witnesses Prior to a Criminal Trial: Practice Guidance', available at <http://www.cps.gov.uk/publications/prosecution/therapychild.html> accessed 13 March 2017.

- The nature of the therapy should be explained so that consideration can be given to whether or not the provision of such therapy is likely to impact on the criminal case ...
- Records of therapy ... and other contacts with the witness must be maintained so that they can be produced if required by the court. They should include, in the case of therapy, details of those persons present and the content and length of the therapy sessions ...
- At the outset of therapy an understanding should be reached with the child and the carers, of the circumstances under which material obtained during therapy might be required to be disclosed.

(v) Provision for defence witnesses at the pre-court stage

3.77 Defence witnesses have the same entitlements as prosecution witnesses to information and support during the pre-court stage, and should be kept informed of case progression by the defence legal team. Defence witnesses should have access to the pre-trial support provided by the Witness Service, including in the form of a pre-trial visit; they should be made aware of the Witness Service by the defence lawyers, who also have responsibility for applying for any necessary special measures.

(c) Trial

3.78 When a witness attends court to give evidence at trial, support may be required from the point of arrival at court and while waiting to be called into the courtroom; the witness may also need support while giving evidence and immediately afterwards.

(i) Attendance at court for trial

3.79 **Safeguarding at court** Arrangements for entry to and exit from the court building for vulnerable and/or intimidated witnesses should be agreed in advance of the trial; this may entail putting specific security measures in place if safety concerns have been raised. In some courts, special entrance arrangements may require advance authorization from a judge, and the Witness Service can assist with this.

3.80 Under the Witness Charter, the court should provide separate waiting areas for defence and prosecution witnesses, ideally within the Witness Service. Where waiting areas are not available, the court can review other options, including the provision of waiting facilities outside the court building.

3.81 **Support from the Witness Service during the waiting period** The Witness Service provides practical and emotional support to witnesses, and particularly those who are vulnerable, while they are waiting at court to give evidence. This can include sitting with a witness and offering information and reassurance, and alerting the court to any specific witness needs that have not previously been identified or addressed. The Witness Service may liaise with the prosecution: for example, advising advocates that a witness has arrived in order that they can meet the witness and fulfil their obligations under the Prosecutors' Pledge; and ensuring that the witness's statement (in written or DVD form) is given to him or her to review in good time.

The Witness Service may also be required to clarify roles and responsibilities **3.82** where a number of supporting agencies are attending court with a vulnerable witness.

Timetabling, waiting, and delay   Timetabling of witness evidence should be **3.83** considered in the light of any known vulnerabilities. The 'Equal Treatment Bench Book' for judges and magistrates recognizes that 'vulnerable people are often more adversely affected by delay, both in terms of their recall and their emotional well-being [and that] timetabling is therefore an issue that impacts upon best evidence and safeguarding'.[22] (See further Chapter 9, 'Case Management' and Chapter 13, 'Trial Management: The Judge's Role'.)

As a matter of good practice, the Witness Service should monitor witness waiting **3.84** times and well-being, and alert the court if a vulnerable witness has waited more than two hours or if the witness is having evident difficulties. A decision can then be made by the court to release the witness if it is unlikely the witness will be heard that day. The Witness Charter (standard 13) requires relevant parties to 'seek to ensure' that any witness is not required to wait at court for more than two hours, while recognizing that some delays are 'unavoidable'.

Where a defendant changes the plea from not guilty to guilty on the first day **3.85** of the trial or over the course of the trial, all witnesses in the case should be informed of this by the prosecution team or the police. Under the Prosecutors' Pledge, the prosecutor should 'wherever possible' speak to any victim and take his or her views into account in deciding whether to accept a plea to a less serious charge.

(ii) Giving evidence

A witness may give evidence in the courtroom (from behind a screen if appropri- **3.86** ate), via video link from a room in the court building, or via video link from a remote location. The witness's evidence-in-chief may take the form of screening a pre-recorded ABE interview, which the witness may view in advance, or at the same time as the jury in the courtroom or from the live-link room. Where cross-examination follows the evidence-in-chief, this must be conducted in accordance

---

[22] Judicial College, 'Equal Treatment Bench Book 2013' (Judicial College, 2013) ch. 5, 'Children and Vulnerable Adults', para. 54.

with any rules agreed at a ground rules hearing. Pre-recorded cross-examination of vulnerable witnesses, under the Youth Justice and Criminal Evidence Act 1999 s. 28, was piloted in three areas from December 2013.[23] At the time of writing (March 2017), a phased expansion of pre-recorded cross-examination to other courts and other (limited) groups of complainants is planned. (For further discussion of cross-examination of vulnerable witnesses, see in particular Chapter 9, 'Case Management', Chapter 12, 'Ground Rules Hearings', and Chapter 16, 'Looking Ahead'.)

3.87 **Use of screens**   Where a witness is to give evidence from behind a screen, unwanted contact between the witness and the defendant (and/or individuals in the public gallery) should be avoided through coordination between the Witness Service and the clerk or usher over the witness's entry to the courtroom. The usual procedure is as given below:

- The jury is removed from the courtroom, the defendant leaves the dock, and the public gallery is cleared.
- Screens are put into place and a 'safe' corridor is identified for the witness to enter the courtroom (sometimes from an alternative route such as the judges' corridor).
- The public gallery is re-opened and the defendant is brought back into the courtroom, followed by the jury.

The above process is repeated after the witness has finished giving evidence and leaves the courtroom.

3.88 With permission from the court, a Witness Service or other supporter may sit with the witness while he or she gives evidence.

3.89 **Support in the live-link room**   A supporter, including a Witness Service volunteer, may sit with the witness in the live-link room. The supporter should be familiar with court procedure, but have no knowledge of the evidence in the case, and is preferably someone with whom the witness has established a bond and is trained in supporting vulnerable witnesses. This is particularly important if an intermediary is not involved. Ultimately, it will be the judge's decision as to who is best placed to provide the support.

3.90 The frequency of breaks while the witness gives evidence should have been agreed in pre-trial preparations, although the supporter can alert the Court to signs of excessive distress or fatigue. These may not always be visible to the court from the live-link room, and witness's welfare should be paramount in any decision on whether to interrupt proceedings.

---

[23] J. Baverstock, *Process Evaluation of Pre-Recorded Cross-Examination Pilot (Section 28)* (MoJ Analytical Series, 2016).

The role of the supporter is distinct from that of the person, usually the usher, who **3.91** is responsible for ensuring the equipment is operating effectively and administering the oath if necessary. Equipment should be tested by court staff in advance of scheduled live-link evidence, to allow for adjustments or courtroom changes if necessary.

Use of remote live links   Increasing use is being made of remote live links away **3.92** from the trial court; these are usually arranged in other courtrooms closer to the witness's home and in Sexual Assault Referral Centres (SARCs), but other venues are possible (e.g. residential care homes). Witnesses are entitled to the same level and type of support in remote locations as in court-based live-link rooms.

An updated risk assessment should be carried out with reference to remote link **3.93** sites. The Witness Service issues clear guidelines to its staff and volunteers about boundaries of support in link rooms, whether at court or off-site.[24]

(iii) After giving evidence

After a witness has finished giving evidence, he or she will be released by the **3.94** court. A witness has the right to stay on to observe the remainder of the proceedings from the public gallery. However, this is sometimes inadvisable where the witness is vulnerable and intimidated: for example, the witness may encounter the defendant and/or defendants' supporters at court.

The Witness Service or other witness supporter should be able to identify ongoing **3.95** needs or concerns through discussion with the witness after completion of evidence. The Witness Service can assist with signposting or referrals for further help to organizations like Citizens Advice, Victim Support, and Women's Aid. The Witness Service can also liaise with court security to facilitate the witness's discreet exit from the court building, where appropriate.

Witnesses should be given information by the CPS about how to claim expenses **3.96** arising from the court attendance.

(iv) Provision for defence witnesses at trial

Witness Service support is available to all defence witnesses, as well as prosecu- **3.97** tion witnesses, who present at court, including any witnesses being held in the cells at court. It is likely that defence witnesses will be aware of the available support through the Witness Service only if they are informed of this by the defence team.

Defence witnesses who are vulnerable are entitled to the same special measures as **3.98** prosecution witnesses while giving evidence—including, for example, the opportunity to give evidence from behind screens or via a live link where appropriate.

---

[24] See also The Advocate's Gateway, 'Toolkit 9: Planning to Question Someone Using a Remote Link'.

The defence team should make the application for special measures or the court may make the order of its own motion. Vulnerable defence witnesses should also be signposted to sources of further support, where necessary, after giving evidence.

3.99 Defence witnesses should be informed by the defence team about how to claim expenses.

(d) Sentencing

3.100 Under the Witness Charter, witnesses should receive updates from the Witness Care Unit, or the police in some cases, about verdict and, if applicable, the sentencing date. This information should be provided by the end of the working day on which the information has been received from the court.

(i) Attendance at court to observe sentencing

3.101 Witnesses may choose to attend court to observe the sentencing, and the Witness Service offers emotional and practical support for those wishing to do so. This may include help to accommodate specific requests through liaison with the court.

3.102 In complex cases involving multiple vulnerable victims, the Witness Service should consider the implications of having several victims attend sentencing who may have been dealt with entirely separately during the trial; any risks associated with victim or witness contact with the defendant or defendant's supporters should also be considered. There may be a need for provision of separate waiting areas, seating plans for the courtroom, and screening from the defendant(s).

3.103 In homicide cases, the Witness Service may be able to provide private rooms for bereaved family members who wish to attend sentence hearing. In these and other serious or high profile cases, the police should liaise with the court and security to allow for particular measures to be put in place.

(ii) Presentation of VPS at sentencing

3.104 Under the Victims' Code, victims are entitled to say if they would like to read out their VPS (if they have made one) at the sentencing hearing or if they would like it to be read for them by someone else, such as the prosecuting advocate or a family member. The police should inform the CPS of victims' preferences in this regard, who should notify the court. The bereaved family of a victim are also entitled to make a VPS and request that it is read at sentencing.

3.105 Unless there is a good reason not to do so, the court will usually accommodate a victim's or family's wishes with regard to reading the VPS—although it will not necessarily be read in full. A vulnerable victim can ask for special measures to assist with reading the statement: for example, such that they read from behind a screen in the courtroom or in the live-link room. A 2014 protocol agreed between the police, the CPS, HMCTS, the Witness Service, and the judiciary on reading VPSs at court[25] states that the Witness Service 'will endeavour' to ensure that a representative is at court to assist a victim with reading out the VPS.

As a statement of the crime's impact on the victim, the VPS should be taken **3.106** into account by the sentencer in the sentencing decision, since the sentence is expected to reflect both the harm caused by the offence and the culpability of the offender (the Criminal Justice Act 2003 s. 143(1)). However, the VPS does *not* provide an opportunity for the victims to give their views on what the sentence should be, and victims should be advised of this when they give the statement. If a VPS does include views on sentence, the sentencer will not take account of these.

(iii) Provision for defence witnesses at sentencing

For information on trial outcome and sentencing date, defence witnesses should **3.107** contact the court or the defence team, if they have not already been informed. Defence witnesses, like prosecution witnesses, may choose to attend court to observe sentencing.

(e) After court

After the court case has concluded, provision for witnesses may extend to offering **3.108** further information and updates on the case, ongoing support, and information and assistance in relation to the defendant's progression on sentence.

(i) Updates on case, including appeals

Under the Witness Charter and Victims' Code, witnesses and victims are entitled **3.109** to information after a case ends, including information on sentence from the Witness Care Unit or police. The Victims' Code imposes an obligation on service providers to offer victims information on restorative justice and how they can participate.

Witness Care Units or the police should notify prosecution witnesses of any **3.110** appeal against conviction or sentence, and inform witnesses of appeal outcomes. It is rare for witnesses to appear at appeals, although they may be called if new evidence has been produced. The Witness Service can provide emotional and practical support for witnesses appearing at appeal hearings. Witness support at the Court of Appeal Criminal Division, at the Royal Courts of Justice, is provided by the Witness Service at the Central Criminal Court.

---

[25] Association of Chief Police Officers, *A Working Protocol between ACPO, the Crown Prosecution Service (CPS), Her Majesty's Court & Tribunals Service (HMCTS), the Witness Service and the Senior Presiding Judge of England and Wales on reading Victim Personal Statements at Court* (2014), para. 2.15.

(ii) Ongoing support

3.111 Where witnesses or victims have further need for support or practical assistance after a case is completed, they should be signposted to appropriate organizations by the Witness Care Unit, the police, the Witness Service, or other witness supporter. Local authorities, specialist victims' services, and other agencies can put safety measures in place for victims who face continuing risks after case completion—such as domestic violence and hate crime victims. Victim Support's national Homicide Service will continue to offer ongoing support to bereaved families.

(iii) Information and support in relation to sentence

3.112 Where victims of violent or sexual offences have opted into the National Probation Service's Victim Contact Scheme, they will be provided with information about the offender's sentence, including notification of pending release from custody or a forthcoming parole hearing. Under the scheme, a victim is also entitled to make representations to the Parole Board about the offender's licence conditions following release from custody.[26]

3.113 Under the Victims' Code, any victim who has suffered harm or economic loss, or bereaved family members, can make a new VPS to describe the continuing impact of the offence and the possible impact that the prisoner's release or move to open conditions might have. The Parole Board is required to read the VPS when making its decision. Victims can ask to attend an oral Parole Board hearing to read out their statement.

(iv) Provision for defence witnesses after court

3.114 Defence witnesses can contact the court or defence team for information on sentence. Where they have ongoing support needs, they may be signposted to appropriate services by the defence team or the Witness Service.

E. Adequacy of Witness Support

3.115 The preceding sections of this chapter have described what support is available to witnesses in general, and vulnerable witnesses in particular, according to current policies, standards, and guidelines. The adequacy of this support—both as it exists in theory and, most critically, in terms of how the theory is translated into practice—is the subject of this concluding section of the chapter.

---

[26] National Offender Management Service, 'Victim Contact Scheme Guidance Manual' (effective 31 October 2013–30 October 2017), available at <http://www.justice.gov.uk/downloads/offenders/probation-instructions/pi-11-2013-vicitim-contact-scheme-guidance.doc> accessed 13 March 2017.

This discussion includes a number of case studies variously illustrating good **3.116** and poor practice in provision of witness support; these case studies are drawn from the direct experiences and observations of one of the authors, Harlow, as a Witness Service manager.

(a) Improved provision for witnesses, including vulnerable witnesses

The past three decades have seen a vast expansion in provision of witness sup- **3.117** port—from a situation in which, as described by academic Paul Rock: 'Witnesses were little considered: they were unproblematic and taken for granted, the "fodder of the criminal courts".'[27]

(i) Overview of improvements

One of the major initiatives has been the establishment of the Witness Service **3.118** across the entire criminal court network in England and Wales for the explicit purpose of providing support to witnesses before, during, and after they give evidence. A growing emphasis on informing and, more broadly, communicating with witnesses throughout the prosecution process—for example, through Witness Care Units, probation-run Victim Liaison Units, and court-based Witness Liaison Officers—has been another significant feature of policy on the judicial process. Also important has been the introduction of adjustments to court proceedings to facilitate participation by vulnerable witnesses—most notably, the 'special measures' introduced by the Youth Justice and Criminal Evidence Act 1999.

Evidence from survey research on court users suggests that, for the most part, **3.119** witnesses are broadly satisfied with their experiences of court. The latest Ministry of Justice Witness and Victim Experience Survey (WAVES), which was conducted annually from 2005/06 to 2010, found that 84 per cent of victims and witnesses were satisfied with their overall contact with the criminal justice system. Of those respondents who had given evidence in court, two-thirds said that they would agree to be a witness again in future, while a sixth said they were not likely to do so, and a further sixth said that it would depend on the circumstances of the case.[28] A survey conducted by the Courts Service for four years from 2007, which covered both professional and lay court users across civil and criminal jurisdictions, also painted a broad-brush picture of general satisfaction with court experiences.[29]

---

[27] P. Rock, *The Social World of an English Crown Court* (Oxford University Press, 1993) 288.
[28] R. Franklyn, *Satisfaction and Willingness to Engage with the Criminal Justice System: Findings from the Witness and Victim Experience Survey 2009–10* (MoJ, 2012).
[29] Ministry of Justice, *Her Majesty's Courts Service Court User Survey 2009–10* (MoJ, 2010).

3.120 More recently, a 2014 CPS survey of victims and witnesses produced a more mixed picture, albeit most respondents indicated general satisfaction. The percentages of witnesses and of victims who were 'very' or 'fairly' satisfied with the CPS totalled 74 and 67 per cent respectively. When asked if they would consent to being a witness in a trial in future, 60 per cent of witnesses said that they would, as did 52 per cent of victims. The percentages of witnesses and of victims who said they would be unlikely to agree to being a witness totalled 5 and 9 per cent respectively, while 35 and 39 per cent respectively said that it would depend on circumstances.[30]

(ii) Contribution of the Witness Service and pre-trial visits

3.121 The Witness Service evolved into a national service from an initial demonstration witness support project implemented at a single Crown Court in 1989.[31] By 2003, an Audit Commission report on victims' and witnesses' experiences of the criminal justice system found quite limited awareness of support organizations, including the Witness Service, and confusion about the respective roles of differing agencies. However, the Witness Service was 'an important positive feature that is consistent to many people's experiences [of court]', with staff providing a 'friendly face' and helping to tackle victims' and witnesses' apprehensions about appearing at court.[32]

3.122 The latest WAVES survey found that almost two-thirds of victims and witnesses who attended court to give evidence remembered having contact with the Witness Service, and almost all (96 per cent) of those who recalled contact with the Witness Service were satisfied with it.[33] Recent qualitative research on Crown Court experiences by Jacobson et al. found that victims and witnesses tended to talk in highly positive terms about the practical and also emotional assistance provided by 'caring' and 'kind' Witness Service staff and volunteers[34]—who were described in similar terms also by respondents in a qualitative study conducted as part of the wider WAVES research.[35]

3.123 Pre-trial visits (PTVs) are central to how the Witness Service helps to prepare witnesses for court, and research evidence suggests they can be valued by those who take part in them. However, levels of awareness and take-up of pre-trial visits

---

[30] M. Wood, K. Lepanjuuri, C. Paskell, J. Thompson, L. Adams, and S. Coburn, *Victim and Witness Satisfaction Survey* (CPS, 2015).

[31] Implementation of the demonstration project was observed by Rock, *English Crown Court*.

[32] Audit Commission, *Experiences of the Criminal Justice System—Victims and Witnesses of Crime: Research Study Conducted for the Audit Commission* (Audit Commission, 2003) 10.

[33] Franklyn, *WAVES*.

[34] J. Jacobson, G. Hunter, and A. Kirby, *Inside Crown Court: Personal Experiences and Questions of Legitimacy* (Policy Press, 2015) 143.

[35] Commissioner for Victims and Witnesses, *Victims' Views of Court and Sentencing: Qualitative Research with WAVES Victims* (MoJ, 2011).

may be limited: only around a third of respondents to the CPS survey said that they were offered a PTV, and 15 per cent of victims and 12 per cent of witnesses undertook one. Of those who did a PTV, over 72 per cent of victims and 65 per cent of witnesses reported that this had been 'very helpful'.[36]

(iii) Positive responses to special measures

As will be discussed below, the implementation of special measures for those wit-   **3.124**
nesses who are entitled to them is sometimes fraught with difficulty. But where appropriate special measures are put in place, they are generally valued by witnesses. Just a few years after special measures were introduced, Hamlyn et al. found that they were beneficial to witnesses: those who received them were less likely to feel anxious or distressed and a third who had used them said that they would not have been willing or able to give evidence without them.[37] Plotnikoff and Woolfson, in an evaluation of government support for young witnesses, found that 88 per cent of the 172 young witnesses in the study gave evidence using special measures—of whom 75 per cent gave evidence via live link and 13 per cent from behind a screen. Overall, 82 per cent of the total sample were happy with the arrangements made for them to give evidence and, of these, 39 per cent said they would have been unwilling to give evidence in any other way.[38]

Another positive picture of the impact of special measures is offered by the CPS   **3.125**
survey, which found that 11 and 3 per cent of victim and witness respondents, respectively, gave evidence from behind a screen, and the large majority of them found this helpful.[39] Similarly, the last WAVES survey found that a low proportion of victims and witnesses took up special measures, but most who did so felt that this had helped them to give their evidence.[40]

(iv) Multi-agency and individualized support

Many agencies and services are potentially engaged in providing support to wit-   **3.126**
nesses who are vulnerable. This in itself can be a source of difficulty, if agencies are jostling with each other and competing for a vulnerable individual's attention. It is even possible for there to be a number of different service providers present with the witness in the live-link room, which can be disconcerting or confusing for the witness and disruptive for proceedings. On the other hand, where agencies are clear about their respective roles and non-territorial in their approach, this can give rise to support that is flexible and tailored to the specific needs and wishes or

---

[36] Wood et al., *CPS Survey*, 46.
[37] B. Hamlyn, A. Phelps, J. Turtle, and G. Sattar, *Are Special Measures Working? Evidence from Surveys of Vulnerable and Intimidated Witnesses* (Home Office Research Study 283, 2004).
[38] J. Plotnikoff and R. Woolfson, *Measuring Up? Evaluating Implementation of Government Commitments to Young Witnesses in Criminal Proceedings* (NSPCC, 2009).
[39] Wood et al., *CPS Survey*, 46–7.
[40] Franklyn, *WAVES*.

expectations of the individual. For example, specialist services such as ISVAs and IDVAs can offer expertise that other agencies will not have, and may provide support to a vulnerable victim throughout the criminal justice process and beyond, while other services may have roles to play at specific stages of the process.

3.127 The Witness Service, as a neutral and independent entity, can have an important part to play in brokering flexible, individualized support and ensuring clarity: clarity which must be conveyed to the witness him or herself, as well as among the agencies involved. In a situation where multiple supporters are available for a vulnerable witness, it is critically important that the court identifies which supporters should (and should not) accompany the witness as he or she gives evidence.

3.128 Case studies 1 to 4, below, provide illustrations of contrasting scenarios in which relevant agencies worked well together in providing support to some highly vulnerable individuals.

Case Study 1

A 12-year-old girl attended court to give evidence in the trial of her parents, who were accused of having committed multiple rapes and sexual assaults against her. She had a dedicated support team comprising two care workers, a legal guardian, a Witness Service volunteer, a specialist police liaison officer, and an intermediary. She was suffering post-traumatic stress disorder, and had behavioural problems and significant care needs. Before and during pre-trial visits, specific roles were allocated and agreed among her supporters, with the Witness Service coordinating court staff involvement—including practice of the live link with a court clerk, security staff assistance with arrangements for discreet access to the court, and provision of a private and secure waiting area in the Witness Service suite.

Case Study 2

A young witness, L, had support from an IDVA, a social worker, Witness Service volunteers, and an intermediary. L was a victim of domestic violence and was due to give evidence against her mother.

One of the volunteers facilitated a pre-trial visit by L and the supporters from outside the court. With input from L herself, the roles and responsibilities of the differing supporters were agreed at the beginning of the visit. The visit included demonstration of and practice with a screen in the courtroom and the live link. L opted to give evidence from behind a screen, although the CPS had assumed that the live link was her preference. During the visit, L also viewed her ABE interview and, with the court's permission, the Witness Service volunteer and specialist police officer sat with her.

On the day of the trial, another Witness Service volunteer provided support at court, including help with safe entry to and exit from the building. While L gave evidence, and with the agreement of the court, the IDVA sat with L behind the screen, and the intermediary assisted with communication.

Case Study 3

A historic sexual abuse case involved multiple complainants, most of whom were highly vulnerable men with mental health problems, post-traumatic stress disorder, and substance dependencies. Counselling and trauma therapy was arranged for the complainants during and immediately after they were due to give evidence. The complainants expressed their preference for support from male Witness Service volunteers, who were resourced from the trial court's Witness Service team of volunteers trained in sexual violence cases and supplemented, as a contingency, with male volunteers from neighbouring courts to ensure that there were sufficient numbers to preserve the integrity of the evidence (e.g. each complainant was supported by a different individual). The Witness Service and the police worked together to identify: (a) a vulnerable victims' facility to use as a temporary trauma centre near the trial court location; and (b) access to ISVAs rape crisis centres which could respond to need at short notice.

Case Study 4

A 15-year-old was acting as a prosecution witness in a case involving various allegations of child sexual exploitation and grooming.

The young witness had previously waited four days to give evidence at the original trial, which had collapsed. She was now attending court for a retrial. She described herself as transgender and made known to the Witness Service that she had severe anxieties about her gender presentation and had been suffering panic attacks—issues which had not been identified during the original trial. The Witness Service advised the judge, police, and prosecution and defence counsel about the witness's situation. The judge then informed the court that the witness's preferred name and pronoun should be used throughout the proceedings. The young person later said, 'I was really well supported at court and it made a huge difference to know that my views had been taken into account.'

(b) Inefficiencies, disorganization, and delay

3.129 The beneficial effects of the increasing availability of support for witnesses appear to be often undermined by inefficiencies, disorganization, and delay at all stages of the criminal justice process. Reducing inefficiency and delay is an abiding concern of government and is central to a variety of recent and current initiatives (including the court digitization programme)—with an important part of the backdrop to these initiatives, in the current era of austerity, being the need to cut public spending on the courts and associated services. There are clear tensions between governmental aspirations to reduce expenditure (including through cutbacks to court staff), to improve communication with witnesses, and to process cases more quickly and effectively.

(i) *Impact of delays*

3.130 Frequent adjournments and delays to court proceedings have an impact on all witnesses and are likely to impact those who are vulnerable the most. As observed by Jacobson et al. in their discussion of what they term the 'structured mayhem' of the court process, witnesses often experience lengthy delays waiting for a case to come to court, and delays at the courtroom once a case has started and they have come to court to give evidence.[41] Timetabling of witness evidence is often undertaken poorly: typically, for example, multiple witnesses are asked to attend court at 10 a.m. on the first day of a trial when it is likely that none will be called until that afternoon at the earliest. The CPS survey found that more than half of victims and witnesses had experienced waiting times longer than the two hours stipulated by the Witness Charter as the maximum they should wait; and around one-quarter had waited for more than four hours.[42]

3.131 A National Audit Office report on *Efficiency in the Criminal Justice System* notes that witnesses who must wait for lengthy periods cannot necessarily recover the costs, such as childcare costs, that they incur when doing so, and that 'extended waits and uncertainty about whether a case will go ahead can be distressing and create a disincentive for witnesses to attend court in future'.[43]

3.132 Case Study 5, below, outlines a case in which extremely lengthy adjournments of a trial had a deleterious effect on a witness's mental health problems.

Case Study 5

A complainant with mental health needs was called to give evidence in a historic rape case. The trial had been adjourned twice before transferring to a new court, where it was adjourned on two further occasions before finally going ahead. During the trial, the complainant took a non-fatal overdose, and it was apparent that her existing mental health issues had been exacerbated by stress and the protracted delays.

The trial resulted in a hung jury. Almost two years had by now passed since the first trial date, and a new trial was scheduled for many months later. The police officer in the case was highly frustrated by what he perceived to be poor case management on the part of the CPS, despite the police having provided frequent reminders of the complainant's needs. For their part, the CPS were frustrated by numerous delays and requests for adjournment from the defence team.

The court's Witness Service notified the listing office and trial judge of concerns about the likely impact on the complainant of further delays to the case. The trial was then brought forward, and full and appropriate support to the complainant was provided by an intermediary, an ISVA, and a Witness Service volunteer. The trial concluded with no further incidents at court.

---

[41] Jacobson et al., *Inside Crown Court*, 114–20.
[42] Wood et al., *CPS Survey*, 50.
[43] The Comptroller and Auditor General, *Efficiency in the Criminal Justice System* (National Audit Office and MoJ, 2016) para. 1.20.

(ii) Late transfers to other courts

Last-minute transfer of cases from one court to another are sometimes unavoid-   **3.133**
able, and can be a means of reducing delay if the new court has the availability to
hear a case which would otherwise be further adjourned. However, late transfers
can also add to witnesses' uncertainty or anxiety: particularly where they are
given inadequate information about the transfer; where they have carried out a
PTV at the original court; or where arrangements (such as for entry to the building or special measures) have been made at the original court and are not in place
or available at the new venue. Case Study 6, below, illustrates some of the possible
repercussions of a late transfer of a hearing.

Case Study 6

A historic sexual assault case was transferred from one court to another overnight.
The second court was not alerted to the needs of a vulnerable and intimidated witness, which only became apparent when the witness arrived at court and was seen
by the Witness Service. The witness had a physical disability which limited her
mobility; she had substance dependency and an anxiety condition exacerbated by
stress; she was also intimidated by virtue of the circumstances of the case, and was
expecting to give evidence from behind a screen.

The case had been listed in a courtroom not suitable for special measures and in
which the witness box could be accessed only via a number of steps. The trial was
delayed by four hours, until an appropriate courtroom became available. The case
then commenced at 2.30 p.m., and by the end of the day the witness had been part-
heard. The witness had to be accommodated overnight in a hotel and was required
to return to court the next day.

(iii) Staff shortages

Public spending cuts have resulted in staffing shortages in many courts. Fewer list-   **3.134**
ing and other court office staff potentially impacts case scheduling, while shortages
of clerks and, particularly, ushers in the courtroom can have a knock-on effect on the
running of hearings and support for and communication with witnesses. Witness
Service staff and volunteers are increasingly being called on to sit with witnesses in
the live-link room because of unavailability of ushers, which can cause practical difficulties as they are not authorized to handle the equipment. Witness Service staff
are in the live-link room frequently. A report by JUSTICE observes that:

> Cutbacks have led to a reduction in the amount of information and assistance
> provided by staff in the courts and tribunals. This has worked to the detriment
> not only of vulnerable, unrepresented court users, but also to the support available
> to users more broadly, including the judiciary and professionals. A flexible and
> dynamic court and tribunal estate can only operate effectively if it is appropriately
> staffed.[44]

---

[44] JUSTICE, *What Is a Court?* (JUSTICE, 2016) para. 2.28.

(c) Shortcomings in responses to vulnerability

3.135 There is wide-ranging research and anecdotal evidence that the extent to which the available support for vulnerable witnesses is put into practice is variable. This reflects shortcomings in the identification of vulnerabilities, in inter-agency communication and coordination, and in the implementation of special measures.

(i) Poor identification of vulnerabilities

3.136 The extent to which and how vulnerabilities in court users are identified is a theme which cross-cuts many of the specific topics addressed by this volume. It is clear that vulnerabilities can be effectively addressed only if they are recognized as such by the authorities.

3.137 The challenges associated with identifying vulnerability are many—and include the fact that there is a wide variety of definitions of what constitutes a vulnerability; that many vulnerabilities may be largely hidden and evident only to practitioners with specialist skills and expertise; that responsibility for assessing and recording witness needs is spread between various agencies and stages of the justice system, meaning that it can easily fall between the gaps; and that, notwithstanding the increasing policy emphasis on tackling vulnerability, criminal justice practitioners do not necessarily recognize that they have a role in this regard—a problem compounded by resource and staffing constraints.

3.138 Just some of the extensive research evidence pointing to poor identification of witness vulnerabilities includes the CPS survey finding that, of those asked to give evidence, only 45 per cent of victims and 35 per cent of witnesses had a needs assessment carried out by the Witness Care Unit.[45] A criminal justice joint inspectorates review of 459 case files found that police investigating officers did not record whether or not a witness had needs requiring support in around one-quarter of the examined cases, and that an assessment for special measures was carried out in only about half of the cases which merited it (and was inadequately conducted in a third of these cases). It was relatively common for witness vulnerabilities to be identified by prosecutors at a late stage of the prosecution process—as the case progressed to trial.[46]

(ii) Lack of inter-agency coordination and communication

3.139 The identification of a witness's vulnerability is a first step towards supporting that witness; but supportive action depends on information about the vulnerability, and the circumstances surrounding it, being shared between relevant agencies

---

[45] Wood et al., *CPS Survey*, 52–3.

[46] Her Majesty's Inspectorate of Constabulary (HMIC), Criminal Justice Joint Inspection, and HM Crown Prosecution Service Inspectorate (HMCPSI), *Witness for the Prosecution: Identifying Victim and Witness Vulnerability in Criminal Case Files* (HMIC, 2015).

(in accordance with data protection principles). The joint inspectorates review cited above did not just note shortcomings in assessment of need, but also found that in 44 per cent of cases in which vulnerability was identified, adequate information was not then passed on to the prosecutor or court. Overall, the review found that of all cases which appeared to involve vulnerability, in only about half was need both identified and managed properly by the CPS.[47]

A case in which inadequate needs assessment along with a lack of inter-agency coordination had tragic consequences was that of Frances Andrade, who committed suicide shortly after giving evidence in a historic sexual abuse trial. A serious case review into the support offered to Mrs Andrade pointed to failings by both mental health and criminal justice services, and observed that those risk assessments that were carried out were 'more like separate snapshots rather than a linked up story'.[48] Her level of vulnerability was not recognized, and she was not provided with adequate care to support her through the trial process. One of many specific issues addressed by the serious case review was her lack of access to pre-trial therapy, and agencies were criticized for having failed to challenge her view that such therapy would 'damage her testimony'.[49] **3.140**

Effective support for witnesses cannot be provided in the absence of communication among the relevant parties on all—and potentially evolving—threats to a witness's welfare over the course of the criminal justice process. This is illustrated by Case Study 7, below, concerning the situation of a heavily pregnant prosecution witness in a murder trial. **3.141**

Case Study 7

A prosecution witness in a murder trial—who was the partner of the victim—was in the advanced stages of pregnancy (and facing pregnancy complications), and had also been designated an intimidated witness.

The witness's due date coincided with the scheduled start date of the trial. The prosecution had been aware of this, but insisted 'we can work around it'. The Witness Service were first alerted to the witness's condition two days before the trial commenced. The witness gave birth when she was due, and the police and CPS were given medical advice that she should be called to give evidence no sooner than two weeks after giving birth, and subject to a GP's agreement.

---

[47] ibid.
[48] Surrey County Council Safeguarding Adults Board, 'The Death of Mrs A: A Serious Case Review', 43, available at <http://www.surreycc.gov.uk/__data/assets/pdf_file/0018/42624/FINAL-Mrs-A-full-report-26.03.14.pdf> accessed 13 March 2017.
[49] ibid. 22–3. Mrs Andrade was said to have believed that the police had advised against her receiving therapy prior to giving evidence, but both police forces involved in the case stated clearly that they had not given this advice.

> Precisely two weeks after the birth, and without having obtained further medical advice, the prosecution called the witness. She presented at court while suffering from a serious infection (the baby was also unwell at the time). The Witness Service alerted the court to the witness's medical condition and, after discussion between the judge and counsel, the witness statement was read and the witness released.

(iii) Poor implementation of special measures

3.142 The subject of special measures and their implementation is considered in detail in Chapter 10, 'Special Measures'. In the context of this more general discussion of witness support, it suffices simply to touch on some of the widespread implementation problems (which have been reported upon in a number of research studies[50]). These difficulties include delays in special measures applications and/or in decision-making on applications. The delays can mean that decisions are made only on the day of the witness's court appearance, which causes unnecessary stress and anxiety. Witnesses—and indeed practitioners—are often inconvenienced and disconcerted by practical hitches which arise when special measures are put in place, particularly at short notice: live-link technology can easily fail, and even screens around a witness box can be of the wrong size or shape. While use of intermediaries is becoming more widespread, this is not always approached in a systematic or consistent fashion—see, for example, Case Study 8. Practitioners often feel inadequately trained in the application of special measures and methods of supporting vulnerable witnesses more generally.[51]

> *Case Study 8*
>
> During trial preparation, the police identified that a prosecution witness had numerous vulnerabilities (some of which had not, however, been noted at the time of the initial police interview), including ADHD, anxiety, Tourette's Syndrome, suicidal tendencies, and being subject to seizures and fainting fits.
>
> An intermediary was appointed, but no ground rules hearing was arranged in advance of the trial, as prosecuting counsel believed this was not necessary. The intermediary was asked to attend court for three consecutive days once the trial had commenced, in anticipation of a ground rules hearing, while the witness was asked to wait 'on standby' each day. On day four of the trial, the court was made aware of the witness's vulnerabilities, and it was then agreed that the witness's evidence would be read and the witness was not called.

[50] See, e.g., Jacobson et al., *Inside Crown Court*; M. Burton, R. Evans, and A. Sanders, *An Evaluation of the Use of Special Measures for Vulnerable and Intimidated Witnesses* (Home Office Findings 270, 2006); and C. Charles, *Special Measures for Vulnerable and Intimidated Witnesses: Research Exploring the Decisions and Actions Taken by Prosecutors in a Sample of CPS Case Files* (CPS, 2012).

[51] R. Ewin, 'The Vulnerable and Intimidated Witness: A Study of the Special Measure Practitioner' (2016) *Journal of Applied Psychology and Social Science*, 2(1), 12–40.

(d) Poor communication with witnesses

Communication with witnesses is central to many of the reforms described over **3.143** the course of this chapter. The Witness Charter sets out witness entitlements to information on case progression and outcomes; the Victim Personal Statements enable victims to explain the impact of the crime and to have this reflected at sentencing; under the Victims' Code and CPS Right to Review Scheme, victims should receive an explanation for why charges have been dropped or amended and can ask for a review of the decisions; and prosecutors are expected to speak to victims at court (under the Prosecutors' Pledge) and to witnesses (under the new CPS Guidance). Notwithstanding these reforms, shortcomings remain in terms of both *extent* and *style* of communication with witnesses.

(i) Limited communication with witnesses

Most victim and witness respondents—around two-thirds—to the recent CPS **3.144** survey reported being 'fairly' or 'very' satisfied that the CPS had kept them informed about their case throughout the prosecution process. In contrast, around one-fifth of victims and 14 per cent of witnesses were dissatisfied with the information they received. Dissatisfaction was highest among the most vulnerable groups, including victims who felt threatened, were persistently targeted, or had a health condition.[52]

The survey found that most victims and witnesses where charges were altered or **3.145** stopped could recall being given an explanation as to why this had happened. 70 per cent of 213 victims in whose cases the charges had been dropped stated that they felt this decision was unfair, but only 10 per cent asked for a review—almost all of whom were dissatisfied with how this request was handled. Of those who did not ask for a review, about half said that they did not know how to do so.[53] A recent CPS Inspectorate investigation found that charging decision explanations to victims were of 'variable and often inadequate quality', and that there was scant evidence of victims being consulted—as they should be—about these decisions.[54]

Face-to-face communication between the prosecution and victims or witnesses **3.146** at court is not yet routine—thanks in part to CPS staff cutbacks,[55] but perhaps also reflecting general failure on the part of many prosecutors to see this communication as a core part of their role. Only around 60 per cent of CPS survey respondents who went to trial were able to ask questions of the legal team or a court official.[56]

---

[52] Wood et al., *CPS Survey*, 58.
[53] ibid. 40–1.
[54] HMCPSI, *Communicating with Victims* (HMCPSI, 2016) paras 1.6, 1.10.
[55] ibid. para. 1.8.
[56] Wood et al., *CPS Survey*, 51.

3.147 While the introduction of Victim Personal Statements (VPSs) was conceived as a means of giving victims a 'voice' in the criminal justice process, the effects of this are so far limited—with, for example, many victims reporting that they did not believe that, or did not know whether, their statement had been taken into account.[57] Thirty-six per cent of victim respondents to the CPS survey had made a VPS, while 35 per cent said they were not offered the opportunity to do so; and more than half who had made a VPS did not know if it had been used.[58] One apparent difficulty with VPSs is that police tend to take them at the same time as they take the general witness statement, and do not necessarily make it clear to victims that the VPS has a distinct and separate function.

(ii) Inappropriate styles of communication

3.148 Communication with witnesses, and particularly those who are vulnerable, is often inappropriate in its style. In the courtroom, interaction among professionals and between professionals and court users tends to be highly formal, elaborate, and therefore exclusionary for the non-professionals.[59] Approaches to cross-examination have been a particular cause for concern, and a wide range of measures have been taken to ensure that vulnerable witnesses are not subjected to cross-examination that is overly complex, demeaning, or aggressive. However, real change in practice appears to be slow-moving and impeded by aspects of legal professional culture,[60] and further reform is called for.[61] Support for vulnerable witnesses before and during cross-examination has become more widely available, but 49 per cent of victims and 36 per cent of witness respondents to the CPS survey did not feel they were given enough support with preparing for cross-examination.[62]

---

[57] J. V. Roberts and M. Manikis, 'Victim Personal Statements in England and Wales: Latest (and Last) Trends from the Witness and Victim Experience Survey' (2013) *Criminology & Criminal Justice*, 13(3), 245–61.

[58] Wood et al., *CPS Survey*, 50.

[59] Jacobson et al., *Inside Crown Court*.

[60] E. Henderson, 'Communicative Competence? Judges, Advocates and Intermediaries Discuss Communication Issues in the Cross-Examination of Vulnerable Witnesses' (2015) *Crim LR* 9, 659–78.

[61] For example, a new approach to interviewing and cross-examining child witnesses in abuse cases is shortly to be piloted in London, where two 'Child Houses' are to be opened which 'will offer medical investigative and emotional support in one place, removing the need for young victims to go through the trauma of repeating their statement several times to different agencies'. Provision will include evidence-gathering interviews to be conducted by child psychologists on behalf of the police, use of video links for court appearances, and after-care (King's College Hospital NHS Foundation Trust, 'UK's First Child Houses to Launch', available at <http://www.kch.nhs.uk/news/public/news/view/21120> accessed 7 April 2017. See further Chapter 16, 'Looking Ahead'.

[62] Wood et al., *CPS Survey*, 49.

Outside the courtroom, communication with victims and witnesses is not **3.149** always undertaken in a style that is appropriate to their needs and expectations. For example, Victim Liaison Units have been criticized for the impersonality and lack of empathy of the letters they send to victims regarding charging decisions.[63]

(e) Limited support for defence witnesses

Much of the provision for witness support described in this chapter applies to **3.150** defence witnesses as it does to witnesses for the prosecution. The Witness Charter, for example, specifies that it covers both prosecution and defence witnesses; the Witness Service is available to offer support to defence witnesses—with the general expectation that it should, wherever possible, provide separate waiting facilities for prosecution and defence witnesses; and defence witnesses are explicitly included within the special measures provisions of the Youth Justice and Criminal Evidence Act 1999 (while defendants are explicitly excluded).

In practice, however, defence witnesses—including the most vulnerable among **3.151** them—often have limited opportunities to access the available support. A particular difficulty is that, for the most part, there are no statutory criminal justice bodies with responsibility for implementing the relevant provisions with regard to defence witnesses. Defence witnesses are largely dependent for their support on individual defence lawyers having the requisite knowledge, skills, and willingness to put that support into place—which therefore tends to be highly inconsistent and ad hoc at best. This is especially clear when it comes to assessment of risk and needs: a defence witness's vulnerabilities are likely to go unrecognized and unaddressed, unless the defence team takes the initiative in both requesting an assessment by relevant services and thereafter making a special measures application.

Defence lawyers do not necessarily know that the Witness Service provides sup- **3.152** port to defence witnesses, and most defence witnesses attend court without having had prior contact with, or even awareness of, the Witness Service (let alone having had a pre-trial visit). Once at court, whether or not they receive help from the Witness Service depends partly on how proactive the service is in publicising its services in the building and engaging with individuals (see Case Study 9 for an example of such engagement)—which varies from court to court. In the latter part of 2016, the Witness Service undertook a number of national and court-level initiatives to promote their services to the defence community. It is also possible for the judiciary to advise defence counsel, at pre-court hearings, of the availability of Witness Service support for defence witnesses, particularly where there are signs of vulnerability.

---

[63] HMCPSI, *Communicating with Victims*, para. 3.7.

Case Study 9

At 3 p.m., a Witness Service volunteer found a defence witness sitting outside a courtroom looking distressed. He had arrived at court at 9.15 a.m., and been advised by defence counsel to wait by the courtroom until the court was ready for him.

The volunteer took the witness to the Witness Service waiting area and advised the court. The witness disclosed that he had mental health problems: he was bipolar, for which he had not taken his medication, and suffered anxiety and panic attacks. He had not left the waiting area outside the court, nor had anything to eat or drink all day, for fear of being missed if called. The court was unaware that he had been waiting, and the defence counsel had failed to update him.

Following liaison with the Witness Service, the court released the witness for the day and the witness order for the following day was amended to allow this witness to give evidence first. The defence counsel told the Witness Service, 'I didn't know you look after defence witnesses.'

Further Reading

Franklyn, R., *Satisfaction and Willingness to Engage with the Criminal Justice System: Findings from the Witness and Victim Experience Survey 2009–10* (Ministry of Justice, 2012).

Jacobson, J., Hunter, G., and Kirby, A., *Inside Crown Court: Personal Experiences and Questions of Legitimacy* (Policy Press, 2015).

Ministry of Justice, *The Witness Charter: Standards of Care for Witnesses in the Criminal Justice System* (MoJ, 2013).

Ministry of Justice, 'Code of Practice for Victims of Crime' (MoJ, 2015).

Wood M., Lepanjuuri, K., Paskell, C., Thompson, J., Adams, L., and Coburn, S., *Victim and Witness Satisfaction Survey* (CPS, 2015).

The second author's contributions are based on personal observations and experiences in her professional capacity as manager of the Witness Service at the Old Bailey. Any views expressed should not be taken as those of Citizens Advice Witness Service.

4

VULNERABLE SUSPECTS
The Investigation Stage

Miranda Bevan

A. Introduction

(a) An overview

4.01 The police custody suite is a challenging place, not only for the vulnerable suspect, but also for those charged with their care. For a suspect who has no pre-existing difficulties, it can be a stressful, confusing, even frightening place. For a vulnerable suspect, the demands made of them both by the investigative process, and by the environment itself, can be overwhelming. For custody officers, and other professionals, whose task is to ensure the welfare of the suspect and the integrity of the investigation, different challenges arise. They operate under significant pressure of time, dealing with individuals often at their most vulnerable and challenging, and frequently without specialist training to address the particular problems with which they are presented.

The Police and Criminal Evidence Act 1984[1] (PACE) and the accompanying Codes of Practice (hereafter 'the Codes'), particularly Code C,[2] provide the core framework for the treatment of suspects in police custody. There is an overriding principle that all suspects should be treated fairly, with respect for their dignity and without unlawful discrimination (Code C 1.0). But PACE and the Codes recognize that certain 'special groups' of vulnerable suspects require additional safeguards.

However, the nature of those safeguards differs dramatically from the sort of accommodations made for vulnerable witnesses (as discussed in Chapter 2, 'Vulnerable Witnesses: The Investigation Stage'). A vulnerable suspect will not routinely be questioned by an officer specially trained to elicit their best evidence. Nor are intermediaries usually available for those with substantial communication difficulties. The most significant adjustment of the custody process to address vulnerability is the provision of an appropriate adult (hereafter 'AA') to provide support, and to advise and assist the suspect. But that individual is more often than not a family member or carer of the suspect, rather than a professional with specific training. Otherwise, Code C requires minimal adjustment of the custody process to take account of vulnerability, whether that arises from youth, mental disorder, or other mental vulnerability.

(b) The approach taken in this chapter

This chapter focuses on the treatment of vulnerable suspects who are in police custody so that their alleged involvement in a criminal offence may be investigated. A suspect may have been arrested and detained for the purposes of investigation, or they may have attended the police station voluntarily (not under arrest) so that they can be interviewed under caution.

PACE and Code C apply to both these groups of suspects (although s. 15 of Code C applies solely to those who have been arrested and are in police detention). However, these provisions refer to 'detainees' rather than 'suspects' because they also apply to individuals who have been removed to a police station as a place of safety under the Mental Health Act 1983 (see paragraph 4.32, '(c) Place of

4.02

4.03

4.04

4.05

---

[1] Police and Criminal Evidence Act 1984 (PACE).
[2] Revised Code of Practice for the Detention, Treatment and Questioning of Persons by Police Officers, Police and Criminal Evidence Act 1984 (PACE)—Code C. Presented to Parliament pursuant to PACE s. 67(7B), 22 November 2016, entered into force 23 February 2017. See also Code D (identification procedures), Codes E and F (audio and visual recording of interviews), Code G (powers of arrest), and Code H (detention, treatment, and questioning of terrorism suspects).

safety: MHA 1983 s. 136'). These other detainees are discussed where relevant, but their position is not considered in detail in this chapter.

4.06 The chapter opens with a review of the legal framework which governs the treatment of vulnerable suspects in the police station. It then considers the 'special groups' of individuals treated as vulnerable within police custody, and how a suspect might be identified as falling into one or more of those groups. The remainder of the chapter then considers the custody process as it unfolds and the particular adjustments to that process which are required for those special groups of vulnerable suspects at each stage.[3]

B. The Legal Framework

(a) The status of the PACE Codes of Practice

4.07 The Secretary of State is required by PACE s. 66 to issue Codes of Practice[4] setting out how the police will exercise their powers under PACE. However, a failure by a police officer or other custody staff to comply with any of the provisions of the Codes does not itself give rise to criminal or civil liability. Instead, the provisions are admissible in any criminal or civil proceedings and will be 'taken into account' where relevant to any question the court may have to decide (PACE, s. 67(11)).

4.08 In criminal proceedings, a failure to comply with the Codes is often raised where the defence argue that the court should exercise its discretion to exclude unfair evidence (PACE, s. 78). Breaches of the Codes are also often relied upon where the court is invited to exclude a confession obtained through oppression, or which is unreliable as a result of something said or done at the time of the confession (PACE, s. 76), or where the need for a special warning is triggered as a result of the confession having been obtained from a 'mentally handicapped person'[5] without an independent person, such as an AA, being present (PACE, s. 77).

4.09 The Codes also contain Annexes and Notes for Guidance[6] (NFG). The Annexes are provisions of the Codes, while the NFG are not (Code C 1.3). However, in

---

[3] Annex E to Code C provides a useful summary of provisions relating to mentally disordered and otherwise mentally vulnerable detainees. There is no similar summary in Code C of the provisions relating to 'juvenile' detainees.

[4] Codes of Practice presented to Parliament pursuant to PACE s. 66.

[5] A 'mentally handicapped person' in PACE s. 77(3) is defined as a person in a 'state of arrested or incomplete development of mind which includes significant impairment of intelligence and social functioning'.

[6] Notes for Guidance contained within the Codes (NFG).

practice, the NFG are considered relevant by the courts and in effect are treated as part of the Codes.[7]

(b) The wider legal framework

The treatment of vulnerable suspects is also governed by a number of other provisions, both national and supranational. The European Court of Human Rights has made plain that a suspect's right to a fair trial under Article 6 of the European Convention on Human Rights[8] (ECHR) extends to the earliest stages of the investigative process, including the police station. The case law has developed in particular in respect of young suspects, but is applicable to vulnerable adult suspects as well:

4.10

> The authorities must take steps to reduce as far as possible his feelings of intimidation and inhibition ... and ensure that the accused minor has a broad understanding of the nature of the investigation, of what is at stake for him or her, including the significance of any penalty which may be imposed as well as of his rights of defence and, in particular, of his right to remain silent ... It means that he or she, if necessary with the assistance of, for example, an interpreter, lawyer, social worker or friend, should be able to understand the general thrust of what is said by the arresting officer and during his questioning by the police.[9]

(c) Particular provisions relating to children

The police have a duty under the Children Act 2004 s. 11(1)(h) to have regard to the need to safeguard and promote the welfare of children,[10] in discharging their functions, including when they detain a child in the police station. Beyond domestic legislation, the UN Convention on the Rights of the Child[11] (UNCRC) is the most important source of human rights protection for children in conflict with the law.[12] Article 37 sets out general principles, including the requirement that detention be used only as a 'means of last resort' and for the 'shortest appropriate period', and that a child be treated with 'humanity and respect and in a manner which takes into account the needs of persons his or her age.' Article 40(2) details more specific safeguards for the treatment of children in detention.[13]

4.11

---

[7] For fuller discussion, see M. Zander, 'If the PACE Codes Are Not Law, Why Do They Have to Be Followed?' (2012) *Criminal Law & Justice*, 176(49), 713.

[8] The Convention for the Protection of Human Rights and Fundamental Freedoms (entered into force 3 September 1953).

[9] *Panovits v Cyprus,* App. No. 4268/04, 11 December 2008 at [67].

[10] Defined for these purposes as an individual under 18 years of age.

[11] The UN Convention on the Rights of the Child (opened for signing 20 November 1989, entered into force 2 September 1990).

[12] The UNCRC should be read in connection with the UN Standard Minimum Rules for the administration of juvenile justice (the Beijing Rules), the UN Rules for the Protection of Juveniles Deprived of their Liberty (the Havana Rules), and the UN Guidelines for the Prevention of Juvenile Delinquency (the Riyadh Guidelines).

[13] For full discussion, see M. Panzavolta, D. de Vocht, M. van Oosterhout, and M. Vanderhallen, *Interrogating Young Suspects: Procedural Safeguards from a Legal Perspective* (Intersentia, 2015) 12 ff.

(d) Particular provisions relating to individuals vulnerable by reason of a disability

4.12 The police, and other agencies engaged in the custody suite, have duties to safeguard and promote the welfare of vulnerable adults under the Care Act 2014, or the Social Services and Wellbeing (Wales) Act 2014. Under the Equality Act 2010 s. 20, the police are also under a duty to provide reasonable adjustments to the custody process to ensure that suspects with disabilities[14] are not disadvantaged.

4.13 Similar duties to ensure equal access to justice arise under the UN Convention on the Rights of Persons with Disabilities[15] (UNCRPD). In particular, Article 12 establishes equal recognition before the law for persons with disabilities, and Article 13(1) requires states to ensure:

> effective access to justice for persons with disabilities on an equal basis with others, including through the provision of procedural and age-appropriate accommodations, in order to facilitate their effective role as direct and indirect participants.

C. Code C and Vulnerability: Special Groups and Identification

4.14 Code C identifies a number of categories of vulnerability referred to as 'special groups'. An individual suspect may fall into more than one 'special group'. Where that is the case, extra care should be taken to ensure that each aspect of the suspect's vulnerability is fully addressed.

(a) Child suspects: 'juveniles'

4.15 Any suspect who 'appears to be' under the age of 18 will be treated as a 'juvenile', in the absence of clear evidence to the contrary, and will enjoy special safeguards by virtue of their apparent youth alone (Code C 1.5, 1.5A, PACE, s. 37(15) NFG 1L).[16]

---

[14] Persons with disabilities are defined as individuals with a physical or mental impairment which has a substantial, long-term adverse effect on their ability to perform day-to-day activities (Equality Act 2010 s. 6).

[15] UN Convention on the Rights of Persons with Disabilities (opened for signature 30 March 2007, entered into force 3 May 2008).

[16] Previously a young suspect would only be treated as a 'juvenile' if he or she appeared to be under the age of 17. The October 2013 revision of Code C required 17 year olds to be treated as 'juveniles' for the first time (following the case of *R(C) v Secretary of State for the Home Department and Another* [2013] EWHC 982 (Admin)). However, the upper age limit of an 'arrested juvenile' in PACE s. 37(15) was not raised from 17 to 18 years until 26 October 2015 when Criminal Justice and Courts Act 2015 s. 42 was entered into force. This change has now been fully incorporated into the latest revision of Code C, entered into force from 23 February 2017.

(i) Identifying child suspects

Code C 3.5(c)(ii) requires the custody officer to identify whether a suspect **4.16** requires an appropriate adult, triggering, if the assessment has not already been made, consideration of whether the individual is to be treated as a 'juvenile' for the purposes of Code C (Code C 1.5, 1.5A). If the suspect refuses to provide their age or has no means of proving their age, the custody officer needs to decide whether they should treat the individual as a 'juvenile' or as an adult. Code C takes a precautionary approach and any person who appears to be 'under 18' should be treated as a 'juvenile' for the purposes of the Codes unless there is clear evidence that they are older. The custody officer can be assisted by a medical professional or a member of the youth offending team to make that judgment, but where doubt remains, the individual should be treated as a 'juvenile'. If charged, the court will formally determine the individual's age.

(ii) Moving away from the term 'juvenile'

Although the term 'juvenile' remains in PACE and Code C, the College of **4.17** Policing and the National Police Chiefs Council are moving away from this term.[17] For the purposes of this chapter, 'child suspect' should be taken to relate to a suspect treated as a 'juvenile' under Code C, unless otherwise indicated.

(b) Vulnerable adult suspects: 'Mentally disordered or otherwise mentally vulnerable' suspects

Code C also identifies as a 'special group' those individuals who are 'mentally dis- **4.18** ordered or otherwise mentally vulnerable'.[18] For this purpose, 'mental disorder' is to be read as defined by Mental Health Act 1983[19] (MHA) s. 1(2), encompassing 'any disorder or disability of the mind' (NFG 1G).

'Mentally vulnerable' is a broader category, applicable to any person who 'because **4.19** of their mental state or capacity may not understand the significance of what is said, of questions or of their replies' (NFG 1G). Although not explicitly referred to in Code C, where a concern about lack of capacity arises, officers and health-care professionals will be assisted by considering the test for lack of capacity set out in the Mental Capacity Act 2005 ss 2–3. That test focuses on the individual's ability to make a decision, which requires the individual to be able to understand the information relevant to the decision in question, retain and use it as

---

[17] See, e.g., 'Authorised Professional Practice, Detention and Custody' (College of Policing, last modified April 2017) (hereafter APP(DC)).
[18] 'Mentally disordered or otherwise mentally vulnerable', Code C.
[19] Mental Health Act 1983.

part of the process of making the decision, and then communicate the decision arrived at.

4.20 For the purposes of this chapter, 'vulnerable adult suspect' or 'vulnerable adult' should be taken to relate to a suspect treated as 'mentally disordered or otherwise mentally vulnerable', unless otherwise indicated.

(i) Identifying vulnerable adult suspects

4.21 Code C explicitly recognizes how difficult it can be for a custody officer to make an accurate assessment of whether a suspect has a mental disorder or some other mental vulnerability. Conditions capable of giving rise to mental vulnerability (e.g. a learning disability or a developmental condition such as an autism spectrum condition) may be very difficult for a custody officer to identify. The suspect themselves may not be aware of their condition, be unable to report any difficulties accurately, or may not wish to disclose their diagnosis.[20] In addition, suspects arriving in the police station may be in distress, intoxicated, or withdrawing from substance use, and this may make identification of other vulnerabilities more difficult.

4.22 Code C takes a precautionary approach, requiring a suspect to be treated as a vulnerable adult suspect if an officer has 'any suspicion, or is told in good faith' that this may be so, in the absence of clear evidence to the contrary (Code C 1.4). NFG 1G reaffirms this stance in respect of mental vulnerability, detailing that a custody officer who has 'any doubt about the mental state or capacity' of an individual should treat them as being mentally vulnerable.[21]

4.23 Initial consideration of the potential vulnerability of a suspect should occur immediately on arrival in custody, when the custody officer is required to assess in particular whether the suspect may be in need of medical treatment or attention and whether he or she requires an AA (Code C 3.5(c)). However, vulnerability is not a fixed status or dependent upon a confirmed diagnosis. Officers should be aware of the potential for a suspect to become mentally vulnerable during the course of their detention, or be alive to the emergence of signs indicating mental disorder or mental vulnerability as the custody process progresses. (Risk assessment is discussed in more detail below at paragraph 4.29, '(a) The importance of immediate risk assessment').

---

[20] See for discussion of these difficulties L. Crane, K. L. Maras, T. Hawken et al., 'Experiences of Autism Spectrum Disorder and Policing in England and Wales: Surveying Police and the Autism Community' (2016) *Journal of Autism and Developmental Disorders*, 46, 2028.

[21] Empirical research identifies that, despite the precautionary approach required by Code C, difficulties of definition, identification, and interpretation of 'mental disorder' and other 'mental vulnerability' (Code C 1.4 and NFG 1G) persist. See R. Dehaghani, 'He's Just Not That Vulnerable: Exploring the Implementation of the Appropriate Adult Safeguard in Police Custody' (2016) *Howard Journal*, 55(4), 396.

(ii) Approach to be taken where the legal representative has concerns, or where vulnerability becomes apparent at a later stage

Occasionally, a legal representative knows or suspects that their detainee client **4.24** may be mentally disordered or otherwise mentally vulnerable, but this is not apparent to the custody officer. The custody officer must act on such information if told in 'good faith', and a subsequent application to exclude interview evidence may fail if the custody officer was not alerted to the issue by the legal representatives, and otherwise the custody officer had no reason to know of or suspect such vulnerability. As a result, in such circumstances, it will generally be in the best interests of the suspect for the legal representative to notify the custody officer of their concerns, triggering a health-care assessment for their client.

However, care must be taken to ensure that the legal representative's duty of **4.25** confidentiality to the suspect is not infringed. Where the legal representative's concerns arise from something said to him or her by the suspect (on that or an earlier occasion), that information can only be disclosed with the suspect's consent. Whatever the source of the concerns, it is important for the legal representative to discuss health-care assessment with the suspect before approaching the custody officer.

The vulnerability of a detainee may only become apparent at a later stage (e.g. **4.26** during interview). The custody officer has a duty to consider whether safeguards are required at whatever point the concerns are raised. If indications of mental disorder or other mental vulnerability emerge during interview, sufficient to give rise to at least a suspicion that the suspect may be a vulnerable adult, the interviewing officer should stop the interview for the custody officer to consider that potential vulnerability, and fitness for interview, where appropriate. Failure to do so may result in the interview being inadmissible. If the interviewing officer does not do so, the legal representative should stop the interview so that the issues can be considered and further assessment obtained where appropriate.

(c) Suspects with language or communication difficulties (not giving rise to concerns of mental vulnerability)

Safeguards are also afforded to a third 'special group' of suspects who appear not **4.27** to speak or understand English, or who have a hearing or speech impediment (Code C 3.12).

(d) Suspects who are blind, seriously visually impaired, or unable to read

Those individuals who are blind, seriously visually impaired, or unable to read **4.28** constitute a fourth 'special group' who are required to receive additional assistance (Code C 3.20).

D. Arrest and Alternatives to Arrest (PACE Code G[22])

(a) The importance of immediate risk assessment

4.29 Officers responding to an incident should conduct an immediate risk assessment. This should consider the individual's appearance and behaviour, including whether they are showing signs of illness or injury, and how they are communicating. This assessment should consider all available information, taking into account the circumstances and environment in which the individual is found.[23] In many areas, street triaging initiatives[24] are in operation providing officers with expert mental health input, especially where there are concerns that the individual may need to be detained under the Mental Health Act 1983 s. 136 (see paragraph 4.32, '(c) Place of safety: MHA 1983 s. 136'). Alternatives to arrest, or granting street bail (PACE s. 30A), may be particularly appropriate for individuals considered to be vulnerable. Note that care should always be taken to ensure that safeguards and support, such as the provision of an AA, will be available should street bail be used.[25]

(b) Arresting children and young people

4.30 Officers are required to consider the age of a child or young person when deciding whether any of the Code G statutory grounds for arrest apply. In particular, they should have in mind the timing of any necessary arrests of children and young people, and make sure that they are detained for no longer than needed (Code C 1.1). Officers should take special care to avoid holding children overnight in police cells unless absolutely necessary.

4.31 Concerns around the unnecessary criminalization of children in care, and the frequency with which police forces are called to respond to domestic incidents in local authority accommodation, have recently been considered in Lord Laming's review.[26] The review recommends collaborative working between the police, local authorities, and accommodation providers to respond effectively to challenging

---

[22] Police and Criminal Evidence Act 1984 (PACE) Code G—Revised Code of Practice for the Statutory Power of Arrest by Police Officers (November 2012).

[23] APP(DC), 'Response, Arrest and Detention', 1.1.

[24] Health professionals work in close liaison with police officers in responding to incidents where it is suspected that a person has mental health problems. See, e.g., B. Reveruzzi and S. Pilling, 'Street Triage: Report on the Evaluation of Nine Pilot Schemes in England' (UCL, 2015), available at <https://www.ucl.ac.uk/pals/research/cehp/research-groups/core/pdfs/street-triage> accessed 9 April 2017.

[25] APP(DC), 'Response, Arrest and Detention', 1.2.5.

[26] 'In Care, Out of Trouble: How the Life Chances of Children in Care Can Be Transformed by Protecting Them from Unnecessary Involvement in the Criminal Justice System', an independent review chaired by Lord Laming (May 2016).

behaviour in a care setting, without recourse to arrest and more formal criminal justice processes. This has been done very effectively in some areas using restorative justice approaches.[27]

(c) Place of safety: MHA 1983 s. 136

If an individual appears to officers to be suffering from a mental disorder, and **4.32** is in immediate need of care or control, the officers may detain that person and transport them to a place of safety, if they think it is necessary to do so in the interests of that person or for the protection of other persons (MHA 1983 s. 136).[28] [29] The individual should be taken directly to a hospital, care home, or other local social services authority provision as a place of safety. A police station should only be used as a place of safety in exceptional circumstances (MHA 1983 Code of Practice (2015) ss 16.36–16.44).[30] The findings of the *Adebowale Report* emphasize that the use of police custody as a place of safety can have both immediate and long-term effects on the health and well-being of an individual.[31] Officers should take particular care if reasonable force is required to restrain an individual detained under the MHA 1983 and should use the least restrictive and stigmatizing approach, considering the dignity of the individual and their particular vulnerabilities.[32]

E. Booking in: Initial Actions in the Custody Suite

(a) Prioritizing vulnerable individuals

APP requires custody staff to prioritize and triage vulnerable individuals on **4.33** arrival at the station. 'Where practicable', officers should call ahead to inform the

---

[27] See submission 196 to the Laming Review from Blaenau Gwent and Caerphilly Youth Offending Service.

[28] This chapter relates predominantly to the treatment of vulnerable suspects rather than individuals detained under the MHA 1983 s. 136. For more information about the treatment in police custody of individuals detained under this section, see the *Mental Health Act 1983: Code of Practice* (Department of Health, 2015) and K. Gledhill, *Defending Mentally Disordered Persons* (Legal Action Group, 2012).

[29] See also the power to obtain a warrant to remove a person to a place of safety where there is reasonable cause to suspect that the individual has a mental disorder and is being ill-treated, neglected, or otherwise is not kept under proper control, or is unable to care for themselves (if living alone) (MHA 1983 s. 135).

[30] From a date to be appointed, the Mental Health Act s. 136A(1) will prevent a police station from being used as a place of safety for a child under the age of 18 years and the period of detention for all individuals under MHA ss 135 and 136 will be reduced to a maximum of twenty-four hours (extendable by a further twelve hours) (amendments made by Policing and Crime Act 2017).

[31] Independent Commission on Mental Health and Policing Report, May 2013 (the 'Adebowale Report').

[32] See, in addition, Authorised Professional Practice, 'Mental Health' (August 2016) (hereafter APP(MH)), 'Mental Health—Detention'.

custody suite of the arrival of a vulnerable suspect.[33] Where there is any delay, it is particularly important that a vulnerable suspect is subject to ongoing risk assessment and that care is taken to ensure that their needs are met.

(b) Rights and entitlements: general support with understanding

4.34 On booking in, every suspect must be informed by the custody officer of their rights and entitlements, including their right to legal advice, their right to have someone informed of their arrest, and their right to be informed about the offence for which they have been arrested. They are also required to be given a notice explaining those rights and entitlements (Code C 3.1–3.2).

4.35 Many suspects may not have such significant difficulties that they fall into one of the 'special groups', but may still struggle to understand their rights and entitlements. Officers should adjust their communication of a suspect's rights and entitlements to facilitate that individual's understanding, consistent with their right to participate effectively in the proceedings from the earliest stage.[34] This might include, for example, an adjusted verbal explanation, the use of an easy-read or translated version of the rights and entitlements notice, or the use of a hearing loop.[35]

(c) Child suspects: ensuring understanding of rights and entitlements

4.36 Research suggests that children may be less aware of their rights and entitlements than adults,[36] and less likely to exercise those rights of which they are aware.[37] It is particularly important, therefore, that custody officers take extra care to ensure that children understand their rights, especially the right to legal advice and the role of the appropriate adult. Children should also be told of their right to make a complaint about their treatment and how to do that. Any complaint made by a child should be referred to the local authority Designated Officer, who has a duty to investigate.[38]

(d) Suspects who are blind, visually impaired, or unable to read: help with documents

4.37 Where the suspect is blind, visually impaired, or unable to read, the custody officer should ensure that someone likely to take an interest in him or her and not

---

[33] APP(DC), 'Response, Arrest and Detention', 2.2.

[34] *Panovits v Cyprus* at [67], and EU Directive 2010/64.

[35] APP(DC), 'Response, Arrest and Detention', 5.

[36] J. Jacobson and J. Talbot, *Vulnerable Defendants in the Criminal Courts: A Review of Provision for Vulnerable Adults and Children* (Prison Reform Trust, 2009). Also E. S. Scott and T. Grisso, 'The Evolution of Adolescence: A Developmental Perspective on Juvenile Justice Reform' (1997) *Journal of Criminal Law and Criminology*, 88(1), 137.

[37] S. Choongh, *Policing as Social Discipline* (Clarendon Press, 1997); and N. Hazel, A. Hagell, and L. Brazier, *Young Offenders' Perceptions of Their Experiences in the Criminal Justice System* (Economic and Social Research Council, 2003).

[38] APP(DC), 'Detainee Care: Children and Young Persons', 3.3.

involved in the investigation of the allegation (e.g. a legal representative, a relative, or an appropriate adult (where one is required)) is available to help check any documentation (Code C 3.5(c)(ii) and 3.20). Such assistance should also be given where that individual is subject to identification or other evidential procedures (Code D 2.13).[39]

(e) Suspects with language or communication difficulties: interpreters

If the suspect appears to be someone who does not understand or speak English, **4.38** or who has a hearing or speech impediment, the custody officer must ensure that an interpreter is called without delay to enable the suspect to understand his or her rights and entitlements, to support them in any subsequent consultation with a legal adviser, and in interview (Code C 3.5(c)(ii) and 3.12, and NFG 13B).

Where the difficulty relates to a hearing or speech impediment, then 'interpreter' **4.39** includes 'appropriate assistance necessary' to enable the person to understand their right and entitlements (e.g. a sign language interpreter). Interpretation may now be provided by live link, where that is considered appropriate (Code C 13.12 and Annex N).

A suspect requiring interpretation assistance must be told of their right to **4.40** interpretation and translation (as set out in Code C (13 and Annex M). They should also be given a notice (in a language they understand) setting out those rights and detailing how the provisions apply to them. This should be explained through interpretation if an appropriate translation of the notice is not available.

(f) Foreign nationals

Where the suspect is a citizen of an independent Commonwealth country, or is **4.41** a foreign national, they must also be informed, as soon as practicable, of their right to communicate with their High Commission, Embassy, or Consulate (Code C 3.12A).

F. Fitness to Be Detained and Risk Assessment

Every arrested suspect's fitness for detention must be assessed, but this will be **4.42** particularly important where the suspect is vulnerable. Whether an arrested individual is fit to be detained is a decision that must be made by the custody

---

[39] Police and Criminal Evidence Act 1984 Code D—Code of Practice for the Identification of Persons by Police Officers (February 2017).

officer. In order to make the decision, the custody officer must conduct a thorough risk assessment, potentially involving assessment by a health-care professional.

(a) Risk assessment

4.43 The purpose of the risk assessment is to identify whether an individual is likely to present specific risks to custody staff, to others in the custody suite, or to themselves. The initial risk assessment should include a check of the Police National Computer. The custody officer should also obtain from the arresting officer any information about mental or physical health issues indicated at the time of arrest, as well as any available information concerning the circumstances of arrest and the use of force (Code C 3.6). Efforts should also be made, where appropriate, to obtain information from family members or carers, the children's services team of the local authority where the child is 'looked after' or otherwise known to the local authority, and the Youth Offending Team (YOT) if the child has had previous contact with the youth justice system.

(b) Seeking medical attention

4.44 Officers are required to seek medical attention if the suspect appears to be suffering from physical illness or a mental disorder, is injured, or appears to need clinical attention (Code C 9.5), whether or not the suspect requests it. Officers are also required to consider medical attention for those suffering the effects of alcohol or drugs (Code C 9.5B and NFG 9C). There is in addition a duty for a health-care professional to be called as soon as practicable where a suspect requests a clinical examination. A suspect can also be examined by a medical practitioner of their choice at their expense (Code C 9.8).

(c) Risk assessment: general issues arising in respect of vulnerability

4.45 It is widely appreciated that the incidence of mental disorder and mental vulnerability among suspects of all ages is much higher than in the general population.[40] Research has also demonstrated that risk assessments in police custody under-identify those suspects with mental health issues, and learning disabilities and difficulties.[41]

---

[40] For a helpful comparison of research into prevalence rates, see National Appropriate Adults Network (NAAN) report, 'There to Help' (March 2015), appended Paper A, 'Literature Review', 1–3.

[41] I. McKinnon and D. Grubin, 'Health Screening of People in Police Custody—Evaluation of Current Police Screening Procedures in London, UK' (2013) *European Journal of Public Health*, 23(3), 399. See also: the Adebowale Report at [48] ff; and the Independent Police Complaints Commission report, 'Near Misses in Police Custody: A Collaborative Study with Forensic Medical Examiners in London' (2008).

In some areas of the country, piloting of improved risk assessment templates **4.46**
is showing better rates of identification of mental illness and suicidal ideation,
promising improved responses.[42] Whatever the template used, it is important
that an environment conducive to disclosures is achieved as far as possible, with
care taken to provide privacy and to handle information sensitively. However,
the layout of many custody suites, and the need for other officers to be present to
address risk issues, makes this difficult to achieve in practice.

APP(DC) emphasizes the importance of identifying and considering with care **4.47**
the individual risk that a particular vulnerable suspect may pose to themselves or
to others, and avoiding generalized responses. It also stresses the need for ongoing
risk assessment, and the importance of taking into account the adverse effect that
the experience of being in a custody suite can have on an individual.[43] In addition, APP(MH) provides detailed guidance on the identification and assessment
of vulnerabilities arising from mental ill-health, learning disability, developmental disorders, and related issues.[44]

(d) Risk assessment: child suspects

The police have a duty under the Children Act 2004 s. 11 to ensure that they con- **4.48**
sider the need to safeguard and promote the welfare of children in their custody.
This includes the identification of concerns about a child's safety and well-being, the
sharing of information, and acting promptly to protect a child where that is needed.
Officers conducting risk assessments of child suspects should be aware that they
may identify a previously unrecognized risk to a child's safety or welfare and should
have sufficient training to enable them to make appropriate referrals, as required by
local child protection arrangements, and in line with statutory guidance.[45]

APP(DC) provides a helpful list of additional factors which may increase risks to **4.49**
the safety and well-being of child suspects.[46]

(e) Recording and handing over risk assessment information

It is essential that the risks identified, a care plan for monitoring those risks, and **4.50**
the level of observation required should be documented at the earliest opportunity and included within the custody record. This should include the health-care

---

[42] I. McKinnon and D. Grubin, 'Evidence-Based Risk Assessment in Police Custody: The
HELP-PC Study in London, UK' (2014) *Policing: A Journal of Policy and Practice* 8(2), 174.
[43] APP(DC), Risk Assessment.
[44] See, in particular, APP(MH) 'Mental vulnerability and illness'.
[45] See: HM Government guidance, 'Working Together to Safeguard Children: A Guide to
Interagency Working to Safeguard and Promote the Welfare of Children' (March 2015, updated
February 2017); and Welsh Assembly Government guidance, 'Safeguarding Children: Working
Together under the Children Act 2004' (April 2007).
[46] APP(DC), 'Detainee Care, Children and Young Persons', 3.1–3.2.

professional's clinical findings relevant to the suspect's custodial health care, with any concerns noted and directions given in respect of frequency of visits. Communication at shift handover should specifically include vulnerabilities, and the medical and welfare needs of suspects.[47]

G. Persons to Be Informed

(a) Child suspects: persons to be informed

4.51 Once the custody officer has determined that the suspect is to be treated as a 'juvenile', a number of duties to inform other persons are triggered, as discussed below.

(i) Duty to identify and inform the person responsible for the child suspect's welfare

4.52 The custody officer must take such steps as are practicable to identify the person or persons responsible for the welfare of the child suspect. The custody officer must inform that person, as soon as is practicable: that the child has been arrested, why they have been arrested, and where they are being detained (PACE s. 57 and Code C 3.13).

4.53 The person responsible for a child suspect's welfare is:

- the child's parent or guardian;
- if the child is in local authority or voluntary organization care or otherwise 'looked after' (under the Children Act 1989), whoever has been appointed by the authority or organization to be responsible for the child's welfare; or
- any other person who has, for the time being, assumed responsibility for the child's welfare.

4.54 Other people who should be identified and informed are as follows:

- if the child is under a court order, reasonable steps should be taken to notify the 'responsible officer' who supervises or monitors the child. This would normally be a member of the YOT (where the child is subject to, for example, a community order) or the contractor providing monitoring (where the child is subject to a curfew order with electronic monitoring) (Code C 3.14, PACE s. 57); and
- if the child's parents are not responsible for the child's welfare (because, for example, the child is in local authority care), they should normally be contacted, even though there is no legal obligation to inform the parents in such a situation (Code C NFG 3C).

---

[47] See APP(DC), 'Risk Assessment', for full guidance on risk assessment.

In many cases, these obligations in fact require the custody officer to contact only **4.55**
a single individual, the child's parent, who may also be called upon to act as AA.
However, custody officers should be alive to the possibility that they may need
to contact a number of individuals. Although time-consuming, making those
contacts also presents an opportunity to ensure that appropriate multi-agency
information sharing and cooperation is triggered at an early stage in the criminal
process.

(ii)   Duty to inform the appropriate adult and require his or her attendance

The custody officer is also required as soon as practicable to inform the AA of the **4.56**
grounds for the detention of the child and their whereabouts, and to ask the AA
to come to the police station to see the child.

These duties to inform are in addition to the child suspect's right, in common **4.57**
with all detainees, to have a person known to them, or likely to take an interest in their welfare, informed of their whereabouts, and their additional right
to make a phone call or write a letter ('Right not to be held incommunicado':
Code C section 5). These rights may be delayed in accordance with Code C
Annex B, but the requirements for the person responsible for the child's welfare
to be informed, and for an AA to be informed and asked to attend (for a child or
vulnerable adult suspect), cannot be delayed.

(iii)   Who is eligible to act as an appropriate adult for a child suspect?

Code C provides that an AA for a child suspect means: **4.58**

- the parent, guardian, or, if the child is in the care of the local authority or a
  voluntary organization, a person representing that authority or organization;
- a social worker of the local authority; or
- failing these, some other responsible adult aged 18 or over who is not a police
  officer, employed by the police, or providing services or support to the police
  on a voluntary or contractual basis (Code C 1.7(a)).

This list is intended to operate as a hierarchy of preference, so that a parent or **4.59**
guardian is asked to act as the AA wherever that person is available and suitable. Failing that, a social worker should be called to act. However, Code C
does not provide any guidance on what efforts should be made to contact or
secure the attendance of the child's parent of guardian before turning to a local
authority AA. This decision will often require the custody officer to balance
the desirability of parental involvement against the need to avoid prolonging
the child's detention. Local authorities have a legal duty under the Crime and
Disorder Act 1998 (CDA 1998) s. 38 to ensure provision of AAs for child suspects, through their YOT. Arrangements vary across the country. Some local
authorities use volunteer appropriate adult schemes; others make use of paid
providers.

4.60 Only if a social worker or social services representative is not available should 'some other responsible adult' be identified. Apart from the restriction on police officers, police staff, and police volunteers and contractors acting in this capacity, under Code C any responsible adult may be selected.

(iv) Who is not appropriate to act as appropriate adult for a child suspect?

4.61 Although eligible, there may be a number of reasons why a particular adult, including a parent or guardian, is not appropriate to act as AA for a child suspect. Code C NFG 1B provides that an adult will not be appropriate if he or she is:

- suspected of involvement in the offence;
- the victim of the alleged offence;
- a witness to the alleged offence;
- involved in the investigation;
- received, or was present for, an admission about the alleged offence from the child prior to attending as the AA (including where the adult in question is a social worker or member of the YOT) (see also Code C NFG 1C); or
- an estranged parent, where the child detainee has 'expressly and specifically' objected to their presence.

In addition, an adult will not be appropriate if he or she is:

- a solicitor or an independent custody visitor who is present at the police station in that capacity (Code C NFG IF); or
- suspected of involvement in the commission, preparation, or instigation of acts of terrorism (in the case of a child suspect arrested under Terrorism Act 2000 s. 41).

4.62 These restrictions are designed to ensure that the AA operates impartially and fairly, undistracted by other duties, and that the child suspect and the court has confidence that they will do so. A care home manager, for example, who calls the police to attend a domestic incident at the home, while he or she may not be a witness, might be considered to be sufficiently 'involved in the investigation' to exclude any possibility of their being able to act as the AA.[48]

4.63 Although not explicitly addressed in Code C, the custody officer will also have to be alive to the possibility that an otherwise eligible AA may be unsuitable by virtue of their own vulnerability. In the case of *Morse and Others* (1991) Crim LR 195, the court rejected the defendant's father as a suitable person to act as AA. He had an IQ of between 60 and 70, was virtually illiterate, and, the court concluded, probably incapable of appreciating the gravity of his son's predicament

---

[48] *DPP v Morris* (1990) 8 October, unreported.

(but see by contrast *W* (1994) Crim LR 130). Decisions as to whether an eligible AA may be inappropriate to act are not always straightforward.[49]

(b) Vulnerable adult suspects: persons to be informed

(i) *Duty to inform the appropriate adult and require his or her attendance*

As with child suspects, where a suspect is a vulnerable adult, the custody officer is **4.64** required to inform an AA as soon as practicable of the grounds for the detention of the vulnerable adult, and their whereabouts, and to ask the AA to come to the police station to see the suspect (Code C 3.15). However, there is no additional requirement for the custody officer to inform any other person responsible for the welfare of a vulnerable adult suspect about that person's arrest and detention.

(ii) *Who is eligible to act as an appropriate adult for a vulnerable adult suspect?*

Code C provides that an AA for a vulnerable adult suspect means: **4.65**

- a relative, guardian, or other person responsible for the suspect's care or custody;
- someone experienced in dealing with mentally disordered or mentally vulnerable people, but who is not a police officer or employed by the police; or
- failing these, some other responsible adult aged 18 or over who is not a police officer or employed by the police, or providing services or support to the police on a voluntary or contractual basis (Code C 1.7(b)).

As with AAs for child suspects, the list at Code C 1.7(b) is drafted as a hier- **4.66** archy for identifying the AA for a vulnerable adult suspect. Officers should begin with identifying a relative, guardian, or other person responsible for the suspect's care, moving finally to some other responsible adult only where the preceding two categories do not yield an eligible and appropriate AA. This is subject, however, to Code C NFG 1D, which suggests that it may be 'more satisfactory' if the AA for a vulnerable adult suspect is someone experienced or trained in the care of that person, rather than a relative lacking such qualifications; but that if the suspect prefers a relative to act as AA, or objects to a particular person identified as a more suitable AA, then his or her wishes should be respected if practicable.

(iii) *Who is not appropriate to act as the appropriate adult for a vulnerable adult suspect?*

The same restrictions (Code C NFG 1B) which apply for AAs for child suspects **4.67** apply for AAs for vulnerable adult suspects. See paragraphs 4.61 et seq. '(iv) Who is not appropriate to act as appropriate adult for a child suspect?' for full details

---

[49] For fuller discussion, see E. Cape, *Defending Suspects at Police Stations* (6th edn, Legal Action Group, 2011).

of those factors which may render an otherwise eligible adult ineligible to act as an AA.

4.68 It is worth noting that, in contrast to the provision of AAs for child suspects, PACE itself includes no requirement for the police to secure AA provision for vulnerable adult suspects. Significantly, there is no statutory requirement for local authorities to have in place provision for AA services for vulnerable adults in the same way as for child suspects under the CDA 1998 s. 38. As a result, the availability and quality of AAs in different areas is highly variable.[50]

(iv) Consequences of failure to provide an appropriate adult for a vulnerable adult suspect

4.69 Despite the mandatory requirement under Code C to provide an AA for a vulnerable adult suspect, the response of the courts to failures to secure such support has been somewhat inconsistent, and to a degree has undermined the importance of the role of the AA for vulnerable adults. In the early years following the introduction of PACE, the Court of Appeal took a robust approach, quashing convictions where confession evidence had been obtained in the absence of an AA where one was required by the Codes (see, e.g., *R v Cox* [1991] Crim LR 276 and *R v Kenny* [1994] Crim LR 284). However, since the late 1990s, the Court of Appeal has taken a rather more pragmatic approach. Following *R v Aspinall* [1999] 2 Cr App R 115 and *R v Gill* [2004] EWCA Crim 3245, the court should ask what had been lost by the absence of the AA, and whether admission of the evidence, as a consequence, would have such an adverse effect upon fairness that it should be excluded (see, e.g., *R v Wilding*[51]). Absence of an AA where a solicitor was present would be unlikely in itself to justify exclusion of an interview (*R v Brown*[52]).

H. The Role of the Appropriate Adult

4.70 The involvement of an appropriate adult for child and vulnerable adult suspects is the only really significant adjustment of the custody procedures for vulnerable individuals. The courts have acknowledged the AA's key role for vulnerable suspects, particularly for child suspects, in acting as the 'gateway to a young person's access to justice' and in making good the power 'imbalance' which is

---

[50] See NAAN, 'There to Help', which identifies the shortcomings in provision of AAs for vulnerable adult suspects and makes recommendations for reform.
[51] [2010] EWCA Crim 2799.
[52] [2011] EWCA Crim 1606.

the 'inevitable result when a child or young person is confronted with criminal justice'.[53]

(a) The scope of the appropriate adult's role

The AA role is not clearly defined in PACE or the Codes. CDA 1998 s. 38(4)(a) **4.71** identifies the purpose of the AA as being to 'safeguard the interests' of a suspect while detained or questioned. Home Office Guidance for AAs suggests that there are four overlapping aspects of the role:

- to assist the individual to ensure that they understand what is happening at the police station during the interview and investigative stages;
- to support, advise, and assist the individual;
- to ensure that the police act fairly and respect the rights of the individual; and
- to help communication between the individual, the police, and others.[54]

Research has repeatedly suggested that the role requires clarification.[55] What is **4.72** clear, however, is that whoever attends is required to be proactive in advocating on behalf of the suspect and will need to be assertive if they are to fulfil the role envisaged by the courts.

(b) Explaining the role for the appropriate adult who is a family member or other untrained adult

Research has raised a number of concerns about how effectively AAs who are fam- **4.73** ily members are able to fulfil all the requirements of the role. In particular, obser- vations in custody suites and examination of interview transcripts have identified that AAs who are family members can be unsupportive of vulnerable suspects, showing distress, hostility, and even violence towards the suspect, particularly where there is a background of family conflict.[56] Conversely, it is widely acknowl- edged that for many vulnerable suspects the familiarity of an AA who is a family member can be a source of considerable reassurance and emotional support.[57]

Although a vulnerable individual is required to be told by the custody officer **4.74** of the AA's duty to give advice and assistance, Code C stipulates no similar

---

[53] *HC v Secretary of State for Home Department* [2013] EWHC 982 (Admin) at [68].

[54] Home Office and National Appropriate Adults Network, 'Guide for Appropriate Adults' (February 2011). See also Youth Justice Board, 'Appropriate Adults: Guide for Youth Justice Professionals' (19 December 2014).

[55] See, e.g., J. Williams, 'The Inappropriate Adult' (2000) *Journal of Social Welfare & Family Law*, 22(1), 43; and H. Pierpoint, 'Extending and Professionalizing the Role of the Appropriate Adult' (2011) *Journal of Social Welfare & Family Law*, 33(2), 139.

[56] T. Bucke and D. Brown, 'In Police Custody: Police Powers and Suspects' Rights under the Revised PACE Codes of Practice', Home Office Research Study No. 174 (Home Office, 1997); and S. Medford, G. H. Gudjonsson, and J. Pearse, 'The Efficacy of the Appropriate Adult Safeguard During Police Interviewing' (2003) *Legal and Criminological Psychology*, 8(2), 253.

[57] See, e.g., NAAN, 'There to Help', 12.

requirement for the custody officer to inform the AA of the scope of their role at that initial stage. The only requirement for the AA to be given information about their role is in respect of the interview (Code C 11.17) (discussed in more detail at paragraphs 4.132 et seq., '(c) The appropriate adult's role in interview'). Although it is undeniable that the scope of the role would be difficult to convey to an AA who has received no training in the task,[58] best practice requires that the custody officer should endeavour, where the AA is untrained, to explain to the AA at least the aspects of the role identified in the Home Office guidance. An untrained AA should be provided with a copy of the guidance and given time to read it. He or she should also be told that the custody officer will be available to answer any questions they may have. Trained AAs should also be offered the guidance.[59]

(c) Legal professional privilege and appropriate adults

4.75 AAs do not enjoy legal professional privilege. Although rarely called upon to do so, an AA could be required to, or voluntarily, give evidence about information provided to them by a vulnerable suspect when speaking alone together about any matter relating to the allegation.[60] However, the presence of an AA in a suspect's consultation with their legal representative does not destroy the legal privilege that otherwise attaches to that exchange,[61] contrary to the impression given in Code C NFG 1E. An AA cannot, therefore, be required by the police or the court to disclose what was said by a vulnerable suspect in a legal consultation. However, there remains some uncertainty as to whether the AA could voluntarily disclose that information.[62]

4.76 It is the decision of the suspect, having received advice from their solicitor, whether the AA should be present in any legal consultation. In practice, legal representatives generally advise against the AA's presence for consultation. This runs the risk of undermining the AA's role in facilitating communication between the suspect and others in police custody, and limits their ability to check the suspect's understanding of the advice they have received. Good practice suggests that the legal representative should tell the AA of the advice given to the suspect in his or her absence so that the AA is able to check understanding and support the suspect in any decision made.

---

[58] See, e.g., Williams, 'The Inappropriate Adult'.

[59] See APP(MH), 'Mental health—detention'.

[60] Perhaps the most well-known example being the appropriate adult who supported Rosemary West who gave evidence on behalf of the Crown at trial (*R v West* [1996] 2 Cr App R 374).

[61] *A Local Authority v B* [2008] EWHC 1017 (Fam) at [25].

[62] See C. Bath, 'Legal Privilege and Appropriate Adults' (2014) *Criminal Law & Justice*, 178(27), 404.

(d) The appropriate adult's involvement at specific stages

(i) Rights and entitlements

If the AA is already present when the suspect is booked in, then the vulnerable **4.77** suspect should be told of his or her rights and entitlements in the presence of the AA. If the AA arrives later at the police station, then the suspect's rights and entitlements should be given again in the AA's presence (Code C 3.17). The AA should also be provided with a copy of the notice of rights and entitlements (Code C 3.17). At this stage, the suspect should also be told that the AA's role includes giving advice and assistance and that they may consult privately with their AA at any time (Code C 3.18).

In practice, in some areas the AA is not required to attend until the police are **4.78** ready to interview the suspect.[63] This inevitably reduces the ability of the AA to support and assist the suspect, especially to ensure that they understand and are afforded their rights and entitlements, prior to interview. There are plainly resource constraints, but ideally the AA would visit the vulnerable suspect in the custody suite as soon as practicable after their arrival so that rights and entitlements can be explained in the AA's presence, or at the very least the vulnerable suspect would have the opportunity to speak on the telephone to the AA at that stage.

(ii) Inspection of the custody record

Code C 2.4 requires the AA (as well as the suspect's legal representative) to be **4.79** allowed to inspect the whole of the custody record 'as soon as practicable after their arrival at the station and at any other time on request'. This includes, in particular, access to:

- information about the circumstances and grounds of arrest; and
- the records of each authorization for further detention (Code C 2.4).

The custody officer is not required to show the risk assessment to the suspect, or **4.80** anybody acting on their behalf, including the AA, save in respect of any information which that person needs to have to prevent them being put at risk (Code C 3.8A).

The custody record is an important source of information in the identification of **4.81** any deficits in the care and treatment of the suspect, and in terms of enabling any challenge to the continued detention of that individual. Although inspection has revealed that in some areas only the front sheet of the custody record is provided to the AA,[64] review of the whole record is important to ensure that the child or

---

[63] See *Who's Looking Out for the Children?* (Criminal Justice Joint Inspectorate, 2011) 3.38. Also *The Welfare of Vulnerable People in Police Custody* (Her Majesty's Inspectorate of Constabulary, 2015) 91.

[64] See CJJI, *Who's Looking Out for the Children?*, 3.21.

vulnerable adult suspect has received their rights and entitlements and that any welfare concerns have been addressed.

(iii) Requests for legal advice

4.82 The AA is not present to provide legal advice, but they are required to consider whether the suspect should have advice from a legal representative, and have the right to ask for a legal representative to attend for the vulnerable suspect, if this would be in his or her best interests (Code C 6.5A). The police are required to act on such a request without delay (Code C 3.19, subject to Annex B). This is an important power, especially given the tendency for some vulnerable suspects to waive their right to legal advice on the basis that this might result in their earlier release. The power can be exercised where the suspect objects to the calling of a legal representative; however, the suspect cannot be forced to see the representative 'if they are adamant that they do not wish to do so' (Code C 6.5A).

(iv) Continued detention

4.83 If the AA is 'available at that time', he or she must be given the opportunity to make representations when an officer is deciding whether to authorize continued detention of a vulnerable suspect (Code C 15.3).

(v) Searches, identification procedures, and interview

4.84 See paragraphs 4.93 et seq., 'J. Searches: PACE ss 54 and 55 and Code C Annex A', paragraphs 4.107 et seq., 'K. Identification and Other Evidential Procedures', and paragraphs 4.132 et seq., '(c) The appropriate adult's role in interview' for the specific duties of an AA role in relation to searches, identification procedures, and interviews respectively.

I. Conditions of Detention, Care, and Treatment

4.85 Custody officers and staff must be alive to the likelihood that vulnerable suspects will need additional support and care during detention. Code C ss 8 and 9 set out the conditions of detention, and detail provisions for the care and treatment of all detainees. Code C NFG 8C directs attention also to more detailed guidance provided in the College of Policing's APP(DC).

(a) Checks and support

4.86 Code C specifically recommends that 'whenever possible' child and vulnerable adult suspects should be visited in their cell or detention room 'more frequently' than other suspects (Code C NFG 9B). In practice, the risk assessment for many such suspects will have identified a more demanding observation and checking schedule than for most suspects in any event.

Participants in vulnerable suspect voice projects, particularly children, have **4.87** described how stressful and disorientating detention in police custody can be,[65] and the difference that can be made by supportive custody staff. The provision of age-appropriate, and accessible, reading materials, and responsiveness to calls for assistance is particularly important for vulnerable suspects.

(b) Visits

In addition, child and vulnerable adult suspects who are likely to be held for **4.88** longer than twenty-four hours (or overnight) should be allowed to have visits from parents or carers.[66]

(c) Particular measures for child suspects

The Children and Young Persons Act 1933 (CYPA 1933) s. 31 requires arrange- **4.89** ments to be made to prevent child suspects, while detained in custody, from associating with any adult charged with an offence. Code C 8.8 goes further, stipulating that a child may under no circumstances be placed in a cell with a detained adult (whether the adult has been charged or not).

Code C 8.8 also stipulates that a child suspect should not be held in a police cell, **4.90** unless no other secure accommodation is available and it is not practicable to supervise them without placing them in a cell (or where a cell is more comfortable than any secure alternative at the station). However, inspection evidence suggests that in practice facilities are often insufficient to enable this to be achieved.[67] If a child suspect is placed in a cell, the reasons should be recorded in the custody record (Code C 8.10). All girl suspects should remain in the care of a female officer while they are detained (CYPA 1933 s. 31). That female carer does not need to be physically present at all times with the girl suspect unless the risk assessment requires that specifically, but the girl suspect should be told that she can see the carer at any time.[68]

(d) Particular measures for vulnerable adult suspects

Under the Equality Act 2010 s. 20, staff have a duty to make reasonable adjust- **4.91** ments for those with a disability to ensure that they are not disadvantaged during detention. Adult suspects who require special provisions for any reason (e.g. disability or health-care requirements) ought not to be kept in multi-occupancy calls, even in exceptional circumstances.[69]

---

[65] See, e.g., HMIC, *The Welfare of Vulnerable People in Police Custody*, 86.
[66] APP(DC), 'Detainee Care', 4.1.2.
[67] HMIC, *The Welfare of Vulnerable People in Police Custody*, 76–7.
[68] APP(DC), 'Detainee Care, Children and Young Persons', 7.1.
[69] APP(DC), 'Response, Arrest and Detention', 3.2.1.

4.92 For all suspects, additional approved restraints in locked cells should not be used 'unless absolutely necessary'. But if a suspect is deaf or a vulnerable adult, particular care must be taken in deciding whether to use such restraints (Code C 8.2).

J. Searches: PACE ss 54 and 55 and Code C Annex A

4.93 Code C Annex A sets out the requirements for intimate searches (examination of a person's body orifices other than the mouth) and strip searches (searches involving the removal of more than outer clothing). Annex A rightly draws attention to the 'intrusive nature' of searches of this sort, and cautions against underestimating the risks of such a search. In respect of both intimate and strip searches, Annex A requires these searches to be conducted 'with proper regard to the sensitivity and vulnerability' of the individual, and for intimate searches 'every reasonable effort' must be made to secure 'cooperation and minimize embarrassment' (Annex A 11(d)), regardless of whether or not the individual falls into one of the 'special groups'.

(a) Specific duty of care to prevent self-harm

4.94 The particular vulnerability to self-harm in police custody of mentally vulnerable individuals is clearly established.[70] In *Reeves v Commissioner of Police of the Metropolis* [2000] 1 AC 360, the House of Lords determined that, in light of the total control exercised by the police over those in their custody, and the inherent stresses on a detainee in police custody, exceptionally the police have a duty to take reasonable care to prevent a suspect from self-harming, whether that individual is of sound mind, mentally disordered, or vulnerable in some other way.

4.95 One particular mechanism adopted by officers to satisfy that duty is the use of PACE ss 54 and 55 to ensure that items which may be used by a suspect to self-harm are removed. However, APP(DC) cautions against officers automatically considering that strip-searching an individual for their own protection is the best way to prevent them from harming themselves.[71]

4.96 The importance of conducting such searches with sensitivity cannot be overstated, particularly in light of suspect voice research with vulnerable suspects conducted on behalf of Her Majesty's Inspectorate of Constabulary (HMIC), which revealed a 'strong view that strip-searches were undignified and degrading'.[72] Following the recent case of *D v Chief Constable of Merseyside Police* [2015]

---

[70] See, e.g., Home Affairs Committee, *Policing and Mental Health: Eleventh Report of Session 2014–15* (The Stationery Office, 2015).

[71] APP(DC), 'Control, Restraint and Searches', 6.2.

[72] HMIC, *The Welfare of Vulnerable People in Police Custody*, 89–90.

EWCA Civ 114, where an officer seeks to remove more than outer clothing from a suspect on the basis that it may be used by the detainee to harm him- or herself (PACE s. 54), the provisions relating to the conduct of strip searches (Code C Annex A paragraph 11) will apply.[73] Although officers in *D* were found to have acted 'reasonably and proportionately' in strip-searching D, a 14-year-old girl, Pitchford LJ expressed concern about the way in which D had been dealt with, particularly the removal of her clothes when she was in a state of distress, 'without thought for alternative and less invasive measures to protect her from herself'.[74]

(b) General safeguards for searches

Code C Annex A details a range of safeguards for all suspects who are to be searched, including searching by an officer of the same gender as the individual suspect, and minimum requirements as to who should be present for the conducting of the search itself. Police officers are required to show particular sensitivity when dealing with transgender individuals (including transsexual and transvestite suspects) in respect of establishing gender for the purposes of searching that person (see Code C Annex L for detailed guidance). **4.97**

Child and vulnerable adult suspects are subject to the same searching procedures as other suspects, save for the following special protections. **4.98**

(c) Special protections for child suspects

(i) Intimate search of a child suspect

In respect of an intimate search, an AA is required to be present: **4.99**

- when a child suspect is told of the authority and grounds for an intimate search (Code C Annex A 2A);
- for the seeking and giving of appropriate consent where the intimate search is a drugs search (Code C Annex A 2(a)(ii)); and
- for the giving of the warning that refusal without good cause to give appropriate consent for a drugs search may harm their case if it comes to trial (Code C Annex A 2B).

Appropriate consent is required in writing where officers propose to conduct an intimate drugs search. What is meant by appropriate consent in such a situation depends on the age of the child, as follows: **4.100**

- aged 14–17 years: the child's consent, and the consent of their parent or guardian, is required;[75]

---

[73] See commentary [2015] CLR 539.
[74] [2015] EWCA Civ 114 at [44] and commentary [2015] CLR 539.
[75] The Policing and Crime Act 2017 s. 73 removed the distinction between 16 and 17 year olds for the purposes of appropriate consent.

- aged 10–13 years: only the parent or guardian's consent is required (although the child's consent should be sought as well) (Code C Annex A 2B).

(Similar protections are available for a child where the police propose to x-ray or ultra-sound scan him or her: see Code C Annex K.)

4.101 An intimate search of a child may be carried out in the absence of the AA, but only where the child has signified in the presence of the AA that they do not want the AA present during the search, and the AA agrees. Such a decision must be recorded in the custody record and signed by the AA. Otherwise, the AA must be present for the intimate search, and must be of the same gender as the child suspect, unless the child specifically requests the presence of a particular adult of the opposite gender and that person is readily available (Code C Annex A 5).

(ii) Strip search of a child suspect

4.102 There is no consent requirement for a strip search. Otherwise, the special protections for child suspects mirror those for intimate searches. The only difference is that, for strip searches, the police can search in the absence of an AA where an 'urgent' search is required—that is, where there is a risk of serious harm to the individual suspect or others (Code C Annex A 11(c)).

(d) Special protections for vulnerable adult suspects

(i) Intimate search of a vulnerable adult suspect

4.103 In respect of an intimate search, an AA is required to be present:

- when the vulnerable adult suspect is told of the authority and grounds for an intimate search (Code C Annex A 2A);
- for the seeking and giving of appropriate consent where the intimate search is a drugs search under Code C Annex A 2(a)(ii) (Code C Annex A, 2B); and
- for the giving of the warning that refusal without good cause to give appropriate consent for a drugs search may harm the suspect's case if it comes to trial (Code C Annex A 2B).

4.104 The requirement for appropriate consent for a drugs search is satisfied by the vulnerable adult suspect's consent alone (Code C Annex A 2(a)(ii)). (Similar protections are available where the police propose to x-ray or ultra-sound scan him or her: see Code C Annex K.)

4.105 The search of a vulnerable adult suspect must take place in the presence of an AA of the same gender as the suspect, although he or she can specifically request the presence of a particular adult of the opposite gender as long as they are readily available. Unlike in the case of a child suspect, a vulnerable adult suspect is not entitled to refuse to have an AA present (Code C Annex A5). It is not clear what the basis of this distinction is, since the AA identified by the police may, as for a child suspect, be someone previously unknown to the suspect concerned.

(ii) Strip search of a vulnerable adult suspect

There is no consent requirement for a strip search. Otherwise, the protections for **4.106** vulnerable adult suspects mirror those for intimate searches of vulnerable adult suspects, with the single exception that the police may strip search a vulnerable adult suspect in the absence of the AA in cases of urgency (Code C Annex A 11(c)).

K. Identification and Other Evidential Procedures

PACE Code D sets out the safeguards for the conducting of identification pro- **4.107** cedures, including physical or video identification parades, the taking of photographs, footwear impressions, DNA samples, examination for marks, and fingerprinting. Where such a procedure requires a child or vulnerable adult suspect to be given or to provide information, this must occur in the presence of an AA (Code D 2.14). Likewise, where the participation of a child or vulnerable adult suspect is required for an identification procedure, the AA must be present (Code D 2.15).

Where consent is required, for vulnerable adult suspects this consent will only **4.108** be valid if given in the presence of the AA (Code D 2.12). The requirements for informed consent from a child suspect are as set out at paragraphs 4.99 et seq., '(i) Intimate search of a child suspect' (Code D 2.12). However, if the parent or guardian refuses to consent, or has not, following reasonable efforts, been located, and this is the only barrier to an identification procedure occurring, the police may conduct a video identification procedure using still images, obtained covertly if necessary (Code D 3.21).

L. Fitness to Be Interviewed

(a) What does fitness to be interviewed mean?

Before any suspect can be interviewed, it is necessary to determine whether he or **4.109** she is fit to be interviewed (Code C 12.3 and Annex G). Code C 12.3 requires the custody officer to determine and consider:

- the risks to the individual's 'physical or mental state' if he or she were to be interviewed; and
- whether any safeguards are required so that the interview can take place.

Code C Annex G provides further guidance as to how a police officer or health- **4.110** care professional should assess whether a suspect might be 'at risk' in an interview. Paragraph 2 of Annex G widens what constitutes 'risk' for the purposes of fitness for interview. In addition to the risk that conducting the interview could 'significantly harm the detainee's physical or mental state' (Annex G 2(a) reflecting Code C 12.3), Annex G 2(b) states that a suspect may also be 'at risk' in an interview if anything he or she says in response to the allegation '*might* be considered unreliable'[76] at trial because of his or her physical or mental state at the time of interview.

4.111 Code C 12.3 (read in conjunction with Code C 11.18) requires the following suspects to be treated as always being at some risk during an interview:

- a child suspect;
- a vulnerable adult suspect;
- anyone who appears to be unable to appreciate the significance of questions and their answers; and
- anyone who appears to be unable to understand what is happening because of the effects of drink or drugs, or an illness or condition.

4.112 Having addressed the question of whether an individual is 'at risk,' Code C Annex G 3 then sets out the factors which must be considered in assessing whether the suspect should be interviewed:

- how the suspect's physical or mental state might affect his or her ability to understand the nature and purpose of the interview, to comprehend what is being asked, and to appreciate the significance of any answers given, and make rational decisions about whether he or she wants to say anything;
- the extent to which the suspect's replies may be affected by his or her physical or mental condition, rather than representing a rational and accurate explanation of his or her involvement in the offence; and
- how the nature of the interview, which could include particularly probing questions, might affect the suspect.

4.113 What is clear is that consideration of fitness for interview, as defined by Code C, is not just about the effect on the suspect of the interview process, but, importantly, requires consideration of the suspect's ability to participate effectively in the interview. This latter requirement includes not just understanding and answering questions reliably, but appreciating the nature and purpose of the interview itself.

4.114 Code C 12.3 makes plain that where the custody officer considers that to interview the suspect would cause 'significant harm' to his or her physical or mental state, then the officer should not allow the suspect to be interviewed.

4.115 However, Code C 12.3 is not so prescriptive where the risks identified relate to the reliability of the suspect's answers in interview or ability to participate effectively in the interview. In such cases, the wording of Code C 12.3 suggests

---

[76] Emphasis in the original.

greater discretion as to whether the individual should be interviewed, depending on whether safeguards can address the risks identified. The only stipulation in this regard is that a child or vulnerable adult may not be interviewed without an appropriate adult being present, save where an urgent interview is required (see below paragraphs 4.126 et seq., '(h) Urgent interviews (Code C 11.18)').

(b) Whose decision?

It is the responsibility of the custody officer to determine fitness for interview. **4.116** However, he or she should consult 'as necessary' with the officer in charge of the investigation and the appropriate health-care professional (Code C 12.3). If the custody officer has any doubts about the suspect's medical fitness for interview, then a health-care professional must assess the suspect before interview, and this may need to be repeated if the suspect's condition changes (Code C 12.3).[77]

(c) The health-care professional's role

When asked to assess an individual for fitness to be interviewed, the health-care **4.117** professional should:

- consider the functional ability of the suspect, rather than relying on a diagnosis (Code C Annex G 4). As the Annex notes, a person who has a mental disorder may still be fit for interview;
- advise on the need for an AA to be present (Code C Annex G 5);
- advise as to whether fitness for interview will need to be reassessed if the interview lasts longer than a specified time (Code C Annex G 5);
- consider whether more specialist opinion is required, and advise the custody officer accordingly (Code C Annex G 5);
- identify and quantify the risks to the individual suspect should he or she be interviewed (Code C Annex G 6);
- identify whether the individual's condition is likely to improve, if it is amenable to treatment, and how long may be required for any improvement in their condition to take effect (Code C Annex G 6); and
- advise the custody officer of the outcome of that assessment (Code C Annex G 7).

The custody officer must record the health-care professional's, and any other **4.118** expert's, assessment in the custody record (Code C Annex G 7) and take that advice into consideration (Code C 12.3). However, the final decision as to whether the interview goes ahead and, if so, what safeguards are required, is for the custody officer alone, subject to the requirement of an AA for a child or vulnerable adult suspect (Code C 12.3).

---

[77] APP(DC), 'Response, Arrest and Detention', 7.

(d) Meeting the challenge of identifying difficulties

4.119 Paragraphs 4.45 et seq., '(c) Risk assessment: general issues arising in respect of vulnerability' discussed the high incidence of mental health issues and mental vulnerability among the suspect population, and the challenges of identifying when an AA should be required to attend. The same challenges arise in respect of determining the separate question of fitness to be interviewed, and whether safeguards might address any risks identified. Many custody officers receive limited training in respect of identifying communication and participation issues. It is important that they are alive to the possibility of issues of unfitness for interview and follow guidance to seek the assessment of a health-care professional where they have any doubts.

4.120 The health-care professionals who advise custody officers are also often lacking in specialist training in identifying the sorts of conditions which may give rise to unfitness for interview. Health-care professionals are typically general nurses or general practitioners, and are not required to have specific training in recognizing mental health, learning disability, and related difficulties. It is important, therefore, for the health-care professional to bear in mind their duty to consider whether a more specialist opinion is required, and to advise the custody officer accordingly (Code C Annex G 5).

(e) Obtaining more specialist assessment

4.121 Where concerns remain that the suspect may not be fit for interview or requires additional safeguards, there are a number of steps that may be taken. Where the custody officer is reluctant to involve a health-care professional in the assessment, the suspect is entitled to request a clinical examination (Code C 9.8). In addition, the suspect also has the right to request independent examination by a medical expert of their choice, but at their own expense (Code C 9.8, PACE Code H[78] 9.10). This is a useful safeguard. Where an appropriate adult or legal representative is concerned that a specific condition of the suspect is not being appropriately assessed, then they may consider exercising this right and obtaining a specialist medical opinion. Where the suspect is legally aided, this should, if reasonably incurred, be recoverable as a disbursement.

4.122 In many force areas there are now liaison and diversion services[79] operating within police custody suites, with forensic mental health practitioners stationed

---

[78] Revised code of practice in connection with: the detention, treatment and questioning by police officers of persons in police detention under s. 41 of, and sch. 8 to, the Terrorism Act 2000. The treatment and questioning by police officers of detained persons in respect of whom an authorization to question after charge has been given under s. 22 of the Counter-Terrorism Act 2008, Police and Criminal Evidence Act 1984 (PACE)—Code H (February 2017).

[79] See, e.g., E. Disley, C. Taylor, K. Kruithof et al., *Evaluation of the Offender Liaison and Diversion Trial Schemes* (RAND Corporation, 2016), available at <http://www.rand.org/pubs/research_reports/RR1283.html> accessed 14 March 2017.

in, or available on call to, custody suites. Although local variations exist, the remit of such services is intended to cover the identification of communication and participation difficulties.[80] In most areas, they accept referrals not only from the police, but from AAs, legal representatives, family members, and suspects themselves.

(f) Safeguards other than the appropriate adult

Code C Annex G states explicitly that the custody officer should not be restricted **4.123** in his or her consideration to those safeguards which are required under the Code. Code C Annex G 8 gives as an example the presence of a health-care professional in interview to monitor the effects of the interview on the condition of the detainee, although anecdotal evidence suggests that such additional safeguards are rarely engaged.

One potential additional safeguard is the use of an intermediary to assist a **4.124** child or vulnerable adult suspect. An intermediary is an independent expert, normally a speech and language therapist, whose role is to facilitate communication and understanding between a vulnerable individual and the police or courts. As discussed in Chapter 11, 'Intermediaries', intermediaries are used to assist young or vulnerable witnesses and defendants to give evidence. The use of intermediaries for suspects is much less common in England and Wales,[81] but does occasionally occur, although no reference to intermediaries is made within Code C. There are two particular barriers to their wider use for vulnerable suspects: the first is identifying who should be responsible for the intermediary's fees; and the second is the time constraints when a suspect is held in custody. Identifying an intermediary with the appropriate specialist experience to support an individual with particular communication difficulties can take some time, and would rarely be achievable within the twenty-four hour initial detention period, under current arrangements. Where an intermediary is being considered, then the individual should be bailed to allow that assistance to be arranged.

---

[80] See NHS England Liaison and Diversion, 'Standard Service Specification 2016', 2.5.1.4 (screening for youths) and 2.5.2.4 (screening for adults) (forthcoming). Criminal Justice Liaison Services provide a comparable scheme in Wales. See Welsh Government, 'Criminal Justice Liaison Services in Wales: Policy Implementation Guidance' (2013).

[81] In Northern Ireland, intermediaries for vulnerable suspects are provided for by legislation and provisions relating to their use are included in Northern Ireland's PACE Codes. See P. Cooper and D. Wurtzel, 'Better the Second Time Around? Department of Justice Registered Intermediaries Schemes and Lessons from England and Wales' (2014) *Northern Ireland Legal Quarterly*, 65(1), 39–61; and DoJ, 'Northern Ireland Registered Intermediaries Schemes Pilot Project Phase II Review' (DoJ, July 2016).

(g) Where concerns remain

4.125 If, despite representations and/or efforts to achieve more expert assessment, a legal representative has concerns that a child or vulnerable adult suspect has been wrongly determined to be fit for interview, then he or she may advise the detainee to answer 'no comment' in interview.[82] Where an AA retains concerns which he or she does not feel have been adequately addressed by the custody officer or interviewing officer, then he or she should ask for their concerns to be noted on the custody record and they may wish to repeat those concerns for the audio/video recording at the outset of the interview.

(h) Urgent interviews (Code C 11.18)

4.126 There are very limited circumstances in which vulnerable suspects can be subject to an 'urgent interview'—that is, interviewed without the usual safeguards. An 'urgent interview' can only take place where an officer of superintendent rank or above is satisfied that the interview would not significantly harm the person's physical or mental state and where that officer considers that delaying the interview will lead to one of the circumstances set out in Code C 11.1:

1. interference with/harm to evidence or other people;
2. serious loss of, or damage to, property;
3. the alerting of other suspects still at large; or,
4. hindering the recovery of property obtained in an offence.

4.127 Where those conditions are met, a child or vulnerable adult suspect may be interviewed without an AA present, and a suspect requiring interpretation may be interviewed without the assistance of an interpreter. These circumstances also allow the interview of a suspect who appears unable to appreciate the significance of questions and their answers, or to understand what is happening because of the effect of drink, drugs, or any illness or condition. An urgent interview must be stopped as soon as enough information has been obtained to avert the consequences set out above (Code C 11.19).

M. Interview

(a) The need for special care

4.128 Clinical research has identified a number of factors which affect the ability of a suspect to cope with the demands and stresses of police interview, and raise the

---

[82] Although he or she will bear in mind that this will not provide an absolute bar to an adverse inference being drawn from their silence in interview under the Criminal Justice and Public Order Act 1994 s. 34 and *Condron and Condron* [1997] 1 Cr App R 185 at [191].

risk of unreliability in a suspect's responses to questioning. These include vulner-abilities which arise from mental disorder, abnormal mental states (such as mood disturbance or intoxication), impaired intellectual functioning (such as low IQ), and personality traits (such as suggestibility or acquiescence).[83] Such vulnerability may also arise as a result of the suspect's youth, immaturity, or lack of life experience. In particular, child suspects have been found to confess more readily and are more likely to make a false confession.[84]

Code C acknowledges the need for special care to be taken when a child or vulner-able adult suspect is interviewed (Code C NFG 11C). It notes that, although such suspects are able to give reliable evidence, they may 'without knowing or wishing to do so, be particularly prone in certain circumstances to provide information that may be unreliable, misleading or self-incriminating'. NFG 11C repeats the precautionary approach adopted in Code C 1.4 and 1.5 (referred to at paragraph 4.21, '(i) Identifying vulnerable adult suspects'), namely that wherever there is any doubt about a suspect's age, mental state, or capacity, an AA should be involved. It also reminds officers of the importance of obtaining corroboration of any facts admitted by a vulnerable suspect whenever possible. APP(DC) also notes that such suspects 'may be more suggestible and require special protection', but provides no further detail as to how this should be addressed in a police interview.[85] **4.129**

(b) Limited guidance for the interviewing of child or vulnerable adult suspects

The approach to be taken when interviewing vulnerable suspects is not set out in detailed guidance in the same way as the approach required when interviewing a child or vulnerable adult as a witness.[86] Nor does The Advocate's Gateway, for example, offer a 'toolkit' specifically addressing the interview of a child or vulnerable adult suspect.[87] Nonetheless, the principles set out in the toolkit guidance for the questioning of vulnerable witnesses and victims are readily applicable to the investigative interviewing of vulnerable suspects.[88] (See also Chapter 2, 'Vulnerable Witnesses: The Investigation Stage'.) **4.130**

In summary, questions should be short and simply phrased (*M v Leicestershire Constabulary* [2009] EWHC 3640 (Admin)). Interviewers should not use **4.131**

---

[83] For discussion, see G. Gudjonsson, 'Psychological Vulnerabilities During Police Interviews: Why Are They Important?' (2010) *Legal and Criminological Psychology*, 15, 161.

[84] For discussion, see M. Lamb and M. Sim, 'Developmental Factors Affecting Children in Legal Contexts' (2013) *Youth Justice*, 13(2), 131.

[85] APP, 'Investigation, Investigative Interviewing'.

[86] MoJ, *Achieving Best Evidence in Criminal Proceedings: Guidance on Interviewing Victims and Witnesses, and Using Special Measures* (MoJ, 2011) (discussed in full at Chapter 2).

[87] See <http://www.theadvocatesgateway.org/toolkits> accessed 14 March 2017.

[88] See, in particular, MoJ, *Achieving Best Evidence* guidance and the Advocates Gateway Toolkits 2 to 6 (available at <http://www.theadvocatesgateway.org/toolkits> accessed 14 March 2017).

complex or problematic question formats, such as tagged or legal-closure questions. Hypothetical questions, while they may lead to admissible responses, should be approached with caution (*R v Stringer* [2008] EWCA Crim 1222). Checking the suspect's understanding and monitoring the pace of questioning, and the duration of the interview, are also of critical importance.

(c) The appropriate adult's role in interview

4.132 Following Code C 11.15, a child or vulnerable adult suspect may not be interviewed in the absence of an AA (save where the interview is urgent: see paragraphs 4.126 et seq., '(h) Urgent interviews (Code C 11.18)').[89] The AA must be told at the outset of the interview that he or she is not expected simply to act as an observer, and that the purpose of their presence is to:

- advise the person being interviewed;
- observe whether the interview is being conducted properly and fairly; and
- facilitate communication with the person being interviewed (Code C 11.17).

4.133 This is a demanding role, especially for a family member, under emotional pressure themselves and acting with no training on how to ensure procedural compliance and fairness. There is no further guidance in Code C as to how the AA should fulfil this role. Unsurprisingly, research has tended to reveal limited, and at times unconstructive, input during interviews from AAs who are family members.[90] However, the courts have been slow to interfere with or question the efficacy and constructiveness of the support afforded by parents. See, for example, the case of *R v Jefferson*[91] at [27], in which a father who had 'intervened robustly from time to time, sometimes joining in the questioning of his son and challenging his exculpatory account of certain events', was found to have fulfilled his role as AA.

4.134 The AA must be present for the giving of a caution or a special warning (Code C 10.11A and 10.12). Code C NFG 10D requires the officer giving the caution, where it appears that the suspect does not understand the caution, to require the suspect to explain what he or she understands by it in their own words. However, the AA's presence for the giving of the caution or warning is meaningless if the AA does not also make the effort to satisfy him- or herself that the suspect has understood the words of the caution and their significance.

---

[89] The provisions requiring an AA to be present for a child or vulnerable adult suspect also apply to those individuals who are not arrested but have attended the police station voluntarily for interview. In addition, there is now a requirement for a child or vulnerable adult suspect to confirm, in the presence of their AA, their willingness to take part in the voluntary interview. For a child suspect, the agreement of a parent or guardian is also required (Code C 3.21).

[90] See, e.g., S. Medford, G. H. Gudjonsson, and J. Pearse, 'The Efficacy of the Appropriate Adult Safeguard During Police Interviewing' (2003) *Legal and Criminological Psychology*, 8(2), 253.

[91] [1994] 99 Cr App R 13.

The AA's role in interview is distinct from that of the legal representative. **4.135**
Although the AA is told by the interviewing officer that part of their role is to
'advise' the interviewee, it is important that the AA does not purport to give
the suspect legal advice, or contradict legal advice given by the legal representative in the presence of the interviewee, for example, on the issue of making
no comment or answering questions put. Should the AA have concerns about
the suspect's understanding of the advice which has been given, then he or she
should ask the interview to be suspended so that he or she can speak privately
to the legal representative, and to the suspect as well if that is appropriate.
Likewise, part of the AA's role is to ensure that questioning is fair and the
interview properly conducted. The AA must be ready to raise concerns during
the interview if he or she considers questions to be inappropriate or unfairly
phrased.

The AA may now be required to leave an interview, 'if their conduct is such **4.136**
that the interviewer is unable properly to put questions to the suspect' (Code C
11.17A). Such a step requires consultation with an officer of at least superintendent rank (or inspector if none is available) who would be required to warn the AA
that they are not entitled to obstruct proper questioning. If the consulted officer
decides to remove the AA, another AA must be obtained before the interview can
continue. NFG 11F provides further clarification of the circumstances in which
this new power may be engaged.

(d) Those requiring interpreters

Where the suspect or a family member acting as AA requires an interpreter, then **4.137**
the interview cannot proceed in the absence of someone capable of interpreting
(Code C 13.2 and 13.2A). The only exception is the holding of urgent interviews
(see paragraphs 4.126 et seq., '(h) Urgent interviews (Code C 11.18)').

N. Charging and Out-of-Court Disposals

(a) Decision-making: child suspects

The Crown Prosecution Service's (CPS) guidance on *Youth Offenders*[92] empha- **4.138**
sizes the importance of prosecutors working with other agencies, and gathering
sufficient information about the young person's home circumstances and background from a range of sources (such as the police, the YOT, and children's services), before making the decision whether to prosecute.

---

[92] CPS, 'Legal Guidance: Youth Offenders', available at <http://www.cps.gov.uk/legal/v_to_z/
youth_offenders/> accessed 14 March 2017.

4.139 That a suspect is under 18 years of age will be a particular consideration for a Crown Prosecutor when deciding whether a prosecution is in the public interest. At paragraph 4.12(d) of the Full Code Test, contained within the Code for Crown Prosecutors,[93] the Crown Prosecutor is required to give particular consideration to the youth of the suspect, having regard to the best interests and welfare of the young person (CYPA 1933 s. 44), and the principal aim of the youth justice system, the prevention of offending by young persons (CDA 1998 s. 37). Prosecutors must also have regard to the obligations arising under the UNCRC. The Full Code Test paragraph 4.12(d) indicates that: 'As a starting point, the younger the suspect, the less likely it is that a prosecution is required.' However, in some circumstances, prosecution may still be in the public interest—for example, where the offence is serious or where suitable alternatives to prosecution are not available.

(b) Charging: child suspects

4.140 Where a child suspect is charged, this should be done in the presence of an AA (Code C 16.1), who should be given a written charge notice providing the particulars of the offence (Code C 16.3). Reasonable efforts should be made to enable the AA to attend for charging, but there is no power to detain a suspect, so that an AA can attend (Code C NFG 16C) for charge. If the AA cannot attend, then the suspect should ordinarily be released on bail to attend for charging when an AA will be available.

(c) Youth cautions and youth conditional cautions: child suspects

4.141 A youth caution (CDA 1998 ss 66ZA and 66ZB) may be given in any situation where a child suspect has admitted an offence and there is sufficient evidence for a realistic prospect of conviction, but it is not in the public interest to prosecute. The police have the final responsibility for making decisions on the suitability of a youth caution, but can ask the YOT to assess the child detainee to inform the decision, under local protocol arrangements. The nature and status of a youth caution should be fully explained to the child when it is delivered, and the appropriate adult should always be present.[94]

4.142 It is important to note that no consent is required for a youth caution to be given, but the young person and the AA should be given information about the options available, so that they can make an informed decision before the question as to whether the child admits the offence is put to him or her. The child may be bailed

---

[93] CPS, 'The Code for Crown Prosecutors' (January 2013).
[94] MoJ/Youth Justice Board, 'Youth Cautions: Guidance for Police and Youth Offending Teams' (effective from April 2013).

for assessment by the YOT, or for delivery of the caution, since a youth caution must be delivered by an officer with special training.[95]

The more robust youth conditional caution (YCC) (CDA 1998 ss 66A–66H) can be **4.143** given where it is considered appropriate to attach one or more conditions to the caution. The giving of a conditional caution stops criminal proceedings for any offence and gives the child an opportunity to comply with the conditions attached. If the child complies, then prosecution is not normally commenced. But where there is no reasonable excuse for non-compliance, criminal proceedings may be commenced for the original offence and the conditional caution will cease to have effect.[96]

YCCs can only be administered in the presence of an appropriate adult. The YCC **4.144** Code of Practice[97] makes plain that significant care should be taken to ensure that a YCC is only given where the child has made a clear and unambiguous admission to the offence, especially where there may be doubt about the child's mental state or capacity. In contrast to the youth caution, a YCC cannot be given unless the child has accepted the YCC, and the YCC Code of Practice sets out the need to explain with care the nature and implications of accepting such a disposal.[98]

(d) Decision-making: vulnerable adult suspects

The CPS's guidance on *Mentally Disordered Offenders*[99] makes plain that all **4.145** available information about any mental health problem, and its relevance to the offence, should be taken into account in making the decision whether to prosecute or not. This guidance echoes statements in Home Office guidelines which suggest that when considering where the public interest lies, it is desirable to consider alternatives to prosecution for mentally disordered or mentally vulnerable suspects, such as cautioning, referral to health and social care services, or voluntary admission to hospital where support is required, before deciding that prosecution is necessary.[100] The importance of diversion has been underlined by the 2009 Bradley report,[101] and the government response to it.[102] The Code for

---

[95] ibid.

[96] MoJ, 'Code of Practice for Youth Conditional Cautions' (March 2013) (hereafter YCC Code of Practice). See also CPS, 'Director's Guidance on Youth Conditional Cautions' (January 2015).

[97] YCC Code of Practice.

[98] YCC Code of Practice, 16.2 and 16.3.

[99] CPS, 'Legal Guidance: Mentally Disordered Offenders', available at <http://www.cps.gov.uk/legal/l_to_o/mentally_disordered_offenders/#a01> accessed 14 March 2017.

[100] See Home Office Circular 66/90, 'Provision for Mentally Disordered Offenders', [2]; and Home Office Circular 12/95, 'Mentally Disordered Offenders: Inter Agency Working'.

[101] 'The Bradley Report: Lord Bradley's Review of People with Mental Health Problems or Learning Disabilities in the Criminal Justice System' (Department of Health, 2009).

[102] See G. Durcan, A. Saunders, B. Gadsby, and A. Hazard, 'The Bradley Report Five Years on: An Independent Review of Progress to Date and Priorities for Further Development' (Centre for Mental Health, 2014).

Crown Prosecutors and Home Office circular 12/95 make plain that there is a balance to be struck between the public interest in diverting an individual with significant mental illness from the criminal justice system and other public interest factors in favour of prosecution, including the need to safeguard the public.

(e) Charging: vulnerable adult suspects

4.146 Where a vulnerable adult suspect is charged, this should be done in the presence of an AA (Code C 16.1), who should be given a written charge notice providing the particulars of the offence (Code C 16.3). As with a child suspect, reasonable efforts should be made to enable the AA to attend for charging, but there is no power to detain a suspect, so that an AA can attend (Code C NFG 16C) for charge. If the AA cannot attend, then the suspect should ordinarily be released on bail to attend for charging when the AA can be present.

(f) Simple cautions and conditional cautions: vulnerable adult suspects

4.147 Simple cautions and conditional cautions for adults require admission of the offence, sufficient evidence to prosecute, and an agreement from the adult suspect to accept the caution or conditional caution.[103] Ministry of Justice guidance[104] requires officers to 'have regard to Code C' in terms of having an AA present for vulnerable adult suspects when a caution or conditional caution is being administered and officers administering a caution must also ensure that 'all matters that need to be explained are explained in a language that the offender can understand'.[105] In addition, both a caution and a conditional caution may, in exceptional circumstances, be administered at the home of an elderly or vulnerable adult.[106]

O. Bail/Remand Decisions: Particular Issues for Vulnerable Suspects

(a) Child suspects: duty to transfer to local authority accommodation where bail refused

4.148 Where a child suspect has been charged, and where the police have decided to remand him or her in custody, PACE s. 38(6) requires the police to arrange for the child to be removed to local authority accommodation pending his or her

---

[103] CPS, 'The Director's Guidance On Charging (Revised Arrangements)' (5th edn, CPS, 2013).

[104] MoJ, 'Simple Cautions for Adult Offenders', effective from 13 April 2015, [81] (hereafter MoJ Caution Guidance); and MoJ, 'Code of Practice for Adult Conditional Cautions' (January 2013), [3.8].

[105] MoJ Caution Guidance, [81].

[106] MoJ Caution Guidance, [79]. MoJ Conditional Caution Code of Practice, [3.2].

appearance in court. This applies whether the remand following charge is to be overnight or during the day. Under the Criminal Justice and Courts Act 2015 s. 42, this now includes all child suspects under the age of 18.

There are only two bases on which a child who has been charged may continue to be detained in the police custody suite: **4.149**

- if it is 'impracticable' for the child to be taken into local authority accommodation; or
- where the custody officer determines that secure accommodation is required to protect the public from 'serious harm' from a child aged 12 years or over (PACE s. 38(6)) and none is available.

The first basis for not transferring the child suspect, that it is 'impracticable to do so', is confined by Code C NFG 16D to difficulties arising in respect of transportation and travel requirements for the individual. It is not applicable to situations where the difficulties arise as a result of a shortage of available beds. This position was reaffirmed by a letter from the Association of Chief Police Officers Lead for PACE Strategy to all forces dated 29 October 2014.[107]   **4.150**

The second basis for not transferring a child suspect is intended to represent an extremely high threshold. It only arises where the child is aged 12 or over, the local authority is unable to provide secure accommodation, and the custody officer determines that non-secure accommodation would be inadequate to protect the public from 'serious harm' at the hands of the child.[108]   **4.151**

This latter determination is the only decision that a custody officer is required to make about the nature of the accommodation required. In all other cases where this threshold is not met, it is for the local authority to decide whether secure or non-secure accommodation is required, in accordance with their separate legal obligations. These dictate that where the child is 12 years or over, secure accommodation would only be appropriate where the child is likely to abscond or injure themselves or others (Secure Accommodation Regulations 1991 reg. 6(1)(a), modifying the Children Act 1989 s. 25(1)). Where the child is under 12 years, in addition to the likelihood of absconding or injuring themselves or others, the child must also have a history of absconding to require secure accommodation. The police, however, have a duty to provide the local authority with full information about the grounds for refusing bail and any relevant information held about the suspect's previous history.   **4.152**

---

[107] Appendix E to HMIC, *The Welfare of Vulnerable People in Police Custody*.

[108] PACE s. 38(6A) defines 'serious harm' in relation to a child charged with a violent or sexual offence as 'death or serious personal injury, whether physical or psychological'.

4.153 Recent reports have revealed that the obligations under PACE s. 38(6) are frequently not met,[109] although the situation is improving. There appear to be several reasons for these failures, including misunderstanding as to when secure accommodation is required and whose decision that is, the lack of effectiveness of multi-agency working in some areas, and the scarcity of both secure and non-secure local authority accommodation.[110]

4.154 Where the custody officer has concluded that it is impracticable to transport the child, or where the custody officer has determined (in respect of a child aged 12 or over) that secure accommodation is required and none is available, the custody officer must produce a certificate to the court confirming the same (PACE s. 38(7) Code C 16.7). The certificate is now required to detail the reasons why it was impracticable to transport the child suspect to local authority care (if that is the reason relied upon). In addition, an officer of at least inspector rank is required to monitor and supervise any such post-charge detention of a child suspect (Code C 16.7).

(b) When PACE s. 38(6) does not apply

4.155 The duty to transfer a remanded child into local authority accommodation does not apply to children who have been arrested for breach of bail (Bail Act 1976 s. 7) or on a warrant not backed for bail (Magistrates' Courts Act 1980 s. 13). In these situations, the arrested child must be detained in the police custody suite until he or she can be produced to court.

(c) Vulnerable adult suspects: remand for the individual's own protection or in their best interests

4.156 There may be exceptional circumstances where the custody officer concludes for an extremely vulnerable suspect that release on bail is unsuitable—for example, where there are real and credible risks to the safety of that individual. This might arise in respect of concerns about self-harm or suicide, or some other feature related to the suspect's vulnerability. The custody officer can refuse bail if he or she concludes that remand is necessary for the individual's protection (PACE s. 38(1)(a)(vi)).

4.157 In exceptional cases, there may be other reasons why it is appropriate for the custody officer to continue to detain the suspect beyond the expiry of the provisions of PACE. This might occur where the individual lacks capacity, and the officer decides against immediate release in the best interests of the individual (Mental

---

[109] HMIC, *The Welfare of Vulnerable People in Police Custody*. See also L. Skinns, *The Overnight Detention of Children in Police Cells* (Howard League for Penal Reform, 2011).
[110] It is hoped that the situation will be improved by the Home Office's forthcoming 'Concordat on Children in Custody'.

Capacity Act 2005 s. 5), or where the custody officer concludes that the suspect needs a mental health assessment and he or she is detained for that to occur (but see *MS v United Kingdom* (2012) 55 EHRR 23). Where a vulnerable detainee is being released to an external agency, it is essential that appropriate communication of information about their risk or vulnerability occurs (see *Webley v St George's Hospital NHS Trust* [2014] EWHC 299 (QB)).[111]

P. Release

(a) Risk assessment for child and vulnerable adult suspects bailed or otherwise released

The police have a common law duty of care to all suspects, and a duty to release **4.158** into a safe environment (*Webley v St George's Hospital*). The custody officer should complete a pre-release risk assessment for each suspect, and this will be particularly important for vulnerable individuals. This should not be left until just before release, but should be an ongoing process throughout the suspect's detention. This assessment should refer to all available risk-assessment information, and the custody officer should speak to the detainee individually. Where specific risks are identified, the custody officer should detail the actions necessary to support the vulnerable individual.

The pre-release risk assessment should also consider whether there is any risk of **4.159** harm to others, or by others, following release. Notification to affected individuals about the suspect's impending release may be appropriate, or the imposition of bail conditions to prevent interference with witnesses or to reduce the risk of further offending.[112]

(b) Addressing identified post-release risks

In particular for child and vulnerable adult suspects, efforts should be made to **4.160** ensure that there is safe transportation home for them, and checks should be made to investigate the suitability of returning them to their home circumstances.

(c) Onward referral

For a child or vulnerable adult suspect, where appropriate, officers should agree **4.161** an exit and after-care strategy on release. This might involve referral to community-based services for treatment care or support. There should be inter-agency

---

[111] *Webley v St George's Hospital NHS Trust and Metropolitan Police Service* [2014] EWHC 299 (QB), (2014) 138 BMLR 190.
[112] APP(DC), 'Risk Assessment', 4.

protocols to enable this to occur.[113] Liaison and Diversion practitioners operating within the custody suite should also be able to assist where a referral is required. Some Liaison and Diversion teams have outreach workers who will follow up and support an individual to access referrals following release.

Further Reading

Adebowale, 'Independent Commission on Mental Health and Policing Report' (May 2013).
Cape, E., *Defending Suspects at Police Stations* (6th edn, Legal Action Group, 2011).
Criminal Justice Joint Inspectorate, 'Who's Looking Out for the Children?' A joint inspection of Appropriate Adult provision and children in detention (December 2011).
Her Majesty's Inspectorate of Constabulary, 'The Welfare of Vulnerable People in Police Custody' (2015).
National Appropriate Adults Network, 'There to Help' (March 2015).
Panzavolta, M., de Vocht, D., van Oosterhout, M., and Vanderhallen, M., *Interrogating Young Suspects: Procedural Safeguards from a Legal Perspective* (Intersentia, 2015).

---

[113] APP(MH), 'Mental Vulnerability and Illness', 4.

5

UNFITNESS TO PLEAD

Miranda Bevan

A. Introduction

(a) An overview

5.01 The law relating to unfitness to plead concerns those vulnerable defendants who have such substantial participation difficulties that they are unable to engage meaningfully in the trial process. This may occur as a result of a range of causes, including difficulties arising from mental illness, learning disability, developmental disorders, and communication impairments. Defendants who are determined to be unfit to plead are not tried in the usual way, on the basis that to do so would be unfair. They are instead subject to alternative procedures for testing the allegation, after which the court has limited scope to put in place arrangements to treat or support the defendant, and to protect the public where necessary.

(b) An outline of the legal framework

The common law test for unfitness to plead was first set down in the case of **5.02**
Pritchard (1836) 7 C & P 303.[1] If, on the basis of expert medical evidence,
the judge concludes that a defendant lacks any one of the capabilities set out
in the *Pritchard* test, he or she will determine that the defendant is unfit to
plead, formally 'under a disability' (Criminal Procedure (Insanity) Act 1964
(hereafter CP(I)A 1964) s. 4).[2]

A jury then considers whether or not the defendant 'did the act or made the omis- **5.03**
sion' charged against him or her (CP(I)A 1964 s. 4A), at a hearing commonly
known as the 'trial of the facts'. If the jury are satisfied that the defendant 'did the
act or made the omission' in respect of at least one allegation, the judge is required
to impose one of three disposals: a hospital order (with or without a restriction
order); a supervision order; or an absolute discharge (CP(IA) 1964 s. 5). If the jury
are not so satisfied, they must acquit the defendant on the particular charge.

(c) Frequency

The threshold for a finding of unfitness to plead is very high and formal findings **5.04**
of unfitness are rare. Between 2002 and 2014, there were on average approximately 100 findings of unfitness to plead per year.[3] However, anecdotal evidence
from judges and criminal practitioners suggests that the issue is being raised more
frequently than has previously been the case.[4] This may be unsurprising given the
increase in historic allegations before the courts. At the same time, the criminal
justice system is becoming better equipped to accommodate significant participation difficulties within the trial process, with the wider use of special measures
and other adjustments to facilitate the effective participation of defendants (see
Chapter 10, 'Special Measures').

(d) Challenges

This is a complex area of law, made the more difficult for judges and prac- **5.05**
titioners by the relative infrequency with which it is employed. Removing a

---

[1] *Pritchard* (1836) 7 C & P 303; 173 ER 135.

[2] Criminal Procedure (Insanity) Act 1964 (CP(I)A 1964) as amended by the Criminal
Procedure (Insanity and Unfitness to Plead) Act 1991 (CP(IUP)A 1991) and the Domestic
Violence, Crime and Victims Act 2004.

[3] R. Mackay, 'Unfitness to Plead—Data on Formal Findings from 2002 to 2014', Appendix
A to Law Commission, 'Report: Unfitness to Plead' (13 January 2016), Law Com No. 364,
available at <http://www.lawcom.gov.uk/wp-content/uploads/2016/01/apa.pdf> accessed 14
March 2017.

[4] See, e.g., the observation in *Walls* [2011] EWCA Crim 443; [2011] 2 Cr App R 6 at [38].

defendant from the full trial process, with its fair trial guarantees,[5] is a 'very serious step' (*Walls* [2011] EWCA Crim 443 at [37]) and the unfitness to plead procedures present significant challenges to all those engaged in a case involving an unfit defendant. A finding of unfitness shields the defendant from conviction, but curtails significantly the defendant's rights and the extent to which the allegation can be tested. Complainants, witnesses, and defendants alike often experience extremely lengthy delays as expert evidence is assembled. In addition, identifying what should be proved, and what evidence is admissible, at the trial of the facts can be extremely problematic. Yet, at the conclusion of the processes, the court's powers to deal with an unfit individual, to support his or her rehabilitation, and to protect the public are very limited.

5.06 As a result of these difficulties, the courts have rightly taken the approach that a finding of unfitness to plead should be a last resort, and that all efforts should be made to enable the defendant to participate fully in the trial if that can, fairly, be achieved. The court has a duty to take 'every reasonable step' to adjust trial proceedings to enable a vulnerable defendant to participate in the hearing (Criminal Practice Directions 3D.2 and 3G,[6] hereafter 'Crim PD'), including the provision of an intermediary where appropriate (see further Chapter 10, 'Special Measures', and Chapter 11, 'Intermediaries').

(e) The approach taken in this chapter

5.07 This chapter considers the legal test for unfitness to plead. It then reviews the procedures set out at CP(I)A 1964 s. 4 for identifying defendants who are unfit to plead, and follows the alternative procedures which are then adopted under ss 4A and 5, examining the 'trial of the facts' hearing and the range of disposals available thereafter. The CP(I)A 1964 however, is only applicable in the Crown Court, and the chapter closes with a consideration of the procedures available for addressing an inability to participate effectively in summary trial in the adult magistrates' court.

5.08 Children and young defendants may be subject to unfitness to plead procedures if they are tried in the Crown Court. However, more commonly participation issues arising in respect of young defendants are dealt with in the youth court. Youth court procedures are considered separately in Chapter 7, 'Youth Courts and Young Defendants'.

---

[5] Under Art. 6 of the Convention for the Protection of Human Rights and Fundamental Freedoms (entered into force on 3 September 1953) (ECHR).

[6] Criminal Practice Directions I General Matters 3D 'Vulnerable People in the Courts' and 3G 'Vulnerable Defendants', Criminal Practice Directions 2015 [2015] EWCA Crim 1567 as amended April, October, and November 2016 and February and April 2017. See <https://www.justice.gov.uk/courts/procedure-rules/criminal/rulesmenu-2015> accessed 25 April 2017.

B. The Legal Test for Unfitness to Plead

(a) The *Pritchard* test: formulation

The test for unfitness to plead is not statutory but common law. It remains that **5.09** set out by Alderson B in the 1836 case of *Pritchard* at 304:

> There are three points to be enquired into:– First whether the prisoner is mute of malice or not;[7] secondly whether he can plead to the indictment or not; thirdly, whether he is of sufficient intellect to comprehend the course of proceedings on the trial, so as to make a proper defence—to know that he might challenge any of you [jurors] to whom he may object—and to comprehend the details of the evidence.

The case of *Davies* (1853) 3 Car & Kir 328 added to this list the ability of the **5.10** defendant to be able to instruct his or her legal adviser. At that point, the *Pritchard* criteria, therefore, required a defendant to be able to: plead to the indictment; understand the course of proceedings; instruct a representative; challenge a juror; and understand the evidence. An inability to do any of these things would result in a finding that the defendant was unfit to plead.

However, the trial process has changed significantly since the late nineteenth **5.11** century. In particular, when *Pritchard* was decided, the defendant could not give evidence in his or her own defence. More recently, the courts have interpreted the *Pritchard* test to take account of the modern trial process. The most widely used formulation of the *Pritchard* test is that approved by the Court of Appeal in the case of *John M* [2003] EWCA Crim 3452,[8] following which a defendant would be found to be unfit to plead (formally 'under a disability', CP(I)A 1996 s. 4) if one, or more, of the following were beyond his or her capability:

1. understanding the charge(s);
2. deciding whether or not to plead guilty;
3. exercising his or her right to challenge jurors;
4. instructing solicitors and/or counsel;
5. following the course of the proceedings;
6. giving evidence in his or her own defence.

The judge at first instance elaborated on some of those capabilities.[9] In respect of **5.12** 'instructing solicitors and/or counsel', the judge observed at [21]:

---

[7] The defendant in *Pritchard* was deaf-mute. Where an individual makes no plea when the indictment is put, a jury must decide whether the defendant is 'mute of malice', in which case a not guilty plea will be entered and the trial proceeds (Criminal Law Act 1967 s. 6(1)(c)), or whether he or she is 'mute by visitation of God', in which case a judge must then determine whether he or she is unfit to plead.

[8] *John M* [2003] EWCA Crim 3452; [2003] All ER (D) 199.

[9] *John M* being decided before the Domestic Violence, Crime and Victims Act 2004, when the issue of unfitness was determined by a jury, not by the judge sitting alone.

This means that the defendant must be able to convey intelligibly to his lawyers the case which he wishes them to advance on his behalf and the matters which he wishes them to put forward in his defence. It involves being able (a) to understand the lawyers' questions, (b) to apply his mind to answering them, and (c) to convey intelligibly to the lawyers the answers which he wishes to give.

5.13 In relation to 'following the course of the proceedings', the judge explained at [22]:

This means that the defendant must be able (a) to understand what is said by the witness and by counsel in their speeches to the jury and (b) to communicate intelligibly to his lawyers any comment which he may wish to make on anything that is said by the witnesses or counsel.

5.14 Finally, in respect of 'giving evidence in his or her own defence', the judge stated at [24] that:

This means that the defendant must be able (a) to understand the questions he is asked in the witness box, (b) to apply his mind to answering them, and (c) to convey intelligibly to the jury the answers which he wishes to give.

The Court of Appeal clarified in *Orr* that the ability to be cross-examined is an integral part of a defendant's ability to give evidence in his or her own defence, and a lack of capacity in that regard would render a defendant unfit to plead.[10] However, such a lack of capacity to be cross-examined is to be distinguished from the situation where 'the physical or mental condition of the accused makes it undesirable for him to give evidence'. The latter position, under the Criminal Justice and Public Order Act 1994 s. 35(1)(a), would not render the defendant unfit to plead, but would protect him or her from an adverse inference being drawn against him or her should the defendant choose not to give evidence at trial.[11]

(b) The *Pritchard* test: scope

(i) Amnesia does not give rise to unfitness to plead

5.15 In the case of *Podola* [1960] 1 QB 325, the Court of Appeal made clear that a case of hysterical amnesia, even where the defendant had a total inability to recall the alleged offending, would not give rise to a finding of unfitness to plead.

(ii) No requirement to be able to act in one's own best interests

5.16 There is no requirement for a defendant to be able to act in his or her own best interests to be fit to plead (*Robertson* [1968] 1 WLR 1767). The case of *John M*

---

[10] *Orr* [2016] EWCA Crim 889 at [23].

[11] *Orr* at [24] and [28]. The distinction between these two states may be narrow: see A. Owusu-Bempah and N. Wortley, 'Case Comment: Unfit to Plead or Unfit to Testify?' (2016) *Journal of Criminal Law* 80(6), 391–6. See also *Hamberger* [2017] EWCA Crim 273.

makes clear that to be fit to plead there is no requirement for a defendant's instructions, or account in evidence, to be 'plausible, believable or reliable'. Nor need the defendant be able to appreciate that his or her instructions are implausible, unreliable, or unbelievable. Likewise, a defendant's comments to representatives on the evidence need not be 'valid or helpful'.[12] The right to instruct a representative to pursue an unreliable or implausible version of events is a general principle of criminal law.[13]

(iii) Difficulties in respect of delusional conditions and mood disorders

There are, however, circumstances in which this can be problematic, especially   **5.17** where the defendant's instructions are affected by a psychotic or delusional condition, or a mood disorder. The *Pritchard* test was first developed at a time when the science of psychiatry was in its infancy, and was formulated in respect of a defendant who was deaf-mute. The test was not, in its foundation, designed to address psychiatric disorders. Rather, it was, and remains, focused on the intellectual abilities of the defendant, and does not require a defendant to be able to engage in rational decision-making processes.[14]

As a result, there are a number of significant limitations to the *Pritchard* test   **5.18** when applied to defendants who suffer from mental illness, particularly delusional or psychotic states, and mood disorders. The extent of these limitations was first made clear in *Robertson* [1968] 1 WLR 1767. The defendant suffered from delusions 'which might at any time interfere with proper action on his part', but nonetheless had a 'complete understanding of the legal proceedings and all that is involved'. The Court of Appeal considered that he was not unfit to plead on that basis.

The Court of Appeal followed *Robertson* in the case of *Berry*.[15] Here, the defend-   **5.19** ant had so 'grossly abnormal' a mental state that while he was aware of the nature of his actions, he was unable to view them in 'any sensible sort of manner'.[16] The court concluded that the defendant ought not necessarily be considered to be unfit to plead on that basis. This approach has been more recently endorsed in a line of authority arising in respect of murder allegations where the defendants were each unable to engage in rational decision-making processes because of delusions or mood disorders.[17] The defendant Moyle, for example,

---

[12]   *John M* at [21]–[24].
[13]   Albeit in some respects subject to certain restrictions, such as the need for credible material before making an allegation of fraud (see Bar Standards Board, *Bar Standards Board Handbook* (3rd edn, 2017) Section C: The Conduct Rules, rC9.2.c).
[14]   In contrast to the definition of lack of capacity in civil matters, which is focused on decision-making capacity (Mental Capacity Act 2005 s. 2(1)).
[15]   (1978) 66 Cr App R 156.
[16]   At 157.
[17]   See *Murray* [2008] EWCA Crim 1792; *Moyle* [2008] EWCA Crim 3059; and *Diamond* [2008] EWCA Crim 923.

was determined to be fit to plead despite expert evidence that the defendant's delusions would have 'significantly impaired his ability to take a proper or valid part in his trial and significantly affected his capacity to be properly defended in legal proceedings'.[18]

5.20   The *Pritchard* test has been heavily criticized in this regard.[19] Toulson LJ in *Murray* observed that 'psychiatric understanding and the law in relation to mentally ill defendants do not always sit comfortably together'.[20] More recently, the Law Commission has called for the *Pritchard* test to be updated to include decision-making capacity as one of the required abilities.[21]

(iv) No requirement for mental disorder or other condition

5.21   Inevitably, given the high threshold for a finding of unfitness, a defendant who is unfit to plead is likely to have a diagnosed, or diagnosable, condition. However, it is important to note that the *Pritchard* test does not require the defendant to be suffering from a mental disorder, or any other condition.[22] It is a legal test to be applied by the judge, rather than a psychiatric test.

5.22   Nonetheless, for the medical expert assessing the defendant a diagnosis will, in many cases, assist in identifying the defendant's capabilities with regard to the trial process. However, it is important that instructions to clinicians for the preparation of reports on a defendant's fitness to plead stress the need to apply the *Pritchard* criteria in their assessment of the defendant. Empirical research reveals that many expert reports fail to address the *Pritchard* criteria in full or at all.[23]

(c) Unfitness 'to plead' and unfitness 'to stand trial'

5.23   Some criminal practitioners and judges make reference to 'fitness to stand trial' as distinct from 'fitness to plead'. However, as formulated in *Pritchard* and interpreted in *John M*, the *Pritchard* test draws no such distinction. The particular abilities which might be associated with either 'standing trial' or being 'fit to plead' (in the narrower sense of entering a valid plea to the indictment) are all

---

[18] *Moyle* [2008] EWCA Crim 3059; [2009] MHLR 91 at [27].

[19] See, e.g., D. Grubin, 'What Constitutes Fitness to Plead?' [1993] Crim LR 748. Also *Attorney General v O'Driscoll* [2003] JLR 390 at [29], where the Royal Court of Jersey declined to apply the *Pritchard* test on this basis.

[20] *Murray* [2008] EWCA Crim 1792 at [6].

[21] See Law Com No. 364, paras 3.108 ff.

[22] In contrast, for example, to a finding of lack of capacity, under the Mental Capacity Act 2005 s. 2, which would require an individual to have an 'impairment of, or a disturbance in the functioning of, the mind or brain'. See, for discussion of the issues, H. Howard, 'Lack of Capacity: Reforming the Law on Unfitness to Plead' (2016) *Journal of Criminal Law* 80(6), 428–35.

[23] R. Mackay, B. J. Mitchell, and L. Howe, 'A Continued Upturn in Unfitness to Plead—More Disability in Relation to the Trial under the 1991 Act' [2007] Crim LR 530, 536.

contained within that single group of abilities prescribed by the *Pritchard* test. It is a 'single, indivisible test which must be met in its entirety'.[24]

However, it might be argued that there is good reason for the distinction drawn   **5.24**
by some practitioners. Often, a defendant who cannot meet one of the *Pritchard* criteria fails to meet them all, but this will not always be the case. This can be problematic where the defendant is able to understand the case against him or her, has a clear appreciation of their own guilt, and understands the consequences of entering a guilty plea, but would not be able to give evidence or, for example, may suffer from a mood disturbance such that they could not follow the course of a trial. Should such a defendant be denied the ability to enter a plea of guilty if that is their informed wish, simply because they would not be able to engage in a trial that they do not seek? In *Marcantonio and Chitolie* at [8] Lloyd Jones LJ questioned, *obiter dicta*, the desirability of an indivisible test which does not allow a plea of guilty in those circumstances.[25]

(d) The *Pritchard* test and the right to 'participate effectively' in trial

The right to a fair trial under Article 6 of the ECHR includes the right of an   **5.25**
accused to 'participate effectively' in a criminal trial. In *SC v United Kingdom*,[26] following *T v United Kingdom* (App. No. 24724/94) and *V v United Kingdom* (App. No. 24888/94),[27] this was described as follows:

> ... 'effective participation' in this context presupposes that the accused has a broad understanding of the nature of the trial process and of what is at stake for him or her, including the significance of any penalty which may be imposed. It means that he or she, if necessary with the assistance of, for example, an interpreter, lawyer, social worker or friend, should be able to understand the general thrust of what is said in court. The defendant should be able to follow what is said by the prosecution witnesses and, if represented, to explain to his own lawyers his version of events, point out any statements with which he disagrees and make them aware of any facts which should be put forward in his defence.[28]

Clear parallels with the *Pritchard* test can be identified in the reference to under-   **5.26**
standing of the process, and the ability to follow the proceedings and instruct representatives. However, it would appear that 'effective participation' as defined in *SC v UK* and *T v UK, V v UK* is more expansive than the *Pritchard* test. For example, the need for the defendant to 'have a broad understanding of the nature of the trial process and of what is at stake for him or her' might arguably be said to go beyond the *Pritchard* criteria. Indeed, in *SC v UK* and *T v UK, V v UK*, the

---

[24] *Marcantonio and Chitolie* [2016] EWCA Crim 14 at [8].
[25] The Law Commission have recently grappled with this issue, recommending that a supplementary test of 'capacity to plead guilty' be introduced. See Law Com No. 364, paras 3.148 ff.
[26] (2005) 40 EHRR 10 (App. No. 60958/00).
[27] 16 December 1999 (hereafter *T v UK, V v UK*).
[28] *SC v United Kingdom* at [29]. See also *T v UK, V v UK*.

defendants, all 11-year-old children being tried in the Crown Court, were not considered to be unfit to plead according to the *Pritchard* criteria, but the court concluded that they had been unable to participate effectively in their trials.

5.27　This line of case law on 'effective participation' has shaped the approach to vulnerable defendants (both adult and child) in terms of trial adjustments (see Chapter 10, 'Special Measures'). [29] However, it remains unclear how the *Pritchard* test aligns with this separately developed concept of 'effective participation'.

(e) Unfitness to plead distinct from 'insanity'

5.28　Unfitness to plead is distinct from the legal concept of 'insanity'. Unfitness to plead concerns the state of mind of the defendant at the time of trial. The issue of 'insanity' considers the state of mind of the defendant at the time of the commission of the offence. [30] A defendant who is unfit to plead is removed from the trial process and cannot be convicted. A defendant who raises the issue of 'insanity' undergoes the full trial process, and can be convicted, acquitted, or, where 'insanity' is established, receive a special verdict of 'not guilty by reason of insanity' (Trial of Lunatics Act 1883 s. 2(1)). However, where a special verdict is returned, the same disposal options are available as where an unfit defendant is found to have 'done the act or made the omission' at the trial of the facts (CP(I)A 1964 s. 5).

5.29　It is not uncommon for a defendant, who may have been legally 'insane' at the time of the offence, to be unfit to plead at the time of trial. In those circumstances, the issue of unfitness to plead should be determined first. If the defendant is determined to be unfit to plead, then the trial of the facts will proceed (CP(I)A 1964 s. 4A), but the defendant may not raise the issue of insanity (*Antoine*[31]). If the defendant is determined to be fit to plead, he or she may then raise the issue of insanity at trial.

C. Expert Evidence on the Issue of Unfitness to Plead

(a) The requirement for expert evidence CP(I)A 1964 s. 4(6)

5.30　The judge may only arrive at a determination that a defendant is unfit to plead on the evidence of two registered medical practitioners (CP(I)A 1964 s. 4(6)). One

---

[29] See: Criminal Procedure Rules 2015 (SI 2015/1490, as amended by SIs 2016/120, 2016/705, 2017/144, and 2017/282), r. 3.9(3)(b) (hereafter 'Crim PR'); and Crim PD I General Matters 3D.2 and 3G.
[30] *M'Naghten's Case* (1843) 10 Cl & F 200. See Chapter 6, 'Vulnerability and Defences', for discussion.
[31] *Antoine* [2001] 1 AC 340; [2000] 2 WLR 703 at [373].

of these two experts must also be approved under s. 12 of the Mental Health Act 1983 (MHA 1983) as having 'special experience in the treatment and diagnosis of mental disorder' (CP(IA) 1964 s. 4(6)), and, as a result, will usually, but not always, be a psychiatrist. This is despite the fact that the *Pritchard* test itself does not require a diagnosis of mental disorder, and unfitness to plead may arise as a result of a participation difficulty outside the field of psychiatry.

The evidence of clinical psychologists is frequently put before the court on the issue of unfitness to plead, especially where the defendant may be unfit to plead due to a learning disability or developmental disorder. Clinical psychologists, however, are not registered medical practitioners and so, while their evidence is frequently relied upon by the court, it is not capable of satisfying the requirement for two registered medical practitioners (CP(I)A 1964 s. 4(6)). As a result, where a clinical psychologist's opinion is required, this will mean that a minimum of three experts will be required before the court can arrive at a determination of unfitness to plead. **5.31**

(b) Avoiding delay in the obtaining of expert reports

Anecdotal evidence from practice suggests that the preparation of an expert report addressing the issue of unfitness to plead generally takes a minimum of six weeks, although it is sometimes possible to expedite the process. In addition, there are a limited number of forensic psychiatrists and it can be difficult to identify a clinician with the relevant expertise who is likely to be available for the hearing. As a result, it is essential that representatives who have concerns over the fitness to plead of the defendant address the issue at the earliest opportunity and do not delay in obtaining prior authority and instructing experts where that is appropriate. **5.32**

In many cases, defence representatives (or indeed the prosecution or court) may have concerns about a defendant's fitness to plead, but lack information to be able to assess whether the difficulties are so significant as to justify instruction of a medical expert to assess unfitness to plead, or whether it may be possible to address any issues by means of special measures, or other adjustments to the trial process. In those circumstances, where Liaison and Diversion Services are operating at the court, the defendant should be referred to them for screening. (See Chapter 4, 'Vulnerable Suspects: The Investigation Stage', paragraphs 4.121 et seq., under '(e) Obtaining more specialist assessment'.) **5.33**

Screening for participation difficulties, including the identification of reasonable adjustments of the process to facilitate participation and referral for specialist assessment, is specifically included within NHS England's Liaison and Diversion service specification.[32] Such a screening process would require

---

[32] See NHS England Liaison and Diversion, Standard Service Specification 2016, at 2.5.1.4

the defendant's consent, and would not be a bar to a defence representative obtaining a fuller report if the screening process did not satisfactorily allay concerns.

(c) Prosecution right to instruct their own expert

5.34 Most frequently, the issue of unfitness to plead will first be raised by the defence, who will begin expert investigation of the issue.[33] The prosecution are entitled to have their own expert examine the defendant if the issue of unfitness is to be pursued. In many cases, the prosecution delay securing their own evidence until served with two reports by the defence supporting a finding of unfitness to plead. This approach can exacerbate the already significant delays in cases of this sort, but it has been condoned by the Divisional Court in the case of *R (Alexander) v Isleworth Crown Court*[34] at [9], on the basis of cost saving and the possibility that the prosecution may not seek to pursue the issue on receipt of two reports from 'reputable' doctors.

(d) Where the defendant will not cooperate with assessment

5.35 Among the most challenging issues which arise in cases involving unfitness to plead is the situation where the parties or court have concerns that the defendant may be unfit to plead, but the defendant will not cooperate with assessment. In the first instance, the court and the defendant's representatives should make every effort to ensure that the defendant has understood the purpose of the assessment, providing any assistance or reassurance the defendant may require to consider whether to cooperate.

5.36 Where that approach is not successful, there is a fundamental tension between the defendant's right to a fair trial (under Article 6 of the ECHR) and the defendant's autonomy rights.[35] There is rarely an easy answer to this issue. While not an ideal solution, it may sometimes be possible to satisfy the requirements for a remand under MHA 1983 s. 35, if that is appropriate (see sections (e) and (f) below), without the need for a formal assessment—for example, by way of a registered medical practitioner observing the conduct of the defendant while at court.

(screening for youths) and 2.5.2.4 (screening for adults) (forthcoming). Criminal Justice Liaison Services provide a comparable scheme in Wales. See Welsh Government, *Criminal Justice Liaison Services in Wales: Policy Implementation Guidance* (2013).

[33] The recent Scottish case of *Murphy (Charles) v HM Advocate* [2016] HCJAC 118 at [67] stresses the importance of defence representatives not relying on their own judgment, and obtaining a medical report 'where any question of mental fitness arises'.

[34] [2009] EWHC 85 (Admin).

[35] Including, for example, under Arts 12 and 13 of the UN Convention on the Rights of Persons with Disabilities (opened for signature 30 March 2007) (UNCRPD).

(e) Remand to hospital for a report to be prepared (MHA 1983 s. 35)

Under MHA 1983 s. 35, the court can remand a defendant to hospital so that a **5.37** report can be prepared on his or her mental condition.[36]

(i) Applicability

A defendant appearing before the Crown Court can be subject to a s. 35 remand **5.38** if he or she:

1. is awaiting trial for an offence punishable with imprisonment, including the offence of murder; or
2. has been arraigned, but has not yet been sentenced or otherwise dealt with for an offence punishable with imprisonment. However, a defendant who is awaiting sentence following a conviction for murder cannot be remanded under MHA 1983 s. 35.

A s. 35 remand can be engaged for any defendant before a magistrates' court **5.39** who:

1. has been convicted by the court of any offence punishable with imprisonment;
2. has had proved against them the act or omission of an offence (MHA 1983 s. 37(3)—see section 5.139 below); or
3. consents to being remanded for a report to be prepared.[37]

(ii) Requirements for a s. 35 remand

The court cannot remand a defendant to hospital under this section unless: **5.40**

1. it is satisfied, on the basis of evidence (in written or oral form) from a registered medical practitioner, that there is reason to suspect that the defendant has a mental disorder, as defined by MHA 1983 s. 1 (MHA 1983 s. 35(3) (a));
2. it is of the opinion that it would be impracticable for the report to be prepared were the defendant to be on bail (MHA 1983 s. 35(3)(b)); and
3. it is satisfied, on the basis of evidence from the clinician responsible for writing the report (or the managers of the hospital), that there is a bed available for the defendant for him or her to be admitted to a particular hospital within seven days (MHA 1983 s. 35(4)).

It is important to note that a s. 35 remand does not confer the power to treat **5.41** without the defendant's consent. Where necessary, the approved clinician would

---

[36] Hereafter a s. 35 remand.
[37] It is assumed that this will require the defendant to have sufficient capacity to give consent.

be required to use MHA 1983 s. 3 to enable him or her to treat the defendant while remanded if the defendant was not consenting.[38]

(iii) Period of a s. 35 remand and renewal

5.42   A s. 35 remand will in the first instance last for up to twenty-eight days. The period of remand can be extended for further periods of twenty-eight days, up to a maximum period of twelve weeks (MHA 1983 s. 35(7)). Further remands require written or oral evidence from the clinician responsible for writing the report that the further remand is necessary for the completion of that report (s. 35(5)).[39] The defendant need not be produced to court for further remand applications to be made, but his or her representative must be able to make submissions when the power to remand further is to be exercised (s. 35(6)).

(iv) Terminating a s. 35 remand

5.43   The court has the power to terminate the remand at any time, should it appear that it is appropriate to do so (MHA 1983 s. 35(7)). The defendant who is remanded under this section is entitled to obtain a report at his or her own expense (from a registered medical practitioner, or a clinician approved to make such reports), to support an application that the remand should be terminated (s. 35(7)).[40]

(f) Remand to hospital for treatment under MHA 1983 s. 36

5.44   MHA 1983 s. 36 gives the court power to remand a defendant to hospital for treatment.[41]

(i) Applicability

5.45   A defendant can be remanded to hospital for treatment under MHA 1983 s. 36 if he or she is:

1. in custody awaiting trial in the Crown Court for an offence punishable with imprisonment, save where the offence is one of murder; or
2. in custody at any time before sentence in the Crown Court for an offence punishable with imprisonment, save where the offence is one of murder (MHA 1983 s. 36(2)).

MHA 1983 s. 36 has no application in the magistrates' courts.[42]

---

[38] See *North West London Mental Health NHS Trust, ex p. Stewart* [1998] QB 628; [1998] 2 WLR 189.

[39] This individual will be an 'approved clinician', but need not be a registered medical practitioner (following amendments to MHA 1983 introduced by the Mental Health Act 2007), where, for example, the report is to be prepared by a clinical psychologist.

[40] However, defendants subject to orders under MHA 1983 ss 35 and 36 do not have the right to apply to a tribunal under MHA 1983 s. 66.

[41] Hereafter a s. 36 remand.

[42] Although the Secretary of State has power to transfer a remand prisoner to hospital under MHA 1983 s. 48.

(ii) Requirements for a s. 36 remand

The court cannot remand a defendant to hospital for treatment unless the court is **5.46** satisfied:

1. on the evidence (written or oral) of two registered medical practitioners that the defendant has a mental disorder of a nature or degree which makes it appropriate for him to be detained in a hospital for medical treatment, and that appropriate medical treatment is available (MHA 1983 s. 36(1)); and
2. on the basis of evidence (written or oral) from the clinician who will have overall responsibility for the defendant's treatment (or the managers of the hospital) that there is a bed available for the defendant for him or her to be admitted to a particular hospital within seven days (MHA 1983 s. 36(3)).

(iii) Period of a s. 36 remand and renewal

As with s. 35 remands, a s. 36 remand will in the first instance last for up to twenty- **5.47** eight days. The period of remand can be extended for further periods of twenty-eight days, up to a maximum period of twelve weeks (MHA 1983 s. 36(6)). Further remands require written or oral evidence from the approved clinician responsible for the defendant's treatment indicating that a further remand is warranted (MHA 1983 s. 36(4)).[43] The defendant need not be produced to court for further remand applications to be made, but his or her representative must be able to make submissions when the power to remand further is to be exercised (MHA 1983 s. 36(5)).

(iv) Terminating a s. 36 remand

The court has the power to terminate the remand at any time, should it appear that it is **5.48** appropriate to do so (MHA 1983 s. 36(6)). The defendant who is remanded under this section is entitled to obtain a report at his or her own expense (from a registered medical practitioner, or a clinician approved to make such reports, of his or her own choosing), to support an application that the remand should be terminated (MHA 1983 s. 36(6)).

D. The Trial of the Issue: The S. 4 Hearing (CP(I)A 1964 s. 4)

(a) Presumption of fitness until established otherwise

A criminal trial proceeds on the assumption that a defendant is fit to plead **5.49** until it is established otherwise (*Ghulam*[44]). There is no statutory presumption of fitness to plead.[45]

---

[43] See observations in fn. 39.
[44] [2009] EWCA Crim 2285; [2010] 1 WLR 891.
[45] In contrast to the position in civil proceedings where, following the Mental Capacity Act 2005 s. 1, an individual is 'assumed to have capacity' unless the contrary is established.

5.50 The requirement for evidence from two suitably qualified medical experts (CP(I) A 1964 s. 4(6)) applies to a finding of unfitness rather than a finding of fitness to plead. Where doubts are raised about the defendant's fitness to plead, falling short of the evidence required under CP(I)A 1964 s. 4(6), the judge is not obliged to hold a formal hearing under CP(I)A 1964 s. 4 (commonly known as the 'trial of the issue'), or to have evidence supportive of a finding of fitness from two medical experts, before proceeding with the trial. In such a situation, the judge has a discretion as to how to proceed, and is entitled to take into account his or her own observations of the defendant where, for example, trial has already begun (*Ghulam* at [15]–[22]).

(b) Who can raise the issue of unfitness to plead?

5.51 The issue of unfitness to plead is most often raised by the defence. However, CP(I)A 1964 s. 4(1) leaves open the possibility that the prosecution may raise the issue of unfitness, or indeed that the court may do so of its own motion. The judge also has a 'separate and distinct' duty to keep a defendant's ability to engage in proceedings under review[46] and to raise the issue of unfitness with the defendant's representatives if any question arises in that regard as the trial proceeds.[47]

(c) When to raise the issue and timely service of reports

5.52 Inkeeping with the parties' duties to prepare and conduct their cases in accordance with the overriding objective (Crim PR rr. 1.1 and 1.2), any party who has a proper basis for concern about a defendant's fitness to plead should raise that issue as soon as possible. The issue can be raised at any time up until the return of verdicts.[48] Once the issue has been raised, as emphasized in *Norman*,[49] it is important that there is 'very careful case management' to avoid undue delay. A clear timetable will need to be put in place to ensure the timely service of expert reports.

(d) Burden and standard of proof

5.53 If the defence raise the issue, the burden of proof lies on the defence to establish on the balance of probabilities that the defendant is indeed unfit to plead (*Podola* [1960] 1 QB 325). Where the prosecution raise the issue, the burden

---

[46] See the judge's duty under Crim PR r. 3.9(3)(b) and Crim PD I General Matters 3D.2 and 3G to take 'every reasonable step' to 'facilitate the participation of any person, including the defendant'.

[47] *Erskine* [2009] EWCA Crim 1425 at [89]; see also *M* [2006] EWCA Crim 2391 at [21].

[48] CP(I)A s. 4(3); see also *Orr* [2016] EWCA Crim 889.

[49] [2008] EWCA Crim 1810; [2009] 1 Cr App R 13 at [34].

lies on the prosecution to establish the defendant's unfitness to the criminal standard of proof (*Robertson* [1968] 1 WLR 1767). Where the court raises the issue, it is not clear where the burden of proof lies and what standard of proof should be applied. *Halsbury's Laws* suggest that the burden lies on the prosecution to disprove the defendant's unfitness.[50] This approach was taken in the case of *Marcantonio and Chitolie* at [96], where the court proceeded on the basis that the burden lay on the Crown to establish the defendant's unfitness to the criminal standard.[51]

(e) When to hold the 'trial of the issue': adjournment to allow for recovery

As discussed in the introduction to this chapter, the consequences of a find- **5.54** ing of unfitness to plead are serious, for the defendant as well as for complainants, witnesses, and the public. The court should only deviate from the usual criminal process where that is absolutely necessary, and every effort should be made to enable the defendant to participate in full trial if that can fairly be achieved.

In many cases, it is apparent from early clinical assessments that the condition **5.55** which renders the defendant unfit to plead may be capable of improvement, or resolution, within a reasonable period of time so that the defendant will become fit to be tried in the usual way. This may be the case where the defendant is, for example, a paranoid schizophrenic whose condition can be stabilized with appropriate medication. In such cases, the court may be persuaded to adjourn arraignment, where there is expert evidence to support this contention, so that the defendant can be given the opportunity to recover and undergo trial in the usual way. Where this approach is taken, the court would not proceed with the trial, or a 'trial of the issue', until the prospect of recovery has been explored. It is good practice for reporting experts to be invited to comment on whether there is a reasonable prospect that the defendant may become fit to plead with appropriate treatment or recovery time, and to indicate what time period is likely to be needed.

(f) When to hold the 'trial of the issue': postponement of the determination

Under CP(I)A 1964 s. 4(4), the question of unfitness to plead should be deter- **5.56** mined 'as soon as it arises'. The determination can plainly not take place

---

[50] *Halsbury's Laws of England and Wales*, vol. 27 (LexisNexis Butterworths, 2015) para. 357, n. 5.

[51] Contrast the Law Commission recommendation that the Crown's burden in such cases should be discharged if unfitness is established on the balance of probabilities (Law Com No. 364, para. 4.24).

until sufficient expert evidence is before the court. However, following CP(I) A 1964 s. 4(2), the court, having received the required evidence, may postpone the determination where the court considers that it is 'expedient to do so and in the interests of the accused'. Under this subsection, the determination can be postponed until 'any time up to the opening of the case for the defence'. In the case of *Norman*, Thomas LJ made plain at [34] that the court should 'consider carefully' whether it is appropriate for the determination to be postponed, given the serious consequences that a finding of unfitness has for a defendant.

5.57 This power to postpone the determination until the opening of the defence case is not designed to explore potential recovery, but rather it enables the defence to require the Crown to establish a case to answer on all elements of the offence where that may be problematic.[52] As discussed in more detail at paragraphs 5.73 et seq. below, the 'trial of the facts' (under CP(I)A s. 4A) does not require the prosecution to establish the mental element of the offence, and there are significant limitations on the defences which are available to the defendant. Where the defence representative considers that there is a reasonable prospect that a submission of no case to answer following the close of the prosecution case will succeed, particularly on a point arising in respect of the mental element of the offence, he or she may wish to invite the court to postpone determination until after that point.

5.58 In *Burles*, Lord Parker CJ proposed at [196] that the court should consider first of all the 'apparent strength or weakness of the prosecution case as disclosed' and then the 'nature and degree of the suggested disability' before considering what would be 'expedient and in the prisoner's interest'. In practice, postponement of the determination rarely occurs. This may be because amendment to the CP(I)A by the introduction of the trial of facts and flexibility of disposal[53] has made this safeguard less critical. However, it nonetheless remains important and is, as Thomas LJ counseled in *Norman*, worth considering with care.

(g) The 'trial of the issue': the determination itself

5.59 It is for the judge sitting alone to determine whether the defendant is unfit to plead (CP(IA) 1964 s. 4(5), as amended by the Domestic Violence, Crime and Victims Act 2004). The formal determination is that the defendant is 'under a disability' such that it would 'constitute a bar' to his or her being tried (CP(IA) 1964 s. 4(1)).

---

[52] See *Antoine* at [375]. See also: *Webb* [1969] 2 QB 278; and *Burles* [1970] 2 QB 191. Although the latter two cases were decided before CP(IUP)A 1991.
[53] Introduced by CP(IUP)A 1991.

(h) The 'trial of the issue': examining the expert evidence

Under CP(I)A 1964 s. 4(6), the court is not required to receive the expert evi- **5.60**
dence orally, and the judge can determine the issue on written evidence alone.
However, in *Walls*, Thomas LJ emphasized at [38] that, save in clear cases of
unfitness, the fact that psychiatrists agree on the question of unfitness is 'not
enough', and the judge should 'rigorously examine evidence of psychiatrists
adduced before them and then subject that evidence to careful analysis against
the *Pritchard* criteria'.

The issue of unfitness to plead is determined by the judge applying the legal **5.61**
test, but informed by the opinion of the medical experts (see *Miller and Miller*
[2006] EWCA Crim 2391 at [17]). The judge is entitled to reject the opinion
of the medical experts, as, for example, happened in *Walls*, and this not infrequently occurs where the expert has failed to apply the *Pritchard* criteria in full.
However, the courts have taken the view that, following CP(I)A 1964 s. 4(6),
the judge would not be entitled to find a defendant 'under a disability' without
having received evidence supportive of that finding from at least two suitably
qualified experts.[54]

(i) Taking into consideration special measures

Thomas LJ stressed in *Walls* at [37] that a finding of unfitness to plead is a 'very **5.62**
serious step', which deprives the defendant of a number of significant rights.
Before taking such a step, the judge should also consider whether the participation difficulties identified in any psychological or psychiatric report might be
accommodated within the trial process by the use of an intermediary[55] or other
adjustments to the process. (See Chapter 10, 'Special Measures'.)

(j) Applying the test in the context of the particular proceedings

Applying the *Pritchard* criteria should involve an assessment of the defend- **5.63**
ant's capabilities, not in the abstract, but in the context of the particular
proceedings. The judge should consider the demands likely to be made of the
defendant at trial, taking into account, for example, the nature and complexity of the issues arising (in so far as they can be identified), the likely duration
of any trial, and the number of parties involved (*Marcantonio and Chitolie*
at [7]).

---

[54] *Borkan* [2004] EWCA Crim 1642; and *Lederman* [2015] EWCA Crim 1308.
[55] Under the court's inherent powers following *C v Sevenoaks Magistrates' Court* [2009] EWHC
3088 (Admin) and *R (AS) v Great Yarmouth Youth Court* [2011] EWHC 2059. See Chapter 11,
'Intermediaries'. But see also Crim PD I General Matters 3F.11 ff.

(k) Procedure where the defendant recovers before the trial of the facts or before disposal

5.64 Very occasionally, a defendant found unfit to plead recovers his or her fitness before the trial of the facts is heard, or before the disposal is imposed. CP(I)A 1964 is silent as to what should occur in such a situation, giving rise to 'an unsatisfactory lacuna in the law'.[56]

5.65 This issue was addressed in *R (Hasani) v Crown Court at Blackfriars*,[57] in which Hooper LJ concluded that it would be consistent with the policy behind the unfitness to plead provisions for a second trial of the issue to be conducted (under CP(I)A 1964 s. 4). Where this occurs and the defendant is found fit to plead, then arrangements would be made for the defendant to be arraigned and tried in the usual way. In the unusual event that the second determination finds the defendant 'under a disability' for a second time, then the trial of facts would follow (or a previous finding of fact would remain in force and the judge proceed to disposal under CP(I)A 1964 s. 5).

(l) Unfitness to plead and abuse of process

5.66 A defendant may wish to argue that the proceedings should be stayed as an abuse of process, on the basis of his or her inability to participate effectively in the proceedings. At common law, a fair trial requires that the defendant be able to participate in the proceedings (*Lee Kun*[58]), and effective participation is an essential component of fair trial guarantees under Article 6 of the ECHR (*SC v UK* and *T v UK, V v UK*) (see paragraph 5.25, '(d) The *Pritchard* test and the right to "participate effectively" in trial').

5.67 However, in *M and Others*,[59] the Court of Appeal considered the relationship between an application to stay proceedings and the unfitness to plead provisions. The Court of Appeal concluded that the defendant's unfitness to plead does not remove his or her right to mount an abuse of process argument, which could be made either before or after the determination under CP(I)A 1964 s. 4. However, Rose LJ giving judgment made plain that the application could not be founded on the defendant's 'disability', since for that to be the basis of the abuse argument would be to 'avoid the whole point of sections 4 and 4A' of CP(I)A 1964:

> An abuse application, whenever made, must be founded on matters independent of the defendant's disability, such as oppressive behaviour of the Crown or agencies of the state, or circumstances or conduct which would deprive the defendant of a

---

[56] *Omara* [2004] EWCA Crim 431 at [17].
[57] [2005] EWHC 3016 (Admin).
[58] [1916] 1 KB 337.
[59] [2001] EWCA Crim 2024; [2002] 1 WLR 824.

fair trial, eg destruction of vital records during a long period of delay or an earlier assurance that he would not be prosecuted.[60]

E. The Trial of the Facts: The S. 4A Hearing (CP(I)A 1964 s. 4A)

(a) Background

As originally enacted, CP(I)A 1964 included no provisions for considering the **5.68** facts of the alleged offence. At that time, a defendant found unfit to plead was subject to mandatory and indefinite hospitalization. However, the Criminal Procedure (Insanity and Unfitness to Plead) Act 1991 amended CP(I)A 1964 to introduce s. 4A, which requires a jury to consider the facts of the allegation before any disposal can be imposed.

(b) The trial of the facts: the determination

Under CP(I)A 1964 s. 4A(2), once a defendant has been found to be 'under a dis- **5.69** ability', full trial cannot proceed, or proceed further (where the issue of unfitness to plead was determined after the trial had begun). Instead, a jury are required to determine whether the defendant 'did the act or made the omission charged against him as the offence'. This hearing is commonly referred to as the 'trial of the facts' or the 's. 4A hearing'.

If the jury are satisfied beyond reasonable doubt that the defendant did the act **5.70** or made the omission charged in respect of one, or more than one, of the alleged offences, then the judge will proceed to consider what disposal is appropriate (CP(I)A 1964 s. 5). If the jury is not so satisfied on any of the charges, then the defendant is acquitted on that charge. If acquitted on all charges, then the defendant will be discharged and cannot be made subject to any disposal under CP(I)A 1964.

An acquittal on a charge at the trial of the facts functions in the same way as **5.71** if the defendant had been acquitted on that charge following full trial (CP(I)A 1964 s. 4A(4)). As a result, prosecution on that charge cannot be resumed on recovery (see paragraph 5.127 below). However, an application for retrial under Part 10 of the Criminal Justice Act 2003 (CJA 2003) would be available in appropriate cases where new and compelling evidence comes to light. Conversely, it is important to note that the trial of the facts does not consider the defendant's culpability in respect of any offence. It cannot, therefore, result in a

---

[60] *M and Others* at [36]–[38]. (See also discussion of the availability of a stay for a defendant with significant participation difficulties falling short of unfitness in *T v UK, V v UK*.) Paragraph 5.154 addresses the position in the magistrates' court.

conviction, nor can the disposal imposed following a finding that the defendant 'did the act or made the omission' be considered to function as punishment for the unfit defendant.[61]

(c) No discretion whether to proceed

5.72 The purpose of the trial of the facts is not to determine culpability. Rather, it is to identify those defendants in respect of whom it may be appropriate to impose a protective disposal (or any ancillary orders), by providing an opportunity for the defendant to be acquitted where the evidence of his or her involvement in the offence is insufficient. Where such a disposal is not required, nor an acquittal likely to follow, there may be little purpose in holding a trial of facts. However, CP(I)A 1964 s. 4A(2) is framed in mandatory terms, and the court has no discretion to decline to proceed with the trial of facts.[62]

(d) What the prosecution must establish

5.73 The House of Lords considered in the case of *Antoine*[63] how 'did the act or made the omission charged against him as an offence' (CP(I)A 1964 s. 4(A)2) should be interpreted. They concluded that to establish that the defendant 'did the act or made the omission', the prosecution would be required to prove only the *actus reus*, the external elements of an offence. These include the conduct elements of an offence (what the defendant must do or fail to do), the consequence elements (the result of the defendant's actions), and the circumstance elements (other facts distinct from the defendant's actions, but required to establish the offence, such as whether or not a complainant in a sexual allegation was consenting). The Crown would not be required to prove the *mens rea*, or fault element of the offence, namely the state of mind which, at full trial, would be necessary to prove the allegation.

5.74 Lord Hutton concluded that this approach struck the necessary 'fair balance between the need to protect a defendant who has, in fact, done nothing wrong and is unfit to plead at his trial and the need to protect the public from a defendant who has committed an injurious act which would constitute a crime if done with the requisite mens rea'.[64]

---

[61] See *M and Others*.

[62] See *Orr* at [29]. Although empirical research has identified that the trial of the facts does not proceed in every case of unfitness, including cases where the judge concluded that to proceed to the trial of the facts was not in the public interest. See Mackay et al., 'A Continued Upturn in Unfitness to Plead', 538.

[63] [2001] 1 AC 340, overturning *Egan* [1998] 1 Cr App R 121.

[64] [2001] 1 AC 340 at [375].

(e) Separating the external and fault elements of an offence

The separation of the external and fault elements of an offence, as required fol-   **5.75**
lowing *Antoine*, is not always straightforward. Some elements of an offence which
would ordinarily be considered to constitute a part of the *actus reus*, such as the
possession of a particular item, imply a mental element in addition to that which
is externally observable. The difficulty that such a strict division can present has
been acknowledged not only by Hutton LJ in *Antoine*,[65] but more recently by Sir
Brian Leveson P in *Wells and Others*[66] at [12], noting that in a number of criminal
offences there is no 'bright line' between the external and fault elements.

This has led to a piecemeal, and sometimes inconsistent, development of the law,   **5.76**
as the task of separating the external and fault elements of particular offences is
addressed by the courts. In *B(M)*,[67] for example, the Court of Appeal considered
what elements of the offence of voyeurism the Crown should be required to prove
in establishing that the defendant 'did the act' at the trial of the facts. The court
concluded that the external elements included the defendant's purpose in observing the private act of another, namely to obtain sexual gratification. This was,
Atkins LJ considered, 'central to the statutory offence of voyeurism' and what
turned the behaviour of the defendant into what Lord Hutton had described in
Antoine as an 'injurious act'. The defendant's knowledge, however, that the person he observed was not consenting, was, the court concluded, part of the fault
element and should not concern the jury at the trial of facts.

This stands somewhat at odds with the earlier decision of the Court of Appeal in   **5.77**
the case of *Young*,[68] which concerned an allegation of dishonest concealment of
a material fact.[69] The defendant's purpose in the concealment and his dishonesty
were, the Court of Appeal concluded, part of the fault element of that offence,
and thus not matters for the jury's consideration at the trial of facts. However,
the issue of whether the defendant had the intention alleged against him, and
whether he had concealed it, were, by contrast, part of the external elements of
the offence required to be proved by the Crown. The court acknowledged that
what the Crown had to prove went beyond 'purely physical acts', but that this
was necessary in order to avoid the finding at the trial of facts being 'utterly
emasculated'.[70]

The consistent thread that can be discerned in these cases where there is no 'bright   **5.78**
line' between external and conduct elements is the importance of retaining for

---

[65] At [376].
[66] [2015] EWCA Crim 2.
[67] [2012] EWCA Crim 770.
[68] [2002] EWHC 548 (Admin).
[69] Now an offence under the Financial Services Act 2012 s. 89.
[70] Observation in the judgment of Leveson J, concurring with the leading judgment of Rose LJ.

the jury's consideration any aspect of the offence which, while going beyond the 'purely physical', is necessary for the jury to be able to distinguish between behaviour on the part of the defendant which might be considered innocuous and behaviour which would constitute, in Lord Hutton's terminology, an 'injurious act' if done with the necessary intent (warranting the imposition of an appropriate disposal). However, the piecemeal development of the law relating to the trial of the facts, as this issue is considered in respect of particular offences, is far from satisfactory.

(f) Defences

5.79 Following *Antoine*, defences will not generally be available to an unfit defendant at the trial of the facts, since they relate predominantly to issues of *mens rea* which are outside the jury's consideration at that hearing. However, in *Antoine*, Lord Hutton identified limited circumstances in which the defences of self-defence, mistake, or accident may be available to an unfit defendant:

> If there is objective evidence which raises the issue of mistake or accident or self-defence, then the jury should not find that the defendant did the 'act' unless it is satisfied beyond reasonable doubt on all the evidence that the prosecution has negatived that defence.[71]

5.80 The same approach would apply, Lord Hutton considered, where the defence raise the issue of involuntary action 'as when a man kicks out and strikes another in the course of an uncontrollable fit brought about by a medical condition'.[72]

5.81 Lord Hutton gave two examples of what might amount to objective evidence for these purposes, both being independent eye-witness accounts of the alleged offending. However, in *Wells and Others* at [15] and [17], Leveson P confirmed that the requirement for objective evidence might be satisfied by a wider range of evidence, including 'CCTV, cell site, scene of crime or expert forensic evidence'. Objective evidence raising the issue of self-defence on an assault charge might also arise, he observed, from 'the background to the incident, the antecedents of the complainants and the circumstances of the fight as evidenced, for example, by the injuries'.

5.82 However, Leveson P stressed that what would not satisfy the category of objective evidence were, 'the assertions of a defendant who, at the time of speaking, is proved to be suffering from a mental disorder of a type that undermines his or her reliability and which itself has precipitated the finding of unfitness to plead', even where these assertions were not obviously delusional.

---

[71] *Antoine* at [376].

[72] ibid. at [377]. But this raises the question of the position where the involuntary action arises as a result of insane automatism. See R. Mackay and G. Kearns, 'An Upturn in Unfitness to Plead? Disability in Relation to the Trial under the 1991 Act' [2000] Crim LR 532, 544.

However, he suggested that, in limited circumstances, what the defendant **5.83** said in interview might be admissible where the issue which caused his or her unfitness to plead was not experienced by the defendant at the time of interview:

> It is not difficult to visualize a defendant of full capacity who is involved in an incident and then provides a full account to the police but thereafter suffers an injury which renders him or her unfit to plead. It is not uncommon for such interviews to be admitted into evidence whatever the strict operation of the principles in *Antoine* might otherwise suggest.[73]

These restrictions on the ability of a defendant to raise a defence at a trial of facts **5.84** have been the subject of criticism.[74] However, Leveson P in *Wells and Others* reasoned that any 'disadvantage' experienced by the requirement is 'balanced by the fact that these are not criminal proceedings and the disposals are accordingly limited'.[75]

(g) Insanity

The defendant would not be entitled to seek a special verdict of not guilty by rea- **5.85** son of insanity (Trial of Lunatics Act 1883 s. 2) at the trial of facts.[76] However, it is not clear whether this prohibition would include insane automatism, which appears, in *Antoine* at [377], to be left open to the defendant, where there is medical evidence to support the contention.[77]

(h) Partial defences

The partial defence to murder of diminished responsibility cannot be advanced **5.86** on behalf of an unfit defendant at a trial of the facts.[78] The case of *Grant*[79] established that provocation is also not available to an unfit defendant. Following the Coroners and Justice Act 2009 s. 54, provocation has been reformulated as loss of control, but it is anticipated that the position with regard to the trial of the facts will remain unchanged.

---

[73] *Wells and Others* at [18]. For further discussion, see K. Kerrigan and N. Wortley, 'Unfitness to Plead: Expanding the Scope of "Objective Evidence" on the "Trial of the Facts"' (2015) *Journal of Criminal Law* 160.

[74] See, e.g., Law Com No. 364.

[75] At [15].

[76] See *Antoine* at [373] ff. However, Lord Hutton's observation in *Antoine* that the defence relates entirely to the defendant's *mens rea*, and is therefore outside the elements required to be considered by the jury under CP(I)A 1964 s. 4A, overlooks the availability of insanity in cases of strict liability.

[77] See n. 72 above.

[78] *Antoine* at [368].

[79] *Grant* [2001] EWCA Crim 2611 at 43 ff. Also ruling out the defence raising an issue of the lack of specific intent in a trial of the facts at [42].

(i) Secondary participation

5.87 An allegation that an unfit defendant participated in an offence as a secondary party also presents some difficulty in terms of what the prosecution must prove at the trial of the facts. In *M(KJ)* [2003] 2 Cr App R 21, CA Potter LJ held that the jury should be directed as to the minimum facts of which they must be satisfied to find 'the act' proved in the particular case:

> If, by reason of the definition of the crime concerned, or the level of the participation required to establish liability, it is necessary for the jury to be satisfied that the defendant had a particular level of knowledge as to the activities of the principal offender and/or the surrounding circumstances, then the judge should so direct. (at [42])

5.88 Potter LJ acknowledged that this approach required the jury to consider the unfit defendant's state of knowledge at the time of the alleged offence. However, in line with Lord Hutton's approach to issues of mistake, accident, and self-defence in *Antoine*, Potter LJ considered that the defendant's state of knowledge could be determined on 'an objective basis by inference from the facts presented in evidence',[80] and not from evidence provided by the defendant or the suggestions of his or her representative. (Although see the application of this principle in *Wells and Others* at [58]–[62].)

(j) Conduct of the hearing

(i) When to hold the trial of the facts

5.89 The trial of the facts should be heard as soon as possible after the determination that the defendant is unfit to plead, in order to avoid the difficulties encountered in cases such as *Omara*[81] and in consideration of the significant delays which often characterize cases involving issues of unfitness to plead.

(ii) Representation for the defendant

5.90 Under CP(I)A 1964 s. 4A(2)(b), the court has a duty to appoint a representative to put the case for the defence at the trial of the facts. In *Norman* at [34], Thomas LJ elaborated on the nature of this duty, observing that in every case the court must 'consider afresh the person who is to be appointed; it should not necessarily be the same person who has represented the defendant to date, as it is the responsibility of the court to be satisfied that the person appointed is the right person for this difficult task'. However, in many cases it will be preferable for the same representative to continue to act on behalf of the defendant, given the rapport which will have been built up. Crim PR r. 25.10(3)(a) sets out the factors to be taken into account by the court in making the appointment.

---

[80] *M(KJ)* [2003] 2 Cr App R 21 at [46].
[81] [2004] EWCA Crim 431.

The representative, as a court appointee, is paid out of central funds and has **5.91** different responsibilities from an advocate representing a defendant in full trial. Although the representative should give effect to the defendant's expressed will and preferences, in so far as they can be identified,[82] the representative is not required to act upon the defendant's 'instructions' if he or she considers that to do so would not be in the defendant's best interests.

(iii)   Adjustments to facilitate the defendant's participation in the hearing

The court should take every reasonable step to adjust the hearing to enable the **5.92** unfit defendant to attend, where that is practicable, and to participate in the hearing, to the extent that that is achievable (in keeping with the approach in Crim PD 3D.2 and 3G).

(k)   Trial of the facts alongside full trial of co-defendants

If a defendant who is determined to be unfit to plead is jointly charged with other **5.93** defendant(s) who are fit to plead, the full trial of the fit defendant(s) and the trial of the facts for the unfit defendant can occur simultaneously before a single jury (*B and Others*[83]). This position is unaffected by the timing of the determination of unfitness, whether that occurs before or after full trial has commenced.

Simultaneous hearings can cause difficulties, both for fit and unfit defendants. **5.94** This may particularly occur where 'cut-throat' defences are deployed, where bad character applications are made, or where the question of adverse inferences in respect of the fit defendants may arise. However, there may also be strong reasons for simultaneous proceedings, not least to prevent delay and to avoid the need for a complainant or other witnesses having to give evidence in two proceedings. In *B and Others*, Toulson LJ observed that the decision whether to hold separate hearings required four sets of interests to be considered: those of the unfit defendants, the fit defendants, witnesses, and the public (at [25]). (See also Crim PR rr. 3.21 and 3.22.)

(l)   Article 6 ECHR not applicable

The House of Lords determined in *H*[84] that hearings under CP(I)A 1964 s. 4A do **5.95** not involve the determination of a criminal charge, for the purposes of Article 6 of the ECHR. In applying the test in *Engel v The Netherlands (No. 1)*[85] at [678]– [679], their lordships focused in particular on the fact that unfitness to plead procedures cannot result in a conviction and that they do not trigger the imposition

---

[82] Consistent with efforts to ensure that the defendant can exercise his or her legal agency to the fullest extent possible. See UNCRPD Arts 12 and 13.
[83] [2008] EWCA Crim 1997; [2009] 1 WLR 1545.
[84] [2003] UKHL 1; [2003] 1 WLR 411.
[85] (1976) 1 EHRR 647.

of punishment. As long as properly conducted, 'with scrupulous regard for the interests of the accused person', unfitness to plead procedures are fair and compatible with the rights of the individual.[86] The Court of Appeal made similar observations in *B*[87] at [15], emphasizing the importance of taking time to ensure that the procedures are 'handled justly and fairly'.

(m) Evidence

5.96 At the trial of the facts, the jury reach their determination as to whether the defendant 'did the act or made the omission' on the basis of evidence adduced by the prosecution or by the representative appointed to put the case for the defence. Where the finding of unfitness to plead occurs after trial has begun, the jury will include in their deliberations any evidence already given in the trial and any further evidence adduced by either side after the trial of the issue (CP(I)A 1964 s. 4A(2)).

5.97 Although, following *H*, trials of the facts do not involve the determination of a criminal charge, they are 'criminal proceedings in relation to which the strict rules of evidence apply' for the purposes of CJA 2003 s. 134. As a result, hearsay provisions apply[88] and either side can adduce bad character evidence in accordance with the provisions of CJA 2003 Pt 11.[89]

5.98 Where it is proposed that the unfit defendant's account in police interview be admitted, the court should be satisfied, on the basis of expert evidence, that the defendant understood the caution at the time of answering questions, and that generally it was safe for him or her to be interviewed (*Swinbourne*[90] at [25]). Where any aspect of the defendant's interview is put before the jury, the judge in summing up should give a specially crafted direction to the jury warning them of the need for particular care to be taken, given the risk that what was said in interview may be the result of the defendant's disability rather than because he or she was lying or otherwise attempting to mislead the police (*Swinbourne* at [30]; see also *Wells and Others* at [18] ff).

5.99 The unfit defendant may give evidence at the trial of the facts, although this will very rarely be appropriate. In *Antoine* at [368], Lord Hutton cautioned that 'careful consideration' should be given by the defendant's representative before allowing an unfit defendant to give evidence. It is suggested that expert evidence as to the defendant's understanding of the caution and the general safety of him or her giving evidence would be required (*Swinbourne* at [25]). No adverse inference may

---

[86] *H* at [20].
[87] [2012] EWCA Crim 1799.
[88] *Chal* [2008] 1 Cr App R 18, CA.
[89] *Creed* [2011] 3 All ER 509, CA.
[90] [2013] EWCA Crim 2329; (2014) 178 JP 34.

be drawn from an unfit defendant's failure to give evidence (Crim PR r. 25.10(3)
(c)(iii)).

F. Disposals

(a) The rationale behind disposals for unfit defendants

Where the jury have found that an unfit defendant has 'done the act or made the **5.100**
omission' in respect of at least one of the charges, then the individual must be
made subject to one of the disposals listed in CP(I)A 1964 s. 5(2). The defendant has not been convicted, nor have the jury determined his or her culpability
in respect of the allegation. As a result, the disposals are not intended to punish
the individual; rather, the purpose of the disposals is to support the person to live
without being involved in criminal behaviour, and to protect the public, where
that is considered necessary. The disposal is therefore imposed 'in respect of the
accused' (CP(I)A 1964 s. 5(2)), rather than in relation to a particular act or omission found proved (but see offences of murder discussed at paragraph 5.106).

(b) Disposal options

CP(I)A 1964 s. 5(2) provides for the following disposals: **5.101**

1. a hospital order (with or without restriction order);
2. a supervision order; or
3. an absolute discharge.

(c) Hospital order: CP(I)A 1964 s. 5(2)(a)

A hospital order imposed under CP(I)A 1964 s. 5(2)(a) has the same meaning as **5.102**
one imposed on conviction under MHA 1983 s. 37,[91] and requires the unfit individual to be admitted to and detained in a hospital which is secure.

In order to make a hospital order, the court would have to be satisfied, on the **5.103**
basis of evidence from two registered medical practitioners, at least one of whom
is approved (under MHA 1983 s. 12) as having special experience in the diagnosis
of mental disorder,[92] that:

1. the individual is suffering from a mental disorder of a nature and degree which
   makes it appropriate for him or her to be detained in a hospital for medical
   treatment;
2. appropriate medical treatment is available to him or her; and

---

[91] CP(I)A 1964 s. 5(4).
[92] As required under MHA 1983 s. 54.

3. in the circumstances of the case, a hospital order is the 'most suitable method' of disposing of the case (MHA 1983 s. 37(2)).

Before making the order, the court must also receive written or oral evidence from an approved clinician with responsibility for the individual's treatment, or from a representative of the hospital's manager, that arrangements have been made for the admission of the unfit individual within twenty-eight days of the order being made (MHA 1983 s. 37(4)).

(d) Restriction order: CP(I)A 1964 s. 5(2)(a)

5.104 Where a hospital order is made under CP(I)A 1964 s. 5(2)(a), the court may also impose a restriction order. CP(I)A 1964 s. 5(4) defines 'a restriction order' for these purposes as having the same meaning as under MHA 1983 s. 41, so that the individual subject to a restriction order cannot be granted leave of absence, transferred to a different hospital, or discharged without the consent of the Secretary of State.[93]

5.105 Following CP(I)A 1964 s. 5(4), it is assumed that the requirements for making a restriction order under MHA 1983 s. 41 also apply. Save in cases of murder (addressed in paragraph 5.106), following MHA 1983 s. 41(1), a restriction order can therefore only be imposed on an unfit individual where it is 'necessary' to protect the public from 'serious harm', having regard to the nature of the offence, the individual's antecedents and the risk that he or she will commit further offences. A restriction order could not be made unless the judge has heard orally from at least one of the two registered medical practitioners whose evidence is before the court in respect of the making of the hospital order (MHA 1983 s. 41(2)). Although the judge is not obliged to follow expert opinion in respect of the restriction order, the assessment of risk being a matter for the court not the medical experts.[94]

(e) Mandatory restriction order for cases of murder: CP(I)A 1964 s. 5(3)

5.106 Where a defendant has been found to have done the act in relation to a murder allegation, and if the court has the power to make a hospital order in respect of that individual, the court must also impose a restriction order (CP(I)A 1964 s. 5(3)). This applies whether or not the court would otherwise have had the power to make a restriction order (under CP(I)A 1964 s. 5(2)(a) and MHA 1983 s. 41).

5.107 This position, introduced by the Domestic Violence, Crime and Victims Act 2004 s. 24, is an improvement on the earlier mandatory requirement for a

---

[93] See MHA 1983 s. 41(3)–(6) for full details of the special restrictions applicable.
[94] Birch (1990) 90 Cr App R 78 at [86].

hospital order with restriction to be imposed on all unfit individuals found to have done the act of murder, whether or not they were suitable for treatment in a hospital. However, it leads to somewhat arbitrary outcomes which could be considered to discriminate against those with a 'mental disorder' for which treatment is appropriate. For the unfit individual found to have 'done the act' of murder and who satisfies MHA 1983 s. 37(2), a restriction order will also follow (and the prospect of resumption, discussed at paragraph 5.127) whether or not they pose a risk of 'serious harm' (otherwise required otherwise under MHA 1983 s. 41). But for an unfit individual found to have 'done the act' of murder who does not satisfy MHA 1983 s. 37(2),[95] only a supervision order or an absolute discharge is available, whatever risk of 'serious harm' he or she may present.

(f) Supervision order: CP(I)A 1964 s. 5(2)(b)

5.108 The nature of the supervision order for an unfit individual, available under CP(I)A 1964 s. 5(2)(b), is set out in detail in Sch. 1A to CP(I)A 1964. An individual subject to such an order must 'keep in touch with' a supervising officer according to the officer's instruction, and must notify the officer of any change of address (Sch. 1A para. 3(5)). The supervising officer must be either a social worker or an officer of a local probation board or probation provider (Sch. 1A para. 1(1)) and must be 'willing to undertake the supervision' (Sch. 1A para. 3(2)(a)).[96] Anecdotal evidence suggests that there have been difficulties in some cases identifying a willing supervisor.[97]

(i) Additional requirements

5.109 A supervision order may include medical treatment requirements. The court can include a requirement that the individual submit to treatment with a view to improving his or her mental condition (CP(I)A 1964 Sch. 1A para. 4). The court would need to be satisfied, on the evidence of at least two registered medical practitioners,[98] that the mental condition of the individual requires, and may be susceptible to, treatment, but is not such as to warrant the making of a hospital order under MHA 1983.

5.110 Alternatively, or in addition, a medical treatment requirement can also be included where, having received the evidence of at least two registered medical practitioners, the court is satisfied that because of a medical condition (other than his or her

---

[95] Because, for example, they do not have a 'mental disorder' or one for which medical treatment is appropriate.
[96] See *City and County of Swansea v Swansea Crown Court* [2016] EWHC 1389 (Admin) (QBD (Admin)).
[97] See Law Com No. 364.
[98] One of whom is 'duly registered', which is taken to be a reference to MHA 1983 s. 12.

mental condition) the individual is likely to pose a risk to him- or herself or others and the condition is susceptible to treatment (Sch. 1A para. 5).

5.111 Treatment under either such requirement is supervised by a registered medical practitioner. The treatment requirement cannot impose residential treatment unless the supervised person consents (Sch. 1A para. 6).

5.112 The court may also include a residence requirement (Sch. 1A para. 8).

(ii) Duration and variations

5.113 The maximum period of any such supervision order is two years (CP(I)A 1964 Sch. 1A para. 1(1)). Before that time, a supervision order may be revoked (Sch. 1A para. 9), or the requirements varied or removed (Sch. 1A paras 10 ff) on application by the supervised person or the supervising officer.

(iii) Limitations of the order

5.114 Even with the additional requirements, the supervision order that is available to be imposed is fairly 'light touch'. In addition, beyond the limited power to revoke or vary the requirements, the court has no other oversight of the order, and there is no mechanism to support an individual's compliance with it.

(g) Absolute discharge: CP(I)A 1964 s. 5(2)(c)

5.115 The only other disposal option available to the court is to absolutely discharge the unfit individual (CP(I)A 1964 s. 5(2)(c)). This would be appropriate for an unfit individual who does not require treatment or supervision in the community.

(h) Notification requirements

5.116 An unfit individual may also be subject to notification requirements:

1. If determined to have done the act in relation to an offence included within the Sexual Offences Act 2003 (SOA 2003) Sch. 3 (covering the majority of sexual offences), the unfit individual will be a 'relevant offender' and subject to notification requirements under SOA 2003 s. 80(1)(c). A failure to notify the police of relevant information without reasonable excuse is a separate criminal offence which can incur up to five years' imprisonment (on indictment) or six months' imprisonment (on summary conviction).

2. If determined to have done the act in relation to an offence (carrying a term of twelve months' imprisonment or more) to which the Counter-Terrorism Act 2008 Pt 4 applies, and given a hospital order, an unfit individual aged 16 or over will be subject to notification requirements under the Counter-Terrorism Act 2008 s. 54. A failure to comply, without reasonable excuse, is a separate criminal offence which can incur up to five years' imprisonment

(on indictment) or twelve months' imprisonment (on summary conviction, subject to the date of the commission of the offence).

(i)   Multi-Agency Public Protection Arrangements

Following CJA 2003 s. 327, an unfit individual will automatically be subject to **5.117** Multi-Agency Public Protection Arrangements if:

1. he or she is subject to notification requirements under SOA 2003 Pt 2 as a result of the proceedings; or
2. he or she has been found to have 'done the act' in relation to a charge of murder, or a specified violent or sexual offence (as listed in CJA 2003 Sch. 15) and has received a hospital order.[99]

(j)   Ancillary orders

There are a number of ancillary orders which may also be made following a finding **5.118** that the unfit defendant 'did the act or made the omission' in respect of particular offences. In each case, breach of the ancillary order is a separate offence punishable with imprisonment:

1. On application by the chief officer of police, a notification order under SOA 2003 s. 97, where the unfit individual has been found to have done the act in relation to an offence contained within SOA 2003 Sch. 3 and the conditions in SOA 2003 s. 97 apply.
2. A sexual harm prevention order under SOA 2003 s. 103A, where an unfit individual is found to have done the act in respect of an offence within SOA 2003 Sch. 3 or 5 and the court is satisfied that such an order is necessary to protect the public, or particular members of the public, from sexual harm.
3. A violent offender order under the Criminal Justice and Immigration Act 2008 s. 98, where an unfit adult is found to have done the act in relation to an offence specified in that section, where he or she received a hospital order or supervision order, and where the court is satisfied that such an order is necessary to protect the public from the risk of serious violent harm.
4. A slavery and trafficking prevention order under the Modern Slavery Act 2015 s. 14, where the unfit individual is found to have done the act in respect of a slavery or human trafficking offence, and the court is satisfied there is a risk that he or she will commit a further offence of that sort and that such an order is necessary to protect the public from the harm that a further such offence is likely to cause.

---

[99] Guardianship orders are also referred to in CJA 2003 s. 327(4), although they are no longer an available disposal under the Domestic Violence, Crime and Victims Act 2004 s. 24.

The court may also make an exploitation proceeds order under the Coroners and Justice Act 2009 s. 155 in respect of an unfit individual determined to have done the act of a 'relevant offence' within the Coroners and Justice Act 2009 s. 159.

(k) Restraining orders not available where the act or omission is found proved

5.119 The court may make a restraining order where an unfit defendant is acquitted of an offence, if it is satisfied that such an order is necessary for the protection of a person from harassment, under the Protection from Harassment Act 1997 s. 5A. However, where the unfit individual is found to have done the act, or made the omission, in respect of an offence, neither s. 5 (order on conviction) nor s. 5A (order on acquittal) of the Protection from Harassment Act 1997 is applicable and so no restraining order can be made.[100]

G. Appeals

(a) Rights of appeal to the Court of Appeal

5.120 An unfit individual can appeal to the Court of Appeal against a finding that he or she was 'under a disability' under CP(I)A 1964 s. 4, or against a determination that he or she 'did the act or made the omission' under CP(I)A 1964 s. 4A, or both (Criminal Appeal Act 1968 (CAA 1968) s. 15).[101] There is also a right of appeal against any hospital order or supervision order imposed under CP(I)A 1964 s. 5 (CAA 1968 s. 16A).

5.121 These rights of appeal are exercisable only where the Court of Appeal has granted leave or where the trial judge has issued a certificate that the case is fit for appeal. The right of appeal is exercisable only by the unfit individual him- or herself, and only at the conclusion of the proceedings (CAA 1964 ss 15 and 16A).

(b) Appeal outcomes

5.122 An appeal will be allowed if the Court of Appeal concludes that the finding is unsafe (CAA 1968 s. 16(1)). If an appeal is allowed in relation to the finding that the defendant was unfit to plead ('under a disability'), the Court of Appeal can remit the appellant to the Crown Court for trial on the original offence (s. 16(3)).

5.123 However, where an appeal is allowed against a finding of fact under CP(I)A 1964 s. 4A, but the finding of unfitness remains in place, the Court of Appeal has

---

[100] *Chinegwundoh* [2015] EWCA Crim 109.
[101] The trial judge may also grant a certificate that the case is fit for appeal under CAA 1968 s. 15(2)(b).

no power to remit the appellant to the Crown Court for the trial of the facts to be reheard. The Court may only enter an acquittal in respect of that charge or charges (CAA 1968 s. 16(4)). This has caused difficulties and raised public protection concerns,[102] resulting in calls for Parliament to amend what has been described as a 'most unfortunate error in the law'.[103]

Where permission to appeal against the decision at the determination of the facts **5.124** has been granted, the unfit individual has the right to pursue that appeal. Any resumption of the proceedings against him or her under CP(I)A 1964 s. 5A will have to await the outcome of the appeal, and will be prevented if the appeal is allowed.[104]

Where appeal against disposal alone is allowed, the Court of Appeal can vary the **5.125** original order or substitute for it any other order which could have been made by the trial judge under CP(I)A 1964 s. 5.

(c) Judicial review and appeal by way of case stated

A finding that a defendant is fit to plead is included within 'matters relating to **5.126** trial on indictment'[105] and so is not susceptible to judicial review or appeal by way of case stated.[106] However, where the judge determines that a defendant is unfit to plead, the trial process is suspended and subsequent decisions are no longer 'matters relating to trial on indictment'. As a result, an unfit individual may seek judicial review (SCA 1981 s. 29(3)) or appeal by way of case stated (SCA 1981 s. 28(1)) in respect of decisions made by the judge during the trial of the facts and on disposal.[107]

H. Remission and Resumption of the Prosecution on Recovery

(a) Limitation to individuals with live restriction orders

There is very limited scope for a prosecution to be resumed against an individual **5.127** who was previously found unfit to plead, but has subsequently recovered. CP(I) A 1964 s. 5A(4) gives the Secretary of State, in consultation with the individual's responsible clinician, power to remit an individual to court or prison for trial, if

---

[102] See *McKenzie* [2011] EWCA Crim 1810.
[103] Per Thomas P in *B* [2012] EWCA Crim 1799 at [19]; see also Thomas LJ in *Norman* at [34].
[104] *MB* [2010] EWCA Crim 1684.
[105] Senior Courts Act 1981 (SCA 1981) s. 29(3).
[106] *Bradford Crown Court, ex p. Bottomley* [1994] Crim LR 753.
[107] See, e.g., *Grant* [2001] EWCA Crim 2611 (appeal by way of case stated); *R (Young) v Central Criminal Court* [2002] EWHC 548 (Admin); and *R (Kenneally) v Crown Court at Snaresbrook* [2001] EWHC Admin 968.

satisfied that the individual can now 'properly be tried'. This is limited to cases where the unfit individual is subject to a hospital order with a restriction order which continues to have effect. There is no other express power for the prosecution to be resumed against an unfit individual who is not subject to a live restriction order.[108]

(b) No power for a recovered individual to seek remission or resumption of the prosecution

5.128 There is no power for an individual to seek remission for trial or resumption of a prosecution against him or her following recovery of fitness, even where that individual remains subject to a live restriction order.[109]

(c) Procedures for remission and resumption of a prosecution

5.129 The Crown Prosecution Service (CPS), the National Offender Management Service, and HM Courts and Tribunals Service have agreed guidance as to how remission for trial, and the resumption of proceedings, should be handled in respect of a recovered individual.[110]

5.130 Although the reinstitution of proceedings against a recovered individual has come to be referred to simply as 'remission', the guidance makes plain that there are two separate functions involved: the Secretary of State's decision whether to remit the individual for trial and the separate decision of the prosecutor, generally the CPS, as to whether or not to resume the prosecution. In order to inform these decisions, the Mental Health Casework Section (MHCS) of the Ministry of Justice monitors the individual's fitness to plead, receiving reports on a yearly basis from the clinician responsible for the individual's treatment.

5.131 The MHCS inform the CPS when the responsible clinician takes the view that the individual is now fit to plead. The CPS then decide whether to resume the prosecution, applying the Code for Crown Prosecutors, and the principles at para. 3 in 'Resuming a Prosecution'. This will include consideration of the availability and admissibility of the evidence, the views of those affected by the offence, the effect of prosecution on the individual's health, and the likely sentence on conviction.

5.132 The Secretary of State then makes his or her independent decision as to whether to remit the individual for trial under CP(I)A 1964 s. 5A(4), although where the

---

[108] *Sultan* [2014] EWCA Crim 2468 at [9].
[109] ibid.
[110] CPS, NOMS, and HMCTS, 'Resuming a Prosecution When a Patient Becomes Fit to Plead' (2013) (hereafter 'Resuming a Prosecution'), available at <https://www.justice.gov.uk/downloads/offenders/mentally-disordered-offenders/resuming-guidance-prosecution-fit-to-plead.pdf> accessed 14 March 2017.

CPS propose to resume proceedings, this will be 'the norm'.[111] However, it is worth noting that the Secretary of State can lift the restriction order, or conditionally discharge a restricted patient, without having to remit the individual for trial (MHA 1983 s. 42).

(d) First appearance on resumption

Where the Secretary of State decides to remit an individual for trial, the hospital **5.133** and restriction orders cease to have effect on arrival at court or prison (CP(I)A 1964 s. 5A(4)). There is no further guidance in CP(I)A 1964 as to what procedure should be followed once the individual is produced to court, nor indeed the status of the indictment following the finding under CP(I)A 1964 s. 4.

Where prosecution is to be resumed, at the first appearance the court will make **5.134** arrangements for the recovered individual (now a defendant again) to be tried on those counts on the indictment on which he or she was found to have 'done the act or made the omission'. The Court will have to consider whether the defendant should be remanded to hospital for reports or treatment (MHA 1983 s. 35 or 36), or remanded in custody or on bail. Custody time limits, however, do not apply.[112]

(e) Approach to be taken if the defendant becomes unfit to plead for a second time

Very occasionally, a defendant, against whom prosecution is resumed, becomes **5.135** unfit to plead for a second time, as a result, for example, of the strain of the new trial proceedings, or a relapse in the defendant's condition. If this occurs, there is no power for the Crown Court to reverse the decision to remit. The court is required to hold a second CP(I)A 1964 s. 4 hearing. If the defendant is formally found again to be 'under a disability', the court cannot rely on the earlier determination(s) at the trial of the facts, but must conduct the hearing afresh, under CP(I)A 1964 s. 4A.[113]

I. Summary Jurisdiction: The Adult Magistrates' Court

(a) Overview

The unfitness to plead provisions of CP(I)A 1964 have no application in magis- **5.136** trates' courts.[114] There is no statutory procedure designed specifically to identify

---

[111] 'Resuming a Prosecution', para. 10.
[112] ibid. para. 14. See also Prosecution of Offences (Custody Time Limits) Regulations 1987.
[113] *R (Julie Ferris) v DPP* [2004] EWHC 1221 (Admin).
[114] *R (P) v Barking Youth Court* [2002] EWHC 734 (Admin); [2002] 2 Cr App R 19, DC.

and respond to participation difficulties in either the adult magistrates' or the youth courts.

5.137 This section considers mechanisms available in respect of adults where participation issues are identified in the magistrates' courts. The approach taken to address similar issues for youths before the youth court is dealt with in Chapter 7, 'Youth Courts and Young Defendants', but there is considerable overlap with the approach taken for adults set out in this section.

5.138 In the adult magistrates' court, there are two statutory powers available to the court when dealing with defendants who have participation difficulties: MHA 1983 s. 37(3) and the Powers of the Criminal Courts (Sentencing) Act 2000 s. 11.

(b) MHA 1983 s. 37(3): power to make a hospital or guardianship order

5.139 MHA 1983 s. 37(3) enables the magistrates' court to make a hospital order (or a guardianship order where the individual is aged 16 years or over) without convicting him or her, as long as the court is satisfied that the defendant 'did the act or made the omission charged'.[115] Following *Barking Youth Court*, this section is applicable in cases where issues relating to unfitness to plead arise.

(i) Limitations on the availability of a s. 37(3) order

5.140 A s. 37(3) order can only be made if the court would otherwise have the power to make a hospital order or guardianship order in respect of the defendant (under MHA 1983 s. 37(1)). This limits the applicability of s. 37(3) orders in two significant ways:

1. The defendant must be charged with 'an offence punishable on summary conviction with imprisonment'. Section 37(3) orders cannot be made in respect of defendants charged with non-imprisonable offences.[116]
2. A s. 37(3) order can only be made in relation to a defendant who has a 'mental disorder' within the meaning of MHA 1983 s. 1. It has no application to defendants who have participation difficulties as a result of conditions not included within that definition—for example, communication impairments, or a learning disability which is not associated with 'abnormally aggressive or seriously irresponsible conduct' (MHA 1983 s. 1(2A)).

---

[115] An order under MHA 1983 s. 37(3) (hereafter 'a section 37(3) order').

[116] Where there is clear evidence of significant participation difficulties, non-imprisonable matters may well be resolvable by defence representatives making representations to the prosecution inviting them to review the case, in light of the defendant's difficulty. Depending on the stage of proceedings reached, the defence may invite the prosecution to discontinue proceedings or offer no evidence. However, plainly, this will not resolve all non-imprisonable matters, especially where the allegation is of repeat offending.

(ii) When should the court move to the procedure under s. 37(3)?

MHA 1983 s. 37(3) is designed to be flexible and to enable the magistrates' court **5.141**
to cater for a range of different issues raised by defendants who have a mental
disorder.[117] However, this presents a difficulty when applied to unfitness to plead,
since MHA 1983 s. 37(3) provides no indication as to the nature or severity of
the participation difficulties which will warrant the court departing from the full
trial process (with the consequent curtailment of the defendant's rights) and moving to a finding that the defendant 'did the act or made the omission'.

(iii) Section 37(3) orders: procedure to be followed

MHA 1983 provides no guidance as to the procedure to be adopted when the **5.142**
court is considering making a s. 37(3) order. There are a number of cases which
have considered how the statutory power might operate: *Lincoln (Kesteven)*
Justices, ex p. O'Connor;[118] *Barking Youth Court; R (Singh) v Stratford Magistrates'*
Court;[119] and *Blouet v Bath and Wansdyke Magistrates' Court*.[120]

It is plain from this line of authority that where the likelihood of a s. 37(3) order **5.143**
is indicated at the outset of the proceedings, the court can move directly to a
fact-finding process without beginning the trial. Indeed, the court can make
a s. 37(3) order without requiring the defendant to consent to summary trial
(*Lincoln (Kesteven) Justices*)[121] or even after the defendant has purported to elect
trial by jury.[122]

Where the possibility of such a disposal does not become apparent until after the **5.144**
trial has begun, the court can convert to the fact-finding process during the trial
itself. Conversion to the s. 37(3) fact-finding process can also occur where effective participation difficulties have been raised on an abuse of process application
and the court has embarked on the trial (following the procedure in *DPP v P*,[123]
discussed at paragraph 5.155 below), but where it has become apparent that the
defendant is unable to participate effectively in the full trial process (applying the
test in *SC v UK*).

The judgment in *Barking Youth Court* makes clear the sequence that should be **5.145**
followed, where the possibility of a s. 37(3) order has been identified. The court

---

[117] See, e.g., *R (Singh) v Stratford Magistrates' Court.*
[118] [1983] 1 WLR 335; [1983] 1 All ER 901.
[119] [2007] EWHC 1582 (Admin).
[120] [2009] EWHC 759 (Admin).
[121] *Lincoln (Kesteven) Justices* was decided in respect of the Mental Health Act 1959 s. 60(2),
a precursor of MHA 1983 s. 37(3), and before the CP(IUP)A 1991, but it is anticipated that the
position remains the same.
[122] *Ramsgate Justices, ex p. Kazmarek* (1985) 80 Cr App R 366. But not where the offence is
indictable only: *Chippenham Magistrates' Court, ex p. Thompson* (1996) 160 JP 207; (1996) 32
BMLR 69.
[123] *DPP v P* [2007] EWHC 946 (Admin); [2008] 1 WLR 1005.

should first determine whether the defendant 'did the act or made the omission' and then proceed to consider, on the basis of medical evidence, whether either of the orders under s. 37(3) should, in fact, be made.

5.146 The finding that the defendant has 'done the act or made the omission' can be arrived at by way of admissions or by the calling of evidence.[124] Given that the finding is worded in the same terms as CP(I)A 1964 s. 4A(2), it is suggested that what must be proved to establish that the defendant 'did the act or made the omission' will be governed by the principles applied at the trial of the facts (CP(I)A 1964 s. 4A), see paragraphs 5.73 et seq. However, there is no requirement for the defendant to be represented by an advocate appointed by the court for the hearing (in contrast to the position in the trial of facts under CP(I)A 1964 s. 4A(2)(b)).

(iv) Requirements to be satisfied before a s. 37(3) order can be made

5.147 Following the finding of fact, the conditions in MHA 1983 s. 37(2) have to be met before a hospital or guardianship order can be made. The court has to be satisfied, on the basis of evidence from two registered medical practitioners, at least one of whom is approved as having special experience in the diagnosis or treatment of mental disorder,[125] that:

1. the defendant is suffering from a mental disorder of a nature or degree which makes it appropriate for him or her to be detained in a hospital for treatment or to be received into guardianship;
2. in all the circumstances of the case, a hospital order (or guardianship order) is the 'most suitable method' of disposing of the case (MHA 1983 s. 37(2)); and
3. the court is satisfied that arrangements are in place for the defendant's admission to hospital, or that a person (or authority) is willing to act as guardian for the defendant (meeting the requirements of MHA 1983 s. 37(4) or 37(6) respectively).

(v) Limitations on disposals under MHA 1983 s. 37(3)

5.148 Where a hospital order is made under MHA 1983 s. 37(3), the magistrates do not have the power to impose a restriction order under s. 41, nor can the court commit the defendant to the Crown Court for a restriction order to be imposed.[126]

5.149 Where a guardianship order is made, the defendant is placed under the responsibility of a local authority, or a person approved by the local authority. The guardian can take decisions on behalf of the defendant, acting in that person's best

---

[124] *Lincoln (Kesteven) Justices; R (Singh) v Stratford Magistrates' Court* at [35].

[125] Under MHA 1983 s. 12, as required under MHA 1983 s. 54.

[126] In contrast to the court's power to commit a defendant to the Crown Court for a restriction order to be imposed where the court considers making a hospital order on conviction (MHA 1983 s. 43).

interests, including directing where the person should reside and requiring them to attend treatment, work, or education (MHA 1983 s. 8 and following).

Section 37(3) provides only for a hospital order or a guardianship order. There is **5.150** no provision for an alternative disposal, such as a supervision order or an absolute discharge to be imposed.

(vi) Where neither order is appropriate

The courts have experienced significant difficulty where, even though the defend- **5.151** ant has been found to have 'done the act' under s. 37(3), neither disposal is suitable or available. In those circumstances, it is suggested that the court would be obliged to make no order. The only alternative is to stay the proceedings as an abuse of process, if the court is satisfied that the defendant is unable to participate effectively in the proceedings (see paragraph 5.154).

(c) Powers of Criminal Courts (Sentencing) Act 2000 s. 11(1): adjournment for reports

Section 11(1) of the Powers of Criminal Courts (Sentencing) Act 2000 provides **5.152** an ancillary power for the court to adjourn for medical reports to be prepared in respect of a defendant being tried for an imprisonable summary offence, where the court has established that the defendant 'did the act or made the omission'.

(d) Alternatives to a s. 37(3) order where participation difficulties arise

Despite Wright J's observation in *Barking Youth Court* at [10] that the statutory **5.153** powers provide a 'complete statutory framework for a determination by the magistrates' court of all the issues that arise in cases of defendants who are or may be mentally ill or suffering from mental impairment', there are, as discussed, significant limitations to the statutory scheme. Where a s. 37(3) order is not applicable or suitable, there are few options for addressing the defendant's participation difficulties.

(i) Application for a stay of the proceedings as an abuse of process

The defendant may apply to the court to stay proceedings as an abuse of process **5.154** on the basis that he or she is unable to participate effectively in the trial. Although the case law in this regard has largely been developed in respect of young defendants,[127] it is applicable to adults in the magistrates' court as well.[128] The requirements for effective participation, set out in *SC v UK*, are discussed at paragraphs 5.25 et seq.

---

[127] See *SC v UK* at [29]; and *R (TP) v West London Youth Court* [2005] EWHC 2583 (Admin). See also Chapter 7, 'Youth Courts and Young Defendants'.

[128] *R (Wotton) v Central Devon Magistrates' Court* [2003] EWHC 146 (Admin).

5.155 The power to stay proceedings is very sparingly exercised in the magistrates' courts.[129] Following *DPP v P*[130] at [51]–[56], where effective participation difficulties are raised on an abuse of process application, the court should begin the trial process, and hear medical evidence as part of the evidence in the case rather than on free-standing application. The court should monitor carefully the defendant's capacity to engage with the proceedings and his or her understanding, and stop the trial if it determines that the defendant is not participating effectively. The court would then have the option of switching to a fact-finding hearing (under MHA 1983 s. 37(3)), as discussed, and only where this would 'serve no useful purpose at all' should proceedings be stayed as an abuse of process. Only in 'exceptional cases' should a stay be imposed before any evidence is heard on the trial.

(ii) Sending for trial: where the charge faced is indictable

5.156 If the defendant's participation difficulties are raised at an early stage, the court may conclude that it is more appropriate for the case to be tried on indictment, where the unfitness to plead provisions under CP(I)A 1964 can be engaged, and send the defendant's case to the Crown Court (Magistrates' Courts Act 1981 s. 21).[131]

5.157 Alternatively, if the magistrates accept jurisdiction, it is open to the defendant to elect Crown Court trial (Magistrates' Courts Act 1981 s. 20). However, this is a problematic course to take for two reasons. First, because the decision to choose Crown Court trial opens the defendant to the Crown Court's greater sentencing powers, and second, because a defendant whose fitness to plead is in doubt may not be able to understand the significance of the decision he or she is asked to make.[132]

5.158 It should be noted that where the court sends a defendant to the Crown Court for trial under the Crime and Disorder Act 1998 s. 51, it can only do so in the presence of the defendant him- or herself. There is no power to proceed in absence.[133]

J. The Law Commission's Proposals for Reform

5.159 Following a thorough and wide-ranging consultation process, the Law Commission have published a report[134] recommending substantial reforms to the

---

[129] *R v Horseferry Road Magistrates' Court, ex p. Bennett* [1994] 1 AC 42, HL; and *R (Ebrahim) v Feltham Magistrates' Court* [2001] EWHC Admin 130.

[130] *DPP v P* [2007] EWHC 946 (Admin); [2008] 1 WLR 1005.

[131] See also Crim PD II Preliminary proceedings 9A.2.

[132] There is also the potential for the court to proceed under MHA 1983 s. 37(3) even where the defendant has elected jury trial (*Ramsgate Justices, ex p. Kazmarek* (1985) 80 Cr App R 366).

[133] See *Lord Janner v Westminster Magistrates' Court* [2015] EWHC 2578 (Admin).

[134] Law Com No. 364.

legal test and procedures for addressing unfitness to plead. The Law Commission proposes modernizing the legal test so that it focuses on the defendant's capacity to participate effectively in the proceedings that he or she faces, including the defendant's ability to make the decisions required of him of her at trial. They also argue that a test of capacity to plead guilty should be introduced for those defendants found to lack the capacity to participate effectively at trial.

In addition, the Law Commission's recommendations call for a fuller examin- **5.160** ation of the allegation following a finding that a defendant lacks capacity for trial, including consideration by the jury of the fault elements of the offence. The Law Commission also recommend changes to the supervision order, and to the process for resuming prosecution should the individual recover the capacity for trial following disposal.

Importantly, the Law Commission's report also engages with the lack of effective **5.161** procedures for addressing participation difficulties in magistrates' courts, particularly the youth court. The Law Commission recommends that procedures for addressing lack of capacity for trial, comparable to those adopted in the Crown Court, should be introduced for all criminal matters in the summary jurisdiction, including in the youth court where reform is most urgently required. At the time of writing, the government's full response to the Law Commission's report is awaited.

Further Reading

Crown Prosecution Service, National Offender Management Service, and Her Majesty's Courts and Tribunals Service, 'Resuming a Prosecution When a Patient Becomes Fit to Plead' (2013), available at <https://www.justice.gov.uk/downloads/offenders/mentally-disordered-offenders/resuming-guidance-prosecution-fit-to-plead.pdf> accessed 14 March 2017.

Gledhill, K., *Defending Mentally Disordered Persons* (Legal Action Group, 2012).

Kerrigan, K. and Wortley, K., 'Unfitness to Plead: Expanding the Scope of "Objective Evidence" on the "Trial of the Facts"' (2015) *Journal of Criminal Law* 79(3), 160.

Law Commission, 'Report: Unfitness to Plead', Law Com No. 364 (HMSO, 2016), available at <http://www.lawcom.gov.uk/wp-content/uploads/2016/01/apa.pdf> accessed 14 March 2017.

Loughnan, A., *Manifest Madness: Mental Incapacity in Criminal Law* (Oxford University Press, 2012).

6

VULNERABILITY AND DEFENCES

Penny Cooper and Felicity Gerry

A. Introduction

6.01 In criminal proceedings, an accused person's 'mental vulnerability'[1] may be relevant to a wide range of matters, including:

1. suspect interview procedures (see Chapter 4);
2. discretion to prosecute;
3. unfitness to plead and stand trial (see Chapter 5);
4. adjustments to the procedures at court (see Chapters 7, 9, 10, 11, 12, 13, and 15);
5. admissibility and/or reliability of confession evidence;
6. admissibility and/or reliability of interview evidence;
7. adverse inferences for no comment interviews and/or failure to give oral evidence at trial;
8. defences of insanity or automatism;
9. partial defences of diminished responsibility and loss of control (in the case of homicide);
10. evaluation of the defendant's presentation at trial;
11. determining if the defendant had the required *mens rea* for the offence charged;
12. sentencing/disposal (see further Chapter 15).

6.02 An accused person's mental vulnerability will therefore be relevant to case preparation, the trial process, criminal responsibility, and defences. As indicated above, a number of these matters are dealt with elsewhere in this book. This chapter is confined to situations where the accused person is fit to plead[2] and can therefore put forward a challenge to the prosecution case or raise a specific defence. In so far as defences are concerned, it is well established that an accused person's mental vulnerability might provide evidence relevant to a partial defence in law to murder,[3] but there are other areas where mental vulnerability might be relevant to the court's determination of guilt—for example, self-defence,[4] where an issue is raised whether there have been mistakes of fact regarding the use of reasonable force as a result of the accused's mental vulnerability; or the Modern Slavery Act 2015, which (in s. 45) provides a defence for human trafficking victims who commit certain crimes and who may well be vulnerable.

---

[1] The term 'mental vulnerability' is used as a wide, umbrella term to cover mental disabilities and disorders.

[2] It is, of course, vital that decisions around unfitness to plead are not taken without assessing whether the accused person could in fact participate with communication assistance. These issues are dealt with elsewhere in this volume.

[3] Either 'diminished responsibility' or 'loss of control'.

[4] For a discussion, see C. Elliott, 'Interpreting the Contours of Self-Defence within the Boundaries of the Rule of Law, the Common Law and Human Rights' (2015) *Journal of Criminal Law*, 79(5), 330–43.

Much depends on the facts, in particular the relationship, if any, between the **6.03** mental vulnerability that the accused person had at the time of the alleged offence and the mental element of the offence of which they are accused. There is no single definition of the mental element of an offence[5] and no two cases or defendants with a mental vulnerability are the same.

The review here is of certain selected cases in common areas of criminal practice **6.04** where the defendant is mentally vulnerable, but nevertheless fit to stand trial. The appellate decisions referred to are a non-exhaustive selection of instances when expert evidence of the defendant's mental state has been relevant to procedural fairness and/or to the determination of guilt for the offence(s) for which they stood trial. It is not possible within the scope of this chapter to cover all mental vulnerabilities and all related defences; however, it is suggested that the examples covered, most of which are less than ten years old, reflect a growing recognition that a defendant's mental vulnerability is not only relevant to procedural fairness, but also to the defendant's culpability.

Thus, this chapter will cover decisions to prosecute, the admissibility and reliabil- **6.05** ity of interviews and confessions, adverse inferences, defences, and the evaluation of the defendant's presentation at trial. The use of expert evidence is addressed first since the opinion of medical expert(s) is likely to be of critical importance to the case. In particular, the defence team will most likely rely on the expert evidence to make crucial and usually irrevocable decisions as to how to put the defence case:

> Criminal litigation is a process in which the defendant is required to make a series of irrevocable (or usually irrevocable) decisions: for example, whether to plead guilty, whether to give evidence and so forth. If things go badly for the defendant, he cannot simply go back to square one and try a different tack. Criminal litigation is not a tactical exercise. It is a serious process conducted to promote the overriding objective set out in rule 1.1 of the Criminal Procedure Rules. This includes, first and foremost, acquitting the innocent and convicting the guilty.[6]

B.   Engaging an Expert Witness to Report on the Defendant

(a) Who is an expert?

Expert witnesses are in a special category of witness; the court may permit the **6.06** expert witness to give opinion evidence to assist the court in matters that are outside the court's own expertise. Expertise may arise from qualifications or experience; it is not simply a matter of whether the proposed expert has a particular title

---

[5] It may be 'intention', 'recklessness', or some other mental state that must be proved.
[6] *R v Smith* [2013] EWCA Crim 2388 at [91].

or set of letters after their name. For instance, police officers have been accepted as expert witnesses in several different contexts, such as investigation and reconstruction of road traffic accidents[7] and drug-dealing practices.[8]

6.07 In relation to the assessment of vulnerable defendants, it is likely that the relevant expertise will be found in a psychiatrist and/or a psychologist. Generally speaking, a psychiatrist is qualified in the study and treatment of diseases of the mind and therefore would be instructed where the defendant has or is thought to have an identifiable mental illness or disorder. Again, generally speaking, a psychologist has expertise in human personality and behaviour and is not usually medically qualified. Sometimes those with mental vulnerabilities have complex issues which require both forms of expert assessment and they may also require a communication assessment by an intermediary.

6.08 Although the role of the intermediary is to facilitate communication, not to act as an expert witness, intermediary assessments are used to inform the parties and the judge about the defendant's communication needs. Although it should not be seen as a precedent, in *R v Beards & Beards*,[9] the defendant's counsel was permitted to adduce, as expert evidence, parts of an earlier assessment conducted by an intermediary (not the intermediary at the trial) which described the accused person's mental vulnerabilities. The intermediary had assessed the defendant 'as having a mild learning difficulty (classified as a person with an IQ of between 50 and 70) and in certain educational respects a level of understanding similar to that of an infant or child of about 9 years old'.[10] The trial judge admitted the intermediary's assessment as expert evidence on the basis that the intermediary's CV demonstrated her 'qualifications and extensive experience in all relevant aspects of communication with individuals with special needs' and was 'a good match' for the defendant's disabilities.[11]

6.09 It is important to note that the two roles of intermediary and expert witness are quite distinct, with different purposes and responsibilities. It is submitted that the intermediary report in *Beards* could not have been admitted as expert evidence had the author still been acting as an intermediary in the case; the two roles are mutually exclusive (see further Chapter 11, 'Intermediaries'). However, sometimes the contents of an intermediary's report can be a useful indicator of the need for expert evidence or can contain specifics which may be capable of being agreed. *Beards* (which is a Crown Court ruling of no binding authority) illustrates a practice that should not be readily followed in which the choice of expert may be determined by the resources that are available. The intermediary

---

[7] *R v Hodges* [2003] EWCA Crim 290.
[8] *Myers v The Queen (Bermuda)* [2015] UKPC 40 at [57]–[58].
[9] *R v Beards & Beards*, unreported ruling, Leicester Crown Court, 23 May 2016 at [20].
[10] ibid. at [2].
[11] ibid. at [22].

system is not a substitute for a full assessment by an appropriate clinical expert. The need for expert evidence should be identified as early as possible prior to trial.

(b) What is the purpose of expert evidence?

When a defendant has or might have a mental vulnerability, up-to-date expert **6.10** evidence is required to identify the vulnerability if any, whether it affected the defendant at the time of the alleged offence, and/or whether it affects the defendant now. A medical diagnosis of a defendant's mental vulnerability may be relevant to the decisions whether or not to prosecute, the relevant mental element for the offence, evidential matters such as the admissibility of interviews, procedural matters such as the adjustment required at trial, and any available defence. These are discussed in detail below.

(c) What is the test of admissibility?

The Criminal Practice Directions (Crim PD) summarize the position with regard **6.11** to admissibility:

> 19A.1 Expert opinion evidence is admissible in criminal proceedings at common law if, in summary, (i) it is relevant to a matter in issue in the proceedings; (ii) it is needed to provide the court with information likely to be outside the court's own knowledge and experience; and (iii) the witness is competent to give that opinion.[12]

The Court of Appeal said in *R v Dlugosz*:

> It is essential to recall the principle which is applicable, namely in determining the issue of admissibility, the court must be satisfied that there is a sufficiently reliable scientific basis for the evidence to be admitted. If there is then the court leaves the opposing views to be tested before the jury.[13]

The Crim PD also remind practitioners that such expert opinion must be sufficiently reliable in order to be admissible and sets out eight factors which the court may take into account when considering reliability:

  (a) the extent and quality of the data on which the expert's opinion is based, and the validity of the methods by which they were obtained;

  (b) if the expert's opinion relies on an inference from any findings, whether the opinion properly explains how safe or unsafe the inference is (whether by reference to statistical significance or in other appropriate terms);

  (c) if the expert's opinion relies on the results of the use of any method (for instance, a test, measurement or survey), whether the opinion takes proper account of matters, such as the degree of precision or margin of uncertainty, affecting the accuracy or reliability of those results;

---

[12] Crim PD 19 A.1.
[13] *R v Dlugosz* [2013] EWCA Crim 2 at [11].

(d) the extent to which any material upon which the expert's opinion is based has been reviewed by others with relevant expertise (for instance, in peer-reviewed publications), and the views of those others on that material;

(e) the extent to which the expert's opinion is based on material falling outside the expert's own field of expertise;

(f) the completeness of the information which was available to the expert, and whether the expert took account of all relevant information in arriving at the opinion (including information as to the context of any facts to which the opinion relates);

(g) if there is a range of expert opinion on the matter in question, where in the range the expert's own opinion lies and whether the expert's preference has been properly explained; and

(h) whether the expert's methods followed established practice in the field and, if they did not, whether the reason for the divergence has been properly explained.[14]

As is clear from Crim PD 19A.1, for expert opinion evidence to be admissible at common law it must be both relevant and necessary, and the witness must be competent to give that opinion.

6.12 As Lord Bingham succinctly stated:

> Any evidence, to be admissible, must be relevant. Contested trials last long enough as it is without spending time on evidence which is irrelevant and cannot affect the outcome. Relevance must, and can only, be judged by reference to the issue which the court (whether judge or jury) is called upon to decide. As Lord Simon of Glaisdale observed in *Director of Public Prosecutions v Kilbourne* [1973] AC 729, 756, 'Evidence is relevant if it is logically probative or disprobative of some matter which requires proof ... relevant (i.e. logically probative or disprobative) evidence is evidence which makes the matter which requires proof more or less probable'.[15]

Expert evidence will be necessary where the nature and impact of the defendant's vulnerability is outside the experience and knowledge of the fact finder, whether that is a jury or a magistrate. In 1974, in *R v Turner*,[16] Lawton LJ said:

> An expert's opinion is admissible to furnish the court with scientific information which is likely to be outside the experience and knowledge of a judge or jury. If on the proven facts a judge or jury can form their own conclusions without help, then the opinion of an expert is unnecessary.[17]

Expert evidence is only admissible if it is needed by the fact finders; if they can form an opinion on the facts in issue without the need for expert evidence, then such evidence will not be admissible.[18] Thus, the party seeking to adduce the evidence will need to satisfy the court that it is on subject matter outside the

---

[14] Crim PD 19 A.5.
[15] *O'Brien v Chief Constable of South Wales Police* [2005] UKHL 26 at [3].
[16] [1975] QB 834.
[17] ibid. at p. 841.
[18] *R v Turner* [1975] QB 834; (1974) 60 Cr App R 80.

assumed competence of a jury. In *Masih*, for example, the Court of Appeal held that if a person's IQ is over 70 (a borderline learning disability), then the experiences of such a person are likely to fall within the experience of a jury.[19]

The relationship between the admissibility of expert evidence and the defendant's IQ **6.13** has resulted in some contrasting cases. In *R v Tracy Jackson-Mason*,[20] the accused person was convicted unanimously of eight counts of fraud by false representation and two counts of possession or control of articles for use in fraud. She had a learning disability and as a child had attended special schools. The offences came about after she had been approached by a gang 'operating a sophisticated fraud syndicate' whereby they persuaded vulnerable people to cash cheques at the post office and obtain duplicate birth certificates from the Registry Office for use in the cheque cashing fraud.

The defence case was that the appellant was out shopping when she was approached by a group of men who asked if she would cash a giro for their cousin who was unwell. She explained that she had never cashed a giro herself before as her mother dealt with all her money as her appointee. Nevertheless, she agreed to help the men. They handed her some papers and showed her where to sign her name. The men waited for her outside the post office while she went in and cashed the cheque. She then got into a car with the men who drove her to a number of other post offices where she cashed more giros for them. In one post office, she was told the cheque was not a giro and it was taken off her. She says she gave all the money to the men and received nothing in return. Her defence was therefore that she was not acting dishonestly; she thought she was helping the men on behalf of their 'cousin'.[21]

The defence had sought to introduce evidence of the accused person's learning dis- **6.14** ability at trial:

> [The accused person's] overall IQ of 77 fell within the borderline learning disability range which is 70–80, but her verbal comprehension was 68, which was within the mild learning disability range. He found that her intellectual function was low and thus she was vulnerable to exploitation. The results of the 'Gudjonnson' test found her suggestibility level was high, making it likely that if requested to act in a certain way by people who may have power over her, she would acquiesce. However her intellectual disability was not so profound that she would have no understanding of the notion of dishonesty.[22]

At trial, the judge ruled that the expert evidence was inadmissible. The Court of Appeal referred to *R v Masih*,[23] *R v Henry*,[24] and *R v Turner*,[25] and the

---

[19] See *R v Masih* [1986] Crim LR 395; and *R v Henry* [2005] EWCA Crim 1681.
[20] [2014] EWCA Crim 1993.
[21] ibid. at [7].
[22] ibid. at [10]. Note that the Gudjonsson test tries to measure how susceptible a person is to coercive interrogation using a standardized suggestibility scale.
[23] [1986] Crim LR 395.
[24] [2005] EWCA Crim 1681.
[25] (1974) 60 Cr App R 80.

principle that it is expected that 'people with an IQ of 69 or over would be within the experience of the jury', hence the evidence would not be necessary.[26] In respect of the evidence of suggestibility and the accused person's 'score on the Gudjonsson test, namely that one would expect one in 25 of the general population to be more suggestible than the appellant', the trial judge concluded that the jury would have come across people in their lives with similar characteristics so that expert evidence was not required. The appeal was dismissed as the conviction was not found to be unsafe. *R v Jackson-Mason* can be contrasted with *R v Antar*,[27] where evidence of the accused person's suggestibility had been admitted. In that case, the defence put forward was one of duress and Antar's IQ was measured at 51. When a court is determining whether the jury should hear expert evidence on the accused's vulnerability, much depends on the specific vulnerability and the issues specific to the case in hand.

6.15 IQ numbers should not be considered as decisive, not merely because research has identified that the margin of error in the assessment of low IQ is much greater than the five points suggested in test manuals.[28] A defendant might well have an IQ in the range of normal, but nevertheless have a mental vulnerability.[29] *Pora* was one such example:

> Although [the appellant] was found to have an IQ of 83 (which is within normal limits), [an expert witness] pointed out that this was not inconsistent with there being significant abnormalities in some areas.[30]

(d) What are the duties of the expert?

6.16 Lord Hughes in the Judicial Committee of the Privy Council provided a reminder of the duties of the expert witness which were 'helpfully set out by Cresswell J in the commercial case of *The Ikarian Reefer* [1993] 2 Lloyds Rep 68 at 81 but apply equally in the criminal context: *R v Harris* [2005] EWCA Crim 1980'.

6.17 The duties are as follows:

> 1. Expert evidence presented to the court should be and seen to be the independent product of the expert uninfluenced as to form or content by the exigencies of litigation.

---

[26] *R v Tracy Jackson-Mason* [2014] EWCA Crim 1993 at [15].

[27] [2004] EWCA Crim 2708.

[28] S. Whitaker, 'Error in the Estimation of Intellectual Ability in the Low Range Using the WISC-IV and WAIS-III' (2010) *Personality and Individual Differences*, 48, 517–21.

[29] A common-sense approach was exemplified by the trial judge, Green J, in *R v Beards & Beards*: 'It may be dangerous to make quick and easy assumptions based upon IQ as laying down hard and fast evidential thresholds. The modern literature suggests that IQ scores have to be construed and understood in context' (at [35]).

[30] *Pora v The Queen* [2015] UKPC 9 at [45].

2. An expert witness should provide independent assistance to the court by way of objective unbiased opinion in relation to matters within his expertise. An expert witness in the High Court should never assume the role of advocate.

3. An expert witness should state the facts or assumptions on which his opinion is based. He should not omit to consider material facts which detract from his concluded opinions.

4. An expert should make it clear when a particular question or issue falls outside his expertise.

5. If an expert's opinion is not properly researched because he considers that insufficient data is available then this must be stated with an indication that the opinion is no more than a provisional one.[31]

6. If after exchange of reports, an expert witness changes his view on material matters, such change of view should be communicated to the other side without delay and when appropriate to the court.[32]

Additionally, the expert's duties are set out at Crim PR 19.2:   **6.18**

(1) An expert must help the court to achieve the overriding objective—
   (a) by giving opinion which is—
      (i) objective and unbiased, and
      (ii) within the expert's area or areas of expertise; and
   (b) by actively assisting the court in fulfilling its duty of case management under rule 3.2, in particular by—
      (i) complying with directions made by the court, and
      (ii) at once informing the court of any significant failure (by the expert or another) to take any step required by such a direction.
(2) This duty overrides any obligation to the person from whom the expert receives instructions or by whom the expert is paid.
(3) This duty includes obligations—
   (a) to define the expert's area or areas of expertise—
      (i) in the expert's report, and
      (ii) when giving evidence in person;
   (b) when giving evidence in person, to draw the court's attention to any question to which the answer would be outside the expert's area or areas of expertise; and
   (c) to inform all parties and the court if the expert's opinion changes from that contained in a report served as evidence or given in a statement.

(e) What are the duties of the parties?

Lawyers are not doctors and cannot be expected to diagnose a mental vulnerability; however, they should identify when a vulnerable individual needs to be medically assessed by an expert. Many mental vulnerabilities are complex. In some cases, accused persons have multiple difficulties.[33]   **6.19**

---

[31] Creswell J in *National Justice Compania Naviera SA v Prudential Assurance Co Ltd ('The Ikarian Reefer')* [1993] 2 Lloyd's Rep 68 at [81] sets out numbers 1 to 5 herein.

[32] *Myers v The Queen (Bermuda)* at [59].

[33] e.g. *R v Cox* [2012] EWCA Crim 549.

6.20 The need for expert evidence can be identified by many means, including evaluation of the defendant's presentation in conference with his or her lawyers, responses and behaviour in police interviews, witness evidence as to events, or the accused's personal history.[34] In such circumstances, there are significant disclosure issues which will need to be completed (see further Chapter 8, 'Disclosure'). Experts instructed will need sufficient information to make an informed opinion.

6.21 If the prosecution realizes that the accused person has a mental vulnerability that they believe is relevant they should make available material, in advance of the first hearing, giving an 'indication of any medical or other expert evidence' they are likely to adduce in relation to the accused person.[35] In practice, the defence will usually be the first to consider adducing expert evidence of the accused person's mental vulnerability, but the duties fall to both parties, in the context of the overriding objective of dealing with cases justly,[36] to identify a participant's mental vulnerability at the earliest opportunity.

> The days of ambushing and taking last-minute technical points are gone. They are not consistent with the overriding objective of deciding cases justly, acquitting the innocent and convicting the guilty.[37]

The Privy Council in *Robinson v The State* underlined the importance of an expert forensic psychiatric assessment of a defendant charged with murder:

> It is an important contribution to this process that every person charged with murder is routinely assessed by such a psychiatrist instructed by the prosecution, and early after arrest, either in prison or, in the relatively few cases in which s/he is on bail, as a condition of bail. So long as this careful consideration is given to each case, it is plainly of public benefit for pleas of guilty of manslaughter to be accepted. This avoids trials on non-issues which will be both expensive to the public and distressing to many of those involved, whether as witnesses, or relatives of the deceased, or as defendants and their families.[38]

Whether the defence decide to adduce such expert evidence is a different matter.

6.22 A decision by a defence team not to adduce evidence of the accused person's mental vulnerability was the subject of appeal in *R v Smith*,[39] where the accused person appealed his conviction for murder of a 10-year-old girl at a Christmas party.

---

[34] See further The Advocate's Gateway, 'Toolkit 10: Identifying Vulnerability in Witnesses and Parties and Making Adjustments' (The Advocacy Training CouncilThe Inns of Court College of Advocacy, 2017).

[35] Crim PD 3A.12(f).

[36] Crim PR 1.2.

[37] *R (DPP) v Chorley Justices* [2006] EWHC 1795 at [26].

[38] [2015] UKPC 34 at [29]. See also: *R v Golds* [2016] UKSC 61; [2016] 1 WLR 5231 at [48]; and *R v Blackman* [2017] EWCA Crim 190 at [79], where the Lord Chief Justice said: 'It would clearly have been much better if there had been an assessment by the prosecution prior to the court martial, but that did not happen.'

[39] *R v Smith* [2013] EWCA Crim 2388.

He had been diagnosed with an autism spectrum condition, as a result of which he had had behavioural problems.

> Neither party called expert evidence concerning the accused person's Asperger's Syndrome, although there were a number of references to it during the trial. Defence counsel relied upon the accused person's vulnerability in order to explain his somewhat unusual manner in the witness box and his flat, unemotional way of talking.[40]

On appeal, it was argued that defence counsel at trial 'omitted to deploy vital **6.23** evidence concerning the applicant's Asperger's Syndrome. This would have explained the way he behaved generally, in particular during his interviews with the police and at trial.'[41] The Court of Appeal rejected this. The expert evidence had also referred to the accused person's 'history of aggression' and 'polarized view towards women'. Providing such information to the jury would have been 'highly damaging' to the accused person's case,[42] thus it was held that it was not unreasonable of his legal representatives at trial to choose not to adduce it. For those people with mental vulnerabilities and challenging behaviours, these are difficult and complex decisions which need to be carefully handled. There is a professional and ethical responsibility on advocates properly to address such issues. Where expert evidence is not adduced for whatever reason, it may be that certain basic facts can be placed before the jury by agreement, such as IQ and level of education and the reasons why the court has adapted procedures.[43]

(f)   What is the procedure for introducing expert evidence?

The Criminal Procedure Rules (Crim PR) set out the applicable procedure when a **6.24** party wishes to introduce expert evidence. Unless the expert's findings are agreed as fact,[44] then the party seeking to rely on the expert evidence must file and serve a report that complies with Crim PR 19.4. If one side supplies an expert's report in relation to the accused person's vulnerability, another party may well seek their own expert opinion on the accused person's vulnerability.

The plea and trial preparation hearing (PTPH) form which is completed online **6.25** at the PTPH provides for the judge to set out a timetable for any fitness to plead hearing (including the exchange of reports). Where psychiatric or medical evidence is to be relied upon outside issues of fitness to plead, the ordinary timescales

---

[40] *R (DPP) v Chorley Justices* at [22].
[41] ibid. at [29, i].
[42] ibid. at [79].
[43] This was done in *R v Cox* [2012] EWCA Crim 549, where there was no challenge to the multiple assessments of the accused person's level of mental vulnerabilities. He was otherwise fit to be tried for rape and put forward a positive defence.
[44] Crim PR 19.3.

are for the defence to serve expert evidence relied upon at stage 2 (twenty-eight days after service of the case papers), and for the prosecution to serve any expert medical or psychiatric evidence at stage 3 (either fourteen or twenty-eight days after stage 2). Although in some very obvious cases (e.g. where the defendant is already receiving treatment and has a named consultant), it will be possible to indicate at the PTPH the nature of the evidence and the issue it is likely to go to; as the PTPH is the first effective hearing, only a few weeks after charge, it would be an exceptional case where the defence would have funding in place already to secure any reports.

(g) What to include in instructions to an expert witness?

6.26 Prior to instructing an expert witness, it is important that a party is satisfied that they have found a suitable expert witness. This does not simply mean an expert with the right qualifications and experience; these ought to be obvious from the expert's curriculum vitae. A party should also be satisfied that the expert witness has appropriate training and professional indemnity insurance for the role of expert witness.[45]

6.27 Although Crim PR 19.4 requires an expert in their report for court to give detail of the expert's 'qualifications, relevant experience and accreditation', it should be noted that there is no requirement for an expert witness to be accredited for the role of expert witness. In fact, there is no standard scheme of training, regulation, or accreditation for expert witnesses; some will be members of expert witness representative and/or regulatory bodies, but others will not.

6.28 Those instructing expert witnesses should include, among other things, in the expert's letter of instruction:[46]

- the issues that the expert is being asked to address;
- the importance of complying with the timetable of the court and being available for court to give testimony;
- a copy of Crim PR Part 19;
- a reminder that the expert's overriding duty is to the court;
- the evidence for the expert to consider (indexed); and
- the relevant legal criteria for the expert to apply.

6.29 It should not be assumed that the expert witness will be familiar with the legal framework to which the evidence relates. In *R v GAC*, the proposed defence was

---

[45] Not least since expert witness immunity from being sued has been abolished: *Jones v Kaney* [2011] UKSC 13.

[46] A 'Letter of Instruction Template' is available with CPS guidance 'Expert Evidence' at p. 41, available via the CPS website at <http://www.cps.gov.uk/legal/assets/uploads/files/expert_evidence_first_edition_2014.pdf> accessed 16 March 2017.

duress, which has four elements that must be present (see paragraph 6.74 below). The Court of Appeal noted that an expert witness should 'test the assertions made [according to the four elements] against the available evidence' before offering an opinion on the defence of duress.[47] If the wrong test is applied and erroneous evidence is placed before the jury, this might result in the quashing of a conviction. For example, in *R v A(G)*,[48] the appeal was allowed because the wrong standard of proof had been applied to the test of the complainant's mental capacity and the erroneous expert evidence on that matter would have prejudiced the jury's consideration of the facts.

In *R v H,* where there were deficiencies in expert reports on the complainant's **6.30** mental vulnerability, the Court of Appeal said:

> ... a new and more rigorous approach on the part of advocates and the courts to the handling of expert evidence must be adopted. That should avoid misunderstandings about what is (and what is not) appropriately included in an expert's report and so either avoid, or at least render far more straightforward, submissions on admissibility such as those made in this case.[49]

C. Relevance of Expert Evidence to the Trial Process

(a) Discretion to prosecute

Decisions to prosecute must pass the CPS's own test. The Full Code Test[50] has **6.31** two stages: (i) the evidential stage, followed by (ii) the public interest stage.

At the 'evidential stage', prosecutors:

> ... must be satisfied that there is sufficient evidence to provide a realistic prospect of conviction against each suspect on each charge. They must consider what the defence case may be, and how it is likely to affect the prospects of conviction. A case which does not pass the evidential stage must not proceed, no matter how serious or sensitive it may be.[51]

Key questions that the prosecutor must ask themselves are whether the evidence **6.32** is to be used in court, whether it is reliable, and whether it is credible. If, for instance, there is expert evidence that the suspect was mentally disordered, but was interviewed without an appropriate adult, the admissibility and reliability of the interview is brought into question and this should factor in the prosecutor's evaluation of the Crown's evidence.

---

[47] [2013] EWCA Crim 1472 at [60].
[48] [2014] EWCA Crim 299; [2014] 1 WLR 2469; [2014] 2 Cr App R 5.
[49] *R v H* [2014] EWCA Crim 1555 at [44].
[50] 'Code for Crown Prosecutors: The Full Code Test', available at <https://www.cps.gov.uk/publications/code_for_crown_prosecutors/codetest.html> accessed 16 March 2017.
[51] ibid. para. 4.4.

6.33 If the 'evidential stage' of the test is passed, the prosecutor must go on to consider the 'public interest stage':

> It has never been the rule that a prosecution will automatically take place once the evidential stage is met. A prosecution will usually take place unless the prosecutor is satisfied that there are public interest factors tending against prosecution which outweigh those tending in favour. In some cases the prosecutor may be satisfied that the public interest can be properly served by offering the offender the opportunity to have the matter dealt with by an out-of-court disposal rather than bringing a prosecution.[52]

6.34 At the public interest stage, prosecutors should consider a non-exhaustive list of questions:[53]

(a) How serious is the offence committed?
(b) What is the level of culpability of the suspect?
(c) What are the circumstances of and the harm caused to the victim?
(d) Was the suspect under the age of 18 at the time of the offence?
(e) What is the impact on the community?
(f) Is prosecution a proportionate response?
(g) Do sources of information require protecting?

Both (b) and (d) in particular require prosecutors to consider the suspect's culpability. This necessarily includes the mental vulnerability of the defendant. In the test, part (b) specifically requires the prosecutor to consider 'the suspect's age or maturity' and:

> … whether the suspect is, or was at the time of the offence, suffering from any significant mental or physical ill health as in some circumstances this may mean that it is less likely that a prosecution is required. However, prosecutors will also need to consider how serious the offence was, whether it is likely to be repeated and the need to safeguard the public or those providing care to such persons.[54]

Part (d) specifically requires the age of the suspect to be considered because:

> … the criminal justice system treats children and young people differently from adults and significant weight must be attached to the age of the suspect if they are a child or young person under 18 … As a starting point, the younger the suspect, the less likely it is that a prosecution is required.[55]

6.35 In *R v A(G)*,[56] the appellant was 22 years of age; he and the complainant were 20 when the incident took place. They had been friends for some time and were

---

[52] ibid. para. 4.8.
[53] ibid. para. 4.12.
[54] ibid. para. 4.12(b).
[55] ibid. para. 4.12(d).
[56] [2014] WLR(D) 55; [2014] 1 WLR 2469; [2014] EWCA Crim 299; [2014] 2 Cr App R 5; [2014] WLR 2469.

both students at a special needs school. They both had learning disabilities and the appellant had an IQ of 51.

They had been watching 'Matilda' on TV together in a bedroom at the complainant's house when: **6.36**

> ... a sexual encounter occurred which at least involved the appellant removing the complainant's trousers and underwear by pushing them down her legs and removing his own, lying on top of her rubbing his penis against her vagina. He ejaculated onto the complainant's underwear and that appeared to be the end of the matter. Subsequently, the complainant was to say that she did not like it and had told him to stop ... The following day, the complainant mentioned to the brother's girlfriend that she had had sex with the appellant the previous day. When asked if she had said 'yes' the complainant said that she did not want to do it and had said 'no'. The complainant's mother was informed and the police were contacted ... the complainant's version of events was obtained and recorded in an ABE (achieving best evidence) interview.[57]

Giving judgment, Lady Justice Macur commented as an 'aside': **6.37**

> We have taxed [prosecuting counsel] to explain the 'public interest' said to be served in prosecuting this appellant in the obvious and particular circumstances of the case. The facts are previously recorded, including the relative disability of the appellant comparative to that of the complainant. The decision to charge him first with rape and then with sexual assault is astonishing. [Prosecuting counsel] frankly acknowledges this. This appellant was a young man of good character, which fact should in our opinion have weighed heavily in the context of the facts as a whole in informing the appropriate course to be followed.[58]

Another example of how the discretion to prosecute might be applied when the **6.38** defendant is vulnerable is *R v A*.[59] In this case, the alleged victim of a sexual assault made a complaint to the police that her husband had raped her:

> In due course she withdrew that complaint. She then proceeded to assert and reassert that her complaint had been false. Proceedings against him were stopped. She was prosecuted for perverting the course of justice by making a false complaint of rape. In due course, having seen counsel and solicitor, she reasserted the truth of the original complaint.[60]

The appellant was then charged with and convicted of making false retractions. It is noted in the judgment that:

> If [the current guidance] had been in force at the date of the appellant's conviction, on the basis of the evidence that she had been raped and subjected to other domestic violence over a long period and that this had had a damaging effect on

---

[57] ibid. at [7]–[10].
[58] At [15].
[59] [2012] EWCA Crim 434.
[60] ibid. at [2].

her health, she would ... the Crown accepted, in all likelihood, not have been prosecuted.[61]

6.39 When the decision to prosecute is being considered, it is of course necessary that the prosecutor has the relevant information, including any information about the defendant's vulnerability, which will affect their assessment of their culpability and which is relevant to public interest stage. The defence team should consider supplying the prosecutor with such evidence as they may have (such as school or medical reports about the defendant's vulnerability) which would help inform the prosecutor's decision.

> Although prosecutors primarily consider the evidence and information supplied by the police and other investigators, the suspect or those acting on his or her behalf may also submit evidence or information to the prosecutor via the police or other investigators, prior to charge, to help inform the prosecutor's decision.[62]

(b) Assistance to the court and parties in dealing with the defendant

6.40 The adaptation of the court processes and the directions given to a jury in any particular case will very much depend on the issues, but they are best achieved through cooperation and where defence counsel has prepared the ground so that the prosecution and the court have sufficient evidence not to dispute the accused person's condition(s). In *R v Cox*, all parties agreed on the approach to the evidence, which included using simple language, having regular breaks, and giving counsel the opportunity to speak to his client. This occurred throughout the prosecution case so that counsel for the defendant could ensure that the defendant understood the evidence and implications of the evidence given by the prosecution witnesses. The defendant had given answers in police interview and the tape was played to the jury so that they could hear what he said at the time. All of this was done by trained advocates who specialized in cases involving vulnerable people and in the light of many expert and intermediary reports. The fact that no intermediary was present at trial was not sufficient to persuade the Court of Appeal that the trial was unfair. The judge was sufficiently interventionist to make sure the advocates kept to the agreed arrangements and did not need to intervene very often. This was a case where counsel on both sides provided maximum assistance to the court and the judge was very experienced in such cases. The same judge took the view in another similar case that it was not sufficient simply to give a 'special arrangements' direction without the jury hearing some

---

[61] ibid. at [7].
[62] Code for Crown Prosecutors The Decision Whether To Prosecute, para. 3.3, available at <https://www.cps.gov.uk/publications/code_for_crown_prosecutors/decision.html> accessed 4 Sept 2016.

evidence of the accused person's mental vulnerabilities. He gave the following direction after consultation with both counsel:[63]

> The evidence of the accused person's [intellectual limitations, vulnerability (or whatever condition)] gives rise to matters of law:
>
> (1) The procedure of the court has been adjusted to make allowance for [factors affecting the accused person].
> (2) You discharge your duty applying the same rules and standards regardless of the arrangements made for the trial.
> (3) If you decide that the accused person did the acts alleged, the factors affecting the accused person [in this case] do not mean he did not have capacity to commit the offence. It is no defence to say that he would not have done things if [less intellectually challenged or less anxious (or whatever factor)].
> (4) When considering his evidence, you should make appropriate allowance to reflect his limitations.

(c) Informed decisions about adjustments to the trial process

Provided proper arrangements are made, a vulnerable accused person can be **6.41** tried. The Criminal Procedure Rules (see, in particular, Crim PR 3.9(3))[64] and Criminal Practice Directions (see, in particular, Crim PD 3G: Vulnerable Defendants) taken together, require the courts to accommodate vulnerable accused persons. Preparing for such a trial, once a mental vulnerability is recognized, requires an assessment in advance of the trial by the appropriate expert(s) (psychiatrist/psychologist/intermediary/speech and language therapist/deaf signer, etc.). The question for the court is whether the accused person can effectively participate in his or her trial. The steps which should be taken should be judged, in any given case, depending on the age and intelligence of the accused, as well as any mental vulnerability of the accused and all the other circumstances of the case.

In order to participate effectively in a trial, a child (or vulnerable adult) need not **6.42** be able to understand every point of law or evidential detail, but should not be intimidated or inhibited and should have a broad understanding of the nature of the trial process and what is at stake for him or her, including the significance of any penalty. With the assistance of an intermediary, interpreter, social worker, or friend, he or she should be able to understand the general thrust of what is said in court. He should be able to follow what is said by the prosecution witnesses and to explain his version of events, thus putting forward the points in his or

---

[63] Substantially taken from a direction given by HHJ Head in *R v Pepper*, 2007, unreported, Leicester Crown Court in which the second author appeared.

[64] Crim PR 3.9(3): 'In order to prepare for the trial, the court must take every reasonable step— (a) to encourage and to facilitate the attendance of witnesses when they are needed; and (b) to facilitate the participation of any person, including the defendant.'

her defence.[65] The minimum requirements for a fair trial have been held to be as follows:[66]

1. The accused person has to understand what he or she is said to have done wrong.
2. The court has to be satisfied that he or she had the means of knowing, when he or she had done an act or omission, that he or she knew that was wrong.
3. The accused person has to understand what, if any defences, are available to him or her.
4. He or she has to have a reasonable opportunity to make relevant representations if he or she so wishes.
5. He or she has to have the opportunity to consider what representations he or she wishes to make once he or she has understood the issues involved.
6. He or she must be fit to plead in the sense that he or she is able to give proper instructions and participate by way of providing answers to questions and suggesting questions to his or her lawyers in the circumstances of the trial as they arise.

6.43 There should be a Ground Rules Hearing (see further Chapter 12, 'Ground Rules Hearings') prior to the start of the trial of a vulnerable defendant to determine what steps need to be taken for the effective participation of the accused. By way of example, the court may direct the following to assist the accused person to receive a fair trial:

- assistance of an intermediary either throughout the trial[67] or for giving evidence only (see Chapter 11, 'Intermediaries');
- giving evidence via live link;[68]
- a court familiarization visit;
- removal of formal court dress—wigs, gowns, bands, etc;
- seating the accused person out of the dock without the attendance of a dock officer and at the same level as the advocates and judge;
- securing the attendance of an interpreter/deaf signer;
- limiting the length of court sessions and allowing frequent breaks;
- ensuring that questioning is phrased appropriately and expressed in a clear, simple, and non-hostile manner;
- clearing the public gallery.
- In *R v Hamberger*,[69] the defendant suffered chronic ill health, but his medical condition was such that he was not eligible to give evidence by live link (Youth Justice and Criminal Evidence Act 1999 s. 33A). However, sometimes an

---

[65] *R(TP) v West London Youth Court* [2005] EWHC 2583; and *SC v UK* [2004] EHRR 10.
[66] *R(TP) v West London Youth Court.*
[67] *R(AS) v Great Yarmouth Youth Court* [2011] EWHC 2059 (Admin). The decision not to allow the accused person to have the benefit of a registered intermediary was quashed.
[68] Youth Justice and Criminal Evidence Act 1999 s. 33A.
[69] [2017] EWCA Crim 273.

account may be given by way of hearsay evidence (Criminal Justice Act 2003 ss 114 and 116)—for example, by a written, audio, or video recording. Successful defendant hearsay applications of this nature will be 'rare and exceptional'.[70]

Even where an intermediary is unavailable, 'it remains the court's responsibility to adapt the trial process to address the defendant's communication needs, as was the case prior to the existence of intermediaries'.[71] In such a case, a ground rules hearing should be convened to ensure every reasonable step is taken to facilitate the defendant's participation in accordance with Crim PR 3.9.[72] It will be a matter for the trial judge in each individual case to decide whether the defendant is capable of effectively participating in the trial and what adjustments, if any, are necessary to achieve this (see also Chapter 10, 'Special Measures').

In many cases (particularly where the defendant has a mental health issue), it will **6.44** not be sufficient to simply give a direction regarding the special arrangements (see further Chapter 14, 'Jury Directions') without the jury hearing some evidence of the accused's incapacity. For example, psychiatric evidence might explain why a defendant might behave or has behaved unusually or unexpectedly at trial.[73] The jury should be directed as to how to use any evidence of vulnerability. Ability to follow a trial is different from state of mind in relation to a criminal offence and careful directions will be needed to avoid error or speculation.

(d) Evaluation of the defendant's presentation at trial

The mental vulnerability of an accused person would need to be understood by **6.45** the fact finders if it is relevant to their evaluation of the defendant's presentation in court—for example, the defendant's body language and reactions. Expert evidence on the defendant's vulnerability should have been before the jury where the defendant (who had Asperger's Syndrome, though undiagnosed at the time) read a book in the dock while the complainant gave evidence.[74]

R v Thompson, like *TS*, also concerned an appellant with Asperger's Syndrome. **6.46** The Court of Appeal observed:

> ... the tendency of the appellant, during his evidence before the Reading jury, to pick arguments with the prosecutor over comparatively trivial detail, while failing, unless re-directed, to confront the underlying and critical question ... In our opinion, the expert evidence would have been of value to the jury in determining whether, on the one hand, the appellant was evading the question or, on the other,

---

[70] ibid. at [44].
[71] *R v Cox* [2012] EWCA Crim 549.
[72] Crim PD F.21.
[73] See, e.g., *R v TS* [2008] EWCA Crim 6, where the defendant was reading a book while the complainant gave evidence.
[74] ibid. at [67]

that he was, as a result of his unusual traits, reluctant to be deflected from his pre-occupation with matters of detail.[75]

D. Relevance of Expert Evidence to Issues at Trial

(a) Issues relating to defences/mental element to be proved

6.47   The defences of insanity, sane automatism, and partial defences to a charge of murder (diminished responsibility and loss of control) will, without doubt, require the defence team to adduce expert evidence of the defendant's mental vulnerability. These defences/partial defences are discussed in detail below. Expert evidence of the defendant's mental vulnerability may also be relevant to whether or not the defendant had the requisite *mens rea*, or guilty mind. Criminal responsibility under English criminal law now requires proof of some subjective application of the mind to the events in hand in the context of intention.[76] Recklessness may have both subjective and objective criteria and even negligence tests may require a comparative exercise with other people's behaviour. This means that courts are often required to consider the defendant's own characteristics. Specific cases of a defendant's mental vulnerability affecting the court's assessment of their *mens rea* are discussed below (see '*G. Mens Rea*').

(b) Limitations of expert evidence (the final issue)

6.48   'The expert witness should be careful to recognize, however, the need to avoid supplanting the court's role as the ultimate decision-maker on matters that are central to the outcome of the case.'[77]

6.49   In *Pora v The Queen*, the appellant, who had a form of foetal alcohol spectrum disorder (FASD), had been convicted of rape and murder. He maintained that he had not committed these offences, but was 'bereft' of an explanation as to why he had confessed. One of the principle grounds of his appeal was that the confessions he made were unreliable. The Privy Council noted that 'the possibility of such [FASD] evidence [including that the appellant had memory deficits and would confabulate[78]] securing a different outcome to the trial cannot be gainsaid'.[79]

---

[75]   *R v Thompson* [2014] EWCA Crim 836 at [33].

[76]   The Criminal Justice Act 1967 s. 8 expressly provides that in relation to proof of criminal intent, 'A court or jury, in determining whether a person has committed an offence (a)shall not be bound in law to infer that he intended or foresaw a result of his actions by reason only of its being a natural and probable consequence of those actions; but (b)shall decide whether he did intend or foresee that result by reference to all the evidence, drawing such inferences from the evidence as appear proper in the circumstances.'

[77]   *Pora v The Queen* [2015] UKPC 9 per Lord Kerr at [24].

[78]   ibid. at [37].

[79]   ibid. at [40].

The Privy Council also said, '[i]t is for the court to decide if the confessions are **6.50** reliable and to reach conclusions on any reasons for their possible falsity.'[80] The Privy Council rejected the opinion of an eminent expert who asserted that the confession was unreliable because, it said, he had gone beyond his role. It would have been open to the expert to give his 'opinion as to why, by reason of his psychological assessment of the appellant, [the suspect] might be disposed to make an unreliable confession but, in the Board's view, it is not open to him to assert that the confession is in fact unreliable'.[81]

(c) Admissibility and reliability of confessions

In *R v Blackburn*,[82] the Court of Appeal quashed the conviction based on con- **6.51** fessions of a 15-year-old interviewed by the police without adequate safeguards where the heart of the Crown's case was constituted by those admissions.[83] The Court of Appeal remarked that: 'No doubt we are more aware today than were courts in the late 1970s of the risks of a combination of factors such as existed here producing false confessions.'[84] Assisted though the appeal court was by the testimony of the expert witness, it would have 'reached the same conclusion as to the unreliability of the admissions even without that assistance'.[85]

Expert evidence that a party seeks to adduce with regard to the admissibility and **6.52** reliability of a confession should be for the purpose of assisting the court to evaluate the reliability of a confession and not an attempt to usurp the court's function of deciding whether or not the confession is in fact reliable. The defence may wish to instruct an expert to provide a detailed expert analysis of the how the accused person's mental vulnerability combined with situational factors' might have had a bearing on the reliability of the accused's confessions; in theory, such expert evidence about the confessions could be admissible.[86]

(d) Admissibility and reliability of interviews

Evidence of a suspect's mental vulnerability might in certain circumstances be **6.53** relevant to the determination of the admissibility of the interviews[87] and the

---

[80] ibid. at [24].

[81] ibid. Although regarding usurping the role of the fact finders, it has been argued that the Privy Council in *Pora* was 'out of step with the weight of academic and judicial opinion'—see R. Roberts, 'Case Comment *Pora v The Queen*' (2015) Crim LR, 11, 884–7, 886.

[82] [2005] EWCA Crim 1349.

[83] ibid. at [64].

[84] ibid. at [61].

[85] ibid.

[86] D. Ormerod, 'Expert Evidence: Where Now? What Next?' (2006) *Archbold News*, 5, 5–9, 7.

[87] If, for example, an application were made to exclude the interviews because 'having regard to all the circumstances, including the circumstances in which the evidence was obtained, the admission of the evidence would have such an adverse effect on the fairness of the proceedings that the court ought not to admit it' (Police and Criminal Evidence Act 1984 (PACE) s. 78).

reliability of the suspect's answers in interview. Even if the interview is deemed admissible, expert evidence may be essential for the fact finders to evaluate how much weight to attach (if any) to the defendant's answers at interview.

6.54 Of course, it is far preferable for the suspects' mental vulnerability to be recognized at the time and for the interviewers to adjust their approach based on expert advice:

> Although juveniles or people who are mentally disordered or otherwise mentally vulnerable are often capable of providing reliable evidence, they may, without knowing or wishing to do so, be particularly prone in certain circumstances to provide information that may be unreliable, misleading or self-incriminating. Special care should always be taken when questioning such a person, and the appropriate adult should be involved if there is any doubt about a person's age, mental state or capacity. Because of the risk of unreliable evidence it is also important to obtain corroboration of any facts admitted whenever possible.[88]

6.55 Police guidance for interviewing suspects highlights the special care that must be taken and the risks of unreliable responses when the suspect is mentally vulnerable (see further Chapter 4, 'Vulnerable Suspects: The Investigation Stage').

(e) Adverse inferences (no comment interviews; failure to give evidence at trial)

6.56 It is not proposed to go into this legislation in detail, but the drawing of adverse inferences from silence remains controversial. However, mental vulnerability does not automatically prevent the court from giving such a direction, particularly where adaptations have been made to the court process to enable a vulnerable defendant to participate effectively. Experience tends to show that such a direction is rarely given when vulnerable people do not answer police questions, but it may be given where the accused person does not give evidence.

6.57 In *R v Dixon*,[89] 'the [trial] judge directed the jury that no adverse inference should be drawn from the fact that the Appellant did not answer questions in interview. However, he did direct the jury that it was open to them to draw an inference from his failure to give evidence.'[90] The judge had looked 'beyond the expert material put before him, including the Appellant's behaviour after the event, the fact that an intermediary had been in place, the anticipated approach of a fair-minded jury, and the nature of the account to be given by the Appellant'.[91]

---

[88] PACE Code C, 30 para. 11C.
[89] [2014] 1 WLR 525; 177 JP 361; (2013) 177 JP 361; [2014] Crim LR 141; [2013] EWCA Crim 465; [2013] 3 All ER 242; [2014] WLR 525.
[90] ibid. at [12].
[91] ibid. at [55].

The Court of Appeal concluded that: **6.58**

> The question for us is whether the judge was wrong to give an adverse inference
> direction. It is recognised that the question for the judge is a broad one with a wide
> margin of appreciation. In our judgment, the judge's approach and assessment of
> the situation resulted in a decision to which he was entitled to come.[92]

The appeal court took the view that the evidence proffered on appeal represented
only 'amplification of materials which were before the court below ... A tactical
decision was made not to adduce certain aspects of the material available to the
defence at trial for fear that it might cast a spotlight on character traits of the
Appellant which would be unhelpful to his defence'.[93]

In *Dixon*, the Court of Appeal distinguished *R v Billy Joe Friend (No. 2)*,[94] in   **6.59**
which the defendant's Attention Deficit Hyperactivity Disorder (ADHD) had
not been diagnosed at trial and his condition had not been recognized:

> The focus of the fresh evidence in *Billy Joe Friend* was not to the effect that the appel-
> lant would be harmed physically or mentally by giving evidence, but that the extent
> of his condition was such that it was undesirable for him to give evidence because
> of his intellectual and cognitive deficits and his ADHD. The appeal court said that
> it was clear that had the judge known the true position, he would not have ruled in
> favour of drawing any adverse inference[95] and thus quashed the conviction.

E. Defences

The defences of insanity and sane automatism, which arise out of mental vulner-   **6.60**
ability, create a complex area of law which the Law Commission has recognized
as being in need of reform.[96] What follows below is an overview.

(a) Insanity (including insane automatism)

A mentally vulnerable defendant is entitled to be found 'Not Guilty by reason   **6.61**
of Insanity' if at the time of the commission of the *actus reus* of the offence, they
were suffering from a 'disease of the mind' which gives rise to a defect of reason
such that they did not know 'the nature and quality of the act' they were doing
or that what they were doing was legally wrong.[97] If the defendant pleads the
defence of insanity, then the burden of proving this defence lies on the defendant.
The defendant must prove this on the balance of probability.

---

[92] ibid. at [57].
[93] ibid. at [73].
[94] [2004] EWCA Crim 2661.
[95] *R v Dixon* [2013] EWCA Crim 465 at [46].
[96] Law Commission, 'Criminal Liability: Insanity and Automatism—A Discussion Paper' (23 July 2013).
[97] *M'Naghten's Case* [1843] 8 ER 718; [1843] UKHL J16.

6.62 The Criminal Procedure (Insanity) Act 1964 s. 6 requires the evidence of at least two registered medical practitioners, at least one of whom is duly approved. It is for the judge to decide if the medical evidence amounts to a defence of insanity[98] and, if it does, it is a matter for the jury to determine if the defendant was in fact insane and return a verdict of Not Guilty by reason of Insanity. Medical evidence will be crucial, not only to assist the jury to determine whether the defendant was suffering from a disease of the mind (the medical evidence is usually not in dispute on that aspect), but also in respect of the usually more challenging issue whether as a result the defendant knew what he or she was doing and/or that what he or she was doing was wrong.[99]

6.63 What is in fact a disease of the mind for the purposes of this defence is a legal question. The Court of Appeal in *R v Coley* concluded that a 'disease of the mind' cannot be caused by an external act such as the defendant taking illegal drugs that cause a psychotic episode.[100]

6.64 A defendant can be treated as insane if the disease of the mind giving rise to a defect of reason 'arises from a medical condition such as diabetes'; in *R v Hennessy*,[101] a diabetic's hyperglycaemic episode fell within insane automatism as it was 'caused by an inherent defect'. Epilepsy,[102] sleepwalking,[103] and a tumour[104] have fallen within the definition of diseases of the mind that allowed the accused to be treated as insane.

> The plea of insanity may take the form of insane automatism (i.e. that the defendant has a total loss of control as a result of some disease of the mind). The defence is mutually exclusive from that of sane automatism which requires that the total loss of control arises from some external factor.[105]

(b) Sane automatism

6.65 The division between insanity and sane automatism creates 'illogical and strange results':

> 'External factor' is not limited to things like a blow to the head ... The upshot is that a diabetic who, without fault, fails to take insulin and then commits an

---

[98] *Dickie* [1984] 3 All ER 173.
[99] Crown Court Compendium 18-20.
[100] *R v Coley; R v McGhee; R v Harris* [2013] EWCA Crim 223; and see R. Mackay, 'Case Comment *R. v Coley; R. v McGhee; R. v Harris*: Insanity—Distinction between Voluntary Intoxication and Disease of Mind Caused by Voluntary Intoxication' (2013) Crim LR, 11, 923–9.
[101] [1989] 2 All ER 9 at 14.
[102] *R v Sullivan* [1984] AC 156.
[103] *R v Burgess* [1991] 2 QB 92. See W. Wilson, I. Ebrahim, P. Fenwick, and R. Marks, 'Violence, Sleepwalking and the Criminal Law: Part 2: The Legal Aspects' (2005) Crim LR, 614–23.
[104] *R v Kemp* [1957] 1 QB 399.
[105] Crown Court Compendium 18-18 para. 6.

allegedly criminal act would be treated as insane. In contrast, a diabetic who took insulin in accordance with a medical prescription would be acquitted if they were an automaton at the time of committing an allegedly criminal act.[106]

The essence of automatism is that the movements or actions of the defendant at the material time were wholly involuntary.[107] For example: **6.66**

> ... a reflex action such as swerving by a driver when a stone smashes through the windscreen is not a result of a recognised medical condition. The accused in such a case might plead automatism and be acquitted outright.[108]

The defence is not available where the expert evidence is that the behaviour was irrational rather than involuntary.

Self-induced automatism may still be a defence: **6.67**

> Automatism which is self-induced (other than by taking alcohol to excess or recklessly taking drugs, whether prescribed or otherwise)—e.g. by taking alcohol while using some types of prescribed drugs or failing to have regular meals while taking insulin—may still provide a defence, provided that [the defendant] was not at fault to the degree required by the offence with which he is charged. In some cases the question of fault may be resolved by considering whether [the defendant] was reckless in causing the state of automatism to exist.[109]

(c) Duress

The Modern Slavery Act s. 45 provides a 'Defence for slavery or trafficking victims who commit an offence'—thus, issues surrounding pressure and coercion may be relevant to a defence of being a human trafficking victim. **6.68**

> Some argue that it should cover every offence committed by a trafficked person, regardless of proximity to the trafficking offence ... Others argue that there must be some restriction on the defence, and that aligning it with a duress defence fits more comfortably. The Act does not define the term 'direct consequence', however, nor is there any definition or guidance in the explanatory note ... In respect of the s. 45 defence, it is assumed that the evidential burden is on the defence—this however is not clear on the current drafting of the legislation.[110]

The Modern Slavery Act 2015 is outside the scope of this chapter and here we focus on the common law defences: **6.69**

> Duress affords a defence which, if raised and not disproved, exonerates the defendant altogether. It does not, like the defence of provocation [now 'loss of control']

---

[106] ibid. pp 9–10, paras 42–4.
[107] Mackay, 'Case Comment *R v Coley; R v McGhee; R v Harris*'.
[108] Law Commission, 'Criminal Liability', 19, para. 89.
[109] Crown Court Compendium 18-6, para. 7.
[110] C. Haughey, 'The Modern Slavery Act Review' (2016), available at <https://www.gov.uk/government/uploads/system/uploads/attachment_data/file/542047/2016_07_31_Haughey_Review_of_Modern_Slavery_Act_-_final_1.0.pdf> accessed 23 March 2017.

to a charge of murder, serve merely to reduce the seriousness of the crime which the defendant has committed ... The only criminal defences which have any close affinity with duress are necessity, where the force or compulsion is exerted not by human threats but by extraneous circumstances, and, perhaps, marital coercion under section 47 of the Criminal Justice Act 1925 s. 47.[111]

6.70 The defence of marital coercion (coercion of married woman by husband was found in the Criminal Justice Act 1925 s. 47) was abolished by the Anti-social Behaviour, Crime and Policing Act 2014 s. 177. In rare and unusual cases, justification and necessity have been raised in circumstances not immediately connected with vulnerability, including protest and driving matters. It is not dealt with in any detail here, since it is not clear that the defence of necessity actually exists in English law.[112] In any event, if it does exist, it is not seen as a defence arising from human frailty, but one arising from circumstances forcing a choice of the lesser of two evils. In practice, such a choice would be most likely recognized in the exercise of a discretion whether to prosecute (see further below) or in sentencing. The partial defence of loss of control is considered later in this chapter.

(d) 'Huge pressure' does not constitute duress

6.71 The Lord Chief Justice said in *R v A*, 'duress should not and cannot be confused with pressure'.[113] In *R v A*, the defendant was vulnerable in the sense that she was a victim of a sexual assault and felt huge pressure to retract the allegation of rape she had made against her husband (see above at 6.38).

6.72 The appellant was then charged with and convicted of making false retractions. The Court of Appeal proceeded on the basis that the appellant had 'enabled her husband to escape justice for the crime of rape for which she was the victim',[114] albeit that her husband had always denied the allegations. The appellant engaged new legal advisers who obtained witness statements supporting her account that she was subjected to ill-treatment by her husband and a report from a consultant forensic clinical psychologist concluding that she had post-traumatic stress disorder (PTSD) and had done so when she retracted the allegations of rape. The appellant argued that crucial evidence was not properly examined or considered before she pleaded guilty, and if it had been the defence of duress would have been open to her. The Court of Appeal also noted that:

> ... unprompted contemporaneous account by the appellant to the writer of the Pre-Sentence Report about the circumstances in which she came to make the false

---

[111] *R v Hasan* [2005] UKHL 22 at [19]. Note also: 'Duress does not afford a defence to charges of murder, attempted murder and, perhaps, some forms of treason' (at [21]).

[112] See further, for instance: *Re A (Children)* [2000] EWCA Civ 254; and *R (Nicklinson) v Ministry of Justice* [2012] EWHC 2381 (Admin).

[113] At [63] per Lord Judge (LCJ).

[114] At [3].

retractions of which she was subsequently convicted are, again, inconsistent with a defence of duress.

The Court of Appeal recognized 'that the appellant felt under huge pressure, **6.73** but although feeling concerned for or even fearful of her husband, or a sense of guilt, or concern about what would happen to her children if her husband was in prison for 10 years or thereabouts, taken in combination, undoubtedly creates difficult problems and provides significant mitigation, does not constitute duress'.[115] This does not close the door to similar cases in the future, but highlights the importance for practitioners to explore issues of vulnerability beyond special arrangements at court.

The elements of the defence of duress were analysed and set out in detail in **6.74** the House of Lords on *Hasan* and are summarized well in the Crown Court Compendium (2016). In short, there are four elements and the jury must find that each is true or may be true for the defence to succeed. The defence fails unless each of the following are present:

1. The defendant reasonably believed that threats of death or serious injury had been made against him- or herself or a member of his or her immediate family or someone for whom he or she might reasonably feel responsible.
2. The defendant reasonably believed the threats would be carried out immediately or almost immediately and the threat was effective in the sense that there was no evasive action he or she could reasonably have been expected to take.
3. The defendant's criminal conduct which it is sought to excuse was directly caused by the threats which are relied upon.
4. A sober person of reasonable firmness of the defendant's age, sex, and character would have been driven to act as the defendant did.

It is submitted that when the defendant's characteristic(s) at the time of the **6.75** alleged offence included a mental vulnerability that affected either their beliefs (first and second elements) or the causal link between the threat and his or her actions (third element) or their firmness (fourth element), then evidence of that characteristic(s) is potentially relevant.

As to the second element and the taking of evasive action, in *R v Hudson and* **6.76** *Taylor*,[116] the Lord Chief Justice stated:

> In the opinion of this court it is always open to the Crown to prove that the accused failed to avail himself of some opportunity which was reasonably open to him to render the threat ineffective, and that upon this being established the threat in question can no longer be relied upon by the defence. In deciding whether such an opportunity was reasonably open to the accused the jury should have regard to

---

[115] At [66].
[116] [1971] EWCA Crim 2, Lord Parker (LCJ) giving judgment.

his age and circumstances, and to any risks to him which may be involved in the course of action relied upon.

6.77 Notably, *Hudson and Taylor* referred to age and circumstances, but not 'characteristics' of the defendant. When the jury considers what evasive action would be reasonable in the circumstances, it is submitted that it would be wrong to exclude evidence of the defendant's characteristics if they affected the defendant's ability to think of a way to avoid the threat. If, for instance, a defendant had a diagnosed mental disorder giving rise to anxiety, particularly acute anxiety when under threat, which would have disabled him of the inability to imagine a way to 'render the threat ineffective', then the defendant's action should not be judged by the standards of an ordinary person with the ability to think of ways to evade the threat.

6.78 It is submitted that the relevance to the fact finders of evidence of a recognized mental illness in relation to the first three elements should be treated according to the principles that would be applied to it in relation to the fourth element.

6.79 The fourth element also requires the jury to consider what a person would have done in the same position that the defendant was in. The jury will be required to ask themselves if an ordinary person sharing the characteristics of the defendant would be able to resist the threats made to him or her?[117] If the defendant's 'characteristics' include mental vulnerability and this was the reason or part of the reason the defendant acted as they did, the defendant's lawyers will no doubt seek a jury direction that the 'ordinary person' is one with the same mental vulnerability as the defendant. However, not all characteristics that could fall under the umbrella term 'mental vulnerability' are relevant.

6.80 In the case of *Bowen*, the court considered the authorities:

> What principles are to be derived from these authorities? We think they are as follows:
>
> 1. The mere fact that the accused is more pliable, vulnerable, timid, or susceptible to threats than a normal person are not characteristics with which it is legitimate to invest the reasonable/ordinary person for the purpose of considering the objective test.
> 2. The defendant may be in a category of persons who the jury may think less able to resist pressure than people not within that category. Obvious examples are age, where a young person may well not be so robust as a mature one; possibly sex, though many women would doubtless consider they had as much moral courage to resist pressure as men; pregnancy, where there is added fear for the unborn child; serious physical disability, which may inhibit self-protection; recognised mental illness or psychiatric condition, such as post-traumatic stress disorder leading to learned helplessness.

---

[117] *R v Bowen* [1996] EWCA Crim 1792.

3. Characteristics which may be relevant in considering provocation, because they relate to the nature of the provocation, itself will not necessarily be relevant in cases of duress. Thus homosexuality may be relevant to provocation if the provocative words or conduct are related to this characteristic; it cannot be relevant in duress, since there is no reason to think that homosexuals are less robust in resisting threats of the kind that are relevant in duress cases.

4. Characteristics due to self-induced abuse, such as alcohol, drugs, or glue-sniffing, cannot be relevant.

5. Psychiatric evidence may be admissible to show that the accused is suffering from some mental illness, mental impairment or recognised psychiatric condition provided persons generally suffering from such condition may be more susceptible to pressure and threats and thus to assist the jury in deciding whether a reasonable person suffering from such a condition might have been impelled to act as the defendant did. It is not admissible simply to show that in the doctor's opinion an accused, who is not suffering from such illness or condition, is especially timid, suggestible or vulnerable to pressure and threats. Nor is medical opinion admissible to bolster or support the credibility of the accused.

6. Where counsel wishes to submit that the accused has some characteristic which falls within (2) above, this must be made plain to the judge. The question may arise in relation to the admissibility of medical evidence of the nature set out in (5). If so, the judge will have to rule at that stage. There may, however, be no medical evidence, or, as in this case, medical evidence may have been introduced for some other purpose, e.g. to challenge the admissibility or weight of a confession. In such a case counsel must raise the question before speeches in the absence of the jury, so that the judge can rule whether the alleged characteristic is capable of being relevant. If he rules that it is, then he must leave it to the jury.

7. In the absence of some direction from the judge ... the jury may be tempted, especially if there is evidence, as there was in this case, relating to suggestibility and vulnerability, to think that these are relevant. In most cases it is probably only the age and sex of the accused that is capable of being relevant. If so, the judge should, as he did in this case, confine the characteristics in question to these.[118]

In *Bowen*, on the particular facts of that case, the Court of Appeal concluded **6.81** that it was irrelevant that the appellant was 'abnormally suggestible and a vulnerable individual'. The court did not see 'how low IQ [68 in the appellant's case], short of mental impairment or mental defectiveness, can be said to be a characteristic that makes those who have it less courageous and less able to withstand threats and pressure'. Thus, the fourth element of duress requires that the evidence of the defendant's character (including vulnerability) is a mental impairment or mental defect. Expert evidence that goes beyond evidence of a low IQ is required.

It is also worth noting that in *R v VSJ*,[119] in the context of human trafficking, the Court of Appeal held that the defence of duress should not be expanded.

---

[118] ibid.
[119] [2017] EWCA Crim 36.

(e) Duress, battered woman syndrome (BWS), and PTSD

6.82 In *R v GAC*, the appellant, C, had been caught at the airport with her co-accused carrying a large quantity of cocaine into the United Kingdom. Her co-accused pleaded guilty. C pleaded not guilty, claiming she was wholly innocent and made no mention at all of being pressured. The jury convicted her. She did not appeal. While she was in prison, W, the father of her child, was convicted of murder. She appealed her conviction via the Criminal Cases Review Commission (CCRC) on the basis of psychiatric evidence that she suffered BWS as a result of her relationship with W. At the appeal, there was also independent evidence that the appellant had had a violent relationship with W and she had sought medical treatment for the resultant stress and depression. The appellant's psychiatrist was of the view that when W told the appellant to commit the offence, she had no option but to obey. The Crown's psychiatrist did not agree that the appellant suffered BWS.

6.83 The issues for the Court of Appeal were:

(i)   whether the appellant may have been suffering from BWS at the time of the offence; and

(ii) if so, was it of a severity and degree that it might have afforded her the defence of duress?[120]

6.84 The court focused on the 'two key features of Battered Woman's Syndrome, namely learned helplessness and traumatic bonding'.[121] After reviewing the evidence in detail, including hearing from the appellant, the Court of Appeal concluded that:

> … fortunately not every woman who suffers from domestic violence goes on to suffer from Battered Woman's Syndrome. Not every woman who suffers from BWS can claim the defence of duress. It is essential to analyse, with some care, the extent and timing of the domestic violence, the impact upon the person concerned and their presentation at the relevant time.[122]
>
> …
>
> However, not every contradiction and inconsistency in their behaviour and accounts can necessarily be attributed to the illness and an accused would have to be suffering from BWS in a severe form to be in a position to claim their will was overborne.[123]

The Court of Appeal took the view that the appellant did not 'come close to establishing she may have been subjected to serious physical violence so bad that she had lost her free will, at any time, let alone before the importation'.[124] The

---

120   ibid. at [31].
121   ibid. at [25].
122   ibid. at [49].
123   ibid. at [51].
124   ibid.

case clearly turned on its facts. While not disputing the factual basis for the decision, one academic has argued[125] that the 'learned helplessness' aspect of BWS may be wrongly regarded as a precondition for success of the defence of duress. Since BWS is recognized as a sub-category of PTSD in the *Diagnostic and Statistical Manual of Mental Disorders*,[126] legal practitioners would be advised to take extra care when asserting the defence of duress on the basis of BWS as opposed to PTSD.

F. Partial Defences

(a) Homicide and diminished responsibility

'The partial defence [to a charge of murder] of diminished responsibility was **6.85** radically altered by s. 52 of the Coroners and Justice Act 2009, and fundamental reformulations became effective on 4 October 2010. The new provision was designed to align the mitigating doctrine with "developments in diagnostic practice".'[127]

Section 52(1) of the Coroners and Justice Act 2009 states: **6.86**

(1) A person ('D') who kills or is a party to the killing of another is not to be convicted of murder if D was suffering from an abnormality of mental functioning which—
   (a) arose from a recognised medical condition,
   (b) substantially impaired D's ability to do one or more of the things mentioned in subsection (1A), and
   (c) provides an explanation for D's acts and omissions in doing or being a party to the killing.

(1A) Those things are—
   (a) to understand the nature of D's conduct;
   (b) to form a rational judgment;
   (c) to exercise self-control.

(1B) For the purposes of subsection (1)(c), an abnormality of mental functioning provides an explanation for D's conduct if it causes, or is a significant contributory factor in causing, D to carry out that conduct.

Thus, to raise diminished responsibility successfully, the defendant must prove, on the balance of probabilities, that at the time of the killing he or she was suffering from an 'abnormality of mental functioning' arising from a 'recognized medical condition'. In most cases, this is generally resolved by the expert opinion.

---

[125] Loveless J, '*R v GAC*: Battered Woman "Syndromization"' (2014) Crim LR, 9, 655–67.

[126] American Psychiatric Association, *Diagnostic and Statistical Manual of Mental Disorders* (5th edn, 2013).

[127] N. Wake, 'Recognising Acute Intoxication as Diminished Responsibility? A Comparative Analysis?' (2012) *Journal of Criminal Law*, 76(1), 71–98, 72.

6.87   In 2015, Catley and Claydon published a review[128] of the extent to which neuroscientific evidence is used in the courtroom by those accused of criminal offences in England and Wales. It was not possible to tell if the number of appeals relying on neuroscientific evidence was increasing or simply that the number of appeals being reported was increasing. However, in several cases relating to alcohol dependence syndrome, neuroscientific evidence had helped lead to the quashing of convictions for murder and the substitution of a conviction for manslaughter on the grounds of diminished responsibility.

6.88   Wake concludes that:

> ... [recent changes to legislation] have potentially far-reaching consequences for accused persons suffering from substance use disorders. It is apparent that states of acute intoxication *may* satisfy the 'recognised medical condition' requirement which has become an integral part of the diminished responsibility plea in England and Wales.[129]

The overlap between alcohol dependence and voluntary intoxication can create complexities at trial. The moral concerns about not absolving someone who commits an offence in drink have to be balanced with any expert opinion that the accused person was suffering as a result of alcohol dependence from a recognized mental condition which substantially impaired their ability to do any of the following: understand the nature of their conduct; form a rational judgment; and exercise self-control.

6.89   In *R v Williams*,[130] the Court of Appeal said the use of drink is not an abnormality of mind:

> That issue in our judgment cannot be sensibly addressed without some consideration of the question what is meant by the term 'mental responsibility'. This has received rather less attention in the cases than the meaning of abnormality of mind. The concept of mental responsibility, quite different of course from moral responsibility, describes in our judgment the extent to which a person's acts are the choice of a free and rational mind ... Such a choice may be inhibited by many things. The effect of drink is plainly one. But ... the use of drink, even excessive use, is not an abnormality of mind. Here, in this case, the preponderance of the evidence however is that there was an abnormality of mind. We have given some of the references to the fresh evidence. Whether that caused a substantial impairment of the appellant's ability to bring a free and rational mind to bear on what he did is not necessarily concluded in favour of the Crown by lies he may have told or did tell or shifts of ground after the event. It is pre-eminently a jury question. We cannot decide pro or con the Crown or the defence. However, in Hughes LJ's words, the fresh material causes us to doubt the safety of the guilty verdict.[131]

---

128   P. Catley and L. Claydon, 'The Use of Neuroscientific Evidence in the Courtroom by Those Accused of Criminal Offences in England and Wales' (2015) *Journal of Law and the Biosciences*, 1–40, 34.

129   Wake, 'Recognising Acute Intoxication', 96 (emphasis in the original).

130   [2013] EWCA Crim 2749.

131   ibid. at [21].

Subject to evidence that the defendant at the time of the offence had a 'recognised **6.90** medical condition', that is, a medical condition that is recognized in law for the purposes of the defence of diminished responsibility, the issue of fault remains a jury question:

> Whether something is a medical condition is capable of being answered by an expert, but the question is not one of medicine but of law. This was confirmed in Dowds,[132] in which the Court of Appeal held that even though voluntary 'acute intoxication' is a medical condition, in that it is recognised as being such by both medical manuals, it is not a 'recognised medical condition' for the purposes of establishing diminished responsibility.[133]

One such recognized (in law, as well as in medicine) medical condition is Asperger's Syndrome.

In *R v Reynolds*,[134] decided under the Homicide Act 1957 before it was amended **6.91** by the Coroners and Justice Act 2009 s. 52, the accused person was convicted of murdering with a claw hammer a pharmacist at the shop where he worked; he was 17 years old at the time. Years later, a medical report to a Parole Board concluded that:

> ... there was sufficient evidence to suggest that [Reynolds] was suffering from what was described as autistic spectrum disorder, sometimes known as Asperger's Syndrome. [The medical expert] considered that it was unlikely that given the nature of the disorder the appellant would be able to make any major gains around, as he put it, 'victim empathy', nor would he be able to display emotions consistent with remorse for the offence.[135]

A clinical psychologist agreed with the diagnosis. The CCRC instructed a con- **6.92** sultant forensic neuropsychiatrist, who confirmed the diagnosis of Asperger's Syndrome and:

> ... was of the view that Asperger's Syndrome was capable of amounting to an abnormality of mind within section 2 of the Homicide Act 1957 and that in those circumstances a plea of guilty to manslaughter on the grounds of diminished responsibility may have been accepted or if the matter had proceeded to trial the judge may well have directed the jury that it was a defence open to the accused person justifying a conviction of manslaughter.[136]

The prosecution expert witness agreed that:

> ... had the vulnerability been recognised and evidence called to that effect at trial, it was highly likely that the jury would have concluded that the appellant's behaviour in attacking the deceased was significantly attributable to his mental disorder

---

[132] [2012] EWCA Crim 281.
[133] Crown Court Compendium 19-2, para. 7.
[134] [2004] EWCA Crim 1834.
[135] ibid. at [6].
[136] ibid. at [8].

and accordingly that the jury would have concluded that his abnormality of mind substantially impaired his responsibility at the time of the killing.[137]

The Court of Appeal concluded that the conviction of murder was unsafe and quashed the conviction, substituting a verdict of manslaughter in place of the verdict of murder.[138]

6.93 Applying the law as it now stands,[139] since Asperger's Syndrome is a 'recognised medical condition' which gives rise to abnormal mental functioning, diminished responsibility would potentially be open to a defendant with this vulnerability who is charged with murder. Whether a defendant could convince the jury that they were suffering an 'abnormality of mental functioning' at the time of the killing and it constituted a defence to murder will very much depend on the facts and circumstances of the alleged offence and the expert evidence about their mental vulnerability.

6.94 In *Blackman*,[140] the defendant's attachment disorder (a recognized medical condition), arising from the stress he was placed under as a frontline combat soldier in Afghanistan, was not detected prior to his trial. The defendant had shot and killed an injured insurgent and consequently was found guilty of murder at a court martial. The incident was captured on a helmet camera. On appeal, arising from a referral by the CCRC, a verdict of manslaughter by reason of diminished responsibility was substituted on account of fresh psychiatric evidence of his attachment disorder and all the other evidence in the case.[141]

(b) Homicide and loss of control

6.95 Sections 54 and 55 of the Coroners and Justice Act 2009 set out the loss of control defence. The defence is available to the defendant charged, as a principal or secondary party, with murder. The Coroners and Justice Act 2009 s. 56 abolished the defence of provocation. In *R v Clinton*, the Court of Appeal noted that:

> ... the new statutory defence is self-contained. Its common law heritage is irrelevant. The full ambit of the defence is encompassed within these statutory provisions. Unfortunately there are aspects of the legislation which, to put it with appropriate deference, are likely to produce surprising results.[142]

---

[137] ibid. at [11].
[138] ibid. at [12].
[139] Homicide Act 1957 s. 2, as amended by Coroners and Justice Act 2009 s. 52.
[140] [2017] EWCA Crim 190.
[141] See also P. Cooper, 'R v Blackman, Case Commentary' (2017) Crim LR (in press).
[142] *R v Clinton* [2012] EWCA Crim 2 at [2]. See also *R v Dawes and Others* [2013] EWCA Crim 322; [2014] 1 WLR 947; *R v Jewell* [2014] EWCA Crim 414; and *R v Gurpinar* [2015] EWCA Crim 178.

The loss of control defence in its entirety is contained in the statute as follows: **6.96**

Section 54

Partial Defence to Murder: loss of control

(1) Where a person ('D') kills or is party to the killing of another ('V'), D is not to be convicted of murder if—
   (a) D's acts and omissions in doing or being a party to the killing resulted from D's loss of self-control,
   (b) the loss of self-control had a qualifying trigger, and
   (c) a person of D's sex and age, with a normal degree of tolerance and self-restraint and in the circumstances of D, might have reacted in the same or in a similar way to D.
(2) For the purposes of subsection (1)(a), it does not matter whether or not the loss of control was sudden.
(3) In subsection 1(c) the reference to 'the circumstances of D' is a reference to all of D's circumstances other than those whose only relevance to D's conduct is that they bear on D's general capacity for tolerance or self-restraint.
(4) Subsection (1) does not apply if, in doing or being a party to the killing, D acted in a considered desire for revenge.
(5) On a charge of murder, if sufficient evidence is adduced to raise an issue with respect to the defence under subsection (1), the jury must assume that the defence is satisfied unless the prosecution proves beyond reasonable doubt that it is not.
(6) For the purposes of subsection (5), sufficient evidence is adduced to raise an issue with respect to the defence if evidence is adduced on which, in the opinion of the trial judge, a jury, properly directed, could reasonably conclude that the defence might apply.
(7) A person who, but for this section, would be liable to be convicted of murder is liable instead to be convicted of manslaughter.
(8) The fact that one party to a killing is by virtue of this section not liable to be convicted of murder does not affect the question whether the killing amounted to murder in the case of any other party to it.

Section 55

Meaning of 'qualifying trigger'

(1) This section applies for the purposes of section 54.
(2) A loss of self-control had a qualifying trigger if subsection (3), (4) or (5) applies.
(3) This subsection applies if D's loss of self-control was attributable to D's fear of serious violence from V against D or another identified person.
(4) This subsection applies if D's loss of self-control was attributable to a thing or things done or said (or both) which—
   (a) constituted circumstances of an extremely grave character, and
   (b) caused D to have a justifiable sense of being seriously wronged.
(5) This subsection applies if D's loss of self-control was attributable to a combination of the matters mentioned in subsections (3) and (4).
(6) In determining whether a loss of self-control had a qualifying trigger—
   (a) D's fear of serious violence is to be disregarded to the extent that it was caused by a thing which D incited to be done or said for the purpose of providing an excuse to use violence;

217

(b) a sense of being seriously wronged by a thing done or said is not justifiable if D incited the thing to be done or said for the purpose of providing an excuse to use violence;

(c) the fact that a thing done or said constituted sexual infidelity is to be disregarded.

(7) In this section references to 'D' and 'V' are to be construed in accordance with section 54.

6.97 The statute does not define the words 'loss of control', but in *R v Jewell*, the Court of Appeal said:

> Loss of control is considered by the authors of Smith and Hogan 13th Edition to mean a loss of the ability to act in accordance with considered judgment or a loss of normal powers of reasoning. The judge readily accepted that definition and so do we.[143]

6.98 In *R v Gurpinar*[144], the Lord Chief Justice said:

> The three principal components of the defence set out in the Act were reviewed by Lord Judge in *Clinton*:

(i) The killing must have resulted from the defendant's loss of self-control: see paragraph 10 of *Clinton*;

(ii) The loss of self-control had a qualifying trigger: see paragraphs 11–29 of *Clinton*;

(iii) A person of the defendant's sex and age, with a normal degree of tolerance and self-restraint and in the circumstances of the defendant might have reacted in a similar way to the defendant: see paragraphs 30–32 of *Clinton*.

As Lord Judge emphasized at paragraph 9 of *Clinton*:

> If one is absent, the defence fails. It is therefore inevitable that the components should be analysed sequentially and separately. However, it is worth emphasising that in many cases where there is a genuine loss of control, the remaining components are likely to arise for consideration simultaneously or virtually so, at or very close to the moment when the fatal violence is used.

6.99 The judge must consider whether to leave the defence of loss of control to the jury, even if the defendant has not raised the issue or given evidence.[145] Unless there is evidence sufficient to raise the issue of loss of control, the judge should withdraw it from consideration by the jury.[146] If the loss of control defence is successful, it results in a manslaughter conviction. The defence may be pleaded alongside diminished responsibility[147] or alongside self-defence. In the case of the latter, the Court of Appeal said in *R v Dawes and Others*[148] that 'even if the defendant may

---

[143] *R v Jewell* at [24].
[144] *R v Gurpinar* [2015] EWCA Crim 178 at [5].
[145] ibid. at [10].
[146] ibid. at [45].
[147] Crown Court Compendium 19-2, para. 1.
[148] At [59].

have lost his self-control, provided his violent response in self-defence was not unreasonable in the circumstances, he would be entitled to rely on self defence as a complete defence'.[149]

In *Dawes*, it was said that: **6.100**

> Unless the defendant has a sense of being seriously wronged s. 55(4) has no appli-
> cation. Even if it does, there are two distinctive further requirements. The cir-
> cumstances must be extremely grave and the defendant's sense of being seriously
> wronged by them must be justifiable.[150]

Whether or not the defendant's sense of being seriously wronged is justifiable is an objective question. However, if there is evidence that the circumstances were extremely grave, and the defendant had a justifiable sense of being seriously wronged, and there was qualifying trigger for the killing, then his or her defence will succeed unless the prosecution can disprove (as per s. 54(1)(c)) that 'a person of D's sex and age, with a normal degree of tolerance and self-restraint and in the circumstances of D, might have reacted in the same or in a similar way to D'. Section 54(3) states:

> In subsection 1(c) the reference to 'the circumstances of D' is a reference to all of
> D's circumstances other than those whose only relevance to D's conduct is that
> they bear on D's general capacity for tolerance or self-restraint.

The Crown Court Compendium suggests that s. 54(3):

> … only appears to exclude a circumstance on which D seeks to rely if its *sole* rel-
> evance is to diminish D's self restraint. The circumstance has to be relevant to
> D's conduct and not to the conduct or words of those that triggered his loss of
> control.[151]

The Court of Appeal said in *R v Asmelash*:

> … if, a defendant with a severe problem with alcohol or drugs was mercilessly
> taunted about the condition, to the extent that it constituted a qualifying trig-
> ger, the alcohol or drug problem would then form part of the circumstances for
> consideration.[152]

G. *Mens Rea*

Save for strict liability offences where evidence of the defendant's vulnerabil-   **6.101**
ity may only go to decision to prosecute or not,[153] the accused person's mental

---

[149] *R v Dawes and Others* at [59].
[150] ibid. at [61].
[151] Crown Court Compendium 19-11, para. 23 (emphasis in the original).
[152] [2013] EWCA Crim 157 at [25].
[153] Only the *actus reus* (the guilty act) needs to be proved; *mens rea* does not have to be proved.

vulnerability at the time of the alleged offence may be relevant to criminal liability. Put simply, the question of whether the accused person applied their mind to the offence gives rise to questions on the effect of the mental vulnerability.

(a) Intent

6.102 In the case of *R v Thompson*, it was alleged that the accused person had engaged in sexual touching of young boys he had taken on trips and acted for as a football coach. Consent was not the issue, but rather whether the accused person's actions had been sexually motivated. Post-conviction, the accused person was diagnosed with Asperger's Syndrome. Two new psychologists' reports about his vulnerability were admitted under the Criminal Appeal Act 1968 s. 23. The Court of Appeal decided that it could have been relevant to three counts on the indictment:

- First, as regards the count alleging inappropriate washing where the complainant protested that it was unnecessary for the appellant to wash and dry him so thoroughly, it was relevant that a 'person like the appellant who was rule-bound and somewhat obsessive about personal hygiene might not be sensitive to any expression of the boy's resistance'.[154]
- Second, as regards another count which involved the accused person's finger rubbing against one boy's anus, the Court of Appeal could 'not exclude the possibility that, had the jury been aware of the admitted features of the appellant's Asperger's, they would have reached a different conclusion, either as to the nature of the act or as to its purpose'.[155]
- Third, the Court of Appeal determined that expert evidence was relevant in relation to the way in which the jury received and understood the appellant's evidence.

The Court of Appeal said that the trial jury,

> … was very much concerned with the issue of interpretation of the appellant's alleged conduct, partly admitted and partly denied. It was to that issue that the expert evidence was primarily, although not exclusively, relevant. We cannot conclude that the decisions made by the jury in 2007 would undoubtedly have survived their consideration of the new evidence.[156]

The verdicts were found to be unsafe and were quashed. The Crown determined that it was not in the public interest for a re-trial to take place.

6.103 In *R v Stewart (Jamie Aaron)*,[157] the accused person had been left with a 3-year-old boy for a short time and it was alleged that he had exposed his penis to the boy and invited him to touch it with a sexual motivation. The accused person was

---

[154] *R v Thompson* at [31].
[155] ibid. at [32].
[156] ibid. at [34].
[157] Court of Appeal (Criminal Division) 11 December 2015 (unreported).

convicted of causing or inciting a child under 13 to engage in sexual activity. The accused person had an autism spectrum disorder. The 3-year-old boy did not give evidence in interview or at trial, but the judge admitted as hearsay the evidence of the boy's father, who said that the boy had told him that the accused person had shown him his penis and invited him to touch it. The Court of Appeal quashed the conviction; it was unsafe because there had been a number of failings in the judge's summing-up, in particular a failure to highlight the appellant's autistic spectrum disorder or to give a direction in relation to whether the appellant's actions had been sexually motivated. The judge had given inadequate direction to the jury with regard to the father's hearsay evidence. Taken together, these deficiencies made the conviction unsafe.

Although not considered here in detail, the authors also note Mahoney's extensive paper on Asperger's Syndrome (AS) and alleged child pornography offences:[158]   **6.104**

> The aptitude and comfort of AS individuals with computers, and the prevalence of pornography as a vehicle for AS individuals to try to learn about sexuality and romance, what neurotypical youth learn from their social interactions, has exposed more than a few AS male individuals to child pornography. Their curiosity, unrestrained by social or legal taboos, of which they are unaware, leads them to view images of 'underage' (i.e., younger than 18-years old) girls who are nearly their own age and years older than the level of their own social adaptation skills. This has resulted in criminal convictions, lengthy mandatory prison sentences, and a lifetime of reporting, ostracization, and residency restrictions as 'sex offenders'.[159]

In light of the decisions in *Thompson* and *Stewart*, a failure to admit expert evidence to assist the fact finders in determining whether the defendant's actions were sexually motivated and to interpret the defendant's behaviour at the time of the alleged offence and subsequently could be enough to render a conviction unsafe.

(b)   Reasonableness of belief—consent and sexual offences

For sexual offences where the complainant's consent is in issue and the accused person's defence is that he had a reasonable belief that the complainant consented, the accused person's mental vulnerability may be relevant: **6.105**

> Deciding whether a belief is reasonable is to be determined having regard to all the circumstances ... It is likely that this will include a defendant's attributes, such as disability or extreme youth, but not if (s)he has any particular fetishes.[160]

---

[158] M. Mahoney, 'Asperger's Syndrome and the Criminal Law: The Special Case of Child Pornography' (2009). See also T. Attwood, I. Henault, and N. Dubin, *The Autism Spectrum, Sexuality and the Law* (Jessica Kingsley Publishers, 2014).

[159] ibid. at [1].

[160] Crown Prosecution Service, 'Rape and Sexual Offences: Chapter 3: Consent', 'Reasonable belief in consent' (2016), available at <http://www.cps.gov.uk/legal/p_to_r/rape_and_sexual_offences/consent/> accessed 16 March 2017.

6.106 These issues were considered in *R v TS*, where the accused person was convicted of rape and indecent assault committed in December 2003 against his estranged wife. He was sentenced to four years' imprisonment. His appeal raised 'the issue of the impact on the safety of his convictions of fresh evidence relating to his psychological vulnerability at the time of the incident ... [namely] ... for the first time a diagnosis of Asperger's Syndrome'.[161] The Court of Appeal considered expert evidence which suggested that:

> ... although the appellant would have been aware that [his wife's] consent was required for sexual contact, his disorder impacted on his ability adequately to determine another's intentions or beliefs or desires in ambiguous situations; and that unless an unequivocal statement or set of actions was made by [his wife] to ensure that he ceased his unwanted attentions and left the premises, he was compromised by his disorder.[162]

The Court of Appeal was unable to affirm that the diagnosis was established,[163] but recognized that the accused person was 'not well'.[164] The Crown challenged the new diagnosis, but agreed that if it was correct, it applied at the time of the incident and its effects were agreed.[165]

6.107 In the Court of Appeal's judgment,

> ... the new evidence could have affected the trial in one or more of three ways. First, it would have enabled a defence for the first time to be based on the requirements of mens rea. Secondly, it would have enabled the jury to view the accused person before them not solely on the basis of whether what he said happened was at all credible, but more importantly on the basis of whether he was honest about what he believed to have been the situation, even if the facts were otherwise as [his wife] said them to be. Thirdly, it might have gone some way to explain to the jury why the appellant was behaving so oddly at trial, such as reading a book during [his wife's] evidence.[166]

The appeal was allowed, the convictions quashed, and a re-trial was ordered. *TS* must now be read in light of *B v The Queen*:[167]

> This appellant was convicted of counts of rape and common assault upon his partner and of a minor offence of criminal damage to her house. There was clear evidence that at the time of the offences he had been mentally ill, affected by paranoid schizophrenia and harbouring a number of delusional beliefs. His appeal certainly raises the question what if any impact his mental illness had on the issues before the jury. It is said more generally to raise the question whether, when considering the issue of a defendant's reasonable belief in the complainant's consent to

---

[161] *R v TS* at [1].
[162] ibid. at [22].
[163] ibid. at [28].
[164] ibid. at [29].
[165] ibid. at [34].
[166] ibid. at [34].
[167] [2013] EWCA Crim 3.

sexual intercourse, account can or cannot be taken of the mental condition of the defendant.[168]

The Court of Appeal concluded that:

> ... unless and until the state of mind amounts to insanity in law, then under the rule enacted in the Sexual Offences Act beliefs in consent arising from vulnerabilities such as delusional psychotic illness or personality disorders must be judged by objective standards of reasonableness and not by taking into account a mental disorder which induced a belief which could not reasonably arise without it.[169]

Or more succinctly: 'A delusional belief in consent, if entertained, would be by definition irrational and thus _un_reasonable, not reasonable.'[170]

This objective approach appears to run somewhat counter to the subjective approach   **6.108**
in homicide, but it is there as a result of the legislative provisions to set standards of sexual behaviour. This approach also leaves open the possibility of a defence when the accused has Asperger's Syndrome. Asperger's Syndrome does not create delusions, or amount to insanity. However, it does impair communication and may mean that someone with this vulnerability often interprets social signals in a way which someone without this mental vulnerability would not. In these circumstances, would the accused person's Asperger's Syndrome be relevant to consent? In light of *B*, it is suggested that it could be:

> It does not follow that there will not be cases in which the personality or abilities of the accused person may be relevant to whether his positive belief in consent was reasonable. It may be that cases could arise in which the reasonableness of such belief depends on the reading by the accused person of subtle social signals, and in which his impaired ability to do so is relevant to the reasonableness of his belief.[171]

(c) Reasonableness of belief—self-defence

The defence of self-defence: **6.109**

> ... takes slightly different forms in different contexts (see below) but these overlap substantially. All share the same basic structure with two crucial limbs (see in particular *Keane and McGrath* [2010] EWCA Crim 2514, para. [4]).
>
> (1) Did D believe or may he have believed that it was necessary to use force to defend himself an attack or imminent attack on himself or others or to protect property or prevent crime? (subjective question); and
> (2) Was the amount of force D used reasonable in the circumstances, including the dangers as D believed them to be? (objective question).[172]

---

[168] ibid. at [1].
[169] ibid. at [40].
[170] ibid. at [35] (emphasis in the original).
[171] ibid. at [41].
[172] Crown Court Compendium 18-1, para. 1.

The issue in *R v SO*[173] was:

> Did an insanely held delusion on the part of the appellant that he was being attacked or threatened, causing him violently to respond, entitle him to an acquittal on the basis of reasonable self-defence?

The Court of Appeal noted:

> The defence of self-defence at common law has, of course, two limbs. In summary, the first is whether the defendant genuinely believed that it was necessary to use force to defend himself. The second is whether the nature and degree of force used was reasonable in the circumstances. It is also elementary that once self-defence has been raised as an issue it is for the prosecution to disprove it to the criminal standard: this therefore is to be contrasted with a defence of insanity, where the burden is on the defendant.

> Leaving aside cases of self-induced intoxication, it has long been established that the first limb of the defence involves assessment of subjective considerations. The state of mind and belief of the defendant is in issue: objective considerations of reasonableness in this context are only relevant as potentially casting light on what the state of mind of the defendant in truth really was. It thus follows that even if the belief is based upon a mistake or a delusion still, if genuinely held, it can operate to satisfy the first limb of the defence. The second limb, however, unquestionably incorporates (by its requirement of reasonableness) objective considerations.[174]

As to the second limb, the Court of Appeal said:

> An insane person cannot set the standards of reasonableness as to the degree of force used by reference to his own insanity. In truth it makes as little sense to talk of the reasonable lunatic as it did, in the context of cases on provocation, to talk of the reasonable glue-sniffer.[175]

6.110   In that case, although the appellant's grounds of appeal were rejected, the court noted 'the greatest unease at the verdicts reached'[176] and concluded the proper verdicts on the two counts of affray and one count of inflicting grievous bodily harm contrary to the Offences Against the Person Act 1861 s. 20 were not guilty by reason of insanity. The Court of Appeal thus substituted these verdicts.

(d) Dishonesty

6.111   As is well known, there are two limbs to the *Ghosh*[177] test for dishonesty: the first is objective (what is dishonest by the ordinary standards of reasonable and honest people); and the second is subjective (did the defendant realize what he or she was doing was dishonest by the standards of reasonable and honest people?).

---

[173] [2013] EWCA Crim 1725 at [2].
[174] ibid. at [38]–[39].
[175] ibid. at [47].
[176] ibid. at [62].
[177] *R v Ghosh* [1982] EWCA Crim 2. The test remains 'good law': *R v Cornelius* [2012] EWCA Crim 500.

For determination of the second limb of *Ghosh*, jurors are required, as Spencer put it, to 'determine what the defendant would have thought the jury would have thought of it, had the matter crossed his mind'.[178]

The second limb of the test implicitly requires a defendant to possess what psy-chologists refer to as unimpaired 'theory of mind' abilities.[179] Theory of mind (ToM) refers to a person's ability to attribute mental states (e.g. beliefs, intents, desires, pretending, knowledge) to him- or herself and others and also the abil-ity to understand that others have beliefs, desires, intentions, and perspectives that are different from their own.[180] Thus, a jury would need to hear expert evi-dence if the defendant charged with an offence of dishonesty had a mental vul-nerability affecting his or her ability to understand what others think. In these circumstances, the fact finders would need to hear expert opinion[181] so that they could evaluate a defence that amounted to 'I did not realise that what I was doing was dishonest [by the standards of reasonable and honest people]'. This issue could arise, for example, when a defendant with Asperger's Syndrome is tried for an offence of dishonesty. Account may have to be taken that individuals with Asperger's Syndrome do not attribute mental states spontaneously, but they may be able to do so in explicit tasks through compensatory learning.[182]

6.112

H. Conclusion

This chapter has given an overview of the instances when expert evidence of particular mental vulnerabilities in an accused person might be relevant. Mental vulnerability is potentially relevant to much more than procedural adjustments.

6.113

There is little dispute that the defences of insanity and sane automatism are in an unsatisfactory state and in need of reform. We also suggest that more needs to be done to recognize the effect of coercion on vulnerable people in more cir-cumstances than the current defences. However, it is a forward step that the Law

6.114

---

[178] J. Spencer, 'Dishonesty: What the Jury Thinks the Defendant Thought the Jury Would Have Thought *R v Ghosh*' (1982) *Criminal Law Journal*, 41(2), 222–5.

[179] P. Cooper and C. Allely, 'The Curious Incident of the Man in The Bank: Procedural Fairness and a Defendant With Asperger's Syndrome' (2016) *Criminal Law and Justice Weekly*, 180, 35, 632–4.

[180] U. Frith and F. Happé, 'Autism: Beyond Theory of Mind' (1994) *Cognition*, 50, 115–32.

[181] P. Cooper, C. Berryessa, and C. Allely, 'Understanding What the Defendant With Asperger's Syndrome Understood' (2016) *Criminal Law and Justice Weekly* 180(35), 792–4.

[182] L. Burdon and G. Dickens, 'Asperger Syndrome and Offending Behaviour' (2009) *Learning Disability Practice*, 12(9), 14–20, 16, citing A. Senju, V. Southgate, S. White et al., 'Mindblind Eyes: An Absence of Spontaneous Theory of Mind in Asperger Syndrome' (2009) *Science*, 325(5942), 883–5.

Commission has prioritized reform of the law related to the closely linked issue of unfitness to plead.

6.115 Mackay goes further than recommending reform of the defence of insanity:

> … there is surely a continued and pressing need not only to rid the law of the term 'insanity', but also to avail ourselves of the opportunity presented by the Law Commission in its Discussion Paper, namely to forge ahead with a new and radical approach to the issue of criminal responsibility.[183]

6.116 An equally challenging area of law is criminal responsibility, where a mental vulnerability falling short of insanity or sane automatism raises the issue of whether or not the accused person had the requisite *mens rea*. This can be important both in relation to principal offenders and mentally vulnerable accessories. The latter, following *R v Jogee*,[184] requires proof of an intent to assist or encourage. Practitioners must be alive to these issues well before the trial and if in doubt as to the mental vulnerability of the defendant, seek appropriate expert advice.

6.117 The appellate courts have emphasized the importance of raising these issues at trial. The Court of Appeal has noted that:

> … the greatest caution should be taken not to allow an appellant to subvert the trial process by permitting him to deploy second time around an expert case which could and should have been deployed before the jury.[185]

6.118 Where the appellant seeks to adduce new evidence before the Court of Appeal, there are legal hurdles to overcome; the Criminal Appeal Act 1968 s. 23(2) sets out the grounds upon which the court is entitled to receive evidence not adduced at trial. The Court of Appeal may do so if it is necessary or expedient in the interests of justice.

> The Court of Appeal shall, in considering whether to receive any evidence, have regard in particular to—
>
> (a) whether the evidence appears to the Court to be capable of belief;
> (b) whether it appears to the Court that the evidence may afford any ground for allowing the appeal;
> (c) whether the evidence would have been admissible in the proceedings from which the appeal lies on an issue which is the subject of the appeal; and
> (d) whether there is a reasonable explanation for the failure to adduce the evidence in those proceedings.

6.119 *R v GAC* (see also above, 'Section E(c) Duress') is a salutary example; the appellant sought to argue duress albeit that she had pleaded guilty at trial. The Court of Appeal said that had the appellant 'wanted to run duress the time to do so

---

[183] Mackay, 'Case Comment *R. v Coley; R. v McGhee; R. v Harris*', 929.
[184] [2016] UKSC 8.
[185] *R v Sultan* at [33].

was at trial. It would have to be an exceptional case for this court to entertain an appeal based on a completely different case advanced years later.'[186] The appellant's counsel 'eloquently and valiantly', but ultimately unsuccessfully, tried to persuade the Court of Appeal that this was an exceptional case.[187]

In *R v Smith*, the Court of Appeal reaffirmed its view that the overriding object-   **6.120**
ive requires issues of mental vulnerability to be dealt with at trial and not left for an appellate decision:

> A further element of the overriding objective is dealing with cases efficiently and expeditiously. The need for finality in litigation is a basic principle, which applies in all areas including criminal justice. In the criminal context the principle of finality has less drastic consequences because there exists a safety net outside the courts. That safety net is the CCRC. If (absent a reference from the CCRC) criminal proceedings drag on interminably, many people suffer. These include the victim's family, the victim (if alive) and others involved in the case. The present application is a good example. It is now nine years since the applicant's conviction. Successive counsel have been engaged, dismissed and criticised. The ordeal for the deceased's family continues, as we can see from the updated victim impact statement.[188]

In *R v Workman*,[189] the court said:

> It is not the system under the law of England and Wales that parties can wait and see if they are convicted at trial and then, if they are, seek to adduce further evidence which could have been adduced at trial but was not. It is thus their responsibility to put their best case at trial. An unrestricted lenience in this regard would render the criminal justice system virtually inoperable. The countervailing consideration, of course, is that a wrongful conviction is abhorrent. (at [59])

Contrast *R v Rahman*,[190] where the Court of Appeal quashed a conviction because the defendant had been wrongly advised not to plead duress. The leading case on whether the Court of Appeal will find it necessary or expedient in the interests of justice to receive evidence which was not adduced at trial is *R v Erskine*,[191] and it was applied in *R v Blackman*.[192] Prior to sentencing, no psychiatric assessment of the defendant was sought and it was unknown that, at the time of the incident, he had a recognized psychiatric condition. This was not regarded as a case of a defendant who, having tactically opted for one strategy at trial which then turned out badly, was seeking a second bite of the cherry. The appeal court received fresh evidence and subsequently quashed his conviction for murder and substituted one of manslaughter.

---

[186] *R v GAC* at [62].
[187] ibid.
[188] *R v Smith* at [92].
[189] [2014] EWCA Crim 575.
[190] [2010] EWCA Crim 235.
[191] [2009] EWCA Crim 1425; [2010] 1 WLR 183.
[192] [2017] EWCA Crim 190.

6.121 The importance of lawyers giving careful consideration to potential mental vulnerability in the accused person and to adducing expert evidence hardly needs reiterating. If lawyers do seek an expert opinion, they must ensure that they are clear as to its relevance to the case—reliability of a confession, adapting trial procedure, a defence, the defendant's presentation, and/or another reason such as fitness to be interviewed (see Chapter 4, 'Vulnerable Suspects: The Investigation Stage') or for mitigation and sentencing (see Chapter 15, 'Sentencing'). Only then is it possible to give clear instructions to the expert witness, including an explanation of the legal framework to which their opinion will apply.

6.122 It is also important to recognize that the categories of expert evidence are never closed so that there will always be a few cases where fresh expert evidence on mental vulnerability will need to be raised on appeal. Advances in neuroscience, for example, over time, will lead to greater understanding about brain function, which may in turn affect the approach to mental vulnerability in court. However, in the meantime, it is vital that criminal courts approach questions of mental vulnerability with caution and ensure that a jury is properly directed on the use to which expert evidence of mental vulnerability should be put.

6.123 One legal academic reaches a conclusion which, although referring specifically to the mentally ill, is applicable to all mentally vulnerable accused persons:

> Mentally ill people are not a discrete category, fundamentally different in kind from the mentally healthy, that can be dealt with by one or two separate, specialised defences. They make up a significant proportion of incarcerated individuals, and it is vital that the criminal justice system makes space for them at every level, with respect to both liability and procedure.[193]

In the final analysis, fair procedures will count for nothing if the law determining criminal liability is not also fair.

---

[193] See C. Hogg, 'The Insanity Defence: An Argument for Abolition' (2015) *Journal of Criminal Law*, 79(4), 250–6, 256.

7

YOUTH COURTS AND YOUNG DEFENDANTS

Emma Arbuthnot and Naomi Redhouse

A. Introduction

In this chapter, we aim to examine how young defendants are dealt with in the   **7.01**
criminal courts. We will consider the history of the youth court and the way
in which the court today reflects the changes in social and political attitudes to
the young defendant. We will set out the aims of the youth justice system and
the ways in which the youth court and the adult court can be distinguished,
in both law and practice. The complex areas of jurisdiction, bail, and effective

229

participation will be examined in detail. The important areas of sentencing and the provisions relating to the special measures available for young witnesses and defendants are dealt with in other chapters.

B. History of the Youth Court

7.02 The magistrates' court is thought to date back to 1285, but until Victorian times there were no separate courts to deal with children and young people and there was no legal distinction between adults and children. Children appeared in the same courts as adults and were given similar sentences. Through the nineteenth century, however, there was an increasing interest in the idea of childhood and how things experienced by children affected their adulthood. The first distinction between adults and children was drawn by the Juvenile Offenders Act 1847, which allowed children under the age of 14 to be tried for some lesser offences in the magistrates' courts. Reformatory schools were introduced in the 1850s and by the 1880s there was increasing interest in setting up a separate court to try young defendants.

7.03 The Children Act 1908 introduced juvenile courts, although the first juvenile court had been established in Birmingham in 1900. The emphasis was on saving 'delinquent' juveniles for the sake of society. The courts were concerned with character, and the wider philosophy concentrated on the lack of male role models and the failure of family. The Probation of Offenders Act 1907 introduced the supervision of 'juvenile delinquents' in the community.

7.04 In the First World War, delinquent crime rose and this was generally thought to have been caused by the loss of male role models and the inability of mothers to cope particularly with their sons at time of war. A committee chaired by Sir Thomas Molony was set up by the then Home Secretary to look at the treatment of young offenders in the criminal justice system.

7.05 In 1927, the Molony Committee produced their report, in which it was suggested that: juvenile courts should sit separately to the adult court; the proceedings should be as simple as possible; young persons before the juvenile court should remain anonymous; and as much information as possible should be provided to the court about the juvenile. Further, the report emphasized probation work with the delinquent to enable him or her to become a good citizen.

7.06 It was this report which led in due course to the Children and Young Persons Act 1933 (CYPA 1933). It was the CYPA 1933 that set out the principle to be observed by all courts in dealing with children and young persons: the 'welfare of the child'. In addition, it abolished the death penalty for juveniles under the age of 18 years and the age of criminal responsibility was increased from 7 to 8. As

well as probation supervision, sentences included corporal punishment, the use of
which greatly increased during the Second World War.[1]

The Children Act 1948 and subsequent Acts reflect the contrasting views in soci-   **7.07**
ety that delinquent children should be either punished or saved. The 1948 Act
abolished the committal of child prisoners under the age of 17 years into adult
prisons. The Children and Young Persons Act 1963 raised the age of criminal
responsibility to 10 years. The Children and Young Persons Act 1969 introduced
care and supervision orders and local authority community homes were replaced
by reform schools. The Children Act 1989 separated youth justice from family
proceedings, and orders for the care and supervision of children were taken out
of the criminal justice system. The juvenile court was then for offenders only. The
Criminal Justice Act 1991 renamed juvenile courts as youth courts and the age
limit was raised so that offenders under the age of 18 years, unless jointly charged
with an adult, appear first in the youth court.

Until 1999, there was a legal presumption (known as *doli incapax*) that children   **7.08**
aged under 14 did not know the difference between right and wrong and were
therefore incapable of committing an offence. This presumption was rebuttable
if the prosecution could satisfy the court that the child knew that what he or she
was doing was seriously wrong, not merely naughty or mischievous. However, the
doli incapax presumption was abolished.[2] The criminal law now applies to children aged 10 to 13 in the same way as to those aged 14 or over. Following a highly
critical review of the youth justice system by the Audit Commission,[3] the Crime
and Disorder Act 1998 introduced 'prevention of offending' as the new principal
aim of the youth justice system alongside the welfare principle of the CYPA 1933.
Youth Offending Teams (YOTs, now often known as Youth Offending Services,
YOS) were introduced, bringing together in one place the various statutory services dealing with the needs of young people. The Youth Justice Board (YJB)
was established to oversee the youth justice system, provide guidance to YOTs,
and manage placement in the secure estate. Successive governments have further
amended existing legislation relating to the sentencing of children and young
people and there is a continuing debate as to the best methods for dealing successfully with young offenders. At its heart is the philosophical tension between
rehabilitation and punishment.

In 2009, the Sentencing Guidelines Council (now the Sentencing Council)   **7.09**
issued 'Overarching Principles: Sentencing Youths', which set out for the first
time the approach to be taken by all criminal courts when dealing with a child or

---

[1] The authors are grateful for the assistance of K. Bradley, 'Juvenile Delinquency and the
Evolution of the British Juvenile Courts c1900–1950', *History in Focus*, Issue 14, October 2008.
[2] By Crime and Disorder Act 1998 s. 34.
[3] *Misspent Youth: Young People and Crime* (Audit Commission, 1996).

young person. A revised and updated definitive guideline,[4] 'Sentencing Children and Young People, Overarching Principles and Offence Specific Guidelines for Sexual Offences and Robbery', has now been published and applies to all children and young people who are sentenced on or after 1 June 2017. Every court sentencing a young person must have regard to this guideline.[5]

(a) The current position

7.10   There are no consistent statutory definitions of the terms 'child', 'young person', 'youth', or 'juvenile', but as a general rule defendants between the ages of 10 and 14 are referred to as 'children' and those between 14 and 17 as 'young persons'.[6] It is, however, common practice among some in the youth justice system to refer to all under-18s as 'children', in line with the UN Convention on the Rights of the Child's definition of a 'child'.[7]

7.11   Reflecting declining rates of offending by children and young people, and the authorities' increasing emphasis on diversion from formal prosecution, there has been a continuing and very substantial fall in both the numbers of young people coming into the youth justice system and the use of custody over at least the past ten years. In the year ending December 2015, there were around 18,900 first-time entrants to the youth justice system,[8] a fall of 11 per cent when compared with the year ending December 2014. The number of first-time entrants has fallen by 83 per cent since its peak level in the year ending December 2006.[9] In March 2016, the number of young people under the age of 18 in custody was 882, down by 12 per cent when compared with the number in March 2015 and by 72 per cent since the peak custody figure of 3,200 in October 2002.[10] While there are now fewer young people offending, these young people have committed more previous offences and may have more complex needs. In the twelve months ending June 2007, the average number of previous offences per young person currently involved in the criminal justice system was 1.60; this rose to 2.53 in the twelve months ending June 2014. An increased focus on diverting low-level offenders from contact with the youth justice system means that those entering the system now tend to have a more serious record of offending, which in turn is linked to a greater likelihood of reoffending.[11]

---

[4] See <https://www.sentencingcouncil.org.uk/wp-content/uploads/Sentencing-Children-and-young-people-Definitive-Guide_FINAL_WEB.pdf> accessed 25 April 2017.

[5] Criminal Justice Act 2003 (CJA 2003) s. 172.

[6] Judicial College, *Youth Court Bench Book* (Judicial College, 2015).

[7] Adopted 20 November 1989, entered into force 2 September 1990, Art. 1.

[8] This includes both young people being issued with a youth caution (reprimand or warning, prior to 8 April 2013) and young people found guilty in all courts.

[9] The Youth Justice Board for England and Wales Annual Report 2015/16.

[10] ibid.

[11] ibid.

(b) Why are children and young people treated separately from adults?

The history of the youth court demonstrates the gradual recognition by society that children and young people are not the same as adults and should be treated differently. It could be said that the separate system of dealing with young defendants is in place because they are vulnerable due to their age. The emphasis of current legislation is on rehabilitation and the Sentencing Guidelines set out some of the vulnerabilities particularly associated with youths. They include: the high incidence of mental health problems; learning difficulties and disabilities; the effect of language or speech difficulties on the ability of the youth to understand the court hearing; their attitude to those they consider to be in authority (which may be hostile); their vulnerability to self-harm; the extent to which changes in adolescence lead to experimentation (particularly so in relation to allegations of drug taking and sexual offences); the effect on young people of loss (particularly of their primary carer); and abuse. More generally, immaturity must be considered by the court and the effect of neglectful or incompetent parenting. Young people are unlikely to have the same experience and capacity as an adult to appreciate the effect of their actions on other people and are less likely to be able to resist temptation, especially where peer pressure is exerted. At the time of sentence, there is an expectation that young people will be dealt with less severely than an adult offender.[12]

7.12

C. Aims of the Youth Justice System

The principal aim of the youth justice system is set out in the Crime and Disorder Act 1998 s. 37(1): 'it shall be the principal aim of the youth justice system to prevent offending by children and young persons'.

7.13

Section 37(2) states that 'it shall be the duty of all persons and bodies carrying out functions in relation to the youth justice system to have regard to that aim'. The 'welfare principle' is set out in CYPA 1933 s. 44:

7.14

> Every court in dealing with a child or young person who is brought before it ... shall have regard to the welfare of the child or young person and shall in proper cases take steps for removing him from undesirable surroundings and for securing that proper provision is made for his education and training.

In making a sentencing or bail decision, the court must always have regard to both of these aims. The requirement to have regard to these two principles is one of the ways in which the youth court fundamentally differs from the adult court: the

---

[12] 'Overarching Principles: Sentencing Children and Young People'.

purposes of sentencing which apply in the adult court include deterrence and punishment alongside rehabilitation;[13] these do not apply in the youth court.

D. Youth Offending Services/Youth Offending Teams

7.15   Section 39 of the Crime and Disorder Act 1998 places a duty on local authorities to set up one or more youth offending teams in each area. The YOT must consist of at least one probation officer, social worker, and police officer, and one person each nominated by the health authority and the Chief Education Officer. In court, there will be at least one member of the YOT team present at the time of plea and/or sentencing. The YOT representative will make proposals to the court where bail is opposed by the Crown Prosecution Service (CPS). Each local authority is required by statute to have available appropriate youth justice services, which will provide, among other things: prevention and early intervention work; the provision of persons to act as appropriate adults; support for young persons while on bail; the placement in local authority accommodation of young defendants; the provision of reports or of information required by the court; the supervision of community and detention and training orders; and the management of referral orders.[14] The YOT role in sentencing is to tailor a sentence around the needs and vulnerabilities of the young defendant according to the seriousness of the offence. The YOT will deal with a limited number of young people, as compared with the Probation Service and the Community Rehabilitation Companies, and, therefore, they are in a position to give very detailed assessments of the needs, vulnerabilities, and circumstances of the defendant.

7.16   A recent review of the youth justice system noted that there are 156 YOTs in England and Wales; each tailors its services to reflect differences in geography, demographics, case loads, and local priorities, as well as local authority structures and finances. All YOTs perform their statutory function of supervising sentences passed by the courts, but the interventions they provide as part of these sentences are often locally designed and delivered. Similarly, the degree to which YOTs engage in work to prevent offending or divert low-level offenders from the system varies. In all areas, multi-agency working is established at some level.[15]

7.17   The YJB, at its inception, pioneered an assessment tool to be used by all those working in the youth justice system. *Asset* is a structured assessment

---

[13]   CJA 2003 s. 142.
[14]   Crime and Disorder Act 1998 ss 38–9.
[15]   Ministry of Justice, *Review of the Youth Justice System* (MoJ, 2016).

tool used by all YOTs in England and Wales on all young offenders who come into contact with the criminal justice system. This comprehensive assessment of a young defendant enables an assessment of the needs, vulnerabilities, and risks of reoffending. It aims to look at the young person's offence or offences and identify a multitude of factors or circumstances, ranging from lack of educational attainment to mental health problems, language difficulties, and domestic circumstances which may have contributed to such behaviour.

The information gathered from *Asset* can be used to inform court reports so that **7.18** appropriate intervention programmes can be drawn up. It also highlights any particular needs or difficulties the young person has, so that these may also be addressed. *Asset* helps to measure changes in needs and risk of reoffending over time.[16] Part of the YJB's role has been to collate and analyse the information obtained by the YOTs in the course of their work and to undertake research as to its effectiveness.

The YJB is currently introducing a revised tool, *Assetplus*, which builds on pre- **7.19** vious assessment tools used in youth justice settings incorporating both the lessons learned from their use since 2000 and new insights from research and the academic literature. It is also designed to reflect the changing context in practice in which greater emphasis is now being placed on flexibility, desistence, and the importance of professional discretion. The development of the new framework reflects lessons learned from the literature on assessment practice in a range of disciplines and contexts, including social work, health care, and probation.[17]

The assessment informs the nature and extent of the work which is to be under- **7.20** taken with a young person as part of a sentence or a bail support programme and incorporates a structured approach to intervention. Different levels of intervention are provided: standard, enhanced, and intensive. The standard level is for defendants who are unlikely to reoffend and are at low risk of causing serious harm. Typically, this will involve an attempt to involve the parents in any order. The enhanced level is for a defendant with a medium risk of reoffending or a medium risk of harm. Typically, this order will involve greater activity in motivating the young defendant and more effort in addressing his or her breaking of the law. The highest level is the intensive level. This is aimed at defendants where there is a high likelihood of reoffending or at least a high risk of serious harm. The order will try to minimize the risks by seeking to control the defendant by restricting him or her and monitoring.

---

[16]   YJB, 'Young Offenders: Assessment Using Asset' (April 2014).
[17]   Dr Kerry Baker, 'Assetplus Rationale' (July 2012, revised October 2014, YJB).

E. The Youth Court—Practice and Procedure

7.21 All criminal charges against a child or young person aged 10 and over but under the age of 18 years are dealt with in the youth court unless there is an adult co-defendant or the young defendant is sent to the Crown Court for trial or for sentence. The legal provisions relating to custodial remands and sentencing are almost entirely different in the adult and youth courts and specialist legal knowledge is necessary for those working in the youth court. Notwithstanding these demands, there are currently no training requirements for advocates appearing in the youth court.

7.22 Section 31 of the CYPA 1933 requires the arrangements for the youth court to be separate from those for the adult court, including separate courtrooms, waiting areas, cells, and secure escort services, to ensure that youths are not in contact with adult defendants.

(a) Training for judges and magistrates

7.23 The district judges and magistrates who sit in the youth court have been specifically trained to sit in that jurisdiction. Before a district judge is trained to sit in the youth court, he or she will have had usually at least six months' experience of full-time sitting (as well as any part-time sitting as deputy district judges), as well as having been appraised. District judges usually sit with court associates. Once sitting in the youth court, district judges have annual updating training. Some more senior judges attend a 'serious sex' training course run by the Judicial College, which enables them to conduct the cases identified in the Criminal Practice Direction (Crim PD) XIII Annex 2 Sexual offences in the youth court.

7.24 Before a lay magistrate can sit in the youth court, they will have attended a six-hour youth court induction course followed by six hours of consolidating training between nine and eighteen months after induction. They will receive youth court 'winger' and chairmanship training every three years. Magistrates sit with a legal adviser. They also have the benefit of use of the *Youth Court Bench Book*[18] and the Youth Court Pronouncement Cards produced by the Judicial College. As well as dealing with legal matters, the training is likely to include specialist training in matters such as child development, speech and language difficulties, and mental health issues of young people.

---

[18] Available to judges via the judicial intranet.

(b) Layout of the courtroom

There is an emphasis on ensuring that the layout of the youth court is not intimi- **7.25**
dating and is more conducive to good communication with the young defendant
and his or her parents. The court is usually set out with the judge or magistrates
sitting on the same or similar level as the defendant, who sits next to or near his
or her lawyer and parents. The court will be presided over by at least two lay magistrates, including at least a man and a woman, or a district judge (magistrates'
courts). Others in court will be the legal adviser or court associate, members of
the YOT, and an usher. The defendant's parent or guardian (or person who has
care of the defendant, including the local authority where the child is in care) is
required to attend if the defendant is under the age of 16 and may be required
if they are over 16 years of age. [19] The youth court is not open to the public,
although bona fide representatives of the press can attend. Other persons can be
present, but only with the permission of the court.

(c) Language and informality

The court is much less formal than the adult court and the defendant and any **7.26**
young person is addressed by his or her first name. The court has been designed
for and is suited to the needs of children and young people. The judges and
magistrates use clear and simple language that a young person can be expected
to understand. They are expected to build up a rapport with the defendant, to
encourage their participation in the court process, particularly at a sentencing
hearing. The court may also hear directly from a parent or guardian.

The young defendant may require frequent breaks during a lengthy hearing or **7.27**
time in which to speak to his or her lawyer and parent or guardian. The court is
focused on ensuring, as far as possible, the effective participation of the young
defendant and adapts its proceedings and the speed of the hearing to the age and
understanding of the defendant and any child witness it hears from. The court is
expected to keep an eye on the defendant and any witness to ensure that he or she
has not lost concentration. Great care is taken by the court to explain each step
in the proceedings to the defendant. It is good practice to check the defendant
has understood any expectations of him or her (e.g. bail conditions or sentencing
expectations).[20]

(d) Fair trial and effective participation

Compared to the adult courts, the youth court has a structure and format that **7.28**
is better suited to the needs of young defendants; and where cases involve young

---

[19] CYPA 1933 s. 34A.
[20] *Youth Court Bench Book.*

witnesses, the youth court's less formal and more supportive environment is likely to be of benefit to them also. Trials in the youth court take place far sooner than ones in the Crown Court and on a fixed date, and the atmosphere, procedures, and layout of the court are more informal. The specialist nature of the tribunal and the ability of the court to adapt its procedures to ensure the effective participation of a vulnerable defendant was considered in *R(TP) v West London Youth Court*.[21] The case involved a 15-year-old defendant with a mental age which was assessed at 8 years. The specialist nature of the youth court was held to be essential in enabling a fair trial to take place.

7.29 The question of ensuring a fair trial for young and vulnerable children was considered by the European Court of Human Rights in *V v UK, T v UK*.[22] The court observed that in the case of a child it is essential that he or she is dealt with in a manner which takes account of age, level of maturity, and intellectual and emotional capacities. Steps must be taken to promote the child's ability to understand and participate in the proceedings, including conducting the hearing in such a way so as to reduce as far as possible feelings of intimidation and inhibition. The importance of the youth court as a specialist tribunal was further emphasized in *SC v UK*.[23] Since the early twenty-first century, the courts have, to a much greater extent, acknowledged the needs of vulnerable witnesses and defendants. The courts' duties are set out in detail in Crim PD I 3D-G. See further Chapters 9, 'Case Management', 10, 'Special Measures', and 13, 'Trial Management: The Judge's Role'.

7.30 In *R(TP) v West London Youth Court*, the High Court approved the minimum requirements for a fair trial which had been adopted by the district judge dealing with the case in the youth court. They were:

1. the defendant had to understand what he is said to have done wrong;
2. the court had to be satisfied that the defendant when he had done wrong by act or omission had the means of knowing that was wrong;
3. he had to understand what, if any, defences were available to him;
4. he had to have a reasonable opportunity to make relevant representations if he wished; and
5. he had to have the opportunity to consider what representations he wished to make once he had understood the issues involved.

Therefore, he had to be able to give proper instructions and to participate by way of providing answers to questions and suggesting questions to his lawyers in the circumstances of the trial as they arose. The case involved a defendant aged 15 with a mental age of 8. It was crucial that the tribunal hearing the case, in this

---

[21] [2005] EWHC 2583 (Admin).
[22] [2000] 30 EHRR 121.
[23] [2005] 40 EHRR 226.

case a youth court, was able to adapt its procedures so that the defendant could effectively participate in the proceedings.

If a defendant is particularly vulnerable (not just because of his or her age), this **7.31** should be drawn to the court's attention at the first hearing so that the court can further adapt its procedures to ensure that the young defendant understands what is happening, using specialist information if appropriate.

(e) Fitness to plead, effective participation, and abuse of process

As discussed in Chapter 5, the fitness to plead procedure that applies in the **7.32** Crown Court has no equivalent in the adult magistrates' and youth courts. The difficulties of dealing with a young defendant aged 12 with learning difficulties and mental health problems were discussed in *R(P) v Barking Youth Court*.[24] The High Court confirmed that the procedures set out in s. 37(3) of the Mental Health Act 1983 (MHA 1983) and s. 11(1) of the Powers of Criminal Courts (Sentencing) Act 2000 would apply in this situation. The court has the power to make 'findings of fact in relation to the act or omissions' of a person charged with a criminal offence, without convicting them. The court then has power to make a hospital order under MHA 1983 if appropriate. Difficulties arise with this procedure as young defendants are rarely recommended to be appropriately dealt with by way of a hospital order by a psychiatrist. In the authors' view, the *Barking Youth Court* case needs to be considered in the light of subsequent decisions which have dealt directly with the issues of effective participation of the defendant and the right to a fair trial. In *CPS v P*,[25] the court was concerned with a young defendant against whom proceedings in the Crown Court had been previously stayed on the basis of medical reports dealing with his intellectual functioning and capacity. The court stated that:

(i) A previous finding that a person is unfit to plead does not make it an abuse of process to try them for subsequent criminal acts. The issue of a child's ability to effectively participate must be decided afresh.

(ii) Where the court is to proceed to decide whether the defendant did the acts alleged, the proceedings are not a criminal trial.

(iii) The court may proceed to decide the facts at any stage. It may decide to do so before hearing any evidence or it may stop the criminal procedure and switch to the fact-finding procedure at any stage.

(iv) The district judge should not have stayed the proceedings at the outset as he did, without considering the alternative of allowing the trial to proceed while keeping the [defendant's] situation under constant review.

---

[24] [2002] EWHC 734 (Admin).
[25] [2007] EWHC 946 (Admin).

(v)   If the court proceeds with fact-finding only, the fact that the defendant does not or cannot take any part in the proceedings does not render them unfair or in any way improper; the defendant's Article 6 rights are not engaged by that process.[26]

7.33   The court also stated that there would be a very small number of cases where it would be right to stay the proceedings at the outset. This would only be where the child was clearly so severely impaired as to be unable to participate in the trial and where there is no useful purpose in finding the facts.

(f) Reporting restrictions

7.34   Proceedings involving children and young people are a statutory exception to the principle of open justice which requires that justice should be administered in public.

7.35   The recently revised provisions apply automatically in the youth court and there is no need to make any specific direction. The prohibition on publication of any information that is likely to lead to the identification of any child or young person in the proceedings (defendant, complainant, or witness) is automatic and the wide definition of communication to the public at large or any section of the public includes publication online.[27] Applications to lift reporting restrictions on sentence require particular care and there is a body of case law providing guidance.[28] There is also provision for the imposition of a lifetime reporting restriction in certain limited circumstances.[29]

7.36   Children and young persons who are defendants, complainants, or other witnesses in the adult magistrates' and Crown Courts do not have the protection of automatic anonymity and the court must make a specific direction.[30] (See further Chapter 13, 'Trial Management: The Judge's Role'.) Such orders are made at the first hearing of a case (which will be prior to the sending of the case to the Crown Court) and the order will remain in force until the child or young person reaches the age of 18, or until further order. The case law, which applied to previous and very similar legislation,[31] will, it is anticipated, apply equally to the current provisions.[32]

---

[26]   ibid. at [61] per Smith LJ.
[27]   Children and Young Persons Act 1933 s. 49 (as amended by Youth Justice and Criminal Evidence Act 1999 (YJCEA 1999) Sch. 2 para. 3).
[28]   e.g. *McTerry v Teesdale and Wear Valley* (2000) 164 JP 355.
[29]   YJCEA 1999 s. 45A.
[30]   ibid. s. 45.
[31]   Children and Young Persons Act 1933 s. 39.
[32]   See, e.g.: *R(Y) v Aylesbury Crown Court* [2012] EWHC 1140 (Admin); and the guidance in 'Reporting Restrictions in Criminal Courts' (Judicial College, June 2015).

F. Allocation of Cases—Where Will the Case Be Heard?

The CPS will be expected to have served the initial details of the prosecution case **7.37**
(IDPC) in advance or to have it available for the defence representative on the
day of the first hearing. There is an expectation that progress will be made at the
first hearing.

MCA 1980 s. 24(1) sets out the presumption that defendants under the age of 18 **7.38**
charged with an indictable offence will, with certain limited exceptions, be tried
summarily in the youth court. The procedure for allocation of cases is set out in
the Crime and Disorder Act 1998 ss 51 and 51A.

A young defendant *must* be sent to the Crown Court if charged with any of the **7.39**
following:

1. homicide;
2. certain firearms offences, to which the statutory minimum sentence provisions may apply;
3. where notice has been served in relation to complex fraud cases;
4. where notice has been served in relation to certain offences relating to children;
5. where the defendant is charged with a specified offence under CJA 2003
   s. 224 and, if found guilty, the criteria for an extended sentence under s. 226B
   would be made out.[33]

Where the case is one that must be sent to the Crown Court, no plea is taken.

A young defendant *may* be sent to the Crown Court where either: **7.40**

1. the defendant is jointly charged with an indictable offence with an adult who
   has been or is being sent to the Crown Court and the youth court decides that
   the cases should be kept together in the interests of justice;[34] or
2. the offence may be a 'grave crime'.

(a) Youths jointly charged with adults

Most of the young defendants who appear in the adult magistrates' court and the **7.41**
Crown Court are jointly charged with an adult defendant. The statutory regime
as to the plea before venue procedure and allocation decision in these circumstances is set out in the Magistrates' Courts Act 1980 ss 24 and 24A and the
Crime and Disorder Act 1998 ss 51 and 51A. The order in which pleas are taken
and the allocation decision is made depends on the nature of the charges faced.

---

[33] Crime and Disorder Act 1998 s. 51A(2), (3)(a) and (c), and (12).
[34] ibid. s. 51(7).

An adult may be charged with an indictable only offence, such as robbery, which has to tried in Crown Court. The youth could be tried in the youth court. A plea is taken from the youth and the court must undertake the 'grave crime' decision before considering whether the 'interests of justice test' applies. In some circumstances, the decision to send a youth facing an offence for which a sentence under PCC(S)A s. 91 is thought likely can mean that an adult co-defendant will be sent to the Crown Court for trial alongside the youth defendant.[35]

7.42 In considering whether a youth should be sent to the Crown Court for trial alongside an adult, the Sentencing Council's Allocation Guideline suggests that the factors to be taken into account could include:

- whether separate trials will cause injustice to the case as a whole;
- the age of the youth (the younger the defendant, the greater the desirability that he or she be tried in the youth court);
- the age gap between the young defendant and the adult (a substantial gap in age militates in favour of the youth being tried in the youth court);
- the lack of maturity of the youth;
- the relative culpability of the youth compared with the adult, and whether the alleged role played by the youth was minor;
- the lack of previous convictions recorded against the youth.[36]

The guideline also states that the court should bear in mind the power of the youth court to commit to the Crown Court for sentence following a trial.

7.43 Where an adult and a youth are jointly charged with an offence which can only be dealt with summarily, there is no power to separate the youth from the adult and they will be tried together in the adult magistrates' court. The youth may be remitted to the youth court for sentence following a guilty plea or finding of guilt.[37]

(b) 'Grave crime' decision

7.44 If a young defendant faces a charge which, in the case of an adult would carry up to 14 years' imprisonment or is charged with a sexual offence as set out in PCC(S) A 2000 s. 91,[38] the court must decide whether it ought to be possible to impose a sentence substantially greater than can be imposed by the youth court, and therefore to send the case to the Crown Court for trial.

Where a charge may fall within the provisions of PCC(S)A s. 91, the procedure is governed by MCA 1980 s. 24A and Crim PR 9.13 and must be carried out

---

[35] CDA 1998 s. 51A(6).
[36] Sentencing Council, Allocation Guideline, March 2016. See <https://www.sentencingcouncil.org.uk/wp-content/uploads/Allocation_Guideline_2015.pdf> accessed 25 April 2017.
[37] PCC(S)A 2000 s. 8.
[38] Under the Sexual Offences Act 2003 ss 3, 13, 25, or 26.

in the presence of the defendant (save in circumstances where the defendant is very disruptive).[39] The charge must be read to the defendant and the court must explain that he may say whether he is going to plead guilty or not guilty. In the case of a 'grave crime' or a 'specified offence' under CJA 2003,[40] he or she must also be warned that he or she could be committed to the Crown Court for sentence after a guilty plea or after conviction at trial. If the defendant pleads guilty, the court goes on to consider where the defendant should be sentenced.

(c) When to commit to the Crown Court for sentence

The youth court may commit the defendant for sentence if it is of the opinion that the offence or the combination of the offence and one or more offences associated with it was such that the Crown Court should have power to deal with the defendant by imposing a sentence under the Powers of Criminal Courts (Sentencing) Act 2000 (PCC(S)A 2000) s. 91.[41] As the youth court has powers of sentence extending up to the imposition of a twenty-four-month Detention and Training Order, a case will only be sent to the Crown Court for sentence if the court is of the view that its powers of sentence are insufficient. The court will obtain a report from the Youth Offending Service and list the matter for sentence. This also applies to offences for which extended detention[42] may be appropriate. The decision as to whether the case should be committed for sentence is unlikely to be taken without pre-sentence reports in which the offence and the background of the offender can be fully explored. The case law referred to in paragraphs 7.47 and 7.48 below will be relevant to this decision. The court has power to commit for sentence if a guilty plea is entered at any time during the proceedings or if there is a finding of guilt at trial.[43]

7.45

For further discussion on sentencing powers, see section I below, and more generally, at Chapter 15, 'Sentencing'.

7.46

(d) When to commit to the Crown Court for trial

If a not guilty plea is entered or no indication is given to the court by the defendant, then the court must consider where the case should be tried. The criterion is 'ought it be possible to sentence the accused to detention under section 91(3) of the PCCSA 2000 for this alleged offence'?[44] The criterion has been considered in a number of High Court decisions. The decision with arguably the most far-reaching consequences was the judgment of Leveson J in *R (H) v Southampton*

7.47

---

[39] Magistrates' Courts Act 1980 s. 24B.
[40] Sch. 15, which sets out the offences for which an extended sentence may be imposed.
[41] PCC(S)A 2000 s. 3B.
[42] ibid. ss 224 and 3C.
[43] PCC(S)A 2000 s. 3B.
[44] Crime and Disorder Act 1998 s. 51A(3)(b) and Magistrates' Courts Act 1980 s. 24A.

Youth Court,[45] in which the specialist nature of the youth court was emphasized: 'it is the court which is best designed to meet their specific needs'.[46] The
court also stated that cases should only be sent to the Crown Court where there
was a 'real prospect'[47] of a sentence under s. 91 or there is 'some other unusual
feature of the case' which justifies the declining of jurisdiction. The court made
it clear that:

> It is the policy of the legislature that generally speaking, first-time offenders aged 12
> to 14 and all offenders under 12 should not be detained in custody … the excep-
> tional power to detain for grave offences should not be used to water down the general
> principle.[48]

This and subsequent cases have led to increasingly serious cases being tried in the
youth court.

7.48   There have been a number of decisions on allocation since *Southampton Youth Court*.
In *CPS v Newcastle Youth Court*,[49] the court discouraged any attempts by the youth
court to predict the actual sentence and emphasized the need to consider whether
there was a real prospect that the case may attract a sentence to which s. 91 would
apply. In *CPS v South Tyneside Youth Court*,[50] it was recognized that the youth court
would frequently have only limited information about the offence available at the
allocation hearing, with the result that the 'real prospect' test would not be met.
The likelihood of cases clearly satisfying this test at an early hearing was probably
rare and the youth court should be ready to use its power to commit for sentence,
'when the court has determined the full circumstances of the offence and has a far
greater understanding of the position of the offender'.[51] The power of the youth
court to commit for sentence following a finding of guilt at trial was, for a period
of time, removed with the introduction of the 'plea before venue procedure' of the
Magistrates' Courts Act 1980 s. 24A[52] and has since been restored by s. 53 of the
Criminal Justice and Courts Act 2015.[53]

7.49   In deciding whether the youth court should retain jurisdiction, the court will
also consider the nature of the evidence to be heard, any previous convictions
of the defendant, and any age-specific sentencing guidelines. Where there is no
age-specific sentencing guideline, the court will have to consider the adult guideline. The court may consider 'a sentence broadly within the region of half to

---

[45] [2004] EWHC 2912 (Admin); [2005] 2 Cr App R (S).
[46] ibid. at [33].
[47] ibid. at [35].
[48] Per Leveson J at [34].
[49] [2010] EWHC 2773 (Admin).
[50] [2015] EWHC 1455 (Admin).
[51] ibid.
[52] November 2012.
[53] In force 13 April 2015.

two-thirds'[54] of that which would have been identified for an adult offender for those aged 15 to 17 years and allow a greater reduction for those aged under 15. 'In most cases when considering the appropriate reduction from the adult sentence the emotional and developmental age and maturity of the child or young person is of at least equal importance as their chronological age.'[55]

(i) Extended sentences/dangerousness

Where a young defendant is facing a charge which is a 'specified offence' as set **7.50** out in CJA 2003 Sch. 15 and it appears to the court that the defendant may satisfy the criteria for extended detention under s. 226B of the Act, he or she should be sent to the Crown Court without a plea being taken.[56] This means that the court would expect a custodial sentence of at least four years to be imposed. However, the court would still have power to commit for sentence under the Powers of the Criminal Courts (Sentencing) Act 2000 s. 3C following conviction for such a sentence to be considered if the case had been retained in the youth court for trial.

There has been helpful judicial guidance on this issue, and in *CPS v Lang*,[57] the **7.51** Court of Appeal set out the kind of information, including a detailed history of previous convictions, which would be required before an informed decision could be taken. In *CPS v South East Surrey Youth Court*,[58] the suitability of the youth court for trial of youth cases was emphasized and courts were encouraged to delay any decision on the question of an extended sentence until detailed reports were obtained following conviction, in most cases.

(ii) Serious sexual offences

A particularly difficult decision for the court is whether cases involving serious **7.52** sexual offences such as rape and assault by penetration should be tried in the Crown Court or the youth court. The most serious sexual offences, including rape, are increasingly tried in the youth court. A protocol applies to the allocation decision and trial process in such cases. Annex 2 of Crim PD sets out the procedure to be applied in the youth court in all cases involving sexual allegations 'which are capable of being sent for trial at the Crown Court under the grave crime provisions'. Among offences covered by this procedure are allegations of sexual touching under the Sexual Offences Act 2003 s. 3.

Paragraph 2 of Crim PD Annex 2 sets out that the Crim PD applies to all cases **7.53** involving such charges, irrespective of the gravity of the allegation, the age of the

---

[54] 'Overarching Principles: Sentencing Children and Young People', para. 6.46.
[55] ibid.
[56] Crime and Disorder Act 1998 ss 51A(2) and 3(d).
[57] [2005] EWCA Crim 2864.
[58] [2005] EWHC 2929 (Admin).

defendant, and/or the history of the defendant. The procedure to be followed is set out at paragraph 6 onwards of Crim PD XIII Annex 2. The test set out is that 'a youth must be tried summarily unless charged with such a grave crime that long term detention is a realistic possibility or that one of the other exceptions to this presumption arises'.[59]

7.54 Paragraph 7 sets out the expectation that wherever possible such cases should be listed before an authorized district judge to decide on the 'grave crime' issue. If jurisdiction is retained and the activity involved actual, or attempted, penetrative activity, the case must be tried by an authorized district judge (magistrates' court). In other cases, the authorized district judge should decide whether the case is so serious that it must be tried by an authorized district judge or whether the case could be heard by any other district judge or a youth court bench.

Serious sex cases are reserved to certain district judges (magistrates' courts) who have been selected, trained, and authorized. At the end of the trial, the judge can retain the case for sentence or commit if the judge considers that his or her powers are insufficient in the circumstances of the case.

7.55 In reality, these cases may come into the court list with very little warning and then Crim PD Annex 2 paragraph 8 applies so that any district judge or bench of magistrates can consider the issue of allocation. If jurisdiction is retained, then the case papers and a note of the representations made should be shown to an authorized district judge to consider whether the trial should be heard by an authorized district judge. It is often preferable to adjourn the case for an authorized judge to deal with the allocation decision. If the decision is made that the case must be tried by an authorized district judge, then any further hearings should be heard by such a judge.

7.56 There are a number of authorities, referred to in paragraphs 7.47 and 7.48 above, where allocation has been considered by the Divisional Court. The view of the senior courts is that children are best tried in the youth court wherever possible. The new offence-specific guideline for sexual offences will be applicable in the allocation decision.[60]

G. Bail

(a) Grant of bail

7.57 The majority of young defendants appear before the youth court having been bailed by the police to attend court, either with or without conditions on their

---

[59] See discussion at paragraphs 7.47–7.49 above.
[60] Sexual Offences Guideline contained within Sentencing Children and Young People—Sentencing Council—1 June 2017.

bail. Some defendants attend in response to postal requisitions or summonses and therefore attend without being on bail. Some defendants will appear before the court having been refused bail by the police on charge, or having failed to appear at court on an earlier date and having been arrested on a warrant.

The Bail Act 1976 applies to young defendants in almost the same terms as it does **7.58** to adults. However, there are additional requirements, considered below, which are in place in recognition of the desirability of restricting the remand of young people to a custodial environment to only those who cannot be kept within the community.

(i) YOT assessment and bail conditions

The YOT will undertake an assessment of every young person who is not bailed **7.59** by the police when they are brought to court. This assessment must be undertaken before the case is brought into court. It will include information already held by the YOT, where appropriate, as well as assessments of risk factors for the defendant if remanded into custody and the support which may be available both within the family and from elsewhere. The YOT may be able to offer bail support or a bail intensive surveillance and support package (ISSP) to assist the court in its decision and make additional provision for conditions which could be attached to bail to increase the confidence of the court in answering the objections made by the Crown. YOTs are under a statutory duty to provide support for children and young persons remanded or committed on bail while awaiting trial or sentence.[61]

Most schemes aim to help the defendants on the programme to comply with **7.60** their conditions of bail and to provide constructive activities to occupy their time and lessen the risk of further offending. The contents of bail support programmes vary across the country, but may include: regular reporting to the youth offending team; monitored attendance at youth activities; monitoring of school attendance; programmes aimed at re-introducing the young defendant to school or to arrange specific educational provision; assistance with arranging training or finding employment; work with families to resolve conflicts and to ensure a continuing home base for the young defendant and to involve the parents in taking more responsibility for their children's behaviour; and placements with volunteers during the evening and weekends.

The ISSP programme may include: any of the activities which might form part of **7.61** bail support, as well as electronic tagging and voice verification; tracking of the young offender by YOT staff; monitoring of young offenders by police; literacy and numeracy programmes; work with families, as well as offending behaviour

---

[61] CDA 1998 s. 38(4)(c).

workshops/cognitive behavioural therapy. These conditions normally involve at least twenty-five hours of activities each week.

7.62 YOTs will only advise courts to consider the option of a bail ISSP where: the defendant fits the criteria for an ISSP; they are not considered to pose an unacceptable risk to the community if placed on an ISSP; the current offence before the court is of sufficient gravity for the court to be considering a custodial remand; and there is a place available.

7.63 The other bail conditions which can be imposed are the same as those which apply to an adult, save that the restriction of electronic monitoring of a curfew requirement is specifically controlled:

(1) A court shall not impose electronic monitoring requirements on a child or young person unless each of the following conditions is met.
(2) The first condition is that the child or young person has attained the age of 12 years.
(3) The second condition is that—
   (a) the child or young person is defendant is charged with or has been convicted of a violent or sexual offence, or an offence punishable in the case of an adult with imprisonment for a term of fourteen years of more; or
   (b) he is charged with or has been convicted of one or more imprisonable offences which, together with any other imprisonable offences of which he has been convicted in any proceedings—
      (i) amount, or
      (ii) would, if he were convicted of the offence with which he is charged, amount, to a recent history of repeatedly committing imprisonable offences while remanded on bail or to local authority accommodation.
(4) The third condition is that the court is satisfied that the necessary provision for dealing with the person concerned can be made under arrangements for the electronic monitoring of persons released on bail that are currently available in each local justice area which is a relevant area.
(5) The fourth condition is that a youth offending team has informed the court that in its opinion the imposition of electronic monitoring requirements will be suitable in the case of the child or young person.[62]

7.64 The legislative restrictions mean that an allegation of serious offending or a substantial offending history must be present before such a restriction of liberty can be imposed. Any offer by the YOT to provide the resource-intensive bail ISSP is also likely to be restricted to such cases.

(b) Refusal of bail

7.65 If bail is refused under the Bail Act, the provisions of the Legal Aid Sentencing and Punishment of Offenders Act 2012 (LASPO 2012)[63] apply to substantially

---

[62] Bail Act 1976 s. 3AA as amended.
[63] LASPO 2012 ss 91–107.

restrict the circumstances under which a custodial remand can be made. It becomes a measure of last resort. The refusal of bail will mean that the court must go on to make a further decision as to whether to remand the defendant into the care of the local authority or whether to remand to youth detention accommodation.

The refusal of bail for a youth triggers an additional set of provisions which **7.66** control the circumstances under which a custodial remand to youth detention accommodation can be made. Where a court deals with a child or young person charged with or convicted of an offence and the child is not released on bail, the court must remand the child to local authority accommodation.[64] The only alternative is a remand to youth detention accommodation where certain conditions are met.[65] Remands to police detention are restricted to twenty-four hours, as opposed to three days for an adult.[66]

(i) Remand to local authority accommodation

A remand to local authority accommodation is a remand to accommodation pro- **7.67** vided by or on behalf of a local authority and the court must designate the local authority which is to receive the child or young person. Where a child is already being looked after, it will be that authority. In any other case, the court should designate the local authority where it appears that the child habitually resides or where the offence was committed.[67] The local authority has discretion to place a defendant at home, although the court can impose requirements stipulating that the child must not be placed with a named person.[68] The court may also impose conditions on remands to local authority accommodation and may require the defendant to comply with any conditions that could be imposed under the Bail Act 1976[69] if the child were then being granted bail. These conditions include electronic tagging, which is subject to the similar restrictions to those which apply to tagging as a condition of bail.[70] It is essential that the court consult with the local authority (which in practice is likely to be with the assistance of the YOT).[71]

(ii) Youth detention accommodation (a custodial remand)

A court may only remand to youth detention accommodation if *either* of the **7.68** following sets of remand conditions are satisfied.

---

[64] ibid. s. 92.
[65] ibid. s. 102, subject to ss 98 and 99.
[66] Magistrates' Courts Act 1980 s. 128(7).
[67] LASPO 2012 s. 92.
[68] By ibid. s. 93(3).
[69] s. 3(6).
[70] LASPO 2012 s. 94.
[71] ibid. s. 92.

The first set of conditions are:

(a) the defendant must have reached the age of 12,
(b) the offence with which the defendant is charged is:
  (i) a violent or sexual offence, or
  (ii) is an offence punishable in the case of an adult with imprisonment for a term of 14 years or more.
(c) The court is of the opinion, after considering all the options for the remand of the child, that only remanding the child to youth detention accommodation would be adequate:
  (i) to protect the public from death or serious personal injury (whether physical or psychological) occasioned by further offences committed by the child, or
  (ii) to prevent the commission by the child of imprisonable offences.[72]

7.69 The alternative second set of conditions are:

(a) the defendant must have reached the age of 12;
(b) it appears to the court that there is a real prospect that the defendant will be sentenced to a custodial sentence for the offence before the court or one or more of those offences;
(c) the defendant is before the court charged with at least one imprisonable offence;
(d) the 'history condition' is fulfilled; this requires that either:
  (i) the child has a recent history of absconding while subject to a custodial remand and the current offence is alleged to be or has been found to have been committed while the child was remanded to local authority accommodation or youth detention accommodation; or
  (ii) the current offence, together with any other imprisonable offences of which the child has been convicted in any proceedings, amount or would, if the child were convicted of that offence or those offences, amount to a recent history of committing imprisonable offences while on bail or subject to a custodial remand.
(e) Additionally the court must be of the opinion, after considering all the options for the remand of the child, that only remanding the youth defendant to youth detention accommodation would be adequate:
  (i) to protect the public from death or serious personal injury (whether physical or psychological) occasioned by further offences committed by him, *or*
  (ii) to prevent the commission by him of imprisonable offences.[73]

The youth defendant must be legally represented save in limited circumstances.[74]

---

[72] ibid. s. 98.
[73] ibid. s. 99.
[74] ibid. s. 100(5) and (6).

The real prospect of custodial sentence in practice means that a detention and **7.70** training order of at least four months or more is a real prospect, as this is the minimum custodial sentence to which a young defendant can be made subject.[75]

(iii)   Placement in youth detention accommodation

A remand to youth detention accommodation may result in the defendant being **7.71** placed in a secure children's home, a secure training centre, a young offender institution, or accommodation 'of a description for the time being specified'.[76]

The placement decision is the responsibility of the Ministry of Justice, but day- **7.72** to-day management is, at the time of writing, delegated to the YJB. This is likely to change as a result of recent government policy decisions. The provisions which required the court to consider whether a young defendant was 'vulnerable' in relation to the placement decision are no longer in force. The placement deci-sion will be an individual exercise based substantially on the *Asset* assessment.[77] A child who is remanded to youth detention accommodation is to be treated as a child who is looked after by the designated local authority.[78]

H.   Trial in the Youth Court

If the youth has pleaded not guilty and the youth court has retained the case for **7.73** trial, a trial date will be fixed. When listing for trial, all parties and the court complete the Case Management Form in accordance with the Crim PR. This should assist in identifying the further directions which may be needed. The pro-cedure is the same as in the adult magistrates' court, save that the issues of special measures for any child witnesses and additional adaptations to the trial process that may be necessary to ensure the effective participation of the defendant are more likely to arise.

(a)   Young witness protocol

There are few statistics available relating to the age of witnesses who appear in **7.74** the courts, but it is generally thought that there is a larger proportion of young witnesses in the youth court than there is in the adult court. The complainants in allegations brought against children and young people are most likely to be other children and young people. The 'Young Witness Protocol' signed up to by the criminal justice agencies on 19 January 2015 is an attempt to expedite cases

---

[75] PCC(S)A 2000 s. 101.
[76] LASPO 2012 s. 102 and PCC(S)A 2000 s. 107.
[77] See paragraph 7.17.
[78] LASPO 2012 s. 104(1).

involving witnesses under the age of 10.[79] It recognizes that very young children are particularly liable to forget the details of what they say happened to them over a relatively short period of time. It applies to young witnesses who have provided either a statement or, as is more likely these days, an ABE interview. From the investigation stage, the case will be identified as one falling under the protocol and the police should be alert to the need for an intermediary. Investigators should be alert to the need for early consultation with the CPS. At charge, the police should set out clearly on the MG2 and MG6 that the case is a protocol one.

7.75 The CPS should ensure their charging advice is provided within seven days of receiving the file and contains an Action Plan with dates agreed with the police. At this stage, the CPS should be considering what supporting evidence is required should there be an application for Special Measures. Where a Full Code Test will be applied, the CPS should seek to ensure that the time period between first complaint and charge does not exceed eight weeks (or four weeks where a Threshold Test is applied). Generally, the police and CPS should try to keep the time taken for investigations to a minimum.

7.76 In terms of the next steps taken, the first appearance at the magistrates' court should be within seven days of charge and if it is a case to be heard by a district judge, the first hearing can be adjourned to another date, within the seven-day period, if at all possible.

7.77 In bail cases, the protocol demands that the file is provided to the CPS no later than forty-eight hours before the first hearing in the magistrates' court or youth court. The file should contain four copies of each video-recorded interview with the complainant or witness, one of which will be for the defence with the IDPC. The police are to notify any intermediary of the date for their report.

Within three weeks of the first hearing, the police will provide the CPS with an Upgrade File whether the defendant is on bail or in custody. The CPS will serve its case within thirty-five days of the initial hearing, although in the youth court the expectation is that it will be done considerably sooner than that.

7.78 In the youth court, the file will be marked to highlight that the case is a protocol one and the prosecutor should draw this to the attention of the court. As at all first hearings, a plea will be entered and case management will take place, including the consideration of Special Measures. In the youth court, the trial will be fixed for a date no more than eight weeks ahead. The court should consider whether a case management hearing/ground rules hearing should take place, which will be held a minimum of fourteen days before the trial.

---

[79] See <http://www.judiciary.gov.uk/wp-content/uploads/2015/03/police-cps-hmcts-ywi-protocol.pdf> accessed 16 March 2017.

(b) Special measures

The principle which applies to adult witnesses is whether the quality of the evi- **7.79**
dence to be given by the witness will be diminished without the making of a
Special Measures Direction, but for witnesses under the age of 18 there is a legislative expectation that special measures will apply and formal written applications are unlikely to be necessary.

Cross-examination will take place by way of live link so that the witness does not **7.80**
enter the courtroom or face the defendant. The advocate will be expected to comply with The Advocate's Gateway (2015), Toolkit 6 of which gives best practice
guidance to advocates on their approach to young witnesses and defendants.

The defendant may be eligible to give evidence by way of a live link if the provi- **7.81**
sions of YJCEA 1999 s. 33A apply. A defendant under the age of 18 whose ability to participate effectively in the proceedings as a witness giving oral evidence
in court is compromised by his or her level of intellectual functioning and who
would be enabled to participate more effectively if allowed to do so by way of live
link would make an application to do so.[80] In most cases, the young defendant
gives evidence in court and live link is rarely used by defendants, although it is
frequently used by young witnesses. All youth courts have live-link facilities of a
similar standard to that in the Crown Court.

There is no obligation to appoint an intermediary for a child; nor, since amend- **7.82**
ments made to the Crim PD in March 2016, is there any longer a presumption
that a young witness or defendant will require an intermediary.

Crim PD 3F.26 states that an intermediary assessment 'should be considered for **7.83**
witnesses and defendants under 18 who seem liable to misunderstand questions
or to experience difficulty expressing answers, including those who seem unlikely
to be able to recognise problematic questions ... and those who may be reluctant
to tell a questioner in a position of authority if they do not understand'.

However, 'in the light of the scarcity of intermediaries, the appropriateness of **7.84**
assessment must be decided with care to ensure the availability for those witnesses and defendants who are most in need. The decision should be made on
an individual basis, in the context of the circumstances of the particular case.'[81]

It is, therefore, a matter for the court: see *R v Cox*[82] and *F v Crown Prosecution* **7.85**
Service.[83] When the application is for an intermediary for a witness, the issue
for the court is whether one or more special measures 'would in its opinion, be

---

[80] Crim PR r. 29.
[81] Crim PD 3F.
[82] [2012] EWCA Crim 549.
[83] [2015] EWHC 2527 (Admin).

likely to improve the quality of evidence given by the witness', and which of those measures 'would in its opinion, be likely to maximise so far as practicable the quality of such evidence'.[84] The court would need to be satisfied that the lack of an intermediary will not cause any loss in the quality of the evidence.[85] When the application is for an intermediary for a defendant, the issue is whether the court can be satisfied that the lack of an intermediary will not result in an unfair trial.[86] See further Chapter 11, 'Intermediaries'.

(c) Adapting the trial process

7.86 The considerations which apply to ensuring a fair trial for vulnerable adult defendants will also apply to young defendants. There will be some defendants for whom no additional provisions are necessary, aside from the more informal and accessible setting of the youth court. The ethos of the youth court recognizes that additional vulnerability may often arise due to immaturity and that this may not be related to the chronological age of the defendant. A defence representative should be able to ask the court to consider, for example, additional breaks to ensure concentration, without the need for specialist reports. In some cases, there will be information already available about the defendant from their existing educational, psychological, or mental health provision. In other cases, a further assessment of the young person may be necessary and an intermediary may be instructed. Any intermediary, psychologist, or psychiatrist instructed to prepare a report about a young defendant should have substantial experience in dealing with children and adolescents. The provisions relating to ground rules hearings and the use of The Advocate's Gateway Toolkits, as examined in Chapter 12, 'Ground Rules Hearings', apply in the youth court.

7.87 However, as in the youth court special measures and other adaptations to language and procedure are commonplace and everyday, the court is unlikely to delay the arrangements for a trial date while reports are obtained and directions as to the future management of the case will be made on trial fixing, usually at the first hearing.

I. Sentencing

7.88 The complex sentencing provisions relating to children and young people are dealt with in full in Chapter 15 of this book. The Human Rights Act 1998 embodied the European Convention on Human Rights in domestic legislation and there

---

[84] YJCEA 1999 s. 19(2) and (b)(i).
[85] *F v Crown Prosecution Service.*
[86] *AS, R (on the application of) v Great Yarmouth Youth Court* [2011] EWHC 2059.

have been a number of important decisions affecting the way in which young people are tried. In *Nortier v Netherlands*,[87] it was stated that:

> ... minors are as entitled to the same protection of their fundamental rights as adults ... but the developing state of their personality—and consequently their limited social responsibility—should be taken into account in applying Article 6 of the Convention.

The Sentencing Council Guideline states that:

> Domestic and international laws dictate that a custodial sentence should always be a measure of last resort for children and young people ... It is important to avoid 'criminalising' children and young people unnecessarily; the primary purpose of the youth justice system is to encourage [them] to take responsibility for their own actions and promote re-integration into society rather than to punish.[88]

With very few offence-specific exceptions, the powers of the court depend on the age of the defendant on the date of the finding of guilt or plea of guilt. If a defendant crosses a significant threshold between the date of the offence and the date of the conviction, the starting point is the sentence the defendant would have been likely to receive at the date of the offence.[89]

7.89 The new definitive guideline 'Overarching Principles: Sentencing Children and Young People' makes it clear that it will be rare for a court to pass a sentence which is more severe than the maximum it could have passed at the time of the offence, even when a defendant has subsequently reached 18 years of age, but a sentence at or close to the maximum may be appropriate.[90]

7.90 The range of available sentences varies greatly according to age at the date of the conviction. In particular, there are restrictions on custodial sentences also dependent on age,[91] and for a first-time offender who pleads guilty to an offence which is imprisonable in the case of an adult, the court is restricted to the making of a referral order or the imposition of a custodial sentence. The court may impose absolute or conditional discharges, fines, compensation orders, referral orders, reparation orders, youth rehabilitation orders, or custodial sentences of up to twenty-four months' detention and training (in contrast to the adult magistrates' court, which has a maximum power of six months' imprisonment per offence, with a total of twelve months in some circumstances). The court has additional sentencing powers as an alternative to a custodial sentence, which include fostering and ISSPs. The sentences are accompanied by a variety of ancillary orders. The sentencing court must consider whether a parenting order should be made.

[87] (1993) 17 EHRR 273.
[88] 'Overarching Principles: Sententencing Children and Young People', paras 1.3 and 1.4.
[89] *R v Ghafoor* [2002] EWCA Crim 1857.
[90] ibid. at [6.3].
[91] Children aged 10 and 11 cannot receive a custodial sentence in the youth court and those aged 12, 13, and 14 only if they are 'persistent' offenders.

For decisions on when to commit to the Crown Court for sentence, see paragraph 7.45 above.

J. Youths in the Crown Court

7.91 Legislation (including the reintroduction of the power to commit for sentence after trial in the youth court)[92] and its interpretation by the courts should mean that the occasions on which children and young people appear in the Crown Court will be few in number. Those that do are likely to face the most serious of allegations. There will also be some young defendants who appear in the Crown Court because it has been decided that it is in the interests of justice that they be tried jointly with an adult.[93]

7.92 The provisions of the Crime and Disorder Act 1998 Sch. 3 which allow the Crown Court to deal with plea and venue for an adult defendant where there are changes of charge after sending for trial do not apply to youths and the provisions of paragraph 13 of the Schedule require that the defendant be remitted to the youth court to be dealt with. The Crown Court has no other power to remit a young defendant to the youth court for trial and where he or she has been sent to the Crown Court for trial alongside an adult under the provisions of the Crime and Disorder Act 1998 s. 51(7), if the adult pleads guilty, the youth must face Crown Court trial alone. This may be a significant consideration at the allocation hearing if the adult's intended plea is known.

7.93 All of the various adaptations to the trial process that might be applied to a vulnerable witness in the Crown Court should be considered for a youth defendant, although the protection of Special Measures when giving evidence does not apply to a defendant in the same way. The court can make a 'defendant's evidence direction' in accordance with the Youth and Criminal Evidence Act 1999 s. 33A and Crim PR r. 29, which would allow a young defendant to give their evidence-in-chief and to be cross-examined by way of a live link. See further Chapters 9 to 13.

7.94 On conviction, the Crown Court has the power to remit a young defendant to the youth court for sentence.[94] When considering whether to exercise this power, the court must balance the need for expertise in sentencing young offenders with the benefits of being sentenced by the court which had determined guilt. See further Chapter 15, 'Sentencing'.

---

[92] Criminal Justice and Courts Act 2015 s. 53, in force 13 April 2015.
[93] See paragraphs 7.41–7.43.
[94] PCC(S)A 2000 s. 8.

K. Conclusion

As made clear in the above discussion, the tension between the contrasting aims of   **7.95**
protecting, rehabilitating, and punishing young people who offend has long been
evident in the state's responses to children and young people who offend. A largely
separate justice system for dealing with young suspects and offenders has gradually
evolved since the mid to late nineteenth century. Today, the youth justice system
seeks to hold young offenders to account for their actions and in so doing provides
for certain punitive responses to offending. At the same time, rehabilitation is central to a system which, by statute, has the prevention of offending by children and
young people as its 'principal aim'. In line with the statutory obligation of the courts
to 'have regard to the welfare' of all children appearing before them, many aspects of
the youth justice system are designed in such a way as to recognize and address the
particular vulnerabilities of young suspects and offenders: that is, the vulnerabilities
that they have by virtue of their age alone, and the additional and often profound
needs and difficulties that many display.

Key components of the youth justice system include a heavy emphasis on the   **7.96**
diversion of young people involved in low-level offending out of the formal prosecution process. The environment and structures of the youth court, which hears
the large majority of cases involving young defendants, are deliberately less formal
and elaborate than those of adult magistrates' and Crown Courts. Multi-agency
and multi-disciplinary YOTs (or YOS) have responsibility for the local delivery
of youth justice services. YOTs assist with ensuring that sentencing decisions can
be tailored to the specific needs of the individual offenders; and the sentencing
framework for young offenders encompasses a distinctive range of penalties and
includes the expectation that, in general, young offenders will be sentenced less
severely than their adult counterparts. It is observed above that one of the most
notable features of the youth justice system in recent years has been the sharp
decline in the numbers of children and young people it is dealing with—with
first-time entrants to the system having fallen by over 80 per cent in the past ten
years, and those held in custody having fallen by over 70 per cent since the custodial population peaked in 2002.

Notwithstanding the range of specialist provision across the youth justice system,   **7.97**
questions continue to be raised about the adequacy of its responses to the vulnerabilities of children and young people in trouble with the law—especially since a
corollary of the overall reduction in numbers in the system is a higher concentration of serious and complex need among those remaining in it.[95] A general and

---

[95] See, e.g., Deloitte, 'Youth Offending Team Stocktake' (2015); and YJB, 'Youth Offending
Teams: Making the Difference for Children and Young People, Victims and Communities—
Final Report' (2015).

long-running point of contention among many penal reformers is the low age of criminal responsibility in England and Wales: at 10, this is a lower age of criminal responsibility than in almost all other European countries.[96] This means that in England and Wales the authorities must deal with a cohort of vulnerable child suspects and defendants who, elsewhere, would simply not fall within the remit of the criminal justice system.

7.98 A recent enquiry, funded by the Michael Sieff Foundation, into the operation and effectiveness of the youth court and chaired by Lord Carlile, raised a number of concerns.[97] Among them was the finding that growing numbers of children and young people are increasingly likely to appear in adult magistrates' courts, following overnight detention in police custody, because youth courts are sitting less frequently. The enquiry report pointed to the lack of engagement with court proceedings of many young defendants, who struggle to understand the language of the courtroom and the process itself, even in the relatively informal setting of the youth court, but particularly in the Crown Court. More generally, the report noted that the criminal courts lack the means to address effectively young defendants' many welfare needs; needs which arise, for example, from emotional or mental health conditions, learning disabilities, speech language and communication problems, and backgrounds of abuse and neglect.

7.99 Another concern raised by the Carlile enquiry, and also in a subsequent Bar Standards Board report on advocacy in youth proceedings,[98] was the lack of availability of specialist youth justice training for advocates in youth proceedings. Both reports recommended the introduction of a training requirement, to cover not only youth justice law, but also the welfare and communication and engagement aspects of legal practice in the youth justice system. The Bar Standards Board research also reflected on the low status accorded to the youth court within the wider criminal justice systems, one of the manifestations of which is the tendency for it to be regarded as a 'training ground' for inexperienced advocates. This low status of the youth court belies the challenges and importance of the work of advocates in the youth court, who represent some of the most vulnerable offenders to come before the courts.

---

[96] See, e.g., <http://www.halsburyslawexchange.co.uk/its-time-to-raise-the-minimum-age-of-criminal-responsibility/>; and <http://www.justforkidslaw.org/news-events/shauneen-in-the-usa-blog/shauneen-lambe-on-human-rights-day-why-the-government-should-raise-the-age-of-criminal-responsibility> both accessed 16 March 2017.

[97] Independent Parliamentarians' Inquiry into the Operation and Effectiveness of the Youth Court, Chaired by Lord Carlile of Berriew CBE QC (2014).

[98] A. Wigzell, A. Kirby, and J. Jacobson, *The Youth Proceedings Advocacy Review: Final Report* (Bar Standards Board, 2015).

Like much of the rest of the criminal justice system, the youth justice system **7.100** continues to evolve and we are aware that, at the time of writing, the youth justice system has recently been reviewed at the request of the Ministry of Justice and the government have responded to the review.[99] No legislative proposals have yet been published, although the government have indicated an intention to follow some of the proposals, particularly those relating to the reform of the secure estate.[100]

Further Reading

The Advocate's Gateway, 'Toolkit 8: Effective Participation of Young Defendants' (The Inns of Court College of Advocacy, 2017).

Ashford, M. and Redhouse, N., *Blackstone's Youth Court Handbook 2014–15* (Oxford University Press, 2013).

Bateman, T., *Children in Conflict with the Law: An Overview of Trends and Developments* (National Association of Youth Justice, 2013).

Bradley, K., 'Juvenile Delinquency and the Evolution of the British Juvenile Courts c1900–1950', *History in Focus*, Issue 14, October 2008, available at <http://www.history.ac.uk> accessed 16 March 2017.

CPS Legal Guidance, 'Youth Offenders', available at <http://www.cps.gov.uk/legal/v_to_z/youth_offenders> accessed 16 March 2017.

Judicial College, 'Equal Treatment Bench Book 2013' (Judicial College, 2013).

Sentencing Council, 'Overarching Principles: Sentencing Youths' (Sentencing Guidelines Council, 2009).

---

[99] See <https://www.gov.uk/government/uploads/system/uploads/attachment_data/file/577103/ youth- justice-review-final-report.pdf> accessed 25 April 2017.

[100] See <https://www.gov.uk/government/uploads/system/uploads/attachment_data/file/576553/youth-justice-review-government-response.pdf> accessed 25 April 2017.

8

DISCLOSURE

Tracy Ayling and Karen Robinson

A. Introduction

The statutory disclosure regime applies in all criminal proceedings in the Crown **8.01**
Court. There is no modification or enhancement to the nature or application

of the statutory regime in a case which involves a vulnerable person, be that a defendant, complainant or other witness. However, the presence of one or other such participant in a criminal trial may well mean that the disclosure exercise to be completed poses more problems in practice than might otherwise be the case.

8.02 This chapter seeks to provide an overview of the following matters:

- the development of disclosure and the origins of the Criminal Procedure and Investigations Act 1996 (CPIA 1996);
- overview of the statutory scheme of disclosure;
- case management insofar as it relates to disclosure;
- specific disclosure issues in cases involving vulnerable persons;
- failures in disclosure;
- obligations of confidentiality;
- limitations on use/disclosure of material disclosed by the prosecution.

B. Development of Disclosure in Criminal Proceedings

8.03 In *R v H*,[1] the House of Lords reviewed the principles behind, and application of, the statutory disclosure regime contained within the CPIA 1996. Lord Bingham of Cornhill set out plainly the overriding concept of that regime:

> Fairness ordinarily requires that any material held by the prosecution which weakens its case or strengthens that of the defendant, if not relied on as part of its formal case against the defendant, should be disclosed to the defence. Bitter experience has shown that miscarriages of justice may occur where such material is withheld from disclosure. The golden rule is that full disclosure of such material should be made.[2]

However, Lord Bingham was quick to observe that the process of disclosure in this jurisdiction was one which had undergone considerable evolution prior to the commencement of the CPIA.

8.04 The rule established in *R v Bryant and Dickerson*[3] is often regarded as the beginnings of the formal process for the disclosure of material which may assist a defendant in criminal proceedings. The rule established that where the prosecution had taken a statement from a person who could give material evidence but decided not to call him or her as a witness, the prosecution was under a duty to make that person available as a witness for the defence. The rule established, however, was a narrow one: the prosecution was not under the further duty of supplying the defence with a copy of the statement taken.

---

[1] [2004] 2 AC 134.
[2] *R v H* at [14] per Lord Bingham of Cornhill.
[3] [1946] 31 Cr App R 146.

Between 1946 and 1981, the common law duty of the prosecution with regard to   **8.05**
disclosure moved forward from that approach. In *Dallison v Caffery*,[4] it was held
that the prosecution had a duty to disclose to the defence the statement of any
credible witness (or call such a witness) who could speak to material facts which
tended to show the defendant's innocence. In *R v Leyland JJ, ex p. Hawthorn*,[5]
it was held that the failure to notify a defendant of the identity of two witnesses
who could give evidence in support of his case amounted to a breach of the rules
of natural justice.

Prior to 1981, the only duty on the prosecutor of disclosure of material that it did   **8.06**
not intend to rely on at trial was to make available to the defence:

1. those witnesses that he did not propose to call him or herself; and
2. any inconsistent statements made by witnesses that he or she was calling to
   give evidence.

In 1981, the then Attorney-General issued formal (although non-statutory) guidance on disclosure.[6] That Guidance was intended to complement the common
law rules on disclosure and, for the first time, provided a definition of 'unused
material' as, inter alia, 'witness statements and documents not included in the
committal bundle' and unedited versions of such items. Disclosure of material
was to be made by the prosecution if the material in question was considered
relevant, that is to say, if the unused material in the possession of the prosecution
had 'some bearing on the offence(s) charged and the surrounding circumstances
of the case.' Whether material held by the prosecution had such a bearing was left
to the judgment of the prosecution and prosecuting counsel.

In the two decades which followed, a series of appeals before the Court of   **8.07**
Appeal alleged that there had been miscarriages of justice due, in part, to failings in disclosure and, in particular, in the exercise of the prosecution's discretion in that regard. A number of appellate decisions were seriously critical of the
manner in which the prosecution had exercised its discretion under the common law rules and/or under the Guidelines. In *R v Ward*[7] (an appeal against
conviction based in part upon the non-disclosure of material matters affecting the scientific case advanced by the Crown at trial and matters relating to
Judith Ward's psychiatric condition which went to the reliability of her confessions), the court expanded the scope of the prosecution's duty of disclosure to
include disclosure of everything gathered by the prosecution in the course of
the investigation:

---

[4] [1965] 1 QB 348, at 369 per Lord Denning MR.
[5] [1979] QB 283.
[6] Attorney-General's Guidelines: Disclosure of Information to the Defence in Cases to be
Tried on Indictment [1982] 1 All ER 734.
[7] [1993] 96 Cr App R 1.

We would emphasise that 'all relevant evidence of help to the accused' is not limited to evidence which will obviously advance the accused's case. It is of help to the accused to have the opportunity of considering all the material evidence which the prosecution have gathered, and from which the prosecution have made their own selection of evidence to be led.[8]

In *R v Ward*, the Court of Appeal also held that it was for the court to determine whether particular information held by the prosecution could be withheld on the grounds of public interest immunity. The prosecution could not be judge in its own cause in that regard.[9]

8.08 In *R v Keane*,[10] the Court of Appeal provided some guidance as to what evidence might be judged to be 'material', approving the test suggested by Jowitt J in *Melvin and Dingle* (judgment 20 December 1993):

I would judge to be material in the realm of disclosure that which can be seen on a sensible appraisal by the prosecution:

(1) to be relevant or possibly relevant to an issue in the case;
(2) to raise or possibly raise a new issue whose existence is not apparent from the evidence the prosecution proposes to use;
(3) to hold out a real (as opposed to fanciful) prospect of providing a lead on evidence which goes to (1) or (2).

However, following the judgment of the Court of Appeal in *R v Ward*, police and prosecutors expressed disquiet at the move towards full prosecution disclosure, complaining that the burden upon the prosecution was excessively onerous and did not serve the ultimate aim of ensuring that the accused had a fair trial.

8.09 In 1996, the CPIA created a statutory duty of prosecution disclosure, but the test was refined, at least in part, to accommodate the issues raised by police and prosecutors.

C. Overview of the Statutory Scheme of Disclosure

(a) Outline

8.10 This section gives an overview of the CPIA disclosure regime, taking into account the Human Rights Act 1998, the Attorney General's Guidelines on Disclosure 2013[11] (hereafter 'the Guidelines'), the Judicial Protocol on the Disclosure of Unused Material in Criminal Cases 2013[12] (hereafter 'the Protocol'), and the

---

[8] ibid. at [25] per Glidewell LJ.
[9] ibid. at [27] per Glidewell LJ.
[10] [1994] 1 WLR 746, at 752 per Lord Taylor of Gosforth CJ.
[11] See <https://www.gov.uk/government/uploads/system/uploads/attachment_data/file/262994/AG_Disclosure_Guidelines_-_December_2013.pdf> accessed 20 March 2017.
[12] See <https://www.judiciary.gov.uk/wp-content/uploads/JCO/Documents/Protocols/Disclosure+Protocol.pdf> accessed 20 March 2017.

Criminal Justice Act 2003 (CJA 2003). Further assistance will be obtained from the Criminal Procedure Rules (Crim PR)[13] and the Code of Practice[14] issued under s. 23(1) of the CPIA. In accordance with Criminal Practice Direction IV (Disclosure) 15A,[15] 29 September 2015, the Code of Practice, Guidelines, and Protocol should be read together as complementary, comprehensive guidance that should be complied with.

Parts I and II CPIA, as amended by CJA 2003, seek to provide a structured **8.11** scheme for the disclosure of unused material in criminal proceedings. Part I (ss 1–21) contains provisions which regulate: the responsibilities of the parties and the court with regard to disclosure; the staged approach to disclosure (initial disclosure, defence disclosure, continual review by the prosecution); the methods of prosecution disclosure; and the nature of prosecution material to be disclosed. Part I additionally outlines consequences for faults in defence disclosure and identifies the defendant's remedy in the event of a complaint about prosecution disclosure. CJA 2003 applies to all investigations commenced on or after 4 April 2005.

Part II of the CPIA provides for a Code of Practice which regulates how rele- **8.12** vant material obtained in a criminal investigation is to be recorded, retained, and revealed to the prosecutor. At the time of writing, there are in existence two Codes which operate in parallel: the first, which applies to investigations which commenced before 19 March 2015; and the second, a revised Code, which applies to all investigations commenced after that date.[16] The revised Code implements some of the recommendations contained in the Magistrates' Court Disclosure Review (May 2014)[17] and the main revision is to implement a streamlined disclosure procedure in those summary cases that are expected to end in a guilty plea, such that a schedule of unused material need not be served in such cases.

(b) Part I of the CPIA

Under the CPIA, prosecution material must be disclosed to the defence if it is **8.13** material which might reasonably be considered capable of undermining the case for the prosecution against the accused or of assisting the case for the accused (hereafter 'the disclosure test'): see ss 3(1) and 7A(2). The prosecution is not

---

[13] See <http://www.justice.gov.uk/courts/procedure-rules/criminal/rulesmenu-2015> accessed 20 March 2017.

[14] Revised Code of Practice which applies to all investigations commenced after 19 March 2015, <https://www.gov.uk/government/uploads/system/uploads/attachment_data/file/447967/code-of-practice-approved.pdf> accessed 20 March 2017.

[15] See <https://www.judiciary.gov.uk/wp-content/uploads/2015/09/crim-pd-2015.pdf> accessed 20 March 2017.

[16] See n. 14 above.

[17] See <https://www.judiciary.gov.uk/wp-content/uploads/2014/05/Magistrates'-Court-Disclosure-Review.pdf> accessed 20 March 2017.

required to disclose material that does not fall within that description. For this purpose, the cases of the parties should be carefully analysed, to ascertain the specific facts the prosecution seek to establish and the grounds on which the charges are resisted. Neutral material need not be disclosed.[18] The disclosure of material which does not meet the disclosure test (sometimes known as 'handing the defendant the keys to the warehouse') does not comply with the statutory scheme and is considered to be an abdication of the statutory responsibility.[19]

8.14 The Guidelines make clear that in deciding whether material satisfies the disclosure test, consideration should be given, among other things, to:

(a) the use that might be made of it in cross-examination;
(b) its capacity to support submissions that could lead to:
  (i) the exclusion of evidence;
  (ii) a stay of proceedings, where the material is required to allow a proper application to be made;
  (iii) a court or tribunal finding that any public authority had acted incompatibly with the accused's rights under the ECHR;
(c) its capacity to suggest an explanation or partial explanation of the accused's actions;
(d) the capacity of the material to have to have a bearing on scientific or medical evidence in the case.

Examples of material that is likely to meet the disclosure test in any case are:

(a) any material which may point to another person, whether charged or not, having involvement in the commission of the offence;
(b) any material which may cast doubt on the reliability of a confession or admission;
(c) any material which goes to the credibility of a prosecution witness;
(d) material relating to the accused's mental or physical health, intellectual capacity, or to any ill-treatment which the accused may have suffered when in the investigator's custody.

The prosecution has an initial duty under s. 3 to make disclosure of any prosecution material that meets the disclosure test, or to provide the accused with a written statement that there is no such material. Thereafter, the prosecution remains under a duty to review the question of whether there is any prosecution material which falls to be disclosed. If there is such material, the prosecution must disclose it as soon as is reasonably practicable: see s. 7A. This duty of disclosure continues until the conclusion of the trial and persists during the currency of confiscation proceedings.[20] In the interests of justice, the prosecutor must consider disclosing

---

[18] *R v H* at [35] per Lord Bingham of Cornhill.
[19] ibid.; and the Protocol at [4] and [13]–[14].
[20] See *R v Onuigbo* [2014] Lloyds Rep FC 302.

any material which is relevant to sentence (e.g. information which might mitigate the seriousness of the offence or assist the accused to lay blame in part upon
another person).[21] Where, after the conclusion of proceedings, material comes to
light that might cast doubt upon the safety of the conviction, the prosecutor must
consider disclosure of such material.[22]

Once the prosecution has complied, or purported to comply, with its duty of ini-   **8.15**
tial disclosure under s. 3, the accused must make compulsory disclosure under
s. 5 by providing to the court and the prosecutor a defence statement. The defence
statement must set out the nature of the accused's defence, including any particular defences on which the accused intends to rely, the matters of fact on which
he or she takes issue with the prosecution, and any point of law which he or she
wishes to take: see s. 6A.

The prosecution must review the question of disclosure in the light of the defence   **8.16**
statement, and make disclosure of material which meets the test or, if it considers
that there is no such material, must give to the accused a written statement to that
effect: see s. 7A(2), (5).

Regulations made under s. 12 specify the time limits within which the defence   **8.17**
must comply with their disclosure obligations (twenty-eight days from receipt of
initial disclosure in the Crown Court).[23] By virtue of s. 13 of the CPIA, the prosecutor's response to the defence statement must be served 'as soon as is reasonably
practicable' after the accused gives the statement in question.

The responsibility for determining whether material falls to be disclosed pursuant   **8.18**
to s. 3 or 7A rests on the prosecution,[24] although the issue of disclosure under
s. 7A is subject to review by the Court under s. 8. The prosecutor is defined in
s. 2 of the Act as 'any person acting as prosecutor, whether an individual or body'.
The Code of Practice defines the prosecutor as 'the authority responsible for the
conduct, on behalf of the Crown, of criminal proceedings resulting from a specific criminal investigation'.

Material is disclosed by the prosecution giving a copy of the material to the   **8.19**
defence or, if the prosecution is of the opinion that providing a copy is not practical or desirable, by allowing the defence to inspect the material: see s. 3(3).
Disclosure need not be in the same format as the form in which the information
is held by the prosecutor. Ultimately, it is for the prosecution to determine the
appropriate manner of disclosure.[25]

---

[21] Guidelines, para. 71.
[22] ibid. para. 72.
[23] Criminal Procedure and Investigations Act 1996 (Defence Disclosure Time Limits)
Regulations 2011 (SI 2011/209), which came into force on 28 February 2011.
[24] *R v H* at [35] per Lord Bingham of Cornhill.
[25] Protocol, at [13].

8.20 If the accused has at any time reasonable cause to believe that there is prosecution material which is required by s. 7A to be disclosed to him or her and has not been, he or she may apply to the court for an order requiring the prosecutor to disclose it to him or her: see s. 8(2). Section 8 only applies where the accused has provided a defence statement and the prosecution has complied with, purported to comply, or failed to comply with its duty under s. 7A(5). There is no provision within the statutory scheme for the making of a court order in relation to the prosecutor's duty of initial disclosure under s. 3.

8.21 The statutory scheme provides that nothing must be disclosed under s. 3, 7A, or 8 to the extent that the Court, on application by the prosecutor, concludes that it is not in the public interest to disclose it and orders accordingly, or to the extent that disclosure is prohibited by s. 17 of the Regulation of Investigatory Powers Act 2000.

(c) Part II of the CPIA

8.22 The Code of Practice issued under s. 23 of the CPIA sets out the manner in which police officers are to record, retain, and reveal to the prosecutor material obtained in a criminal investigation and which may be relevant to the investigation. The investigator must retain material obtained in a criminal investigation which may be relevant to the investigation. The code sets out that material may be 'relevant to an investigation' if it appears to an investigator, or to the officer in charge of an investigation, or to the disclosure officer, that 'it has some bearing on any offence under investigation or any person being investigated, or on the surrounding circumstances of the case, unless it is incapable of having any impact on the case'.[26] Where information which may be relevant is obtained, it must be recorded at the time it is obtained or as soon as practicable after that time.[27]

8.23 The Code states that in conducting an investigation, the investigator should pursue 'all reasonable lines of inquiry, whether these point towards or away from the suspect'.[28] What is reasonable in each case will depend on the particular circumstances.

D. Case Management in so far as It Relates to Disclosure

(a) General

8.24 The appropriate disclosure regime in all cases, regardless of the involvement of vulnerable persons in them, is that contained within the CPIA. It is essential to

---

[26] Revised Code of Practice, para. 2.1.
[27] ibid. para. 4.4.
[28] ibid. para. 3.5.

the fair and effective presentation of criminal cases that the statutory scheme is properly applied by the prosecution, the defence, and the Court. The Guidelines state as follows:

> Properly applied, the CPIA should ensure that material is not disclosed which over-burdens the participants in the trial process, diverts attention from the relevant issues, leads to unjustifiable delay, and is wasteful of resources. Consideration of disclosure issues should be an integral part of a good investigation and not something that exists separately.[29]

Under Crim PR Rule 3.2(1), the court must further the overriding objective by **8.25** actively managing the case. Rule 3.2(2) identifies various factors which, together, comprise active case management, including: the early identification of the real issues; the early identification of the needs of witnesses; achieving certainty as to what must be done, by whom and when, in particular by the setting of a timetable for the progress of the case; and monitoring the progress of the case and compliance with directions. By virtue of Rule 3.3(1), each party must actively assist the court in fulfilling its duty under Rule 3.2, without or if necessary with a direction. This includes effective communication between the parties' representatives in order to establish, among other things, what information, or other material, is required of one party by another, and why (Rule 3.3(2)(c)). (See further Chapter 9, 'Case Management' and Chapter 13, 'Trial Management: The Judge's Role'.)

(b)   The prosecutor's responsibility

The prosecutor is defined in s. 2 of the CPIA as 'any person acting as prosecutor, **8.26** whether an individual or body'. The Code of Practice defines the prosecutor as 'the authority responsible for the conduct, on behalf of the Crown, of criminal proceedings resulting from a specific criminal investigation'.

The Crown is indivisible. In *Attorney-General's Reference (No. 44 of 2000)*, albeit **8.27** in the context of a plea bargain arrangement, the Court of Appeal held as follows:

> It does not seem to us that there is, so far as the prosecution of criminal offences in the name of the Crown are concerned, any sensible distinction to be drawn between the Crown Prosecution Service, the Customs and Excise or the Inland Revenue. In our judgment, if the Crown, by whatever means the Crown is prosecuting, make representations to a defendant on which he is entitled to rely and on which he acts to his detriment by, as in the present case, pleading guilty in circumstances in which he would not otherwise have pleaded guilty, that can properly be regarded as giving rise to a legitimate expectation on his part that the Crown will not subsequently seek to resile from those representations, whether by way of the Attorney-General exercising his personal statutory duties under section 36 or otherwise. For this purpose the Crown and its agents are indivisible.[30]

---

[29] Guidelines, para. 3.
[30] [2001] 1 Cr App R 27 at [35].

The Guidelines outline the principles to be followed by investigators, prosecutors, and prosecution advocates when applying the statutory disclosure regime and recognize that, within a prosecution team, each member may have a different role and responsibility so far as disclosure is concerned.[31] However, there is a collective responsibility upon the prosecution as a whole to ensure that proper disclosure is effected in a particular case.

8.28 The prosecutor must act as a minister of justice. Included within this must be the requirement, set out in the Guidelines, to take all reasonable steps to facilitate the proper operation of the disclosure regime in order to ensure that proceedings are conducted fairly and in accordance with the interests of justice. There is a requirement to be proactive. Prosecution advocates should ensure that all material that ought to be disclosed under the Act is disclosed to the defence. However, prosecution advocates cannot be expected to disclose material if they are unaware of its existence. As far as possible, prosecution advocates must place themselves in a fully informed position to enable them to make decisions on disclosure. It is essential that prosecution advocates at court are properly and fully instructed as to disclosure issues: it is the duty of the prosecution advocate to keep decisions regarding disclosure under review until the conclusion of the trial, whenever possible in consultation with the reviewing prosecutor. It is frequently the case that the prosecution advocate is the person best placed to carry out the continuing duty of review, as they will be present throughout the trial when the reviewing prosecutor may not be.

8.29 Prosecutors, including prosecution advocates, must review schedules prepared by disclosure officers thoroughly and must be alert to the possibility that relevant material may exist which has not been revealed to them or material included which should not have been. If no schedules have been provided, or there are apparent omissions from the schedules, or documents or other items are inadequately described or are unclear, the prosecutor must at once take action to obtain properly completed schedules.[32]

8.30 The online CPS Disclosure Manual[33] contains operational instructions which are designed to provide a practical guide to disclosure principles and procedures which will assist investigators and prosecutors to perform their disclosure duties. While it has no statutory footing, the Foreword to the Manual provides some indication of its status to the CPS prosecutor:

---

[31] For the various roles of disclosure officer, prosecutor, and advocate, see Guidelines, paras 29–38. See also the CPS Disclosure Manual, chs 3 and 10.

[32] See <http://www.cps.gov.uk/legal/d_to_g/disclosure_manual/disclosure_manual_chapter_3/; and <http://www.cps.gov.uk/legal/d_to_g/disclosure_manual/disclosure_manual_chapter_1> both accessed 20 March 2017.

[33] See <http://www.cps.gov.uk/legal/d_to_g/disclosure_manual/> accessed 20 March 2017.

The Disclosure Manual reflects the Prosecution Team approach to our respective disclosure obligations and is to be regarded as the authoritative guidance on practice and procedure for all police investigators and CPS prosecutors.

Prosecutors are required by the Disclosure Manual[34] to record their decision-making on a disclosure record sheet. Such an audit trail will assist in charting decisions, enquiries, or requests (and the date on which they are made) relating to the discharge of prosecution disclosure obligations, particularly in cases where the disclosure exercise is a substantial one. CPS Disclosure Guidelines state that there is an obligation for the prosecution advocate to consider the disclosure record sheet at all conferences and before all court hearings.

(c) Prosecution disclosure strategy

The larger and/or the more complex the case, the more important it is for the prosecution to adhere to the overarching principle and ensure that sufficient prosecution attention and resources are allocated to the disclosure task. The CPIA does not require the prosecution to examine every item individually in order to ascertain whether there is any material which meets the disclosure test (in some cases, such an exercise would be impossible owing to the quantity of material held by the prosecution), nor does it require (or, indeed, permit) blanket disclosure of items which have not been examined individually. Rather, in cases which might be considered particularly large and/or complex, the prosecution is encouraged to form a strategy for its approach in relation to the examination of unused material, set out in a 'Disclosure Management Document'.[35] The strategy must include (so far as is relevant in an individual case) the overall disclosure strategy, the test applied, the method by which material which may be subject to legal professional privilege will be identified and isolated, and the search terms to be used for (and the parameters of) the review of any electronically held material. The compatibility of such practice with the prosecution's duty under the CPIA has been addressed in the Protocol (at [15]) and the Guidelines (at [48]).

8.31

In *R v R and Others*,[36] the Court of Appeal considered a case which had been proceeding for some five years in the Crown Court, and had reached the stage of primary disclosure. The issue involved the operation of the disclosure regime where the unused material comprised vast quantities of electronic files which would be impossible to read and assess in the usual way. The prosecution appealed against

8.32

---

[34] ibid. para. 11.14.

[35] Disclosure Management Documents were recommended by Lord Justice Gross in his *Review of Disclosure in Criminal Proceedings* (Judiciary of England and Wales, September 2011) and the recommendation is now embodied in the 2013 Judicial Protocol on Disclosure, at [39] (part of Large and Complex cases in the Crown Court): 'A disclosure-management document, or similar, prepared by the prosecution will be of particular assistance to the court in large and complex cases.'

[36] [2015] EWCA Crim 1941.

the judge's decision to stay the whole of a draft indictment as an abuse of process. The Court of Appeal allowed the prosecution's appeal and gave guidance as to the proper approach to disclosure and abuse of process. Having reviewed the statutory framework on disclosure and the court's case management powers, the Court of Appeal identified a number of principles:

- the prosecution must be in the driving seat at the stage of initial disclosure;
- the prosecution must then encourage dialogue and prompt engagement with the defence;
- the law is prescriptive of the result, not the method;
- the process of disclosure should be subject to robust case management by the judge, using the full range of case management powers;
- flexibility is critical.

In particularly large cases involving multiple allegations of child sexual exploitation (and in other large cases or complex cases which do not necessarily involve the participation of vulnerable persons), it has become the practice of the CPS to appoint 'disclosure counsel' to examine and make decisions on unused material either alone or in conjunction with the reviewing lawyer. In essence, the decision to appoint 'disclosure counsel' is taken where the volume or complexity of the material is such that it is inappropriate for the prosecutor to carry out the disclosure task alone, bearing in mind the time constraints which operate in proceedings before the Crown Court. In addition, disclosure counsel may be appointed where counsel has a degree of expertise, for example, because of the specialized nature of the material or because of knowledge of a linked operation. Counsel is instructed to advise the prosecutor and may be instructed to endorse the disclosure schedules as to his or her assessment of the disclosure decisions. Instructions to disclosure counsel cover sensitive and non-sensitive material. The Disclosure Manual is clear, however, that whatever role or responsibility is given to disclosure counsel, the ultimate responsibility for all aspects of the case remains with the reviewing prosecutor.[37]

8.33 'Disclosure counsel' may be instructed solely to conduct the disclosure review, or may be instructed additionally to appear at trial as junior counsel. The Disclosure Manual states that 'irrespective of this, [disclosure counsel] should be instructed for the duration of the case'.[38] The potential for problems to arise if 'disclosure counsel' is not briefed for trial is obvious. Although of course there is an obligation for all prosecution advocates in a given case to be familiar with disclosure material, it is the (specifically briefed) disclosure counsel who has conducted the more detailed and nuanced review. In the absence of disclosure counsel at trial,

---

[37] See <http://www.cps.gov.uk/legal/d_to_g/disclosure_manual/> accessed 20 March 2017, para. 29.43.
[38] See ibid. para. 29.42.

the process by which the prosecution may comply with its ongoing duty of disclosure becomes more difficult.

The Manual states: **8.34**

> It should be made clear in the instructions that counsel will be expected to be disclosure counsel in any forthcoming trial. In the normal course it would be very exceptional reasons that would prevent counsel's attendance at the trial, and accordingly counsel should make the necessary arrangements to make himself or herself available as early as possible.[39]

On a practical note, in some of the early multi-handed child-grooming cases[40] in which disclosure was made of significant quantities of unused material, the unused material was served unpaginated and virtually unindexed. In due course, defence practitioners making applications to cross-examine a complainant on his or her previous sexual history[41] each served on the court a bundle of supporting documentation, indexed and paginated differently. The importance of proper indexing and pagination in the disclosed unused material cannot be over-emphasized.

(d) Early defence engagement

It is acknowledged in the Guidelines and in the Protocol that defence engage-   **8.35**
ment in the disclosure process is vital. Case management powers can and should be used to require defence engagement in the prosecution disclosure exercise, as defined within the prosecution 'Disclosure Management Document'. It should be noted that defence engagement in the process is not limited to the period after proceedings have commenced before the Court. The defence can be invited to engage in the process at the investigation stage, particularly important in cases where the defence assert that there is (potentially exculpatory) material which warrants investigation by the prosecution.

While defence engagement on the question of disclosure is often essential, it must   **8.36**
be borne in mind that the judgment as to how to apply the disclosure test remains vested by statute in the prosecution. As is clearly set out in the Guidelines, defence engagement is 'key to ensuring prosecutors make informed determinations about the disclosure of unused material'.[42]

(e) Judicial case management

The Review of Efficiency in Criminal Proceedings (2015)[43] considered how best   **8.37**
the courts could deal with failings in pre-trial preparation, including disclosure

---

[39] See ibid. para. 29.55.
[40] e.g. Operation Bullfinch at the Central Criminal Court, 2013.
[41] See the Youth Justice and Criminal Evidence Act 1999 s. 41.
[42] n. 11, [5].
[43] Review of Efficiency in Criminal Proceedings by The Rt Hon Sir Brian Leveson.

failings which have the real potential to cause delay, increase costs, and obstruct justice:

> The police, CPS and defence practitioners must be held accountable for repeated default. Courts should therefore maintain a record of failures to comply with the Criminal Procedure Rules and insist on a compliance court appearance once a pattern of failure is identified: Presiding and Resident Judges should consider how best this can be achieved locally, ensuring that the focus of this mechanism addresses the real problem of delay and non-disclosure and is not a means by which tactical advantage may be taken by one party from technical failures to comply that are inconsequential to the real issue.[44]

The Protocol recognizes the need for robust judicial case management of the disclosure process in order to ensure that delays and adjournments are avoided, given that failures by the parties to comply with their obligations may disrupt and frustrate the course of justice. The purpose of active judicial case management is to ensure that each party complies with its statutory duties in order to ensure efficient progress of the case to trial. Judicial case management should not depart from the disclosure scheme contained within the CPIA. Applications by the parties or decisions by judges based on misconceptions of the law or a general laxity of approach (however well-intentioned) which result in an improper application of the disclosure regime have proved costly and have obstructed justice: see Protocol at [3].

(f) Plea and Trial Preparation Hearing (PTPH)

8.38 All cases must be listed for first hearing in the Crown Court within twenty-eight days of being sent from the magistrates' court. If a not guilty plea is entered at the PTPH, case management should take place in preparation for trial. This should be done using the PTPH form which will have been completed by the parties and served on the court in advance of the hearing. In the Crown Court, once the PTPH has occurred, the expectation is that there will be no further pre-trial hearings, save in identified complex cases or if a judge decides that the interests of justice require a further hearing. Thereafter, the next appearance in court should be for trial.

8.39 The PTPH form in use in all cases at the time of writing invites the prosecution to identify whether it is believed that any third party holds potentially disclosable material and, if so, whether the prosecution will be making enquiries to review that material. The form requires the court to set a date for the following matters, relevant to the disclosure exercise in all cases:

Stage 1 (within fifty days (custody cases) or seventy days (bail cases) after sending):

---

[44] ibid. recommendation 41.

- initial disclosure;
- the prosecution to make requests to a relevant third party, or notify the defence in writing that it does not intend to make any application for third-party disclosure;
- the prosecution, if pursuing third-party disclosure, to serve a report in writing on the outcome of efforts to identify potentially disclosable materials held by third parties and any ongoing enquiries not yet completed;

Stage 2 (ordinarily twenty-eight days after stage 1):
- defence statement (including requests for disclosure);

Stage 3 (ordinarily fourteen or twenty-eight days after stage 2):
- further disclosure (items required to be disclosed under CPIA resulting from or requested by the defence statement);

Stage 4 (ordinarily fourteen or twenty-eight days after stage 3):
- complaint about prosecution non-disclosure;
- application(s) for witness summons for third-party disclosure if the prosecution indicates at PTPH that it will not be pursuing any third-party disclosure issues or the defendant is dissatisfied with the outcome of prosecution enquiries.

8.40 In document-heavy cases, a bespoke case-management regime has been developed and is the subject of a pilot at four Crown Courts (Birmingham, Manchester, Kingston upon Thames, and Southwark). The regime envisages that the CPS will conduct a detailed review of the case, including all case management issues, by way of the Notification Form (to be served seven days in advance of the PTPH). Thereafter, the CPS will regularly review disclosure by updating a Disclosure Management Document. All defence requests or suggestions relating to disclosure must be served in writing in accordance with the CPIA and must be served on the prosecution and the Court.

E. Specific Disclosure Issues in Cases Involving Vulnerable Persons

8.41 In cases involving vulnerable complainants and/or other witnesses, there are likely to be particular categories of unused material which may fall to be considered by the prosecutor which are unlikely to feature in cases which do not involve such participants. Examples of those categories of material are as follows:

1. medical records and psychiatric records which might go to the credibility of the account of a complainant or other prosecution witness;
2. third-party material, e.g. social services records or educational records, which might go to the credibility of the complainant or other prosecution witness;
3. material relating to past or current Family Court proceedings;

4. information that the complainant is pursuing a civil claim for compensation;
5. information relating to previous complaints made by the complainant;
6. telephone evidence, especially the content of SMS or similar messages passing between the complainant and the suspect;
7. scientific or scenes of crime findings.

The most frequently encountered of those categories are considered below.

(a) Medical and counselling records

8.42 Frequently, in cases involving allegations of sexual offences, the unused material includes complainant's medical records and/or counselling notes. In the first instance, it will be necessary to identify whether or not the police have obtained an individual's consent to disclosure of their records and/or notes.

8.43 It may be the case that the papers received by the prosecutor do not reveal on their face whether consent has been received. It should not be assumed that consent has been obtained merely because the material may be listed on the non-sensitive schedule of unused material. To the extent that a consent form is available, it should be checked to ascertain whether a complainant has consented to disclosure to the defence, rather than a more limited consent to revelation to the CPS only. If it is contemplated that the involvement of a Registered Intermediary may be of assistance, it will be necessary to obtain a further consent from the individual for the Registered Intermediary to have access to relevant records and reports (and to speak to those who may be able to assist in his or her task, e.g. doctors, psychologists).

8.44 In *R (on the application of B) v Stafford Combined Court*,[45] the claimant, a young girl, was the main prosecution witness in the trial of a man charged in the Crown Court with sexual offences in relation to her. In the run-up to the trial, the claimant had received psychiatric counselling treatment from an NHS Trust. The defence asked for a witness summons directed to the Director of the Child and Mental Health Services of the Trust requiring the production of the claimant's medical and hospital records. The grounds given by the defence were that a history of self-harm and mental illness might undermine her credibility as a witness. At a hearing at which the Trust was represented, the judge ordered disclosure of the records. The Trust contacted the Official Solicitor, who immediately notified the Crown Court, the Crown Prosecution Service, and defence solicitors that she represented the claimant in connection with a possible infringement of her rights under Article 8 of the European Convention on Human Rights. The judge did not want the trial to be delayed and invited the claimant to attend court. She did so, although there was no opportunity for her to be represented,

---

[45] [2006] 2 Cr App R 34.

and she reluctantly agreed to disclosure. She applied for judicial review seeking a declaration that she had been entitled to service of the application for the witness summons, and that she had a right to make representations as to what order should be made, and that the Crown Court had acted unlawfully in proceeding as it had done.

The Divisional Court held that the medical records of a complainant were 'confidential between the medical practitioner and the patient' and that the patient had a 'right of privacy' under Article 8 of the ECHR. Procedural fairness demanded that the claimant should have been given notice of the application and the opportunity to make representations to the court before the order was made. It was not sufficient for the court to delegate her representations to the person holding the documents (the Trust). The court could only order disclosure in breach of confidentiality of the claimant's medical records if it was proportionate, in accordance with the law and necessary for the prevention of crime, for the protection of health or morals or for the protection of the rights and freedoms of others. It required a balance between the claimant's rights of privacy and confidentiality and the defendant's right to have his defence informed of the content of her medical records. Although the existing legislation and rules did not expressly oblige the court to give notice of an application for a witness summons to a person in the claimant's position, the overriding objective required it.

8.45

Available guidance for prosecutors[46] envisages three scenarios:

8.46

1. full, informed consent has been provided

In the event that full, informed consent has been provided by the witness/victim allowing the police access to the medical records/notes and service of the material as additional evidence or unused material, any portion of the records/notes considered to meet the disclosure test may be disclosed as appropriate.

2. qualified consent

In the event that the victim or witness allows their medical/counselling records to be disclosed to the police and prosecutor, but not the defence, a staged approach is necessary. The prosecutor must first assess the records to ascertain whether any/all of them meet the disclosure test. In the event that at least some portion of the records meet the test, the prosecutor should inform the victim or witness of that decision and ask for consent to disclose the material. If consent continues to be refused, the prosecutor must consider whether to make an application for non-disclosure on the grounds of public interest immunity (PII), or to discontinue with the prosecution. In the event that a PII application is made by the

---

[46] See <http://www.cps.gov.uk/legal/p_to_r/rape_and_sexual_offences/disclosure_and_third_party_material/#a1> accessed 20 March 2017.

prosecution, the views of the witness or victim may be placed before the court, either by the prosecutor on the individual's behalf, or by the witness or victim in person or in writing, or through a representative. It is a matter for the court to determine whether the material in question, which meets the disclosure test, can properly be withheld on the grounds of PII.

3. refusal of consent

In the event that a victim or witness declines to consent to the release of their records at all, and where there are reasonable grounds to believe that disclosable material is contained within the medical/counselling records, it will be for the prosecutor to decide whether it is appropriate to use the witness summons procedure to gain access to these records. The victim or witness has a right to make representations to the court as to why such records should not be provided.

8.47 It is important to bear in mind that medical notes and/or counselling records should be considered under the CPIA regime in the normal way, in order to assess whether any or all of them meet the disclosure test. As with all material considered for disclosure purposes, it is not appropriate to take an 'all or nothing' approach. It may be the view of a prosecutor that some material contained in a particular document meets the disclosure test, while the remainder does not.[47] In such a case, only that material which meets the disclosure test may be disclosed. Appropriate disclosure can be made using redactions (blocking out entries which are not disclosable so that they may not be read). Any disclosure beyond that which meets the test is a breach of the complainant's right to respect for their private and family life, under Article 8 of the ECHR.

(b) Third-party disclosure: procedure

8.48 In many criminal cases involving vulnerable witnesses, it will be necessary to consider the issue of third-party material. Third-party issues arise commonly in cases involving allegations of historic sexual abuse and child sexual exploitation. In these cases, the essential starting point is the Guidelines (paragraphs 53–8). The Crown's obligation to disclose material in the hands of third parties only arises if and when the material comes into the possession of the prosecutor.

8.49 Where the investigator, disclosure officer, or prosecutor 'believes' that a third party (e.g. a local authority, social services department, hospital, school) has material or information which might be relevant to the prosecution case, the investigator, disclosure officer, and prosecutor 'should take reasonable steps' to

---

[47] In the HM CPS Inspectorate review of CPS compliance with rules and guidance in relation to the disclosure of complainants' medical records and counselling notes in rape and sexual offence cases, July 2013, it was found that in seven of thirty-two sampled cases, more material was disclosed than was justified by reference to the disclosure test contained within the CPIA.

identify, secure, and consider material held by the third party where it appears to the investigator, disclosure officer, or prosecutor that: (a) such material exists; and (b) it may be relevant to an issue in the case.[48] It is not incumbent upon the prosecution to make speculative enquiries as to the existence of relevant material, but often the fact that such material exists can be ascertained from information already in the hands of the police. By way of example, where a complainant in a historic sex case who tells an investigating officer during her Achieving Best Evidence (ABE) interview[49] that she has undergone significant counselling in respect of her experiences, the relevant counsellor may have relevant material (material likely to have touched upon the subject matter of the investigation).

In *R v Alibhai*,[50] the Court of Appeal held that before taking steps to obtain third-party material, it must be shown (under the Attorney-General's Guidelines then in force) that there was not only a suspicion that the third party had relevant material, but also a suspicion that the material held by the third party was likely to satisfy the disclosure test. The Court of Appeal went on to state that even if there was a suspicion which might trigger the obligation under the Guidelines, the prosecutor is not under an absolute obligation to secure disclosure of the material, enjoying instead a 'margin of appreciation' as to the steps which he or she regards as appropriate in the particular case. However, the court's analysis in that case was based upon a consideration of the Attorney-General's Guidelines then in force which, and in contradistinction to the equivalent part of the current Guidelines, stated that steps should be taken to obtain material 'if the material or information *is likely to undermine the prosecution case, or assist a known defence*'[51] (as opposed to the current requirement to take steps to obtain it if it appears that it exists and that it may be 'relevant to an issue in the case'). **8.50**

There is no obligation (in the CPIA or elsewhere) upon a third party to record, retain, or reveal to the prosecution, material which may be relevant to the investigation. However, if it is believed that a third party holds material which may be relevant to the investigation, the third party should be told of the fact of the investigation and should be alerted to the need to preserve relevant material. **8.51**

If the relevant material is obtained by police from a third party, that material becomes unused material within the terms of the CPIA. This is because the material would then become 'prosecution material' which, as defined in s. 2 of the Act, is material which is in the prosecutor's possession and came into their possession in connection with the case for the prosecution against the accused. This applies to written, audio, or visual records obtained from a third party, and information **8.52**

---

[48] Guidelines, n. 11, para. 56.
[49] More formally known as the Video Recorded Interview or simply VRI.
[50] [2004] EWCA Crim 681.
[51] Emphasis added.

obtained orally from a third party (e.g. information obtained by police at a child protection conference). The Code of Practice provides that if material which may be relevant to the investigation consists of information which is not recorded in any form, the officer in charge of the investigation must ensure that it is recorded in a durable or retrievable form.[52] If the prosecutor takes the view that unused material obtained from a third party meets the disclosure test, good practice would dictate that there should be consultation with the third party before disclosure is made in order that proper account is taken, by the prosecution and the third party, of any rights of confidentiality which may attach to the material.

(c) Third-party disclosure: witness summons

8.53 If the third party declines to allow access to the material, and it is still believed that it is reasonable to seek production of the material, the prosecutor or investigator should apply for a witness summons causing a representative of the third party to produce the material to the court, if the requirements of s. 2 of the Criminal Procedure (Attendance of Witnesses Act) 1965 or s. 97 of the Magistrates' Courts Act 1980 (as appropriate) are satisfied.

8.54 It should be observed that the statutory requirements of both s. 2 of the Criminal Procedure (Attendance of Witnesses) Act 1965 and s. 97 of the Magistrates' Courts Act 1980 are more stringent than the disclosure test. Material sought under a witness summons must be 'likely to be material evidence'. In *R v Derby Magistrates' Court, ex p. B*,[53] the House of Lords interpreted that as meaning 'immediately admissible per se'.

8.55 That interpretation poses a problem. Where material may be sought in order that it may be used in cross-examination in respect of issues going to credibility, it would appear that such material would not be 'immediately admissible per se' and so would fail the test of materiality contained in s. 97 of the MCA 1980 or s. 2 of the Criminal Procedure (Attendance of Witnesses) Act 1965. In *R v Brushett*,[54] the Court of Appeal considered the conflict between the principles governing disclosure by the prosecution and the (narrower) principles governing disclosure by a third party. The court held that PII might attach to documents seen by the police or prosecution, but the more stringent test of materiality applied to uninspected documents remaining in the possession of a third party like social services.

8.56 Part 17 of the Criminal Procedure Rules sets out the procedure to be adopted in applying for a witness summons. The rules apply whether the application for a witness summons is made by the prosecution or defence. Rule 17.5 requires

---

[52] Revised Code of Practice, para. 4.1.
[53] [1995] 4 All ER 526.
[54] [2001] Crim LR 471.

the court to take adequate account of the duties and rights, including rights of confidentiality, both of the proposed witness who would produce in evidence the material (or give evidence about information apparently held in confidence) and of any person to whom the proposed evidence relates, before it may issue a witness summons. Rule 17.6 states that in order to assess the objection of any person served with an application for a witness summons to produce in evidence a document or thing, the court 'may' invite the proposed witness or the person to whom the document or thing relates to help the court assess the objection.

(d) Third-party disclosure: PII

Sections 3(6), 7A(8), and 8(5) of the CPIA provide that material must not be **8.57** disclosed to the extent that the court, on an application by the prosecutor, concludes that it is not in the public interest to disclose it. Section 21(2) of the CPIA preserves the rules of the common law as to whether disclosure is in the public interest.

During an investigation, the prosecution may come into possession of sensitive **8.58** material (potentially, but not always, from a third party). Even if that material meets the disclosure test, there may nonetheless be public interest reasons which justify withholding disclosure. In those circumstances, the prosecutor will make an application to the court to withhold disclosure on the grounds of public interest immunity. Only material which meets the disclosure test should be placed before the court in a PII application.

Part 15 of the Criminal Procedure Rules requires the prosecution to make any **8.59** application for material to be withheld on the grounds of PII to make the application in writing, to be served on the court, any person who the prosecutor thinks would be directly affected by disclosure of the material, and the defendant 'only to the extent that serving it on the defendant would not disclose what the prosecutor thinks ought not be disclosed'. The application must describe the material and explain why the prosecutor considers that it is material they would have to disclose. The application must also set out why the prosecutor contends that it would not be in the public interest to disclose the material and why disclosure short of full disclosure would not adequately protect the public interest and the defendant's right to a fair trial.

The House of Lords in *R v H*[55] set out the principles and procedure to be adopted **8.60** by a court in determining an application that material be withheld on the grounds of PII:

> 36 When any issue of derogation from the golden rule of full disclosure comes before it, the court must address a series of questions.

---

[55] [2004] 2 AC 134 at [36]–[37].

1. What is the material which the prosecution seek to withhold? This must be considered by the court in detail.

2. Is the material such as may weaken the prosecution case or strengthen that of the defence? If No, disclosure should not be ordered. If Yes, full disclosure should (subject to (3), (4) and (5) below) be ordered.

3. Is there a real risk of serious prejudice to an important public interest (and, if so, what) if full disclosure of the material is ordered? If No, full disclosure should be ordered.

4. If the answer to (2) and (3) is Yes, can the defendant's interest be protected without disclosure or disclosure be ordered to an extent or in a way which will give adequate protection to the public interest in question and also afford adequate protection to the interests of the defence? This question requires the court to consider, with specific reference to the material which the prosecution seek to withhold and the facts of the case and the defence as disclosed, whether the prosecution should formally admit what the defence seek to establish or whether disclosure short of full disclosure may be ordered. This may be done in appropriate cases by the preparation of summaries or extracts of evidence, or the provision of documents in an edited or anonymized form, provided the documents supplied are in each instance approved by the judge. In appropriate cases the appointment of special counsel may be a necessary step to ensure that the contentions of the prosecution are tested and the interests of the defendant protected (see para 22 above). In cases of exceptional difficulty the court may require the appointment of special counsel to ensure a correct answer to questions (2) and (3) as well as (4).

5. Do the measures proposed in answer to (4) represent the minimum derogation necessary to protect the public interest in question? If No, the court should order such greater disclosure as will represent the minimum derogation from the golden rule of full disclosure.

6. If limited disclosure is ordered pursuant to (4) or (5), may the effect be to render the trial process, viewed as a whole, unfair to the defendant? If Yes, then fuller disclosure should be ordered even if this leads or may lead the prosecution to discontinue the proceedings so as to avoid having to make disclosure.

7. If the answer to (6) when first given is No, does that remain the correct answer as the trial unfolds, evidence is adduced and the defence advanced?

It is important that the answer to (6) should not be treated as a final, once-and-for-all, answer but as a provisional answer which the court must keep under review.

37 Throughout his or her consideration of any disclosure issue the trial judge must bear constantly in mind the overriding principles referred to in this opinion. In applying them, the judge should involve the defence to the maximum extent possible without disclosing that which the general interest requires to be protected but taking full account of the specific defence which is relied on. There will be very few cases indeed in which some measure of disclosure to the defence will not be possible, even if this is confined to the fact that an ex parte application is to be made. If even that information is withheld and if the material to be withheld is of significant help to the defendant, there must be a very serious question whether the prosecution should proceed, since special counsel, even if appointed, cannot then receive any instructions from the defence at all.

Under s. 16 of the CPIA, where an application is made under s. 3(6), 7A(8), 8(5), 14(2), or 15(4) of the Act, and a person claiming to have an interest in the material applies to be heard by the Court, and he shows he was involved (whether alone or with others and whether directly or indirectly) in the prosecutor's attention being drawn to the material, the court may not make an order for disclosure unless the person applying under s. 16 has had an opportunity to be heard.

(e) Child abuse cases: the 2013 Protocol and Good Practice Model

Experience had shown that although the law regarding information exchange **8.61** between the local authority and Family Courts, and the CPS, remained the same in criminal and Family Court jurisdictions throughout England and Wales, the approach to information exchange varied across the country, which was not always in the best interests of the child subject of the proceedings.[56]

Since 1 January 2014, in child abuse cases, there has been a Protocol in place **8.62** called the '2013 Protocol and Good Practice Model: Disclosure of information in cases of alleged child abuse and linked criminal and care directions hearings'. The 2013 Protocol applies to all cases involving criminal investigations into alleged child abuse (child victims who were aged 17 or under at the time of the alleged offending) and/or Family Court proceedings concerning a child (aged 17 or under). The protocol applies from the moment the police commence an investigation into alleged child abuse (sexual or non-sexual) or from the moment that a local authority contemplates proceedings in the Family Court involving a child. The aim is that the disclosure exercise begins far earlier than previously, so as to avoid delay and/or late and rushed applications.

The 2013 Protocol concerns information exchange between local authorities and **8.63** Family Courts on the one hand and the Criminal Justice System (the police and CPS) on the other. It seeks to eliminate localized differences in the approach to disclosure of this kind, and to eradicate the obstruction from local authorities which was often met by prosecutors in this type of case. The Protocol encourages joint management of cases by the criminal and family courts and is now the starting point for disclosure in child abuse cases. It is outside the scope of this book to provide a detailed analysis of each part of the 2013 Protocol, which has a significant number of aims and objectives. Those parts relevant to contemplated or pending criminal proceedings are summarized. It should be borne in mind that the 2013 Protocol applies only to the exchange of information as described above and that there will remain areas of disclosure in cases involving allegations of child abuse (e.g. medical records, counselling records, school records if the school

---

[56] See <https://www.judiciary.gov.uk/wp-content/uploads/JCO/Documents/Guidance/protocol-good-practice-model-2013.pdf> accessed 20 March 2017.

is not governed by a local authority) which are not regulated by the Protocol and which must be considered in the usual way.

8.64 Part B of the 2013 Protocol, at paragraph 9, deals with disclosure from the local authority/family justice system into the criminal justice system. The 2013 Protocol seeks to ensure that the police gain access to relevant local authority material at the outset of a criminal investigation. Following the commencement of a police investigation, the police must provide to the local authority a prescribed form which will include details of the investigation (and prosecution if commenced). The same form will include requests for disclosure of material which 'must be as prescriptive and detailed as possible and necessary for the pursuit of reasonable lines of enquiry'. It is for the local authority to identify and collate relevant material from Children's Services or other files as appropriate, and additionally to identify the school attended by the subject of the investigation so as to enable the police to approach the school directly. Save for documents lodged at court or used in proceedings, which already existed, the local authority must ensure that documents relating to Family Court proceedings are not included in the files to be examined by police. Where there are documents relating to Family Court proceedings, the local authority will provide a list of that material without describing what it is, in order for the police or CPS to apply to the Family Court for disclosure.

8.65 Where new issues arise in the criminal case (e.g. after receipt of the defence statement), the police will submit a further form requesting access to material not previously examined. Similarly, where further relevant local authority material comes to light after the initial police/CPS examination of the material, the local authority must contact the police/CPS to arrange an examination of the new material.

8.66 The 2013 Protocol provides that the CPS will not disclose any local authority material to the defence in a criminal case without the agreement of the local authority or a court order.

8.67 Section 11 of the Protocol deals with applications by police and the CPS to the Family Court for disclosure of material relating to Family Court proceedings. The 2013 Protocol seeks to summarize the rules about whether material used in Family Court proceedings can be disclosed to the police or CPS. Applications by the CPS must specify the purpose and use to which the material is intended to be put and should seek leave to share the material with the police and with the defence and (subject to s. 98(2) of the Children Act 1989, which renders inadmissible in evidence in all criminal proceedings, save those for perjury, statements made by an individual in Children's Act proceedings) to use the material in evidence at the criminal proceedings. The application must be made by prescribed form, and must be served on all parties to the Family Court proceedings. The application will be determined at a hearing at the Family Court and the CPS (and/or police) will not attend the hearing unless directed to do so by the Family Court. Where it is possible, the police and/or CPS should ask the local authority allocated lawyer to request that the Family Court considers the issue of disclosure to the police/CPS at the hearing, allowing the Family Court to make any orders which may be appropriate without the need for police/CPS to make an application to the Family Court. In making the request through the local authority allocated lawyer, it is of course essential that all relevant information pertaining to the nature and scope of the prosecution case, the nature of the defence, and the issues in the criminal case are before the Family Court in order that decisions with regard to the disclosure of material are made on a properly and fully informed basis.

Paragraph 19.1 of the 2013 Protocol provides that local agencies in each of the **8.68** thirteen CPS areas in England and Wales were to agree and adopt a local protocol to implement the 2013 Protocol before 1 January 2014. Prosecuting advocates should refer to the relevant local protocol in cases involving material of this type.

In *Re X (Children) (Disclosure of Judgment to Police)*,[57] the Family Division held **8.69** that an unredacted judgment which recorded that, during care proceedings, a father had admitted assaulting one of his children could be disclosed to the police and CPS subject to a condition that they could not disclose it or its contents elsewhere without the court's permission. Family law recognized that it was in the public interest for information to be shared between child protection agencies and for barriers between different branches of the justice system to be removed. While the Children Act 1989 s. 98(2) prevented a confession made in family proceedings from being admissible in evidence in court proceedings, save on a count of perjury, it did not preclude the police, to whom the evidence of the confession was disclosed, from using that evidence to shape the nature and range of the enquiries they undertook in the investigation of the alleged criminal offences. If the police, for example, put the confession to a suspect in a further interview and he or she accepted its truthfulness, that response might itself become admissible in the criminal proceedings.

Where material has been obtained following an application by police to the **8.70** Family Court, the police must indicate to the CPS whether the Family Court has given permission for the material to be shared with the CPS and the defence. Further application to the Family Court may be required by the police and/or CPS as appropriate.

The local authority is required to forward to the police/CPS copies of relevant **8.71** Family Court judgments in its possession, redacted if necessary. If the local authority is not in possession of a judgment which appears to be relevant to the

---

[57] [2015] 1 FLR 1218.

concurrent criminal proceedings, it will notify the CPS in order that the CPS may apply for the judgment directly from the Family Court.

8.72 The Protocol states that applications to the criminal court for the withholding of sensitive material should be rare, and that there is no basis for making a PII application except where the prosecutor has identified material that fulfils the disclosure test, disclosure of which would create a real risk of serious prejudice to an important public interest.

(f) Family Court proceedings

8.73 Material held by a local authority might relate to other civil proceedings in the Family Court. The Family Procedure Rules, in force since 6 April 2011, provide a new code of procedure for family proceedings in the High Court, county courts, and magistrates' courts and replace various rules, including the Family Proceedings Rules 1991. Rule 12.73 of the Family Procedure Rules restricts the circumstances in which information relating to proceedings held in private may be communicated to others:

(1) For the purposes of the law relating to contempt of court, information relating to proceedings held in private (whether or not contained in a document filed with the court) may be communicated—
  (a) where the communication is to—
    (i)   a party;
    (ii)   the legal representative of a party;
    (iii) a professional legal adviser;
    (iv)   an officer of the service or a Welsh family proceedings officer;
    (v)   the welfare officer;
    (vi)   the Director of Legal Aid Casework (within the meaning of section 4 of the Legal Aid, Sentencing and Punishment of Offenders Act 2012);
    (vii) an expert whose instruction by a party has been authorised by the court for the purposes of the proceedings;
    (viii) a professional acting in furtherance of the protection of children;
    (ix)   an independent reviewing officer appointed in respect of a child who is, or has been, subject to proceedings to which this rule applies;
  (b) where the court gives permission; or
  (c) subject to any direction of the court, in accordance with rule 12.75 and Practice Direction 12G.
(2) Nothing in this Chapter permits the communication to the public at large, or any section of the public, of any information relating to the proceedings.
(3) Nothing in rule 12.75 and Practice Direction 12G permits the disclosure of an unapproved draft judgment handed down by any court.

Practice Direction 12G[58] provides that a party to Family Court proceedings may communicate to a police officer the text or summary of the whole or part of a

---

[58] See <https://www.justice.gov.uk/courts/procedure-rules/family/practice_directions/pd_part_12g> accessed 20 March 2017.

judgment given in proceedings for the purposes of a criminal investigation. The same Practice Direction provides that a party or any person lawfully in receipt of information from family proceedings may communicate that information to a member of the CPS to enable the CPS to discharge its functions under any enactment. The Practice Direction enables a local authority, by way of example, to disclose material to the CPS in order to enable the CPS to discharge its disclosure obligations under the CPIA. However, in the event that the CPS seeks to make further disclosure of that material to the defence, or to deploy the material received in any criminal proceedings, it would be necessary for the CPS to obtain the permission of the Family Court.

Where it appears to a prosecutor that relevant material which should be obtained **8.74** relates to family proceedings, the prosecutor must make an application to the Family Court to access such material and make use of it in criminal proceedings.

A Family Court considering any such application for disclosure to criminal pro- **8.75** ceedings must balance the importance of maintaining confidentiality in family proceedings against the public interest in seeing that the ends of justice are properly served.[59] In *Re X (Children) (Disclosure of Judgment to Police)*,[60] the Family Division held that the court, when deciding whether to order disclosure to the police of information relating to care proceedings, had to consider the factors identified in *Re C (A Minor) (Care Proceedings: Disclosure)*.[61] The court continued that the public interest in the sharing of information between the agencies involved in child protection, and the removal of barriers between different branches of the justice system, had been recognized by the terms of the Family Procedure Rules Practice Direction 12G and were underlined by the terms of the 2013 Protocol and Good Practice Model.

In *Re C (A Minor) (Care Proceedings: Disclosure)*,[62] Swinton Thomas LJ set out a list of criteria (although he does not suggest it is definitive) of matters to be considered by a judge when exercising his or her discretion whether to order disclosure:

> In the light of the authorities, the following are among the matters which a judge will consider when deciding whether to order disclosure. It is impossible to place them in any order of importance, because the importance of each of the various factors will inevitably vary very much from case to case.
>
> (1) The welfare and interests of the child or children concerned in the care proceedings. If the child is likely to be adversely affected by the order in any serious way, this will be a very important factor.
> (2) The welfare and interests of other children generally.
> (3) The maintenance of confidentiality in children cases.

---

[59] *Re A (Criminal Proceedings: Disclosure)* [1996] 1 FLR 221.
[60] [2014] EWHC 278 (Fam).
[61] [1997] Fam 76.
[62] At [85].

(4) The importance of encouraging frankness in children's cases. All parties to this appeal agree that this is a very important factor and is likely to be of particular importance in a case to which section 98(2) applies. The underlying purpose of section 98 is to encourage people to tell the truth in cases concerning children, and the incentive is that any admission will not be admissible in evidence in a criminal trial. Consequently, it is important in this case. However, the added incentive of guaranteed confidentiality is not given by the words of the section and cannot be given.

(5) The public interest in the administration of justice. Barriers should not be erected between one branch of the judicature and another because this may be inimical to the overall interests of justice.

(6) The public interest in the prosecution of serious crime and the punishment of offenders, including the public interest in convicting those who have been guilty of violent or sexual offences against children. There is a strong public interest in making available material to the police which is relevant to a criminal trial. In many cases, this is likely to be a very important factor.

(7) The gravity of the alleged offence and the relevance of the evidence to it. If the evidence has little or no bearing on the investigation or the trial, this will militate against a disclosure order.

(8) The desirability of co-operation between various agencies concerned with the welfare of children, including the social services departments, the police service, medical practitioners, health visitors, schools, etc. This is particularly important in cases concerning children.

(9) In a case to which section 98(2) applies, the terms of the section itself, namely that the witness was not excused from answering incriminating questions, and that any statement of admission would not be admissible against him in criminal proceedings. Fairness to the person who has incriminated himself and any others affected by the incriminating statement and any danger of oppression would also be relevant considerations

(10) Any material disclosure that has already taken place.

(g) Technology and media

8.76 In a speech given in April 2016, the Lord Chief Justice, Lord Thomas of Cwmgiedd, warned that the disclosure of online material is 'probably the biggest problem that all parts of the common law justice system faces'. Speaking days after four students had been acquitted of rape when it became apparent that police had failed to disclose texts from the complainant which might have appeared to suggest she consented to sexual activity, Lord Thomas added:

> I did not appreciate how important it is in sexual offending until I realised what people put on their smartphones or how they use social media. I am not used to seeing described what happens in such detail for the benefit of other people.

Investigators and prosecutors are well used to dealing with cases which involve telephone billing records and information recovered from the downloading of telephone handsets and SIM cards. Such records may well reveal calls made or received, the fact of and (potentially) the content of SMS messages, photographs, and WhatsApp exchanges, all of which may be relevant to an issue in a given case. However, Facebook and Twitter postings, and those on other social media platforms, may well contain information which might be probative of one or more issues in a given case. This much was recognized by the Court of Appeal in *R v Salt*,[63] a case in which the Crown appealed against a decision to stay proceedings against two defendants charged with serious sexual offences against two women. The prosecution's appeal was allowed. Lord Thomas of Cwmgiedd, the Lord Chief Justice, dealing with one of a number of alleged failings on the part of the police and prosecution, stated:

> It has always been apparent in cases of historic sexual abuse that disclosure will be important and proper steps [should] be taken to ensure that it is dealt with in an orderly manner. [50]

> It should have been apparent to the North Yorkshire Police, given the widespread use of social media, that it is likely that in many cases of sexual offending which arise contemporaneously that what is contained on social media is likely to be relevant and sometimes of great importance. Moreover the volume of such material can be significant, given the ability of 'smart phones' and other hand held mobile devices to contain so much information, quite apart from the records held by the mobile phone network providers. [51]

The Court of Appeal identified that in that case, the Vodafone call records of T's telephone amounted to some 502 pages of A3 paper, which were placed onto the unused material schedule at the end of the first day of the trial. While the Court of Appeal considered that the failure to disclose the records was significant, it was material only relevant to issues of credibility. The Court of Appeal observed that this was the second prosecution appeal in two months brought to the Court of Appeal as a result of the failure to provide materials. The Court invited the Criminal Procedure Rules Committee to consider whether sanctions can be imposed through new rules on those charged with the prosecution of a case who fail in their duties of disclosure.

Understandably, word and date searches are used as a way of complying with disclosure. These have proved in the past to be wholly inadequate. The reason is a matter of common sense. Young and vulnerable witnesses may get dates wrong, they may use different names for each other, they may possess several phones. And as a great many of them are permanently 'glued' to their mobile devices, the number of calls and texts can be enormous. **8.77**

It is submitted that despite the proliferation of online material and postings, there does not exist a general duty to investigate online forums in every case. Only if it appears to the investigator, disclosure officer, or prosecutor that relevant postings may exist and that those postings may be relevant to an issue in the case does **8.78**

---

[63] [2015] 2 Cr App R 27.

there arise any obligation to take reasonable steps to identify, secure, and consider such material.

(h) Scientific materials

8.79 As observed elsewhere in this chapter, the CPIA imposes disclosure obligations on the 'prosecutor' and not upon any third party who may hold material relevant to an investigation. Neither the CPIA nor the Code of Practice imposes any duty upon an expert regarding the retention of material or records, but good practice would dictate that records should be made and retained in respect of material gathered or generated in the course of the examination, notes made during the examination, and the results of tests conducted during the examination. The material held by the expert should be listed, with each item described accurately in order that informed decisions on disclosure may be made if and when a prosecutor comes to consider the list. Upon receipt of the list, the prosecutor should review the items in the usual way in order to assess whether any or all meet the disclosure test.

8.80 A duty of disclosure of material or information which supports the opinion of the expert producing the expert report for the prosecution is set out in Rules 19.3 and 19.4 of the Criminal Procedure Rules. In short, the party wishing to rely on an expert report must give the other party a copy of, or reasonable opportunity to inspect, a record of examination, measurement, test, or experiment on which the expert's findings and opinion are based, or that were carried out in the course of reaching those findings and opinion.[64]

(i) Ongoing disclosure: contact with police officers

8.81 In cases where the credibility of a complainant or other witness is an issue in the case, almost anything said or done by the complainant—particularly in connection with the investigation—falls to be considered under the disclosure test.

8.82 During a police investigation, it is to be expected that the contact between the complainant/other witness and the police will not be limited to the provision of their recorded account. Rather, it may well be the case that the individual's contact with the investigating team began with an initial meeting at which the generality of the allegation was discussed with the recorded account being provided some time later. Thereafter, there may be further contact between the individual

---

[64] See *R v Ward* [1993] 1 WLR 619 at p. 674. 'An incident of a defendant's right to a fair trial is a right to timely disclosure by the prosecution of all material matters which affect the scientific case relied on by the prosecution ... This duty exists whether or not a specific request for disclosure of details of scientific evidence is made by the defence.' See also *R v Sally Clark* [2003] EWCA Crim 1020, in which it was held that the failure to disclose the results of microbiological tests conducted upon Sally Clark's second son might reasonably have affected the jury's decision to convict. The Court of Appeal was critical of the pathologist who did not disclose the microbiological reports.

and the police on a variety of topics (e.g. the progress of the investigation, the provision of further information or detail, general welfare liaison, witness familiarization visit, viewing the ABE interview for the purpose of memory refreshing). All contact between the police and the individual should be recorded in a form of contact log. This log (or logs) should form part of the unused material in a case which must be assessed in order to ascertain whether any portion meets the disclosure test. Any portion which does meet the test must be disclosed.

8.83 There may be cases in which the witness/complainant requests a meeting with the prosecutor to discuss the decisions made (or to be made) regarding special measures. The police should offer such meetings to vulnerable and intimidated witnesses. ISVAs, IDVAs, or other specialist support services may also request such a special measures meeting for the witness.

8.84 Guidance from the CPS states that it is important that the prosecutor, and where possible, the trial advocate, meets with a vulnerable or intimidated witness at a special measures meeting at the earliest opportunity, in order that any application for special measures is informed and has the fullest information with regard to the witness's views. A full record must be maintained of matters discussed at the meeting, and there must be no discussion as to the evidence in the case (if the witness wishes to discuss an evidential matter, the prosecutor must be clear that this must be discussed with the police). The record should be signed and dated by all meeting attendees save for the witness. The note or record is unused material which should be assessed in accordance with the disclosure test in the usual way.

(j) Ongoing disclosure: intermediaries

8.85 Intermediaries facilitate communication with vulnerable people in the justice system, and the primary responsibility of the intermediary is to enable complete, coherent, and accurate communication to take place between a witness and any other relevant participant in the justice system (see Chapter 11, 'Intermediaries'). This includes communication at meetings between the witness and the police and/or the CPS, in the ABE interview, during identification procedures, and during the trial process. It may include communication at meetings between the defence solicitor and a defence witness. An intermediary is independent, impartial, and owes their primary duty to the court.

8.86 The Procedural Guidance Manual for the Registered Intermediary[65] sets out the following within the Code of Practice for Registered Intermediaries:

> 2. Intermediaries must have a clear and comprehensive understanding of the responsibilities and duties of their role within the CJS, including their primary responsibility to the court.
>
> …

---

[65] The Registered Intermediary Procedural Guidance Manual (2015).

20. They must recognise that an intermediary's duty to the court remains paramount. They must understand the different obligations regarding disclosure of information between the prosecution and the defence legal teams and must maintain their professional integrity in relation to these different obligations.

The Manual provides guidance to the Registered Intermediary (assisting with a prosecution witness) in so far as their involvement may give rise to disclosure issues for the prosecution:

> The Registered Intermediary must keep full records of their involvement throughout the process including notes of assessments. These are disclosable by the prosecution to the defence. The notes must be kept safe and comply with MoJ guidance on data protection as well as the law on data protection and confidentiality (cf. the Data Protection Act 1998).

> The Registered Intermediary must inform the officer-in-charge of the case of anything to which they become aware which could potentially undermine the case for the prosecution against the accused or which might assist the case for the accused, e.g. anything said by the witness in respect of the allegation. In respect of a defence witness, however, the Registered Intermediary must not disclose anything said by a defence witness or defendant to anyone other than the defendant's legal representatives without the express consent of the defendant.

(k) Ongoing disclosure: viewing the ABE interview

8.87 In cases involving allegations of sexual misconduct, it is the norm for the complainant to provide their account by way of ABE interview. A video-recorded interview with a vulnerable or intimated witness to any offence may be admitted by the court as the evidence-in-chief of that witness (see further Chapter 10, 'Special Measures').

8.88 As with any witness in any criminal case, it is necessary for the witness to refresh his or her memory from the account provided to police by way of the ABE interview. There is no legal requirement that the witness should watch their ABE interview(s) at the same time as the jury in a case; indeed, best practice dictates that the witness's first viewing of their ABE interview should not take place just before he or she testifies. Clearly, it is essential that the circumstances in which the witness refreshes his or her memory are monitored. The Advocate's Gateway Toolkit 1(a)[66] advises that the officer (or investigator equivalent) should be present and record any comment that the witness makes when viewing the ABE. That record should be passed to the prosecutor.

8.89 Ministry of Justice *Achieving Best Evidence* guidance states:

> It is the responsibility of the police to arrange for prosecution witnesses to read their statements or view video-recorded interviews. They should consult the prosecution

---

[66] See <http://www.theadvocatesgateway.org/images/toolkits/1a-case-management-in-criminal-cases-when-a-witness-or-a-defendant-is-vulnerable-2017.pdf> accessed 25 April 2017.

about where this should take place and who should be present, and keep a record of anything said at the viewing. In exceptional cases, such as those involving very young children or children with learning disabilities, the prosecutor should consider whether a video recording should be made when the witness refreshes their memory from the video-recorded interview.[67]

Any record of comments made by the witness during the memory-refreshing exercise form part of the unused material in a case, and must be assessed in the usual way with the disclosure test in mind.

(l) Ongoing disclosure: SARCS, ISVA, and IDVA

Independent Sexual Violence Advisers (ISVA) and Independent Domestic   **8.90**
Violence Advisers (IDVA) provide support and practical assistance to victims of sexual or domestic violence. Their assistance may be provided to victims regardless of whether criminal proceedings are ongoing. The assistance which may be provided can include the following: risk assessment; provision of support in reporting an offence to police; provision of support during police interviews and court proceedings; assistance in accessing counselling or health screening; and assistance with criminal injuries compensation.

Some ISVA and IDVA services state that they are confidential and that informa-   **8.91**
tion provided to them by victims will not be shared without consent unless that information involves matters of vulnerable adult or child protection or identifies persons at risk of serious harm. Some of those services advise further that, where there is a police investigation, the ISVA service may be legally obliged to share information for the purpose of third-party disclosure. It is submitted that in all cases where the services of ISVAs or IDVAs have been utilized, the records held by those advisers may properly be considered to be third-party material and ought to be dealt with in accordance with the procedures and principles applicable to all third-party material.

Sexual Assault Referral Centres (SARCS) provide services to victims of rape   **8.92**
or other sexual offences, regardless of whether or not the victim has elected to report the matter to police. SARCS can provide immediate medical care, forensic medical examinations, emergency contraception, counselling services, and onward referral to an ISVA. Notes held by SARCS, in respect of victims whose allegations are before the criminal courts, may properly be considered to be third-party material. Even in the absence of victim consent, such notes may fall to be disclosed to the defence in a trial by order of the Court.

---

[67] Ministry of Justice, *Achieving Best Evidence in Criminal Proceedings Guidance on Interviewing Victims and Witnesses, and Guidance on Using Special Measures* (MoJ, 2011) 4.51.

(m) Ongoing disclosure: contact with the prosecution advocate

8.93 In March 2016, the CPS issued guidance to prosecuting advocates on the topic of speaking to witnesses at court.[68] In broad terms, the guidance sets out both what is permissible in this regard and, additionally, what is expected. The guidance sets out in terms that it is now expected (if it was not expected before) that the prosecuting advocate at court should meet all witnesses before they give evidence at court. Among other matters, the advocate should provide the witness with assistance on general court procedure (including the roles of those present in court), the giving of evidence (highlighting the need to answer questions truthfully), and the nature of cross-examination.

8.94 The guidance specifically permits the prosecuting advocate to inform the witness of the following matters:

(i) the general nature of the defence case where it is known (e.g. mistaken identification, consent, self-defence, lack of intent). The prosecutor must not, however, enter into any discussion of the factual basis of the defence case;

(ii) that third-party disclosure pertaining to that witness has been disclosed to the defence as being capable of undermining the prosecution's case or assisting the defence case (such as social services, medical, or counselling records). The details and the impact on the defence cross-examination should not be discussed;

(iii) that leave has been granted for that witness to be cross-examined about an aspect of his or her bad character under CJA 2003 s. 100 or his or her sexual history under s. 41 of the Youth Justice and Criminal Evidence Act 1999.

The guidance states:

> Advocates in the Crown Court should ensure that, during these conversations, they are accompanied by a CPS member of staff based at court to assist with recoding the meeting and conversation ...

> A note of the fact that the prosecutor has spoken to the witness should be made by the prosecutor or by the CPS paralegal in the Crown Court. If the witness makes any comment which is disclosable to the defence under the CPIA then a note of the comment must be made immediately and the note disclosed accordingly.

Those familiar with practice in the courts will be aware that there may not always be time to make a note of a conversation, let alone a member of CPS staff available to make the required note. Although the scheme is in its early stages and the guidance exhorts the prosecutor to set clear limits as to what can and cannot be discussed, there remains the real possibility that witnesses will say more than they ought with the potential for difficulty. In the first instance, if resources are simply insufficient to allow for a member of CPS staff to take the required note,

---

[68] Speaking to Witnesses at Court, CPS Guidance, March 2016.

the burden of notetaking will inevitably fall to the prosecution advocate, with little time or assistance to get agreement as to its contents. That runs the risk of placing the advocate in the evidential chain and may well expose the advocate to complaint and criticism in higher courts and before their professional bodies.

In *R v Momodou and Limani*,[69] Lord Justice Judge confirmed that witness **8.95** training was prohibited in this jurisdiction because of the risk that training might adversely affect the accuracy of the witness's evidence, but observed that pre-trial arrangements to familiarize witnesses with the layout of the court, the likely sequence of events, and a balanced appraisal of the different responsibilities of the various participants were not precluded by that prohibition. There may properly be out-of-court familiarization to improve the manner in which the witness gives evidence—for example, by reducing nervous tension as a result of inexperience. Lord Justice Judge continued that the familiarization process should be supervised by a solicitor or barrister (or someone who is responsible to a solicitor or barrister with experience of the criminal justice process, and preferably by an organization accredited for the purpose by the Bar Council and Law Society). Records should be maintained of all those present and the identity of those responsible for the familiarization process, whenever it takes place. The details of the witness familiarization should be retained, together with all the written material (or appropriate copies) used during the familiarization sessions. None of the material should bear any similarity whatever to the issues in the criminal proceedings to be attended by the witnesses, and nothing in it should play on or trigger the witness's recollection of events. All documents used in the process should be retained and, if relevant to prosecution witnesses, handed to the CPS as a matter of course, and in relation to defence witnesses, produced to the court. Such material, it is contended, should be assessed in order to ascertain whether it meets the disclosure test in the normal way.

F. Failings in Disclosure

(a) Application under CPIA s. 8

As set out above, where the prosecutor has complied with, purported to comply **8.96** with, or failed to comply with s. 7A of the CPIA, and the accused has 'at any time reasonable cause to believe that there is prosecution material which is required by s. 7A to be disclosed to him and has not been', his or her statutory remedy is an application to the court for an order requiring the prosecutor to disclose it to him or her: see s. 8 of the CPIA.

---

[69] [2005] 2 Cr App R 6.

(b) Abuse of process

8.97 The power of the court to stay proceedings as an abuse of process exists in two categories of cases: where it would be impossible for the defendant to have a fair trial; and where it is necessary to protect the integrity of the criminal justice system. It is a power, however, to be most sparingly used. An analysis of the case law would tend to suggest that in the absence of bad faith, it will be a rare case indeed in which it will be found that even serious failings on the part of the police or prosecution (including with regard to disclosure) make it unfair to try a defendant.

(c) Abuse of process: missing material

8.98 In *R (Ebrahim) v Feltham Magistrates' Court*,[70] the Divisional Court stated that, in an application for a stay on the grounds of abuse of process where the complaint relates to non-availability of material, the first step was to identify the nature and extent, in the particular circumstances, of the duty (if it existed) of the investigator/prosecutor to obtain and/or retain the material in question. In this respect, it was important to have regard to the Code of Practice issued under the CPIA and the Attorney-General's Guidelines on Disclosure. If there was no duty to obtain and/or retain the material before the defence first sought its retention, there can be no question of the subsequent proceedings being considered unfair. If there has been a breach of a duty to obtain and/or retain, it will be for the defence to show on the balance of probabilities that owing to the absence of the material, the defence will suffer prejudice of such a degree that he or she cannot have a fair trial. The Divisional Court stated that it should be borne in mind by courts faced with abuse of process applications that the trial process is equipped to deal with the bulk of complaints on which applications for a stay are founded.

(d) Abuse of process: delay

8.99 In *R v F (S)*,[71] it was confirmed that a stay on the grounds of delay should only be employed in exceptional circumstances and only if a fair trial is no longer possible owing to prejudice caused by the delay which cannot fairly be addressed in the trial process. Normally, the trial process can ensure that all relevant factual issues arising from delay will be placed before the jury, together with appropriate directions from the judge in summing-up. These are essential considerations in the assessment of whether or not a defendant will suffer serious prejudice.

8.100 In *R v RD*,[72] the appellant appealed against his conviction, contending that proceedings ought to have been stayed by the court as an abuse of process. In this

---

[70] [2001] 2 Cr App R 23.
[71] [2011] 2 Crim App R 28.
[72] [2013] EWCA Crim 1592.

case, the delay between the allegations and the start of the trial was between thirty-nine and sixty-three years. The appellant contended, in support of the argument, that documents which would have assisted him in his defence were unavailable owing to the passage of time. These included documents showing the defendant's shift pattern and his military service records. The electoral role was unavailable, as were medical records, and other witnesses were dead.

8.101 The Court of Appeal, dismissing the appeal, held that although this matter required careful scrutiny because of the very substantial delay in this case, it was entirely satisfied that the trial process could properly cope with the difficulties faced by the appellant and that there was no prejudice to him of a type which would mean that he could not and did not get a fair trial. On an analysis of the missing material and of the evidence given at the trial and the issues before the jury, the court was satisfied that this appellant received a fair trial, and was not disadvantaged in a way that could properly be described as amounting to serious prejudice to his ability to mount a proper defence to the allegations brought against him.

(e) Abuse of process: failure to comply with disclosure obligations

8.102 In *R v O*,[73] the prosecution applied for leave to appeal against a decision of the Crown Court to stay an indictment for abuse of process in respect of failures of disclosure. The Court of Appeal, allowing the prosecution's appeal, held that whether there had been a wholesale failure of disclosure had to be examined on the basis of identified failures and their scope, the importance of the material in question, and the effect on the trial of the defendants. The Court of Appeal held that the case had called for active case management in order to ensure that requests for disclosure were focused and proportionate, and that where further grounds for disclosure were established, those were similarly focused. While deficiencies in disclosure might be properly censured, that was a long way short of establishing that the defendants could not have a fair trial. Late disclosure was not the same as non-disclosure. It was not unusual for disclosure to take place during a trial, and the question would then arise whether it could be coped with during the trial with or without an adjournment. It would require an exceptional case to go further than to discharge the jury and to make a terminating ruling.

8.103 Where a defendant asserts that the prosecution has failed to disclose material which is still in existence and which should have been disclosed, it is unlikely that the defence will be able to show that the effect of the late disclosure would be to render it impossible for the accused to receive a fair trial. The appropriate course is likely to be an adjournment.

---

[73] [2011] EWCA Crim 2854.

8.104 In *R v Salt*,[74] the defendants were charged with rape, false imprisonment, and assault by penetration. After eight days of the trial, the judge acceded to the defendants' application that the proceedings be stayed as an abuse of process, finding that the Crown's failure to make proper disclosure of unused material had been so fundamental that, although a future trial could be held fairly and notwithstanding the seriousness of the charges, the court ought to mark its condemnation by allowing a stay. The prosecution appealed against the ruling.

8.105 The Court of Appeal allowed the appeal. Where the court was considering acting in such a way as to bring a prosecution to an end as a result of the Crown's failures, whether by refusing to admit evidence or staying the proceedings as an abuse of process, it should approach its decision by determining whether it was in the interests of justice that the proceedings should be allowed to continue. The court had to balance the public interest in ensuring that those charged with grave crimes should be tried and the rights of the complainants to have their allegations determined at trial against the need to ensure the proper integrity of the criminal justice system and the fairness of any future trial. In the present case, the Court of Appeal held that the material considerations were the gravity of the charges, the denial of justice to the complainants, the necessity for proper attention to be paid to disclosure, the nature and materiality of the Crown's failures, the waste of court resources and the effect on the jury, and the availability of other sanctions, including a wasted costs order. Taking account of all those considerations and the fact that the material documentation which had not been disclosed was restricted to telephone records and was relevant only to the issue of credibility, it would not be in the interests of justice to stay the proceedings. The Court of Appeal stated:

> The obligations of the parties under r.1.1 of the Criminal Procedure Rules are clear. To differentiate between a failure to abide by a specific direction and a failure to follow the Rules would be to place an undue premium on the court making an order rather than expecting the parties to carry out their duties without such an order. Nor is it right to make a distinction in principle between a failure by the prosecution to serve evidence on time and the failure to make proper disclosure. Both have the potential to affect the fairness and orderly conduct of a trial and to undermine public confidence in the integrity of the criminal justice system.[75]

8.106 Where the unused material schedule is deficient in that it does not include items that clearly exist and which should be listed on the schedule, it may be an indication that the prosecution has failed to manage the disclosure process properly and that the court can have no confidence in the disclosure exercise. The ultimate remedy for the defence may be to apply to the court for a stay of the indictment as an abuse of process as a result of the prosecution's failure to comply with its

---

[74] *R v Salt* [2015] 2 Cr App R 27.
[75] ibid. at [42].

obligations to gather, retain, and scrutinize unused material in accordance with the CPIA and the Protocol.

G. Confidentiality

(a) Confidentiality within the trial process

In *R v J (DC)*,[76] the Court of Appeal upheld the convictions of a foster carer for **8.107** offences of indecent assault, sexual activity with a child, and rape of a child under 13. At pre-trial hearings, the defence applied for disclosure of documents from social services files in order to demonstrate that the complainants were persons of bad character. The judge ordered disclosure of approximately twenty documents from social services files. The appellant sought to rely on those documents as evidence of bad character on the basis that they showed that the complainants, in respect of the allegations in 1994 to 1996, had made false complaints of sexual abuse, told lies, and had been using controlled drugs at the time. At trial, the complainants were cross-examined on the basis of the documents; some of the matters were accepted, some were denied. The judge ordered that the defence and prosecution should put matters into a schedule setting out what had been accepted and what had been denied. The advocates discussed the order and decided to ignore it; the jury were given the documents and the judge criticized the appellant's advocate in front of the jury for doing so.

The Court of Appeal held that in any case where it was sought to place before **8.108** the jury material from social services files relating to a person who is not a defendant, an application had to be made to the court and the judge was required to give a clear ruling on the matter. Bad character evidence of a person who was not a defendant could be admitted by agreement pursuant to CJA 2003 s. 100. However, when an order was made for the disclosure of matters in social services files that related to a person who was not a defendant, the documents released by the judge were ordinarily released only for the purpose of enabling instructions to be taken from the defendant (or witnesses to be called) and for the matters contained in the documents to be put to the witnesses in the course of cross-examination. Their provision to the prosecution was similarly limited. The order did not entitle either the Crown or the defence to use the documents in any other way, unless the judge made an express order. That was because documents held by social services were generally subject to public interest immunity and the rights of the social services (as holders and guardians of the material) and of the persons who were the subject of the documentation had to be respected.

---

[76] [2010] 2 Cr App R 2.

8.109 There might be cases where it was considered necessary by the defence or the prosecution that wider use be made of the documentation or information. In such a case, it was necessary for the defence or the prosecution to apply to the judge for an order to extend the use which might be made. The judge would then consider the balance between the respective interests. If, for example, there was an application to put a document before the jury on the basis that its contents were admissible under the hearsay provisions of the Criminal Justice Act 2003, then the judge would have to consider the contents of the entire document to see what other matters were contained in the document, whether there should be redactions, or whether there were other ways in which the information could be placed before the jury. This required the judge to make a careful balance of the respective interests; this could not be circumvented by agreement between the advocates.

H. Limitations on Use of Material Disclosed by the Prosecution

(a) CPIA ss 17 and 18

8.110 Under CPIA s. 17, the accused to whom disclosure is made (under s. 3, 4, 7A, 8, 14, or 15) may only use or disclose the information (a) in connection with the proceedings for whose purposes he or she was given the object or allowed to inspect it; (b) to the extent to which the information was displayed or communicated publicly at a hearing; or (c) with the leave of the court.

8.111 Rule 15. 7 of the Crim PR provides that in determining any application by a defendant for leave to use disclosed material otherwise than in connection with the case in which it was disclosed, or beyond the extent to which it was displayed or communicated publicly, the court must consider any representations made by the prosecutor and must be satisfied that it has been able to take adequate account of any rights of confidentiality that may apply to the material.

8.112 It is a contempt of court for a person knowingly to use or disclose information if the use or disclosure is in contravention of CPIA s. 17. Such information would be inadmissible as evidence in civil proceedings if to adduce it would, in the opinion of the court before which the civil proceedings are being taken, be likely to constitute a contempt: see s. 18(9). A person guilty of such a contempt under s. 18 may be sentenced, in a magistrates' court, to a term of imprisonment not exceeding six months, a fine not exceeding £5,000, or both, and in a Crown Court, to a term of imprisonment not exceeding two years, a fine, or both: see s. 18(3). On finding that a contempt has been committed, the court making such a finding may order that the information/material be forfeited and dealt with in such manner as the court may order.

In *Taylor v Director of the SFO*,[77] the House of Lords held that disclosure in **8.113** criminal proceedings, which does not fall within s. 17(1) (such as that made under common law principles prior to the enactment of the CPIA), generated an implied undertaking not to use the material for any purpose other than the conduct of the defence in those criminal proceedings. Such an implied undertaking sought to ensure that the privacy and confidentiality of those who made, and those who were mentioned in, statements contained in unused material which had come into existence as a result of a criminal investigation were not invaded more than was absolutely necessary for the purposes of justice.

(b) Sexual Offences (Protected Material) Act 1997

The Sexual Offences (Protected Material) Act 1997 was introduced as a meas- **8.114** ure to prevent the circulation of disclosure material in sex cases as 'gaol pornography'. It makes provision for regulating access by defendants and others to certain categories of 'protected material' (in essence, statements by, photographs of, or medical reports concerning alleged victims of sexual offences) disclosed by the prosecution or by the CCRC in connection with proceedings relating to certain sexual and other offences. The Act creates offences, punishable by up to two years' imprisonment, of having or disclosing protected material otherwise than in accordance with the Act.

Section 9(3) provides that ss 17 and 18 of the CPIA (confidentiality of disclosed **8.115** information) shall not apply to any material disclosed under the Sexual Offences (Protected Material) Act 1997 in accordance with s. 3(2) or (3) of that Act.

The Act received Royal Assent on 21 March 1997, but some twenty years later, **8.116** it is not yet in force. As drafted, those acting for, or instructed by, the accused in criminal proceedings are at risk of committing offences because there is an absolute prohibition on disclosing protected material for whatever reason, save where the person making the disclosure has given certain statutory undertakings.

I. Conclusion

As criminal prosecutions grow in volume and complexity, so the disclosure exer- **8.117** cise in those cases will grow in scale and difficulty. The modern requirement to maintain written records, together with the proliferation of social media, undoubtedly means that the areas ripe for the application of the disclosure exercise have grown.

---

[77] [1999] 2 AC 177.

8.118 Case management rules now require the active participation in the disclosure exercise of all participants in a criminal prosecution. Gone are the days when the defence could wait for the Crown to identify relevant material, and make complaint at trial if they failed. The various Guideline and Protocol documents make clear that the defence are required to engage early in the process, and that the court must actively manage the discharge of the parties' disclosure obligations.

8.119 The disclosure exercise in every case is different. Under the statutory regime, the relevance and disclosability of material will be a matter for the judgment of the prosecution. The great dangers that exist in the failure to exercise that judgment appropriately or at all are obvious. It is imperative, therefore, that the highest standards of education and teaching are provided to all those with a role in the disclosure exercise.

9

CASE MANAGEMENT

Angela Rafferty, Rosina Cottage, Joshua Normanton, and Simon Taylor

A. Preliminary Issues

(a) Early identification of vulnerability

Early identification of vulnerability is essential to the effective management of **9.01** cases involving vulnerable witnesses. As has been noted throughout this book, vulnerability may derive from a variety of factors such as age, adverse physical and mental health, learning disabilities, and social impairments. Consequently, the way in which vulnerability is dealt with in court requires a flexible, imaginative approach that will be informed by command of law and practice and driven by careful planning and cooperation between the parties, including the judge, but which, above all, must be tailored to the particular circumstances of the vulnerable person and the case as a whole.

9.02 Parties should be alert to potential 'hidden' vulnerabilities and actively consider any warning signs that appear in the papers. While the age of a child witness will often be apparent and highlighted at an early stage, learning disabilities and social inhibitions will be less obvious. Unless the vulnerability is identified, none of the measures identified in this chapter, the Criminal Procedure Rules, or Criminal Practice Directions can be given effect.

(b) The framework

9.03 The starting point for managing cases of this type is Part 3 of the Criminal Procedure Rules[1] (Crim PR). The Crim PR, combined with the Criminal Practice Directions[2] (Crim PD), paragraphs 3D to 3G, give the advocate and court ample flexibility to adapt the preparation and presentation of the case in such a way as to facilitate the effective participation of vulnerable witnesses.

9.04 The Advocate's Gateway Toolkits provide essential reading for advocates engaged in cases involving vulnerable witnesses; they represent best practice and should be followed.[3] Toolkit 1A, which deals specifically with case management, states that 'individuals will vary hugely in their needs, wishes and preferences; any adjustments made must be tailored to respond to these individual requirements'.

(c) Early identification of the needs of witnesses

9.05 Once the vulnerability has been identified, the focus of the preparation will shift to the consideration of how best to ensure the effective participation of the witness. Under Part 3 of the Crim PR, the court must identify the needs of witnesses at an early stage.[4] This may require the parties to identify arrangements to facilitate the giving of evidence and participation in the trial.[5]

9.06 There are various statutory special measures that the court may utilize to assist a witness who is eligible for assistance under ss 16 and 17 of the Youth Justice and Criminal Evidence Act 1999 (YJCEA 1999) in giving evidence, and the necessity for a special measures direction should be considered in every case; however, it is important to note, as paragraph 3D.2 of the Crim PD does, that other

---

[1] See <https://www.justice.gov.uk/courts/procedure-rules/criminal> accessed 21 March 2017.
[2] ibid.
[3] The Advocates Gateway, 'Toolkit 1A: Case Management in Criminal Cases When a Witness or a Defendant Is Vulnerable', available at <http://www.theadvocatesgateway.org/images/toolkits/1a-case-management-in-criminal-cases-when-a-witness-or-a-defendant-is-vulnerable-2017.pdf> accessed 26 April 2017.
[4] Crim PR 3.2(2)(b).
[5] Crim PR 3.11(c)(iv) and (v).

participants in a case, whether witnesses who do not fall within the categories of eligible witnesses, or defendants, may require assistance outside the terms specifically provided for in Chapter 1 of the YJCEA 1999. The court is required to take 'every reasonable step' to facilitate the attendance of witnesses and to facilitate the participation of any person;[6] and it follows that the parties will need to be in a position at an early stage to assist the court with what those steps might be in each individual case. (See further Chapter 3, 'Witness Support'; Chapter 10, 'Special Measures'; Chapter 11, 'Intermediaries', and Chapter 12, 'Ground Rules Hearings'.)

(d) Early identification of the issues

The Ministry of Justice, in a statement issued with the Crim PR,[7] made it clear **9.07** that 'fairness is best served when the issues between the parties are identified as early and clearly as possible'. This will require considerable preparation by both sides in the early stages of each case. The parties will be expected to be able to identify the relevant issues at the Plea and Trial Preparation Hearing (PTPH) and to be able to provide assistance to the court with timetabling for the service of—for example—psychiatric or other expert evidence, third-party disclosure issues, intermediary applications, and the necessity for and identification of the matters to be dealt with at further case management hearings, including a pretrial review and ground rules hearing. This requires early service of both evidential and unused material that may be relevant.

(e) Cooperation between the parties

Rule 3.2(2)(g) of the Crim PR includes (as part of active case management) **9.08** encouragement to the participants to cooperate in the progression of the case. This will include serving reports quickly and efficiently, cooperating in the arrangements for hearings and the rulings sought, and sending proposed questions to intermediaries and the judge for inspection and analysis. The overall aim is a more collaborative approach than has generally been seen in the adversarial process hitherto.

In this regard, the phrase 'participants' ought to be taken to include the judge and **9.09** list office who can effectively assist in the management of pre-trial issues and in some circumstances do so in a manner to avoid unnecessary hearings.

To this end, the early allocation of trial judge is an important feature in cases of **9.10** this type. The judge has much to oversee and early awareness of the issues that

---

[6] Crim PR 3.9(3)(a) and (b).
[7] Ministry of Justice, 'The objectives and content of the first Criminal Procedures Rules' (March 2005, updated on 21 September 2015), available at <https://www.justice.gov.uk/courts/procedure-rules/criminal/notes> accessed 21 March 2017.

may affect the case will assist the trial judge in fulfilling the responsibility for setting ground rules, controlling questioning, and ensuring effective participation.

9.11 If it proves that it is impossible to guarantee continuity of judge (and indeed advocate), the parties ought to strive to make the 'picking up' of a case as easy as possible. Case summaries, hearing agendas, and written disclosure requests should be produced throughout the case in order to facilitate effective case management.

(f) Disclosure issues

9.12 Parties need to be alert to potential disclosure issues and their obligations in respect of them, from the outset of proceedings. The requirement to prioritize cases involving vulnerable people, and the very short timescales that can apply—particularly where the case involves a child under 10—means that disclosure, particularly third-party disclosure, needs to be obtained, considered, and disclosed as soon as possible in accordance with the Criminal Procedure and Investigations Act 1996 (CPIA 1996), the Judicial Protocol on the Disclosure of Unused Material in Criminal Cases, December 2013,[8] and the Attorney-General's Guidelines on Disclosure, December 2013.[9]

9.13 Where the case involves allegations of child abuse, the 2013 'Protocol and Good Practice Model—Disclosure of information in cases of alleged child abuse and linked criminal and care directions hearings' applies.[10] Each CPS area will have a locally agreed protocol produced to give effect to the terms of the national Protocol and Good Practice Model to which reference should be made. It is important to note that: (a) the Protocol applies to all criminal investigations into alleged cases of child abuse—not just those where there are Family Court proceedings, but that (b) the terms of the protocol only cover the disclosure of material to and from the Family Court and local authority. Medical records, or school records if the school is not under local authority control, will still have to be applied for, via the court if an order is required, in the usual way.

(g) Listing of cases and delay

9.14 It is important to understand that in cases involving a vulnerable person, delay is likely to cause real difficulty and distress which can have significant

---

[8] See <https://www.judiciary.gov.uk/wp-content/uploads/JCO/Documents/Protocols/Disclosure+Protocol.pdf> accessed 21 March 2017.

[9] See <https://www.gov.uk/government/publications/attorney-generals-guidelines-on-disclosure-2013> accessed 26 April 2017.

[10] See <http://www.cps.gov.uk/publications/docs/third_party_protocol_2013.pdf> accessed 21 March 2017.

adverse consequences, both for the individual concerned and for the wider trial process.

Toolkit 1A emphasizes the need for priority listing in a case involving a vulnerable person, and the responsibility on the advocates to remind the court that such cases should be prioritized.[11]   **9.15**

Where the case involves a witness under 10 years of age, the young witness protocol applies, under which a provisional trial date should be set no more than eight weeks from the date of plea (ordinarily, the PTPH date).[12]   **9.16**

Ensuring that cases involving vulnerable people are prioritized and not subject to delays extends beyond simply ensuring an early trial date. Trials involving vulnerable people should not be listed as floaters and careful consideration should be given to timetabling of the case (and other cases in the court list) to ensure that vulnerable witnesses give their evidence at a set time and without avoidable delay. Generally, it will be desirable for a vulnerable witness to give their evidence during the morning session.   **9.17**

(h) Pre-trial visits

The witness is entitled to have a pre-trial court familiarization visit. This visit is of enormous assistance to the witness and those presenting the case.[13] (See further Chapter 2, 'Vulnerable Witnesses: The Investigation Stage' and Chapter 3, 'Witness Support'.) Where an intermediary has been appointed, he or she should also attend the visit if possible and speak with the Witness Service. Usually, the officer in the case will also attend.   **9.18**

In particularly sensitive cases, if it is possible for the prosecution advocate to attend this visit it can be immensely reassuring to the vulnerable witness and helpful to the advocate. There may be other issues, not highlighted in any reports, that become clearer on such an occasion and it can help to confirm the areas for discussion at any ground rules hearing. If such a hearing has already taken place, and if thought necessary, a further hearing may be convened to develop the directions originally sought or to change them.   **9.19**

---

[11] The Advocate's Gateway Toolkit 1A, paras 4.1–4.5.

[12] 'Protocol to Expedite Cases involving Witnesses under 10 Years' (19 January 2015), available at <https:www.judiciary.gov.uk/wp-content/uploads/2015/03/police-cps-hmcts-ywi-protocol.pdf> accessed 21 March 2017.

[13] See further: CPS, Legal Guidance, 'Special Measures', available at <http://www.cps.gov.uk/legal/s_to_u/special_measures> accessed 21 March 2017. See also victims' entitlements at Ministry of Justice, 'Code of Practice for Victims of Crime' (London: MoJ, 2015) 25, para. 2.14, available at <https://www.gov.uk/government/uploads/system/uploads/attachment_data/file/476900/code-of-practice-for-victims-of-crime.PDF> accessed 21 March 2017; and service standards for witnesses in the criminal justice system in MoJ, 'The Witness Charter' (MoJ, 2013) 12, Standard 11, available at <https://www.gov.uk/government/uploads/system/uploads/attachment_data/file/264627/witness-charter-nov13.pdf> accessed 21 March 2017.

(i) The prosecutor's duties towards victims and witnesses

9.20   In the preparation of any case, and in particular cases involving vulnerable witnesses or defendants, the prosecution advocate must be aware of their duties towards witnesses and the court. Those duties are principally to be found in the Code for Crown Prosecutors,[14] but it is also essential to be aware of the Casework Quality Standards where the advocate is reminded to take 'account of the rights, interests and needs of victims and witnesses'.[15] Advocates should also consider the Code of Practice for the Victims of Crime, which details what a victim (including the young or otherwise vulnerable) should expect at all stages pre-, during, and post-trial from the Crown Prosecution Service (CPS), the advocate, and others involved in the investigation and proceedings. All Codes and Guidance are set out on the CPS website and are available to download.[16]

(j) Meeting witnesses

9.21   In the event that a pre-trial visit has not been held, the prosecution advocate has a duty where circumstances permit to introduce themselves to witnesses or complainants prior to them giving evidence at trial. In March 2016, the CPS issued Guidance on speaking to witnesses at court.[17] Paragraph 3.4 of the guidance suggests that the prosecutor should meet all witnesses before they give their evidence and that the prosecutor should help the witness with the following matters: (a) introductory matters; (b) providing assistance about procedure; (c) providing assistance on giving evidence; (d) providing assistance for cross-examination; (e) updating on progress; (f) speaking to the witness after they have given evidence; and (g) victim personal statements.

9.22   The prosecution advocate must have in mind the rules and duties of a Crown Prosecutor when meeting the witness. Prosecutors must not train or coach the witness or ask any questions that may influence or affect the nature or content of the witness's evidence (*R v Momodou* and *R v Limani*[18]).

9.23   Paragraph 3.6 of the CPS Guidance suggests that prosecutors can have confidence that providing their discussion with a witness is aimed at assisting the witness to give their best evidence and avoids rehearsing them as to the evidence they should give, there should be no risk that coaching has occurred.

---

[14] CPS, 'The Code for Crown Prosecutors' (2013), available at <https://www.cps.gov.uk/publications/docs/code_2013_accessible_english.pdf> accessed 21 March 2017.

[15] CPS, 'Casework Quality Standards', 2nd edn, Standard 1, Benchmark 3, available at <https://www.cps.gov.uk/publications/casework_quality_standards/> accessed 21 March 2017.

[16] See <http://www.cps.gov.uk> accessed 20 March 2017.

[17] See <http://www.cps.gov.uk/legal/assets/uploads/files/13007%20Special%20measures%20CPS%206th.pdf> accessed 21 March 2017.

[18] [2005] EWCA Crim 177.

The guidance also sets out that prosecutors should be accompanied by a CPS member of staff to assist in keeping a record of what is discussed with the witness at the meeting.

Again, issues as to flexibility may arise when it comes to meeting witnesses. In **9.24** circumstances where the vulnerable witness cannot attend court for either the pre-trial visit or if the evidence is to be taken remotely at trial, consideration will have to be given to how best to assist to familiarize the witness who is at a remote location. If particularly unusual arrangements are put in place, the defence may be put on notice as to the proposal in advance of the meeting.

B. Special Measures

(a) ABE video-recorded interviews

The quality and clarity of the evidence presented in ABE interviews varies enor- **9.25** mously. Matters are complicated by the fact that the recordings themselves serve a dual purpose, in that they are both an investigative tool used by the police and a method of presenting evidence utilized by the advocate. The traditional approach of advocates to the editing of interviews has not always enhanced the quality of the product placed before the jury. Too often, the focus of editing has been restricted to cutting out the rapport section and any inadmissible material, rather than considering what evidence is required to properly reflect the witness's evidence in a manner which will be most intelligible and helpful to the jury. Consequently, in far too many cases, the ABE evidence placed before the jury continues to be over-long, repetitive, and difficult to follow—even after editing.

As the video stands as the witness's evidence-in-chief, it is primarily the prosecu- **9.26** tor's duty to ensure that the interview is properly edited so as to avoid irrelevant matters being included and/or otherwise relevant matters being repeated in an unproductive way. It follows that, subject to defence invitations to exclude inadmissible matters, decisions as to what should be edited are for the prosecutor. The benefit of adopting this approach is that it allows for the early and significant editing of the interview.

In the event that material that has been edited becomes relevant, it can be dealt **9.27** with by: (a) admission; (b) reading the edited part to the jury; or (c) playing the edited part to the jury at an appropriate time in the trial.

There are circumstances where the video-recorded interview is inadequate, either **9.28** wholly or in part. This may be due to technical difficulties or because the content is lacking. Where the inadequacy is due to technical failure (e.g. where the sound is poor), consideration should be given to enhancing the audio.

9.29 Where the content is lacking, consideration ought to be given to: (a) having another short ABE prepared; (b) having a statement taken; or (c) asking supplemental questions.

(i) Case management issues relating to refreshing the memory of a witness whose evidence is video-recorded

9.30 Planning for the stage at which a witness should refresh their memory from a recording should be raised at the PTPH and confirmed at the PTR, taking account of the advice of any intermediary instructed for trial and, if appropriate, the officer in the case or Witness Care. Consideration will need to be given as to when and where memory-refreshing should take place, who should be present, and how a record is kept. Often, there has been editing of the recording which needs to be explained to the witness. It should be remembered that some witnesses will not be able to view all the material on one day.

9.31 It will rarely be appropriate for the recording to be viewed for the first time on the day of trial. It is now the practice in most courts for vulnerable witnesses to view their recording a day or so before the trial.[19]

(b) Advocate's input re. special measures

9.32 When obtaining the views of the witness on special measures, it is essential that the prosecution advocate is satisfied that those views are based on proper information. It is important for the advocate to ensure that the witness is made aware of all of the special measures that are available, and their respective advantages and disadvantages (e.g. facilities for live-link between court centres and offices or even connection via Skype from the home of the witness). There are a plethora of possibilities each suitable either individually or collectively for a particular set of circumstances.

9.33 Often, child witnesses and others are afraid of being seen by the defendant over the live-link. When seeking the witness's views on the use of special measures, if a live-link is being considered, the witness must be told that the defendant will be able to see them on the court monitor. It may be that the use of screens is in fact a more appropriate measure. It may also be possible to partially shield the screen in the courtroom to prevent the defendant from seeing the witness.

9.34 In cases where there are complex needs, information will need to be gathered regarding the abilities and requirements of the witness (provided typically by carers, social workers, and medical staff). This should include information on

---

[19] In accordance with Annex G, Crown Prosecution Service Special Measures Guidance, available at <http://www.cps.gov.uk/legal/s_to_u/special_measures/#a19> accessed 21 March 2017.

cognitive and linguistic ability, range of behaviours, and emotional state. It may be that the witness has not been fully assessed previously. In those circumstances, a report will be required from a psychologist to inform any decision to apply for special measures. Such a report may also indicate that the use of an intermediary[20] at court may be appropriate.

(c) Intermediaries for witnesses

The need for an intermediary should be identified early for witnesses. An intermediary may be instructed either by the Police or the CPS utilizing the matching service under the governance of the National Crime Agency. **9.35**

Intermediaries have different skills and professional backgrounds, for example in occupational health or mental health. At the time of writing, there were only three deaf intermediaries in the country. Whoever is matched to the case, it is still necessary to check that the intermediary's qualifications are appropriate to the communication needs of the particular witness. There may have been an intermediary at the original interview that may not be suitable/available for the trial. The witness and their ability to communicate is key and if there must be a change of intermediary, the sooner that is dealt with, the better. **9.36**

The intermediary will prepare a report. This will assist the prosecution advocate to prepare a plan for what will need to be covered at the ground rules hearing which will feed into plans to assist the witness in communicating their evidence. In the report, there may be any number of helpful practical suggestions on timetabling and how best the witness may refresh their memory and when. Not all suggestions will work. Flexibility is the key. The report is also likely to give a clear idea of how the advocate should phrase questions. This must be taken in the spirit it is intended: as assistance. **9.37**

The defence advocate will need to consider if there is to be any argument about the use of the intermediary or the extent of their involvement. The earlier this argument is flagged up and conducted, the better. The intermediary is neither an expert, nor a witness to be cross-examined. They will attend to explain the report and its recommendations, but the process is not adversarial. The argument itself is based on submissions and the evidence in the case. It is important to remember that 'counsel should only raise such grounds in opposition as are properly arguable and not pursue a hidden agenda simply to deprive the witness of the opportunity of giving evidence effectively'.[21] (See further Chapter 11, 'Intermediaries'.) **9.38**

---

[20] YJCEA 1999 s. 29.
[21] Special Measures Guidance, Bar Council.

(d) 'Special measures' for defendants

9.39 Vulnerable defendants are excluded from the special measures provisions available to vulnerable witnesses under YJCEA 1999, save for a limited access to live-link. YJCEA 1999 s. 33A[22] permits defendants under the age of 18 and those over 18 suffering from a mental disorder to give evidence by live link under appropriate conditions.

9.40 Nevertheless, as has been recognized in a series of cases, and emphasized in Part 3D of the CPD, it is fair that vulnerable defendants should be afforded the same right to effective participation in the trial process as is afforded to witnesses. Part 3G of the Crim PD[23] details trial arrangements for vulnerable defendants. In a multi-handed case, consideration should be given to severing the vulnerable defendant's case if this is consistent with a fair trial and other special measures are not appropriate.[24]

9.41 As with vulnerable witnesses, a vulnerable defendant should be given a court familiarization visit, which may deal with seating, court layout, and functions of those in court, as well as basic court procedure and courtroom facilities.[25] If an intermediary has been instructed, they should accompany the defendant on this visit.[26]

9.42 In some circumstances, particularly if the vulnerable defendant is a young child, then having regard to security and any other relevant factors, consideration should be given to whether it is appropriate to permit them to sit outside of the dock with family or appropriate supporters. The aim is to encourage 'easy, informal communication with legal representatives'.[27]

9.43 If the defendant's use of the live link is being considered, he or she should have an opportunity to have a practice session.[28]

9.44 If any case against a vulnerable defendant has attracted or may attract widespread public or media interest, the assistance of the police should be enlisted to try and ensure that he or she is not harassed or abused while at court.[29]

(e) Defendant intermediaries

9.45 Judges have previously permitted defendants to have the assistance of intermediaries using their inherent powers and funded from the court budget. However,

---

[22] Created by the Police and Justice Act 2006 s. 47.
[23] [2015] EWCA Crim 1567, Part 3, as amended in April 2016.
[24] ibid. at para. 3G.1.
[25] ibid. at para. 3G.2.
[26] ibid. at para. 3G.3.
[27] ibid. at para. 3G.8.
[28] ibid. at para. 3G.4.
[29] ibid. at para. 3G.5.

amendments made to the Crim PD in April 2016 may change this radically. There is no presumption that a defendant will be assisted by an intermediary, and even where it would improve the trial process appointment of a defendant's intermediary is not mandatory. Applications for the entire trial will be 'extremely rare'.

In *R v Rashid*,[30] it was held that the 'overwhelming majority of cases, competent legal representation and good trial management' will provide that a defendant gives best quality evidence, participates in his trial, and has a fair trial. In the rare cases where a defendant nevertheless requires an intermediary,[31] the court approved the distinction between two types of assistance, that is, throughout the trial or only when giving evidence, and that the court must determine what is necessary for the particular defendant. The court confirmed that it would be a 'rare' case where the threshold of disability is crossed such that an intermediary is required when the defendant gives his evidence and 'very rare' for an intermediary to be present for the whole trial.[32]   **9.46**

With defendants under the age of 18, careful assessment is required, but again there is no presumption in favour of appointment of an intermediary and 'the decision should be made on an individual basis in the context of the circumstances of the particular case'.[33]   **9.47**

Given the new approach heralded by the amendment to the Crim PD, it is likely that judges will have to step into the breach and support vulnerable witnesses or defendants. This approach is not new: see *R v Cox*,[34] where the judge said that he would 'take on the role of an intermediary' for the vulnerable defendant.   **9.48**

If it is thought that an intermediary may be required, the defence will need to seek prior authority from the Legal Aid Authority for funding for an intermediary assessment. Even if an assessment results in a recommendation that an intermediary be utilized, it is for the court to determine whether or not an intermediary should be appointed and, if so, for what purpose.[35]   **9.49**

(f) Pre-trial cross-examination—YJCEA 1999 s. 28

In 1989, the Pigot report[36] made recommendations which led to the enacting of s. 28. It is a special measure. It provides for pre-recording of a witness's cross-examination before trial.   **9.50**

---

[30] [2017] EWCA Crim 2.
[31] Para. 73.
[32] Para. 84.
[33] [2016] EWCA Crim 97 at para. 3F.5.
[34] [2012] EWCA Crim 549.
[35] Crim PD 3F.12.
[36] T. Pigot, *Report of the Advisory Group on Video-Recorded Evidence* (Home Office, 1989).

9.51 The section has never been fully implemented. There were three pilot schemes. These began in December 2013 at the Crown Courts in Kingston upon Thames, Leeds, and Liverpool. Eligibility for vulnerable adults remained the same as for other special measures in the 1999 Act, but inclusion of young people was restricted to those under the age of 16 (it is those under 18 who are covered by the Act). A process evaluation assessing the three pilots was published by the Ministry of Justice in 2016.[37] The evaluation relied on statistical data as well as interviews with judges, practitioners, and s. 28 witnesses. Only a handful of witnesses were interviewed as part of the process evaluation. The witnesses still described cross-examination as stressful, unsettling, and difficult, whereas practitioners opined that the s. 28 process reduced the trauma and distress of witnesses. However, both the time the witnesses had to wait until their cross-examination (within the entire trial process) and the length of their cross-examination was significantly shortened. The significant increase in workload was noted, particularly in relation to expedited time frames at the outset of cases and the additional hearings required.

9.52 The legislation was enacted to reduce delay for the witness and to allow the witness's evidence to be captured in full at an early stage in the proceedings. The trial process could then continue without the witness being inconvenienced and distressed by delay. If there was a re-trial, the witness would not have to attend again because the recording may be reused. Recent cases as to delays in proceedings and the treatment of witnesses have provided an impetus to progress implementation of the provisions.

9.53 A judicial protocol (now somewhat out of date) has been issued for the management of s. 28 cases,[38] which aims to consolidate current best practice in case management of cross-examination and is explicit about the need for all advocates to be familiar with The Advocate's Gateway toolkits. It is also explicit that paragraph 3E of the Crim PD[39] must be followed.

9.54 Each s. 28 case must have a ground rules hearing conducted by the same judge who presides at the pre-trial recording. This should take place at least a week before the pre-recording. Prior to the ground rules hearing, the advocates and the judge will need to view the ABE evidence. The defendant's advocate attending the hearing must be the same advocate who will be conducting the recorded cross-examination (and the subsequent trial). The registered intermediary should also attend the ground rules hearing. Topics for discussion and agreement will depend on the individual needs of the witness and the judge will set the ground

---

[37] J. Baverstock, *Process Evaluation of Pre-Recorded Cross-Examination Pilot (Section 28)* (MoJ Analytical Series, 2016).

[38] Judicial Protocol on the implementation of section 28 of the Youth Justice and Criminal Evidence Act 1999: 'Pre-recording of cross-examination and re-examination' (September 2014).

[39] Now available at [2015] EWCA Crim 1567.

rules. The aim is also to reach agreement as to how and when limitations ordered in relation to questioning should be communicated to the jury.

C. Pre-Trial Hearings

(a) Competency of witnesses

One of the issues which may arise pre-trial is the competency of witnesses. This **9.55** is an issue that should be identified as early as possible. The legal test for competence is set out in YJCEA 1999 s. 53. In essence, it provides that a person, whatever their age, is competent to give evidence unless they are not able to understand questions put to them as a witness and give answers to them that can be understood.[40] The former Lord Chief Justice, Lord Judge explained further in *R v B*[41] that the competence test in each case 'is entirely witness or child specific. There are no presumptions or preconceptions.'

It is for the party who seeks to call the witness to satisfy the court on the balance **9.56** of probabilities that with the benefit of any special measures that are proposed, the witness is competent.[42] An expert may be called and cross-examined,[43] as can the witness in question with the benefit of any special measures ordered.[44] This must be done in the presence of all parties.[45]

When considering whether or not a witness is competent, it is important to **9.57** remember that, for example, a child's evidence is not to be judged by the same standards as an adult. The fact that a child may have difficulties in recall, consistency, or communication does not mean that he or she is likely to be judged incompetent. As emphasized by Lord Justice Treacy in *R v F*,[46] where the competence hearing was held to be flawed, it was the court and advocates who needed properly to prepare for such hearings and adapt questions and tests for the witness.

It should now be rare that such a hearing is needed as judges and advocates **9.58** have become more experienced in the necessary modifications to questioning and preparation for vulnerable witnesses, adapting to the witnesses' needs and communication difficulties, rather than the other way round.[47]

---

[40] YJCEA 1999 s. 53(1)(a) and (b).
[41] [2010] EWCA Crim 4 at [38].
[42] YJCEA 1999 s. 54(2).
[43] ibid. s. 54(5).
[44] ibid. s. 54(3).
[45] ibid. s. 54(6).
[46] [2013] EWCA Crim 424 at [24] and [27].
[47] For a detailed discussion of this topic, see P. Cooper, 'Witness Competency Hearings— A Test of Competence' (2013) *Criminal Bar Quarterly*, 2, 5–6.

9.59 In the joined appeal of *R v JP* (heard with *Lubemba*[48]), the trial judge had gone to see a young witness with no advocates present. The judge was unable to get the witness to communicate properly with him and consequently ruled that she could not be cross-examined at all. No consideration was given as to the legal test of competency. The Court of Appeal in overturning the conviction said:

> With respect to the judge, who no doubt had the child's best interests at heart, we simply do not understand what he was saying as a matter of law, why he concluded the child could not be cross examined and why he did not allow defence counsel to try a few sensitively phrased questions. It is not clear to us whether he had concluded the child was not competent to give evidence, not fit to give evidence, or it would not be good for her to give evidence. These difficulties might not have arisen had it been arranged for him to introduce himself to the witness at the same time as the advocates did.[49]

(b) Ground rules hearings

9.60 Ground rules hearings may be held for both vulnerable witnesses and defendants. Where an intermediary has been instructed, the intermediary must attend. Parties should expect the judge to require the parties to provide cross-examination plans in an appropriate case for discussion with the intermediary. Directions may be given concerning the approach to questioning, including length, content, and—where there is more than one defendant—the division of topics of cross-examination between the parties. Ground rules hearings are not restricted to consideration of questioning, but will have a detailed and comprehensive approach to the needs of witnesses and defendants. Paragraph 3E of the Crim PD is the starting point.

9.61 Matters which may be dealt with at the ground rules hearing and throughout the management of the trial include arrangements for memory refreshing and watching ABE interviews, timetabling of witnesses and arrangements for attendance at court and meeting the judge and advocates, court dress, special requirements for each individual, aides to be used during evidence, and final special measure orders.

9.62 A ground rules hearing should be held for defendants at the appropriate time in the trial. This may be before the trial and/or at the time the defendant chooses to give evidence if it is likely that standard cross-examination will not be suitable to allow the defendant to communicate effectively. A ground rules hearing before a defendant gives evidence should be held where it is likely that 'traditional' questioning and cross-examination techniques will cause difficulty. It is fair that defendants who have communication and other vulnerabilities should

---

[48] [2014] EWCA Crim 2064.
[49] ibid. at [47].

be afforded the same treatment as witnesses. (See further Chapter 12, 'Ground Rules Hearings'.)

(c)   Cross-examination plans

As previously stated, a judge may require a cross-examination plan to be prepared **9.63** for discussion at a ground rules hearing or at any other stage prior to the questioning of prosecution or defence witnesses. Given that the reason for requiring a cross-examination plan is to ensure that questions are tailored to the vulnerability and communication needs of the person to be questioned, there is no reason in principle why a cross-examination plan should not also be required in cases involving vulnerable defendants. In cases involving a vulnerable witness or defendant, such a requirement will most commonly arise where:

1. the vulnerable person has communication difficulties (whether with the assistance of an intermediary or not) so as to ensure appropriate phraseology;
2. there is a concern that the cross-examination will not be sufficiently focused or in accordance with the rules of admissibility; and/or
3. there is some other reason for limiting cross-examination, such as to ensure that the distress caused by the questioning of the witness is proportionate to the forensic value of the questioning.

The parameters of cross-examination plans will be adapted to the circumstances of the case.[50] In cases with an intermediary, it will ordinarily be necessary for each question to be written out in full and shown to the judge and intermediary for comment on phraseology and length.[51]

In other cases where the need for a ground rules hearing does not derive from the **9.64** witness's communication difficulties, where, for example, the witness is fearful or distressed or the witness is a complainant in a sexual offence case, the cross-examination plan may take the form of headlines/topics.

Where questions are written out in full, the ground rules hearing ought to con- **9.65** sider the issue of additional questioning and departure from plan. The advocate, judge, and intermediary ought to be clear before cross-examination starts as to the permitted level of departure/flexibility. This decision is likely to be informed by the quality of the initial cross-examination plan, i.e. if it shows that the planned questioning is appropriate and avoids the mischief sought to be avoided it is likely that greater flexibility can/ought to be sanctioned prior to the witness giving evidence.

---

[50] B. Leveson, 'Review of Efficiency in Criminal Proceedings' (Judiciary of England and Wales, 2015) 266, available at <https://www.judiciary.gov.uk/wp-content/uploads/2015/01/review-of-efficiency-in-criminal-proceedings-20151.pdf> accessed 21 March 2017.
[51] The Advocate's Gateway Toolkit 1, para. 3.1.

(i) Disclosure of cross-examination plans

9.66   The decision as to the appropriateness of the proposed question is a decision for the judge after consultation with the advocate and the intermediary. It follows that the cross-examination plan will need to be disclosed to the judge and intermediary.

9.67   In multi-handed cases, it may be necessary for each defendant's legal representative to set out the questions that are going to be asked or the topics that are to be covered in order to avoid unnecessary repetition.

9.68   Complications may arise in 'cut-throat' defences or where the judge has required the prosecution to provide a cross-examination plan for a defendant. Each of these scenarios will require discussion by the court and parties. However, ultimately the court's case management powers under Crim PR 3.5(1) make it clear that, in furtherance of the overriding objective, the court may give any direction and take any step actively to manage a case unless that direction or step would be inconsistent with legislation, including the Crim PR. It follows that the court may well direct the service of cross-examination plans upon co-defendants and, where it is necessary, the party whose witness it is.

D. Evidential Issues at Trial

(a) Putting the case

9.69   In *Lubemba*,[52] the Court of Appeal held that:

> Advocates must adapt to the witness, not the other way round. They cannot insist upon any supposed right 'to put one's case' or previous inconsistent statements to a vulnerable witness. If there is a right to 'put one's case' (about which we have our doubts) it must be modified for young or vulnerable witnesses.

Lubemba is a case which makes it clear that 'putting the case' is not a sacrosanct right, nor is it a fundamental principle of advocacy in cases involving young or vulnerable witnesses. However, the issues surrounding challenging vulnerable witnesses are not straightforward and must be scrutinized carefully in each individual case.

(i) A historical perspective

9.70   The principle of 'putting the case' is also referred to as the 'rule in *Browne v Dunn*'.[53] In this House of Lords case, Herschell LJ expressed the following oft-quoted opinion

---

[52] [2014] EWCA Crim 2064 at [51].
[53] (1893) 6 R 67.

on the question of whether the case should be put to a witness whose evidence is challenged:

> I cannot help saying that it seems to me to be absolutely essential to the proper conduct of a cause, where it is intended to suggest that a witness is not speaking the truth on a particular point, to direct his attention to the fact by some questions put in cross-examination ... My Lords, I have always understood that if you intend to impeach a witness you are bound, whilst he is in the box, to give him an opportunity of making any explanation which is open to him; and as it seems to me, that is not only a rule of professional practice in the conduct of a case, but is essential to fair play and fair dealing with witnesses.[54]

It follows that challenging a witness has traditionally been viewed as not only about **9.71** fairness to the defendant, but also fairness to the witness: the witness is entitled to have the opportunity to answer the assertions a defendant makes which affect the witness's standing with the court. This point is reflected in the second speech made in *Browne v Dunn* by Lord Halsbury:

> To my mind, nothing would be more absolutely unjust than not to cross-examine witnesses upon evidence which they have given, so as to give them notice and to give them an opportunity of explanation, and an opportunity very often to defend their own character, and not having given them such an opportunity, to ask the jury afterwards to disbelieve what they have said, although not one questions has been directed either to their credit or to the accuracy of the facts they have deposed to.

The point is also reflected in *Fenlon*,[55] a criminal case in which Lane LCJ considered *Browne v Dunn* in determining whether the prosecution or a co-defendant had to put his case to a defendant. The court found:

> It is the duty of counsel who intends to suggest that a witness is not telling the truth to make it clear to the witness in cross-examination that he challenges his veracity and to give the witness an opportunity of replying. It need not be done in minute detail, but it is the duty of counsel to make it plain to the witness ... that his evidence is not accepted and in what respects it is not accepted.[56]

(ii)   Code of Conduct

The fundamental nature of the principle led to its incorporation (for a time) into **9.72** the Code of Conduct of the Bar of England and Wales.[57] Paragraph 708(i) held that counsel:

> Must not by assertion in a speech impugn a witness whom he has had an opportunity to cross-examine unless he has given the witness an opportunity to answer the allegation.

---

[54] *Browne v Dunn* as quoted in *Director of Public Prosecutions & Another v Burke and Another* [2014] IEHC 483. For an in-depth analysis of the origins and development of the rule, see J. Welsh, 'To Put, or Not to Put' [2016] Crim LR, 4, 245–65.
[55] [1980] 71 Cr App R 307.
[56] [1980] 71 Cr App R 307 at [313].
[57] Code of Conduct of the Bar of England and Wales, 3rd edn (April 2017).

The Code of Conduct was replaced by the BSB handbook on 6 January 2014. This contains a narrower interpretation of the rule. Rule C 7.2 provides:

> You must not make a serious allegation against a witness whom you have had an opportunity to cross-examine unless you have given that witness a chance to answer the allegation in cross-examination.[58]

(iii) Putting the case to vulnerable witnesses

9.73 In vulnerable witness cases, the Court of Appeal has consistently held that there is no requirement to put the case to a witness who will not understand it or who is incapable of dealing with such a challenge. In certain cases, the advocate may in fact be prevented from putting the case by direction of the judge. The Crim PD[59] provides that:

> For adult non-vulnerable witnesses an advocate will usually put his case so that the witness will have the opportunity of commenting upon it and/or answering it. When the witness is young or otherwise vulnerable, the court may dispense with the normal practice and impose restrictions on the advocate 'putting his case' where there is a risk of a young or otherwise vulnerable witness failing to understand, becoming distressed or acquiescing to leading questions.

The objective of the rule is not to vitiate the defendant's right of challenge, but to protect the vulnerable from confusion and distress. The rule resets the balance between defendants and that small group of witnesses for whom it would be unfair to put the case.

9.74 *R v E*[60] provides a practical perspective on this rebalancing of the principles of fairness. *R v E* involved the cross-examination of a 5-year-old in a case involving allegations of child cruelty, specifically punching of the child in the stomach by the appellant. Given the age of the complainant, the judge placed limitations on how he would be cross-examined by defence counsel. He directed that defence counsel could ask questions to which he wanted 'actual answers, but ... the nature of the defence in this case has been set out writing and [defence counsel was] neither required [nor permitted] to put that to the witness'.[61] Directions were given to the jury to the effect that the witness would not be challenged in the traditional way. Defence counsel embarked on cross-examination, but was frequently stopped or interrupted by the judge, who prevented counsel from exploring inconsistencies, credibility, and reliability with the witness. He did not put the essential elements of his case to the witness.

---

[58] *Bar Standards Board Handbook*, 2nd edn (30 April 2015).
[59] Crim PD at para. 3E.4.
[60] [2011] EWCA Crim 3028.
[61] ibid. at [7].

The appellant appealed. The Court of Appeal described the core argument of on appeal thus: 'the real complaint here, in our view, is that the defence was deprived of the opportunity to confront C in what we might venture to call "the traditional way" '.[62] The court went on to observe: **9.75**

> The jury knew that the defendant disputed the evidence of C. The judge clearly explained his decision as to cross-examination technique and why he had taken it. In addition, the jury was specifically directed 'to make proper fair allowances for the difficulties faced by the defendant in asking questions about this'.[63]

It was held that there was no unfairness to the defendant in not permitting his advocate to 'put the case' to a young, vulnerable witness.

(iv)   No general prohibition on putting the case

Some vulnerable witnesses will be able to deal fairly with challenge in an appropriate way. Formulation of questions can often be devised which allow the witness to address the challenge, even with vulnerabilities and communication issues. *R v Lubemba* should not be thought to have established a contrary principle to that articulated in *Browne v Dunn,* i.e. that the defendant's case should *never* be put to a vulnerable person. This is far from the position in law. **9.76**

In *R v B*,[64] the Lord Chief Justice stated: **9.77**

> When the issue is whether the child is lying or mistaken in claiming that the defendant behaved indecently towards him or her, it should not be over-problematic for the advocate to formulate short, simple questions which put the essential elements of the defendant's case to the witness, and fully to ventilate before the jury the areas of evidence which bear on the child's credibility.

Prohibitions on putting the case should only apply where a particular witness's vulnerabilities are such that putting the case would cause unfairness. However, in cases where those circumstances do not arise, some advocates may seek to obtain an advantage by not putting the case to the witness. After all, it is often damaging to a defendant's position when the witness is able to give compelling responses to challenging questions. **9.78**

If it is the view of the judge (having considered—where applicable—the conclusions of any intermediary assessment about the communication needs and abilities of the witness) that the witness can cope with having the case put to them (or put to them in a suitably modified way), then the principle of fairness to the witness means it will be appropriate that the defence case be put to them. This **9.79**

---

[62] ibid. at [28].
[63] ibid.
[64] [2010] EWCA Crim 4 at [42].

gives them a fair opportunity to answer it. If permitted to do so, it is the duty of the advocate to put the case in a way that is comprehensible to the witness.

(b) Inconsistencies

9.80 As with putting the case, advocates may also be prevented from putting relevant and admissible inconsistencies or previous accounts to a vulnerable witness or defendant. As the Lord Chief Justice made clear in *R v B*:[65]

> Aspects of evidence which undermine or are believed to undermine the child's credibility must, of course, be revealed to the jury, but it is not necessarily appropriate for them to form the subject matter of detailed cross-examination of the child and the advocate may have to forgo much of the kind of contemporary cross-examination which consists of no more than comment on matters which will be before the jury in any event from different sources ... Comment on the evidence, including comment on the evidence which may bear adversely on the credibility of the child, should be addressed after the child was finished giving evidence.

9.81 Many vulnerable witnesses will find it either extremely difficult or impossible to deal with detailed and lengthy cross-examination about events which may have occurred some time ago or involve their reports to other witnesses. Furthermore, the exploration of these types of issues in cross-examination be distressing and have a concomitant effect on the witness's communicative ability. This is particularly the case where sexual offences are alleged. However, the defendant is entitled to have the material before the jury so that a fair and informed analysis of the witness's evidence and credibility can be made.

9.82 Practical assistance on the issue is derived from paragraph 3E.4 of the Crim PD:

> Instead of commenting on inconsistencies during cross-examination, following discussion between the judge and the advocates, the advocate or judge may point out important inconsistencies after (instead of during) the witness's evidence. The judge should also remind the jury of these during summing up. The judge should be alert to alleged inconsistences that are not in fact inconsistent, or are trivial.

(i) Admissibility

9.83 Admissibility issues should be considered as early as possible. Only admissible and relevant evidence should go to the jury. Issues around bad character and the provisions of the Criminal Justice Act 2003, previous sexual behaviour and YJCEA 1999 s. 41, and hearsay should be resolved before cross-examination commences. Any inconsistencies to be relied on must be real inconsistencies and not trivial matters.

9.84 The Practice Direction provides that the advocate or judge may point out 'important' inconsistencies. *Lubemba* provides that 'it is perfectly possible to ensure the

---

[65] ibid. at [42].

jury are made aware of the defence case and of significant inconsistencies without intimidating or distressing a witness'.[66] A skilled advocate would not seek to draw out every single trivial or unimportant inconsistency in a witness's evidence or in the material which surrounds it. The emphasis is on important and significant inconsistencies. The court will seek to prevent exhaustive lists of every minor contradiction in the witness's account or life going before the jury.

(ii) Timing

The Crim PD indicates that in some cases the process of informing the jury as to inconsistencies is to occur 'after' the witness gives evidence.[67] Best practice dictates that this translates to 'immediately after' the witness gives evidence. As stated in *R v Wills*:[68] **9.85**

> This case highlights that, for vulnerable witnesses, the traditional style of cross-examination where comment is made on inconsistencies during cross-examination must be replaced by a system where those inconsistencies can be drawn to the jury at or about the time when the evidence is being given and not, in long or complex cases, for that comment to have to await the closing speeches at the end of the trial. One solution would be for important inconsistencies to be pointed out, after the vulnerable witness has finished giving evidence, either by the advocate or by the judge, after the necessary discussion with the advocates.

It can be undesirable to wait until the end of the trial to highlight important inconsistencies. It is preferable to do it when the evidence of the witness is fresh in the jury's mind and it may be important for the jury to hear material which undermines the witness at the time that the witness would have been cross-examined in a 'traditional' case. **9.86**

Discussion between the trial advocates and the judge is important when deciding how and when to deal with inconsistencies. It may be possible to deal with some matters of inconsistency through other witnesses in the trial and draw them to the jury's attention by this method. It is important that all advocates know what approach is to be taken so that no important and relevant evidence is overlooked. This is an area where cooperation between all parties is required. **9.87**

(iii) Format

The Crim PD and authorities state that inconsistencies could be highlighted after the witness gives evidence. They do not provide practical guidance on approach and format. **9.88**

The approach the advocate will take may depend on the particular circumstances of the case. A relevant consideration is the number of matters relied on and the **9.89**

---

[66] [2014] EWCA Crim 2064 at [45].
[67] Crim PD at para. 3E.4.
[68] [2011] EWCA Crim 1938 at [39].

density of the material containing them. In cases involving many issues, it is submitted that best practice is likely to require the preparation of a schedule of inconsistencies. However, where there are only a few inconsistencies, defence counsel may prefer the opportunity to deal with these orally. This is a matter which should be discussed with the judge and between the trial advocates as early as possible.

9.90 The Practice Direction also provides that the judge may highlight the inconsistencies. As a matter of fairness in almost all cases, the judge will highlight important and significant inconsistencies in the summing-up. It is a matter for discussion whether the judge is to do so immediately after the witness gives evidence.

9.91 It will be important for the judge to direct the jury as to the legal status of any document or disclosure revealing inconsistencies and directions should be carefully tailored to the circumstances of each case. While the Crown may agree and/or the judge may rule that important inconsistencies should go before the jury, the legal status of the evidence must be made clear, with fairness to both sides.

(iv) Preparation and analysis of material

9.92 Preparation of a schedule of inconsistencies takes significant time and analysis from an early stage. All parties should engage in the process, including the prosecution. The prosecution's role is to ensure that all third-party material has been identified and where it meets the disclosure test, disclosed. Disclosure must be in hand well in advance of trial. It will only be possible to deal with the topic of inconsistencies when the defence advocate has had sight of all the evidence and unused material which may bear upon the issue. This requires careful preparation and analysis by all.

(c) The continued importance of cross-examination

9.93 A particular set of circumstances peculiar to the vulnerable witness or defendant (as discussed above) may justify a radical departure from the traditional way of putting certain matters. However, this does not mean that the relevant witness should not be cross-examined at all. The purpose of the alternative approach to highlighting inconsistencies is to prevent unnecessary distress, unfairness, or confusion. There will remain other matters that can and should be dealt with in cross-examination. It is the duty of the judge to ensure that fairness to both sides is achieved in the particular circumstances of each case.

9.94 In *R v JP*,[69] the importance of cross-examination was emphasized. The appellant was convicted of three counts of sexual assault of a child. He was accused

---

[69] [2014] EWCA Crim 2064, a case heard with *Lubemba*.

of sexually assaulting an 8-year-old, but had maintained in trial that innocent physical contact had been misinterpreted. At the plea and case management hearing, the judge directed that the child was to give her evidence by live link and be cross-examined by the defence advocate on a live link. All parties agreed that the complainant, who was described as an intelligent and capable witness, was willing and able to attend court and that the services of an intermediary were not required. At trial, both advocates met with the child, who was described as calm and willing to give evidence. The child watched her video interview at court. After watching the interview, the judge visited the child without counsel. On his return to court, the judge refused to allow cross-examination of the child as she was 'not even managing to communicate in monosyllables ... on neutral subjects'. In his opinion, the child could not participate in cross-examination, however sensitively done.

9.95 The judge indicated to the defence advocate that he would be allowed the rest of the day to prepare a document to be placed before the jury, containing any points the defence would have wished to have made to the witness. The trial proceeded and the video interview was played as the witness's only evidence. In directing the jury, the judge invited them to give appropriate allowance for the fact that the defence advocate had not been permitted to question the witness.

9.96 The appellant appealed on the basis that the judge erred in preventing cross-examination of the complainant so that the defendant did not have a fair trial and his convictions were unsafe. The advocate for the Crown sought to persuade the Court of Appeal that the appeal should not be allowed. One of the arguments was that the judge remedied the potential for unfairness by allowing the defence the advantage of putting the document before the jury.

9.97 The appeal was allowed. The judge's ruling that the witness should not give evidence was criticized and the court held:

> Finally, and most importantly, the judge should have openly and clearly given far greater consideration to the impact on the fairness of the trial of prohibiting the defence from testing the evidence of the main prosecution witness.[70]

It follows from *JP* that a list of matters which the advocate wished to put to the vulnerable witness is not a *replacement* for cross-examination. As with putting the case, this alternative method to cross-examination is to be employed only when necessary. *JP* reinforces the importance of the process of cross-examination. It emphasizes that approaches such as the ones identified in this chapter are ancillary rather than alternative regimes.

---

[70] [2014] EWCA Crim 2064 at [49].

E. Non-Compliance and Consequences

(a) The judge's duty

9.98 *Lubemba* emphasized the judge's duty to ensure compliance with ground rules and directions in these terms:

> As we have already explained, a trial judge is not only entitled, he is duty bound to control the questioning of a witness. He is not obliged to allow a defence advocate to put their cases. He is entitled to and should set reasonable time limits and to interrupt where he considers questioning is inappropriate.[71]

(b) *R v Wills*: a case study

9.99 In *R v Wills,* the Court of Appeal commented:

> We consider that in cases where it is necessary and appropriate to have limitations on the way in which an advocate conducts cross-examination, there is a duty on the judge to ensure that those limitations are complied with.[72]

9.100 The concern of many advocates is that the restrictions placed on them lead to unfairness to the defendant as he or she loses the opportunity to actively challenge and discredit the witness in cross-examination.

9.101 *Wills*[73] was a case involving serious sexual allegations and multiple vulnerable witnesses. One advocate did not follow the ground rules set by the judge and cross-examined the witnesses in the 'traditional' way. An advocate for a co-defendant followed the ground rules. This appellant was convicted and the other acquitted.

9.102 One of the two grounds of appeal related to the judge's direction as to cross-examination of young complainant witnesses. The complaint was that while the appellant's counsel had complied with the judge's direction in relation to cross-examination of the complainants, counsel on behalf of the co-defendant did not. The judge's direction was that counsel should not challenge the witnesses and should not put the appellant's case. Counsel for the appellant followed this direction. He asked short, open questions. He did not use tag questions. Counsel for the co-defendant was described by the court as using a 'less constrained and more traditional approach to cross-examination' of the witness.[74] The judge gave a direction referring to the manner of cross-examination by counsel for the co-appellant. The appellant submitted that the judge should have discharged the jury and the direction was not adequate to deal with the unfairness which occurred.

---

[71] ibid. at [51].
[72] [2011] EWCA Crim 1938 at [36].
[73] [2011] EWCA Crim 1938.
[74] ibid. at [19].

In its judgment, the court considered the report: 'Raising the Bar: The Handling   **9.103**
of Vulnerable Witnesses, Victims and Defendants in Court'.[75] The court highlighted a theme which had emerged in consultations for that report: there was
an urgent need to address significant problems associated with the inconsistency and weakness of some advocates in handling and questioning vulnerable
people.[76]

The Court of Appeal, in analysing recordings of the cross-examination of the   **9.104**
witness, found that counsel for the appellant had complied with the direction of
the judge. The court commented:

> Those extracts indicate in our judgment that cross-examination within the limita-
> tions directed by the judge can elicit evidence as effectively as the more traditional
> approach to cross-examination in criminal cases.[77]

The court also found that counsel for the co-defendant did not comply with   **9.105**
the direction of the judge. The court noted that the judge had to intervene on a
number of occasions to stop long questions and inappropriate comment during
cross-examination by that counsel.

The court then asked itself: **9.106**

> ... whether the fact that [the defence advocate] was limited when conducting
> cross-examination on behalf of the appellant, whilst counsel for the co-defendant
> was not, rendered the trial so unfair that the judge ought to have acceded to [the
> defence advocate's] application to discharge the jury.[78]

In finding that the trial was not unfair, the court held:

> The importance of the limitation on cross-examination in cases such as this is to
> protect the vulnerable witnesses and enable them to give the best evidence they
> can. We do not take the view that it follows that the type of cross-examination per-
> mitted means that the questions asked by counsel will be less effective in adducing
> the necessary evidence for the jury. Some of the most effective cross-examination
> is conducted without long and complicated questions being posed in a leading or
> 'tagged' manner.[79]

The court also held that a direction given by the Judge at the end of the trial cured
any unfairness, although stated 'it would have been better if some direction had
been given at an early stage, as is done in other circumstances, to deal with the
position at the time'.[80]

---

[75] 'Raising the Bar: The Handling of Vulnerable Witnesses, Victims and Defendants in Court'
(Advocacy Training Council of England and Wales, March 2011).
[76] [2011] EWCA Crim 1938 at [22].
[77] ibid. at [26].
[78] ibid. at [29].
[79] ibid. at [26].
[80] ibid. at [34].

9.107 Part of the reason that no unfairness arose was because the court effectively found there was no disparity at all. The judgment in *Wills* is support for the contention that, at least in the eyes of the appellate courts, cross-examination of the style which is appropriate in vulnerable witness cases can be every bit as effective as 'traditional' style cross-examination. Any residual concern can be cured by a direction.

9.108 Despite the court's support for the new style of cross-examination, the outcome in *Wills* may cause the advocate concern about unscrupulous advocates abusing the ground rules system to their client's advantage. Advocates should remember that the count against the co-defendant in *Wills* was considered the weakest count. The Court of Appeal also held that the effect of the difference in cross-examination styles was more limited given the age of the witness (a 15-year-old rather than a much younger witness).

(c) Future training for advocates

9.109 The spectre of unscrupulous or substandard advocates remains a source of concern. In September 2014, the Ministry of Justice made an announcement stating that specialist training would be mandatory for all publicly funded advocates carrying out work involving vulnerable witnesses.[81] This has not yet come into force, but the Ministry's position reflects a public concern about the treatment of vulnerable witnesses in English courts.

9.110 A pan profession course designed by a committee chaired by HHJ Peter Rook QC, 'Advocacy and the Vulnerable', is being rolled out nationally during 2017 and 2018 by the Bar Council and Inns of Court College Advocacy with a view to full implementation of training by the end of 2018. It will train advocates in England and Wales how to deal with vulnerable people in the courts.

9.111 One anomaly which may arise is the likely absence of any government requirement that privately funded advocates must receive specialist training. It is hoped that the increasingly robust approach to the treatment of vulnerable witnesses adopted by the judiciary will cure or ameliorate any disparity of this kind.

(d) Consequences for non-compliance

9.112 For those who believe there may be an advantage to not following the rules, it is important to reflect on the sanctions available to the trial judge. They range from robust directions to referral to an advocate's professional body.

---

[81] MoJ, 'Our Commitment to Victims' (2014), available at <https://www.gov.uk/government/uploads/system/uploads/attachment_data/file/354723/commitment-to-victims.pdf> accessed 21 March 2017. See also P. Cooper, 'Ticketing Talk Gets Serious', *Counsel*, November 2014, 12–13.

The judge has a discretion to stop cross-examination in breach of ground rules **9.113** where the witness is confused, unnecessarily distressed, or otherwise unfairly compromised.

In *R v Pipe*,[82] the appellant was convicted of sexual offences on a child. In trial, **9.114** he had denied the offences and said they were fabricated. The child gave evidence-in-chief by way of video-recorded interview. She was cross-examined over the live link system, but was described as finding the process extremely distressing. The judge concluded that the cross-examination should not continue, but permitted the trial to continue. The appellant appealed his conviction on the grounds that unfairness arose because he was stopped from cross-examining the witness.

At the time the complainant's cross-examination was stopped, the critical ele- **9.115** ment of the appellant's defence had been put to her. The cross-examination was described by the trial judge as 'substantially complete'.[83] The witness had been repeatedly accused of lying among other matters. The defence advocate told the Court of Appeal that 'the remaining questions would have gone to the complainant's medical records and possible inconsistencies between them and what the complainant said in her evidence'.[84]

The court considered its decision in *PM v The Queen*,[85] in which similar cir- **9.116** cumstances arose. In that decision, the court said that the judge was in the best position to determine whether a fair trial was possible. His judgment should not be interfered with unless it was outside the range of reasonable conclusions the court could make.[86] Importantly, the court in *PM* held that it was for the jury to form a judgment on whether the factors from independent sources undermined the credibility of what the witness said in evidence; and the truth of the allegations could be tested by means other than cross-examination and did not depend entirely on who was to be believed.[87]

In dismissing the appeal in *Pipe*, the court found that, as the principal defence **9.117** had been explored with the complainant, there was more than enough material to assist the jury on the question of whether the complainant was telling the truth. Furthermore, the court agreed with the judge's analysis that the cessation of cross-examination would not affect the appellant's ability to rely on alleged inconsistencies. Instead, it deprived the complainant of the opportunity to explain the inconsistencies. It follows that the decision to stop the cross-examination could not prejudice the appellant.[88]

---

[82] [2014] EWCA Crim 2570.
[83] ibid. at [19].
[84] ibid. at [18].
[85] [2008] EWCA Crim 2787.
[86] ibid. at [18].
[87] ibid. at [32].
[88] ibid. at [28].

9.118 The court also noted that the complainant's evidence was not the only evidence in the case. There was other evidence in the case which bore on the defendant's guilt, such as an admission to his ex-wife.

9.119 The decision in *Pipe* demonstrates the careful balance which must be struck by the trial judge. These decisions will be fact specific. Advocates who breach orders of the judge which result in a vulnerable person being unable to continue with his or her evidence is unlikely to receive a sympathetic hearing in the court of appeal.

(i) Disciplinary referral

9.120 Failure to adhere to the ground rules and adopt an appropriate style of questioning tailored to the witness is not merely a question of following the judge's rules: it is capable of being a question of ethics. Each Advocates Gateway toolkit provides:

> Questioning that contravenes principles for obtaining accurate information from a witness by exploiting his or her developmental limitations is not conducive to a fair trial and would contravene the Codes of Conduct.[89]

9.121 It is submitted that that type of conduct would fall under rule c7 in the Bar Handbook which details the advocate's duty not to abuse his or her role.[90] Such an advocate would also plainly not be acting in the interests of justice in accordance with rule c3.[91]

9.122 It would be proper and appropriate in the case of flagrant breaches of ground rules by an advocate (leading inevitably to injustice) for judges or even other advocates in the case to make the necessary referral to the Bar Standards Board for disciplinary action.

9.123 In *R v Rashid*,[92] the Lord Chief Justice, Lord Thomas, stated (at para. 80) that:

> In considering what is needed in a particular case, a court must also take into account the fact that an advocate, whether a solicitor or barrister, will have undergone specific training and must have satisfied himself or herself before continuing to act for the defendant or in continuing to prosecute the case, that the training and experience of that advocate enabled him or her to conduct a case in accordance with proper professional competence. Such competence includes the ability to ask questions without using tag questions, by using short and simple sentences, by using easy to understand language, by ensuring that questions and sentences were grammatically simple, by using open ended prompts to elicit further information and by avoiding the use of tone of voice to imply an answer. These are all essential requirements for advocacy whether in examining or cross-examining witnesses or in taking instructions. An advocate would in this court's view be in

---

[89] See <http://www.theadvocatesgateway.org/toolkits> accessed 21 March 2017.
[90] *Bar Standards Board Handbook*, 3rd edn (April 2017), rule c7.
[91] ibid. rule c3.
[92] [2017] EWCA Crim 2.

serious dereliction of duty to the court, quite apart from a breach of professional
duty, to continue with any case if the advocate could not properly carry out these
basic tasks.

The circumstances of the case of *R v Farooqi*[93] should be borne in mind by all   **9.124**
advocates. It is perhaps an extreme example. It was a case which did not involve
vulnerable witnesses. However, the advocate for one defendant acted in direct
contravention of the judge's directions made at an early stage of the trial. This
culminated in a defence speech which contained personal insults to the judge and
the giving of evidence on behalf of a defendant who had not taken the stand. The
judge was invited on the application of the prosecution to discharge the jury. He
refused, but instead gave a lengthy direction as part of his summing-up correct-
ing the assertions made by defence counsel.[94] The Court of Appeal found that
the appellant suffered no unfairness and approved the approach of the judge. In
particular, the court said:

> One further aspect of the principle that the trial process is not a game is that the
> advocate must abide, and ensure that his professional and lay clients understand
> that he must abide, by procedural requirements and practice directions and court
> orders. The objective is to reduce delay and inefficiency and enhance the prospect
> that justice will be done.[95]

Any trial judge has the power to correct any unfairness arising out of the way   **9.125**
an advocate decides to cross-examine a vulnerable witness with a lengthy direction which is, if necessary, critical of the advocates' conduct. The unfairness may
arise out of both a decision to contravene the rules set by the judge at an early
stage of the process or a decision not to adopt an appropriate tone and style of
cross-examination with a vulnerable witness. It is submitted that unfairness is
significantly limited and the judge's powers to police the advocates significantly
assisted where there is an agreed list of questions; deviation being the first sign of
non-compliance.

---

[93] [2013] EWCA Crim 1649.
[94] Excerpts of the direction can be found at ibid. at [93].
[95] ibid. at [114].

10

SPECIAL MEASURES

Ruth Marchant

A. Introduction

10.01   This chapter explores the evolution of special measures in England and Wales, sets out the current arrangements, summarizes some 'extra special' or additional adjustments that have been made to court processes to meet particular needs, and reflects on the new concept of 'every reasonable step' and how this may evolve in practice.

B. A Brief History of Special Measures and Other Adjustments

10.02   The concept of special measures was first introduced in law in the Youth Justice and Criminal Evidence Act 1999 (YJCEA 1999), but for centuries prior to this the courts had quietly made adjustments to meet the needs of individual witnesses or defendants, particularly children and those with communication impairments.

10.03   Some of the 1999 special measures had been created by earlier legislation for children, and some had previously evolved within practice under common law.

10.04   For example, records show young children giving evidence directly to the courts as far back as 1675,[1] and the courts have been adapting processes to enable children to give evidence for centuries, for example from 1778:

COURT TO CHILD: How old are you?

CHILD: Nine years old.

COURT: Do you know for what purpose you are brought here now?

CHILD: Yes.

COURT: Do you know that you are to give evidence upon oath?

CHILD: Yes.

COURT: Do you know what an oath is?

CHILD: No; I do not know what an oath is.

COURT: You have heard that there is a God that governs this world; What do you think will happen to people that are wicked, that tell lies, and do bad things?

CHILD: I know where they go to.

COURT. Where do they go to?

CHILD: To hell.

COURT: Are you sensible it is a very wrong thing to tell a lie?

---

[1] E. Coker, 'Sexual Offences, Rape, Breaking Peace, Assault', case reference t16750115-3, available at <https://www.oldbaileyonline.org/browse.jsp?id=t16750115-3&div=t16750115-3&terms=coker#highlight> accessed 21 March 2017.

CHILD: Yes; I am sure it is.

COURT: Then if it is a wrong thing to tell a lie, it is still worse to tell a lie when you have taken an oath to tell the truth; therefore, you must take care to say nothing, but what is true.[2]

Other measures have evolved to enable children's evidence: for example, in 1919, **10.05** a defendant accused of mistreating his 11-year-old daughter was ordered to sit upon the stairs leading to the dock, out of her sight, so as to avoid her being intimidated. The appeal court ruled that a judge could, using the court's own powers to regulate its own proceedings, remove the accused from the sight of a witness whom his or her presence might intimidate.[3]

In the early part of the twentieth century, a high court judge explained some of **10.06** his own special measures, decades before the intermediary special measure:

> I have also at times made use of a woman juror when a little child of either sex, and especially a little girl, seems too dazed or frightened to answer questions at all. In such a case I have asked the woman juror to let the child stand or sit next to her so that she can hold the child's hand and then act as a sort of interpreter to and for the little one. I have no doubt that many others who happen to have presided when a like difficulty has arisen have adopted similar methods.[4]

Court processes have also long been adapted for adults who would now be **10.07** defined as vulnerable witnesses. For example, in 1817, a young mother described as 'deaf and dumb' was accused of throwing her 3-year-old boy into a river. At the trial a Master from the Edinburgh School of the Deaf and Dumb (as it was then known) was brought in to assist understanding for the counsel and jury. The defendant explained in sign that the child was on her back and as she reached into her pocket the child had fallen. She was later acquitted.[5]

The Interpretation Act 1889 allowed for those who did not speak the language of **10.08** the court to be granted an interpreter. In 1916, a Chinese defendant was sentenced to death; the trial was held in English. The charge and the pre-trial evidence were interpreted. This became a landmark case in interpretation for defendants.[6]

Similarly, arrangements to protect the privacy of witnesses in specific circum- **10.09** stances date back many decades. Section 37 of the Children and Young Persons Act 1933 gave the court the power to clear the courtroom of non-essential persons

---

[2] ibid.

[3] *R v Smellie* (1919) 14 Cr App R 128.

[4] T. Humphreys, *Criminal Days* (Hodder & Stoughton, 1946) 176.

[5] Published in the Dublin Penny Journal 1832 cited by H. D. W. Stiles, 'Interpreter in Court, 1817: The famous case of Jean Campbell, alias Bruce in a deaf history review' (2014), available at <http://blogs.ucl.ac.uk/library-rnid/2014/01/> accessed 21 March 2017.

[6] *Lee Kun* [1916] 1 KB 337; [1916] 11 CrAppR 293, cited with approval in *Kunnath v the State* [1993] 1 WLR 1315.

when a child was giving evidence in a case involving offences against morality or indecency.

10.10 YJCEA 1999 is often cited as 'introducing' a range of special measures to facilitate the gathering and giving of evidence by vulnerable and intimidated witnesses. The reality is that almost all of these measures had already evolved in court practice in some form, and YJCEA 1999 effectively formalized these. Special measures have thus been in use for centuries, although the current legislation is not yet twenty years old. Practice has continued to evolve and many new measures that have become accepted practice are not found in the legislation.

C. Are Special Measures Still Special?

10.11 The former Lord Chief Justice, Baron Judge of Draycote, has questioned whether special measures should still be described as 'special':

> I am no longer very happy with describing them in this way. That was fair enough when we were trying to bring home the importance of addressing these new measures which were, at that time, special. Now they are a perfectly normal ordinary part of the procedural safeguards provided for vulnerable witnesses.[7]

(a) Is 'special measures' a helpful term?

10.12 It may be appropriate to reconsider the term 'special measures' for two other reasons.

Within the field of disability, the term 'special' has been strongly challenged for decades. For example, the concept of 'special educational needs' has been criticized for unhelpfully framing the 'problem' as within the child, meaning that insufficient attention has been given to the barriers to all children's learning and inclusion in our schools. The term 'special' has also become a fairly widespread colloquial insult. More generally, there has been a sustained challenge to models of disability which focus on individual deficits and the social model of disability has gained ground internationally.[8] This approach challenges barriers to inclusion, breaking these down to increase access for everyone.

---

[7] I. Judge, 'Half a Century of Change: The Evidence of Child Victims—Toulmin Lecture in Law and Psychiatry' (King's College London, 2013), available at <https://www.judiciary.gov.uk/wp-content/uploads/JCO/Documents/Speeches/lcj-speech-law-and-psychiatry.pdf> accessed 31 July 2016.

[8] J. Swain, S. French, C. Barnes, and C. Thomas, *Disabling Barriers, Enabling Environments* (Sage, 2004); R. Marchant, 'Preventing the Abuse of Disabled Children' and 'What Is Disability?' in *Safeguarding Deaf and Disabled Children* (NSPCC/Triangle, 2011); T. Shakespeare, 'The Social Model of Disability', in L. J. Davis (ed.), *The Disability Studies Reader* (2nd edn, Routledge, 2006) 197–204.

Completely separately, in the United Kingdom, the term 'special measures' is **10.13** also a status applied by regulators of public services to providers who fall short of acceptable standards (e.g. in the NHS and education). The idea of schools or hospitals being 'in special measures' because they are failing is a familiar concept to many, which creates additional scope for confusion.

D. Evolution of the Current Legislation on 'Special Measures'

In 1998, the Home Office published 'Speaking Up for Justice'—the report of **10.14** the Interdepartmental Working Group on the Treatment of Vulnerable and Intimidated Witnesses in the criminal justice system. The seventy-eight recommendations made by this report were intended to improve the way in which vulnerable or intimidated witnesses were dealt with by the criminal justice system and help them give best evidence in criminal proceedings. Those measures that required legislation were included in Part II of the YJCEA 1999. The impetus for legislation for special measures can be traced back to an Advisory Group chaired by His Honour Judge Pigot (1989).[9]

YJCEA 1999 extended many of the measures previously available only to chil- **10.15** dren to vulnerable and intimidated adult witnesses. The first measures in this Act came into force in 2002.[10] In 2007, a consultation paper, 'Improving the Criminal Trial Process for Young Witnesses', was published and made thirty-one recommendations to improve the process.[11] Progress was reviewed by independent researchers in 2009 and again in 2011.[12] The Coroners and Justice Act 2009 added some new special measures and extended the application of others (described below).

The Victim's Code came into legislation in December 2013, as part of the **10.16** Domestic Violence, Crime and Victims Act 2004. Certain victims automatically

[9] T. Pigot/The Advisory Group on Video Evidence, 'Report of the Advisory Group on Video Evidence' (Home Office, 1989).

[10] P. Roberts, D. Cooper, and S. Judge, 'Coming to a Court Near You! Special Measures for Vulnerable and Intimidated Witnesses: Part 1' (2005) *Justice of the Peace*, 169, 748–51; Roberts et al., ' Coming to a Court Near You! Special Measures for Vulnerable and Intimidated Witnesses: Part 2' (2005) *Justice of the Peace*, 169, 769–75; M. Burton, R. Evans, and A. Sanders, 'Are Special Measures for Vulnerable and Intimidated Witnesses Working? Evidence from the Criminal Justice Agencies' (Home Office, 2006); D. Cooper, 'Special Measures for Child Witnesses: A Socio-Legal Study of Criminal Procedures Reform', unpublished Doctor of Philosophy degree thesis (2010), available at <http://eprints.nottingham.ac.uk/11319/1/DC_Complete_Thesis.pdf/> accessed 21 March 2017.

[11] Home Office, *Improving the Criminal Trial Process for Young Witnesses* (Home Office, 2007).

[12] J. Plotnikoff and R. Woolfson, *Measuring Up? Evaluating Implementation of Government Commitments to Young Witnesses in Criminal Proceedings* (Nuffield/NSPCC, 2011).

became eligible for enhanced rights under the legislation. Each victim should go through a needs assessment; they should be told that if they provide a statement they may be required to give evidence in court; special measures should be explained to them and they should be given the opportunity to provide a victim personal statement, and be allowed to refresh their memory prior to giving evidence.[13] (See further Chapter 2, 'Vulnerable Witnesses: The Investigation Stage' and Chapter 3, 'Witness Support'.)

10.17 Around the edges of the legislation, many other adaptations and additional measures have been sanctioned in individual trials, some only once and others many times.

E. Reasonable Steps and Special Measures

10.18 Since 2013, the Criminal Procedure Rules (Crim PR) have stated:

> In order to prepare for the trial, the court must take every reasonable step—
>
> (a) to encourage and to facilitate the attendance of witnesses when they are needed; and
> (b) to facilitate the participation of any person, including the defendant.[14]

The 'Equal Treatment Bench Book 2013' sets out a flexible approach to facilitate best evidence:

> Courts and tribunals are expected to adapt normal trial procedure to facilitate the effective participation of witnesses, defendants and litigants.[15]

These principles have also been reflected in criminal and family appellate decisions—for example, in *R v Cox*,[16] where it was stated that: 'When necessary, the processes have to be adapted to ensure that a particular individual [in this case, a defendant with complex needs] is not disadvantaged as a result of personal difficulties, whatever form they may take.'

10.19 In *In The Matter of M (A Child)*, a case in which a father of 'limited capacity' gave evidence in family proceedings with only 'unsatisfactory makeshift' arrangements in place despite a report recommending the use of special measures, the court found that the father's Article 6 rights had been breached. It was stated that the judge's general duty to manage all cases to achieve targets 'cannot in any circumstance override the duty to ensure that any litigant ... receives a fair trial and is guaranteed what support is necessary to compensate for disability'.[17]

---

[13] Ministry of Justice, *Code of Practice for Victims of Crime* (MoJ, 2013).
[14] Crim PR 3.9(3).
[15] Judicial College, 'Equal Treatment Bench Book 2013' (Judicial College, 2013) 46.
[16] [2012] EWCA Crim 549 at [29]. See also *R v B* [2010] Crim 4.
[17] [2012] EWCA Civ 1905 at [21].

Special measures are a series of statutory provisions designed to help vulner-   **10.20**
able and intimidated witnesses give their best evidence in criminal cases and to
help relieve some of the stress associated with giving evidence. Special measures
apply to prosecution and defence witnesses, and to some categories of defendants
in some circumstances. Other complementary statutory measures may also be
implemented to support witnesses to give their best evidence, and/or additional
adjustments put in place that, while not set out in legislation, have been regarded
as 'reasonable steps'.

F. Eligibility for Special Measures

Access to special measures is subject to a three-stage test, as set out in s. 19 of the   **10.21**
1999 Act. This three-stage test can be framed as three questions:

1. Is the (potential) witness *vulnerable* due to age or incapacity[18] or *intimidated*[19]
   on account of fear or distress (as defined by ss 16 and 17 respectively)?
2. If yes: is the quality of evidence given by the witness likely to be diminished
   by reason of their vulnerability or fear/distress?
3. If yes: which of the available special measures (or combination of them) is
   likely to maximize the quality of the witness's evidence?

Special measures in ss 23 to 30 are available in relation to vulnerable witnesses
and ss 23 to 28 are available in relation to intimidated witnesses.[20] The accused
is not an eligible witness, with the exception of live link in some circumstances
(see below).

(a) Vulnerable witnesses

There are, broadly, two categories of vulnerable witness: child witnesses who are   **10.22**
vulnerable by virtue of their age, and adult witnesses by virtue of a mental or
physical disorder or disability.

Vulnerable witnesses are defined by YJCEA 1999 s. 16 as: **10.23**

- All child witnesses (under 18 at the time the trial begins, or under 18 when
  evidence-in-chief or cross-examination was video-recorded before the
  trial); and
- Any witness whose quality of evidence is likely to be diminished because they:
- are suffering from a mental disorder (as defined by the Mental Health Act
  1983); or
- have a significant impairment of intelligence and social functioning; or

---

[18] As defined in YJCEA 1999 s. 16.
[19] As defined in YJCEA 1999 s. 17.
[20] YJCEA 1999 s. 18.

- have a physical disability or are suffering from a physical disorder.[21]

In determining whether it is likely that the quality of such a witness's evidence is likely to be diminished, the court must take account of any views expressed by that witness.[22]

(i) Identifying vulnerability

10.24 Some disabilities are obvious, some are hidden. Witnesses may have a combination of disabilities. They may not be aware of their disability, or may not want others to be aware.

10.25 Identifying a vulnerable or intimidated witness at an early stage of an investigation will improve the quality of an investigation by assisting the witness to give information to the police; it will assist the legal process by helping the witness to give their best evidence in court and ensure they are appropriately supported. Some groups of witnesses need particular care. Adults or children who have been victimized may have special difficulties as witnesses in criminal proceedings. They may need some help to overcome the feeling that *they* are on trial rather than the accused. People with mental health issues can also find the criminal justice system especially stressful. Those with post-traumatic anxiety disorders can have special problems prior to and during the trial, particularly if their problem is related to the alleged offence.[23]

(b) Intimidated witnesses

10.26 Intimidated witnesses are defined by YJCEA 1999 s. 17 as those whose quality of evidence is likely to be diminished due to fear or distress in relation to testifying in the case.

10.27 In determining whether or not a witness falls into this category, the court is required to take into account both the circumstances of the witness and the context in which the offence took place.[24]

10.28 Typically, witnesses who fall into this category may include victims of and witnesses to domestic violence, racially motivated crime, crime motivated by reasons relating to religion, homophobic crime, gang-related violence, and repeat victimisation, and those who are elderly and frail.[25]

---

[21] YJCEA 1999 s. 16(1)(b).

[22] YJCEA 1999 s. 16(4).

[23] MoJ, *Vulnerable and Intimidated Witnesses: A Police Service Guide* (MoJ, 2011). See also on the problems identifying vulnerability: G. Gudjonsson, 'Psychological Vulnerabilities During Police Interviews. Why Are They Important?' (2010) *Legal and Criminological Psychology*, 15, 161–75, 170. L. Bunting, D. Hayes, and G. Clifford, *Special Measures for Vulnerable Witnesses in Northern Ireland* (Department of Justice, 2013) 3–4.

[24] YJCEA 1999 s. 17(2).

[25] MoJ, *Vulnerable and Intimidated Witnesses: A Police Service Guide*.

A witness who is a complainant in a sexual offence or an offence under s. 1 or **10.29** 2 of the Modern Slavery Act 2015 will be considered to fall into the category of intimidated witness and thus eligible for assistance, as will witnesses to certain offences where it is alleged that a firearm or knife was used, unless the witness expresses a wish not to be so considered.[26]

(i) Special measures and the quality of a witness's evidence

Wherever a reference is made in the legislation to the 'quality of a witness's **10.30** evidence' for the purposes of determining eligibility for special measures for a vulnerable or intimidated witness, YJCEA 1999 s. 16(5) states that:

> … references to the quality of a witness's evidence are to its quality in terms of completeness, coherence and accuracy; and for this purpose 'coherence' refers to a witness's ability in giving evidence to give answers which address the questions put to the witness and can be understood both individually and collectively.

G. The Eight Special Measures in YJCEA 1999

(a) Screening a witness from the accused (s. 23)

There is some ambiguity about this measure, because the title of the measure **10.31** suggests screening the witness (from being seen) by the accused, but the wording within the Act is the other way around, i.e. witness 'prevented by means of a screen or other arrangement from seeing the accused' or that screens may be authorized 'to shield a witness from seeing the defendant'.

However, for many witnesses, *being seen by* the defendant is as concerning as *see-* **10.32** *ing* the defendant and screens effectively prevent both, whereas live link does not.

The screen is normally placed around the witness rather than the defendant. It **10.33** must not prevent the judge, magistrates, or jury and at least one legal representative of each party to the case from seeing the witness, or the witness from seeing them. If an intermediary or an interpreter or supporter is appointed to assist the witness, they too must be able to see the witness and be seen by the witness.

In most Crown Courts, screens are curtains. For some witnesses, the temptation **10.34** to pull back the curtain is great. Alternatives (e.g. fixed screens or portable rigid screens) are sometimes available.

Screens may sometimes be placed around the defendant (e.g. because the witness **10.35** does not understand the necessity to stay behind the screen, or because screens are being used in combination with live link), but such a course would only be taken exceptionally in the absence of any alternative means of shielding the witness.

---

[26] YJCEA 1999 s. 17(5), as inserted by the Coroners and Justice Act 2009 s. 99.

In such circumstances, further adaptations may be required—for example, ensuring that a break in the witness's evidence is taken so that the defendant can consult with his or her legal representative.

10.36 Where a decision has been taken to screen the defendant rather than the witness, a strong direction will have to be given to the jury by the judge to counteract the potential prejudice that such an adaptation may cause.

10.37 Depending on the layout of the courtroom, alternative arrangements may be able to be put in place which have the same effect of preventing a witness from seeing or being seen by the defendant—for example, turning off the screen above the jury, angling a screen away from the dock, or changing seating arrangements, such as moving the defendant to one end of the dock or from the dock to a position in court where they cannot see or be seen by the witness.

10.38 Screens are not necessarily an inferior alternative to the use of live link. Screens are flexible, easy to use, and permit the witness to stay in court. It is also easier for the jury or magistrates to gain an impression of some physical attributes of the witness where this is relevant.[27]

(b) Evidence by live link (s. 24)

10.39 'Live link' usually means a closed circuit television link, but also applies to any technology with the same effect. A live link enables the witness to be absent from the courtroom where the proceedings are being held, but at the same time to see and hear, and be seen and heard by, the judge, the magistrates, or the jury, at least one legal representative of each party to the case, and any intermediary. Where a live link is used, the remote link room should be treated as an extension of the courtroom and the same rules and procedures observed.

10.40 The main advantages of live link are in the reduction of stress by protecting witnesses from the actual courtroom. However, there can be negative impacts of the use of live link. Even when the technology works perfectly, live link can impede or disrupt communication, thus defeating the objective of improving the quality of the witness's evidence. This is particularly so for children, deaf witnesses, and learning disabled witnesses, who are more dependent on non-verbal communication to understand and be understood.[28]

10.41 Although the live link is a measure which may be available for any witness who is vulnerable or intimidated under YJCEA 1999 s. 16 or 17, the 'primary rule' (which is now in fact a presumption rather than a rule) is that all witnesses—whether prosecution or defence—who are aged under 18 should give their evidence by live

[27] MoJ, *Achieving Best Evidence in Criminal Proceedings: Guidance on Interviewing Victims and Witnesses, and Guidance on Using Special Measures* (MoJ, 2011) B.9.8.
[28] G. Doherty-Sneddon, *Children's Unspoken Language* (Jessica Kingsley, 2003).

link. However, it should be borne in mind that some children do not cope well with live link. In such circumstances, one solution which has been found to work well in a number of cases is for the advocate(s) to enter the live link room and to ask questions of the witness in that room, with the examination being screened to the judge, the jury, and other parties in court over the live link.

The following extract is from an anonymized intermediary report which recom- **10.42**
mended that the advocates were in the live-link room with the witness:

> The quality of [A]'s communication deteriorated significantly when she was asked questions across the live link. She found it more difficult to attend and to listen; she misunderstood or misheard questions; she needed multiple repetitions and it became necessary to direct her attention to the screen. She also hid behind a chair, raced around the room and tried to leave the room, behaviours not otherwise seen at assessment.

> [A] is a much more effective communicator when she is in the same room as those communicating with her, therefore I am recommending that the barristers come to the live link room to question A, using the live link to show the interaction to the court rather than expecting A to communicate across the link. There are now many precedents for this.[29]

(i) *Witness supporters in the live-link room*

Section 24(1)A of the YJCEA 1999 (as inserted by the Coroners and Justice Act **10.43**
2009 s. 102) gives the court power to direct that 'a specified person' can accompany the witness while they are giving evidence by live link. This can be anyone known to and trusted by the witness who is not a party to the proceedings and has no detailed knowledge of the evidence in the case.[30] Ideally, it should be the person who is preparing the witness for court.

> The presence of a supporter is designed to provide emotional support to the witness, helping reduce the witness's anxiety and stress and contributing to the ability to give best evidence.[31]

If evidence is to be given by live link an application for a supporter should be made to the court at the same time as the live link application. In determining who this should be, the court must take the witness's wishes into account.[32]

The supporter may be a member of the Witness Service, but need not be an usher **10.44**
or a court official. Someone else may be appropriate.[33] However, some courts continue to prefer witnesses in the live-link room to be accompanied only by

---

[29] From an intermediary report by the author concerning a 4-year-old child. See also D. Wurtzel, 'Time to Change the Rules?', *Counsel Magazine* (2011), available at <http://www.counselmagazine.co.uk/articles/time-change-the-rules> accessed 21 March 2017.
[30] Crim PD 18B.2.
[31] Crim PD 18B.1.
[32] YJCEA 1999 s. 24(1)B.
[33] Crim PD 18B.2.

the usher, rather than also by a named supporter. It is suggested that this is not always the best approach, since ushers cannot offer emotional support to the witness and are not trained to do so. Witness Service volunteers may be trained to take the supporter role both in the lead up to and during the trial and in some areas are provided with specific training to support children. In one case, the classroom assistant of a 6-year-old with autism and learning disability acted as witness supporter, working alongside an intermediary. The child's needs required the two adults to work closely together to keep him safe in the live-link room and settled enough to listen to and respond to questions.

(c) Evidence given in private (s. 25)

10.45 The principle of open justice normally requires that evidence is given in open court—in other words, in the presence of representatives of the press and of members of the public who wish to attend. There are long-standing exceptions to this for children, and more recently for witnesses giving evidence about sexual offences or an offence under s. 1 or 2 of the Modern Slavery Act. In sexual offences cases, a further exception is justified, partly because the evidence may be of an intimate nature, and partly because the presence of the defendant's supporters or of members of the public with a prurient interest in the proceedings may make the giving of evidence exceptionally difficult.[34] Another exception is made in cases where the court believes that someone, other than the accused, may take advantage of their entitlement to attend the proceedings in order to intimidate the witness.[35]

10.46 Section 25 of the YJCEA 1999 permits the courtroom to be cleared of everyone apart from the accused, the legal representatives, and anyone appointed to assist the witness. The special measures direction will describe individuals or groups of people who are excluded. It is not 'envisaged that the media should routinely be excluded alongside the rest of the public'.[36] The court must allow at least one member of the press to remain, if one has been nominated by the press.[37] The freedom of any member of the press excluded from the courtroom under this section to report the case will be unaffected, unless a reporting restriction is imposed separately.

10.47 The court has the power under the Children and Young Persons Act 1933 s. 37 to clear the public gallery when a person under the age of 18 gives evidence in proceedings relating to conduct that is indecent or immoral. There are also statutory restrictions on attendance and reporting in the youth court for the protection of

---

[34] MoJ, *Achieving Best Evidence*, B.9.13.
[35] ibid. B.9.14.
[36] Judicial College, *Reporting Restrictions in the Criminal Courts* (Judicial College, 2014) 8.
[37] YJCEA 1999 s. 25(3).

children and young people.[38] A court may also use its inherent powers to restrict the numbers and categories of members of the public in the courtroom where the defendant is vulnerable.[39]

(d) Removal of wigs and gowns (s. 26)

It has long been the practice of the courts to dispense with the wearing of wigs and gowns by the judge and by legal representatives when the witness is a child.[40] The power to direct this has now been included in YJCEA 1999 and is available for all vulnerable or intimidated witnesses. **10.48**

Subject to the views of the defendant, the court may additionally make a direction that wigs and gowns are to be dispensed with when the defendant is vulnerable. Moreover, in such a situation, the judge may direct that dock officers or other security staff are not in uniform and that there should be no recognizable police presence in the courtroom.[41] **10.49**

This is another measure which must respond to individual needs and wishes, and where witnesses may need information in order to make a meaningful choice. Not all witnesses want wigs and gowns removed: some feel more comfortable or more confident if the judge and legal representatives are dressed traditionally. **10.50**

One child explained, 'I want their wigs on so I know who's allowed to ask me questions', and a teenage witness observed, 'I wouldn't be happy if I called 999 and the fireman arrived in jeans and a t shirt.' Younger children may have different needs. A judge in a 2015 trial suggested that removal of wigs and gowns did not go far enough, and ordered that counsel wear 'plain clothes' when questioning a 4-year-old. Questioning took place with the barristers in the live-link room, and after some discussion counsel wore smart casual clothes 'as an infant school teacher might wear'.

(e) Video-recorded evidence-in-chief (s. 27)

A video-recorded interview can take the place of a vulnerable or intimidated witness's evidence-in-chief (s. 27). The situation is different for adults and for children. **10.51**

The law presumes that child witnesses under the age of 18 will normally give their evidence outside the courtroom by playing a video-recorded interview as **10.52**

---

[38] MoJ, *Achieving Best Evidence*, B.9.15 and B.9.12.
[39] Crim PD 3G.13-14.
[40] See further MoJ, *Achieving Best Evidence*, B.9.16.
[41] Crim PD 3G.12.

evidence-in-chief and cross-examination via live link unless this will not improve the quality of their evidence. Subject to the agreement of the court, children may opt out of either or both.[42] The factors which the court must take into account along with any others that it considers relevant when deciding whether or not to allow the child to opt out are set out at s. 21(5)(4C):

   (a) the age and maturity of the witness;

   (b) the ability of the witness to understand the consequences of giving evidence otherwise than in accordance with the requirements in subsection (3) or (as the case may be) in accordance with the requirement in subsection (4A);

   (c) the relationship (if any) between the witness and the accused;

   (d) the witness's social and cultural background and ethnic origins;

   (e) the nature and alleged circumstances of the offence to which the proceedings relate.

10.53   To make an informed decision about this requires children and their parents or carers to understand the purpose of the video-recorded interview. Guidance within *Achieving Best Evidence* suggests that an explanation should include the following, at a level appropriate to the child's age and understanding:

- the benefits/disadvantages of having or not having the interview video-recorded;
- who may see the video-recorded interview (including the alleged offender both before the trial and at court);
- the different purposes to which a video-recorded interview may be put; and
- that the child may opt out of video-recorded evidence-in-chief if they wish to do so. The child should be advised that, should the case proceed, whether a video-recording is made or not, they may be required to attend court to answer further questions directly.[43]

10.54   Vulnerable adults and intimidated adults are also eligible to give video-recorded evidence-in-chief.

10.55   In addition, s. 101 of the Coroners and Justice Act 2009 inserted a new s. 22A into YJCEA 1999 making special provision for adult complainants in sexual offence trials in the Crown Court. The section provides, on application by a party to the proceedings, for the automatic admissibility of a video-recorded statement as evidence-in-chief under YJCEA 1999 s. 27, unless this would not be in the interests of justice or would not maximize the quality of the complainant's evidence.

---

[42] The Coroners and Justice Act 2009 s. 100 amended YJCEA 1999 s. 21, the 'primary rule' that applies to child witnesses. This rule (before amendment) required all child witnesses to give evidence-in-chief by a video-recorded interview, then any further evidence by live link, unless (except for child witnesses in need of 'special protection' in certain sexual and other offence cases) the court was satisfied that to do so would not improve the quality of that child's evidence.

[43] Home Office, *Achieving Best Evidence in Criminal Proceedings* (Home Office, 2011) 2.33.

A video recording may not be admitted if 'the court is of the opinion, having **10.56** regard to all the circumstances of the case, that in the interests of justice the recording, or that part of it, should not be so admitted' and the court must also consider 'any prejudice to the accused' which might result from the admission of the video recording.[44] This might occur where the interviewer has—without a reasonable rationale—departed from *Achieving Best Evidence* guidance. 'If there has been a substantial failure to comply with the guidance, the consequence may well be that video evidence is excluded altogether, or the relevant parts edited out.'[45]

Some commentators want to see greater use of video-recorded interviews, **10.57** pointing out that 'if all (vulnerable and intimidated) witnesses were video interviewed then all options for special measures would be open'.[46] Temperton also observes that if a video interview is conducted and the witness later chooses to give live evidence, then their video evidence can be translated into a statement. He refutes the argument that video interviewing for all vulnerable and intimidated witnesses would be too costly and time-consuming, pointing out the shift towards digital recording already underway and noting that to take a comprehensive statement you would still have to ask all the same questions and complete an interview plan and then complete a written statement from the notes you have taken, which if completed in the correct manner would be a lengthier process.

Concerns have been raised about the quality of interviews conducted within **10.58** *Achieving Best Evidence* guidance:

> In short, the inspection found that the Guidance is not achieving what it set out to do, which is achieving the best evidence. This is due in part to poor compliance by interviewers and the failure to properly record decisions and actions, with the rationale underpinning these.[47]

See further Chapter 2, 'Vulnerable Witnesses: The Investigation Stage'.

(f) Video-recorded cross-examination or re-examination (s. 28)

This is the last of the YJCEA 1999 special measures to be implemented. The **10.59** Commencement Order for s. 28 (SI 3236/2013) applied only to three Crown Courts: Kingston upon Thames, Leeds, and Liverpool. A pilot began in these

---

[44] YJCEA 1999 s. 27(2) and (3). See also *R v Krezolek and Luczak* [2014] EWCA Crim 2782.
[45] MoJ, *Achieving Best Evidence*, B.9.18 and B.9.19.
[46] S. Temperton, 'An Examination of the Police's Discretionary Use of Special Measures', unpublished manuscript (2014) 16, available to download at <http://library.college.police.uk/docs/theses/TEMPERTON-use-of-special-measures-2015.docx> accessed 25 April 2017.
[47] HM Crown Prosecution Service Inspectorate and HM Inspectorate of Constabulary, *Achieving Best Evidence in Child Sexual Abuse Cases—A Joint Inspection* (HMCPSI and HMIC, 2014) 7.

courts in April 2014 (cases having been identified by the police from December 2013) and an evaluation was conducted. At the time of writing, indications had been given that a national roll-out of the s. 28 procedure would commence in 2017.

10.60 One of the intentions of this special measure was to speed up the various stages of a case so that cross-examination could take place closer in time to the allegation. The investigation stage proceeds as usual (almost all 's. 28 witnesses' give video-recorded evidence-in-chief). Cross-examination and re-examination take place prior to the trial and are video-recorded. Both videos are played at trial.

10.61 The cross-examination is carried out at court in the usual way, save that it is video-recorded. The witness will be in the link room, but visible to participants in the courtroom over the live link. The defendant is in the dock. Counsel and the judge may be in court or in the live-link room. An intermediary may assist.

10.62 A witness in the pilot areas is eligible if:

- he or she is under 16 at the time of the special measures hearing; or
- he or she suffers from a mental disorder within the meaning of the Mental Health Act 1983 or has a significant impairment of intelligence and social functioning or has a physical disability or a physical disorder, and the quality of his or her evidence is likely to be diminished as a consequence.

There have been indications that those criteria will be extended when the procedure is adopted nationally.[48]

10.63 Conflicting views have been expressed—often based on anecdotal evidence—about the effectiveness of pre-recorded testimony and the potential difficulties that may arise from dealing with such an important part of the case in advance of the trial. For example:

> The scheme can obviously present challenges. New evidence can emerge during the s 28 timetable (in one case another complainant emerged). In a multi-hander several defendants may have a legitimate interest in cross-examining the witness. The Ground Rules procedure envisages one advocate being appointed to do this. But what if the defendants are running different defences? One consequence of s 28 is a feeling, anecdotally, that sometimes the witness can appear 'removed' from the case. For certain witnesses who should not be in the Crown court in the first place, such as children, this is a good thing. Others argue that there is no substitute

---

for having the witness in front of the jury. Every case is different. It is certainly the case under s 28 that the jury hears no testimony from the witness which is actually current and immediate. They get a pre-recording of cross-examination some weeks prior, and an even older ABE.[49]

However, there is no research to suggest that pre-recorded testimony is less effective than having a witness in court. Following a study of the application of special measures in Northern Ireland, Bunting et al. conclude:

> In some cases this [practitioner concern about the use of special measures] is clearly related to a belief that special measures detract from the immediacy and emotional impact of evidence and make securing a conviction more difficult ... this report reviewed the research literature relating to the impact of special measures on jurors' perceptions and case outcomes and concluded that such concerns and fears expressed by legal professionals have little or no foundation in practice.[50]

In those areas where s. 28 has been piloted, it has been found that the progression of trials has been speeded up, there has been an increase in the guilty plea rate, and (as of July 2016) there had only been one instance where a vulnerable witness had had to be recalled.

(g) Examination of a witness through an intermediary (s. 29)

Intermediaries are one of the statutory special measures for vulnerable witnesses. **10.64** They are communication specialists whose primary responsibility is to facilitate the best quality evidence, in other words complete, coherent, and accurate communication. They are expected to prevent miscommunication from arising and 'actively to intervene when miscommunication may or is likely to have occurred or to be occurring'.[51]

Intermediaries can assist the judiciary to monitor the questioning of vulnerable **10.65** witnesses and defendants, but responsibility to control questioning remains with the judge or magistrates. Intermediaries are impartial, neutral officers of the court. They are not expert witnesses. Their reports provide a guide to enabling an individual's best evidence. An intermediary can be requested at trial even if no intermediary was involved at interview. (See further Chapter 11, 'Intermediaries'.)

(h) Communication aids (s. 30)

This provision applies to vulnerable witnesses. It permits a witness 'to be pro- **10.66** vided with such device as the court considers appropriate with a view to enabling

---

[49] A. Ford, 'Pre-Record (Not Fade Away): The Use of s 28 of the Youth Justice and Criminal Evidence Act', Counsel, March 2015.

[50] Bunting et al., *Special Measures for Vulnerable Witnesses in Northern Ireland* (2013) 79–81.

[51] *R v Cox* [2012] EWCA Crim 549 at [28].

questions or answers to be communicated to or by the witness despite any disability or disorder or other impairment which the witness has or suffers from'. A communication aid may augment or replace oral testimony. The witness may already use aids to communication in their daily life—for example, a communication board or book, lightwriter, tablet device, laptop, or mobile phone.

10.67 Courts have permitted a wide range of communication aids (e.g. pen and paper, models representing people or places, maps, photographs, picture cards, symbol boards, visual timetables, human figure drawings, and technology). Quiet, calming objects to enable witnesses to settle and focus may also be defined as communication aids.

10.68 Communication aids may be introduced specifically for the court process: visual timetables, body maps,[52] human figures, small furniture, photographs of items or places, event labels, or timelines of events. Intermediaries can also assist in recommending and producing appropriate communication aids—for example, the development of a visual timeline to support questions about several alleged incidents over time.

10.69 The witness may produce their own communication aids (e.g. drawings or diagrams or coloured figures or event label cards). Everything produced or used at interview becomes an exhibit and should generally be made available to the witness when viewing and when giving his or her evidence at trial.

10.70 Aids have helped improve the quality of evidence and given access to justice to some witnesses previously excluded.[53] There are some signs that the courts are recognizing the value of communication aids—for example, the provision of break cards in most live-link rooms is now common, and a judge's failure to adopt a recommendation from an intermediary that pictures be used to aid communication was the subject of criticism by the Court of Appeal in *R v F*.[54]

10.71 The Advocate's Gateway has a comprehensive toolkit on communication aids.[55]

(i) Combining special measures

10.72 Special measures need not be considered or ordered in isolation. The needs of the individual witness should be ascertained, and a combination of special

---

[52] Crim PD (2015) 3E.6 states: 'In particular in a trial of a sexual offence, "body maps" should be provided for the witness' use. If the witness needs to indicate a part of the body, the advocate should ask the witness to point to the relevant part on the body map.'

[53] *R v Watts* [2010] EWCA Crim 1824.

[54] [2013] EWCA Crim 424.

[55] M. Mattison, 'Using Communication Aids in the Criminal Justice System' (The Advocate's Gateway, 2015).

measures—such as the use of screens to shield the live link from the defendant and the public—may be appropriate.[56]

H. Other Measures in YJCEA 1999

In addition to special measures, YJCEA 1999 also contains the following provisions intended to enable vulnerable or intimidated witnesses to give their best evidence: **10.73**

- mandatory protection of witness from cross-examination by the accused in person for child and adult victims in certain classes of cases involving sexual offences (ss 34 and 35);
- discretionary protection of witness from cross-examination by the accused in person in other types of offence (s. 36);
- restrictions on evidence and questions about complainant's sexual behaviour in cases of rape and other sexual offences (s. 41); and
- reporting restrictions. YJCEA 1999 provides for restrictions on the reporting by the media of information likely to lead to the identification of certain adult witnesses in criminal proceedings (s. 46). See below for reporting restrictions in relation to children.

(a) Live link for a vulnerable defendant and for other witnesses

Although a defendant may be a witness for the defence, the special measures for vulnerable or intimidated witnesses do not apply to a person who is on trial.[57] However, YJCEA 1999 s. 33A makes provision for a live-link direction to be given for certain young or vulnerable defendants when giving oral evidence. **10.74**

The procedure to be followed when making a defendant's evidence application is set out in Crim PR 18.14–18.17. In accordance with Crim PD 3G.11, the court must be 'satisfied that it is in the interests of justice [to make such a direction] and that the use of a live link would enable the defendant to participate more effectively as a witness in the proceedings'.[58] **10.75**

---

[56] Crim PD 18A.2.

[57] YJCEA 1999 ss 16(1), 17(1), and 19(1).

[58] See also *Hamberger* [2017] EWCA Crim 273: When considering the ambit of YJCEA 1999 s. 33A, the trial judge had not sufficiently explained the basis on which the defendant suffered from a mental disorder or the causal link with the defendant's inability to participate effectively in the proceedings as a witness giving oral evidence in court was not clear (para. 36). The Court of Appeal also found that if a defendant cannot give sworn testimony and cannot be cross-examined, in rare and exceptional circumstances, upon proper application being made, a judge would be entitled to admit the defence statement and/or the proof of evidence as hearsay evidence pursuant to the Criminal Justice Act 2003 s. 116(2)(b) (para. 45).

10.76 Section 51 of the Criminal Justice Act 2003 enables the court to allow witnesses (other than the defendant) in the United Kingdom to give evidence by live link if the court is satisfied that giving evidence in this way is in the interests of the efficient or effective administration of justice. The witness does not have to be a special 'category' of witness (for instance, vulnerable or intimidated as defined by YJCEA 1999). Live links will be particularly helpful for witnesses with limited availability, such as professional witnesses, or those with mobility issues who do not qualify for live links under the 'special measures' provisions of YJCEA 1999. It may also assist in cases involving police officers who have to travel some distance to a Crown Court. The Crown Prosecution Service (CPS) website provides online guidance.[59]

I. Measures from Other Legislation

(a) Reporting restrictions on the identification of children under 18

10.77 Reporting restrictions on the identification of children under the age of 18, previously provided by the Children and Young Persons Act 1933 ss 39 and 49, have since April 2015 been governed by the Criminal Justice and Courts Act 2015 ss 78–80.

10.78 Reporting restrictions for under 18-year-olds involved in criminal proceedings (other than in the youth court) will now be governed by YJCEA 1999 s. 45. Section 39 orders will only apply in civil and family cases. YJCEA 1999 s. 45A enables courts to grant lifelong anonymity to child witnesses and victims. Reporting restrictions have been expanded to cover all online content in addition to print and broadcast media.

J. Special Measures Applications

(a) Who applies for special measures?

10.79 Applications for a special measures direction for either the defence or prosecution should be made on a prescribed form, in advance of the trial.[60] The court will expect to deal with any such application at the Plea and Trial Preparation Hearing.

---

[59] Crown Prosecution Service, 'Live Links—Section 51 of the Criminal Justice Act 2003', available at <http://www.cps.gov.uk/legal/l_to_o/live_links_-_section_51_of_the_criminal_justice_act_2003/> accessed 21 March 2017.

[60] Criminal PR, Part 18, Measures to assist a witness or defendant to give evidence.

The police have authority to decide—without prior court approval—on several special measures at interview stage: whether an interview should be video-recorded, and whether an intermediary and/or aids to communication and/or a witness supporter are needed at interview. (See further Chapter 2, 'Vulnerable Witnesses: The Investigation Stage'.) At trial, these measures still require court approval. In other words, while the police can decide whether or not to video record an interview, whether or not the recording is used in court is a matter for the judiciary. Similarly, while the police can decide whether or not to instruct an intermediary for interview, only the court can direct the use of an intermediary at trial. **10.80**

Police decision-making at an early stage in the investigation thus has consequences at trial stage, and it has been recently observed that: 'When a police officer makes a decision in relation to a vulnerable or intimidated witness, they must have an understanding of the possible consequences of that decision.'[61] There is strong encouragement for the police to seek an early special measures discussion with CPS where there may be an issue about whether to implement any special measure.[62] **10.81**

(b) Who grants or directs special measures?

The court determines whether a witness is eligible for special measures and directs the use of those measures (or combination of measures) which would be likely to maximize so far as practicable the quality of the witness's evidence.[63] Being eligible for special measures does not mean that the court will automatically grant them. The court has to satisfy itself that the requested special measure or combination of special measures is likely to maximize the quality of the witness's evidence before granting an application. **10.82**

(c) Who decides what special measures to recommend?

The aim is to enable the best evidence of this witness in this trial. Recommendations must be based on an assessment of needs. **10.83**

This assessment of need may be undertaken by the police, witness care, the witness service, or an intermediary. The CPS and counsel may also be involved in deciding which measures would be appropriate. The assessment may be informed by an expert report (e.g. from a psychiatrist or psychologist). A special measures meeting with a prosecutor may be arranged to explore options further. The views of the witness should be central to the assessment (see below). **10.84**

---

[61] Temperton, 'An Examination of the Police's Discretionary Use of Special Measures', 15.
[62] MoJ, *Achieving Best Evidence*.
[63] YJCEA 1999 s. 19(2).

10.85   Research suggests that the police still struggle to identify some categories of vulnerable and intimidated witnesses.[64] Young witnesses and adult victims of sexual offences are easy to identify, but some mental health issues and communication impairments can be less obvious.

10.86   Some witnesses are thus not identified as vulnerable pre-trial, hence the potential role of counsel and the judiciary in assessment:

> Legal representatives must assist the court, at any hearing where the matter arises, to make informed decisions about any Special Measures directions or other steps which it may be necessary to take, to assist a particular witness. Both prosecution and defence legal representatives are expected to inform the judge of the special needs or requirements of any vulnerable or intimidated witnesses they intend to call.[65]

YJCEA 1999 also imposes an obligation on judges and magistrates to raise of their own motion the question of whether special measures should be used if the party has not applied for them (s. 19(1)).

(d)   The views of the witness about special measures

10.87   'Emphasis is now given to the witness's viewpoint because witnesses are likely to give better evidence when they choose how it is given.'[66] This is only likely to be the case if the person's choices are meaningful and informed. Asking someone to choose between options they have never heard of or are unfamiliar with in relation to a process they have never experienced is unlikely to lead to better choices or better evidence.

10.88   As one 15-year-old witness put it, after being 'told' by the police about special measures and asked to give a view:

> It is like someone saying we are going to land you on another planet, and then asking if you would like bits of that planet to be different. On this other planet I don't even know which way is up yet.[67]

It is essential to talk with the witness about special measures in ways that make sense, and where appropriate to involve their family and/or others in their life. It can help to have the pre-trial visit and/or the prosecutor's special measures meeting with a witness before finalizing the special measures application. For many young or vulnerable witnesses, showing the options is essential—seeing

---

[64] M. Burton, R. Evans, and A. Sanders, 'Vulnerable and Intimidated Witnesses and the Adversarial Process in England and Wales' (2007) *International Journal of Evidence and Proof*, 11, 1–23; Cooper, 'Special Measures for Child Witnesses'; and G. Radice, 'Special Measures Issue Paper' (MoJ, 2014).

[65] MoJ, *Achieving Best Evidence*, para. 5.15.

[66] 'Equal Treatment Bench Book 2013', 9, para. 32.

[67] From personal communication with the author.

wigs and gowns, and trying out screens and live link and seeing how these appear to the jury.

It is important that witnesses understand that they can express preferences, but that decisions about special measures are made by the judge or magistrates. This can be hard to explain simply, for example: **10.89**

> We can show you the different places you can be when you give your evidence. You can try out the live link room and the screens. People can wear wigs and gowns, or not. We might be able to use these communication aids, or not. It is up to the judge, but the judge wants to know what you think. If the judge says yes, we can be in here and I can sit next to you. If the judge says yes, we can use this time line and stop go cards.[68]

For very young children and those with significant learning disability, explaining the 'maybe' is an additional challenge. Some of this can be resolved if the special measures application, or at least the initial application, can precede the pre-trial visit, and the ground rules hearing can follow.

Flexibility could potentially be built in—for example, the trial judge could grant live link and/or screens and/or an intermediary if required. The pre-trial visit explorations would then become much simpler—for example: 'The judge says I can sit with you at the trial. We can sit in the live link room or in court, let me show you.' **10.90**

There are tricky dilemmas where views about special measures do not align, as this example illustrates:

> A 13-year-old complainant, who at the time of trial was as an inpatient in a secure psychiatric unit, wanted to give her evidence in court without screens so she could 'look the defendant in the eye'. The police and CPS felt that remote live-link from the unit was the only safe option. The intermediary supported an extended pre-trial visit and after discussion between the witness, the police and CPS, facilitated by the intermediary, it was arranged that the witness give her evidence by remote live-link from another court. The defendant's view of the witness during cross-examination was screened, and the complainant gave her evidence calmly and clearly.[69]

(e) Early Special Measures Discussions

These discussions, between the police, the CPS, and/or an intermediary (if there is one) can take place in person or by phone or email. **10.91**

Where there is any doubt as to whether an interview should be video-recorded, or where an intermediary or aids to communication are involved, or where there might be an issue about the use of a supporter during an interview, the police **10.92**

---

[68] Example of an explanation by the author, struggling to be both accurate and clear.
[69] From the author's experience.

investigator should request an Early Special Measures Discussion (ESMD). The CPS can also call an ESMD if they consider it necessary after reviewing a case file. Intermediaries may recommend an ESMD where issues are complex.[70]

(i) Can special measures be changed or added to later?

10.93 Applications for a special measures direction can be made and granted at any stage up to and including during the trial itself.

10.94 Special measures directions are binding until the end of the trial, although courts can alter or discharge a direction if it seems to be in the interests of justice to do so. Either party can apply for the direction to be altered or discharged (or the court may do so of its own motion), but must show that there has been a significant change of circumstances since the court made the direction or since an application for it to be altered was last made.[71]

10.95 This provision is intended to create some certainty for witnesses, by encouraging the party calling the witness to make applications for special measures as early as possible and by preventing repeat applications on grounds the court has already found unpersuasive.[72]

10.96 The court must state in open court its reasons for giving, altering, or discharging a special measures direction or refusing an application, so that it is clear to everyone involved in the case what decision has been made and why it was made (YJCEA 1999 s. 20). This is intended to include, for example, the court's reasons for deciding that a witness is ineligible for help.

10.97 While it is important that directions be made in advance of trial where possible, it may be necessary for a court to react to a situation at a later stage of proceedings by making a direction to assist a witness to give evidence. For example:

> On the first day of trial a teenage witness threw a chair at the TV, ran out of the live link room and hid under the stairs. He was assessed by an intermediary the following morning and strategies were put in place to help him stay calm and pace the questioning.[73]

> An eight-year-old girl giving evidence in a rape trial was very disoriented that the usher in the live link room was male. No female usher was available. The child whispered to the intermediary 'well he's going to have to put a cushion over his face every time I say fanny'. The intermediary requested this as an extra special measure, a cushion was located and cross-examination could then begin.[74]

---

[70] MoJ, *Achieving Best Evidence*, Appendix B, 160, 'Early Special Measures Discussions', B.5.1.
[71] CPS Legal Guidance, available at <http://www.cps.gov.uk/legal/s_to_u/special_measures/> accessed 21 March 2017.
[72] Home Office, *Achieving Best Evidence in Criminal Proceedings* (Home Office, 2011) B.7.1.
[73] From the author's experience.
[74] ibid.

New directions are needed for a retrial or appeal. The same measures may be appropriate, or it may be that experience in the first trial leads to a change of plan:

> A six-year-old gave evidence by live link and had significant difficulty responding to cross-examination questions. She did not seem able to understand that she could be seen across the live link so stopped using her hands and face to explain. She was reluctant to look at the screen and therefore her face could not be seen on camera. There was a hung jury on all counts. At the retrial the intermediary requested that counsel come to the live link room to ask their questions. Communication with the child was much more effective. There were unanimous verdicts on all counts.[75]

K. Other Measures or Adaptations

(a) Fast tracking

In April 2015, a protocol for the expedition of cases involving witnesses under the age of 10 was introduced.[76] This recommends that the time period between first complaint and charge should not exceed eight weeks and the trial date should be set no more than eight weeks from the date of plea. In the author's experience, in some CPS areas, this has dramatically reduced delays to trial for young children.   **10.98**

(b) Bringing counsel to the live-link room

This is a provision which is utilized where a witness finds communication over live link difficult, and is now also common in some s. 28 trials. The first recorded use of this additional measure was in 2010.[77]   **10.99**

(c) Screening the defendant's view of the screen during cross-examination

As discussed above, this effectively combines two special measures—live link and screens—and is specifically mentioned in the current Criminal Practice Directions: **10.100**

> For example, if a witness who is to give evidence by live link wishes, screens can be used to shield the live link screen from the defendant and the public, as would occur if screens were being used for a witness giving evidence in the court room.[78]

---

[75] ibid.

[76] ACPO, CPS, and HM Courts & Tribunals Service, 'A Protocol between the Association of Chief Police Officers, the CPS and HMCTS to Expedite Cases Involving Witnesses under 10 Years' (2015), available at <https://www.judiciary.gov.uk/wp-content/uploads/2015/03/police-cps-hmcts-ywi-protocol.pdf> accessed 21 March 2017.

[77] D. Wurtzel, 'Time to Change the Rules?' *Counsel Magazine* (2011), available at <http://www.counselmagazine.co.uk/articles/time-change-the-rules> accessed 21 March 2017.

[78] Crim PD (2015) 29A.2.

(d) Avoiding confrontation outside the courtroom

10.101 Standard 12 of the 2013 Witness Charter[79] requires the court to have separate waiting areas and advises that vulnerable or intimidated witnesses may be allowed to wait on standby near the court, and/or use an alternative entrance.

10.102 Where the witness and defendant are screened from one another in court, if it is not feasible also to shield the witness from the dock and public gallery while entering court, he or she should be behind the screen before the defendant and members of the public are seated and leave at a different time during adjournments. Other ways to achieve the same outcome are:

- screening the route in and out of the witness box and ensuring separate entrances and exits to the courtroom and the court building; and
- keeping the defendant in the dock for fifteen minutes at the end of cross-examination while the witness leaves the building.

See also Chapter 3, 'Witness Support'.

(i) Anonymity and witness protection

10.103 Although outside the scope of this chapter, it should be noted that the Coroners and Justice Act 2009 ss 74–85 makes provision for anonymity in investigations and anonymity of witnesses.[80] CPS guidance is available on 'Witness protection and anonymity'.[81]

(e) Remote live link

10.104 A remote live link means a live link away from the court where the trial is taking place. A remote link may be needed for very different reasons: the witness cannot leave their home, residential setting, or hospital; the witness cannot travel the distance required; the witness is too fearful to be in the same building as the defendant(s), even with additional security or additional special measures; the witness presents too high a risk to be contained safely in a court building; the needs of the witness cannot be met in the court building where the trial is being held; or the witness is too disturbed or too young or otherwise too vulnerable for the experience of a court building to be tolerated, even with additional supportive measures.

10.105 A remote link could be at another court or a separate 'remote' facility which has live-link capability, or links can be set up in homes, hospitals, or schools. Great

---

[79] MoJ, *The Witness Charter Standards of Care for Witnesses in the Criminal Justice* (MoJ, 2013).
[80] See further D. Ormerod QC (Hon) and D. Perry QC, *Blackstone's Criminal Practice* (Oxford University Press, 2016) D.14.49 ff.
[81] See <http://www.cps.gov.uk/legal/v_to_z/witness_protection_and_anonymity/> accessed 21 March 2017.

care should be taken to make informed decisions about putting a remote link into a familiar setting for any witness, but particularly for children, who are unlikely to be able to make informed decisions about the possible 'contamination' of a safe space.

> A teenager with complex needs (severe learning disability, autism, ADHD and post-traumatic stress disorder) was interviewed with mobile equipment at his residential school. The option of remote live link from the same location was not pursued because that area of the school had effectively become 'out of bounds' for the witness as he became so distressed and violent, even when passing the corridor leading to the room.[82]

Use of a remote link is likely to require considerable planning and organization. There is an Advocates Gateway toolkit that sets out a range of considerations: ensuring privacy and security; clarity about roles; how to communicate between the remote site and the trial court before the link is established and if there is a problem with the link; and how exhibits and other documents (e.g. the oath) will be provided to the remote site.[83]

(f) Memory refreshing

There is no legal requirement for witnesses to watch their video interview at the same time as the jury do so. Watching can be distressing or demanding, so watching at a different time from the jury can have several advantages: the witness can control the pacing, watching important or traumatic sections more than once or taking breaks as needed; and it avoids overloading the witness on the day of questioning. **10.106**

Decisions about how, when, and where refreshing should take place should be made on a case-by-case basis and arrangements should be judicially led.[84] It is the police's responsibility to arrange this, with the permission of the court. An intermediary may need to be present, but should not be the person designated to record anything said at the viewing.[85] Someone (usually a police officer, not an intermediary) should be designated to take a note and report to the judge if anything is said. In the case of a very young child, it may be appropriate to record the viewing. If the DVD is ruled inadmissible, an alternative method of refreshing needs to be identified. **10.107**

> A four-year-old was filmed viewing her evidence. She spontaneously made several comments confirming that she had a memory of the event separate to the interview (mentioning parts of her account before they were shown). She also spontaneously

---

[82] From the author's experience.
[83] 'Planning to Question Someone Using a Remote Link' (The Advocates Gateway, 2017).
[84] See further Crim PD 18C.
[85] MoJ, *Achieving Best Evidence*, ibid.

added to her account and two additional charges were added to the indictment as a result.[86]

If watching is too distracting or distressing, alternative methods of refreshing of testimony should be explored.

> A child rape complainant found it very difficult to see himself on video as a much younger child, becoming extremely distressed at how small he had been at the time of the interview. He was able to settle to reading through the transcript while listening to the recorded interview, being asked by the intermediary to look at the screen only when he was demonstrating an action in the recorded interview.[87]

(i) Adapting the live-link environment

10.108 Adaptations might include:

- reducing distractions (putting the phone/oaths/pictures out of sight) or reducing risks (removing fans, water, Bible);
- adjusting room layout (e.g. so that the witness cannot be alarmed by being approached from behind);
- turning off or covering the 'picture in picture' on the witness's TV screen (so that the witness does not have to look at an image of themselves);
- providing chairs that fit children and tables at an appropriate height;
- reducing sound distortion by placing the live-link room microphone on a towel;
- changing the lighting;
- arranging immediate access to bathrooms, medical facilities, shower, inhaler, nebulizer; setting up places to retreat or hide, etc;
- setting up a simple den/small tent in the live-link room for a very traumatized child to calm him- or herself in during breaks.

(ii) Adjustments to pacing

10.109 Adjustments to the pacing of the trial events may be required. For example:

- scheduling an adult with autism to give evidence for short periods, with breaks, in the morning over several days;
- agreeing immediate toilet breaks for a child with continence issues;
- allowing witnesses unable to give evidence (e.g. because of distress due to a delayed start or as a result of inappropriate questioning) to come back the next day if necessary, following a further ground rules discussion between the judge and advocates rather than dismissing the case immediately;
- allocating a female judge and counsel to a trial with an adult witness who refused to speak to a man about the alleged offence;

---

[86] From the author's experience.
[87] ibid.

- allowing an intermediary to relay the answers of witnesses who whisper, write, draw, or type;
- allowing a fearful 8-year-old to calm herself quickly by taking herself out of sight of the main live-link camera, but still visible to the judge on the overview camera. (The child and intermediary practised these 'in room' breaks beforehand, using a large thirty-second sand timer. The judge requested everyone to wait, rather than adjourning the court. The child took around fifteen brief breaks across two hours of evidence. Only one complete break and adjournment was required.)

(g) Ground rules hearings

The necessity for any adjustments such as those outlined would be discussed in **10.110** advance of the trial at a ground rules hearing. The hearing is a mechanism through which trial processes can be adapted to meet individual needs and through which the court can give directions for the appropriate treatment and questioning of a vulnerable witness or defendant. The court must include the parties and the intermediary (if there is one) in the ground rules discussion. There may be directions about relieving a party of putting their case, the manner of questioning, the duration of questioning, the topics that may or may not be covered, allocations of questions among co-defendants, and the use of communication aids.[88]

See further Chapter 12, 'Ground Rules Hearings'. **10.111**

(h) Looking ahead beyond special measures

Current special measures legislation has been criticized by lawyers for being **10.112** 'needlessly complex, in parts almost impenetrable' and 'unduly inflexible'[89] and by the police for being 'complex and difficult to navigate … this works to prevent officers using it to its full advantage'.[90]

The changes in the Coroners and Justice Act 2009 have also been criticized, both **10.113** for not going far enough with defendants, and for going too far in introducing anomalies in the treatment of different categories of intimidated witnesses.[91]

The current regime is without doubt complex. There would be less need for special **10.114** measures and other adjustments if all courts were fully accessible, if all live-link rooms could be easily adjusted to suit different witnesses, if simple adaptations

---

[88] Crim PD 3E.

[89] A. Keane and P. McKeown, *The Modern Law of Evidence*, 11th edn (Oxford University Press, 2016) 154.

[90] S. Temperton, 'An Examination of the Police's Discretionary Use of Special Measures', 31, ibid.

[91] L. C. H. Hoyano, 'Coroners and Justice Act 2009: Special Measures Directions Take Two: Entrenching Unequal Access to Justice?' (2010) Crim LR, 345–67.

to court processes were routine, and if all trials were conducted in clear, straight-forward language.

Further Reading

HM Crown Prosecution Service Inspectorate and HM Inspectorate of Constabulary, Joint Report on the Experience of Young Victims and Witnesses in the Criminal Justice System (HMCPSI and HMIC, 2012).

Judge, I., 'Half a Century of Change: The Evidence of Child Victims', Toulmin Lecture in Law and Psychiatry, King's College London (2013), available at <https://www.judiciary.gov.uk/wp-content/uploads/JCO/Documents/Speeches/lcj-speech-law-and-psychiatry.pdf> accessed 21 March 2017.

Websites with information for witnesses

<http://www.youandco.org.uk/going-court/support-court/what-special-measures-are-right-me> accessed 21 March 2017.

<https://www.cps.gov.uk/victims_witnesses/going_to_court/vulnerable.html> accessed 21 March 2017.

<http://www.triangle.org.uk/page/young-triangle> accessed 21 March 2017.

11

INTERMEDIARIES

David Wurtzel and Ruth Marchant

A. Introduction

11.01 The use of intermediaries under s. 29 of the Youth Justice and Criminal Evidence Act 1999 (YJCEA 1999) has been the most innovative of the special measures. Most of what an intermediary does in a case has evolved through their training and the development of good practice. Only a small part is found in statute. The intermediaries as a body may have done more than anyone to effect a culture change in the way in which the courts deal with vulnerable witnesses and defendants. Some of their proposed strategies have become commonplace. When the Judicial College advises and updates the judiciary on ways in which trials can be handled more flexibly, most of the examples come from cases involving intermediaries.

11.02 Prosecution and defence witnesses may take advantage of the Ministry of Justice's Witness Intermediary Scheme of Registered Intermediaries. A parallel system of intermediaries for defendants has developed ad hoc. Advocates, police, the Crown Prosecution Service (CPS), and defence solicitors all need to understand how these two systems work, what the Court of Appeal and the Criminal Practice Rules and Directions have said about them, and how the use of an intermediary can help to ensure that a witness can give their best evidence.

11.03 Since August 2009, 15,274 witnesses[1] have been seen and/or assisted in some way by an intermediary. The numbers are rising. In the year May 2015 to April 2016, there were 5,879 requests for an intermediary; 85 per cent of these were for children and/or those with learning difficulties. About 10 per cent of these requests came from the West Midlands and 8.6 per cent from London. Over 99 per cent of the requests have been for prosecution witnesses, 93 per cent of whom were the alleged victim in the case. Since August 2009, there have been only 101 requests from solicitors; in 2015–16, there was one request for a defence witness.

11.04 The National Crime Agency, which maintains the 'matching service' for the Ministry of Justice, keeps records for the use of registered intermediaries (RIs). Since 2011, when defendants were no longer able to access the register of RIs, there has been no central body which can compile the figures for use by defendants.

(a) Background

11.05 Intermediaries had not existed in England and Wales before the Act. The English model cannot be found elsewhere apart from Northern Ireland and a pilot scheme in New South Wales.[2] The intermediary scheme for prosecution

---

[1] Statistics provided to the author by the National Crime Agency, June 2016.
[2] P. Cooper and D. Wurtzel, 'Better the Second Time Around? Department of Justice Registered Intermediaries Schemes and Lessons from England and Wales' (2014) *Northern Ireland Legal Quarterly* 65(1), 39–61; and P. Cooper, 'A Double First in Child Sexual Assault Cases in New

and defence witnesses was piloted in 2004. It was rolled out nationally in September 2008. Defendants and suspects are excluded from the special measures regime in the Act. However, judges have since 2007 made orders for the use of an intermediary for a defendant. These orders were and are based on common law and on the court's inherent jurisdiction to ensure that the defendant has a fair trial.

(b) Purpose

The purpose of using an intermediary is to maximize the quality of the witness's evidence and/or to enable a defendant to participate effectively in his or her own trial. Quality is defined by YJCEA 1999 s. 16(5) as 'quality in terms of completeness, coherence and accuracy'. 'Coherence' refers to 'a witness's ability in giving evidence, to give answers which address the questions put to the witness and can be understood both individually and collectively'. Effective participation was defined in *SC v United Kingdom*;[3] the European Court of Human Rights required that proper allowance was made for the difficulties of a young defendant to ensure effective participation in the trial process. In explaining what was meant by this, the Court said: **11.06**

> Given the sophistication of modern legal systems, many adults of normal intelligence are unable fully to comprehend all the intricacies and exchanges which occur in the courtroom: this is why the Convention, in Article 6(3)(c), emphasises the importance of the right to legal representation. However, 'effective participation' in this context presupposes that the accused has a broad understanding of the nature of the trial process and of what is at stake for him or her, including the significance of any penalty which may be imposed. It means that he or she, if necessary with the assistance of, for example, an interpreter, lawyer, social worker or friend, should be able to understand the general thrust of what is said in court. The defendant should be able to follow what is said by the prosecution witnesses and, if represented, to explain to his own lawyers his version of events, point out any statements with which he disagrees and make them aware of any facts which should be put forward in his defence.[4]

(c) What is a registered intermediary?

The legislation uses the word 'intermediary'. However, as the means of providing a scheme the Ministry of Justice (MoJ) maintains a register of registered intermediaries for the Witness Intermediary Scheme. A registered intermediary has been through MoJ recruitment and selection procedures, successfully completed the MoJ-accredited, assessed training course, is subject to the Registered **11.07**

South Wales: Notes from the First Witness Intermediary and Pre-Recorded Cross-Examination Cases' (2016) *Alternative Law Journal* 41(3), 191–4.

[3] [2005] 40 EHRR 10 at [35].

[4] ibid. at [29].

Intermediary Code of Practice and Code of Ethics, and has to fulfil Continuing Professional Development requirements. There is a Quality Assurance Board which can deal with any complaints. The RI is paid by the 'end user', which is the police or the CPS depending on the stage of the case. The rate of pay is set by the MoJ in respect of the work performed by the RI.

The typical professional background of a RI is a speech and language therapist, psychologist, or teacher.[5] Within that they would have specialized in communication with people in specific groups, such as children or people with learning disabilities, autism, or mental ill-health.

(d) What is a non-registered intermediary?

11.08   Under YJCEA 1999 s. 29, the court may appoint anyone as an intermediary if they have the necessary skills to maximize the quality of the evidence of the vulnerable witness; however, in practice, the court will always prefer to appoint a registered intermediary if one is available.

11.09   Defendants were excluded from YJCEA 1999. The provisions in s. 104 of the Coroners and Justice Act 2009 which allow for an intermediary for a defendant when giving evidence have not yet been brought into effect. Defence solicitors are therefore not able to access the register of RIs for the accused. The court may appoint as an intermediary for a defendant anyone who has the necessary skills to assist them and the court. These intermediaries have become known as 'non-registered intermediaries'. There are some organizations which provide them and may have their own systems of recruitment, training, assessment, registration, and monitoring. The court decides whether the intermediary will assist throughout the trial or only when (and if) the defendant gives evidence. Intermediaries for defendants are discussed below in detail.

(e) The matching

11.10   The police officer (or in the case of a defence witness, the solicitor) requests the service of a RI through the matching service.[6] This service has been outsourced by the MoJ to the National Crime Agency (NCA).[7] This process is called a 'referral'. The police send in a request form which sets out their understanding of the nature of the witness's vulnerability. The NCA matches this to a RI who is

---

[5] Registered intermediaries come from a broad range of professional backgrounds, including social work, nursing, and occupational therapy. Most are postgraduates and all have significant expertise in facilitating communication in their specialist area.
[6] The Witness Intermediary Team which runs the matching service is contactable at wit@ nca.x.gsi.gov.uk/0845 000 5463.
[7] See <http://www.nationalcrimeagency.gov.uk/about-us/what-we-do/specialist-capabilities/specialist-operations-centre> accessed 21 March 2017.

on the register, on the basis of the RI's professional experience, availability, and geographical location. RIs, who come from various professional backgrounds, provide the NCA with a list of their specialisms based on their professional experience (e.g. working with very young children or with adults with acquired brain injury).

B. Intermediaries for Prosecution or Defence Witnesses

(a) Statutory basis

YJCEA 1999 s. 29(1)–(3) states that: **11.11**

(1) A special measures direction may provide for any examination of the witness (however and wherever conducted) to be conducted through an interpreter or other person approved by the court for the purposes of this section ('an intermediary').
(2) The function of an intermediary is to communicate—
   (a) to the witness, questions put to the witness, and
   (b) to any person asking such questions, the answers given by the witness in reply to them, and to explain such questions or answers so far as necessary to enable them to be understood by the witness or person in question.
(3) Any examination of the witness in pursuance of subsection (1) must take place in the presence of such persons as rules of court or the direction may provide, but in circumstances in which—
   (a) the judge or justices (or both) and legal representatives acting in the proceedings are able to see and hear the examination of the witness and to communicate with the intermediary, and
   (b) (except in the case of a video recorded examination) the jury (if there is one) are able to see and hear the examination of the witness.

(b) Function

The core function of an intermediary is to facilitate communication between the   **11.12**
witness or defendant and anyone who needs to question or speak with them, such as the police, advocates, the judge or magistrates, the court staff, and the Witness Service. Despite the wording of s. 29(1), they are not interpreters in the ordinary sense of the word. 'Communication' should be given a broad meaning: the intermediary will advise on appropriate vocabulary and other linguistic difficulties, but may also make suggestions, say, for ways to enable the witness or defendant to remain calm and attentive, for breaks, pacing and timetabling of evidence, and the use of communication aids. There are good practice examples of this in The Advocate's Gateway Toolkits 6 ('Planning to Question a Child or Young Person'), 7 ('Additional Factors Concerning Children under 7 or Functioning at a Very Young Age'), 8 ('Effective Participation of Young Defendants'), and 16 ('Intermediaries Step by Step').

(c) The need for transparency

11.13 The RI's role must be transparent throughout. For that reason, and also in order to be able to monitor the witness's communication needs, they normally sit or stand next to the witness and within view of anyone observing the evidence. This means that they should appear within the picture in any video-recorded evidence, on the screen if the witness is giving evidence from a live-link room, or be visible next to the witness if the witness is giving evidence from the witness box. The court must see that the evidence is coming from the witness without prompting.

C. Eligibility for Prosecution and Defence Witnesses

(a) Statutory definition

11.14 YJCEA 1999 defines who is eligible for special measures. Intermediaries are only available for those who fall within the definition set out in YJCEA 1999 s. 16 (as amended by the Coroners and Justice Act 2009), namely:

> Section 16(1)(a) if under the age of 18 at the time of the hearing or
>
> (b) if the court considers that the quality of evidence given by the witness is likely to be diminished by reason of any circumstances falling within subjection (2)
> Section 16(2) The circumstances falling within this subsection are—
>> (i) that the witness (i) suffers from mental disorder within the meaning of the Mental Health Act 1983 or
>> (ii) otherwise has a significant impairment of intelligence and social functioning
> (b) that the witness has a physical disability or is suffering from a physical disorder

(b) Eligibility vs entitlement

11.15 As with other special measures, eligibility should not be confused with entitlement. Before a court makes a special measures order, s. 19 requires the court to go through the following three steps:

- to determine (s. 19(2)(a)) whether one or more measures 'would, in its opinion, be likely to improve the quality of evidence given by the witness' (s. 19(2) (a));
- to determine which of those measures 'would in its opinion, be likely to maximize so far as practicable the quality of such evidence' (s. 19(2)(b)(i)); and
- only then to make the relevant special measures direction (s. 19(2)(b)(ii)).

11.16 The involvement of an intermediary during an Achieving Best Evidence (ABE) interview does not require an order prior to the interview; it is a 'judgment call' by the police. A court may in due course and retrospectively allow for the intermediary's participation (s. 29(6)). It is important that the intermediary has complied with his or her obligation to make the intermediary declaration at the start of the video-recorded interview (s. 29(6)(a)).

See also Chapter 10, 'Special Measures'.

(c) Further criteria

Under s. 19(3), the court must take account of 'any views expressed by the wit- **11.17**
ness' and also 'whether the measure or measures might tend to inhibit such evidence being effectively tested by a party to the proceedings'. If a judge is satisfied that the lack of an intermediary would not cause any loss in the quality of the evidence, he or she is entitled to permit the trial to take place without the intermediary's assistance.[8]

(d) Inhibiting evidence being tested

The words 'inhibit such evidence being effectively tested by a party to the proceed- **11.18**
ings' need to be seen in the light of judicial authority about the advocate's role in testing the evidence. In *R v Edwards*,[9] the Court of Appeal upheld a judge's restrictions on the manner of counsel's cross-examination of a 6-year-old child, saying that the defendant's right to a fair trial was not 'in any way compromised' because counsel was not allowed to ask 'Simon did not punch you in the tummy, did he?' In *R v Lubemba, R v JP*,[10] the Court of Appeal was blunter: 'Advocates must adapt to the witness, not the other way round. They cannot insist upon any right "to put one's case" or previous inconsistent statements to a vulnerable witness.' Intermediaries, however, can advise counsel on how they can put their case to the witness in a way the witness can deal with: section 5 of The Advocates' Gateway Toolkit 1, 'Ground Rules Hearings and the Fair Treatment of Vulnerable People in Court', sets out an example of how this can be done. (On 'putting the case', see further Chapter 9, 'Case Management' and Chapter 12, 'Ground Rules Hearings').

(e) Crim PD 2016 and the question of resources

A 2016 amendment[11] to the Criminal Practice Directions (Crim PD) at 3F.5 **11.19**
states:

> In the light of the scarcity of intermediaries the appropriateness of assessment must be decided with care to ensure their availability for those witnesses and defendants who are most in need. The decision should be made on an individual basis, in the context of the circumstances of the particular case.

---

[8] *F v Crown Prosecution Service* [2015] EWHC 2527 (Admin).
[9] [2011] EWCA Crim 3028.
[10] [2014] EWCA Crim 2064.
[11] Amendment No. 1 to the Criminal Practice Directions 2015 [2016] EWCA Crim 97.

At the same time, the earlier presumption that an intermediary assessment should be considered for all children aged 11 and under has been abolished. Instead, the decision 'should be made on an individual basis'.[12] 'Consideration should be given to the communication needs of all children',[13] but 'the appropriateness of an intermediary assessment for witnesses and defendants under 18 should be decided with care'.[14] Consideration should be given to an assessment where the child seems 'liable to misunderstand questions or to experience difficulty expressing answers including those unlikely to be able to recognise a problematic question'.[15]

(f) The effect of the Crim PD

11.20 There is evidence of a shortage of intermediaries. In the year May 2015 to April 2016, 82 per cent of referrals for a registered intermediary were matched (NCA statistics), but in 12 per cent of referrals a suitable intermediary was not found (other referrals were cancelled). Similarly two organizations which provide non-registered intermediaries for defendants, reported that in the same period, due to high demand, they were also unable to match a number of referrals for defendants.[16]

11.21 Although it goes without saying that an intermediary should only be brought into a case where there is some evidence that they might be needed, and that special measures should not be used without care, the wording of the 2016 Crim PD ('scarcity of intermediaries') introduces a factor which is not based on a witness's communication needs. The task of deciding who is 'most in need' would largely fall to the police (who ought to take advice from the CPS on special measures), who in 76 per cent of cases[17] are the ones who ask for a referral. The difficulty for the police is that they have to deal with witnesses on an individual basis, not knowing whether the person in question is more or less in need than someone they might encounter in a month's time. An example of how this might work is found in *R v Boxer*,[18] where a police officer carried out her own assessment and concluded that an intermediary was not required for the ABE interview. The judgment does not set out what this assessment consisted of. The Court of Appeal found nothing wrong in the admissibility of the ABE interview or, considering the absence of an intermediary in the ABE, in the use of a RI during the trial itself.

---

[12] Crim PD (2015) (as amended) 3F.25.
[13] ibid. 3F.24.
[14] ibid.
[15] ibid. 3F.26.
[16] Email correspondence with the first author from Communicourt and Triangle.
[17] Statistics provided to the author by the NCA.
[18] [2015] EWCA Crim 1684.

D. The Application Process for Prosecution and Defence Witnesses

The rules relating to an application by the prosecution or the defence for a special   **11.22**
measure direction under s. 29 are found in Part 18 of the Criminal Procedure
Rules 2015. They are the same as for any other special measure. The question
of whether the court should make an order for special measures is part of the
Plea and Trial Preparation Hearing (PTPH). The intermediary's report should be
attached to any application as it explains why an intermediary is needed for this
witness. If the application is contested, the intermediary should be asked to attend
the hearing in order to assist the court about his or her findings and conclusions.

E. Principles of Registered Intermediary Practice

'The Registered Intermediary Procedural Guidance Manual (2015)'[19] sets out the   **11.23**
principles of RI practice.

(a) Neutrality

The RI is impartial and neutral. Their paramount duty is to the court.[20] Their   **11.24**
'primary responsibility' is to the court 'and to upholding the overriding objective
that criminal cases are dealt with justly'.[21]

The RI cannot be a witness for either side. They should not be asked to make a   **11.25**
witness statement, even to the extent of exhibiting their report (which is in fact a
free-standing document and not an exhibit). Although an intermediary report in
R v Beards and Beards[22] was used as expert evidence about the vulnerable defendant's condition, this was for unusual reasons and importantly the intermediary
was no longer acting as the intermediary in the case. (See further Chapter 6,
'Vulnerability and Defences', in particular the discussion about the use of expert
evidence.)

RIs should not be asked to be a witness of fact in respect of anything they have   **11.26**
heard or seen. If for any reason they do become a witness of fact, then they must
cease to be the RI in the case.

---

[19] Available at <http://www.theadvocatesgateway.org/images/procedures/registered-intermediary-
procedural-guidance-manual.pdf> accessed 21 March 2017.
[20] 'The Registered Intermediary Procedural Guidance Manual' (MoJ, 2015) 3.14.
[21] ibid. 3.96.
[22] [2016] EW Misc B14 (CC).

(b) What they are not

11.27   The RI is not a witness supporter, a counsellor, a legal adviser, an appropriate adult, an expert or lay witness, or an interpreter.[23] It follows that they should not be asked to express an opinion as to whether the witness fulfils the test for competence to give evidence under YJCEA 1999 s. 53.

They should not express any opinion on the truth or reliability of anything the witness has said.

(c) Not being alone

11.28   The RI should not be alone with the witness.[24] A responsible third party should be present during the assessment and also when the RI is otherwise with the witness.[25] This rule also applies if the RI is there during the court familiarization visit. If there is an issue about anything the witness has said or done while with the intermediary, it is the third party who should be questioned about it.

(d) Consent

11.29   The witness must consent to the RI's involvement throughout the process. If the witness is a child who does not have capacity to consent, the consent of the person with parental responsibility will be necessary. If the witness is an adult without capacity to consent, a 'best interests' decision will need to be taken in relation to the involvement of the RI.

(e) Disclosure

11.30   In the case of a prosecution witness, the RI is obliged to inform the officer in charge of the case or the CPS of anything which comes to their attention (e.g. something which the witness says) which potentially undermines the case for the prosecution against the accused or which might assist the case for the accused.[26] The Crown then deals with the disclosure issue.

11.31   In the case of a defence witness or of a defendant, the intermediary must not disclose anything said by the witness, the defendant, or the legal representatives other than to the defence solicitors or with the express consent of the defendant. They should treat what is said to them as confidential.[27]

---

[23]   Crim PD (2015) (as amended) 3F.1.
[24]   'The Registered Intermediary Procedural Guidance Manual', 3.14.
[25]   ibid. 3.38.
[26]   ibid. 3.14.
[27]   ibid. 3.83.

F. What an Intermediary Does

These steps can also be found in detail in The Advocate's Gateway Toolkit 16, **11.32** 'Intermediaries Step by Step'; sections 7 and 8 deal with defendants. They are also in the 'Registered Intermediary Procedural Guidance Manual (2015)'. The latter includes the Registered Intermediaries Code of Practice and Code of Ethics.

(a) Recognizing vulnerability

In the case of prosecution witnesses, it is most often the police officer who first **11.33** recognizes that the witness has a vulnerability which causes a communication issue: this may well be due to the simple fact that it is the police who have the initial and continuing contact with the witness. NCA statistics confirm that three-quarters of referrals come from the police. Some witnesses can identify their own communication needs. In some instances, the disability may be obvious, for example if the witness is a young child. There may be reports from doctors or teachers; families and carers may be able to assist. Sometimes the disability is only recognized or diagnosed in the course of the case, such as after the ABE interview has taken place. The CPS may request an intermediary assessment pre-trial; nearly a quarter of all NCA-matched referrals since 2009 came from the CPS.

Anyone involved in a case, such as counsel, can raise the question of whether **11.34** a witness should be assessed by an intermediary. Advocates have a duty and responsibility to identify vulnerability in witnesses and defendants (see further The Advocate's Gateway Toolkit 10, 'Identifying Vulnerability in Witnesses and Defendants'). YJCEA 1999 provides that special measures can arise from the judge's own initiative. However, of the nearly 16,000 referrals since August 2009, only twenty have come from the court.[28]

(b) Competent but needs an intermediary vs not competent

It should be recognized that someone who appears to cope in their daily life **11.35** may not be able to communicate effectively unaided in the environment of the criminal justice system, where they may be expected to recall events and dates, and to construct a narrative when questioned, both by those who are trying to adduce their account and those who are tasked with challenging its reliability. A major purpose of the intermediary scheme is to overcome the old assumption that someone who is unable to communicate unaided on the same level as a robust adult or who cannot 'stand up' to 'traditional cross-examination' is not able to give evidence at all. As the Court of Appeal said in *R v B*:[29]

---

[28] Statistics provided by the NCA to the first author.
[29] [2010] EWCA Crim 4 at [38].

The question in each case is whether the individual witness, or, as in this case, the individual child, is competent to give evidence in the particular trial. The question is entirely witness or child specific. There are no presumptions or preconceptions. The witness need not understand the special importance that the truth should be told in court, and the witness need not understand every single question or give a readily understood answer to every question … provided the witness can understand the questions put to him and can also provide understandable answers, he or she is competent.

Whether or not the involvement of an intermediary makes the difference between a witness or a defendant being competent or not is something a court may have to decide.

(c) Matching the witness to the intermediary

11.36   The method of matching is set out in section A(e) above.

(d) Assessment

11.37   If the RI accepts the referral, they are put in contact with the police officer. The officer provides information about the witness, though not the details of any allegation. They should also obtain the witness's consent for the RI to see any relevant reports.[30] Such reports will be referred to in the RI's reports, but they are not annexed to them. The officer arranges for an assessment to take place in the presence of a responsible third party. If pre-interview, then ideally that should be the officer who is going to conduct the ABE interview. The reason is to give them the opportunity to see how one can communicate with the witness. It is left to the RI to devise the most effective method of assessing the witness's communication skills—for example, their ability to settle and maintain attention, to understand questions, and to give an account of events. The intermediaries have been trained that the focus of their assessment is to see how best the witness can deal with questions and to give answers that relate to the questions. If the referral is after the ABE interview has taken place, the RI assesses the witness and then watches the ABE interview. If the RI is unable to establish rapport with the witness and/or feels that they lack the necessary skills to assist them, then they hand the matter back to the matching service to find a different RI.

(e) Keeping records

11.38   From the time they accept the referral until the conclusion of the case, the RI keeps notes of everything they do. These notes are disclosable.

---

[30] This might be, for example, a treating speech and language therapist, occupational therapist, or educational psychologist report.

(f) The ABE interview

Following the assessment, the RI provides a preliminary report to the officer **11.39**
about the witness's communication needs and abilities. This is usually an oral
report if the ABE interview takes place the same day as the assessment and a
written report if it takes place subsequently. In addition, the RI and the officer
plan the interview. This includes consideration of timing, pacing, appropriate
questioning styles, room lay-out, whether communication aids will be needed,
who else will be there, etc. The intermediary is present during the interview and
can intervene to check understanding and can also assist to enable communication in either direction.

Table 11.1 is an example (based on an actual case) of recommendations about the
phrasing of questions for that particular witness.

However, the intermediary is not a second interviewing officer. If the intermedi- **11.40**
ary is not seen to intervene much or at all during the interview, this may be a
function of a successful planning meeting with the officer. The fact that the RI
has not intervened much or at all in the course of interview does not in itself
mean that the RI is not needed at trial during the entirely different atmosphere
and demands of court and cross-examination.

Table 11.1 Example recommendations about the phrasing of questions

Strategy	Example	Rationale
Plan questions in topics and in a logical order. Confirm when a topic is finished.	First I'm going to ask about x. Now I'm going to ask about y.	This will help X to make sense of the process and to attend.
Refer to her birth family and previous home clearly to avoid confusion.	'old mum', 'old dad', and 'grandad'; 'old home'	X calls her adoptive parents mum and dad and her current home is home.
Ask all questions about past events in the past tense.	'What happened' not 'what happens'; 'did' not 'does'.	X is still learning the grammatical rules for verb tenses, therefore present tense questions could be confusing and possibly unsettling
Use short, simply constructed sentences and age-appropriate vocabulary.	'Ask about' instead of 'take you back'.	X will not understand multipart sentences or complex vocabulary or non-literal language.
Limit questions to five information carrying words.	Use human figure drawings or dolls to enable clarity about people, positions, actions or body parts.	X's auditory working memory is limited and it is important that she processes the whole question.

(g) The report

11.41 Following the assessment, the RI will write a report for the court, which is attached to the application for special measures. The report has three purposes: (i) to be taken into consideration when the court decides whether or not to order the use of an intermediary; (ii) to inform those who question the witness how best to communicate with them; and (iii) to help shape the discussions and directions made at the ground rules hearing.[31] The report is sent to the CPS, the court, and the defence. The report is written on the assumptions that the case is proceeding, the RI has established rapport, and there is consent to the RI acting. It is not a conflict of interest for the RI to say that they should or should not be the RI in the case.

(i) Template for the report

11.42 Guidance and a template for reports are found in the 'Registered Intermediary Procedural Guidance Manual'.[32] The report will set out whether the RI has spoken to people who know the witness and which if any documents (such as medical reports) about the witness he or she has read. Those documents are not annexed to the report.

The five main headings of the RI report are as follows:

- Summary of the RI's qualification and experience;
- Background instructions and chronology;
- Summary of conclusions and recommendations;
- Details of the witness assessment; and
- Conclusions and recommendations.

(ii) Recommendations

11.43 The recommendations which appear in a table or schedule in the report are one of the most important intermediary functions. They are practical tips and strategies for the questioner based on what the intermediary learned during the assessment. They are witness-specific; there should be nothing generic about them. At their simplest, they may ask that the questioner takes things at a slow pace, preface each question with the witness's name in order to keep their attention, and/or use the witness's particular vocabulary for body parts, places, or people. See, for example, Table 11.2.

11.44 Recommendations on question structure should deal with the individual witness's communication needs (both cognitively and linguistically) rather than relying on blanket labels or assumptions. There should not be a debate over what

---

[31] 'The Registered Intermediary Procedural Guidance Manual', 4.4.
[32] ibid. Part 4.

Table 11.2 Example recommendations for two different witnesses

Strategy	Example	Rationale
Work with Y's pacing needs	Count silently to 5 before repeating or rephrasing a question.	Y needs extra time to process language; interrupting will disrupt her thinking.
Work with X's pacing needs	Ask the next question as soon as you have X's attention.	X is not good at waiting!

Table 11.3 Example recommendation without tag questions

Strategy	Example	Rationale
If X's account is to be challenged, this must be done in a way she can understand. Questions must be clearly questions and not statements.	Instead of: 'X didn't happen did it.' Try: 'You said x happened. D says x didn't happen. Did x really happen?'	X is not reliably processing statement or tag questions, but is responding to simple suggestive questions if asked in a questioning tone.

is a leading question. For example: 'Tag' questions may be entirely too difficult for very young children; other witnesses may be able to deal with one or two tag questions, but not with six in a row. Still others may be able to understand agreeing tags (e.g. 'then you went to the shops, yes?'), but not make any sense of opposing tags (e.g. 'you went to the shops, didn't you?').

11.45 Where appropriate, it is possible to put a challenge to the witness's account without any tag questions at all. For example, Table 11.3 shows what might be one of the recommendations in the table of proposed ground rules in the intermediary report.

11.46 Other recommendations can be more complex in terms of communication aids (such as using pictures to point to), allowing in-room breaks so the court doesn't have to adjourn every time the witness needs a break in the questioning, allowing the witness to write or type their answers, covering a TV screen so the defendant cannot see the witness in the live-link room, or counsel going into the live-link room for questioning. The recommendations in the report form the basis of discussion in the ground rules hearing, with the judge ultimately deciding.

See also Chapter 10, 'Special Measures'.

(h) The ground rules hearing

11.47 The intermediary must be present at the ground rules hearing (GRH), together with the trial judge and trial counsel. The intermediary is a person whose representations must be invited by the court when setting ground rules for the conduct of the questioning.[33] Good practice in GRHs are set out in Chapter 12. The difference between a GRH with an intermediary and a GRH without one is that in the former one of the participants knows the witness, has assessed them, and has provided the court with a report which makes recommendations which should form the basis of the GRH. The court should therefore take full advantage of the intermediary's attendance. The intermediary may request a further GRH if they become aware of further issues regarding the witness's communication—for example, if something emerges during the course of the court familiarization visit.

(i) Other pre-trial involvement

11.48 Giving best evidence involves more than merely appearing at trial. It is good practice for all witnesses to attend a court familiarization visit. Since the witness is unlikely to have had previous experience of talking to someone through a television screen, it follows that those who will be doing so should be able to practise this from the live-link room, with someone (often a court staff member) asking them neutral questions which have been vetted by the CPS to ensure that they bear no relation to anything in the case. It was through such a practice that one RI discovered that a young child's communicative competence deteriorated when using the live link; she then suggested, at a further GRH, that counsel conduct their examination in the live-link room with the child. This recommendation was accepted by the court.[34]

11.49 Every witness has the right to refresh their testimony from their written statement or recorded interview. Crim PD (2015) goes on to say that this should not happen just before giving evidence at the trial, and that the assistance of an intermediary may be needed to establish 'exactly how memory refreshing should be managed'.[35] The memory they are refreshing is what they communicated in interview. The RI may be present at this viewing, along with a third party, who should note anything said or done by the witness during this session. Finally, the RI must advise the Witness Service of any needs of the witness of which they have become aware so that the Witness Service can make appropriate arrangements. As the RI is not a supporter, it is not their duty to respond to needs that do not relate to communication.

(j) Vetting of questions

11.50 This practice of advocates submitting their proposed questions ahead of time to the judge and intermediary was adopted in the pilots under YJCEA 1999 s. 28,

---

[33] Crim PR (2015) 3.9(7).
[34] See <http://www.counselmagazine.co.uk/articles/time-change-the-rules> accessed 21 March 2017.
[35] 18.C.1.

and has become commonplace in trials involving vulnerable witnesses, particularly where an intermediary is involved. The Crown Court Compendium issued by the Judicial College in May 2016 sets out what orders should take place at the PTPH.[36] These include the date by which advocates must file their questions with the intermediary and the court, arrangements for the advocates and intermediary to discuss the questions before the date of the GRH, and an order that the intermediary must attend the GRH.

The practice of vetting questions has also been approved by the Court of Appeal. **11.51**
In *R v Lubemba, R v JP*,[37] the Court of Appeal said: 'So as to avoid any unfortunate misunderstanding at trial, it would be an entirely reasonable step for a judge at the GRH to invite defence advocates to reduce their questions to writing in advance.' In *R v FA*,[38] the Court of Appeal noted with approval that the intermediary's 'sensible expert suggestions were unhesitatingly adopted'. In *R v Michael Boxer*,[39] cross-examination questions 'were agreed in advance by all concerned with the assistance of the intermediary'. The Court of Appeal added that that would have been appropriate as well had the witness given 'live' evidence-in-chief.

The mechanics of the process of vetting questions is a matter for the trial judge. **11.52**
Generally, the task should be divided between the RI concentrating on the form of the questions (including the best way the advocate could introduce a topic which was not covered in the ABE interview), while the judge decides whether the overall questioning is too long and whether or not certain topics ought to be dealt with differently or at all. The Crown Court Compendium clearly envisages the vetting to take place before the GRH with any further discussion or orders to take place at the GRH. It is worth remembering that in a multi-handed case, counsel are obliged among themselves to divide up topics so that the witness is not questioned about the same thing by different advocates.[40]

In practice, advocates and intermediaries have worked collaboratively and out-of- **11.53**
hours in order to fulfil the spirit of the judge's order. The success of this reinforces the importance of the RI remaining neutral and independent. Intermediaries have been advised to treat these discussions with advocates as confidential until such time as the judge allows the questions to be disclosed to other counsel. It is also a reminder that advocates can question and challenge the evidence of vulnerable witnesses. The appeal in *R v JP* arose when the judge (wrongly in the view of the Court of Appeal) disallowed any cross-examination of an 8-year-old child on the grounds that she could not be expected to answer questions from 'people

[36] *The Crown Court Compendium* (Judicial College, 2016) 3–22, para. 7.
[37] At [43].
[38] [2015] EWCA Crim 209 at [13].
[39] [2015] EWCA Crim 1684 at [15].
[40] Crim PD (2015) 3E.5.

Table 11.4 Other example recommendations

Strategy	Example	Rationale
For an 11-year-old with severe learning disability: Ask one question at a time.	Instead of: 'Did you tell your Dad that you hit your head on the corner of the table and that's how you got the bump on your head?' Break this into two questions: 'Did you tell your Dad that you hit your head on the corner of the table?' 'Did you tell your Dad that's how you got the bump on your head?'	X may respond to just one part of a double question.
For a 4-year-old with age-related communication issues: Ask questions simply and in a logical order.	'You told Mummy that Uncle John put his willy up your bum. Before you told Mummy that, did your sister tell you that Uncle John put his willy up her bum?'	To fully understand this whole question requires processing 21 information-carrying words and this child just can't. Also there's a backwards sequence in there—did this happen before that instead of in chronological order. Please can we go through together tomorrow because if I understand what is being put I may be able to be more helpful.

like us'.[41] Advocates themselves should not fall back on the idea that because they cannot 'put their case' in the traditional way, they cannot question the vulnerable witness at all, thus potentially reducing the weight of the witness's evidence in the eyes of the jury.

11.54 Table 11.4 shows another example of recommendations in the table of proposed ground rules in the intermediary report.

(k) During evidence

11.55 The role of the RI during evidence is one of the matters which is discussed in the GRH. Normally, the RI will sit next to the witness in the live-link room or stand by them in the witness box. The reason for this as already stated is for transparency and to enable the RI to be able to monitor the communication, to observe the witness, and to assist with communication if necessary. Although the question of breaks (and how often) is also discussed in the GRH, the RI may have to alert the court that the witness is tired or distressed and needs a break outside the agreed times.

[41] *R v Lubemba, R v JP* at [15].

In *R v Christian*,[42] the witness had been diagnosed with an emotionally unstable **11.56** personality disorder. During her evidence, the RI put her arm around her while the ABE video was being played and later told her to take time to breathe when she became upset. She continued to allow the witness to lie up against her during cross-examination. The RI also told defence counsel that her questioning 'was coming over in a little harsh manner and I think to be able to control her for the rest of the trial it would be helpful if we could just go a little slower and at a different inflection'. The Court of Appeal held that in the light of the judge's proper warning to the jury about sympathy towards the witness, there was no 'sensible prospect of unfairness' in this and that the jury 'would have understood the situation as a matter of common sense where they were observing a very obviously vulnerable woman'. Where there is a question of physical contact between the RI and the witness, it is best to seek the trial judge's approval in advance and preferably at the GRH.

Most notably, the RI may intervene during the questioning itself if the question **11.57** in any of its aspects may cause difficulty for the witness. At the GRH, it must be discussed how any intervention is to take place (e.g. by raising their hand or saying 'Your Honour' or even addressing counsel directly). In the ideal case, the appropriateness of questioning style for a particular witness would be taken on board so thoroughly by counsel that it will not be necessary for the RI to intervene. If indeed that is what happens, then the RI will have fulfilled his or her role; but the fact that the RI does not intervene is not evidence that he or she was not needed in the first place. Again, in *R v Lubemba, R v JP*, the Court of Appeal stated: 'Advocates must adapt to the witness, not the other way round.'[43] In *R v B*, it was pointed out that although matters which undermine the credibility of a child witness must be revealed to the jury, 'it is not necessarily appropriate for them to form the subject matter of detailed cross-examination of the child, and the advocate may have to forego much of the kind of contemporary cross-examination which consists of no more than comment on matters which will be before the jury in any event from different sources'.[44]

Even when questions are vetted ahead of time, the RI remains entitled to inter- **11.58** vene if communication issues nevertheless manifest themselves. The actual questions might in the event be asked differently or counsel might ask follow-up questions arising out of an answer or the witness in the event struggles with the question.

Interventions may simply identify the potential difficulty (e.g. that the question **11.59** is too complex), but it is more helpful if the RI can also provide a solution, for

---

[42] [2015] EWCA Crim 1582.
[43] At [45].
[44] [2010] EWCA Crim 4 at [42].

example, 'could counsel please rephrase that statement as a question?' or 'please can we clarify what counsel means by "revelation"?'

G. Intermediaries for Defence Witnesses

11.60 There are similarities between the role of the intermediary for a prosecution witness and the role of the intermediary for a defence witness. Although the defence solicitors should be able to access the matching service at the National Crime Agency for a RI, in practice such requests are often routed through the MoJ to check on funding issues. Once there has been a successful referral, the RI meets with and assesses the witness; they assist during any interview or discussion between the witness and the defence solicitor; they write a report which justifies the application for special measures for the witness; they take part in any GRH; they assist in a court familiarization visit; and they assist when the witness gives evidence.

(a) Differences for defence witnesses

11.61 There are also differences. It is the defence solicitor who seeks the referral. If the defence wish to apply for special measures under s. 27 (video-recorded evidence-in-chief), then there needs to be an ABE interview. Solicitors will not have received the training that police have in dealing with vulnerable witnesses in interview in accordance with ABE Guidance, so they may well wish to seek the help of a trained forensic interviewer who would be informed by the assessment and the planning meeting with the intermediary. The solicitor can be the responsible third party during the assessment. It may also be necessary to engage a third party to film the interview and, for instance, to require them to enter into a confidentiality agreement. The defence would need to decide when to make the application for special measures, since the decision whether or not to call evidence may not be taken until the close of the prosecution case.

11.62 From the statistics quoted above (101 referrals in seven years; one in the last year) it may be that defence solicitors are seeking intermediary assistance outside the Witness Intermediary Scheme in respect of vulnerable defence witnesses.

H. Intermediaries for Defendants

11.63 YJCEA 1999 excluded suspects and defendants from s. 29. The Coroners and Justice Act 2009 s. 104 allows for the examination of an accused through an intermediary. It has not been brought into effect in England and Wales, although the equivalent has been brought into effect in Northern Ireland.[45] However, from 2007 and on an ad hoc basis, the defence have applied for the use of an intermediary to assist a defendant, relying on the court's inherent jurisdiction to ensure a fair trial for the defendant. Judges have had to reach their decisions based on the facts and evidence placed before them by the defence. As a general rule, the test inherent in s. 104 is a useful one: does the defendant need an intermediary in order effectively to participate in the proceedings? If the court does allow the use of a defendant intermediary, that person is commonly known as a 'non-registered intermediary', since they are acting outside the Witness Intermediary Scheme.

(a) Role and function

The fundamental role of the defendant intermediary is the same as that of a   **11.64**
RI, namely, to assist in communication between the defendant and anyone who needs to speak with, advise, or question him or her. They assess the defendant for that purpose, as they would a prosecution or defence witness. The defendant intermediary is independent; neutrality and impartiality are maintained. Their primary duty is to the court. They are not legal advisers or appropriate adults or supporters and they are not part of the 'defence team'. If they assist during a trial, they may well check the defendant's understanding of the process and of the vocabulary used in a trial, and advise on strategies for maintaining the defendant's attention. They may assist in conference between counsel and the defendant—for instance, assisting the giving of advice and taking of instructions when the defendant decides whether or not to give evidence at the trial. If they assist during evidence, then they do so in the same way they would for a prosecution or defence witness, advising on questioning styles, dealing with the vetting of questions, and intervening during questioning where appropriate. They express no opinion on the reliability or veracity of any witness or on whether or not the defendant is guilty.

(b) Not necessary in every case

In *R v Cox*,[46] the defendant had 'complex psychiatric difficulties' and a judge had   **11.65**
approved the use of an intermediary. None, however, could be found. The trial judge took a number of steps to ensure that the defendant would be able to follow the proceedings. The Court of Appeal felt that the trial judge had done everything he could to assist the defendant and upheld the conviction, saying that if an intermediary could not be found in the circumstances, the next stage is not to stay the proceedings, 'but for the judge to make an informed assessment of whether the absence of an intermediary would make the proposed trial an unfair

---

[45] DoJ, Northern Ireland Registered Intermediaries Schemes Pilot Project PHASE II REVIEW (DoJ, 2016).
[46] [2012] EWCA Crim 549.

trial. It would, in fact, be a most unusual case for a defendant who is fit to plead to be found to be so disadvantaged by his condition that a properly brought prosecution would have to be stayed.'[47]

(c) The initial judicial attitude towards the use of intermediaries for defendants

11.66 Within a few years of the WIS being rolled out nationwide, judges began to exercise their inherent jurisdiction to order the use of an intermediary to assist the defendant. This practice was approved in *C v Sevenoaks Youth Court*,[48] where Openshaw J said that it is the court's duty to ensure that the defendant had a fair trial 'not just during the proceedings but beforehand as he and his lawyers prepare for the trial'. This view was reinforced by Mitting J in *R (AS) v Great Yarmouth Youth Court*,[49] where he stated: 'There is a right, which may in certain circumstances amount to a duty, to appoint a registered intermediary to assist the defendant to follow the proceedings and give evidence if without assistance he would not be able to have a fair trial.'[50] In *Jordan Dixon v R*, the Court of Appeal noted 'the real assistance to the Appellant in explaining to him what was happening and simplifying the trial process' where an intermediary acted for a defendant throughout his trial for murder.[51]

11.67 A random shift in judicial attitude came with *R (OP) v Secretary of State for Justice*[52] (see below). Evidence was presented to the court that between August 2009 and August 2011, the last period when the Ministry of Justice allowed defence solicitors to access the register of RIs, there were eighty-three requests for an intermediary for the full duration of the trial, and four for the defendant giving evidence alone. The relative financial implications of this can be noted.

(d) Carlile and the Law Commission

11.68 In June 2014, the 'Independent Parliamentarians' Inquiry into the Operation and Effectiveness of the Youth Court'[53] chaired by Lord Carlile of Berriew CBE QC made a series of recommendations to assist young defendants. These included bringing into force s. 104 and to extend it 'by means of new legislation, to enable child defendants to have an intermediary to provide communication support

---

[47] ibid. at [30].
[48] [2009] EWHC 3088 (Admin).
[49] [2011] EWHC 2059 (Admin).
[50] ibid. at [6].
[51] [2013] EWCA Crim 465 at [96].
[52] [2014] EWHC 1944 (Admin).
[53] 2014, available at <http://www.icpr.org.uk/media/37698/YOUTH%20COURT%20REPORT%20-%20final%20version%20DK.pdf> accessed 21 March 2017.

throughout their case and not just for the giving of evidence. This should be achieved within two years.'

In January 2016, the Law Commission report on 'Unfitness to Plead' No. 364[54] **11.69** recommended 'a statutory entitlement be created for a defendant to have the assistance of an intermediary, both for the giving of evidence and otherwise in trial proceedings, where that is required'.[55] To achieve quality assurance and to enable the cost of such assistance to be 'properly regulated', they further recommended the 'creation of a registration scheme for defendant intermediaries, similar to that which regulates the training, qualification and conduct of witness intermediaries'.

(e) *OP* and the Crim PD

The judgment in *R (OP) v Secretary of State* and the 2016 Crim PD was handed **11.70** down some time before the Law Commission report was published. The 2016 Crim PD was already in draft and was issued shortly afterwards. Both implicitly reject the Law Commission's recommendations. The applicant in *OP* brought the action on a narrow point: the magistrates had ruled that he should be allowed the assistance of a RI, but the Ministry of Justice refused to provide one. The court, however, looked further than that and drew a distinction between two intermediary roles, one to assist the defendant through the trial and one to assist him only when (and if) he gave evidence. It declared that assistance to a defendant during the trial was 'founded in general support, reassurance and calm interpretation of unfolding events'. That did not require an intermediary. It could be achieved 'by an adult with experience in life and the cast of mind apt to facilitate comprehension by a worried individual on trial. In play are understandable emotions: uncertainty, perhaps a sense of territorial disadvantage, nervousness and agitation.'[56] No mention is made of the likelihood that the issue for the defendant was more fundamental than his nervousness or disempowerment, but instead that, for example, his learning difficulties or ADHD or autism severely hampered his ability to participate in the proceedings, or that any expertise in such issues were required of the adult with experience in life. Assistance while the defendant was giving evidence, however, the court went on, required 'skilled support and interpretation with the potential for intervention and on occasion suggestion to the Bench'.[57] That would require the skills of an intermediary 'at the point of maximum strain' when the defendant submits to cross-examination.[58]

---

[54] Law Commission, 'Unfitness to Plead', Law Com No. 364 (Law Commission, 2016) available at <http://www.lawcom.gov.uk/project/unfitness-to-plead/> accessed 21 March 2017.
[55] ibid. 1.33.
[56] [2014] EWHC 1944 (Admin) at [35].
[57] ibid. at [34].
[58] ibid. at [36].

11.71 The Crim PD which cites this judgment states that, '[t]he court should adapt the trial process to address a defendant's communication needs and will rarely exercise its inherent powers to direct appointment of an intermediary', even where the intermediary 'would improve the trial process'.[59] 'Directions to appoint an intermediary for a defendant's evidence will thus be rare, but for the entire trial extremely rare.'[60] The Crim PD also cites *R v R*,[61] where the Court of Appeal approved the way in which a trial judge went about assessing whether a defendant needed an intermediary throughout the trial. It is worth noting that the Court of Appeal at the same time ruled that the judge's decision was not appealable under s. 35(1) of the Criminal Procedure and Investigation Act 1996.

(f)   *R v Rashid*

11.72 *R v R* (mentioned above) returned, following conviction, to a different Court of Appeal as *R v Rashid*.[62] That Court of Appeal endorsed the distinction between the two roles set out in *OP*. 'In the overwhelming majority of cases, competent legal representation and good trial management' will suffice to ensure that the defendant 'gives best quality evidence, participates in his trial and receives a fair trial'. An intermediary may be required, but only in 'very rare' cases. 'In rare cases where the threshold of disability is crossed', an intermediary might be needed during the defendant's evidence.

11.73 Significantly, the Court of Appeal went on to say that, when 'determining what is necessary for the particular defendant', the judge must take into account certain things about the advocates. The first is that the advocate 'will have undergone specific training and must have satisfied himself or herself' before acting for the Crown or for the defence 'that the training and experience' enabled them 'to conduct the case with proper professional competence'. The latter is defined as including the ability to ask questions that are not tag questions, by using short and simple sentences, by using easy to understand language, and by avoiding the use of a tone of voice which implies an answer. It would be a 'serious dereliction of duty' and 'a breach of professional duty' to continue with the case if the advocate cannot carry out these 'basic tasks'. If the advocates are in such breach, then the answer is not to engage an intermediary, but to go back to those instructing the advocates who are obliged to ensure that only those who are qualified do these cases. The Court did not define what the 'specific training' would consist of, nor how those instructing the advocates should make a judgment about the competence and qualifications of the advocates.

---

[59] Crim PD (2015) (as amended) 3F.12.
[60] ibid. 3F.13.
[61] [2015] EWCA Crim 1870.
[62] [2017] EWCA Crim 2.

(g) Assessment and at trial: the application

An intermediary assesses a defendant in the same way that they would a pros- **11.74**
ecution or defence witness, but with the difference that they would also keep in
mind the question of how the trial process needs to be adapted for the defendant's
needs (not just the examination-in-chief and cross-examination), whether or not
an intermediary is assisting him or her. The report, which may follow the template for registered intermediary reports, would be attached to the application[63]
for the use of an intermediary in accordance with Part 18. Crim PD 3F.16 states
that an application should be made to the Legal Aid Agency for prior authority
to fund a pre-trial assessment. An appeal against a refusal should be made to the
court. It further states that arranging payment from Central Funds if the application for use of an intermediary is successful is the responsibility of court staff who
have internal guidance. The rate of pay is unregulated.[64] If the application for the
use of an intermediary is contested, then the proposed intermediary should be
asked to attend in order to assist the court with the reasons why they are recommending that one is needed.

(h) Ground rules hearing

If the application is granted, then the court must hold a GRH: Crim PR 3.9(7) **11.75**
treats defendants in the same way as other witnesses when it comes to the court's
powers to control questioning and the requirement to have a GRH with the
intermediary present. If an intermediary is assisting the defendant throughout
the trial, then there needs to be a GRH at the start to consider how the trial
process is to be adapted (e.g. length of sittings, vocabulary used by participants,
breaks) and how the intermediary should indicate it when there is an issue for the
court to note. Even if the judge refuses an application for use of an intermediary
throughout the trial, the findings of the assessment and the recommendations in
the report can help to inform the court when adapting the trial process. See further Chapter 12, 'Ground Rules Hearings'.

I. Conclusion

In the eight years since the intermediary scheme was rolled out nationally, it has **11.76**
evolved into being a crucial participant in the criminal justice system. It was
intermediaries who, following their training and procedural guidance, brought
GRHs into the trial process, and who inventively suggested ways to enable a
witness to give their best evidence and for a defendant to participate in their

---

[63] Crim PD at 3F.14.
[64] See also The Advocate's Gateway, 'Toolkit 16: Intermediaries Step by Step'.

trial. When judges began to order advocates to submit their questions ahead of time, it was intermediaries, who had already assessed the witness's communication needs, who were best placed to help the court and the advocates. In the past, some judges have questioned whether they were needed and some advocates have resented their 'interfering' with the cross-examination, but steadily, the intermediaries have overcome doubts about their role.

11.77 The success of the scheme in the criminal courts has paved the way to their use in civil and family proceedings. They have also acted in the Coroner's Court, Court of Protection, a Mental Health Tribunal, and when a vulnerable witness gave evidence to the Court of Appeal.

11.78 Intermediary-led adaptations to trial processes for individual witnesses or defendants have led to wider changes to the trial processes in general. Some strategies such as planning questions in clear topics and non-adjourned breaks have become commonplace. Others, such as bringing counsel to the live-link room or screening the defendant's view of the live-link screen, are less commonly applied. Several of these innovations appear in the list of 'examples of a more flexible approach' which the Judicial College recommend to judges in the 'Equal Treatment Bench Book'.

11.79 Like others, intermediaries are subject to the financial constraints put on the criminal justice system. There have rarely been enough of them to match the demand. The unregulated fees of non-registered intermediaries have been criticized. As those whose role it is to question witnesses become more adept at recognizing vulnerabilities and better able to adapt their style of questioning accordingly, there may be a temptation to use the intermediary's report to assist in planning how to question the witness, but to dispense with the intermediary, leaving it to the judge through their case-management powers to monitor the questioning to ensure fairness. The more trials are conducted in straightforward, simple language, the more the threshold of who needs an intermediary may change. It remains to be seen whether the dicta of the Lord Chief Justice in *Rashid* regarding the need for an intermediary to assist a defendant when giving evidence is applied in respect of a registered intermediary assisting a prosecution or defence witness. Superficially, the argument is the same for all, but the necessary skills set out in the judgment in fact are identical to the recommendations of Mr Rashid's intermediary. It could be argued that one of the surviving roles of the intermediary will always be to assess the witness or defendant and to recommend what is needed for that particular person.

11.80 It would be a mistake though to underestimate the contribution which is made in having an independent person at trial who comes to the case with an expertise and who has assessed the communication needs of this witness. Whoever they are assisting, they can, as the Court of Appeal said in *FA*, 'promote the interests of justice in the conduct of the case', both the welfare of the witness and the interests of the defendant.

Further Reading

Cooper, P., (2014) 'Highs and lows: The 4th Intermediary Survey' (London: Kingston University), available at <https://www.city.ac.uk/__data/assets/pdf_file/0011/280496/INTERMEDIARY-SURVEY-REPORT-5-July-2015.pdf> accessed 22 March 2017.

Marchant, R., 'Age Is Not Determinative' (2016) *Criminal Law and Justice Weekly*, 180(12 & 13), 223–30.

O'Mahony, B. M., 'Accused of Murder: Supporting the Communication Needs of a Vulnerable Defendant at Court and at the Police Station' (2012) *Journal of Learning Disabilities and Offending Behaviour*, 3(2), 77–84.

Wurtzel, D., 'The Youngest Witness in a Murder Trial: Making It Possible for Very Young Children to Give Evidence' (2014) Crim LR, 12, 891–9.

12

GROUND RULES HEARINGS

Penny Cooper and Laura Farrugia

A. Introduction

12.01 It is now generally accepted that if justice is to be done to the vulnerable witness and also to the accused, a radical departure from the traditional style of advocacy will be necessary. Advocates must adapt to the witness, not the other way round.[1]

The concept of the 'vulnerable witness' took root in the 1998 Home Office report, 'Speaking Up for Justice'.[2] The report identified measures which would improve the treatment of vulnerable witnesses, including those who would be likely to be intimidated. Recommendations included better pre-trial support for witnesses and applications for a range of 'measures'. The report led to the range of special measures for children and vulnerable adult witnesses in the Youth Justice and Criminal Evidence Act 1999 (YJCEA 1999). The 'Speaking Up for Justice' report recognized that its 'Matrix of Court Measures' was illustrative only and that each witness's needs are unique. Case law now also recognizes that there must be a formal hearing to discuss and direct fair treatment and questioning. This hearing is called the ground rules hearing (GRH).

12.02 The court is required to take every reasonable step to encourage and facilitate the attendance of vulnerable witnesses and their participation in the trial process. To that end, judges are taught, in accordance with the Criminal Practice Directions, that it is best practice to hold hearings in advance of the trial to ensure the smooth running of the trial, to give any special measures directions and to set the ground rules for the treatment of a vulnerable witness. We would expect a ground rules hearing in every case involving a vulnerable witness, save in very exceptional circumstances.[3]

The creation of the 'ground rules' approach for vulnerable witnesses can be traced back to early intermediary training and practice. Intermediaries were advised[4] to include in their court reports a section entitled 'ground rules'[5] listing the intermediary's recommendations as to the dos and don'ts for the most effective communication with the particular witness, including how the intermediary would signal if a communication issue arose. Intermediaries were taught to discuss and agree the ground rules for questioning the witness with the advocates at court and this advice

---

[1] *R v Lubemba; R v JP* [2014] EWCA Crim 2064 at [45].

[2] Home Office, 'Speaking Up for Justice: Report of the Interdepartmental Working Group on the Treatment of Vulnerable or Intimidated Witnesses in the Criminal Justice System' (1998).

[3] Hallett LJ in *R v Lubemba* [2014] EWCA Crim 2064 at [42].

[4] Training in 2004 by the first author for the Office for Criminal Justice Reform for the then new registered intermediary role.

[5] The term 'ground rule' refers to an agreed principle about behaviour and is said to have originally been a term used in baseball; each baseball ground had its own unique layout and thus its own set of rules. The term has previously been widely adopted in education to articulate expected behaviour in the classroom.

was reiterated in the first *Intermediary Procedural Guidance Manual*.[6] However, a study by the first author in 2009[7] revealed that intermediaries were encountering significant problems at court since, despite their pre-trial discussions, advocates were not adhering to supposedly agreed ground rules. Studies by the first author revealed a patchy application of the ground rules approach and that some hearings were no more than a 'perfunctory' nod to active judicial management of the adjustment for a vulnerable person.[8] As a result of the first author's research and recommendations, a ground rules procedure was introduced into the Criminal Procedure Rules (Crim PR) in 2015.[9] Guidance can also be found in the Criminal Practice Directions (Crim PD),[10] which also cites[11] the guidance in Toolkit 1 on The Advocate's Gateway.[12] Accompanying Toolkit 1 is a non-exhaustive checklist (replicated at the end of this chapter) of matters which the court should consider and discuss at a GRH.[13] Taking a lead from the criminal justice system, the practice of holding a GRH when a witness or party is vulnerable has now been implemented in other parts of the justice system, including, for instance, family courts and employment tribunals.[14]

The ground rules approach has also been identified by the Court of Appeal **12.03** in Northern Ireland, as one of the principles to be applied to achieve procedural fairness when a litigant is vulnerable as a result of a disability.[15] In *Galo v Bombardier Aerospace Ltd*, where the claimant appealed the decision of the Industrial Tribunal, Gillen LJ described a GRH as involving 'a preliminary consideration of the procedure that the tribunal or court will adopt tailored to the particular circumstances of the litigant'.[16] The judgment also gives examples of matters which the tribunal may consider:

---

[6] *Intermediary Procedural Guidance Manual* (Office for Criminal Justice Reform, October 2005). See section 2, p. 14: 'It is essential that ground rules are agreed before the trial so that all parties and the intermediary have a common understanding …'.

[7] For instance, P. Cooper, 'Tell Me What's Happening 2: Registered Intermediary Survey 2010' (City University London, 2011); and P. Cooper, 'Highs and Lows: The 4th Intermediary Survey' (Kingston University London, 2014).

[8] Cooper, 'Highs and Lows', p. 21.

[9] Crim PR 3.9(7).

[10] Crim PD (2015), [2015] EWCA Crim 1567 (as amended April 2016), 'General matters 3E Ground rules hearings to plan the questioning of a vulnerable witness or defendant'.

[11] ibid. 3F.23.

[12] The Advocate's Gateway, 'Ground Rules Hearings for the Fair Treatment of Vulnerable Witnesses and Defendants' (2016), available at <http://www.theadvocatesgateway.org/images/toolkits/1-ground-rules-hearings-and-the-fair-treatment-of-vulnerable-people-in-court-2016.pdf> accessed 13 April 2017.

[13] The Advocate's Gateway, 'Ground Rules Hearings Checklist' (2016), available at <http://www.theadvocatesgateway.org/images/toolkits/ground-rules-hearings-checklist-2016.pdf> accessed 13 April 2017.

[14] For instance, see *Re WSCC v H and Others (Children) (Care proceedings: Brain Injury)* [2015] EWHC 2439 (Fam); and *J W Rackham v NHS Professionals Ltd* [2015] UKEAT 0110_15_1612.

[15] *Galo v Bombardier Aerospace Ltd* [2016] NICA 25. The appeal was heard by Morgan LCJ, Gillen LJ, and Weatherup LJ.

[16] ibid. at [53(7)].

- The approach to questioning of the claimant and to the method of cross-examination by him/her. Adaptions to questioning may be necessary to facilitate the evidence of a vulnerable person.
- How questioning is to be controlled by the Tribunal.
- The manner, tenor, tone, language and duration of questioning appropriate to the witness's problems.
- Whether it is necessary for the Tribunal to obtain an expert report to identify what steps are required in order to ensure a fair procedure tailored to the needs of the particular applicant.
- The applicant under a disability, if a personal litigant, must have the procedures of the court fully explained to him and advised as to the availability of pro bono assistance/McKenzie Friends/voluntary sector help available.
- Recognition must be given to the possibility that those with learning disabilities need extra time even if represented to ensure that matters are carefully understood by them.
- Great care should be taken with the language and vocabulary that is utilised to ensure that the directions given at the ground rules hearing are being fully understood.
- As happened in the *Rackham* case [*J W Rackham v NHS Professionals Ltd* [2015] UKEAT 0110_15_1612], consideration should be given to the need for respondent's counsel to offer cross-examination and questions in writing to assist the claimant with the claimant being allowed some time to consult, if represented, with his counsel. These were deemed 'reasonable adjustments'.
- The Tribunal must keep these adjustments needed under review.[17]

12.04 The judge is responsible for controlling questioning[18] and a GRH is a key mechanism by which the judge can set the parameters for the fair treatment and questioning of vulnerable witnesses and defendants. Many judges find them an invaluable case management tool, particularly as they may forestall problems at trial.[19] The use of a ground rules discussion is also likely to reduce the chances of an appeal based on an argument that a judge was too interventionist.[20] '[G]round rules hearings should cover and decide upon in detail the scope and content of cross-examination. General assurances from counsel and rough time estimates are a hostage to fortune.'[21]

12.05 By way of example, judges at GRHs have achieved the following through ground rules directions:[22]

---

[17] ibid.
[18] Crim PD (2015) 3E.1.
[19] E. Henderson, 'Jewel in the Crown?', *Counsel*, November 2014, 10–12.
[20] P. Cooper, 'Case Comment, *R. v Jonas (Sandor)*: Trial—Judge—Restrictions on Cross-Examination on Issues of Credibility' (2015) Crim LR, 9, 742–6.
[21] ibid. 745.
[22] With thanks to registered intermediary Ruth Marchant for these examples.

- fixing the timing of the testimony of a young child to match her usual nursery hours, specifically avoiding their 'nap' time;
- scheduling the start times of a vulnerable adult witness's testimony to accommodate their travel requirements and physical care needs;
- setting a maximum time limit on cross-examination;
- identifying vocabulary that should (as well as words that should not) be used to ensure that the witness understands the questions; and
- ensuring the pace of questioning is suitable for the witness (for some witnesses, a pace which is too slow can be as bad as a pace which is too fast).

Crim PR 3.9(3) sets out the obligation of the court, when preparing for trial, to take 'every reasonable step' to (a) to encourage and to facilitate the attendance of witnesses when they are needed; and (b) to facilitate the participation of any person, including the defendant. It is within this general context that the GRH takes place and it is necessary for the court to:

- ensure effective discussions at the GRH;
- make ground rules direction(s) for the appropriate treatment and questioning of the vulnerable person; and
- use the GRH to check that the advocates have planned their questions carefully.

Effective discussions, making directions, and checking the wording of questions will now be considered in detail.

B. Effective Discussions at the Ground Rules Hearing

Crim PR 3.9(7) obliges the court to invite representations from the parties and **12.06** the intermediary (if there is one) and to set ground rules for questioning. Treating a GRH as a mere 'tick box' exercise is inimical to the fair treatment and questioning of a vulnerable person; the GRH is an opportunity for a detailed planning discussion. In many instances, the advocates and the intermediary will have been in contact before the GRH to begin to discuss proposed ground rules and how they will apply to cross-examination. Advocates should collaborate with the intermediary and work together with the aim of achieving the best evidence.

In 2013, one experienced intermediary described a GRH as follows: **12.07**

> In my mind there are two kinds of [ground rules hearings]; 1. where the judge just skips through the recommendations and barristers play lip service to agreeing to them and, 2. where there is a genuine discussion between all parties about the witness and the [intermediary] recommendations.[23]

---

[23] Cooper, 'Highs and Lows', 16.

It is the latter kind of GRH that reflects good practice. Crim PR changes, which came into force in April 2015, set out what is required of the judge and advocates. The court is required to invite representations and set ground rules where required. The Crim PR also sets out what ground rules directions 'may include'. This leaves the court with flexibility to set the ground rules that are appropriate for a particular witness or defendant.

12.08   Crim PR 3.9

> (7) Where directions for appropriate treatment and questioning are required, the court must—
>   (a) invite representations by the parties and by any intermediary; and
>   (b) set ground rules for the conduct of the questioning, which rules may include—
>   (i)   a direction relieving a party of any duty to put that party's case to a witness or a defendant in its entirety,
>   (ii) directions about the manner of questioning,
>   (iii) directions about the duration of questioning,
>   (iv) if necessary, directions about the questions that may or may not be asked,
>   (v)   where there is more than one defendant, the allocation among them of the topics about which a witness may be asked, and
>   (vi) directions about the use of models, plans, body maps or similar aids to help communicate a question or an answer.

Sub-paragraphs (i) to (vi) are considered in detail below at paras 12.21–12.36.

12.09   Careful planning for the GRH is essential. Intermediary reports should include recommendations on questioning of the witness, and may also include recommendations which would enable better communication.[24] It should be possible for advocates to use the intermediary table of recommendations in the report as a guide to the agenda for the discussion at the GRH. The purpose of these discussions is to determine what conditions should be put in place when the witness gives testimony to maximize the potential for achieving the best quality evidence from that witness.

12.10   Even where there is no intermediary, if a witness or defendant is vulnerable, there must be a GRH save in 'very exceptional circumstances'.[25] It is suggested that a very exceptional circumstance might be where, after collaborative decisions, counsel agree the directions and place these in draft form before the judge, who approves and orders them without the need for a hearing.

12.11   When there is a hearing, the Ground Rules Hearing Checklist (written by the first author) on The Advocate's Gateway provides a framework for matters which

---

[24] *Intermediary Procedural Guidance Manual* (MoJ, 2015) 55.
[25] *R v Lubemba* [2014] EWCA Crim 2064 at [42].

should be covered;[26] the checklist is reproduced at the end of this chapter. 'If there are any doubts on how to proceed, guidance should be sought from those who have the responsibility for looking after the witness and or an expert.'[27] In addition, there is a range of toolkits available at <http://theadvocatesgateway. org> which provide guidance on treatment and questioning and represent best practice;[28] advocates should read the relevant toolkits in preparation for a GRH and approach the hearing with a clear idea of what ground rules they are seeking the judge to direct and why. A GRH cannot be conducted properly without detailed preparation on the part of the advocates. Prior to the GRH, advocates should discuss with each other the directions that are sought, and draft a list for the court making it clear which are agreed and those that are not. It is likely to assist efficient case management if this is submitted in writing to the judge in advance of the hearing.

(a) When the ground rules hearing should be held

The GRH takes place after the Pleas and Trial Preparation Hearing (PTPH). **12.12** A GRH is a form of further case management hearing and is one of the exceptions to the rule that after the PTPH there will be no further case management hearings.[29] The Crim PD recommend that: 'Discussion before the day of trial is preferable to give advocates time to adapt their questions to the witness's needs.'[30] In practice, the timing of the GRHs varies considerably; in some cases, it will be listed several days before the witness is due to give their evidence and, in other cases, it will not have been listed and so takes place a matter of minutes before the witness is due to give their evidence. In one Crown Court, judges and the list office ensure that GRHs are held at 9 a.m. to ensure that trial counsel can attend. Since this is the commonly agreed practice at that court, all judges are aware that advocates may arrive late to other trials if the ground rules hearing lasts longer than an hour.[31]

Whatever the timing, GRHs should not be rushed; the issues are far too import- **12.13** ant and go to the heart of the conduct of a fair trial. A rushed GRH is unlikely to result in the most effective questioning of a vulnerable person or the most effective use of the intermediary (if there is one). Matters such as ensuring the proper use of communication aids (which are unlikely to be familiar to the advocates and the court) will require careful planning.

---

[26] See <http://www.theadvocatesgateway.org/images/toolkits/ground-rules-hearings-checklist-2016.pdf> accessed 13 April 2017.
[27] *R v Lubemba* [2014] EWCA Crim 2064 at [42].
[28] Crim PD (2015) 3D.7.
[29] MoJ, 'PTPH—Introduction and Guidance' (2015) 10, available at <https://www.justice.gov.uk/courts/procedure-rules/criminal/docs/october-2015/cm007-eng.pdf> accessed 22 March 2017.
[30] Crim PD (2015) 3E.3.
[31] As reported by an intermediary in a recent GRH survey, discussed in more detail below.

In reality, it may have been impossible to schedule a time when the trial judge, advocates, and intermediary are all available together to have the necessary planning discussion well in advance of the witness's testimony. Nevertheless, at whatever stage the GRH is held prior to the vulnerable person giving evidence, advocates should have carefully planned their questions in advance and consulted the intermediary where there is one. To that end, it is now increasingly the case that judges expect advocates to come to the GRH with their questions for the witness drafted and, if possible, already seen by the intermediary. Prior to the GRH, advocates may, therefore, make contact with the intermediary and email their draft questions to them in advance of the GRH to seek their advice. The intermediary will check that the questions as drafted are likely to be understood completely and accurately. The intermediary may, for example, suggest different vocabulary, a different order of topics, or a different sentence construction. Advocates should find the intermediary's email contact details in the intermediary report.

12.14 Although the Crim PD suggest that it may be *helpful* for a note to be made of the ground rules, the authors suggest that such a note is in fact *essential* to avoid subsequent misunderstandings. This is discussed further below. This is particularly useful if the GRH takes place some time before the trial and particularly if, in the intervening period, the advocate or the trial judge changes.

(b) Who should attend the ground rules hearing

12.15 The trial judge and trial counsel should be present at the GRH. The intermediary, if there is one, should also be present. The intermediary can go through, and explain where necessary, the recommendations in their report. 'The intermediary must be present but is not required to take the oath (the intermediary's declaration is made just before the witness gives evidence).'[32] This is not an opportunity to treat the intermediary as a witness—in any event they are not. The intermediary is an impartial facilitator of communication whose overriding duty is to the court. (See Chapter 11, 'Intermediaries'.)

12.16 If there is a new judge and/or advocate after the GRH, there should be a further hearing, however brief.[33] This is to ensure that there is a meeting of minds for the actual trial about the ground rules and how they will be implemented.

12.17 It is not usually a requirement that the defendant attends the GRH. Unless a good reason is provided, a defendant in custody will not be produced specifically for a GRH, nor will an interpreter be booked for a defendant on bail who wishes

---

[32] Crim PD (2015) 3E.2.
[33] *Intermediary Procedural Guidance Manual* (MoJ, 2015) 39.

to attend.[34] Given that the personal difficulties of a vulnerable person are being discussed, the court should also consider clearing the public gallery.[35]

(c) Where the ground rules hearing should be held

Initially, when the procedure was new, some GRHs took place in chambers. **12.18** However, it is now advised that they take place in open court given that this is a formal case management hearing that should be recorded just like any other hearing.[36]

(d) Number of ground rules hearings

Ordinarily, one GRH to discuss the questioning of a witness should be suffi- **12.19** cient. However, after a witness's testimony has begun, a new communication issue might arise. Unless it can be dealt with succinctly, judge, counsel, and the intermediary (if there is one) should have a further discussion, in effect a supplementary ground rules hearing.

In the case of a vulnerable defendant, usually at least two GRHs are required. **12.20** The first takes place before the commencement of the trial in order to set the ground rules for the fair treatment of the defendant during the trial. For example, there might be a direction regarding where the defendant will sit (in the case of a young and vulnerable defendant, this might be next to his or her legal team as opposed to in the dock), what communication aids will be used, when breaks will occur, etc. The second GRH would take place later if the vulnerable defendant elects to give evidence. At the second GRH, directions will be made about the conduct of questioning of the defendant.[37]

C. Making Ground Rules Directions

Crim PR (2015) 3.9(6) underscores the need for the court to make directions, **12.21** especially where the questioning will be facilitated by an intermediary:

> (6) Facilitating the participation of any person includes giving directions for the appropriate treatment and questioning of a witness or the defendant, especially

---

[34] MoJ, 'PTPH—Introduction and Guidance', 10.

[35] The Advocate's Gateway, 'Toolkit 1: Ground Rules Hearings and the Fair Treatment of Vulnerable People in Court' (Advocacy Training Council, 2016), para. 1.6.4.

[36] ibid.

[37] As occurred, for example, in the case of *R v Piggin* 2014 (unreported) at the Central Criminal Court, when the defendant with Asperger's Syndrome was cross-examined by the QC for the prosecution in a very calm and deliberate manner, being careful to avoid complex and tagged questions which might have confused the defendant. The defendant was assisted in the witness box by an intermediary.

where the court directs that such questioning is to be conducted through an intermediary.

12.22 In *Chaaban*,[38] in 2003, the Court of Appeal recognized the trial management responsibility of the trial judge and a need to be alert to the needs of those involved:

> The trial judge has always been responsible for managing the trial. That is one of his most important functions. To perform it he has to be alert to the needs of everyone involved in the case. That obviously includes, but it is not limited to, the interests of the defendant. It extends to the prosecution, the complainant, to every witness (whichever side is to call the witness), to the jury, or if the jury has not been sworn, to jurors in waiting. Finally, the judge should not overlook the community's interest that justice should be done without unnecessary delay. A fair balance has to be struck between all these interests.[39]

12.23 It has been said that 'to ask a question is to apply one of the most powerful tools in communication'.[40] Research previously conducted by sociolinguistic experts has highlighted that the way in which power is exercised in court is fundamentally related to the syntactic forms of questions.[41] The language of law and questioning that takes place as part of the trial process, therefore, is of vital importance. In 2014, the Court of Appeal said it was the judge's *duty* to control questioning: 'a trial judge is not only entitled, he is duty bound to control the questioning of a witness'.[42] Crim PR 3.9(7) sets out in six sub-paragraphs what may be included in ground rules directions and each of these is now considered in detail.

(a) Crim PR 3.9(7)(i)—'a direction relieving a party of any duty to put that party's case to a witness or a defendant in its entirety'

12.24 Aspects of evidence which undermine or are believed to undermine the child's credibility must, of course, be revealed to the jury, but it is not necessarily appropriate for them to form the subject matter of detailed cross-examination of the child and the advocate may have to forego much of the kind of contemporary cross-examination which consists of no more than comment on matters which will be before the jury in any event from different sources.[43]

These words of the then Lord Chief Justice, Lord Judge, are from the now well-known, pivotal judgment in *B* in 2010. The principles apply equally to vulnerable adult witnesses. A judge is not obliged to allow a defence advocate to put their case[44] and it is by no means certain that advocates have a 'right "to put [their]

---

[38] *R v Chaaban* [2003] EWCA Crim 1012.
[39] ibid. at [35].
[40] K. Hawkins and C. Power, 'Gender Differences in Questions Asked During Small Decision-Making Group Discussions' (1999) *Small Group Research*, 30, 235–56.
[41] D. Eades, *Sociolinguistics and the Legal Process* (Multilingual Matters, 2010).
[42] *R v Lubemba* [2014] EWCA Crim 2064 at [51].
[43] *R v B* [2010] EWCA Crim 4 at [42].
[44] *R v Lubemba* [2014] EWCA Crim 2064 at [51].

case" or previous inconsistent statements to a vulnerable witness', but, even if there is such a right, 'it must be modified for young or vulnerable witnesses'.[45] Where a court directs that a party should not put their case, the jury should be made aware of the defence case:

> Instead of commenting on inconsistencies during cross-examination, following discussion between the judge and the advocates, the advocate or judge may point out important inconsistencies after (instead of during) the witness's evidence. The judge should also remind the jury of these during summing up. The judge should be alert to alleged inconsistencies that are not in fact inconsistent, or are trivial.[46]

How this may be done is demonstrated in the Criminal Bar Association training **12.25** film, *A Question of Practice*.[47] It suggested that judges should, generally speaking, be slow to direct that the defence case need not be put to the witness; a witness has a right to the opportunity to explain their version of events when an opposing version of the truth is put to them.[48] One of the aims of a GRH is to seek to determine how questions may be put so that the witness is afforded the opportunity to understand the questions and respond.

(b)   Crim PR 3.9(7)(ii)—'directions about the manner of questioning'

Recent Court of Appeal decisions about vulnerable witnesses have stressed the **12.26** need to modify questioning so that it is conducted in a manner that is fair to the witness. This is a right of the witness which can be traced back to *Browne v Dunn*:

> My Lords, I have always understood that if you intended to impeach a witness you are bound, whilst he is in the box, to give him an opportunity of making any explanation which is open to him; and, as it seems to me, that is not only a rule of professional practice in the conduct of a case, but is essential to fair play and fair dealing with witnesses.[49]

The Crim PD remind practitioners that:

> All witnesses, including the defendant and defence witnesses, should be enabled to give the best evidence they can. In relation to young and/or vulnerable people, this may mean departing radically from traditional cross-examination. The form and extent of appropriate cross-examination will vary from case to case.[50]

---

[45] *R v Lubemba; R v JP* [2014] EWCA Crim 2064 at [45].
[46] Crim PD (2015) 3E.4.
[47] Available at <http://theadvocatesgateway.org> accessed 22 March 2017.
[48] A right which can be traced back to *Browne v Dunn* (1894) 6 R 67.
[49] *Browne v Dunn* from *Markem Corporation and Another v Zipher Ltd* [2005] EWCA Civ 267, citing at [57] Hunt J in the Australian case of *Allied Pastoral Holdings v Federal Commissioner of Taxation* (1983) 44 ALR 607 because '*Browne v Dunne* [sic] is only reported in a very obscure set of reports' [58] and 'the decision is so difficult to lay hands on' [59].
[50] Crim PD (2015) 3E.4.

12.27 In addition, '[o]ver-rigorous or repetitive cross-examination of a child or vulnerable witness should be stopped'.[51] 'It will never be in the interests of justice that witnesses should be subjected to bullying and intimidatory tactics by counsel or to deliberately and unnecessarily prolonged cross-examination.'[52]

(c) Crim PR 3.9(7)(iii)—'directions about the duration of questioning'

12.28 The trial judge in *Butt* was justified in imposing a time limit on the cross-examination of the complainant; the Court of Appeal 'will not interfere with a decision made by the judge when exercising this function unless it is plain that it has resulted in unfairness'.[53] The judge 'is entitled to and should set reasonable time limits and to interrupt where he considers questioning is inappropriate'.[54] Lord Judge said in *B*:

> ... it should not be over-problematic for the advocate to formulate short, simple questions which put the essential elements of the defendant's case to the witness ... it should not take very lengthy cross-examination to demonstrate, when it is the case, that the child may indeed be fabricating, or fantasising, or imagining, or reciting a well-rehearsed untruthful script, learned by rote, or simply just suggestible, or contaminated by or in collusion with others to make false allegations, or making assertions in language which is beyond his or her level of comprehension, and therefore likely to be derived from another source. Comment on the evidence, including comment on evidence which may bear adversely on the credibility of the child, should be addressed after the child has finished giving evidence.[55]

12.29 Notwithstanding a direction about the duration of questioning, it may be necessary for the judge to bring the cross-examination to an end—for example, if the witness becomes too distressed to continue. 'The fact that a complainant is unable to complete his or her evidence is not necessarily a bar to the trial continuing.'[56] The issue will be whether or not the defendant can have a fair trial if questioning were to be cut short. This will depend on the circumstances of the particular case, including whether the defence case and any apparent inconsistencies in the witness's evidence have been put to the witness and what opportunity the defence has had to do so. If the defence has not had the opportunity to put salient points to the witness, the court will consider whether it is necessary for these matters to be put before the jury in an alternative way, thereby avoiding prejudice to the defendant. Thus, for example, rather than 'dragging' a witness through detailed

---

[51] Crim PD (2015) 3E.1.

[52] B. Leveson, 'Review of Efficiency in Criminal Proceedings by The Rt Hon Sir Brian Leveson, President of the Queen's Bench Division' (2015) at 8.3.1, 'Ground Rules Approach', para. 264, p. 70.

[53] *R v Butt* [2005] EWCA Crim 805 at [16].

[54] *R v Lubemba* [2014] EWCA Crim 2064 at [51].

[55] *R v B* [2010] EWCA Crim 4.

[56] *R v Pipe* [2014] EWCA Crim 2570 at [20]. However in some circumstances if a witness is distressed, as opposed to vulnerable, an adjournment to allow the witness to regain their composure will be the appropriate course of action: *R v SG* [2017] EWCA Crim 617.

records, the agreed inconsistencies in those records might be reduced to written admissions and placed before the jury in writing as agreed facts.[57] The trial judge should give the jury clear directions on how they should approach their task.

(d) Crim PR 3.9(7)(iv)—'if necessary, directions about the questions that may or may not be asked'

If questions can be adapted so that the defence case can be put to the witness, **12.30** then those questions should be put. Although a judge has no power to insist on defence cross-examination of the witness, once the defence has made the decision to cross-examine the witness the judge has a duty to control that questioning. It is not unusual for 'tag' questions to be prohibited by a ground rules direction: 'It is generally recognized that particularly with child witnesses short and untagged questions are best at eliciting the evidence.'[58] The Lord Chief Justice in *Rashid* said this:

> [Professional] competence includes the ability to ask questions without using tag questions, by using short and simple sentences, by using easy to understand language, by ensuring that questions and sentences were grammatically simple, by using open ended prompts to elicit further information and by avoiding the use of tone of voice to imply an answer. These are all essential requirements for advocacy whether in examining or cross-examining witnesses or in taking instructions. An advocate would in this court's view be in serious dereliction of duty to the court, quite apart from a breach of professional duty, to continue with any case if the advocate could not properly carry out these basic tasks.[59]

In *E*,[60] the defendant denied punching C, a witness aged 6, at trial. The Court of **12.31** Appeal said, 'we struggle to understand how the defendant's right to a fair trial was in any way compromised simply because [the defendant's counsel] was not allowed to ask: "Simon did not punch you in the tummy, did he?" '[61] In that case, the 'jury knew that the defendant disputed the evidence of C. The judge clearly explained his decision as to cross-examination technique and why he had taken it. In addition, the jury was specifically directed "to make proper fair allowances for the difficulties faced by the defence in asking questions about this".'[62]

Where there is an intermediary, their advice should be sought as to how the wit- **12.32** ness's evidence may be questioned in a way that facilitates complete, accurate, and coherent answers.[63] In another case with a 6-year-old prosecution witness, on

---

[57] ibid. at [25]–[28].
[58] *R v W and M* [2010] EWCA Crim 1926 at [30].
[59] *R v Rashid* [2017] EWCA Crim 2 at [80].
[60] *R v E* [2011] EWCA Crim 3028.
[61] ibid. at [28].
[62] ibid.
[63] As in YJCEA 1999 s. 16(5): 'In this Chapter references to the quality of a witness's evidence are to its quality in terms of completeness, coherence and accuracy; and for this purpose "coherence" refers to a witness's ability in giving evidence to give answers which address the questions put to the witness and can be understood both individually and collectively.'

intermediary advice, the judge required the defence to reword the questions. The following is based on the case note of the intermediary:[64]

> Defence counsel wanted to put to the witness the defendant's case [which was] that the incident had not happened at all. The intermediary advised on how this could be done in a way that the witness could deal with.
>
> Q: D didn't put his willy in your mouth, did he?
> Q: D didn't put his willy in your bottom, did he?
>
> On the advice of the intermediary, defence counsel's questions were reframed. The traditional statement-plus-tag form was avoided. Instead, two simple statements were followed by a simple question for each of the above, e.g.:
>
> Q: You said D put his willy in your mouth.
> D says he didn't put his willy in your mouth.
> Did D really put his willy in your mouth?

12.33   Defence counsel may be concerned that the vulnerable witness's evidence-in-chief in the form of an Achieving Best Evidence (ABE) interview will be substantially longer than a focused cross-examination of that witness. 'If there is thought to be any seeming disproportion such as might influence a jury the counterbalance is provided by an appropriate judicial direction.'[65] There may also be limitations discussed at the GRH that relate to legislative restrictions; YJCEA 1999 ss 41–3 restrict cross-examination on the complainant's sexual history without leave of the court. After cross-examination, the judge (or the prosecutor in re-examination) may ask a question to give the witness 'the chance to deal with the implication in the cross-examination'.[66]

(e) Crim PR 3.9(7)(v)—'where there is more than one defendant, the allocation among them of the topics about which a witness may be asked'

12.34   The Court of Appeal decision in *R v Jonas* highlights the benefits of allocating questions when there is more than one defendant separately represented and each advocate intends to cross-examine the vulnerable witness.

> Advocates must accept that the courts will no longer allow them the freedom to conduct their own cross-examination where it involves simply repeating what others have asked before, or exploring precisely the same territory. For these

---

[64] The Advocate's Gateway, 'Toolkit 1: Ground Rules Hearings and the Fair Treatment of Vulnerable People in Court' (The Inns of Court College of Advocacy, 2016) 8–9. A slightly longer version of this exchange can be found in P. Cooper, P. Backen, and R. Marchant, 'Getting to Grips with Ground Rules Hearings: A Checklist for Judges, Advocates and Intermediaries to Promote Fair Treatment of Vulnerable People in Court' (2015) Crim LR, 6, 420–35, 429.
[65] *R v RL* [2015] EWCA Crim 1215 at [18].
[66] *H v R* [2014] EWCA Crim 1555 at [63].

purposes defence advocates will now be treated as a group and, if necessary, issues divided amongst them, provided, of course, there is no unfairness in so doing.[67]

This decision has led in some cases to the identification of a single advocate to cover areas of common ground among multiple defendants.

(f)   Crim PR 3.9(7)(vi)—'directions about the use of models, plans, body maps or similar aids to help communicate a question or an answer'

'Aids to communication' are the special measure at YJCEA 1999 s. 30. If the use of a communication aid is to be used, then an order should be made under s. 30 of the 1999 Act and a ground rules direction should be made regarding how the communication aid will be used. The GRH provides the best opportunity for the judge and counsel to see the communication aid and plan how it will be used— for example, at what point in the witness's evidence it will be available, how it will be produced, and how it will be explained to the jury. The vulnerable person might need assistance from someone such as a witness supporter or an intermediary to access and use the communication aid. If so, this should be specified in the ground rules directions.   **12.35**

The Advocates' Gateway provides the only available guide, in the form of a comprehensive toolkit, for advocates planning to use a communication aid. If there is an intermediary for the vulnerable person, the advocates should carefully plan in advance how the aid will be used; this should form part of the discussion at the GRH. In any event, the advocates should use the toolkit to prepare as it brings together, for the first time, legislation, case law, rules, directions, and, importantly, empirical research on communication aids for vulnerable witnesses and defendants.[68]   **12.36**

(g)   Interpreters

Being unable to understand or speak the language of the courtroom creates vulnerability. Crim PR 3.9(3) sets out what must be done if a defendant needs an interpreter or documents need translating because he or she does not speak or understand English or has a hearing or speech impediment. One hundred years ago, the Court of Appeal said this about the use of interpreters and it is still good law: **12.37**

---

[67] [2015] EWCA Crim 562 at [34].
[68] M. Mattison, 'Putting Theory into Practice: A Comparison of the Guidance Available to Investigative Interviewers and Advocates when using Communication Aids in the Criminal Justice System' in P. Cooper and L. Hunting (eds), *Addressing Vulnerability in Justice Systems* (Wildy, 2016) 137.

To follow this practice [of providing a foreign language interpreter so that that the accused can understand the evidence and the case] may be inconvenient in some cases, and may cause some further expenditure of time; but such a procedure is more in consonance with that scrupulous care of the accused's interest which has distinguished the administration of justice in our criminal courts, and therefore it is better to adopt it.[69]

12.38 If the vulnerable witness has an interpreter, then their role should be discussed at the GRH. If there is also an intermediary for the witness, there should be a detailed discussion about how the intermediary and the interpreter will work together. Practical matters such as where they will both sit in relation to the witness should not be left to chance/ad hoc arrangements on the day of the hearing.

(h) Recording the ground rules directions

12.39 'It may be helpful for a trial practice note of boundaries to be created at the end of the discussion. The judge may use such a document in ensuring that the agreed ground rules are complied with.'[70] Boundaries in this context is referring to the directions that a court makes about the treatment and questioning of a vulnerable witness. As discussed above, it is suggested that such a note is necessary as opposed to merely desirable. GRHs in the Crown Court will be digitally audio recorded by the court (although not usually in the magistrates' court); however, as Crown Court transcripts are not routinely ordered, usually the judge and advocates will be relying on their own written records. It is not the responsibility of the intermediary to prepare the note; however, the intermediary report recommendations may provide something akin to an agenda for the discussion. Some intermediaries create a table in the recommendations section of their report with a blank column left free so that the judge and parties can make a note of whether a particular recommendation was directed or not. Of course, there may also be further directions made that are not recommendations in an intermediary report.

12.40 The responsibility of preparing this note falls to the parties' representatives. The note should be agreed and provided to the court so that it can go in the court file and be referred to later as necessary. Listed below are some of the ground rules in a case where the Court of Appeal heard fresh evidence, including from a vulnerable witness.[71] In this case, the intermediary,[72] prosecution counsel, and defence

---

[69] Lord Reading CJ in *Lee Kun* [1916] 1 KB 337; [1916] 11 CrAppR 293, subsequently cited with approval in *Kunnath v the State* [1993] 1 WLR 1315, *Cuscani v UK* [2002] ECHR 630, and *R v Zakowski* [2011] EWCA Crim 1734. See also Directive 2010/64/EU of the European Parliament and the Council of 20 October 2010 on the right to interpretation and translation in criminal proceedings.
[70] Crim PD (2015) 3E.3.
[71] *Re FA* [2015] EWCA Crim 209. See also P. Cooper, 'Clear Direction', *Counsel*, June 2015, 26–8.
[72] The registered intermediary in this case was Kate Man, who kindly provided these examples.

counsel 'worked as a team, the better to promote the interests of justice in the conduct of this case'.[73]

(i) Examples of ground rules in one particular case   **12.41**

(a) Questions in cross-examination to be supplied in advance and provided to all parties, including the RI.
(b) Parties will meet the witness in advance.
(c) She will be supported by her social worker/key worker.
(d) The witness's first name to be used at the start of each question and when possible eye contact made.
(e) Notes to be looked at only if essential.
(f) Speech to be clear and slow.
(g) Topics of questions will be introduced.
(h) Nouns and proper names will be used [not pronouns].
(i) All questions will be single part with a maximum 5 key words, in active form, in everyday language.
(j) Negatives, tags, passive and statements should be avoided.
(k) Counsel maintain a calm manner and steady pace and where necessary pause and re-phrase.
(l) The witness must have a red card to show if she needs a break and feels unable to ask for one.

Trial advocates should have a copy of the directions for their case in their brief and they have a duty to abide by directions of the court;[74] this, of course, includes ground rules directions.

D. Checking that the Advocates Have Planned Their Questions Carefully

Generally speaking, the more preparation that is carried out before the question- **12.42** ing of a vulnerable witness or defendant, the less likely it is that the advocate will contravene a ground rule. A recent development in judicial case management is the direction that advocates write their questions out in advance: 'So as to avoid any unfortunate misunderstanding at trial, it would be an entirely reasonable step for a judge at the ground rules hearing to invite defence advocates to reduce their questions to writing in advance.'[75]

As can be seen in the example above, the ground rules included that: 'Questions **12.43** in cross-examination [are] to be supplied in advance and provided to all parties,

---

[73] *Re FA* [2015] EWCA Crim 209 at [13].
[74] *R v Farooqi and Others* [2013] EWCA Crim 1649.
[75] *R v Lubemba; R v JP* [2014] EWCA Crim 2064 at [42].

including the [intermediary].' In this example, the requirement was placed on defence counsel since it was they who would be cross-examining the vulnerable witness.

12.44 Such a requirement could also apply to prosecution counsel, or co-defence counsel, if they were going to be cross-examining a vulnerable defence witness. If the intermediary were to unilaterally foreworn the witness or opposing counsel of the contents of cross-examination, this would be, at the very least, highly unprofessional. Advocates will wish to be confident that the intermediary is not going to telegraph cross-examination questions to the witness (or to opposing counsel). Advocates may wish to confirm this with the intermediary, especially since intermediaries for defendants are not trained, regulated, or accredited by the Ministry of Justice (see paragraph 12.45 below). The intermediary's paramount duty is to the court. The purpose of sharing the questions (this includes examination-in-chief as well as cross-examination) in advance is that the intermediary can advise the advocate on the most suitable way to pose the questions to achieve the best quality evidence.

12.45 There are additional considerations when the proposed cross-examination questions are for a vulnerable defendant. Although the intermediary should not supply the questions in advance to the vulnerable defendant, there is no code of conduct or ethical guidance for intermediaries for defendants. It is also at least arguable that the defendant's counsel, having seen the questions, would be obliged to share them with their client. As such, it might not be in the interests of justice for defence counsel to become aware of the proposed cross-examination (whether by the prosecution or a co-defendant) of their client. It will be for the trial judge to determine in the circumstances of the particular case, the merits of collaboration and the extent (if any) of the sharing of vulnerable defendant cross-examination questions. Similarly, practical issues may arise about who should be present where there is to be a ground rules hearing discussion about cross-examination of the vulnerable defendant; in these circumstances, the judge might determine that it is not in the interests of justice for detailed discussions about the wording of questions to take place in the presence of the defendant.

12.46 The answer may be for the judge to direct that cross-examining counsel liaises with the intermediary to obtain advice on their proposed questions for the vulnerable defendant, but that they need not share the proposed cross-examination questions with the other parties and the intermediary must not share the proposed cross-examination questions with anyone else.

12.47 Some examples of questions before and after the intermediary's involvement are listed below; the vulnerable witness had learning disabilities and a developmental age much lower than his chronological age of 17.

Counsel's draft	Intermediary's suggested rewording
X used to live with you?	Did X used to live with you?
X used to buy you sweets didn't he?	Did X buy you sweets?
X came into your room?	Did X come into your room?

Advocates should have already planned their questions before attending the **12.48** ground rules hearing. To an extent, what the advocate says to the witness in cross-examination will depend on the answers given and it is understood that no advocate is expected to work to a script. However, writing out questions in advance requires an advocate to think carefully about rapport-building questions, the order of topics, how each topic will be introduced, how their questions will be phrased, the vocabulary to be used, and so on. The advocate should check that their draft questions are in line with the recommendations in the intermediary report, or in the absence of an intermediary report, in line with the relevant toolkits on The Advocate's Gateway and what could be described as *universal ground rules* (discussed further below in section G).

In *R v RL*,[76] in advance of the GRH, counsel provided a list of the questions **12.49** which he proposed to ask two boys.

> In the course of the ground rules hearing the learned judge considered those proposed questions. He had the assistance of an intermediary, who was to assist the younger of the two boys to give evidence. The intermediary was able to assist the court in relation to both boys on questions such as whether they would have difficulty understanding questions asked in particular terms.[77]

Writing out questions in advance is not only a mark of good preparation for the **12.50** trial, but also increasingly expected by the court for the GRHs. Anecdotal evidence from advocates suggests that, despite some early misgivings on the part of some advocates, on the whole the advice of the intermediary has proved to be very helpful. Even if there is no intermediary, advocates should write out their questions, as many judges will require sight of the questions in order to check that they are expressed in a way which is suitable for the vulnerable witness.

E.   Ground Rules Hearings and the Unrepresented Defendant

If there is an intermediary report on a prosecution witness, this should have **12.51** been served with the application for special measures. It follows that a defendant

---

[76] *R v RL* [2015] EWCA Crim 1215.
[77] ibid. at [6].

(whether represented or not) should already have a copy of any intermediary report. Registered intermediary guidance cautions intermediaries about including personal confidential information about the witness:

> It should be noted that the RI's court report is attached to the application for special measures and that these are served on the other party/ies and the court. The RI should therefore only include personal confidential information in so far as it is necessary for their report and must not include information which could further identify or endanger the witness, for instance details that would identify the location (place of residence, name of school, name of day care centre etc.) of a witness. The effect of this is, for example, that they should simply refer to obtaining information from a child witness's school rather than naming the school and the person from whom they obtained that information.[78]

12.52 YJCEA 1999 prevents complainants in proceedings for sexual offences, child witnesses, or 'protected witnesses' from being cross-examined by the accused.[79] Where those provisions do not apply, the Act gives the court power to direct that the defendant is prohibited from cross-examining a particular witness[80] if the quality of that particular witness's evidence is likely to be diminished if the defendant cross-examines and it would not be contrary to the interests of justice to give such a direction. Where the defendant is unrepresented and the judge prohibits the unrepresented defendant from cross-examining the vulnerable witness, cross-examination on behalf of the defendant would be conducted by a legal representative appointed by the court. The court-appointed advocate would be expected to prepare their cross-examination in writing, attend the GRH, and engage in the discussions in accordance with good practice described elsewhere in this chapter.

12.53 However, a person charged in the proceedings is not a witness for the purposes of the judge's discretion to prohibit cross-examination by the unrepresented defendant.[81] This is an anomaly; the legislation does not give the court power to prohibit the unrepresented defendant from cross-examining a vulnerable co-defendant who chooses to give evidence. In such circumstances, the unrepresented defendant would be required to attend the GRH and to be part of the ground rules discussion, and the judge may direct the defendant to reduce his or her cross-examination to writing so that the questions may be submitted to the judge who would vet them. The judge may then allow the defendant to ask those judge-vetted questions of his co-defendant in cross-examination, the judge being ready to step in if required and take over if the unrepresented defendant did not comply with the ground rules.

---

[78] MoJ, *Registered Intermediary Procedural Guidance Manual* (MoJ, 2015) 52.
[79] YJCEA 1999 ss 34 and 35.
[80] YJCEA 1999 s. 36.
[81] YJCEA 1999 s. 36(4).

Alternatively, the judge may decide to ask all the cross-examination questions from the outset.

If there is an intermediary for the vulnerable co-defendant, the judge must also **12.54** invite the intermediary to be part of the ground rules discussion. The judge may direct that the intermediary reviews the unrepresented defendant's proposed, written cross-examination questions and they would also be vetted by the judge. A judge might consider directing that the intermediary (if they were prepared to do so) asks the cross-examination questions; however, this would be an unusual, ad hoc, and untested procedure. Detailed advance discussion would be required about who would ask supplementary questions (if they were required) and how this would be determined. A suggested solution, as set out in Chapter 13, 'Trial Management: The Judge's Role', is for the unrepresented defendant to put his questions into writing, and for those questions to be asked of the witness by the judge.[82]

F. A Recent Survey

This chapter has highlighted the rules, practice directions, and case law govern- **12.55** ing GRHs. However, and in line with the first author's previous research survey findings, many intermediaries and advocates report varying experiences in practice. A subsequent small-scale GRH survey conducted by the authors revealed some interesting results.[83]

(a) Stage and duration of ground rules hearings in proceedings

Many intermediaries and advocates highlighted that the timing of the GRH **12.56** depended largely on the judge involved in the trial. This ranged from a few weeks prior to trial to the day of the vulnerable witness providing their evidence. When asked how long GRHs usually took, intermediaries and advocates gave a variety of answers and this ranged from three minutes to five hours; however, the majority of answers tended to indicate that the GRH usually lasted between thirty and forty-five minutes.

---

[82] *R v Smith* [2004] EWCA Crim 2414; and *Re K (Children) (Unrepresented father; cross-examination of a child)* [2015] EWCA Civ 543.

[83] The survey by online questionnaire contained fifteen questions and was made available at <http://theadvocatesgateway.org> accessed 22 March 2017. Forty-two responses were received between December 2015 and January 2016. Twenty-seven respondents identified themselves as intermediaries, nine as advocates, and there were six others comprising two judges, three legal managers/advisers, and one paediatrician. The survey was conducted with ethical approval given by the first author's institution, Institute for Criminal Policy Research, Birkbeck, University of London.

(b) Parties present and location of ground rules hearing

12.57   Although there is no requirement for the defendant to be present during the GRH, the majority of those who completed the survey made reference to the defendant being present, although this may depend on whether the GRH was being conducted for the purposes of a vulnerable witness or a vulnerable defendant. Some intermediaries made reference to experience involving one judge at a GRH and another for the trial, with no additional GRHs being conducted when the judge had changed. Implications of this for the smooth running of the case have already been discussed above.

12.58   In terms of the location of the GRH, most intermediaries and advocates reported that GRHs are usually heard in court, with few references made to them being held in chambers. Other experiences include the GRH being conducted with the intermediary over video link. This seems an efficient strategy which could avoid a lengthy journey and waiting time for the intermediary for what might be a short GRH; it could also avoid having to reschedule a hearing if the intermediary is already elsewhere in court that day.

(c) Positive and negative experiences of ground rules hearings

12.59   Intermediaries reported mixed experiences (some positive, some negative). All but one of the nine advocates reported positive experiences of GRHs. The more positive experiences reported by the intermediaries make reference to all advocates 'being on-board' and a hearing which 'reinforced that the ground rules must be followed throughout the trial'. However, some intermediaries have also reported that they can be largely ignored, with one reference made to a perception of being dismissed '[s]ometimes off-handedly with an attitude of "we are experienced and know what we're doing thank you" '.

12.60   Responses of intermediaries illustrate how their experiences in GRHs can differ from case to case:

- 'All very differently; one went through all the cross-examination questions, the other was more informal and was more of a discussion.'
- 'It can be difficult as there is still no standard way. But it is becoming more methodical.'

When asked how GRHs are conducted, one advocate commented:

- 'With competency and interest requiring explanation but with sympathy to witness, intermediary, and unusually the Advocates!'

Another reported:

- 'Most Judges approached [the GRH] in a flexible manner.'

The only advocate who reported a negative experience said this, perhaps referring to discussions about the cross-examination questions that were planned by the advocate:

- 'I think it is far too prescriptive at the moment, with Judges treating it as an opportunity to say, "I wouldn't do it like this so therefore this is not the way to do it".'

12.61 Participants were asked to indicate[84] levels of compliance with ground rules directions set by trial judges. Twenty-two respondents in total indicated either 'full compliance' (n = 4) or compliance to a large extent (n = 18).

12.62 The survey results suggest there may be a disparity between the experiences of intermediaries and advocates at GRHs. However, many respondents recognized the importance of the ground rules. GRHs are part of the solution to effective treatment and questioning of vulnerable people in court, as these three comments from intermediary respondents illustrate:

- 'GRHs help but are not a fix it solution to some of the problems encountered with trials involving vulnerable witnesses. In fact they can sometimes be a tick box experience (along with the dreaded question "I am sure we have all read the toolkits haven't we?" from the judge) and mask some of the real attitudinal and skill issues inherent in questioning vulnerable witnesses effectively.'
- 'The success of the GRH depends on the willingness of the advocates to engage and follow recommendations afterwards. In my experience this year I would say there has been a change in the way cross examination is handled. Prosecution and defence advocates make huge efforts to make sure they are putting their case but fairly. Some find it much easier than others. Advocate training is therefore hugely welcomed.'
- 'A good GRH, well timed (i.e. a few days from the date of trial, and with the trial judge and advocates present) makes the whole process go so smoothly, that I hardly have to intervene during questioning.'

G. Looking Back and Looking Ahead

12.63 The way in which vulnerable witnesses and defendants are treated in the criminal courts has substantially changed over the past two decades and the introduction of the ground rules approach has had a significant impact on judicial case management. The ground rules approach has become widely accepted practice and its use has spread not only beyond cases where there is an intermediary, but beyond the criminal justice system of England and Wales. The approach complements a

---

[84] The question used a five-point scale ranging from 'Full Compliance' to 'No Compliance'.

judge's duty to carefully and assiduously manage the treatment and questioning of vulnerable people.

12.64 Most research on GRHs is based on intermediary perceptions; however, further research is required before a clear picture emerges of what is happening at GRHs where there is no intermediary present. Are GRHs as effective without the input of an intermediary who has assessed and reported on the vulnerable person's communication needs and abilities? We know that practitioners think that they need more training to determine what special measures may be needed, and guidance for advocates on identifying vulnerability does not appear to be reflected in practice, although practitioners do purport that special measures have a positive impact on witnesses.[85] Until we are better informed about the extent of court-user vulnerability and about the range and adequacy of provisions put in place for addressing vulnerability, GRHs may not be as effective as they could be or indeed the best solution at all.

12.65 The traditional style of advocacy has been called into question for vulnerable witnesses and has led to a greater focus on training for advocates on working with vulnerable witnesses and defendants.[86] The recent increased awareness of the need for advocates to adapt to witnesses and the detailed focus on questioning ought to give rise to what could be termed *universal ground rules*. These might raise standards of advocacy generally, improve the quality of all questioning, and promote the attainment of the best evidence from all witnesses, whether or not they are deemed to be vulnerable. Case law already points the way towards what should be universally accepted and, more importantly, universally applied ground rules:

12.66 Lord Judge, then Lord Chief Justice, in *Farooqi* in the Court of Appeal Criminal Division in 2013:

> Although the judge is ultimately responsible for the conduct of the proceedings, the judge personally, and the administration of justice as a whole, are advantaged by the presence, assistance and professionalism of high quality advocates on both sides.[87]

> What ought to be avoided is the increasing modern habit of assertion, (often in tendentious terms or incorporating comment), which is not true cross-examination. This is unfair to the witness and blurs the line from a jury's perspective between evidence from the witness and inadmissible comment from the advocate.[88]

With echoes of *Farooqi*, but even more firm, are the words of the present Lord Chief Justice, Lord Thomas, in *Rashid*[89] (see above at paragraph 12.30).

---

[85] R. Ewin, 'The Vulnerable and Intimidated Witness: A Study of the Special Measure Practitioner' (2016) *Journal of Applied Psychology and Social Science*, 2(1), 12–40.

[86] P. Cooper, 'Ticketing Talk Gets Serious', *Counsel*, November 2014, 11–12.

[87] Per the then Lord Chief Justice, Lord Judge, in *Farooqi* [2013] EWCA Crim 1649 at [109].

[88] ibid. at [113].

[89] P. Cooper, 'R v Rashid (Yahya)' [2017] *Criminal Law Review* 5, 420–1, 421.

Parker J in *Re PB* at the Court of Protection said: **12.67**

> Effective steps must be taken to reduce evidence to the essential. In Farooqi Lord Judge emphasized the requirement that cross-examination should proceed by short, focussed question rather than by comment, opinion and assertion. I also note that in The Law Commission lecture given last year Lord Judge stated (as I was taught) that in principle no question should be longer than one line of transcript. In any event, the judge is interested in the answer, not the question.
>
> Advocates need to be able to control the witness by the form and structure of their questions and not permit discursive replies or to allow the witness to ramble (particularly if the witness has the tendency to be prolix). There is no necessity for a long introduction: apart from anything else it may distract and confuse the witness and the judge.
>
> Examination must not proceed by way of 'exploration' of the evidence: i.e. a debate, or by putting theory or speculation, rather than by properly directed questions which require an answer.
>
> This is all the advocates' responsibility. However hard a judge tries to speed the process, this takes up time and interrupts the flow, and often leads to a debate with the advocate. Also it can give the wrong impression to the lay client about the judge's view of them or their case.
>
> Where two parties have the same case to put, the same points must not be repeated.
>
> Finally the advocate needs, if facts are challenged, to put the client's case.[90]

Lord Carloway, then Lord Justice Clark, in *Begg v Her Majesty's Advocate* in   **12.68**
2015 said:

> Due regard must be had to the right or privilege under domestic law to test a witness's evidence by properly directed and focused cross-examination. That right, however, does not extend to insulting or intimidating a witness (*Falconer v Brown* (1893) 21 R (J) 1, LJC (Macdonald) at 4). It also requires to be balanced against the right of a witness to be afforded some respect for her dignity and privacy.[91]

Case law gives us the makings of *universal ground rules which reflect good questioning practice with any witness*. When a witness or defendant is vulnerable, the parties and the court will need to consider what additional, specific ground rules are required for that particular witness or defendant. Usually cross-examination should:

- 'Be short and focus on one point.
- Use simple vocabulary.
- Use simple sentences. (Not 'tag' questions, that is statements with a generic question tacked onto the end. Avoid for example: 'You would agree wouldn't you, [statement]?' or '[Statement], that's right isn't it?')
- Properly direct the witness to the matter which requires their answer; a question should not invite the witness to speculate or debate.
- Not contain preamble. (For example, a preamble 'In light of your previous answers, let me ask you about this, if I may …' should be dispensed with altogether.)

---

[90] *Re PB* [2014] EWCOP 14; [2015] COPLR 118 at [141]–[146].
[91] [2015] ScotHC HCJAC 69.

- Not contain comment on the evidence. (If it is a good comment, save it for the speech.)
- Not use intonation to imply a question. For example, do not say: 'You were unhappy about that?' Instead ask, 'Did that make you unhappy?' or 'Were you unhappy?'[92]

FURTHER READING

Cooper, P., Backen, P., and Marchant, R., 'Getting to Grips with Ground Rules Hearings: A Checklist for Judges, Advocates and Intermediaries to Promote Fair Treatment of Vulnerable People in Court' (2015) Crim LR, 6, 420–35.

Mattison, M., (2016) 'Putting Theory Into Practice: A Comparison of the Guidance Available to Investigative Interviewers and Advocates When Using Communication Aids in the Criminal Justice System', in P. Cooper and L. Hunting (eds), *Addressing Vulnerability in Justice Systems* (London: Wildy, 2016).

Ground Rules Hearing Checklist

12.69 The Advocate's Gateway produces a toolkit checklist (written by the first author) for ground rules hearings. These and other resources are available at no charge at <http://theadvocatesgateway.org> and are regularly updated. Readers should consult the website of The Advocate's Gateway for the most up-to-date, online version.

Section 1: facilitating the role of the intermediary

If there is an intermediary they must be included in the GRH discussion and, in particular, their report(s) considered and discussed, especially if a report recommendation is disputed. Some cases will require an addendum to the original intermediary report, particularly if the witness's/defendant's needs have changed since the initial assessment and the report is many months old by the time of the trial. For more information on intermediaries, see Toolkit 16 Intermediaries: step by step.

The intermediary is not a witness and is not required to be in the witness box for the GRH. The hearing is a discussion and the hearing is not for cross-examination of the intermediary. The intermediary is not required to make the intermediary declaration at this stage.

At the GRH, where relevant, discuss:

1. Whether advocates have shown the intermediary the wording of their proposed questions and taken advice on the suitability of the wording and communication style.
2. Where the intermediary will stand/sit during the trial during the vulnerable person's testimony so that the intermediary is able to observe and intervene to assist with communication whilst all the time being visible to the judge, advocates and jury.
3. If for a defendant during a trial, where the intermediary will sit in relation to other defendants (if any) and officers in the dock.
4. Where and when the intermediary will make the intermediary declaration (Youth Justice and Criminal Evidence Act 1999 (YJCEA), section 29(5), requires the intermediary to make the declaration as specified). See Toolkit 16 Intermediaries: step by step.

---

[92] P. Cooper, 'Moving the Bar: Is Cross-Examination Any Good?', *Mental Capacity Report: Practice and Procedure*, Issue 74 (March 2017) 3–6, 6, available at <http://www.39essex.com/content/wp-content/uploads/2017/03/Mental-Capacity-Report-March-2017-Practice-and-Procedure.pdf> accessed 26 April 2017.

5. If the intermediary and witness will be in a remote location, practical issues such as who will administer the oath(s) and how exhibits would be made available to the witness. See also Toolkit 9 Planning to question someone using a remote link.
6. How the intermediary will be addressed in court in front of the vulnerable person—for example, it might be by the intermediary's first name if that is how the witness knowsthem.
7. How the intermediary will intervene/get the judge's attention if there is a communication issue or the intermediary needs to discuss a communication issue with the judge and counsel in the absence of the jury.
8. How the role of the intermediary will be explained to the jury in a way that makes clear that the intermediary is not a witness but that their role is to assist everyone in achieving complete, accurate and coherent communication with the vulnerable person.
9. If communication aids are to be used, how the intermediary will assist with these.
10. Which toolkits the advocates should consult (if they have not done so already) to assist with questioning.
11. Any other recommendations in the intermediary's report.

Section 2: participation of the vulnerable defendant

If the defendant is vulnerable and, in so far as this has not been covered above, discuss (including with the intermediary if there is one):

12. Whether an interpreter is required for the trial.
13. Where the defendant will sit during the trial, for example, in the dock or next to the defence lawyers/if anyone will accompany the defendant in the dock—if they need the support of a nurse, for example.
14. Whether the vulnerable defendant will need assistance in the dock to access/follow written evidence and, if so, how this will be achieved.
15. Start and end times of the trial days.
16. Scheduled breaks during the trial day, including, for example, time to take medication, extra time to go through papers with a defendant who cannot read and extra time to allow counsel to take instructions. (Criminal Practice Directions (CPD) 2015 Amendment No 1, 3F.22) How a request for an unscheduled break will be notified, if required.
17. Whether all testimony should be adduced using modified questions and answers: '… to help the defendant follow proceedings the court may require evidence to be adduced by simple questions, with witnesses being asked to answer in short sentences'. (CPD 2015 Amendment No 1, 3F.22).
18. Use of communication aids, for example, iPad/tablet, hearing loop, stress/concentration aids, break cards, visual timetable and writing/drawing materials.
19. Whether it will be necessary to provide the jury with an explanation about the defendant's condition and its effect on his or her behaviour so as to avoid that behaviour being misinterpreted (for example, see *R v Thompson* [2014] EWCA Crim 836 and the defendant with Asperger syndrome). This might be achieved by calling expert witnesses or prosecution and defence agreeing a set of simple and clear agreed facts which can be read to the jury.

Good practice example

Ground rules may need to be revisited if during the trial the defendant's effective participation is still not being achieved. Then, if the defendant later elects to give evidence, there would normally be a further GRH specifically to discuss how questioning should be conducted (see section 3).

Section 3: fair questioning of a vulnerable person (witness or defendant)

Discuss (including with the intermediary if there is one):

20. Whether an interpreter is required for the person's testimony.

21. Whether it is necessary to appoint a lawyer for an unrepresented defendant to conduct any cross-examination on behalf of the defendant. (YJCEA, sections 34–40.)
22. Whether the person will give evidence on oath or not and any assistance they might need to take the oath.
23. Whether the person will give evidence in court or over a live link. (YJCEA, section 33A, for an eligible defendant, and YJCEA, section 24, for an eligible witness.)
24. How other special measures which may have previously been directed for a witness, will be implemented—for example, a screen, evidence given in private, evidence prerecorded, wigs and gowns removed by judge and advocates, a witness supporter, use of communications aids (see Toolkit 14 Using Communication aids in the criminal justice system), such as models of maps, timelines, charts, pictures etc. Use of communication aids, such as body maps, for trial of a sexual offence (CPD 2015 3E.6) should also be considered.
25. How special measures and other adjustments may be combined: '[a] combination of special measures may be appropriate. For example, if a witness who is to give evidence by live link wishes, screens can be used to shield the live link screen from the defendant and the public, as would occur if screens were being used for a witness giving evidence in the court room.' (CPD 2015 18A.2)
26. Where the advocates will be when they conduct their questioning, for example, in court over live link or in the live link room.
27. How long cross-examination is likely to take and how long it will be permitted to last, taking into account relevant matters such as the witness's concentration abilities, effects of prescribed medication etc.
28. When there will be scheduled breaks during the trial day, including duration and nature of breaks.
29. How a request for an unscheduled break will be notified, for example, arising from an urgent medical need.
30. Whether all breaks should involve adjourning the court or whether brief breaks may speed proceedings for all. Many courts have agreed breaks of up to three minutes for young children; during a short, non-adjourned break (the court stays sitting), the microphones and cameras to the live link room are temporarily made visible only to the judge, enabling the witness to take a few minutes in the live link room to re-orientate or calm themselves. This avoids the need for the jury to be sent out and brought back which would be unnecessarily time-consuming.
31. Whether the judge has seen the advocates' proposed questions and determined if they are appropriate (if there is an intermediary they should also have been reduced to writing and shown to the intermediary).
32. How repetitious questioning will be avoided when there are separately represented defendants (CPD 2015 3E.5).
33. If limitations are going to be placed on crossexamination, how these will be explained to the jury (CPD 2015 3E.4).
34. How and when the vulnerable person will be familiarised with the court and the witness box/live link room/remote live link site, if this has not happened already. This should include practising communicating over live link—see CPD 2015 18B.4 (witnesses) and 3G.4 (defendants).
35. How and where and when the person will have their memory refreshed by watching the DVD recording of their achieving best evidence (ABE) interview, if any (CPD 2015 18C). Note that there is no requirement for the witness to watch their ABE at the same time as the jury.
36. Whether and how the judge and advocates (preferably together) will meet the vulnerable person beforehand. Discussion may include matters such as whether the judge/advocates will be robed. 'In general, experts recommend that the trial judge should introduce him or herself to the witness in person before any questioning, preferably in the presence of the parties. This seems to us to be an entirely reasonable step to take to put the witness at their ease where possible.' (*R v Lubemba* [2014] EWCA Crim 2064 para 43)
37. The best time of day for the person's testimony to start.

38. Whether the person will need assistance during testimony, for example, referring to/accessing written material, maps, photos, diagrams, transcripts etc.
39. How the court will be enabled to access the person's non-verbal communication, for example, indicating, pointing, drawing, writing.

In due course, consideration should be given to whether or not this [ground rules hearings] approach may sensibly be extended to other areas of cross-examination in which it may take place (for example, with expert witnesses). Review of Efficiency in Criminal Proceedings by The Rt Hon Sir Brian Leveson, President of the Queen's Bench Division (2015), para 8.3.1 'Ground rules approach'.

13

TRIAL MANAGEMENT
The Judge's Role

Heather Norton

A. Introduction

The overriding objective, as set out in the Criminal Procedure Rules (Crim PR),[1] is that criminal cases should be dealt with justly. **13.01**

This includes: **13.02**

• dealing with the prosecution and the defence fairly;

---

[1] See <https://www.justice.gov.uk/courts/procedure-rules/criminal> accessed 23 March 2017.

- recognizing the rights of a defendant, particularly those under Article 6 of the European Convention on Human Rights;
- respecting the interests of victims; and
- dealing with the case efficiently and expeditiously.[2]

13.03 This chapter is primarily concerned with the judge's case management powers and responsibilities to ensure that the trial can best be managed in accordance with the overriding objective when a party to it—whether defendant or witness—is vulnerable through age, circumstance, or physical or mental disability.

B. Case Management and the Criminal Procedure Rules

13.04 The Crim PR and the Criminal Practice Directions (Crim PD) (as amended in April 2017) have a combined length of nearly 800 pages. Whether because of that, or for other reasons, they have not always been given the close attention by the parties, or by the judge, that they deserve and require. Good case management starts with the Crim PR, compliance with which is—as was noted in the Leveson Review—'not optional, but mandatory'.[3]

13.05 Part 3 of the Crim PR sets out the rules for case management. Those rules are instructive, informative, and, above all, sensible; they impose upon the court not only the duty to engage in active case management, but also provide the tools with which to do so.

13.06 Active case management includes:

- the early identification of the real issues;
- the early identification of the needs of witnesses;
- monitoring compliance with directions; and
- ensuring that evidence is presented in the shortest and clearest way.[4]

13.07 Of fundamental importance in cases which involve a vulnerable person, the court is required to take every reasonable step:

- to encourage and facilitate the attendance of witnesses when they are needed; and
- to facilitate the participation of any person, including the defendant.[5]

---

[2] Crim PR 1.1(2).
[3] Rt Hon Sir Brian Leveson, 'Review of Efficiency in Criminal Proceedings', para. 7.3., available at <https://www.judiciary.gov.uk/wp-content/uploads/2015/01/review-of-efficiency-in-criminal-proceedings-20151.pdf> accessed 23 March 2017.
[4] Crim PR 3.2.
[5] Crim PR 3.9(3).

Facilitating participation includes ensuring that the defendant is able to understand and follow proceedings through the provision where necessary of an interpreter, and giving appropriate directions for the treatment and questioning of a witness or the defendant to enable that person to give their best evidence. What directions are required will of course be case-specific, but courts should be prepared to adopt a flexible approach, adapting the normal trial process as necessary to meet the needs of the individual.

13.08 This requires active engagement at an early stage, not only by the parties, who will be expected to identify what arrangements are necessary to facilitate effective participation, but also by the judge. Not only does the judge have a duty to manage the trial process and to give directions which will further the overriding objective and facilitate effective participation, but he or she also has a role to play in safeguarding vulnerable people at court in ways which further the overriding objective, and which do not interfere with judicial independence.[6]

C. Case Management and the Plea and Trial Preparation Hearing

13.09 The plea and trial preparation hearing (PTPH) is the first (and, in many cases, the only) pre-trial hearing for trials on indictment. Although cases which involve a vulnerable witness or a defendant who is 'a child, or otherwise under a disability, or requires special assistance' fall into the category of cases listed in Crim PD 3A.21 which may require a further pre-trial hearing, the PTPH provides an opportunity for effective case management which risks being overlooked if the PTPH hearing is reduced to a tick-box or date-filling exercise.

13.10 The digital PTPH form in its current incarnation[7] contains numerous automatic directions to standardize orders for vulnerable witnesses. 'Standard orders for witnesses' include directions that:

- any Achieving Best Evidence (ABE) interview recorded by any witness should automatically stand as that witness's evidence-in-chief unless otherwise ordered;
- the ABE is to be viewed in the week preceding trial in the presence of the officer in the case (or suitable alternative), who should record any comments made and pass them to the prosecution;
- any application for screens or live link should be made after a court visit and include details of the witness's reasons for preference;

---

[6] Judicial College, 'Equal Treatment Bench Book' (Judicial College, 2013) para. 45, available at <https://www.judiciary.gov.uk/wp-content/uploads/JCO/Documents/judicial-college/ETBB_all_chapters_final.pdf> accessed 23 March 2017.

[7] As of April 2017. It is expected that the PTPH form will be subject to regular revision.

- the witness's attendance must be timetabled for the time when the witness is expected to commence examination; and
- young or vulnerable witnesses to whom an Advocate's Gateway Toolkit applies are to be examined or cross-examined in accordance with the toolkit unless superseded by specific ground rules.

13.11 Elsewhere on the PTPH form can be found sections dealing with the timetabling of s. 28 hearings (pre-trial cross-examination), further case management and ground rules hearings; and space to make directions for the dates of service of any special measures or third-party disclosure applications (stage 1), applications for special measures for the defendant or defence witnesses (stage 2), the service of psychiatric evidence, intermediary reports, and draft ground rules (stage 3), and service of any defence intermediary report (stage 4). All of these are clearly matters that need to be considered at the PTPH stage, but, as ever, flexibility is key. Orders sought need to be considered in context, and directions tailored to the individual case.

(a) Listing

13.12 The trial date will be determined at the PTPH. It is likely that most, if not all, cases which involve a vulnerable person will require a fixed date for trial unless the only vulnerable participant is a witness whose cross-examination is pre-recorded under YJCEA 1999 s. 28.

13.13 Listing is a 'judicial function', and the judge should ensure that proposed trial dates do not conflict with times of public examinations, birthdays, or other significant anniversaries; this may ordinarily be expected to apply to any witness, but is particularly important where the witness or defendant is vulnerable.

13.14 Where the case involves a witness under 10 years of age, the young witness protocol[8] applies, by which a trial date should be set no more than eight weeks from the date of plea (ordinarily the PTPH hearing). Where at all possible, and to ensure consistency in management, the case should be allocated to a named trial judge at this stage, if not before.

(b) Self-represented defendants (litigants in person)

13.15 Self-represented defendants (litigants in person) may present a challenge, particularly where they are themselves vulnerable or where a vulnerable person will be cross-examined. It is important, however, for the court to understand that for

---

[8] See <https://judiciary.gov.uk/wp-content/uploads/2015/03/police-cps-hmcts-ywi-protocol.pdf> accessed 23 March 2017.

such defendants it is the trial process and court procedures that present the difficulty, and that they will be, or may at the very least perceive themselves to be, at a disadvantage due to their lack of knowledge about or familiarity with court rules and procedures. The judge is a 'facilitator of justice'[9] and as such should at each hearing, including the PTPH and any further pre-trial hearings, use clear everyday language to ensure that the defendant understands the purpose of the hearing and to explain any directions made.

At the time of writing, no guidance had been given as to how to adapt the **13.16** digital case system to self-represented defendants; pending any such guidance it is likely that paper copies of all documents will need to be provided to such a defendant. The judge should encourage cooperation between the defendant and the prosecuting authority and ensure that appropriate contact details are exchanged between the parties and provided to the court in order that this can be facilitated.

On occasion, concerns may arise about the mental health or fitness to plead **13.17** of an unrepresented defendant. If the defendant consents, then the judge may consider adjourning the case for the preparation of a court-ordered psychiatric report. Alternatively, in areas where it is available, the court could refer the defendant to the NHS England Liaison and Diversion Service for assessment.[10] Of more difficulty is the situation where the defendant refuses consent. In that situation, the judge could request that a registered medical practitioner attend to observe the defendant at court. Evidence from the practitioner of his or her observations may then pave the way in appropriate circumstances for a remand under s. 35 of the Mental Health Act 1983 for a report on the defendant's mental condition to be prepared. (See further Chapter 5, 'Unfitness to Plead'.)

The judge should additionally consider using the court's inherent powers to order **13.18** an intermediary assessment for any defendant that he or she considers may benefit from such a measure. Again, the defendant's consent will be required, so the judge should take care to explain to the defendant what the intermediary's role is, and how he or she may help the defendant with different aspects of the trial process. (See further Chapter 11, 'Intermediaries'.)

---

[9] 'Equal Treatment Bench Book 2015', para. 44.

[10] See <https://england.nhs.uk/commissioning/health-just/liaison-and-diversion> accessed 23 March 2017. Where in operation, NHS England Liaison and Diversion Services exist to identify mental health and other vulnerabilities that an offender may have, such as a learning disability or substance misuse. The aim is 'to improve health outcomes, reduce re-offending and identify vulnerabilities earlier, thus reducing the likelihood that offenders will reach crisis-point'.

D. Case Management and the Pre-Trial Hearing

(a) When should a pre-trial hearing be held?

13.19 A pre-trial hearing must be held in all cases in which a ground rules hearing is required, and should be held in all cases which involve a vulnerable witness or defendant, most if not all of which will require adaptations to be made to the normal trial process in order to meet the needs of the individual(s) concerned.[11] [12]

(b) How many pre-trial hearings may be required?

13.20 The number of hearings should be kept to a minimum. In the vast majority of cases, a single pre-trial hearing combined with a ground rules hearing (where applicable) will be sufficient. Where issues arise as to which (if any) special measures are appropriate, they can be resolved at the pre-trial hearing, with the assistance of any intermediary appointed. Where there is an issue regarding whether an intermediary is required, that will ordinarily require the attendance of the intermediary to speak to her assessment of the vulnerable witness or defendant in any event; it therefore makes most practical sense to deal with such issues first and to hold any ground rules hearing immediately thereafter.

(c) Who should attend the pre-trial hearing?

13.21 The pre-trial hearing should be conducted by the allocated judge and trial counsel should attend. If an intermediary has or may be appointed for either a witness or the defendant, his or her attendance is essential for any issues to be resolved, whether and if so to what extent the intermediary will be required, and if an intermediary direction is given, for effective ground rules to be established.[13] Where the case involves a vulnerable witness, it may well be helpful for a representative from the Witness Service to be in attendance as the most direct means of ensuring that they understand the measures put in place to support that witness. Whether the defendant is required to attend is a matter for the discretion of the trial judge; however, in those cases where it is a witness who is vulnerable, and particularly where an intermediary is involved and is therefore required to attend court for the ground rules hearing, it is often the case that the pre-trial court familiarization visit and watching the ABE interview is arranged for the same day. Care will therefore be required to ensure that the witness and the defendant (if on bail) do not inadvertently come into contact.

---

[11] Crim PD 3A.21.
[12] *R v Lubemba* [2014] EWCA Crim 2064 at [42].
[13] Crim PD 3F.27.

(d) Timing of the pre-trial hearing

In order to ensure that the most up-to-date information is available for the court, **13.22** but to allow sufficient time for any amendments necessary as a result of directions given, it is suggested that a pre-trial hearing should ideally be listed between two and four weeks before the trial date (or YJCEA s. 28 hearing to pre-record cross-examination and re-examination where appropriate). It is essential that sufficient time is allocated for the pre-trial hearing; attempting to push such a hearing into a crowded list is not likely to result in an effective hearing.

(e) Ground rules

Where directions are required to ensure the appropriate treatment and question- **13.23** ing of a vulnerable witness or defendant, the judge will need to hold a ground rules hearing in which he or she may give directions about:

- the manner of questioning;
- the duration of questioning;
- the questions/topic areas that may be the subject of examination;
- the avoidance of repetition in cases where there is more than one defendant;
- the use of special measures, reasonable adjustments, and communication aids; and
- the necessity of applying the relevant ATC toolkits.

In order for a ground rules hearing to be effective, it is essential that the parties **13.24** should have complied with the Crim PR (or any court orders if there has been an earlier PTPH) for service of special measures applications, intermediary and any other relevant reports, draft ground rules, draft cross-examination plan, defence case statement, and prosecution opening where appropriate. The ground rules hearing is an essential part of good trial management, but will only achieve its purpose if all parties cooperate to ensure that by that stage the issues are clear, the needs of the witness or defendant have been properly assessed, and the necessary adaptations to the trial process considered. The judge should be robust in ensuring that orders have been complied with to enable an effective ground rules hearing to take place. In particular, any cross-examination plan that has been ordered at the PTPH should be available for consideration at the ground rules hearing so that all parties can be clear about the scope of limitations on questioning; any amendments necessary to comply with directions from the trial judge or suggestions from the intermediary can then be considered and made in advance of the trial.

Although cross-examination plans and limitations on questioning are most **13.25** commonly expected where there is a vulnerable witness, there would seem to be no reason in principle why the same should not apply to vulnerable defendants. Although Crim PD 3E.4 generally refers to young or otherwise vulnerable witnesses when considering restrictions on questioning, it is the vulnerability of the person to be cross-examined which gives rise to the necessity to adapt or restrain cross-examination, not their status as a witness as opposed to a defendant who is, after all, a witness in his or her own case.

13.26 (See further section F(d), 'Questioning the vulnerable person', below, and Chapters 9, 'Case Management', 10, 'Special Measures', 11, 'Intermediaries', and 12, 'Ground Rules Hearings'.)

(f) Special measures

13.27 Any applications for special measures should have been made, and granted where appropriate, in accordance with the directions given at the PTPH and in advance of the pre-trial hearing, but the judge should confirm with the parties that this is the case, check that any practical issues have been resolved, and consider whether any further adaptations are required.

In particular, the judge should check the following:

- *The ABE interview*[14]—Have all necessary edits been made and checked? Has the DVD been tested using the same equipment that will be used to play the recording at trial? If there are issues with sound and picture quality, it is essential that these are discovered—and rectified where possible—in advance of trial. Problems which are only discovered on the day of trial are likely to lead to lengthy delays, the necessity to provide transcripts to enable the jury to follow the ABE interview, or in some cases, the abandonment of the ABE recording altogether.

- *Memory refreshing*—What arrangements have been made for the witness to refresh his or her memory from the ABE? The Crim PD makes it clear that decisions about how, when, and where memory refreshing should take place should be 'court-led'.[15] Although it would in nearly all cases be thought undesirable and unnecessary for the witness to watch his or her ABE interview(s) at the same time as the jury, decisions such as this should always be made on a case-by-case basis according to the needs of the witness. Where the witness has an intermediary, their view should be sought.

- *Court familiarization*—What arrangements have been made for a court familiarization visit? The witness is entitled to have a pre-trial court familiarization visit and to have the opportunity to practise using the live link or screens.[16] The same applies to a vulnerable defendant where a defendant's evidence direction has been made under YJCEA 1999 s. 33A.[17]

---

[14] Commonly referred to as the ABE interview or simply the ABE, it is more formally known as the Video Recorded Interview or VRI for short.
[15] Crim PD 18C.3.
[16] Crim PD 18B.4.
[17] Crim PD 3G.2–4.

- *Remote link*—Have all necessary arrangements been made for any remote link? The necessary details need to be provided to the court in order that the link can be made. Where the remote link location is a private address, a pre-trial visit should be conducted to enable any mobile equipment to be tested in situ and to ensure that the location is free from anything visible which might either distract the viewer, or lead to the location being identified (e.g. personal photographs, ornaments, elaborate or expensive furnishings). The judge should ensure that the parties have liaised over what exhibits, photographs, or other documents may need to be shown to the witness and that arrangements have been made for them to be present at the link location. The judge should remind the parties of the need to comply with the Remote Link Toolkit.[18]
- *Additional adjustments*—Are any further adjustments/adaptations to the trial process required? Where an intermediary is instructed, the intermediary's report should set out any additional adjustments required. Whether or not that is the case, the judge should consider—for example—such matters as the timing of evidence, the timing and frequency of breaks, whether any communication aids are required, whether wigs and gowns should be worn, what arrangements should be made for the judge and advocates to meet the witness, and any other matters relevant to that particular witness and particular case.

(g) Vulnerable defendants

Defendant's evidence direction[19]—Any application for a defendant's evidence direction should have been made prior to the pre-trial hearing (usually at stage 2). Such a direction, by which the defendant gives evidence through the live link, is the only 'special measure' that is available to a defendant under YJCEA 1999. To qualify, at the time of application the defendant must either be: **13.28**

(a) under 18, and compromised in his or her ability to participate effectively in the proceedings due to his or her 'level of intellectual ability or social functioning'; or

(b) over 18, with a mental disorder or other significant impairment of intelligence and social function, for which reason he or she is unable to participate effectively as a witness giving oral evidence in court; and in either case

(c) the use of the live link would enable him or her to participate more effectively in the proceedings as a witness.

The defence are required under Crim PR 18.15 to identify an appropriate person to accompany the defendant on the live link; however, it is likely that if the defendant meets the criteria in YJCEA 1999 s. 33A as set out above, he or she will **13.29**

---

[18] See <http://theadvocatesgateway.org/images/toolkits/9-planning-to-question-someone-using-a-remote-link-2017.pdf> accessed 14 April 2017.

[19] YJCEA 1999 s. 33A.

have the benefit of an intermediary. It should be noted that there is no power to grant a live-link application under these provisions on the basis of age alone, or fear or distress: 'If the defendant's use of the live link is being considered, he or she should have an opportunity to have a practice session.'[20]

13.30 *What other adjustments can be made for a vulnerable defendant?*—The fact that there is only one measure for vulnerable defendants provided by statute does not prevent the court from using its own inherent powers to adapt the court process and procedure to effectively facilitate the defendant's participation in the trial. To the contrary, the court is required to take 'every reasonable step to encourage and facilitate the participation of any person, including the defendant. This includes enabling a witness or defendant to give their best evidence, and enabling a defendant to comprehend the proceedings and engage fully with his or her defence. The pre-trial and trial process should, so far as necessary, be adapted to meet those ends.'[21]

13.31 This was reiterated in *R v Cox,* when it was stated that:

> ... as part of their general responsibilities, Judges are expected to deal with specific communication problems faced by any defendant or any individual witness ... as part and parcel of their ordinary control of the judicial process. Where necessary, the processes have to be adapted to ensure that a particular individual is not disadvantaged as a result of personal difficulties, whatever form they may take. In short, the overall responsibility of the trial judge for the fairness of the trial has not altered because of the increased availability of intermediaries, or indeed the wide band of possible special measures now enshrined in statute.[22]

13.32 Adapting the trial process may require consideration to be given to the number and frequency of breaks, the language to be used, whether wigs and gowns should be worn, whether there should be restrictions on access to the courtroom by members of the public and press, and the court layout. It is important that any adjustments required are identified pre-trial in order that those adjustments can be put in place without delay at trial.

13.33 *Adjustments to the court layout*—The necessity to make adjustments to the normal layout of the court is not unusual in a case which involves a vulnerable defendant. It is wise to consider such issues pre-trial in order that any security implications can properly be evaluated, appropriate arrangements can be put in place before the trial starts, and to alleviate any anxiety that might otherwise be felt by the defendant.

13.34 *Juvenile defendants*—A young defendant should not be required to sit in the dock, but rather should be permitted to sit with an appropriate adult supporter

---

[20] Crim PD 3G.4.
[21] Crim PR 3D.2.
[22] *R v Cox* [2012] EWCA Crim 549 at [29].

in a position from which he or she can easily communicate with his or her legal representatives.[23] Ultimately, however, this must be a matter for the discretion of the judge taking account of the extent of vulnerability of the defendant, his or her needs, and the wider context of the trial as a whole, including any security concerns. (See further Chapter 7, 'Youth Courts and Young Defendants'.)

Defendants with disabilities—Many defendants, particularly elderly defendants, **13.35** present with disabilities which need to be accommodated by adjusting the court layout. With the increase in historic sexual allegations, it is now not uncommon for a defendant to be facing trial in his or her 80s or even older. Such defendants may have multiple medical needs which have to be accommodated. Where those needs are complex, it is essential that the judge is provided with up-to-date medical evidence specifically directed to the adjustments that will need to be made to the court process; these may include limiting evidence to the morning only and frequent breaks where the defendant struggles to focus or maintain concentration for lengthy periods, or where he or she suffers from pain, discomfort, or stress. Physical immobility may make it difficult, if not impossible, for the defendant to get into the dock or the witness box; in such circumstances, particularly if the defendant is confined to a wheelchair, the judge will need to consider positioning a table behind which the defendant can sit when listening to or when giving evidence. Similar adjustments may be required for a defendant who has impaired hearing or vision. Additional complications can arise when the witness has the benefit of special measures such as screens, or where an interpreter or palantypist is also required who needs to be accommodated.

(h) Self-represented defendants (litigants in person)

Vulnerable self-represented defendants—With all litigants in person the import- **13.36** ance of effective communication cannot be overstated. Such a defendant is likely to be unfamiliar with the applicable law, the procedures, and the language used in court. With a vulnerable self-represented defendant, such problems are magnified. The judge should take time and care to explain the relevant processes to the defendant in language appropriate to their needs, aiming to 'ensure that litigants in person understand what is going on and what is expected of them at all stages of the proceedings—before, during and after any attendances at a hearing'.[24] With a vulnerable self-represented defendant, the judge's responsibilities in this regard are even more important.

If an order has been made for an intermediary but the vulnerable self-represented **13.37** defendant does not have an intermediary (either because it is not possible to obtain one, or because the defendant has refused one), then in an appropriate

---

[23] Crim PD 3G.8.
[24] 'Equal Treatment Bench Book 2013', para. 19.

case consideration should be given to permitting a suitable adult (a carer, support worker, or close family member who is not also a witness in the case) to sit with the defendant to provide support and reassurance and to assist the defendant's understanding.

13.38   *Self-represented defendants and restrictions on cross-examination*—Where the defendant is self-represented, the judge will need to consider whether the defendant should be restricted from cross-examining any witness in person.

13.39   YJCEA 1999 ss 34 and 35 prohibit cross-examination by a defendant in person in certain circumstances. Section 34 prohibits the cross-examination of a complainant in a sexual offence by an unrepresented defendant. Section 35 deals with the prohibition of unrepresented defendants from cross-examining 'protected witnesses'. In essence, a 'protected witness' is a child complainant or child witness who 'witnessed the commission of the offence' in relation to certain offences. These offences are set out in s. 35(3), but may be taken to broadly include offences of violence and cruelty. Section 35(4) defines a child as being under the age of 18 when the allegation is of a sexual offence and under the age of 14 for each of the other offences covered.

13.40   Where neither s. 34 nor s. 35 operates, the court may, of its own motion or on application by the prosecutor, make a direction prohibiting an unrepresented defendant from cross-examining a witness under s. 36 if it appears to the court that:

(a)   the quality of evidence given by the witness on cross-examination is likely to be diminished if conducted by the defendant in person;

(b)   the quality of evidence is likely to be improved if a direction prohibiting such cross-examination is given; and

(c)   it would not be contrary to the interests of justice to give such a direction.[25]

Under s. 38 where such a direction is made, the court must invite the accused to arrange representation and in the event that this is not done must consider appointing a legal representative to cross-examine the witness. The duties of the appointed advocate are limited to the proper cross-examination of the witness, but this may include making applications to adduce bad character of the witness or making requests for disclosure of material relevant to the cross-examination of the witness.

13.41   Where a prohibition applies under ss 34 and 35, or is imposed under s. 36, the court must invite the defendant to arrange for a legal representative to act for him or her for the purposes of cross-examining the witness. If he or she fails to notify the court that he or she has done so within a specified period, then

---

[25] YJCEA 1999 s. 36.

the court must consider whether it is necessary in the interests of justice for the court to choose and to appoint a qualified legal representative to carry out the cross-examination.[26]

There is no statutory power to prohibit the cross-examination of a vulnerable co-defendant by an unrepresented accused.[27] Nevertheless, although the defendant's entitlement to examine or have examined witnesses against him or her is a constituent ingredient of a fair trial under Article 6, that does not mean that he or she has an unfettered right to cross-examine a witness him or herself; moreover, the judge has a duty to protect the interests of all parties. In the absence of any power to direct the appointment of a legal representative in these circumstances, it is suggested that should a situation arise where this is considered desirable, a possible solution would be for the unrepresented defendant to produce the questions that he or she would wish to put in writing, and for those questions then to be asked of the witness by the judge.[28] (See further Chapter 12, 'Ground Rules Hearings'.) **13.42**

(i) Witness care

The judge should take the opportunity presented by the pre-trial hearing to check **13.43** what arrangements have been made for witness care at court.

What arrangements have been made for the vulnerable person to get to court/the **13.44** *remote link facility?*—Witnesses are often anxious about travel arrangements and their arrival at court. In particular, they may have justifiable concerns about accidental contact with the defendant or his or her supporters. Timings, routes to court, and appropriate entrance and exit points may need to be considered. It is not necessary for the judge to know the details unless the judge's consent is required for the witness to access the court via a secure route to which the public would not ordinarily have access; it is necessary, however, for the judge to clarify that someone has properly considered the issue and that those responsible for witness care are in possession of the appropriate information to convey to the witness.

Who will have responsibility for the vulnerable person's welfare at court?—Some **13.45** vulnerable witnesses may have received contact and support from a number of different agencies in the course of the investigation and as the case has progressed through the system: the police, the Crown Prosecution Service, witness care, witness support, an ISVA or IDSVA; the witness may have an interpreter and/

---

[26] YJCEA 1999 s. 38.
[27] YJCEA 1999 s. 36(4) makes it clear that a 'witness' does not include any other person who is charged with an offence in the proceedings.
[28] *R v Smith* [2004] EWCA Crim 2414; *Re K (Children) (Unrepresented father; cross-examination of a child)* [2015] EWCA Civ 543.

or an intermediary. Particularly where there are multiple agencies involved, it is important that thought is given to identifying an appropriate supporter who will take responsibility for the witness's welfare at court, who can then liaise between the court and the witness if issues arise such as unforeseen delays, or matters relating to the witness's vulnerability (e.g. medical needs). As is stated in the 'Equal Treatment Bench Book', in which the judge's role in safeguarding is made clear, 'safeguarding is most at risk when responsibilities are unclear and there is a breakdown in communication'.[29]

13.46 *What arrangements have been made for the advocates and judge to meet the vulnerable person?*—In most cases, a child witness will be put at ease if they are able to meet the advocates and judge before giving evidence. Where a vulnerable adult witness requests to meet the parties, as a general rule that should be facilitated.[30] A judge should never meet a witness (child or adult) alone, save in exceptional circumstances and with the consent of all the parties; such a situation might arise if it is assessed that the witness would become distressed meeting more than one person at a time. The judge should discuss with the parties how the situation should be best managed—for example, the parties could observe the judge meeting the witness over the video link.

13.47 Careful consideration should be given to how a meeting should be facilitated where a witness will give evidence from a remote location; ordinarily this would be done over the video link in the absence of the jury, but other arrangements may be appropriate on a case-by-case basis.

13.48 *Who will accompany the vulnerable person when giving evidence?*—Consideration should be given to the identity and number of supporters that would be appropriate to accompany the witness when giving evidence. A member of the witness service will generally be present as an independent supporter who has knowledge of court procedures, and any intermediary assigned will also, of course, need to be present. It is not infrequently the case that the witness requests the presence of the ISVA or IDVA, or a supporter who he or she trusts, such as a carer or social worker. Ultimately, it is a matter for the judge's discretion who he or she allows to accompany the witness when giving evidence, but in making that decision, the court must have regard to the wishes of the witness.[31] [32] Care should be taken not

---

[29] 'Equal Treatment Bench Book 2013', para. 49.
[30] 'In general, experts recommend that the trial judge should introduce him or herself to the witness in person before any questioning, preferably in the presence of the parties. This seems to us to be an entirely reasonable step to take to put the witness at their ease where possible.' Per Hallett LJ in *R v Lubemba* [2014] EWCA Crim 2064 at [43].
[31] YJCEA 1999 s. 24(1A).
[32] Crim PD 18B.

to overload the witness with supporters, which can be distracting for the jury and counterproductive for the witness.

(See further Chapter 3, 'Witness Support'.)

(j) Timetabling

Trials involving vulnerable witnesses or defendants should ordinarily have a **13.49** fixed date set at the PTPH. At the pre-trial hearing, the judge should use the opportunity to apply his or her case management powers to the timetabling of the trial and evidence to be given in order to ensure that adjournments are avoided and delays kept to a minimum. The judge is entitled to expect that the parties have full details of the needs of any individual witness or defendant (with supporting evidence if necessary) to support the judge in the exercise of this function.

Children and other vulnerable witnesses—It is now generally accepted that usu- **13.50** ally children should, where at all possible, give their evidence in the morning when they are fresh and their concentration is highest. There is no reason why the same approach should not be taken to an adult vulnerable witness. In order to ensure that the witness is not kept waiting, it will ordinarily be appropriate for the witness to be scheduled to give evidence on the morning of day 2 of the trial (assuming that the vulnerable person will be the first witness), with the first day of the trial set aside for empanelling the jury, the opening, playing the ABE interview to the jury, and legal argument (if any). There may, of course, be exceptions to this 'rule'—for example, it may be appropriate for a witness to give evidence over more than one day, but in small sections. As ever, advice should be sought from the intermediary or any other appropriate professional and the judge should adopt a flexible, case-by-case approach based on the witness's needs.

Vulnerable defendants—Crim PD 3G.10 states that 'a trial should be conducted **13.51** according to a timetable which takes full account of a vulnerable defendant's ability to concentrate. Frequent and regular breaks will often be appropriate'. Where a defendant is a young person, it may be helpful to think in terms of the school day when assessing concentration spans. Other defendants may have physical disabilities which make it uncomfortable to remain seated, or other conditions which affect their ability to concentrate. These are all factors which may impact on the length of time the case takes.

Listing—Although the practical realities are such that most courts cannot avoid **13.52** listing additional cases during the currency of a trial, in so far as possible, scheduled start times should be adhered to in order to avoid any delay to a vulnerable person's evidence. This may mean listing additional cases at the end of the day rather than at the beginning.

(k) Reporting restrictions

13.53 Reporting restrictions should be considered at each stage of the trial process. Restrictions may be either automatically applied or, where not automatic, appropriate to apply in the following circumstances:[33]

13.54 *Complainants of sexual offences*—By s. 1 of the Sexual Offences (Amendment) Act 1992, anonymity is automatically provided to victims of certain sexual offences as set out in s. 2 of the Act. The statute does not enable the court to make an order prohibiting identification of the defendant to protect the identity of the victim; it is for the press to decide how to report a case so as to comply with the legislation (*Re Press Association*[34]). There is a power to displace s. 1 set out at s. 3 of the Act; however, it is only in very limited situations that a court would be likely to displace the anonymity of the complainant in such cases.

13.55 *Persons under 18*—The court may make an order prohibiting the publication of any matters which are likely to lead to the identification of a person under the age of 18 concerned in criminal proceedings under YJCEA 1999 s. 45(3). Section 45 came into force on 13 April 2015; similar provisions contained in s. 39 of the Children and Young Persons Act 1933 continue to apply to civil and family proceedings and to criminal proceedings brought before that date. A person 'concerned in the proceedings' may be a witness or an accused; 'publication' means publication in any media (including online). The court may relax the restrictions which would otherwise be imposed by making an 'excepting direction' where the effect of the restrictions would 'impose a substantial and unreasonable restriction on the reporting of the proceedings', and/or where it is necessary in the public interest to do so.

> When deciding whether to impose reporting restrictions under s. 45(3) or to make an 'excepting direction' the court must have regard to the welfare of the person concerned.
>
> An order under s 45(3) only applies whilst the person is under the age of 18; however, s 45A provides the power to make a reporting restriction for life in respect of a victim or witness (but not a defendant) who is under 18 during the proceedings. The court must be satisfied that the quality of any evidence or level of co-operation to any party's preparation of the case is likely to be diminished by their identification. The court must consider the welfare of the person, the interests of justice and the public interest in avoiding a substantial and unreasonable restriction on the reporting of proceedings.

13.56 Where reporting restrictions have been imposed in respect of a defendant under the age of 18 who is convicted, the court must weigh the principle of

---

[33] See further: Judicial College, 'Reporting Restrictions in the Criminal Courts', revised May 2016.
[34] [2013] 1 Cr App R 16, CA.

balanced open justice against the principle of offending prevention, the welfare of the child, and Articles 8 (privacy) and 3 (best interests of the child) when deciding whether or not to lift the reporting restrictions. Release of the details of the young person is not to be for the purpose of 'naming and shaming'.[35]

Persons over 18—YJCEA 1999 s. 46 enables a party to apply for a reporting **13.57** restriction in relation to a witness other than the accused who is over the age of 18 and in need of protection. The reporting direction extends for the witness's life (s. 46(6)). Eligibility for protection is defined in s. 46(3) in relation to the quality of their evidence and their willingness to assist with the preparation of the case being diminished by fear or distress in being identified. The court must take into consideration the interests of justice and the public interest in restricting reporting of the proceedings. In the same way as with ss 45 and 45A above, the court or a court on appeal may make 'an excepting direction' (subs. 11) varying or lifting the restrictions altogether—either at the time of the proceedings or any time thereafter.

If the case is one which may attract high media interest, the judge should add- **13.58** itionally have regard to Crim PR 3G.5:

> If any case against a vulnerable defendant has attracted or may attract widespread public or media interest, the assistance of the police should be enlisted to try and ensure that the defendant is not, when attending the court, exposed to intimidation, vilification or abuse.

In addition, s. 41 of the Criminal Justice Act 1925 prohibits the taking of photographs of defendants and witnesses in the court building or in its precincts, or when entering or leaving.[36]

(l) Trial practice note

A 'trial practice note' should be created at the conclusion of any ground rules **13.59** hearing or pre-trial hearing setting out the directions of the judge in terms of the limitations that have been imposed on questioning, and any other matters agreed or ruled upon. This has the dual purpose of providing a useful aide memoire for the advocates to ensure that they keep within the agreed boundaries, and for use by the judge to ensure compliance with the directions given.[37] [38] (See further Chapter 12, 'Ground Rules Hearings'.)

---

[35] *McKerry v Teesdale and Wear Valley Justices* [2001] EMLR 5.
[36] This is an entirely separate consideration to the power of the Resident Judge to allow photographs or other visual recordings of court facilities in accordance with Crim PD 3F.29, to assist vulnerable or child witnesses to familiarize themselves with the setting so as to be enabled to give their best evidence.
[37] Crim PD 3E.4.
[38] *R v Wills* [2011] EWCA Crim 1938.

E. Pre-Trial Cross-Examination

13.60 YJCEA 1999 s. 28 provides that where a special measures direction has been made providing for a video-recording to be admitted under s. 27 as evidence-in-chief, the direction may also provide for any cross-examination and re-examination to be recorded, and for that recording to be admitted in evidence.

13.61 The section was partially brought into force on 30 December 2013, but only for the purposes of pilot schemes in Kingston upon Thames, Leeds, and Liverpool Crown Courts, and only for the purposes of the cross-examination or re-examination of a witness who either:

(a) is under the age of 16; or

(b) suffers from mental disorder as defined by the Mental Health Act 1983, or has a significant impairment of intelligence and social functioning or a physical disability or physical disorder, and the quality of his or her testimony is likely to be diminished as a consequence.

13.62 A phased roll-out to all courts of s. 28 pre-recorded cross-examination for a wider group of complainants is anticipated; however, at the time of writing (April 2017), only the pilot schemes are in operation, to which a Judicial Protocol (YJCEA s. 28 Protocol) dated September 2014 applies.[39] That Protocol has itself been overtaken by the introduction of Better Case Management and the introduction of the PTPH. A new Protocol will undoubtedly be produced, and amendments made to the Crim PD when s. 28 is introduced nationally. Some general points can, however, be made which will no doubt continue to be universally applicable.

13.63 First, for the s. 28 procedure to work, both parties must expect and be expected to cooperate and to work expeditiously. The defence will be required to identify the real issues in the case at the PTPH and provide a defence case statement promptly; it is essential that the prosecution use the applicable disclosure protocols to fulfil their disclosure obligations under the Criminal Procedure and Investigations Act 1996 without delay. (See further Chapter 8, 'Disclosure'.) In appropriate cases, an intermediary suitable to the needs of the witness may need to be instructed and an assessment carried out.

13.64 Second, a ground rules hearing will be required in every case. It is essential that whoever is instructed as trial advocate attends both the ground rules hearing and the s. 28 procedure. It is highly desirable that both hearings are conducted by the allocated trial judge. The intermediary and the officer in the case should both

---

[39] Ministry of Justice, Judicial Protocol on the implementation of section 28 of the Youth Justice and Criminal Evidence Act 1999: 'Pre-recording of cross-examination and re-examination' (MoJ, 2014).

attend. In addition to the usual issues considered at a ground rules hearing, any bad character or YJCEA 1999 s. 41 applications[40] relating to the witness should be made and determined at this hearing.

Third, the witness is entitled to have a court familiarization visit and to practice **13.65** using the link equipment prior to the s. 28 hearing.[41] Directions will be given for this and for memory refreshing at the PTPH and will be confirmed at the ground rules hearing.

Fourth, s. 28 hearings may be expected to take precedence over other cases listed **13.66** at the court.

Fifth, neither the original ABE, nor the recording of cross-examination, can be **13.67** edited without the approval of the judge.

F. Trial

If there has been effective case management at the pre-trial hearings, the likeli- **13.68** hood of unforeseen difficulties arising on the day of trial should be reduced, but can never be completely negated. The needs of a vulnerable witness or defendant may have changed, and directions given at the pre-trial review—even if recently conducted—may need to be reviewed and amended.

(a) Vulnerable defendants at trial

The judge should check that any necessary adjustments to the court layout—such **13.69** as the position of the defendant—have been made, that the defendant is comfort- able and can see and hear the judge, jury, advocates, and (where appropriate) the witness, and should ensure that the defendant knows how to ask for breaks when needed. Clear, simple, and direct language should be used—especially where the defendant is a young person—and the defendant's understanding of any expla- nations should be checked. The duty on the court to ensure that the defendant understands what is happening continues throughout the course of the trial.[42]

(b) Use of the TV link/remote link

An enormous amount of court time is lost when equipment does not work as **13.70** expected. Not only are the consequent delays costly, they are frustrating for the parties and the jury and can be distressing for a defendant or witness. The judge

---

[40] YJCEA 1999 s. 41 prohibits a party from adducing evidence or asking questions in cross- examination on behalf of the defendant about the sexual behaviour of the complainant.
[41] Crim PD 18B.4.
[42] Crim PD 3G.9.

should ensure that the advocates have checked and double-checked that any ABE or other DVD is playable and audible; if there are problems with the sound quality, transcripts may have to be provided to assist when listening to the recording. The judge should check with the court staff that they have been provided with the correct details to link with any remote site.

13.71 Before a witness is called to give evidence over the link, the judge should ensure that the sound quality is satisfactory and the camera angles have been properly checked and adjusted if necessary to give the best picture of the witness. Those responsible for adjusting and operating the equipment should be aware that if the witness is a child, the correct camera angle is likely to be different from that used for an adult. Chairs should be positioned in the link room so that both the witness and intermediary (if there is one) can be clearly seen. Any documents or exhibits that may be shown to the witness should be taken to the link room in advance rather than during the witness's evidence.

(c) Meeting the witness

13.72 Who should meet the witness and how that should be facilitated are matters that should have been canvassed at the pre-trial review, taking account of any views expressed by the intermediary (if there is one) or witness supporter. The purpose of the meeting is to enable the witness to meet the judge and those who will be asking questions and thereby help to put the witness at ease; evidence should not be discussed. Any decision about whether wigs and gowns should be worn may be made at this meeting.

13.73 As previously stated, the judge should not ordinarily meet the witness in the absence of the advocates.

(d) Questioning the vulnerable person

13.74 Any limitations on the length or form of questioning should have been established at the ground rules or other pre-trial hearing, and a trial practice note prepared to remind all parties—including the judge—of the directions given.

13.75 The reason why limitations on cross-examination may be imposed was made clear in *R v Wills*:[43] it is 'to protect the vulnerable witnesses and enable them to give the best evidence they can'.

The Court of Appeal have made it abundantly clear in a series of judgments stretching back to *R v B*[44] that questioning should be adapted to the needs of the witness and that the court can and should impose restrictions to ensure that. So, in *R v IA*,[45] it was held that:

---

[43] [2011] EWCA Crim 1938 at [30].
[44] [2010] EWCA Crim 4.
[45] [2013] EWCA Crim 1308.

… there is a need, both for advocates' techniques and court processes to be adapted to enable the witness to give his or her best evidence. That will involve a degree of persistence and patience by all concerned. A witness found competent is entitled to have the best efforts made to adduce his or her evidence before the court, notwithstanding the difficulties that may exist.[46]

And in *R v Lubemba*,[47] it was made clear that 'advocates must adapt to the witness, not the other way around'.[48]

What restrictions will be required to enable a witness to give his or her 'best evidence' will, of course, vary from witness to witness. As it is put in the Criminal Practice Direction: **13.76**

> All witnesses, including the defendant and defence witnesses should be enabled to give the best evidence they can. In relation to young and/or vulnerable people, this may mean departing radically from traditional cross-examination. The form and extent of appropriate cross-examination will vary from case to case. For adult non vulnerable witnesses an advocate will usually put his case so that the witness will have the opportunity of commenting upon it and/or answering it. When the witness is young or otherwise vulnerable, the court may dispense with the normal practice and impose restrictions on the advocate 'putting his case' where there is a risk of a young or otherwise vulnerable witness failing to understand, becoming distressed or acquiescing to leading questions.[49]

It follows that what limitations (if any) are imposed on cross-examination will be entirely case- and witness-specific and will vary according to the needs and limitations of the witness, the nature of the defence, and the availability of other evidence through which the reliability and credibility of the witness can be tested. **13.77**

Limitations that are commonly imposed may include: **13.78**

- restrictions on the length of cross-examination;
- a prohibition on questions which amount to little more than a comment on the evidence;[50]
- preventing alleged inconsistencies from being put to the witness in cross-examination; any important inconsistencies can be pointed out to the jury at the conclusion of the witness's evidence;[51] and
- where there is more than one defendant, requiring the advocates to divide topics of cross-examination between them to avoid repetition.[52]

---

[46] ibid. at [72].
[47] [2014] EWCA Crim 2064.
[48] ibid. at [45].
[49] Crim PD 3E.4.
[50] *R v B* [2010] EWCA Crim 4.
[51] *R v Wills* [2011] EWCA Crim 1938.
[52] *R v Jonas* [2015] EWCA Crim 56.

13.79   In an appropriate case—for example, where a young witness may become distressed, or where the prosecution are simply being put to proof—the judge may impose restrictions on the advocate 'putting their case'; however, there is no blanket rule that a case should *never* be put to a vulnerable witness, and it is submitted that where a 'positive' case is being asserted, ordinarily the witness should have the opportunity to comment on, refute, or explain what is being put forward.[53] The responsibility is on the advocate to adapt the questions to meet the needs and capabilities of the witness. (See Chapters 9, 'Case Management' and 12, 'Ground Rules Hearings'.)

13.80   Where any limitations have been imposed, the judge should explain those limitations and the reason for them to the jury. (See Chapter 14, 'Jury Directions'.)

13.81   For guidance on the appropriate way to question a witness with specific vulnerabilities, and for advice on case management, the judge and advocate will find significant assistance available in the The Advocate's Gateway 'toolkits'.[54] Toolkits currently available include:

- 'Planning to Question Someone with an Autism Spectrum Disorder, Including Asperger Syndrome';
- 'Planning to Question Someone with a Learning Disability';
- 'Planning to Question Someone with 'Hidden' Disabilities: Specific Language Impairment, Dyslexia, Dyspraxia, Dyscalculia and ADHD';
- 'Planning to Question a Child or Young Person';
- 'Effective Participation of Young Defendants';
- 'Planning to Question Someone Who Is Deaf';
- 'General Principles When Questioning Witnesses and Defendants with Mental Disorder';
- 'Witnesses and defendants with autism: memory and sensory issues'; and
- 'Working with Traumatized Witnesses and Defendants'.

13.82   The toolkits have been specifically endorsed in the Crim PD as representing best practice: 'Advocates should consult and follow the relevant guidance whenever they prepare to question a young or otherwise vulnerable witness or defendant.'[55]

(e) Judicial intervention

13.83   Judges have a clear duty in all cases to control questioning in furtherance of the overriding objective. Where limitations have been imposed on questioning, the judge has a duty to ensure that the limitations are to be complied with, should

---

[53] *Browne v Dunn* [1893] 6 R 67.
[54] See <http://theadvocatesgateway.org> accessed 23 March 2017.
[55] Crim PD 3D.7.

intervene to prevent further questioning that does not comply with them, and explain to the jury why he or she has done so. In *R v Wills*,[56] it was held that:

> ... in cases where it is necessary and appropriate to have limitations on the way in which the advocate conducts cross-examination, there is a duty on the judge to ensure that those limitations are complied with. This is important to ensure that vulnerable witnesses are able to give the best evidence of which they are capable.
>
> Where appropriate the judge, in fairness to defendants, should explain the limitations to the jury and the reasons for them. It is also important that defendants do not perceive, whatever the true position, that the cross-examination by their advocate was less effective than that of another advocate in eliciting evidence to defend them on allegations such as those raised in the present case. This means that the limitations must be clearly defined. One way of achieving this, as suggested in the Advocacy Training Counsel's [sic] report, is for a practice note or protocol to be drafted for use by advocates and the trial judge containing the relevant matters set out in paragraph 15 of part 5 of that Report.
>
> Secondly, we observe that if there is some lapse by counsel in failing to comply with the limitations on cross-examination, it is important that the judge gives a relevant direction to the jury when that occurs, both for the benefit of the jury and any other defendant. To leave that direction until the summing up will in many cases mean that it is much less effective than a direction given at the time.

The Court of Appeal have made it clear that they will support judges who act **13.84** robustly to prevent the repetitive, oppressive, or intimidating questioning of a vulnerable person.

In *R v Lubemba*, the Court of Appeal held that:

> ... a trial judge is not only entitled, he is duty bound to control the questioning of a witness. He is not obliged to allow a defence advocate to put their case. He is entitled to and should set reasonable time limits and to interrupt where he considers questioning is inappropriate.[57]

This was affirmed in *R v Jonas*,[58] in which the Court of Appeal rejected the sub- **13.85** mission of the defence advocate that she had been unfairly fettered in the way in which she conducted her cross-examination of the complainant. The court noted that:

> At the plea and case management hearing, and at trial, counsel had been reminded of the necessity to avoid repetitive questioning on areas that were common to the defendants. The trial judge was therefore duty-bound to comply with the Criminal Procedure Rules and with the Criminal Practice Directions to ensure that the questioning of the witness was controlled. The court is required to take every reasonable step to encourage and facilitate the attendance of witnesses and to facilitate their participation. This includes enabling a witness to give their best evidence. As was explained in *R v Lubemba and Pooley* [2014] EWCA Crim 2064, the judge has a

---

[56] [2011] EWCA Crim 1938.
[57] ibid. at [51].
[58] [2015] EWCA Crim 562.

duty to control questioning ... we reject the criticism that the judge intervened when she should not have done and that she in any way prevented the appellant from receiving a fair trial. On the contrary, in our view her timely and sensible interventions ensured that the whole process was fair to everyone. She protected the witness from unnecessary and oppressive questioning, but not at the expense of a fair trial for the defendants.[59]

13.86 Where the case involves a vulnerable person, the judge should be able to identify when someone is, or may be, at a disadvantage owing to a personal attribute; judicial intervention may be required to remedy that disadvantage and to enable them to play a full part in the proceedings.[60] This requirement may mean that the judge needs to take a more interventionist approach than would previously have been expected, and to step in to prevent repetitive, oppressive, or intimidating questions. This is the case whether or not an intermediary is engaged; the judge cannot delegate his or her responsibility to control questioning to the intermediary, whose role is to facilitate communication.

13.87 Although the intermediary cannot and should not assume the judge's responsibility to control questioning, the judge may need to take on the mantle of the intermediary where that is necessary to ensure fairness.

13.88 In *R v Cox*,[61] the appellant had what were described as 'complex psychiatric difficulties', as a result of which it was determined that he would benefit from having an intermediary at trial. Despite concerted efforts, no suitable intermediary was available. The trial judge considered that notwithstanding the absence of an intermediary, the defendant would be able effectively to participate in his trial taking into account what was described as a 'raft of procedural modifications' directed by the judge as appropriate to the situation presented. The judgment of the Court of Appeal records that:

> The judge concluded that the interests of justice required him to maintain a close control over the questioning, to intervene where any possible unfairness might arise, and to ensure that the appellant was not unduly stressed by the proceedings. He would have to be 'rather more interventionalist' than normal. He would play 'part of the role which an intermediary, if available, would otherwise have played'. He recognized the continuing obligation on him to monitor his 'initial conclusion' on these issues.[62]

13.89 The Court of Appeal approved the judge's actions, stating that:

> We immediately acknowledge the valuable contribution made to the administration of justice by the use of intermediaries in appropriate cases. We recognize

[59] ibid. at [30]–[37].
[60] 'Equal Treatment Bench Book 2013', paras 2.22 and 2.28. See also *R v JD* [2013] EWCA Crim 465.
[61] [2012] EWCA Crim 549.
[62] ibid. at [22].

that there are occasions when the use of an intermediary would improve the trial process. That, however, is far from saying that whenever the process would be improved by the availability of an intermediary, it is mandatory for an intermediary to be made available. It can, after all, sometimes be overlooked that as part of their general responsibilities judges are expected to deal with specific communication problems faced by any defendant or any individual witness (whether a witness for the prosecution or the defence) as part and parcel of their ordinary control of the judicial process. When necessary, the processes have to be adapted to ensure that a particular individual is not disadvantaged as a result of personal difficulties, whatever form they may take. In short, the overall responsibility of the trial judge for the fairness of the trial has not been altered because of the increased availability of intermediaries, or indeed the wide band of possible special measures now enshrined in statute.[63]

Given the continuing shortage of intermediaries, and the change in emphasis away from a presumption that a young child or vulnerable defendant will require an intermediary,[64] judges may find themselves increasingly called upon to step into the arena in this way in order to ensure fairness. **13.90**

(f) Dealing with witness difficulties in the course of giving evidence

Giving evidence is a stressful experience for most witnesses; where the witness has a vulnerability, the anxiety, stress, and distress may be exacerbated. Where there has been an intermediary assessment, it is likely that the judge and the advocates will have been provided with information about the witness's ability to concentrate, the frequency of breaks that may be required, and the signs that the witness may display when becoming tired or anxious. These are all matters that should have been covered at the ground rules hearing. The judge may gain additional insight when meeting the witness prior to giving evidence. The judge (and the advocates) need to be alert to signs of tiredness and distress when the witness is giving evidence, but should recognize that, particularly where the live link is being utilized, those signs may not always be apparent to those in court. The judge should therefore take advice from the intermediary (or other supporter where appropriate) who is likely to be in a better position to ascertain any difficulties that the witness is having. **13.91**

Where a witness does become distressed, it is important that the judge takes a calm, patient, and flexible approach. Often, at the first sign of distress the questioning advocate will immediately suggest a break; but it is for the judge to control the court, not the advocate or, for that matter, the witness. It is perhaps worth stating the obvious that a witness describing upsetting events is likely to become upset. The witness's welfare is paramount, but having a break is not always in the witness's best interests—repeated breaks can be disruptive to the evidence, **13.92**

---

[63] ibid. at [29]. Re-affirmed in *R v Rashid* [2017] 1 Cr App R 25.
[64] Crim PD 3F.25.

prolong the amount of time that the witness is 'in the box', and potentially increase the distress. Conversely, a witness may unwisely refuse a break because he or she wants to get the 'ordeal' finished as soon as possible. It is for the judge, taking advice from any intermediary and taking into account the witness's own views, to make a judgment regarding whether a break should be taken.

13.93 Where a break is required, frequently, all that is necessary is a few minutes for the witness to collect themselves. Where the witness is appearing on live link, that can be an 'in-room' break; the screens are turned off or blanked and the sound muted, the court remains in situ, and the witness supporter alerts the court when the witness is ready to continue. On other occasions, a longer break will be required, possibly even until the following day. Ordinarily, abandoning proceedings at the first sign of distress will rarely be helpful—either for the witness or the trial prospects.

13.94 In the rare case when cross-examination cannot be completed due to the distress of the witness, it does not necessarily follow that the defendant has been denied a fair trial. The central consideration for the judge will be whether the defendant has been given an adequate and proper opportunity to challenge or contest the evidence on which the allegation faced was based. That may depend on the extent to which challenge to the witness's evidence has already been put. In certain cases, where there has only been partial challenge to the witness, it may still be possible to achieve fairness through challenge of other witnesses, or the admission of other evidence. If fairness can be achieved through such means, then coupled with a strong direction to the jury, the trial may continue and the Court of Appeal will not interfere unless the decision to continue was outside the range of reasonable conclusions that the judge could have reached.[65]

13.95 Two cases which fell on either side of the line were *R v Pipe*[66] and *R v JP*.[67] In the former case, the majority of cross-examination had been completed when the witness became too distressed to continue. The judge ruled that that which remained could be dealt with in another way. The Court of Appeal upheld the conviction; the critical issue was the extent to which the defendant could have a fair trial.

13.96 In *JP*, however, the linked case with *Lubemba*, in which the complainant had not been called to give evidence at all following an erroneous decision from the judge that the complainant would not be able to cope with questioning, the Court of Appeal reached the opposite conclusion. In particular, the court noted that there had been a failure on the part of the judge to consider the effect of YJCEA 1999 s. 27(5)(a) that where an ABE recording is to be played, the witness must be called to give evidence.

---

[65] *R v M* [2008] EWCA Crim 2787.
[66] [2014] EWCA Crim 2570.
[67] [2014] EWCA Crim 2064.

What is unclear is how the potential tension between YJCEA 1999 s. 27(5)(a)   **13.97**
and Criminal Justice Act 2003 s. 114 should be resolved. In *R v M*, the Court
of Appeal, having stated that 'it does not seem to us that s. 114 of the 2003
Act is relevant', drew a distinction between the impact on the jury of seeing
a witness, and a statement being read. The Court in *R v JP* does not appear
to have considered the issue at all. Nevertheless, even if CJA 2003 s. 114 does
apply, the issue would still be the extent to which the defendant could have a
fair trial; to which issue the extent to which he or she can, or has been able to,
challenge the witness (whether directly or through other means) is likely to be
determinative.

G.   Conclusion

Although the judge's role differs from that of the advocates, all parties have the   **13.98**
same responsibility to ensure that the management of cases involving vulnerable
people—whether witnesses or defendants—is carried out in such a way that both
furthers the overriding objective and enables the effective participation of the
vulnerable person to be facilitated. That requires a new way of thinking, particularly on the part of the judge who may find him or herself far more actively
involved in the trial process than has historically been the case; whether in terms
of case management, safeguarding, active intervention to control questioning,
or even involvement in asking questions of the witness him or herself. This may
be unfamiliar territory and it is tempting in such circumstances to reach for the
latest Court of Appeal case and assume that whatever was decided therein reflects
the steps that must be taken or the restrictions imposed in every case; but that
would be fallacious. The whole point of adaptations to meet the needs of a particular vulnerable person—whether that be the complainant, a witness for either
side, or the defendant—is that each individual, each case, is different. What is
required is not a rigid approach, but a flexible one tailored to the particular person and context that is presented. It has often been stated that the advocate must
adapt his or her questions to the needs of the person being questioned; but that
is too often a throw-away line. Requiring an advocate to adapt their questioning is to require them to find a way of putting a question so that the witness *can*
answer it, not to allow them to avoid asking the question, or, worse, stopping the
question being asked at all on the basis that it is 'too difficult'. If we truly want to
enable vulnerable people, to facilitate their participation and allow them access
to justice, surely rather than talking about the 'right' of the defence to 'put their
case', we should focus on the right of the vulnerable witness to answer the allegation or suggestion being made—not by preventing the case being put at all, but
by requiring the advocate to put it in a way which the witness can understand
and can answer.

13.99 Neither should the focus be entirely on the vulnerable witness (whether complainant or otherwise) excluding the vulnerable defendant. Adaptations (of whatever kind) are made because of the person's vulnerability and to enable them to participate in the trial process notwithstanding that vulnerability—not because of their particular status in the trial or which side they are on. If in an appropriate case restrictions may be applied to the style, tone, and content of questions put to a vulnerable witness, similar restrictions should also be applied to the questioning of a vulnerable defendant.

Further Reading

Rt Hon Sir Brian Leveson, 'Review of Efficiency in Criminal Proceedings' (January 2015).
Judicial College, 'The Crown Court Compendium—Part 1: Legal Summaries, Directions and Examples' (May 2016).

14

JURY DIRECTIONS

Heather Norton

A. Introduction

In March 2015, in the case of *R v NKA*,[1] the Court of Appeal, presided over by **14.01** the Lord Chief Justice—Lord Thomas of Cwmgiedd, criticized a trial judge who had split his summing-up into two parts: giving directions on the law prior to closing speeches, and summing-up the facts of the case after those speeches had

---

[1] [2015] EWCA Crim 614.

been delivered. Giving the judgment of the court, Mr Justice Macduff observed that this was:

> … contrary to the express provisions of the Criminal Procedure Rules which lay down the order in which events take place in a Crown Court Trial. None of the members of this court has experienced this practice previously. Counsel tells us that neither has she. This is not something that should be repeated. It could in many cases lead to considerable confusion. This court takes the view that in all cases judges in a criminal trial should sum up the law and the facts at the conclusion of counsel's speeches in the normal way.[2]

14.02   Whether there is still a 'normal way' for directions to be given to the jury is perhaps open to debate. As Professor David Ormerod noted in his commentary on this case in the *Criminal Law Review*,[3] the law and practice governing the manner and timing of directions, instructions, and information provided by the judge to the jury are developing rapidly.

14.03   Shortly before the Court of Appeal delivered their judgment in *R v NKA*, Lord Justice Leveson published his 'Review of Efficiency in Criminal Proceedings'[4] (hereafter the Leveson Review). He recommended not only that a summing-up could and should be split, with directions on law (burden and standard of proof, separate verdicts, ingredients of the offence, and route to verdicts) provided to the jury by the judge prior to closing speeches,[5] but also that the judge should be able to provide appropriate directions, 'at whatever stage of the trial he or she considers it appropriate to do so',[6] whether that be at the outset of the trial after the opening in order to alert the jury to the specific issues that they will be required to decide, or in the course of the trial at the time at which evidence to which the direction relates is given.

14.04   Exactly twelve months after the decision in *NKA*, Lord Justice Leveson's recommendations were incorporated into the Criminal Practice Directions[7] (Crim PD), providing the judge with a far greater degree of flexibility than had hitherto been the case to tailor the provision of directions and guidance to the particular needs of an individual case.

14.05   As well as a sea change in the way in which directions can be given to the jury, in cases in which a vulnerable person in particular has been involved—whether as a defendant or as a witness—the need to make adjustments to the trial process

---

[2] ibid. at [19].
[3] [2015] Crim LR 654.
[4] 'Review of Efficiency in Criminal Proceedings' (January 2015), available at <https://www.judiciary.gov.uk/publications/review-of-efficiency-in-criminal-proceedings-final-report/> accessed 16 April 2017.
[5] ibid. [302].
[6] ibid. [282].
[7] Crim PD VI—Trial 26K: Juries, Directions, Written Materials and Summing Up—Criminal Practice Directions 2015—Amendment No. 1, [2016] EWCA Crim 97.

(whether through the use of special measures or by any other means) together with continued research into the way in which juries approach evidence, has led to an increase in the number of directions that a judge has to give the jury, as well as guidance based on the experience of the courts to counteract the risk that the jury would otherwise make 'unwarranted assumptions' in their approach to the evidence.

It is worth repeating the obvious point that the purpose of any direction or guid-   **14.06** ance given by the judge is to assist the jury: to explain to the jury what their task is and how to approach it; to explain the legal framework within which they must carry out their task; to enable the jury to approach and evaluate the evidence in its proper legal context; and to counsel the jury against using evidence in an inappropriate way. It follows that when considering which directions to give in addition to the mandatory directions that apply to all cases (e.g. burden and standard of proof, elements of the offence(s), separate consideration of counts/defendants), the judge must keep to the forefront of their mind whether the direction will help the jury with an issue in the case and, if it will, when it will best assist the jury to give that direction.

All directions and the timing of them should be tailored to the facts of the par-   **14.07** ticular case; all should be discussed with the advocates prior to delivery.

The aim of this chapter is to set out the main areas that the judge trying a case   **14.08** involving a vulnerable person is likely to need to cover, and provides suggestions for when those directions might most usefully be provided. It is not intended to be an exhaustive list of all directions that could possibly arise in any particular case, nor to provide precedents for the wording of directions that might be given; for a full and comprehensive guide to judicial directions, the reader is referred to 'The Crown Court Compendium Part 1: Legal Summaries, Directions and Examples 2017',[8] which contains worked-through illustrative examples of directions.

B.   Directions to Be Given at the Start of the Trial

(a)   Introductory remarks

In the introductory remarks given to the jury at the outset of a trial, the judge has   **14.09** the task of explaining to the jury in clear terms that they, like the advocates and the judge, have a job to fulfil; to explain what that job entails; and to provide clear instructions about how they should carry out their task.

---

[8]   See <https://www.judiciary.gov.uk/publications/crown-court-bench-book-directing-the-jury-2/> accessed 23 March 2017.

14.10 To that end, the judge should in every case:[9]

- direct the jury that the verdict(s) that they will be required to deliver must be the verdicts reached collectively by the twelve of them uninfluenced whether directly or indirectly by any other person; consequently, they must not discuss the case with anyone else outside their number or allow anyone else to communicate with them (by whatever means) about the case that they are trying. Should someone make an approach towards them, they should immediately alert a member of court staff;
- direct the jury that they must be true to their oaths to try the case only on the evidence and that they must therefore reach their verdicts on, and only on, the evidence that is placed before them in court; they must not carry out any form of research, whether via the internet or through visiting a scene or by any other means;[10]
- direct the jury to disregard any media reports about the case;
- direct the jury to report any concerns, whatever they may be, that they may have as the trial progresses in order that the judge may deal with any problems arising or give reassurance; and
- direct the jury to keep an open mind until they have heard all of the evidence, speeches, and summing-up and have retired to consider their verdict(s).

(b) Distressing or emotional evidence

14.11 In a case that involves a vulnerable witness or defendant, it is likely that this last direction will require expanding. Cases of this sort will often involve allegations of a sexual nature or domestic violence and/or may involve children, sometimes very young children. Such evidence can be distressing, both for the witness who is giving the testimony and for anyone listening to it. It is important that the jury are not only forewarned of the fact that they will be hearing such evidence, but should also be given a clear direction on how to deal with their understandable reactions to it.

14.12 The judge should therefore warn the jury that they may find some of the evidence distressing, but remind them that their job is to evaluate and analyse the evidence presented to them in a calm and objective way and that they should not be swayed by feelings of emotion, sympathy, or prejudice.

(c) Adjustments to the court process

14.13 Where adjustments have been made to the normal court procedures in order to enable a vulnerable defendant to participate—such as adjustments to the layout

---

[9] See also Crim PD 26G.
[10] Since 13 April 2015, it has been an indictable offence punishable with up to two years' imprisonment for a juror to carry out any form of research into a case that he or she is trying (Juries Act 1974 s. 20A).

of the court, frequent breaks, or other alterations to the usual timetable—the jury should be told about them at the outset and given an explanation for those adjustments. This may involve outlining to the jury any particular difficulties that the defendant may have—for example their age, physical or mental disability, or any communication needs. The extent to which it is appropriate to go into detail will depend upon the facts of the case and should always be discussed in advance with the advocates. Particular care over the form of words used will be necessary where the defendant's difficulties may be relied upon by either party as relevant to an issue in the case. It should be made clear to the jury that any necessary adjustments have been made to ensure fairness and to enable the defendant to participate in the trial process (see section D below).

(d) Intermediaries for a defendant from the start of the trial

Where an intermediary or any other special measure is granted to a witness, the judge is required under s. 32 of the Youth Justice and Criminal Evidence Act 1999 (YJCEA 1999) to give such warning to the jury as the judge considers necessary to ensure that no prejudice is caused to the accused. It may be thought appropriate to give this warning at the outset, or—more helpfully—just before the jury hear evidence from or relating to that witness. **14.14**

Where the court has used its own inherent jurisdiction to grant a defendant the use of an intermediary, s. 32 does not apply; nevertheless, the judge should obviously explain to the jury why an intermediary is being used, and explain the intermediary's role. The jury should be told that: **14.15**

- the intermediary is independent;
- the intermediary is not an expert;
- the role of the intermediary is to facilitate two-way communication between the defendant and the court; and
- the intermediary will intervene if there is a communication issue.

The jury should be told why it has been decided that the defendant needs to have an intermediary; precisely what the jury are told should be agreed with the advocates in advance. **14.16**

If the intermediary is to be used for a defendant throughout the trial, the jury should be given the explanations for their presence both at the outset of the trial, before opening, and immediately before the defendant gives evidence; if the intermediary is only being utilized for the defendant's evidence, then it would normally make more sense for the direction to be given at that stage of the trial. **14.17**

(e) Interpreters

If the defendant has any other form of visible support, either instead of or in addition to an intermediary, such as an interpreter or carer (e.g. a nurse or social **14.18** worker) sitting alongside them in the dock, that person's presence should be made known to the jury and their role explained. Where the defendant has an interpreter, the jury should be warned that there will be continuous translation contemporaneous with the evidence, but that they should not allow themselves to be distracted and should concentrate on the evidence being given in court.

14.19   In the case of a deaf defendant, there may be a number of interpreters present in court, commonly two teams each containing a sign language interpreter and a relay interpreter; one pair will be actively translating, while the other pair check that the interpretation is correct, with regular swaps between the teams. They will almost certainly be standing in different positions in the court, depending on available sight lines and whether equipment such as video links are being utilized. In order to avoid confusion and distraction, the jury should be given an explanation not simply of the fact that there are deaf interpreters being used, but also how they work together and why they are positioned where they are in the courtroom. For these purposes, it is often helpful to ask one of the hearing interpreters to explain to the jury how they will be working together to provide interpretation. Similar considerations will apply to lip readers/lip speakers.

(f) Litigants in person

14.20   According to the latest official figures available, approximately 6 per cent of defendants in the Crown Court are unrepresented for at least one hearing,[11] but anecdotally, the number of defendants who now represent themselves is expected to rise, whether because of restrictions on the availability of legal aid (due to income or the type of offence involved), or because they have dispensed with their lawyers or for any other reason. For the litigant in person, the criminal court can be a bewildering and alien place even where they have the assistance of a McKenzie friend.[12] They may struggle to understand the language used, the legal concepts that apply, lack the necessary detachment from their case to be able to present it in the best light, and lack the skills of advocacy that might be expected of the trained lawyer.

14.21   The judge should explain to the jury that the defendant is representing him or herself and that it is open to any defendant to do so. In addition, the judge should advise the jury that it can be difficult for an unrepresented defendant to properly present their case, and that they should keep in mind the difficulties that the defendant may have when they are considering the evidence.

---

[11] See <https://www.gov.uk/government/uploads/system/uploads/attachment_data/file/437677/annex-b-legal_representation.pdf> accessed 23 March 2017.

[12] A litigant in person is entitled to receive assistance in court from a layperson often referred to as a McKenzie friend. A McKenzie friend may provide support, practical assistance, and provide advice, but may not act as an advocate or conduct litigation.

C. Directions Following the Prosecution Opening

In the Leveson Review, it was recommended that following the prosecution **14.22** opening, the defence should be required to publicly identify the issues in the case. Such an approach, it was suggested, would also 'provide an opportunity for the Judge to provide certain directions at the beginning of the trial … alerting the jury to what they should be looking out for while the evidence is being called, but before it is called'.[13]

This recommendation has now been incorporated into the Criminal Procedure **14.23** Rules[14] (Crim PR) and Crim PD,[15] which state that: 'The court is required to provide directions about the relevant law at any time that will assist the jury to evaluate the evidence.'

Thus, where, for example, in a sexual case the sole issue is lack of consent, it may **14.24** well be of assistance for the judge to give the jury a direction on consent at the very outset rather than waiting until the summing-up, as would previously have been the case.

Providing an early direction will enable the jury (and the advocates) to focus on the relevant issues in the case from the outset and will assist in dispelling some of the preconceptions and stereotypes that the jury may otherwise have in mind, thereby promoting a 'fair and effective trial'.[16]

In order for the judge to be able to give early directions, however, it is clearly **14.25** essential that pre-trial case management has been robust (see further Chapter 9, 'Case Management'), that the prosecution has fully complied with their duty of disclosure (see further Chapter 8, 'Disclosure'), and that a properly focused prosecution case opening has been provided and an appropriately detailed defence statement served.

D. Directions in the Course of the Evidence

The injunction to provide directions 'at any time that will assist the jury' should **14.26** be taken at face value. Judges will be accustomed to giving directions to the jury when special measures are used, but Crim PD 26K.10 envisages that directions may be given in respect of many categories of evidence such as expert evidence,

---

[13] Leveson Review, [276].
[14] Criminal Procedure Rules 2015 (SI 2015/1490) as amended by the Criminal Procedure (Amendment) Rules 2016 (SI 2016/120) 25.14(2).
[15] Crim PD 26K.8.
[16] Crim PD 25A.3.

or hearsay, or which will involve 'legal concepts' such as voluntary intoxication or consent.

14.27   In a case which involves a vulnerable person, the judge is likely to give explanations (whether they amount to full directions or not) in respect of some or all of the following matters during the course of the evidence:

(a) Special measures

14.28   There is a statutory requirement for judges to give 'such warning (if any) as the judge considers necessary to ensure that the fact that the [special measures] direction was given in relation to the witness does not prejudice the accused'.[17]

14.29   This applies to evidence given:

- from behind screens (YJCEA 1999 s. 23);
- through the live link—the witness may be accompanied by a supporter in the live-link room (YJCEA 1999 s. 24);
- in private, or where specified persons have been excluded from the court (YJCEA 1999 s. 25);
- when the judge and advocate have removed wigs and gowns (YJCEA 1999 s. 26);
- by pre-recorded evidence-in-chief (ABE interview) or cross-examination (YJCEA 1999 ss 27–8);
- through an intermediary (YJCEA 1999 s. 29); and
- with the use of communication aids (YJCEA 1999 s. 30).

14.30   In practice, the judge is likely to explain that certain measures are standard for children and commonplace for adults, particularly in circumstances where the witness will be describing intimate or sensitive details. The purpose of the special measures should be explained to the jury in general terms (e.g. to allow the witness to concentrate on the questions and answers without having to worry about seeing or being seen by members of the public). Most importantly, the jury should be told in clear terms that the use of special measures is not a reflection on the defendant or their case, and that they should not be prejudiced against them because of it; it is the evidence that matters, not the means by which that evidence is given. In order to carry the greatest weight, the warning should be given to the jury immediately before the witness to whom the special measure applies gives evidence.[18]

(b) ABE recordings/s. 28 recordings/transcripts

14.31   Where evidence is given by means of a pre-recorded video recording, the jury should be warned that the recording stands in place of the witness's evidence-in-chief

---

[17] YJCEA 1999 s. 32.
[18] *Brown and Grant* [2004] EWCA Crim 1620.

(and for cross-examination where YJCEA s. 28 is being utilized) and that they should therefore concentrate on watching and listening to the recording in the same way that they would listen to any other witness giving live evidence in court. They should be warned that save in very exceptional cases, they will not be able to see the recording again.[19]

Ordinarily, transcripts will not be provided to the jury, but if exceptionally **14.32** transcripts are provided for any reason (e.g. because the quality of the sound recording is poor or to enable the jury better to follow cross-examination), it should be explained to the jury that they have only been provided with the transcripts for that limited purpose, and that the transcripts will be collected up after the witness has concluded their evidence, but should be reassured that the judge will be reminding them of the main points of the evidence in summing-up.[20]

(c) Meeting the witness

If the judge and/or the advocates have met the witness before they give evidence, **14.33** then it should be made clear to the jury that this has occurred, and the explanation given that the purpose was to introduce them to the judge and the advocates in a less formal setting so that the witness would be more at ease when giving evidence.

(d) Intermediaries for witnesses

If not done at an earlier stage (e.g. because the defendant has an intermediary), **14.34** the judge should explain to the jury what the intermediary's role is, and why an intermediary is required. The judge should explain the role of the intermediary, in particular that he or she:

- is not an expert;
- is independent;
- is present to assist with communication; and
- will intervene if any communication difficulties are identified.

The judge should additionally identify and explain any particular difficulties that the witness has, and warn the jury that the use of an intermediary should not prejudice the defendant.

A suggested form of words can be found in 'Toolkit 1: Ground Rules Hearings **14.35** and The Fair Treatment of Vulnerable People in Court' (1 December 2016).[21]

---

[19] *R v Mullen* [2004] EWCA Crim 602; *R v Rawlings (Royston George)* [1995] 1 WLR 178.
[20] *R v Popescu* [2010] EWCA 1230; *R v Sardar* [2012] EWCA Crim 134.
[21] See <http://www.theadvocatesgateway.org/toolkits> accessed 23 March 2017.

(e) Restrictions on cross-examination

14.36 In accordance with Crim PR 3.9(7) and Crim PD 3E, a ground rules hearing must be held in advance of the relevant evidence being given in all cases in which an intermediary is to be used, and is good practice in all other cases in which a witness or defendant has communication needs.[22] At the ground rules hearing, the judge may impose restrictions on the length and content of cross-examination.[23] Such restrictions may include:

- a direction restricting the advocate from 'putting their case';[24]
- a direction that inconsistencies (if any) in the witness's evidence should be identified to the jury through means other than by direct challenge to the witness;[25] and
- where there is more than one defendant, a direction preventing repetition of topics or of questions already asked, but instead a requirement that the advocates divide the necessary questions between them.[26]

14.37 In most cases where a witness is particularly young or vulnerable, or where an intermediary is being used, the judge will have required the advocate to submit a cross-examination plan for consideration by the court and the intermediary; the advocate may be required to comply with any amendments made on the advice of the intermediary and direction of the judge.

14.38 It is good practice for a trial practice note to be drawn up setting out clearly the boundaries that have been imposed at the ground rules hearing, with which the advocates should comply and which the judge should enforce.

14.39 The Crown Court Compendium states:

> … the Ground Rules Hearing and the orders made at it … will inform, the directions to be given to the jury at the outset of the trial, before the child or vulnerable witness gives evidence and in summing up.[27]

14.40 Where any restrictions to cross-examination have been imposed, the judge should explain to the jury what those restrictions are and why they have been made just before the witness gives evidence. If an advocate fails to comply with the restrictions imposed, the judge should prevent further questioning that is non-compliant and explain to the jury what has happened. In *R v H*,[28] where the judge felt it necessary to intervene in cross-examination of a vulnerable witness, the Court of Appeal approved of the approach of the trial judge; he

---

[22] cf. Chapter 12, 'Ground Rules Hearings'.
[23] *R v Wills* [2011] EWCA Crim 1938.
[24] *R v Barker* [2010] EWCA Crim 4.
[25] *R v Pipe* [2014] EWCA Crim 2570.
[26] *R v Jonas* [2015] EWCA Crim 562.
[27] Judicial College, 'The Crown Court Compendium' (Judicial College, 2017) 10–19.
[28] [2014] EWCA Crim 1555.

dealt with the possibility that his interventions might have signalled a view to the jury 'by providing the standard direction that any view of his that the jury might have detected should be ignored unless it coincided with their view reached independently'.[29]

If a direction is made limiting the extent to which the witness could be chal- **14.41** lenged on any inconsistencies in their evidence, the judge and advocates should agree an alternative way for those inconsistencies to be placed before the jury—whether by the advocate or the judge—at the conclusion of the witness's evidence.[30]

(f) Record-keeping

Where directions have been given to the jury in the course of the trial, a full and **14.42** accurate record must be kept of the date, time, and subject of any such directions by both the court and the parties.

It is now routinely the case that a written 'route to verdict' (a series of questions **14.43** tailored to the issues and the evidence in the case, to be worked through by the jury in retirement in order to reach the appropriate verdict) is given to the jury. Directions on law may be reduced to writing, as may other material where it will assist the jury to have it before them in writing.

Where any directions or other material has been given to the jury in writing, cop- **14.44** ies should be retained by the parties and also uploaded onto the digital case or, if a paper file, on the court file.[31]

Where any legal directions have been given in the course of the trial, or where **14.45** there has been a split summing-up, the judge should list (but not repeat) those directions prior to beginning or resuming the summing-up.[32]

E. Directions and Guidance in Summing-Up

The 2010 edition of the 'Crown Court Bench Book' (now superseded by the **14.46** 'Crown Court Compendium') stated that:

> The task of the trial judge in summing up is to present the law and a summary of the evidence in such a way as best to enable the jury to reach a just conclusion.

---

[29] ibid. at [71].
[30] See *R v Wills*; and also: *R v Simon Edwards* [2011] EWCA Crim 3028; and *R v Lubemba* [2014] EWCA Crim 2064.
[31] Crim PD 26K.2.
[32] Crim PD 26K.19.

That can be achieved only if the trial judge communicates effectively to the jury the issues which they need to resolve and their legitimate approach to the evidence relevant to those issues.[33]

This requires the trial judge to focus their summing-up on the relevant issues that the jury will have to determine, but also enables him or her in an appropriate case to provide guidance to the jury about their approach to the evidence on those issues. This is particularly so where there is a risk that absent such guidance the jury may resort to their own assumptions, often based upon prejudiced or unwarranted stereotypes, about how and why alleged victims or perpetrators of particular offences behave and thus reach an unjustified conclusion. This is a particular risk in cases which involve sexual offending or children. The purpose of judicial comment, therefore, is to warn the jury about making unwarranted assumptions about issues of behaviour or demeanour and to emphasize that cases should be tried upon the evidence, and not upon preconceived ideas about that evidence which may lead to unfairness.

14.47   In *R v D*[34] (a rape case), it was held that:

> The judge is entitled to make comments as to the way evidence is to be approached particularly in areas where there is a danger of a jury coming to an unjustified conclusion without an appropriate warning.

However, the court warned, 'any comment must be uncontroversial': in a case in which delay in making a complaint was raised as an issue undermining the credibility of the complainant, it was sufficiently well known that feelings of shame or embarrassment caused by trauma might inhibit an early complaint to justify comments to that effect from the judge.[35]

Comments must not only be uncontroversial, but also balanced.

14.48   *R v GJB* concerned historic sexual allegations.[36] One of the issues was why the complainant (MT) had delayed until he was an adult before making allegations about abuse allegedly perpetrated on him when he was a child.

14.49   In his summing-up, the trial judge commented that:

> [MT] said, 'I didn't tell anyone about what had happened although I was aware something wrong had occurred but I didn't understand.' Now he would have been five then so it may have been just a few days after his birthday, it was the day of

---

[33] Judicial Studies Board, *Crown Court Bench Book Directing the Jury* (Judicial Studies Board, 2010) 1.

[34] [2008] EWCA Crim 2557; [2009] Crim LR 591.

[35] See also *R v M* [2010] EWCA Crim 1578; [2011] Crim LR 79: 'In recent years the courts have increasingly been prepared to acknowledge the need for a direction that deals with what might be described as stereotypical assumptions about issues such as delay in reporting allegations of serious crime, and distress.'

[36] [2011] EWCA Crim 867.

his birthday party and you've got to try, a very difficult thing to do, a very difficult thing, you've got to try and put yourself in the mind of a 5 year old who has just experienced that and ask yourself well, is it right that a child would actually inevitably say to somebody what had happened, or may some children speak, some children not and what are the consequences of not speaking?

When you don't speak about something that's profoundly affected you, how is that going to affect you as you go through life? Does it make it more likely or less likely that you're going to speak?

It was submitted on appeal that the judge's direction to the jury about why a complaint may not be made for some time was flawed for two reasons (a) it was predicated on an assumption that D was guilty; and (b) the judge did not remind the jury of the defence case on the point.

The Court of Appeal agreed. They stated that: **14.50**

We entirely accept that in a suitable case, and this was one, the judge is entitled to and should comment on the reluctance or difficulty of the victim of sexual abuse to speak about it for long afterwards ... However, it is important that the comment should not assume the guilt of the defendant and that his case should be made clear.

In a more recent case from Northern Ireland, *R v Creaney*,[37] having reviewed the   **14.51**
authorities, the Court inter alia set out the following general propositions about the content and scope of a summing-up:

The judge must strike a fair balance between the prosecution and defence cases; particularly where the defence case is weak, the trial judge must be scrupulous to ensure that the defence case is presented to the jury in an even-handed and impartial manner;

Provided that the judge emphasises to the jury that they are entitled to ignore his views he may comment on the evidence. The judge may do so robustly ... but the judge must not be so critical as to effectively withdraw the issue of guilt or innocence from the jury;

The judge is not confined to the arguments advanced by the prosecution or defence. He is entitled to make uncontroversial comments as to the way the evidence is to be approached particularly where there is a danger of the jury coming to an unjustified conclusion without an appropriate warning. Such remarks may be particularly appropriate in complaints of sexual abuse where feelings of shame, embarrassment or vulnerability may need to be taken into account in considering the explanation for any delay in reporting the matter.

The emphasis on the requirement that any comments should be uncontroversial and balanced illustrates the importance of discussing any proposed comments with the advocates prior to speeches. Comments should be referable to the facts in the case, but should be carefully structured so that they do not endorse, or appear

---

[37] [2015] NICA 43.

to endorse, the argument for one side or another; the sole purpose of comment is to warn the jury about the unfairness of approaching evidence with any pre-conceived ideas about behaviour or demeanour, and to avoid the risk of applying unwarranted stereotypes to particular offences, or alleged offenders or victims.

14.52 Where there may be a risk that the jury will apply an unwarranted assumption to the evidence to decide an issue in the case such as the credibility of complaint or a complainant, or consent and/or belief in consent, judges may find it necessary to give appropriate guidance in accordance with the above guidelines. Areas in which judges have found it necessary to give guidance to the jury include the following:[38]

(a) Avoidance of stereotypes (sexual offences)

14.53 Every case is different: there is no such thing as a typical offender or a typical victim. Neither is there a 'right' way for someone who has been the victim of a sexual offence to behave. The circumstances in which a sexual offence may take place are infinitely varied, as are the reactions of those who have been the victim of a sexual offence.

14.54 Where the evidence in the case warrants it, the jury should be warned against the 'rape myths'—that is, stereotypes which do not accord with the experience of the courts, including erroneous assumptions that:

- the complainant must have wanted sex if he or she: wore provocative clothing; got drunk or took drugs; was flirtatious;
- the complainant must have consented if he or she was or had been in a relationship with the alleged offender/the offender was attractive;
- a victim of a sexual attack will always shout for help/fight back;
- a victim of a sexual attack will always have injuries.

14.55 The jury should be warned not to apply generalizations or stereotypes that they may have gleaned from media reports about other similar cases, but to consider the evidence on its merits and without prejudice.

(b) Avoidance of assumptions where the parties are known to each other/in a relationship (sexual offences)

14.56 Sexual offences can and do take place in many different circumstances and involve people of all different backgrounds, ages, and relationships—between

---

[38] These are not an exhaustive list of situations where guidance may be required; although the author has drawn on the excellent examples provided in the 2010 *Crown Court Benchbook* and the 2017 *Crown Court Compendium*, they are not intended to be (and should not be read as) specimen directions which, in any case, would always need to be tailored to the particular facts of the case as has been made clear throughout this chapter. For worked examples of the guidance which may be appropriate in various given situations, see 'The Crown Court Compendium'.

strangers, acquaintances, work colleagues, friends, partners, or spouses. Just because the complainant has had consensual sexual intercourse with the defendant on a previous occasion does not mean that they must have consented to sexual intercourse on the occasion being considered by the jury or that this would of itself give the defendant reasonable grounds for believing that they did. A person who gives free consent to sexual activity with a person on one occasion may withhold that consent on another. The jury are looking at a specific incident set within the context established by the evidence placed before them.

(c) Delay in reporting

It is the experience of the courts that there is no one classic response to the trauma of a sexual assault; different people react differently, whether that is at the time of the assault or when giving evidence about it. Some people may make an immediate complaint, others, whether through shame, embarrassment, fear, shock, or some other reason, may say nothing for some time. A late complaint is not necessarily a false complaint. Whether or not to believe the complainant is a matter for the jury to decide considering all the relevant evidence, including the context in which the alleged incident(s) took place, and reasons given (if any) for the timing of the complaint. **14.57**

(d) Lack of resistance

Common sense and our knowledge of human behaviour tells us that different people have different reactions to stressful or traumatic situations. Where that situation is a sexual assault, experience has shown that while some people may put up resistance and fight back, others may submit to what is happening, still others will simply blank it out. The prosecution do not have to prove that the complainant said no, or that he or she resisted; neither is it necessary to show that force was used or that he or she was injured. **14.58**

(e) Demeanour when giving evidence

When assessing a witness's evidence, the jury will also be assessing the way in which the witness gave that evidence and their demeanour in court. However, just as different victims of a sexual assault react to what has happened to them in different ways, so too can the way in which they give evidence about their experiences also differ. One person may be visibly distressed, another may appear to be calm, or even cold. Everyone has their own way of dealing with traumatic or stressful situations, whether that be an assault, or giving evidence. It follows that a distressed person is not necessarily telling the truth, just as a calm person is not necessarily telling lies; it all depends upon the character and personality of the witness. **14.59**

14.60 A vulnerable defendant's demeanour might also require a direction to the jury—this is discussed in detail in Chapter 6, 'Vulnerability and Defences'.

(f) Child witnesses

14.61 The judge will commonly feel it is appropriate to give the jury some guidance to assist them with their approach to a child's evidence based on the common experience of the courts of the way in which children experience events in different circumstances and their ability to recall them. Guidance may therefore be given on the following areas.

(g) A child's understanding is not the same as an adult's

14.62 As a result of their age and immaturity, a child may not have the same levels of reasoning, knowledge, and understanding as an adult might be expected to have. They may not understand what has happened and find it difficult to put it into words or to describe it. That may be even harder to do when they are asked questions by an adult in authority such as a police officer, or by an advocate or judge in court, particularly if they do now realize that something bad has happened. The jury should be advised to be cautious before judging a child by the same standards that would apply to an adult; nevertheless, the standard of proof remains the same, whether it is a child or an adult who is the complainant.

(h) Difficulties in recall of detail and inconsistencies

14.63 Children do not have the same levels of understanding, reasoning, and knowledge as adults, and accordingly may not realize the significance of events that take place; this may be reflected in the ways in which they remember events or describe them. A child may have difficulty remembering when and in what order events occurred, or struggle to describe the context in which events took place. As with any witness, the jury's task will be to determine whether the evidence that the witness has given is truthful, credible, and reliable—this applies to the evidence of a child as it does to the evidence of adults. However, with a child, errors and inconsistencies may be a reflection of the child's lack of maturity and understanding rather than signifying untruthfulness or unreliability. If the jury are sure that the essential parts of the child's evidence are reliable and truthful, then they are entitled to act upon it.

(i) Abuse in a family setting

14.64 Experience has shown that a child will accept as normal behaviour that which takes place at home; if that behaviour is regular and routine, then it may not stand out to a child as particularly memorable. Children do not always appreciate that something which is happening to them in their own home does not happen to other children and may only come to that realization when they are older.

When considering a child's evidence, or evidence made by an adult about events alleged to have occurred when he or she was a child, the jury should assess the evidence within the context of that particular child's life making such allowance as the jury feel proper for the immaturity or dependency of the child at that time. Having done so, if the jury are sure that the child has given reliable and truthful evidence on the essential issues, then they are entitled to act upon it; if they are not sure, they should not.

(j) Grooming

'Grooming' describes the process by which abuse takes place gradually in incremental stages to engender trust and familiarity, starting with befriending by, for example, buying the child small treats or takeaways or giving cigarettes to teenagers and what may appear to the child to be normal harmless touching—for example, a pat, a hug, a tickle. By the time that sexual activity has become more advanced, the child may, as a result of the grooming process, accept it as normal within the context of that relationship. Where that happens, experience has shown that it can be harder for a child to remember at a later stage how and when the touching started or sequences of events. It is for the jury to decide whether they are sure that that is what happened in cases where the prosecution suggest that grooming has taken place. **14.65**

(k) A child's reason for silence

Unlike a typical adult, who may be expected to realize very quickly that a sexual assault has occurred and the implications of it, children may not have the same levels of understanding; they may not understand that what has happened is wrong, or may be confused about it. When they do realize that something bad has occurred, experience shows that they may not speak out about it for days, weeks, or years. There may be many reasons why a child remains silent: a child may blame themselves; they may be embarrassed or ashamed; they may be fearful of the consequences of speaking out—whether for themselves or for the person who has abused them. This latter concern may be a particular issue where what has occurred has taken place within a family setting and where the child may feel love, affection, or loyalty for the abuser or other family members who may be affected if they speak out. **14.66**

Experience shows that children do not always react in the same way as adults to events that take place, as their responses are governed by their own experiences and levels of maturity and understanding. The judge should therefore caution the jury to examine the evidence in context. **14.67**

(l) Directions or guidance?

A warning to the jury to put to one side any stereotypes or preconceived ideas about the types of people and issues involved in cases such as these amounts to a direction; advice about the way in which they should approach the evidence and **14.68** the particular considerations that they should have in mind when considering evidence from a child or adult complainant in a sexual case in particular, is guidance based upon the experience of the courts. As such, guidance on the jury's approach to areas of evidence such as those outlined above should not be given in writing to the jury, as to do so would potentially give it undue prominence.

F. Conclusion

14.69 In recent years, the scope, content, and delivery of the summing-up has changed dramatically. Routes to verdict and other directions on law are now routinely given to the jury in writing, the summing-up is now expected to focus on the issues in the case rather than comprise merely of a rehearsal of the evidence witness by witness, and judges are now permitted, indeed encouraged, to assist the jury with their approach to the evidence where there is a risk that they may otherwise unfairly bring to bear their own preconceived ideas, stereotypes, or prejudices. But as Lord Justice Leveson recognized in his Review, there is still considerable room for improvement and modernization.

14.70 In a case that may involve a number of vulnerable witnesses describing events which occurred when they were children, the sheer number of directions on law required and guidance on the approach to be taken to the evidence presents the judge with an extremely complex task. A not untypical case involving two defendants and two or more complainants in a historic sexual case now requires the judge to give a multiplicity of directions or guidance in addition to summarizing the evidence which the jury have not only heard themselves, but about which they will already have been reminded by at least two if not more advocates. Although directions are increasingly given in writing, the summary of the evidence is not, and juries will commonly have to sit and listen for hours to a judge rehearsing it all over again. It is questionable whether this really provides the assistance to the jury (which is, after all, the primary purpose of the summing-up) which they need. In the modern age, might there not be better and more helpful ways in which a judge can equip the jury for their task? As more research is carried out into the ways in which victims of traumatic events respond to them, might there be scope in the future for a standard agreed position based upon the most up-to-date research to be given to juries in place of the guidance outlined above? Is a rehearsal of the evidence really helpful or necessary—after all, in many jurisdictions, the judge does not sum up the evidence at all; if it is, why cannot an agreed summary of the relevant evidence be given to the jury in writing—why do they have to remember it? Is there scope for the route to verdict to be developed so that it does not merely set out the legal elements of the offence, but contains questions specifically relating to the facts and issues in the particular case?

Certainly, in some quarters, it is clear that there is enthusiasm for a significant **14.71** change of approach as is made clear in the Leveson Review, and the Criminal Procedure Rules and Practice Direction have been amended to give effect to some of his recommendations; but as he recognized, achieving real change will require training and 'tangible support from the Court of Appeal (Criminal Division)'.[39]

In the meantime, judges should: **14.72**

- ensure that the relevant issues are made clear at the outset of the trial to enable the jury to understand what it is that they should be looking for in the evidence and for the judge to be able to tailor his or her directions or guidance to the jury accordingly;
- give directions to the jury—whether that is at the beginning or end of the trial or at the time that they hear the evidence to which the direction relates—at whatever point those directions will be of most benefit to the jury in enabling them to consider the evidence and their approach to the evidence in the appropriate legal context;
- ensure that direction and guidance on any procedural adjustments, including special measures, is ordered at the ground rules hearing;
- ensure that directions and guidance on the approach to the evidence are fair, and balanced and tailored to the issues and evidence in the case;
- discuss directions and guidance with the advocates in advance, save where they are standard and uncontroversial directions (e.g. the use of special measures);
- ensure that a record is kept of the date and time at which directions or guidance is given and ensure that a copy is kept on the court file of any directions or route to verdict given in writing; and
- keep at the forefront of their mind that the purpose of any directions, guidance, or summary of evidence in summing-up is to assist the jury with their approach to the evidence, to enable them to view that evidence in its proper factual and legal context, and to reach fair and just conclusions on the evidence.

Further Reading

Judicial College, 'The Crown Court Compendium: Part 1' (2017), available at <https://www.judiciary.gov.uk/publications/crown-court-bench-book-directing-the-jury-2/> accessed 17 April 2017
'Review of Efficiency in Criminal Proceedings' (January 2015) (The Leveson Review), available at <https://www.judiciary.gov.uk/wp-contents/uploads/2015/01/review-of-efficiency-in-criminal-proceedings-20151.pdf> accessed 17 April 2017

---

[39] Leveson Review, [305].

15

SENTENCING

Heather Norton

A. Introduction

The statutory purposes of sentencing depend upon the age of the offender. Where the offender is aged 18 or over at the date of sentence, the court must have regard to the following purposes of sentencing:[1]

15.01

- punishment;
- the reduction of crime (including by deterrence);
- reform and rehabilitation of offenders;
- public protection; and
- reparation by offenders to persons affected by their offences.

---

[1] Criminal Justice Act 2003 (CJA 2003) s. 142.

15.02 Where the offender is under 18, the statutory principles of sentencing are different.[2] As discussed below, welfare, rehabilitation, and the prevention of further offending are the focus of the sentencing court.

15.03 In any case, however, the sentencing judge will need to determine both the seriousness of the offence (including any aggravating factors) and the culpability of the offender, as well as any mitigation available, which may include the offender's personal circumstances.

15.04 Vulnerability may derive from youth or old age; from mental disorder or physical disability. Each has been held to be, or is expressly stated in sentencing guidelines to be, a feature of the offender which may either affect his or her culpability, or provide an element of mitigation. Depending on the circumstances of the individual case, an offender's vulnerability may affect both the length of sentence and the type of sentence imposed.

15.05 This chapter considers the approach to take where vulnerability is a factor in sentencing, and the main sentences or disposals under the Mental Health Act 1983 (MHA 1983) that the sentencing court is likely to consider.

B. Young Offenders

(a) Overarching principle

15.06 When determining the appropriate sentence for an adult offender, the sentencing court is required to assess the culpability of the offender and the harm caused by the offence, taking into account both aggravating and mitigating factors and allowing the appropriate discount for any guilty plea. The starting point, though, will always be the seriousness of the offence.

15.07 When sentencing an offender aged under the age of 18, the focus shifts from the offence to the offender. The approach when sentencing a child or young person is set out in the Sentencing Council's definitive guideline—'Sentencing Children and Young People'—effective from 1 June 2017. Judges and advocates alike are expected to be familiar with its provisions and to follow the approach to sentencing set out therein (see further, Chapter 7, 'Youth Courts and Young Defendants').

15.08 The sentencing judge must keep at the forefront of their mind:

- the principal aim of the youth justice system—namely, to prevent offending by children and young persons;[3] and

---

[2] Children and Young Persons Act 1933 (CYPA 1933) s. 44; Crime and Disorder Act 1998 (CDA 1998) s. 37.
[3] CDA 1998 s. 37(1).

- the welfare of the young offender,[4] including any:

  - mental health problems;
  - learning disabilities;
  - any brain injury or traumatic life experience;
  - communication difficulties;
  - vulnerability to self-harm; and
  - exposure to neglect or abuse.

When assessing culpability, courts should have regard to the immaturity of the **15.09** offender, not just the chronological age, and take into account the extent to which the offending behaviour may be reflective of normal adolescent behaviour/ experimentation. As stated by the then Lord Chief Justice, Lord Judge in *R v. N, D and L:*[5]

> ... the youth of the offender is widely recognised as requiring a different approach from that which would be adopted in relation to an adult. Even within the category of youth, the response to an offence is likely to be very different, depending on whether the offender is at the lower end of the age bracket, in the middle or towards the top end. In many cases the maturity of the offender will be at least as important as the chronological age ... There will from time to time be individual offenders whose maturity levels are well in advance of most youths of a similar chronological age. All these decisions are specific and individual. They must reflect all the material available to the sentencing judge, including the circumstances of the offence and the behaviour of the offender whose case is under consideration in the context of that offence. If justified, the maturity of the youth is a factor to which weight should properly be given because on this basis such mitigation arising from the youth of the offender is or would be properly reduced or diminished, sometimes (on rare occasions) to virtual extinction. [155]

Sentences should always be tailored to the individual offender, should be deter- **15.10** mined having regard to the principal aims of the youth justice system, and should where possible be rehabilitative, rather than merely punitive. Many young offenders are, because of age and/or circumstance, particularly vulnerable, and courts should bear in mind the potentially disproportionate effect that a criminal sanction may have on a young person.

(b) Relevant age and availability of sentence

(i) Basic rule: age at the date of conviction determines availability of sentence

As a general rule, it is the age of the offender at the date of conviction that deter- **15.11** mines which sentencing options are applicable and the maximum length of any custodial term.

---

[4] CYPA 1933 s. 44(1).
[5] [2011] 1 Cr App R (S) 22.

15.12 The date of conviction is the date upon which the defendant either pleads or is found guilty. In *R v Danga*,[6] the Court of Appeal held that:

> As a matter of statutory construction … the age of the offender is his or her age at the date of conviction, that is the day when a jury pronounces a verdict of guilty or when the plea of guilty is entered. This conclusion also makes practical sense. Most defendants are sentenced on the day that they are convicted. It is only for administrative reasons or to enable the court to acquire more information that sentences are passed at a later date.

This construction and the practical effect of it was confirmed in *R v Robson*:[7] 'As a matter of statutory construction, we conclude that the age of the offender for the purpose of determining which of the statutory regimes … applies to him is the offender's age at the date of conviction'; and more recently in *R v Morgan*:[8] 'It is age at the date of conviction, not at the date of sentence, which determines the available custodial sentencing options.'

(ii) Exceptions to the basic rule

15.13 There are some exceptions to the basic rule. These exceptions are largely confined to offences for which minimum prescribed custodial sentencing provisions apply. The following sentences depend on the offender's age at the date of the commission of the offence, rather than the date of conviction:

- a sentence of detention during Her Majesty's pleasure for an offence of murder—offender under 18 at date of offence;[9]
- minimum prescribed term for a third offence of domestic burglary—offender 18 or over at date of offence;[10]
- minimum prescribed term for a third offence of class A drug trafficking—offender 18 or over at date of offence;[11]
- minimum prescribed term for offences of:
  - possession of an offensive weapon (PCA 1953 s. 1);
  - possession of a bladed article (CJA 1988 s. 139);
  - having a bladed article or offensive weapon on school premises (CJA 1988 s. 139A).

Where the offender is 16 or over at date of offence and has a previous conviction for a 'relevant' offence:

---

[6] [1992] 13 Cr App R (S) 408.
[7] [2006] EWCA Crim 1414 at [13]–[14].
[8] [2014] EWCA Crim 2587.
[9] PCC(S)A 2000 s. 90.
[10] PCC(S)A 2000 s. 111.
[11] PCC (S)A 2000 s. 110.

- minimum prescribed term for certain firearms offences[12]—offender 16 or over at date of offence;[13]
- minimum prescribed term for using someone to mind a weapon—offender 16 or over at date of offence.[14]

(iii) Approach when offender crosses a relevant age threshold

Although in the majority of cases it is the age at the date of the conviction which determines the statutory regime applicable and the availability of sentence type, where an offender crosses a relevant age threshold between the date of the commission of the offence and the date of conviction, he or she may be liable to receive a greater sentence than that which would have been available at the time he or she committed the offence. **15.14**

In such circumstances, 'the court should take as its starting point the sentence likely to have been imposed on the date on which the offence was committed'.[15] This principle is of particular importance where a young offender crosses the threshold from 14 to 15. As a custodial sentence can only be imposed upon a young offender under 15 if he or she is a persistent offender or has committed a 'grave crime' warranting detention for a period of at least two years, then unless the offender falls into either of those categories, if he or she was 14 at the date of the commission of the offence but turns 15 before sentence, the starting point will be a non-custodial sentence.

In *R v Ghafoor*,[16] the Court of Appeal, having affirmed that the form of sentence available is dictated by the age of the defendant on conviction, stated that: **15.15**

> The approach to be adopted where a defendant crosses a relevant age threshold between the date of the commission of the offence and the date of conviction should now be clear. The starting point is the sentence that the defendant would have been likely to receive if he had been sentenced at the date of the commission of the offence. It has been described as a 'powerful factor'. That is for the obvious reason that, as Mr Emmerson points out, the philosophy of restricting sentencing powers in relation to young persons reflects both (a) society's acceptance that young offenders are less responsible for their actions and therefore less culpable than adults, and (b) the recognition that, in consequence, sentencing them should place greater emphasis on rehabilitation, and less on retribution and deterrence than in the case of adults. It should be noted that the 'starting point' is not the *maximum* sentence that could lawfully have been imposed, but the sentence that the offender would have been likely to receive.[17]

---

[12] Firearms Act 1968 ss 5(1)(a), (ab), (ac), (ad), (ae), (af), and (c), 5(1A)(a), 16, 16A, 17, 18, 19, and 20.

[13] FA 1968 s. 51A(1).

[14] Violent Crime Reduction Act 2006 s. 29.

[15] Sentencing Council, 'Sentencing Children and Young People: Definitive Guideline' (June 2017), 6.2.

[16] [2002] EWCA Crim 1857.

[17] ibid. at [31] (emphasis in the original).

Although the court went on to state that there would 'have to be good reasons for departing from the starting point', they made clear that the approach to be taken was not an inflexible one. The seriousness of the offence, the need for deterrence, and information coming to light about the culpability of the offender in between the date of the commission of the offence and the date of conviction have all been cited as examples of when it might be appropriate to apply a greater starting point.[18]

(iv) Determining the offender's age

15.16 There will be occasions when the offender's age is either unknown or is in dispute. Where the offender is or appears to be a 'child or young person', CYPA 1933 s. 99(1) requires the court to 'make due inquiry as to the age of that person, and for that purpose shall take such evidence as may be forthcoming at the hearing of the case'.

15.17 Similar provisions can be found in the Powers of Criminal Courts (Sentencing) Act 2000 (PCC(S)A 2000) s. 164(1): 'For the purposes of any provision of this Act which requires the determination of the age of a person by the court ... his age shall be deemed to be that which it appears to the court ... to be after considering any available evidence'; and the Magistrates' Courts Act 1980 s. 150: '[a person's] age shall be deemed to be or to have been that which appears to the court after considering any available evidence to have been his age at that time'.

15.18 The nature of the evidence that will be required and the extent of the investigations that should be carried out in order to ascertain age were considered in *R(B) v London Borough of Merton*[19] and *R v L*.[20] In the former case, which concerned an asylum seeker, the High Court observed that:

> ... the assessment of age in borderline cases is a difficult matter, but it is not complex. It is not an issue which requires anything approaching a trial ... it is a matter which may be determined informally, provided safeguards of minimum standards of inquiry and of fairness are adhered to ... Except in clear cases, the decision maker cannot determine age solely on the basis of the appearance of the applicant. In general, the decision maker must seek to elicit the general background of the applicant, including his family circumstances and history, his educational background, and his activities during the previous few years. Ethnic and cultural information may also be important. If there is reason to doubt the applicant's statement as to his age, the decision maker will have to make an assessment of his credibility, and he will have to ask questions designed to test his credibility. [36]–[37]

15.19 In *R v L*, a conjoined appeal concerning human trafficking, the Lord Chief Justice giving the judgment of the court stated that, where the issue of the defendant's

---

[18] *R v Bowker* [2007] EWCA Crim 1608; and *R v G* [2010] EWCA Crim 1062.
[19] [2003] EWHC 1689 (Admin).
[20] [2013] EWCA Crim 991.

age arises, the requirement of CYPA 1933 s. 99(1) and other similar legislative provisions to make 'due enquiry' into age:

> ... requires much more than superficial observation of the defendant in court or in the dock to enable the judge to make an appropriate age assessment ... when an age issue arises, the court must be provided with all the relevant evidence which bears on it. Although the court may adjourn proceedings for further investigations to be conducted, these have to be undertaken by one or other or both sides, or by the relevant social services. The court is not vested with any jurisdiction, and is not provided with the resources to conduct its own investigations into the age of a potential defendant until after the investigation has completed its course and the individual in question is brought before the court.

There is no onus of proof on the defendant to prove their age.

As a consequence of 'deeming' provisions set out at CJA 1982 s. 1(6) and CYPA 1933 s. 99(1), even where a determination as to age is subsequently shown to be incorrect, the sentence passed will not therefore be unlawful. Moreover, CYPA 1933 s. 48 states that a youth court may proceed with the hearing and determination of a charge against a person believed to be a child or young person, 'notwithstanding that it is discovered that the person in question is not a child or young person'.

(c)   Categories of young offender

The categories of young offender are as follows: **15.20**

- <u>Adult offenders</u>: For the purposes of criminal procedure and mode of trial, an adult offender is a person aged 18 or over; however, it is only when the adult attains 21 that he or she becomes liable to a sentence of imprisonment.
- <u>Juvenile offenders</u>: A juvenile offender refers to any person under the age of 18. Juveniles may be subdivided into:
  - ◦ <u>Young persons</u>: offenders aged 14–17;[21] and
  - ◦ <u>Children</u>: offenders aged 10–13.

The age of criminal responsibility is 10 years. Therefore, 'it shall be conclusively presumed that no child under the age of ten years can be guilty of an offence'.[22]

(i)   Persistent offenders

In respect of youths under the age of 15, certain sentences are only available for   **15.21** 'persistent offenders'. They are:

- a Youth Rehabilitation Order with Intensive Supervision and Surveillance, or Fostering;[23] and
- a Detention and Training Order.[24]

---

[21] CYPA 1933 s. 107.
[22] ibid. s. 50.
[23] Criminal Justice and Immigration Act 2008 (CJIA 2008) s. 1(4)(c).
[24] PCC(S)A 2000 s. 100(2).

15.22 There is no statutory definition of a 'persistent offender', although useful guidance can be found in the Sentencing Council's 'Sentencing Children and Young People: Definitive Guideline' at paragraph 6.4. In *R v M*,[25] the Court of Appeal stated that: '"Persistence" is a creature which, perhaps like an elephant, should be capable of being recognized when it is encountered without further definition'. It is for the court to determine on a case-by-case basis whether a young person falls into this category; however, the following general points can be stated:

- A persistent offender will have a history of previous offending. This may be demonstrated by not only previous convictions, but reprimands, final warnings, or conditional cautions.[26]
- There is a difference between a 'repeat' offender and a 'persistent' offender; a young person who has committed only one previous offence cannot properly be termed a 'persistent' offender.[27]
- The court should take into account not just the number of previous offences, but also the nature of the offences, the lapse of time between offences, and any changes in patterns of offending.[28]

(ii) Dangerous offenders

15.23 A young offender will only be liable to be sentenced as a dangerous offender where:

- the offender is convicted of a specified violent or sexual offence;[29] and
- the court is of the opinion that there is a significant risk of serious harm from future specified offences committed by the offender; and
- the court considers that a custodial sentence of at least four years would be justified for the offence.

When considering future conduct, and whether it may give rise to significant risk of serious harm, the court should bear in mind a young offender's levels of maturity and the fact that a young person will change and develop more rapidly than adults.[30]

(d) Procedure

(i) Where to sentence

15.24 The starting point is that a child or young person should be tried and sentenced in the youth court; however, there are certain circumstances in which a juvenile defendant must or may be committed to the Crown Court.

---

[25] [2008] EWCA 3329.
[26] *R v D* [2001] 1 Cr App R (S) 59; *R v B* [2001] 1 Cr App R (S) 113.
[27] *R v M* [2008] EWCA 3329.
[28] ibid.
[29] As listed in CJA 2003 Sch. 15.
[30] *R v Lang* [2005] EWCA Crim 2864.

(ii) When to commit to the Crown Court

The process for determining where a juvenile defendant's case should be heard **15.25**
is not straightforward. The procedure for allocation of cases is set out in CDA
1998 ss 51 and 51A and is discussed in Chapter 7, 'Youth Courts and Young
Defendants'.

In broad terms, however, a child or young person must be sent to the Crown
Court to be dealt with where charged with:

- homicide;
- certain firearms offences subject to a mandatory minimum sentence of three
  years and where the offender is over the age of 16 at the time of the offence;
- certain cases of complex fraud;
- a specified offence under CJA 2003 s. 224 where, if found guilty, the criteria
  for an extended sentence under s. 226B would be made out.

A young defendant may also be sent to the Crown Court where either: **15.26**

- the defendant is jointly charged with an adult who has been or is being sent
  to the Crown Court and the youth court considers that it is in the interests of
  justice that the cases are kept together; or
- the offence meets the criteria for a 'grave crime'.

In addition, where a young defendant indicates a guilty plea, the youth court
may commit the defendant to the Crown Court for sentence if it is of the opinion
that its powers of sentence (up to twenty-four months' Detention and Training
Order) are insufficient, and that either a sentence under PCC(S)A 2000 s. 91 or
an extended sentence of detention under CJA 2003 s. 226B is likely.

(iii) When to remit to the youth court

When a juvenile is convicted in the Crown Court of an offence other than homi- **15.27**
cide, the court must remit the offender to the youth court for sentence, unless
satisfied that it would be undesirable to do so.[31]
Relevant factors may include:

- the desirability that the judge who presided over the trial and who will therefore
  have a detailed knowledge of the facts of the case should also determine sentence;
- where there is more than one defendant, the risk of disparity were the defendants to be sentenced by different courts;
- the increased delay and expenditure incurred by further hearings;
- the expertise of the youth court in dealing with young offenders; and
- (in an appropriate case) the non-availability in the Crown Court of a referral
  order as a means of disposal for a first-time offender who has pleaded guilty.

---

[31] PCC(S)A 2008 s. 8.

15.28 When a juvenile is convicted in the adult magistrates' court, he or she must be remitted to the youth court unless dealt with by way of a fine, an order binding over his or her parents or guardians, or, where applicable, a referral order.

(iv) Requirement for legal representation

15.29 Any court should be slow to pass sentence on a vulnerable defendant in the absence of legal representation, especially if that sentence is a custodial one. Where a defendant is under the age of 21, however, there is a statutory bar on the magistrates' or Crown Courts passing a custodial sentence in the absence of legal representation, unless:

- a representation order was made, but subsequently withdrawn due to his or her conduct;
- his or her financial resources were such that he or she was not eligible for representation; or
- having been informed of his or her right to apply for representation, and having the opportunity to do so, he or she either refused or failed to apply.

15.30 The sentences to which this rule applies are:

- detention under PCC(S)A s. 91;
- custody for life under either PCC(S)A s. 93 or 94;
- detention in a young offender institution;
- a Detention and Training Order;
- a Youth Rehabilitation Order containing either a local authority residence requirement or a fostering requirement.

(v) Attendance of parents or guardians

15.31 There is a statutory requirement for parents or guardians of a young person aged under 16 to attend all court proceedings, unless the court is satisfied that this would be unreasonable having regard to the circumstances of the case.
Where the young offender is aged 16 to 17, the court may require the parents or guardians to attend if it is deemed desirable.[32]

(vi) Reports

15.32 Where the offender is under the age of 18, the court must obtain and consider a pre-sentence report before imposing either a custodial sentence or a Youth Rehabilitation Order.[33] In respect of custodial sentences, the court will require a report in order to assess whether:

- the offence(s) is so serious that neither a fine nor a community sentence can be justified for it;[34]

---

[32] ibid. s. 34A.
[33] CJA 2003 s. 158(1).
[34] ibid. s. 152(2).

- the custodial sentence must be for the shortest period of time commensurate with the seriousness of the offence;[35]
- the 'dangerousness' test is met—detention for life;[36]
- the 'dangerousness' test is met—extended determinate sentence.[37]

In respect of community sentences (Youth Rehabilitation Order), the report will enable the court to assess whether: **15.33**

- the offence(s) is serious enough to warrant a community order;[38]
- the restrictions on liberty imposed by the order are commensurate with the seriousness of the offence;[39]
- the necessary pre-conditions are met for imposing a youth rehabilitation order with intensive supervision and surveillance, or with fostering;[40]
- the offender is suitable for the proposed requirement(s) to be imposed by a youth rehabilitation order.[41]

The court does not have to obtain a pre-sentence report if it decides that it is unnecessary to do so; however, in the case of an offender under the age of 18, it can only reach such a decision if there is a previous report in existence and the court has considered the information contained within it.[42] **15.34**

Any report, which is required before the court passes a custodial sentence on an offender under 18, must be in writing.[43] **15.35**

A full copy of the report must be given to the prosecution and to the offender's legal representative. A copy must also be given to the offender's parent or guardian (or local authority with parental responsibility) present in court, but may be redacted if it contains information, the disclosure of which would be likely to create a risk of significant harm to the offender.[44] **15.36**

(e) Sentencing guidelines

The Sentencing Council has issued a definitive guideline setting out the overarching principles to be followed when sentencing youths: 'Sentencing Children and Young People: Overarching Principles and Offence Specific Guidelines for Sexual Offences and Robbery', effective from 1 June 2017.[45] **15.37**

---

[35] ibid. s. 153(2).
[36] ibid. s. 266(1)(b).
[37] ibid. s. 226B(1)(b).
[38] ibid. s. 148(1).
[39] ibid. s. 148(2)(b).
[40] CJIA 2008 s. 1(4)(b) and (c).
[41] CJA 2003 s. 156(3).
[42] ibid. s. 156(5).
[43] ibid. s. 158(1B).
[44] ibid. s. 159(2) and (3).
[45] See <http://www.sentencingcouncil.org.uk/wp-content/uploads/Sentencing-Children-and-young-people-Definitive-Guide_FINAL_WEB.pdf> accessed 17 April 2017.

15.38   Save for where offence-specific guidelines for juvenile offenders are provided (robbery and sexual offences), if a custodial sentence cannot be avoided, the sentencing court should utilize the adult sentencing guidelines and apply a sentence which is reduced proportionally.[46]

(f) Non-custodial sentences

(i) *Absolute or conditional discharge*

15.39   The details pertaining to absolute or conditional discharge[47] are as follows:

- <u>Age</u>: Available at any age.
- <u>Length of order</u>: Not exceeding three years (conditional discharge).
- <u>Restrictions</u>: A conditional discharge is not available for an offender who has been convicted of an offence within two years of receiving a second youth caution, save in exceptional circumstances.[48]
- <u>Combination with other orders</u>: May not be combined with a fine or referral order.
- <u>Breaches</u>: Where a further offence is committed during the period of the conditional discharge, the court may (but does not have to) re-sentence for the original offence. If the court does proceed to re-sentence, it does so on the basis of the offender's age at the date of re-sentencing, not the date of conviction.

(ii) *Reparation order*

15.40   The details pertaining to reparation orders are as follows:

- <u>Age</u>: Under 18.
- <u>Length of order</u>: The order must not require the offender to work for more than a total of twenty-four hours.[49] Reparation must be made within three months of making the order.[50]
- <u>Reports</u>: The court must obtain a written report from probation or the local youth offending team (YOT) setting out the type of work that is suitable for the offender to undertake in reparation, and the attitude of the victim(s) to the proposed requirements.[51]
- <u>Restrictions</u>: The person to whom reparation is to be made must consent to the order.[52] The requirements specified in the order must, in so far as is practicable,

---

[46] The 2017 guidelines suggest a sentence of between a half and two-thirds of the length of that which would be applied to an adult offender. The guidelines emphasize that this reduction 'is only a rough guide and must not be applied mechanistically'.

[47] PCC(S)A 2000 s. 12.

[48] CDA 1998 s. 66ZB(5) and (6).

[49] PCC(S)A 2000 s. 74(1)(a).

[50] ibid. s. 74(8).

[51] ibid. s. 73(5).

[52] ibid. s. 74(1)(b).

avoid any conflict with the offender's religious beliefs, and must not interfere with the times at which the offender normally works or attends school or any other educational establishment.[53]

- <u>Combination with other orders</u>: A reparation order cannot be combined with a custodial sentence, a youth rehabilitation order (whether made at the time or to which the offender is already subject), or a referral order.
- <u>Breaches</u>: Where the court is satisfied that there has been a failure to comply with any requirement of a reparation order, the court may impose a fine of not more than £1,000, or revoke the order and re-sentence for the original offence.
- <u>Additional note</u>: If a reparation order is not made where it would be open to the court to make such an order, reasons must be given.[54]

(iii) Fine

The details pertaining to fines are as follows: **15.41**

- <u>Availability</u>: In the magistrates' or Crown Court.
- <u>Age</u>: Available at any age.
- <u>Restrictions</u>: Maximum fine when offender is under 14 = £250; maximum fine when aged 14–18 = £1,000.[55]

Where the offender is aged under 16, the court must order the fine to be paid by the offender's parent or guardian, and may make such an order if the offender is aged between 16 and 18, unless the parent or guardian cannot be found or it would be unreasonable to make that order in all the circumstances.[56]

An order requiring a parent or guardian to pay the fine can only be made if they have been given the opportunity to be heard.[57]

(iv) Referral order

The details pertaining to referral orders[58] are as follows: **15.42**

- <u>Availability</u>: Available in the youth court and magistrates' court, but only in the Crown Court on appeal; a referral order is mandatory for first-time offenders in the circumstances set out below.
- <u>Age</u>: Under 18.
- <u>Mandatory order</u>: The youth or magistrates' court *must* make a referral order where:
  - the offender is aged under 18;

---

[53] ibid. s. 74(3).
[54] ibid. s. 73(8).
[55] ibid. s. 135.
[56] ibid. s. 137(1).
[57] ibid. s. 137(4).
[58] ibid. s. 16.

- o the offender pleaded guilty to each offence for which he or she is to be sentenced;
- o the offender has never been convicted by or before a court in the United Kingdom or another Member State of any offence;
- o the offence for which he or she is to be sentenced is punishable with imprisonment, but neither the offence nor any connected offence is one for which the sentence is fixed by law;
- o the court does not intend to deal with the case by way of a discharge, hospital order, or custodial sentence.
- Reports: Although reports are not mandatory, for many first-time offenders aged 15 or over, the court will be facing a stark choice between making a referral order and passing a custodial sentence. The court is likely to require at least a pre-sentence report, and very possibly further information from any specialist agencies involved with the child; particularly where the decision may be finely balanced. In such a situation, the YOT may convene a panel to make a more robust suggestion for the possible referral order in the hope of persuading the sentencing court that such an order is a real alternative to custody.
- Discretionary order: The court *may* make a referral order where:
  - o the offender is under 18; and
  - o the offender pleaded guilty to at least one offence for which he or she is to be sentenced.
- Length of order: Not less than three and not more than twelve months.
- Making the order: The court must:
  - o specify the YOT responsible for implementing the order;
  - o require the offender to attend meetings of a youth offender panel to be established by the YOT; and
  - o specify the period for which the youth offender contract is to have effect.
- Terms: Under a referral order, the offender is required to attend meetings with the youth offender panel, and to enter into a 'youth offender contract'. The contract is a 'programme of behaviour' intended to prevent reoffending.[59] PCC(S)A 2000 s. 23(2)–(4) sets out the terms that may be included in such a contract. The court may—and if the offender is aged under 16, must—make an order requiring the offender's parent or guardian, or a representative of the local authority, to attend meetings of the youth offender panel.[60]
- Combination with other orders: Where an offender sentenced to a referral order is also sentenced for a connected offence, the court must in respect of that other offence either make a referral order or an absolute discharge. The court must not impose:
  - o a Youth Rehabilitation Order;

---

[59] ibid. s. 23(1).
[60] ibid. s. 20.

- a fine;
- a reparation order;
- a conditional discharge; or
- a bind over (whether of the offender or his or her parents or guardians).
- Breaches: If the offender breaches the order (by, for example, failing to enter into the youth offender contract, or by failing to comply with the terms of the contract), the offender may be referred back to the court by the youth offender panel.

The court may then revoke the order and re-sentence the offender, impose a fine of up to £2,500, allow the order to continue with the existing contract, or extend the period for which the contract has effect for a maximum of three months (provided that the total period does not exceed twelve months).
- Commission of further offences: If the offender is convicted of a further offence committed after the referral order was made, the court may revoke the order and re-sentence the offender, or extend the period of the order to a total maximum of twelve months.

(v) Youth Rehabilitation Order (YRO)—basic order

The details pertaining to YROs,[61] basic order, are as follows: **15.43**

- Availability: Available in any court, save for a first-time offender sentenced in the youth or magistrates' court who qualifies for a mandatory referral order, or where a mandatory custodial sentence is required.
- Age: Under 18 at date of conviction.
- Length of order: Up to three years.
- Reports: Before making the order, the court must obtain and consider information about the offender's family circumstances and the likely effect of such an order on those circumstances.[62] The court must also be satisfied that where more than one requirement is attached to the order, those requirements are compatible with each other and (in so far as is practicable) that they do not conflict with the offender's religious beliefs, or attendance for work or education.[63]
- Restrictions: A YRO is a community order, and as such can only be made where the court considers that:
  - the offence, or combination of offences, are serious enough to warrant such a sentence;
  - the requirements forming part of the order are the most suitable for the offender; and
  - the restrictions on liberty imposed by the order are commensurate with the seriousness of the offence(s).[64]

---

[61] CJIA 2008 s. 1.
[62] ibid. Sch. 1, para. 28.
[63] ibid. Sch.1, para. 29.
[64] CJA 2003 s. 148.

- <u>Requirements</u>: The requirements that may be attached to a YRO are as follows:
  - activity requirement—up to ninety days;
  - curfew—two to sixteen hours per day for up to twelve months;
  - must be electronically monitored unless court considers it inappropriate or householder refuses consent;
  - drug treatment (and drug testing)—may be residential, or non-residential
    - must be recommended;
    - court must be satisfied that the offender is dependent on, or has a propensity to misuse drugs, which dependency or propensity requires and may be susceptible to treatment;
    - court must be satisfied that arrangements for treatment can or have been made;
    - offender must consent.
  - education requirement—must not extend beyond compulsory school age
    - court must consult with the local education authority;
    - court must be satisfied that arrangements have been made for the offender to receive appropriate full-time education;
    - court must be satisfied that such a requirement is necessary for securing the good conduct of the offender or to prevent the commission of further offences.
  - exclusion from a specified place—up to three months
    - must be electronically monitored unless arrangements cannot be made or it is otherwise inappropriate.
  - intoxicating substance treatment requirement
    - must be recommended;
    - court must be satisfied that the offender is dependent on, or has a propensity to intoxicating substances, which dependency or propensity requires and may be susceptible to treatment;
    - court must be satisfied that arrangements for treatment can or have been made;
    - offender must consent.
  - local authority residence requirement—up to six months or until reaches 18, whichever is the shorter
    - must be satisfied that the offending behaviour was due to a significant extent to the circumstances in which the offender was living;
    - must be satisfied that the imposition of the requirement will aid rehabilitation;
    - must consult with the local authority and parent or guardian.
  - mental health treatment requirement
    - must be under the direction of a registered medical practitioner or psychologist;

- court must be satisfied that the mental condition of the offender is such as requires and may be susceptible to treatment, but is not such as to warrant the making of a hospital order or guardianship order;
- court must be satisfied that arrangements have been, or can be made for treatment;
- offender must consent.
  - programme requirement
    - must be recommended.
  - prohibited activity requirement
    - must be recommended.
  - supervision—for a period equal in length to the term of the order

The following requirements are age restricted:
  - Attendance Centre—twelve to thirty-six hours, depending on age at the time of conviction
    - under 14—up to twelve hours
    - under 16—twelve to twenty-four hours
    - 16 or over—twelve to thirty-six hours
  - Residence—only available where aged 16 or over at date of conviction
    - court must consider the offender's home surroundings before making the order;
    - place of residence specified cannot be a 'hostel or other institution' unless recommended.
  - unpaid work—only available where aged 16 or 17 at the time of conviction; 40–240 hours to be completed within twelve months
    - court must be satisfied that the offender is a suitable person to work under such a requirement.

- <u>Breaches</u>: If the court is satisfied that the offender has failed without reasonable excuse to comply with the terms of the order, it may allow the order to continue unaltered; impose a fine; amend the terms of the order; or revoke the order and re-sentence.

  If there has been a wilful and persistent failure to comply with the order, the court may impose a Youth Rehabilitation Order with intensive supervision and surveillance.

- <u>Commission of further offences</u>: The court may revoke and deal with the offender for the original offence unless it considers that it would not be in the interests of justice to do so, having regard to the circumstances that have arisen since the YRO was made.

- <u>Revocation and amendment</u>: The court may revoke (and, if appropriate, re-sentence) the offender on application by the offender or the responsible officer if it appears to the court to be in the interests of justice to do so.

(vi) Youth Rehabilitation Order and Intensive Supervision and Surveillance (ISS)

15.44 The details pertaining to YROs and ISSs are as follows:

- Availability: Only available if a custodial sentence would otherwise have been appropriate and offender is over 15 at the date of conviction or is a 'persistent offender'.[65]
- Age: Over 15, unless a persistent offender.
- Length of order: Six months to three years.
- Requirements: A YRO and ISS must include:
  - an extended activity requirement—90–180 days;
  - a supervision requirement; and
  - a curfew requirement (+ electronic monitoring).

  It may also include any of the other requirements that may be attached to the basic order, but may not include a fostering requirement.
- Breaches: If the court is satisfied that the offender has failed without reasonable excuse to comply with the terms of the order, it may allow the order to continue unaltered; impose a fine; amend the terms of the order; or revoke the order and re-sentence.

  If the court revokes the order and re-sentences the offender, and if the original offence was punishable with imprisonment, the court may impose a custodial sentence.

  If the YRO+ISS was imposed following an earlier breach, and the original offence was not punishable with imprisonment, the court may impose a Detention and Training Order for a period not exceeding four months.
- Commission of further offences: As for basic order.

(vii) Youth Rehabilitation Order and fostering

15.45 The details pertaining to YROs and fostering are as follows:

- Availability: Only available if a custodial sentence would otherwise have been appropriate and offender is over the age of 15 at the date of conviction or is a 'persistent offender'.[66]
- Age: Over 15, unless a persistent offender.
- Length of order: Maximum of twelve months or until reaches the age of 18, whichever is shorter.
- Criteria and restrictions: The court must be satisfied that the offending behaviour was due to a significant extent to the circumstances in which the offender was living, and that a fostering requirement will aid rehabilitation.

  The court must consult the offender's parents or guardians and the local authority.

---

[65] See paragraph 15.21, 'Persistent offenders', above.
[66] cf. paragraph 15.21 above.

A fostering requirement may not be made unless the offender is legally represented (where eligible and entitled to funding).

- Requirements: The court must, in addition to the fostering requirement, impose a supervision requirement, and may impose any other requirement(s) that could be attached to the basic order.
- Breaches and Commission of further offences: As for basic order.

(g) Custodial sentences

No custodial sentence is available in the youth court for an offender aged 10 to 11. Where a young offender is aged 12 to 14, a custodial sentence can only be imposed if the child is either a persistent offender or has committed a 'grave crime' warranting detention for a period of at least two years.   **15.46**

Where a custodial sentence is imposed in the youth court, it must be a Detention and Training Order (DTO). The minimum length of time for which a DTO can be imposed is four months—a longer minimum term than that which can be imposed for an adult offender. Consequently, the threshold for imposing a custodial sentence should be higher. A DTO can only be imposed for a term of four, six, eight, ten, twelve, eighteen, or twenty-four months.   **15.47**

A custodial sentence in the Crown Court can range from a DTO to the maximum for the offence. The starting point for an offender aged 15 to 17 is likely to be between one-half to two-thirds of the appropriate starting point for an adult offender; a child aged under 15 should receive a still greater reduction.[67]   **15.48**

Any custodial sentence should be regarded as the sentence of last resort, where the offence is 'so serious that neither a fine alone, nor a community sentence can be justified'.[68] Any custodial sentence passed must be the shortest commensurate with the seriousness of the offence.   **15.49**

(i) Detention and Training Order

The details pertaining to Detention and Training Orders[69] are as follows: **15.50**

- Availability: Where the offence of which the offender is convicted is punishable with imprisonment, and the offence is so serious that only custody is justified or the offender has breached a YRO+ISS imposed for wilful and persistent breach of a YRO.

---

[67] 'Sentencing Children and Young People: Definitive Guideline', 6.46.
[68] CJA 2003 s. 152(2).
[69] PCC(S)A 2000 ss 100–7.

- Age:[70] offenders aged 15 to 17 at the date of conviction, and 12 to 14 if a persistent offender.[71] Not available for a child under 12.
- Length of order: Four, six, eight, ten, twelve, eighteen, or twenty-four months. The term must not exceed the maximum period that the Crown Court could impose for an adult offender (21 or over); consequently, there are a number of offences—such as criminal damage—for which a DTO could not be imposed as the offence carries a maximum sentence of less than four months.

  Consecutive orders can be imposed up to the maximum period of twenty-four months, but in a magistrates'court, cannot exceed the maximum that that court could impose for summary offences.[72]

  In determining the appropriate term of the order, the court must take account of any time spent in custody on remand or subject to a qualifying curfew and reduce the sentence accordingly, as unlike all other custodial sentences, time served is not automatically deducted.
- Effect of order: The offender will spend half the term in custody before being released; time spent on remand or subject to a qualifying curfew is not deducted. Following release, the offender will remain under supervision for the remainder of the term. Where the offender is aged 18 when released from custody, and where the term of the order is less than twelve months, an additional twelve-month period of supervision will be imposed.
- Breaches: If the offender fails to comply with a supervision requirement, the court may order the offender to be detained for the remainder of the order or a period not exceeding three months (whichever is shorter); order the offender to be subject to supervision for the remainder of the order or a period not exceeding three months (whichever is shorter); impose a fine of up to £1,000; or take no action.
- Commission of further offences: If the offender commits a further offence punishable with imprisonment while subject to supervision, the sentencing court may order the offender to be detained for all or part of the period of the order which remained at the date of the commission of the new offence. Any new DTO may be ordered to run concurrently or consecutively.

---

[70] PCC(S)A 2000 s. 100(2)(b) provides for a DTO to be passed on an offender under the age of 12 if: (i) the court is of the opinion that only a custodial sentence would be adequate to protect the public from further offending by him or her; and (ii) the offence was committed on or after such a date as the Secretary of State appoints. No such date has been appointed and it follows that, as of the time of writing, a DTO remains unavailable for offenders aged under 12.

[71] See paragraph 15.21, 'Persistent offenders', above.

[72] *B v Leeds Crown Court* [2016] EWHC 1230.

(ii) Section 91 detention

The details pertaining to s. 91 detention[73] are as follows: **15.51**

- <u>Availability</u>: Only available in the Crown Court and where the offence is a grave crime, that is:
  - an offence punishable in the case of an adult (21 or over) with imprisonment for fourteen years or more;
  - an offence contrary to the Sexual Offences Act 2003 s. 3, 13, 25, or 26; or
  - the offender is aged 16 to 18 and the offence is a firearms offence subject to minimum sentencing provisions, but where exceptional circumstances have been found justifying a lesser sentence; and
  - the court is of the opinion that neither a YRO nor a DTO is suitable.
- <u>Age</u>: 10 to 18 save in respect of certain firearms offences as above.
- <u>Duration of order</u>: There is no minimum length, save that a sentence of detention will rarely be passed for a period of less than two years; in such circumstances, a DTO is likely to be more appropriate. The maximum length is that available for the offence.
- <u>Multiple offences</u>: The proper approach will be to pass a single sentence of detention appropriate for the totality of offending and order no separate penalty for any lesser offences.
- <u>Effect of sentence</u>: An offender sentenced to a period of detention under s. 91 will serve half the sentence in custody before being released, whereupon he or she will remain on licence for the remainder of the period. If, exceptionally, the term of sentence passed was less than twelve months, the minimum period of licence on release will be three months.

(iii) Detention in a young offender institution

Details pertaining to detention in a young offender institution are as follows: **15.52**

- <u>Availability</u>: Where the offence of which the offender is convicted is punishable with imprisonment, and the offence is so serious that only custody is justified. This form of sentence is abolished 'from a date to be appointed' by the Criminal Justice and Court Services Act 2000 s. 61; however, this section is not as yet in force.
- <u>Age</u>: 18–21.
- <u>Duration of order</u>: Minimum length is twenty-one days; maximum is that available for the offence; this sentence can be suspended.

(iv) Extended sentence of detention

Details pertaining to extended sentence of detention[74] are as follows: **15.53**

---

[73] PCC(S)A 2000 s. 91.
[74] CJA 2003 s. 226B.

- Availability: Only available in the Crown Court and where:
  - the offender is convicted of a specified offence under CJA 2003 Sch. 15;
  - the court considers that there is a significant risk of serious harm occasioned by the commission by the defendant of further specified offences (the 'dangerousness condition');
  - the court is not required to impose a sentence of either custody for life (where aged 18 to 21) or detention for life under s. 91 (where aged under 18);
  - the custodial term would be at least four years; or, where the offender is 18–21; and
  - at the time the offence was committed, the offender had been convicted of an offence under CJA 2003 Sch. 15B.
- Age: Under 21.
- Duration of order: Unless the offender is 18 or over and has committed a previous Sch. 15B offence, the minimum custodial term must be four years. The four-year minimum must apply to at least one offence for which the offender is to be sentenced; where there are multiple offences, it is not permissible to pass consecutive sentences to reach the four-year minimum period; however, the court can consider the totality of the offending behaviour and where appropriate aggregate the sentences that would otherwise be passed by imposing a sentence of at least four years on one offence, and pass concurrent sentences on the others.[75]

  The extension period must be for such length as is necessary for the purpose of protecting members of the public from serious harm occasioned by the offender of further specified offences; but must in any event be for a minimum of one year up to a maximum of five years for a violent offence, or eight years for a sexual offence.
- Effect of sentence: Where the sentence is imposed on or after 13 April 2015, the offender will be referred to the Parole Board for consideration for release when two-thirds of the custodial term have been served. If not released at an earlier stage, the offender must be released at the expiry of the custodial term.

  Following release, the offender will be on licence for the remainder of the custodial term (if any) and for the extended licence period.

(v) Life sentence (discretionary)

15.54 The details pertaining to life sentence (discretionary) are as follows:

- Availability: Only available in the Crown Court, and where:
  - the offender is convicted of a 'serious offence';[76]

---

[75] *R v Pinnell* [2010] EWCA Crim 2848.

[76] A 'serious offence' is one which is listed in CJA 2003 Sch. 15, and which would be punishable in the case of an adult, with imprisonment for life or a determinate sentence of at least ten years.

○ the court considers that there is a significant risk of serious harm occasioned by the defendant of further specified offences;

○ the offence is one in respect of which the offender would be liable to imprisonment for life/detention for life under s. 91 (if under 18); and

○ the seriousness of the offence(s) is such as to justify the imposition of a sentence of custody for life (aged 18–20) or detention for life (under 18).

• <u>Duration of order</u>: The court must set the minimum term which must be served before consideration for release on licence.

(vi) Custody for life

The details pertaining to custody for life[77] are as follows: **15.55**

• <u>Availability</u>: Only in the Crown Court, and where the offender has been convicted of a Sch. 15B offence for which a sentence of at least ten years would be justified and who at the time the offence was committed had previously been convicted of a Sch. 15B offence and received either a life sentence with a minimum term before release of five years, or a determinate or extended sentence with a custodial term of at least ten years.
• <u>Age</u>: 18–20.

(vii) Mandatory life sentences

The details pertaining to mandatory life sentences are as follows: **15.56**

• <u>Availability</u>: Only in the Crown Court where convicted of murder.
• <u>Age</u>: If under 18 at the date of the offence, the offender is sentenced to be detained during Her Majesty's Pleasure (irrespective of age at the date of conviction or sentencing).
  If aged 18 to 20 both at the date of the commission of the offence and at the date of conviction, the sentence is one of custody for life.

(h) Mandatory sentences for young offenders

Prescribed custodial sentences apply to offenders aged 16 or over in the following circumstances: **15.57**

• Threatening with an offensive weapon in a public place[78]—minimum sentence of four months' DTO where aged 16 or 17; six months' custodial sentence if 18 years or over.
• Threatening with an article with a blade or point, or offensive weapon[79]—minimum sentence of four months' DTO where aged 16 or 17 at date of conviction; six months' custodial sentence if aged 18 or over.

---

[77] CJA 2003 s. 224A.
[78] Prevention of Crime Act 1953 (PCA 1953) s. 1A.
[79] CJA 1988 s. 139A.

- Possession of an offensive weapon;[80] possession of a bladed article;[81] having a bladed article or offensive weapon on school premises[82]—where the offender was (a) 16 or over at date the offence was committed and (b) had a previous conviction for a relevant offence,[83] minimum sentence of four months' DTO where aged 16 or 17 at date of conviction; six months' custodial sentence if 18 years or over.
- Certain firearms offences to which s. 51A(1) applies—minimum sentence of three years' detention where aged 16 or 17 at the date of the offence; five years where aged 18 or over.

15.58 The court must apply the prescribed minimum sentence unless the circumstances in relation to the offence or the offender (which must be exceptional in so far as firearms offences are concerned) are such that it would be unjust to do so in all the circumstances.

(i) Orders against parents

15.59 The details pertaining to orders against parents are as follows:

(i) Bind over of parent/guardian

15.60 The details pertaining to bind over of parent/guardian[84] are as follows:

- Availability: If the court is satisfied that it would be desirable to make such an order in the interests of preventing the commission of further offences, it may do so where the offender is aged 16 to 17, and must do so where the offender is aged under 16 at the date of sentence.
- Age: Under 18.
- Duration of order: Up to three years or the offender's 18th birthday, whichever is shorter.
- Effect of order: The parent or guardian enters into a recognizance not exceeding £1,000 to take proper control over the offender, and/or (where a YRO has been imposed) to ensure that the offender complies with the requirements of that order.
  The parent or guardian must give their consent to the order, but if they do not do so, and the court considers that the refusal is unreasonable, it can fine the parent or guardian up to £1,000.

(ii) Parenting order

15.61 The details pertaining to parenting orders[85] are as follows:

---

[80] PCA 1953 s. 1.
[81] CJA 1988 s. 139.
[82] ibid. s. 139A.
[83] Contrary to PCA 1953 ss 1, 1A, and 1ZA; CJA 1988 ss 139, 139A, 139AA, and 139AZA.
[84] PCC(S)A 2000 s. 150.
[85] CDA 1998 s. 8.

- Availability: Where a child or young person has been convicted of an offence, or made subject to a criminal behaviour order or a sexual harm prevention order, and the court considers that a parenting order would be desirable to prevent the commission of any further offence by the child or young person, or any repetition of the kind of behaviour which led to the criminal behaviour order or the sexual harm prevention order being made. A parenting order is mandatory where the child is aged under 16, save where a referral order is made.
- Effect of order: The order requires the parent or guardian to comply with such requirements as are specified in the order and to attend such counselling or guidance programme as may be specified in directions given by the responsible officer.
- Duration of order: Up to twelve months; any counselling or guidance programme should be concurrent and not exceed three months' duration.
- Reports: The court is required to obtain information about the family circumstances and the likely effect of the order.

(j) Ancillary orders

The details pertaining to ancillary orders are as follows: **15.62**

(i) Criminal behaviour order

The details pertaining to criminal behaviour orders[86] are as follows: **15.63**

- Availability: On the application of the prosecution where the offender has been convicted of an offence for which proceedings were commenced after 20 October 2014, and where the court imposes a sentence or conditional discharge.[87] The views of the local YOT must be sought prior to any application being made.[88]
- Age: Available at any age.
- Test: The court must be satisfied beyond reasonable doubt that:
  ○ the offender has engaged in behaviour that caused or was likely to cause harassment, alarm, or distress to any person; and
  ○ making the order will help in preventing the offender from engaging in such behaviour.[89]
- Length of order: For offenders aged under 18, a fixed period of between one and three years.[90]

---

[86] Anti-social Behaviour, Crime and Policing Act 2014 s. 22.
[87] ibid. s. 22(1) and (6).
[88] ibid. s. 22(8).
[89] ibid. s. 22(3) and (4).
[90] ibid. s. 25(4).

- <u>Restrictions</u>: In so far as is practicable, any prohibitions or requirements made as part of the order must not interfere with the times at which the offender normally works or attends school or any other educational establishment.[91]
- <u>Reports</u>: The court must hear evidence from the supervising officer about suitability and enforceability before including any requirement in the order.[92]
- <u>Additional notes</u>:
  - the order should be reviewed every 12 months;[93]
  - the order may be varied or discharged on application by either side;[94]
  - interim orders may be imposed;[95]
  - breach of the order is an offence.[96]

(ii) Sexual offenders—notification requirements

15.64   Where a person who has been convicted of an offence or found to have done an act to which the notification requirements of the Sexual Offences Act 2003 apply is aged under 18 on the date of conviction or finding, the notification periods applicable are one-half of those that would otherwise apply to an adult offender.[97]

15.65   Where an offender is sentenced to a DTO, the relevant period for the purposes of determining the applicable notification requirements is the custodial element of the order—that is, half the length of the order made. So, for example: an adult sentenced to eight months' imprisonment would be subject to the notification requirements for a period of ten years. If a young offender aged under 18 is sentenced to a DTO for eight months, the custodial element would be four months. Four months would normally result in a notification period of seven years, however, as the young offender is aged under 18, that period is halved and he or she would therefore be subject to the notification requirements for a period of three-and-a-half years.

15.66   The court may direct that in the case of a person aged under 18, the obligation to comply with the notification requirements should be treated as the parents' obligation.

C. Mentally Disordered Offenders

(a) Unfit to plead/not guilty by reason of insanity

15.67   Where a finding is made that the offender did the act or made the omission charged or a special verdict is returned of 'not guilty by reason of insanity', the

---

[91]   ibid. s. 22(9).
[92]   ibid. s. 24(1) and (2).
[93]   ibid. s. 28(2).
[94]   ibid. s. 27(1).
[95]   ibid. s. 26(2).
[96]   ibid. s. 30(1).
[97]   Sexual Offences Act 2003 s. 80.

court does not sentence the offender; rather, the court must dispose of the case by making:[98]

- a hospital order (with or without a restriction order); or
- a supervision order; or
- an order for an absolute discharge.

In addition, any of a number of ancillary orders designed to manage future risk may be made.

Each of the orders available to the court are discussed in detail in Chapter 5, **15.68** 'Unfitness to Plead'.

(b) Fit to plead

There are no sentencing guidelines for dealing with offenders who, while fit to **15.69** plead, are found to have a mental disorder. Nevertheless, the fact that an offender has a mental disorder or learning disability is recognized to be a relevant factor in sentencing, which in many cases will reduce the seriousness of the offence or reflect personal mitigation. Thus, in a number of Definitive Guidelines issued by the Sentencing Council, a mental disorder or learning disability is listed as a factor which may indicate lower culpability where that disorder or disability is linked to the commission of the offence, or which may reduce the seriousness of the offence or be taken into account as a matter of personal mitigation where not so linked.

This may be the case even where the mental disorder is arguably self-induced, **15.70** such as in *R v Edwards*,[99] where it was held that the fact that the offender had been suffering from a drug-induced psychosis at the time of the offence (burglary) was to be taken into consideration as a mental disorder indicating lower culpability.

While a mental disorder may be taken into account as a mitigating factor, it **15.71** does not permit the sentencing court to depart from the Coroners and Justice Act 2009 s. 125(1), which provides that a court when sentencing an offender must follow any relevant sentencing guidelines that apply, unless the court is satisfied that it would be contrary to the interests of justice to do so. This is so notwithstanding s. 125(7) of the same, which states that: 'Nothing in this section … is to be taken as restricting any power (whether under the Mental Health Act 1983 or otherwise) which enables a court to deal with a mentally disordered offender in the manner it considers to be most appropriate in all the circumstances.'

---

[98] Criminal Procedure (Insanity) Act 1964 s. 5(2).
[99] [2016] EWCA Crim 1226.

15.72 In *R v Balogh*,[100] the Court of Appeal stated that:

> There are no guidelines for dealing with mentally disordered offenders, although several of the guidelines refer to mental disorder as a mitigating factor, particularly when linked to the commission of the offence. The guidelines provide levels of sentencing both custodial and non-custodial (fine, community order, custody). They do not in their terms contemplate an order specifically designed to deal with a mentally disordered offender who requires treatment. In our view, s 125(7) simply expresses what would, arguably, be implicit, namely that the new requirement to follow a guideline is not intended to interfere with the court's continuing power to pass sentences designed to provide treatment for a mentally disordered offender. It was not, in our view, the intention of Parliament simply to abandon guidelines in the cases of mentally disordered offenders. There may be many mentally disordered offenders who have committed very serious offences and who are not susceptible to treatment. The guidelines apply to such offenders unless the court is contemplating, in an appropriate case, making an order designed to secure treatment for the offender, usually, but not always, in a residential setting and sometimes subject to a restriction under s 41 of the Mental Health Act 1983.

15.73 In any case in which the offender is or appears to be mentally disordered,[101] the court must obtain and consider a medical report before passing a custodial sentence (other than one fixed by law) unless in the opinion of the court it is unnecessary in all the circumstances to do so.[102]

15.74 *Power to remand to hospital for a medical report—s. 35 MHA 1983*

The details pertaining to the power to remand to hospital for a medical report are as follows:

- Availability: In a Crown or magistrates' court after conviction in order to obtain a report on the offender's medical condition.
- Test: (a) The court must be satisfied on the written or oral evidence of a registered medical practitioner that there is reason to suspect that the offender is suffering from a mental disorder; and (b) it would be impracticable for a report on the offender's mental condition to be made if he or she were remanded on bail.
- Duration: Twenty-eight days. Further remands may be made, each of up to twenty-eight days to a maximum of twelve weeks.

15.75 *Power to remand to hospital for treatment—s. 36 MHA 1983*

The details pertaining to the power to remand to hospital for treatment are as follows:

- Availability: In the Crown Court at any point before sentence (including pre-trial) as an alternative to a remand in custody, for treatment.
- Test: The court must be satisfied on the written or oral evidence of two registered medical practitioners that: (a) the accused person is suffering from a

---

[100] [2015] EWCA Crim 44.
[101] Within the meaning of MHA 1983.
[102] CJA 2003 s. 157.

mental disorder of a nature or degree which makes it appropriate for him or her to be detained in hospital for medical treatment; and (b) appropriate medical treatment is available.

- <u>Restrictions</u>: The court must be satisfied on written or oral evidence that arrangements have been made for the accused person's admission to a specified hospital within seven days beginning with the date of the remand. Pending admission, the accused person may be remanded in custody or detained in another place of safety.
- <u>Duration</u>: Twenty-eight days. Further remands may be made, each of up to twenty-eight days to a maximum of twelve weeks.

(c) Hospital orders

(i) Approach to take

15.76 In a case concerning a mentally disordered defendant, where neither a suspended sentence or community order (with or without a mental health treatment requirement) nor a fine or discharge is deemed appropriate, the options available to the sentencing judge are as follows:

- a determinate or indeterminate sentence allowing the Secretary of State to exercise his or her powers of transfer to hospital under MHA 1983 s. 47 (with or without a limitation order under s. 49);
- a determinate or indeterminate sentence and direction for admission to hospital under s. 45A;
- an interim hospital order under s. 38; or
- a hospital order under s. 37 (with or without a restriction order under s. 41).

15.77 The mere fact alone that an offender has a mental disorder does not mean that a hospital order or mental health treatment requirement will be necessary or appropriate in every case, even where such a disposal is recommended. The responsibility to determine the appropriate means of disposal belongs to the judge, who should not devolve decisions on sentencing to medical practitioners.

15.78 In *Vowles, R (on the application of) v Secretary of State for Justice,*[103] it was held that:

> It is important to emphasise that the judge must carefully consider all the evidence in each case and not, as some of the early cases have suggested, feel circumscribed by the psychiatric opinions. A judge must therefore consider, where the conditions in s. 37(2) are met, what is the appropriate disposal. In considering that wider question the matters to which a judge will invariably have to have regard to include (1) the extent to which the offender needs treatment for the mental disorder from which the offender suffers, (2) the extent to which the offending is attributable to the mental disorder, (3) the extent to which punishment is required and (4) the protection of the public including the regime for deciding release and the regime after

---

[103] [2015] EWCA Crim 45.

release. There must always be sound reasons for departing from the usual course of imposing a penal sentence, and the judge must set these out. [51]

> ... the fact that two psychiatrists are of the opinion that a hospital order with restrictions under s. 37/41 is the right disposal is therefore never a reason on its own to make such an order. The judge must first consider all the relevant circumstances ... and consider the alternatives. [53]

15.79 The court went on to set out the order in which a court should approach sentence where: (1) the medical evidence suggests that a defendant is suffering from a mental disorder; (2) the offending is wholly or in significant part due to that disorder; (3) treatment is available; and (4) a hospital order may be appropriate.

First, where the defendant is aged over 21, the judge should consider whether the mental disorder can be appropriately dealt with by a hospital and limitation order under MHA 1983 s. 45A; if it can, that is the order that should be made.

15.80 Second, if a s. 45A order is not appropriate (or not available in the case of an offender aged under 21), the judge should consider whether a s. 37 order (with or without restriction) is the most appropriate method of disposal; in making that decision, the court should consider any other available means of dealing with the case and other relevant factors such as the power under s. 47 to transfer an offender to prison for treatment.

15.81 One such case where it was concluded that imprisonment was appropriate, notwithstanding a mental disorder, was *R v Morgan*,[104] in which the Court of Appeal upheld an immediate sentence of imprisonment passed on an offender who had been diagnosed with schizophrenia, was receiving medication for anxiety and depression, and who self-harmed when under stress. The court, both at first instance and on appeal, took into account that medication can and will be dispensed in prison, and that in an appropriate case, the Secretary of State can direct the transfer of a serving prisoner to hospital for mental health treatment. They concluded that: '[I]t does not by any means necessarily follow that a diagnosis of schizophrenia will lead to a non-custodial sentence. That is a matter for the judgment of the court in every case where the issue arises, and on the facts of this case the sentence was not wrong in principle.'

15.82 When determining whether a sentence of imprisonment or a hospital order is the appropriate disposal, the court should consider the effect of the disposal against the circumstances of the offence and the offender, particularly as it will affect the provisions of release. For example, where a defendant has been assessed as dangerous and therefore falls within the dangerousness provisions and liable to an extended sentence or sentence for life, but where the offending is entirely due to

---

[104] [2014] EWCA Crim 2814.

the mental disorder, the mental disorder is treatable, treatment is available, and once treated there is no evidence that the defendant would be dangerous in any way, then a hospital order under s. 37, with or without a restriction order, is likely to be the correct disposal.[105]

In *R v Ahmed (Imtiaz)*,[106] on the other hand, the Court of Appeal found that sometimes a court may consider that having regard to the nature of the offence and the character and antecedents of the defendant, the s. 37 order is not suitable, even for somebody who is suffering from a mental disorder, and even though the conditions are in principle applicable. It may be, for example, that the court considers that there is an element of culpability which requires punishment. A s. 37 order would then be inappropriate because it could lead to a medical discharge at some point prior to the appropriate sentence having been served.   **15.83**

Where a hospital order is made, the court should bear in mind the powers to combine it with other orders. A hospital order cannot be combined with imprisonment, a community order, referral order, or bind over of parents or guardians, but MHA 1983 preserves the court's power to make other orders.   **15.84**

Interim hospital orders—s. 38 MHA 1983   **15.85**

The details pertaining to interim hospital orders are as follows:

- Availability: Where convicted of an offence punishable with imprisonment other than where the sentence is fixed by law. An order may be made where the defendant would otherwise be liable to be sentenced to a minimum or prescribed custodial sentence.
- Age: 14 or over.
- Length of order: Initial order can be made for up to a maximum of twelve weeks' duration. Thereafter, the order may be renewed every twenty-eight days up to a maximum length of twelve months. The order may be renewed in the absence of the defendant provided he or she is represented.
- Test to be applied: The court must be satisfied on the evidence (written or oral) of two medical practitioners—one of whom must be employed at the hospital to be specified—that the defendant is suffering from a mental disorder, and that the disorder may make it appropriate for a hospital order to be made.
- Restrictions: An interim hospital order can only be made if a hospital place is available, or will be available within twenty-eight days of the order being made.

---

[105] *Vowles*. And see to similar effect: *R v Smalley* [2016] EWCA Crim 1186, in which a sentence for imprisonment for public protection (IPP) for a mentally disordered offender was quashed and replaced with a hospital order with a s. 41 restriction order, the court noting that the regime applicable to those subject to hospital orders was sufficient and designed to protect the public, that the offender would continue to benefit from treatment, and that her supervision under s. 41 would be more stringent than under an IPP.

[106] [2013] EWCA Crim 99.

- <u>Directions</u>: The court must give directions for the defendant's detention pending admission to hospital.

15.86 *Hospital and limitation directions—s. 45A MHA 1983*

The details pertaining to hospital and limitation directions are as follows:

- <u>Availability</u>: Only available in the Crown Court when a sentence of imprisonment is passed other than a mandatory life sentence for murder.
- <u>Age</u>: Over 21 at the date of conviction.
- <u>Test to be applied</u>: The court must be satisfied on the evidence of two registered medical practitioners (at least one of whom must have given evidence orally) that the defendant is suffering from a mental disorder of a nature or degree which makes it appropriate for him or her to be detained in hospital for medical treatment, and that the appropriate medical treatment is available for him or her.
- <u>Restrictions</u>: The court must be satisfied that arrangements have been made for the defendant's admission to a named hospital within twenty-eight days of the order.
- <u>Effect</u>: The order directs that the defendant must be removed to hospital and be subject to a s. 41 restriction order.

If the defendant ceases to need treatment before the expiration of the sentence, he or she is returned to prison.

If the defendant is still in hospital at the expiration of the sentence, he or she is detained in hospital as an unrestricted patient.

15.87 *Hospital orders—s. 37 MHA 1983*

The details pertaining to hospital orders are as follows:

- <u>Availability</u>: Where convicted of an offence punishable with imprisonment other than where the sentence is fixed by law. An order may be made where the defendant would otherwise be liable to be sentenced to a minimum or prescribed custodial sentence.
- <u>Age</u>: 14 or over.
- <u>Duration</u>: Without limitation.
- <u>Test to be applied</u>: The court must:
  - be satisfied on the evidence of two registered medical practitioners, at least one of whom must be approved under MHA 1983 s. 12(2), that the defendant is suffering from a mental disorder, and that the disorder is of a nature or degree which makes it appropriate for him or her to be detained in hospital for treatment; and
  - be satisfied that, with regard to all the circumstances including the nature of the offence, the character and antecedents of the offender and any other available means of dealing with him or her—such as a s. 45 hospital and limitation order—a hospital order is the most suitable method of disposing of the case.

- Restrictions: The court must be satisfied that arrangements have been made for the defendant's admission to a named hospital within twenty-eight days of the order.
- Terms of the order: The order must specify the mental disorder from which the defendant is suffering, and the name of the hospital to which the defendant is to be admitted.
  The order may be made in the absence of the defendant, provided he or she is represented.
- Combining orders: Cannot be combined with a sentence of imprisonment/detention, fine, community order, referral order, or order binding over a parent or guardian, but the court may make any other order it has power to make.

Restriction orders—s. 41 MHA 1983   **15.88**

The details pertaining to restriction orders are as follows:

- Availability: Only available in the Crown Court in conjunction with a hospital order.
- Age: 14 or over.
- Test to be applied: That having regard to the nature of the offence, the antecedents of the offender and risk of committing offences if at large, a restriction order is necessary for the protection of the public from serious harm. The court is concerned with the seriousness of the harm that will result from further offending, rather than with the risk of reoffending itself. It is sufficient if the danger posed is only to a section of the public or even a particular person rather than to the public at large.

At least one medical practitioner who has provided evidence (for the purpose of making a hospital order under s. 37) must give evidence orally; it is, however, for the court to determine whether or not a restriction order is necessary, not the medical practitioners.

Guardianship orders—s. 37 MHA 1983   **15.89**

The details pertaining to guardianship orders are as follows:

- Availability: As for a hospital order under MHA 1983 s. 37.
- Age: Over 16 at date of conviction.
- Test to be applied: The court must:
  - be satisfied on the evidence of two registered medical practitioners, at least one of whom must be approved under MHA 1983 s. 12(2), that the defendant is suffering from a mental disorder, and that the disorder is of a nature or degree which warrants his or her reception into guardianship; and
  - be satisfied that, with regard to all the circumstances including the nature of the offence, the character and antecedents of the offender, and any other available means of dealing with him or her, that a guardianship order is the most suitable method of disposing of the case.

- <u>Restrictions</u>: The court must be satisfied that the local social services authority, or any other person with whom it is proposed to place the offender, is willing to receive the offender into guardianship.
- <u>Combining orders</u>: As for a hospital order under s 37 MHA 1983.

(ii) Ancillary orders

15.90   See Chapter 5, 'Unfitness to Plead'.

D. Old Age, Ill Health, and Disability

(a) Old age

15.91   Old age, like youth, is capable of amounting to a mitigating feature. However, the mitigation derives from the fact that the effects of imprisonment on an elderly offender may be greater than those on a younger person. Old age will rarely act to reduce the culpability of the offender and never where the offence is a historic one for which the offender has escaped justice for a period of years if not decades—see *AG's Ref No. 38 of 2013 (R v James Stuart Hall)*:[107]

> [The appellant's] age and level of infirmity are relevant to the sentencing decision, but need to be approached with a degree of caution. In reality, the offender has got away with his offending for decades.

15.92   Where the offence itself has been committed by an elderly person, age cannot be expected to excuse their behaviour: see *R v Evans*,[108] where it was observed that a court will only send individuals in their 80s to prison as a last resort and with great reluctance. Nevertheless: 'Old age is not a licence to disregard the law or the requirements of decent behaviour towards others in the community.'[109]

15.93   The circumstances of the offence and the offender—including old age—may, however, permit the court to reduce or pass a different form of sentence from that which would otherwise be appropriate as a matter of mercy. For example, *R v Beaver*,[110] in which a term of imprisonment imposed for an offence of the manslaughter of his wife by an 82-year-old man with dementia, was suspended as a matter of mercy.

(b) Reduced life expectancy

15.94   Submissions of a reduced life expectancy may be founded on the basis of old age or ill health. It has been held that it is not for the court to 'manipulate a

---

[107] [2013] EWCA Crim 1450.
[108] [2007] EWCA Crim 1158.
[109] ibid. at [10].
[110] [2015] EWCA Crim 653.

sentence to achieve a social end', which is something for the royal prerogative. Adjustments to a sentence can be made as a matter of mercy, but it would not be right to change radically what would otherwise be a perfectly proper sentence.[111]

(c) Ill health and disability

The extent to which the medical condition of a defendant is relevant to either the **15.95** nature or length of sentence will be case-specific: in some cases, it may not be relevant to sentence at all; in others, it may be relevant if as a result the sentence passed is a significantly greater punishment for the offender than it would be for other people who do not have that medical condition or disability.[112]

The limitations on the extent to which the court should take into account the **15.96** effects of ill health and the correct approach to sentencing were considered in detail in *R v Bernard*[113] and *R v Qazi*.[114] In *Bernard*, it was held that:

(i)   a medical condition which may at some unidentified future date affect either life expectancy or the prison authorities' ability to treat a prisoner satisfactorily may call into operation the Home Secretary's powers of release by reference to the Royal Prerogative of mercy, or otherwise, but is not a reason for this court to interfere with an otherwise appropriate sentence;

(ii)   the fact that an offender is HIV positive or has a reduced life expectancy is not generally a reason which should affect sentence;

(iii) a serious medical condition, even when it is difficult to treat in prison, will not automatically entitle an offender to a lesser sentence than would otherwise be appropriate;

(iv)   an offender's serious medical condition may enable a court as an act of mercy in the exceptional circumstances of a particular case, rather than by virtue of any general principle, to impose a lesser sentence than would otherwise be appropriate.

In the later case of *Qazi*, the Court of Appeal considered the duty of the sentenc- **15.97** ing court and set out the correct approach to sentencing as follows:

1.   The court is entitled to take into account the fact that there are arrangements in place to ensure that prisoners with severe medical conditions in public-sector prisons are treated in accordance with their Convention rights. There is a duty on the Secretary of State to release a prisoner if that is the only way a breach of Article 3 can be remedied.

---

[111] See, e.g., *R v Stark* [1992] Crim LR 384—a case in which the appellant had AIDS and as a result a reduced life expectancy of between one and one-and-a-half years.

[112] See, e.g., *R v Draper, Easterbrook and Frost* [2008] EWCA Crim 3206.

[113] [1997] 1 Cr App R (S) 135.

[114] [2010] EWCA Crim 2579.

2. On the basis of those arrangements and their continued operation in practice, a sentencing court does not need to be concerned in the allocation of a prisoner to a specific prison in the discharge of its duties under Article 3. Furthermore, provided that arrangements for the provision of health care are maintained and work in practice, a sentencing court does not need to enquire into the facilities in prison for the treatment of a medical condition.

3. It is only in circumstances where the very fact of imprisonment itself might expose the individual to a real risk of an Article 3 breach, that the court will be called upon to enquire into whether a custodial sentence will breach Article 3; such a situation will be exceptionally rare.

4. If such circumstances should arise, then the sentencing court has to be provided with detailed medical evidence with an attached statement of truth by a properly qualified medical expert, setting out the ground why imprisonment will cause a breach of Article 3.

5. Once a sentence of imprisonment has been imposed, unless it is contended on appeal that the judge should not have imposed such a sentence because imprisonment itself would cause a breach of Article 3, the relevance of an appellant's medical condition relates solely to the assessment of the overall length of the sentence in accordance with the principles in *Bernard*.

6. Any issues as to breach of the duties of the Secretary of State in relation to medical treatment and conditions in prison are matters for civil remedies and not for the criminal division of the Court of Appeal.

15.98 *R v Hall*[115] was a highly publicized case in which Hall was sentenced to a term of imprisonment for the importation of drugs concealed in the wheels of his wheelchair. He suffered from progressive and irreversible medical conditions as a result of which he had a reduced life expectancy, was confined to a wheelchair, and required twenty-four-hour care. He appealed his sentence on the basis that any sentence of imprisonment was wrong in principle as it would subject him to inhuman or degrading punishment in breach of his Article 3 rights.

15.99 Following *Qazi*, it was held that a sentencing court should not concern itself with the adequacy of medical arrangements in prisons unless the mere fact of imprisonment would expose the defendant to inhuman or degrading treatment contrary to Article 3 and arrangements could not be made to avoid that consequence. However, a sentencing court was fully entitled to take account of a medical condition by way of mitigation as a reason for reducing the length of the sentence, either on the ground that imprisonment would have a greater impact on the offender, or as a matter of mercy in the particular circumstances of the case. However, serious illness or disability could not be a passport to

---

[115] [2013] EWCA Crim 82.

absence of punishment, including imprisonment, where serious offences had been committed.

This latter observation will be particularly relevant where there is evidence before the court that the defendant's disabilities did not prevent him or her from carrying out a serious offence.[116]   **15.100**

---

[116] See, e.g., *R v Arshad* [2015] EWCA Crim 1111.

16

LOOKING AHEAD
Changing Language and Changing Procedures

Penny Cooper, Michelle Mattison, and Heather Norton

At the very beginning of her book *Sociolinguistics and the Legal Process*, Diana **16.01**
Eades notes:

> Language is central to the legal process: written laws, judicial decisions, police
> interviews, competing claims in a dispute, courtroom evidence, legal argument,
> mediation hearings, all of these events or products of the legal process are carried
> out through language, whether written or spoken or both. Lawyers have to be
> 'good with language' to succeed in their profession.[1]

Today, in the Criminal Justice System in England and Wales, lawyers have to be **16.02**
better with language than ever before. They must demonstrate a high degree of
adaptability to enable effective participation of those who are vulnerable; as has
been made clear throughout this book, advocates must adjust to the witness and
not the other way round.[2] This can mean adjusting pace, tone, vocabulary, gram-
mar, and more; but adjusting language is only part of the issue.

The chapters in this book have illustrated in detail how the courts not only **16.03**
expect language to be adjusted, but also procedures. There is no 'one size fits all'

---

[1] D. Eades, *Sociolinguistics and the Legal Process* (Multilingual Matters, 2010) 4.
[2] *R v Lubemba; R v JP* [2014] EWCA Crim 2064 at [45].

approach. While chapters of this book provide a framework of essential know-ledge, they cannot be prescriptive; each vulnerable person participating as a wit-ness or defendant has a unique set of needs. This will affect the directions that the court gives regarding how they refresh their memory of their testimony, where they give their evidence from, who is with them when they give it, what commu-nication aids, if any, they will use, and much more besides.

16.04 Some vulnerable witnesses will have been assessed by an intermediary who, if involved early enough in the process, will have advised the police officers on how to achieve the best communication at the 'ABE interview' before providing a report for the judge and advocates. However, where there is no intermediary assessment of the vulnerable person's communication needs and abilities, it is incumbent on investigators and lawyers to identify vulnerabilities where they exist and seek advice so that the appropriate steps are taken to remove barriers to their participation.

16.05 There is extensive legislation and guidance in this field (outlined in Chapter 1, 'Introduction') which has been woven into each chapter of this book. Each year brings changes, some of which have widespread significance. For instance, in 2015, the Criminal Procedure Rules were amended so as to provide for the ground rules approach and in that same year a new case management procedure was introduced in the Crown Court. In 2016, there were major changes to the Criminal Practice Directions (Crim PD) regard-ing intermediaries for vulnerable defendants and at the time of writing the Ministry of Justice (MoJ) is on the cusp of issuing updated ABE guidance. In 2017, we may see a 'Victim's Law' in draft legislation,[3] as well as the national roll-out of 's. 28', pre-recorded cross-examination and re-examination for witnesses vulnerable under s. 16 YJCEA 1999, the only special measure not yet fully implemented.[4] The need for ongoing specialist training for police, lawyers, and judges is recognized and, notwithstanding the severe limitations on the public purse, is available.

A. A Quarter of a Century of Change?

16.06 Of all the potential changes on the horizon, arguably the most significant will be the introduction, nationally, of s. 28 pre-recorded cross-examination and re-examination. When implemented, it will apply to all child witnesses (aged under 18) and adult witnesses who fall within s. 16(2) of the Youth Justice and Criminal

---

[3] See <http://researchbriefings.parliament.uk/ResearchBriefing/Summary/SN07139> accessed 24 March 2017.

[4] Youth Justice and Criminal Evidence Act 1999 (YJCEA 1999) s. 28.

Evidence Act 1999 (YJCEA 1999) (mental or physical incapacity). A pilot scheme is planned to extend s. 28 to s. 17(4) intimidated witnesses in sexual and modern slavery cases.

The main advantage of s. 28 is that the witness is able to give their evidence **16.07** much sooner than if they had to wait to be called at trial. Removing the vulnerable witness from the substantive trial process makes listing easier and shortens the trial length. Moreover, in the event of a re-trial, there is no need to recall the vulnerable witness whose evidence has already been captured and can be replayed. Those involved in the pilot scheme have reported that cross-examination conducted under the scheme has usually been very short (perhaps as a result of carefully managed ground rules hearings), that defendants are more likely to plead guilty prior to trial, and that fears that a vulnerable witness will have to be recalled at a later date (e.g. because of late disclosure) have been largely misplaced.

However, the way in which s. 28 has been implemented is arguably not as good **16.08** as it could have been. Pre-recording of child witness evidence was first suggested in 'The Pigot Report' back in 1989. In that report, it was suggested that the pre-recording of child witness evidence would take place:

> ... outside the courtroom in informal surroundings and ... video recorded. Nobody should be present in the same room as the child except the judge, advocates and a parent or supporter, but the accused should be able to hear and view the proceedings through closed circuit television or a two way mirror and communicate with his legal representatives. ('Summary of Recommendations', 4)

Contrary to this recommendation, s. 28 hearings take place in court and the **16.09** witness therefore still has to cope with any anxiety related to giving evidence in a court building, despite the increase in provision of specially adapted remote witness suites across the country. Instead, cross-examination and re-examination (if any) are usually conducted by the advocates from the courtroom over the live link in the same way as they would in the absence of s. 28. If the judge directs it, the advocate and the judge may be present in the live-link room for the questioning as is sometimes the case when witnesses give evidence from the live-link room. Judges and advocates must be flexible in their approach because sometimes live link hinders rather than helps.

Another recommendation in the Pigot Report, which has not been implemented, **16.10** was that:

> ... the court should have discretion to order exceptionally that questions advocates wish to put to a child should be relayed through a person approved by the court who enjoys the child's confidence. ('Summary of Recommendations', 6)

At a time when the judiciary and advocates alike are being encouraged to be flex- **16.11** ible and to adapt the processes of the court in the way which best facilitates each witness to give their evidence, it may be thought that the failure to implement such recommendations has been something of a missed opportunity. Despite the significant changes detailed in this book, including s. 28, it is argued by some that major change to the way in which witnesses are treated during a police investigation and at court is still required. Such change might be achieved through the introduction of the 'Barnahus' model.

B. Barnahus/Children's Houses

16.12 In March 2015, a review report published on behalf of the National Health Service (NHS)[5] described the pathway of services available to children and young people following disclosure of sexual assault. The review sought to explore and better understand the obstacles that children and young people face when they are engaged with local services in London. The findings of the review reveal geographical inequity in the provisions currently available within the capital.

16.13 The report suggests that the care and support needs for children and young people who experience sexual assault are not being appropriately met.[6] For instance, the Havens,[7] which provides forensic medical examinations and immediate aftercare for victims of all ages, are currently only commissioned to provide follow-up medical care for those aged 13 and older, not younger. Furthermore, the review suggests that Havens sites are not regarded as child-friendly. Also under scrutiny is accessibility to mental health services for children and young people who experience sexual assault, as well as the support available to parents and caregivers. Reference was also made to the findings produced in the recent Criminal Justice Joint Inspection report (2014)[8] concerning the quality of investigative interviewing, and the treatment of sexually assaulted children by the criminal justice system in England and Wales.

16.14 Approximately 200 stakeholders involved in the care of sexual abuse victims in London were interviewed as part of the aforementioned NHS (2015) review. The participants provided suggestions for an ideal pathway of services. Paediatricians were specifically asked for their views, and they were asked to rank, in order of preference, a number of options presented as potential ways to address the challenges and gaps in the current service pathway for sexually assaulted children in London. Adopting the 'Barnahus' ('Children's House') model was selected as

---

[5] A. Goddard, E. Harewood, and L. Brennan, 'Review of Pathway Following Sexual Assault for Children and Young People in London' (NHS England, 2015).

[6] ibid.

[7] The Havens, Specialist Centres in London for People who have been sexually assaulted, available at <https://www.thehavens.org.uk/> accessed on 24 March 2017.

[8] Criminal Justice Joint Inspection, 'Achieving Best Evidence in Child Sexual Abuse Cases: A Joint Inspection' (HMCPSI Publications, 2014).

first choice.[9] The review presents the reader with an overview of how the model works in practice in its home country,[10] Iceland, and also reports that it has had a positive impact in the Icelandic justice system since its introduction. In order to address the failures in the current system, the principal recommendation of the NHS review is to adopt the Children's House model in England.[11]

Clear momentum has gathered since this recommendation was presented in March 2015: The Mayor's Office for Policing and Crime (MOPAC) and NHS England (London) successfully applied to the Home Office Police Innovation Fund for financial support in the implementation of the Children's House model and piloting of the service in County Durham and Greater London from 2016.[12] **16.15**

Based upon the model of Child Advocacy Centres (CACs) in the United States, the Icelandic Government set up a Children's House in November 1998. The Children's House comprises a multidisciplinary team of government agencies relating to social services, law enforcement, and health care, all operating from under one roof. The Children's House serves the population of Iceland (approximately 320,000) and is covertly located in a residential area, negating the need for children to make multiple visits to police stations, hospitals, and court buildings—settings that are typically not considered child-friendly. The agencies operate collaboratively to investigate allegations of child sexual assault concerning children aged 3.5 to 18 years old. The services provided include: (i) conducting investigative interviews; (ii) conducting medical examinations; and (iii) delivering therapeutic support to children and their families. **16.16**

Once social services or the police are contacted about a clear and certain disclosure of child sexual abuse, the case is referred to a judge who assumes responsibility for the interview process. Prosecution and defence lawyers are appointed, and arrangements are made for an interview to be conducted at the Children's House. The investigative interview takes place within a specially equipped suite that is fitted with discrete microphones and cameras. The interview is conducted by a child psychotherapist and projected live to an observation room located within the Children's House. Although it is the child psychotherapist who conducts the interview, they wear an earpiece and the interview is led by the judge who presides over the process from a nearby observation room within the Children's House. Also observing the interview are the prosecution and defence lawyers, who may **16.17**

---

[9] Goddard et al., 'Review of Pathway'.
[10] Bragi Guðbrandsson, 'Barnahus—Children's House: A Child-Friendly, Interdisciplinary and Multiagency Response to Child Abuse and Services for Child Victims', the European Forum of the Rights of the Child, Brussels, 2–4 June 2015, available at <http://ec.europa.eu/justice/fundamental-rights/files/rights_child/9th_b_gudbrandsson.pdf> accessed 24 March 2017.
[11] Goddard et al., 'Review of Pathway'.
[12] Mayor's Office for Policing and Crime, 'Home Office Police Innovation Fund—Child House', available at <https://www.london.gov.uk/what-we-do/mayors-office-policing-and-crime-mopac/governance-and-decision-making/mopac-decisions-209> accessed 24 March 2017.

communicate (with permission from the judge) questions for the interviewer to ask or information to clarify. Each child is typically only interviewed once, and interviews are reported to last no longer than one hour.[13] The interview serves as testimony for trial, and the assumption of interview responsibility by the judge, as well as the input from prosecution and defence lawyers, removes the need for children to attend court at a later date. Such is the case that approximately 80 per cent of referrals lead to testimony being gathered within less than two weeks. In instances where initial disclosures are less clear or less certain, the Child Protection Services can arrange for an 'exploratory interview' to be conducted. Exploratory interviews take place at the Children's House. If warranted, a judge is appointed to the case, and a full forensic interview (as described above) occurs.

16.18   In addition to investigative interviews, medical examinations also take place at the Children's House in a specially equipped examination room, and treatment, as necessary, is provided. For children whom need acute forensic medical examinations, these take place at the child's local hospital. The Children's House is also the location where therapy and support is provided to sexually abused children and their families. Therapy starts soon after the interview takes place, thereby aiming to address the common misconception that therapy can only start post-trial. The psychotherapist who provides the therapy observes the interview, but does not conduct it.

Children's Houses are described as a child-friendly response to a judicial system that fails to meet children's needs and rights,[14] and their premise has since been adopted in other Scandinavian countries (e.g. Sweden, Norway, and Denmark).[15]

16.19   The recent plans for Children's Houses to be piloted in England,[16] and calls for the model to also be adopted in Scotland,[17] are indicative of ongoing concerns

---

[13] G. Gudjonsson, T. Sveinsdottir, J. F. Sigurdsson, and J. Jonsdottir, 'The Ability of Suspected Victims of Childhood Sexual Abuse (CSA) to Give Evidence. Findings from the Children's House in Iceland' (2010) *Journal of Forensic Psychiatry & Psychology*, 21, 569.

[14] S. Johansson, 'Diffusion and Governance of "Barnahus" in the Nordic Countries: Report from an On-Going Project' (2012) *Journal of Scandinavian Studies in Criminology and Crime Prevention*, 13, 69.

[15] ibid.

[16] Children's Commissioner, 'Barnahus: Improving the Response to Child Sexual Abuse in England', available at <https://www.childrenscommissioner.gov.uk/sites/default/files/publications/Barnahus%20-%20Improving%20the%20response%20to%20child%20sexual%20abuse%20in%20England.pdf> accessed 24 March 2017; see also a speech given by Alison Saunders DPP, 'Children and Young People as Witnesses', St Mary's Sexual Assault Referral Centre annual conference (21 April 2016), available at <https://www.cps.gov.uk/news/articles/children_and_young_people_as_witnesses_-_alison_saunders_dpp/> accessed 14 April 2017.

[17] NSPCC, 'How Safe Are Our Children?' Report briefing: Scottish context 2016, available at <https://www.nspcc.org.uk/globalassets/documents/policy/scotland-briefing-how-safe-2016.pdf> accessed 24 March 2017. In March 2017, the High Court of Justiciary Practice Note No. 1 of 2017, Taking Evidence of a Vulnerable Witness by a Commissioner, was issued. Available at <http://www.scotcourts.gov.uk/docs/default-source/rules-and-practice/practice-notes/criminal-courts/criminal-courts---practice-note---number-1-of-2017.pdf?sfvrsn=4> accessed 14 April 2017.

about the impact of the adversarial justice system on those who are already vulnerable. However, adopting a model that currently operates in other countries will require very careful planning if it is to function effectively and accomplish the desired results in England and Wales. That said, the Children's House model has distinct parallels with child-centred, multidisciplinary services already operating in England and Wales.

C. Existing Multi-Disciplinary Services for Vulnerable Witnesses in England and Wales

The St Mary's Sexual Assault Referral Centre (SARC) in Manchester, established **16.20** in 1986, has specialist accommodation where forensic medical examinations are conducted, where aftercare support and therapy is provided, and where children can provide evidence to court via their remote live-link facilities. The St Mary's multidisciplinary team has forged a collaborative partnership with Greater Manchester Police, Greater Manchester Police Authority, and Central Manchester University Hospitals Trust. The first of its kind in the United Kingdom, St Mary's has arguably set the standard for sexual assault services across the country.[18]

Also delivering services in a radically different way is Triangle. Triangle is an independent organization working across the United Kingdom, with bases in Brighton and Teesside. Triangle has provided skilled support to enable children and young people's best evidence since 1997, including forensic interviewing and intermediary support. Triangle has particular expertise with very young children (gathering evidence from children as young as 20 months) and those with complex communication needs arising from impairment, neglect, or trauma. Triangle has been involved in many landmark procedural developments for gathering children's evidence, and has contributed to national policy and guidance about effective communication in the criminal justice system.[19]

D. Vulnerable Defendants

Understanding how better to improve responses to cases of child sexual abuse **16.21** or other types of cases in which the witnesses are very young is clearly extremely important. However, the focus must be wider than that; it must be the fair treatment of all vulnerable witnesses and also vulnerable defendants.

---

[18] St Mary's Sexual Assault Referral Centre, available at <http://www.stmaryscentre.org/> accessed on 24 March 2017.

[19] See the Triangle website, <http://triangle.org.uk/> accessed on 24 March 2017.

16.22 It is difficult, if not impossible, at present to ascertain how many people who come into contact with the police or the criminal justice system have either a mental or physical disorder or a learning disability. First, it is not always easy to identify those who have such a disorder or disability, particularly in the early stages of the offender pathway. Second, at present there are no obligations to maintain statistics on the number of suspects who may have a vulnerability, many of whom may be refused charge or acquitted after trial. Research into the prison population over the course of the last ten years has, however, consistently revealed that there are significantly higher rates of mental health problems, personality disorders, and learning disabilities among prisoners than in the wider public.

16.23 In 2009, the Bradley Report was published following an independent review by Lord Bradley of people with mental health problems or learning disabilities in the criminal justice system.[20] It was noted that it was essential that professionals in the criminal justice system should have information about the needs of offenders in order to determine their immediate needs, whether they were fit to plead, whether they should be transferred to hospital, whether they would need support through the court process, and to inform decisions about remand and sentencing. He recommended that each police custody suite should have access to liaison and diversion services which would: enable the proper identification and assessment of those with mental health issues or learning disabilities; enable the police to make properly informed risk assessments; provide information to decision-makers; and allow for the possible diversion from the criminal justice system to appropriate health providers and social care services. In addition, he recommended that consideration should be given to extending to vulnerable defendants the special measures available to vulnerable witnesses, and emphasized the importance of training in awareness of mental health and learning disabilities for the police, probation services, magistrates, and judges, stating (in respect of the latter categories) that:

> ... as with other professionals in the criminal justice system who come into contact with offenders with mental health problems or learning disabilities, training for magistrates and judges on mental health and learning disability issues is crucial. In addition to the training, it is also vitally important for them to have access to information on the offender and available local services in order to inform their decisions in court.

16.24 Lord Bradley's recommendations resulted in the creation of the Liaison and Diversion Service in 2010. The following year, the Secretaries of State for Health and Justice announced their joint commitment to developing National Liaison and Diversion services in police custody suites and in the criminal courts for vulnerable suspects and defendants. Provision has so far been piecemeal, with Liaison and Diversion services (which are funded by the NHS England, not the

---

[20] See <http://www.rcpsych.ac.uk/pdf/Bradleyreport.pdf> accessed 24 March 2017.

MoJ) only available in certain trial areas in England. In a speech given in 2014,[21] Rt Hon Theresa May MP, then Home Secretary, stated that:

> Vulnerable people suffering mental crises are not best served in jail; those suffering mental illness or learning difficulties should not be kept at police stations for want of somewhere else to go; and the best use of police time is not attending to people who would be much better dealt with by healthcare professionals ... I want to see a criminal justice system where offenders' mental health needs are identified, where treatment is provided at the earliest opportunity, and where sentencing is appropriate. And I want to see more cases where cycles of offending caused by underlying mental health issues are broken, and offenders are able to rebuild their lives free of crime ... People with mental health issues who are arrested or held in custody, deserve proper assessment of their needs and the appropriate care and support.

On 12 July 2016, it was announced that there would be a full roll-out of Liaison and Diversion services in all police custody suites and prisons by 2020. The need is acute. The most recent statistics issued by NHS England showed that 50,000 people a year are assessed by Liaison and Diversion services following arrest, of whom almost 70 per cent require mental health support. A MoJ survey into disability among prisoners in 2012 revealed that 36 per cent were estimated to have a physical or mental disability. In his 2016 review, the Prisons and Probation Ombudsman noted that in 2014 to 2015, there had been a 34 per cent rise in self-inflicted deaths in custody; 70 per cent of those who died had been identified as having mental health needs, but concerns about mental health had only been identified in about half of those cases, and one in five of those diagnosed with a mental health problem received no care from a mental health professional in prison. There were over 34,000 incidents of self-harming in the same period.[22]   **16.25**

Clearly, there is a need for awareness training, but to date, the emphasis in training needs has been firmly focused on vulnerable witnesses, and little if any has been directed towards managing vulnerable defendants, some of whom may be self-represented. How is the judge, in the absence of training, to manage fairly the trial of the unrepresented defendant with a significant personality disorder who is fit to plead, but who because of his or her disorder refuses to engage in the trial process?   **16.26**

Neither has Lord Bradley's recommendation that special measures be extended to vulnerable defendants been acted upon. Indeed, following the 2016 amendments to the Crim PD, even the courts' inherent powers to appoint a defence intermediary in appropriate cases have been restricted; rather, Crim PD 3F.12 states that: 'The court should adapt the trial process to address a defendant's communication needs and will rarely exercise its inherent powers to direct appointment   **16.27**

---

[21] 10 July 2014, available at <https://www.gov.uk/government/speeches/care-not-custody-speech> accessed 24 March 2017.
[22] MoJ, 'Safety in Custody Statistics Bulletin' (July 2016).

of an intermediary ... even where the intermediary ... would improve the trial process'.

16.28 Defendants' vulnerability is not limited to mental disabilities. Although the number of children in the criminal justice system has fallen,[23] research reveals that a disproportionate number had been in care,[24] and two-fifths had been on the child protection register or had experienced neglect or abuse.[25] One in five reported learning disabilities.[26]

16.29 Although the number of children in custody has fallen, conversely, offenders aged 60 or over are now the fastest growing sector in the prison population.[27] According to the most recent figures published by the MoJ at the time of writing, there were 4,373 offenders in custody aged over 60; 134 were aged over 80. Most of these elderly offenders have been convicted of historic sexual offences, the number of prosecutions of which show no sign of slowing down; indeed, in 2016, a 101-year-old man achieved the dubious sobriquet of being the 'oldest defendant in British legal history' when he was charged with historic child sex offences. The challenges posed by elderly defendants, often frail and with complex needs, provides a challenge for the courts and (in many cases) prisons alike. As the Prisons and Probation Ombudsman commented in his 2016 Report: 'prisons designed for fit, young men, must adjust to the largely unexpected and unplanned roles of care home and even hospice. Increasingly, prison staff are having to manage not just ageing prisoners, but the end of prisoners' lives and death itself.'

E. Conclusion

16.30 In the quarter century that has elapsed since the publication of the Pigot Report in 1989, there has undoubtedly been a sea change in the approach to vulnerable people in court. When the Pigot Report was published, a child witness was required to give evidence in the courtroom and there was still a requirement for the evidence of children or of complainants in sexual cases to be corroborated. The rules requiring corroboration from such witnesses were abolished in a series of Acts between 1988 and 1994. In 1999, YJCEA introduced the concept of the vulnerable witness and a raft of special measures to enable them to give their best evidence. Then came the judgment in *R v B*[28] which emphasized that it was

---

[23] MoJ, 'Youth Justice Statistics 2014–15' (2016).
[24] A. Redmond, 'Children in Custody 2014–15' (HM Inspectorate of Prisons, 2015).
[25] J. Jacobson, 'Punishing Disadvantage: A Profile of Children in Custody' (Prison Reform Trust, 2010).
[26] Department of Education, 'Statistics' (2015).
[27] MoJ, 'Offender Management Statistics' (2016).
[28] [2010] EWCA Crim 4.

not age that determined whether a witness was competent, but their ability, in broad terms, to understand questions and to provide understandable answers; and, further, that it was for the advocate to adapt their questions to the needs of the witness and not the other way round. As a consequence, child witnesses who only a few years ago would have been assumed to be too young to give evidence, now do so on a regular basis. The advent of s. 28 is just the latest in a series of advances designed to facilitate young and vulnerable witnesses to give their best evidence in court.

But there is still a long way to go. Although adaptations have been made to pro- **16.31** cedures, and technology has been brought into the courtrooms, in essence the formal trial process is little changed. Training has been slow and piecemeal with, until recently, no standard vulnerable witness training for advocates and such training is not mandatory. Too often, ABE interviews are lengthy, unfocused, and unhelpful, conducted by police officers without intermediary assistance even for the youngest of witnesses. A lack of resources has led to substandard equipment in many courts for playing the ABE interview and a dearth of available intermediaries. In the laudable drive to improve the facilitation of vulnerable witnesses in the trial process, the vulnerabilities of many defendants have arguably been overlooked. Many have mental disorders or learning disabilities and an increasing number are self-represented, but the measures available to assist such defendants are being squeezed. Training in how to identify, assess, and manage vulnerable defendants through the criminal justice system is all but non-existent for many professionals, including the judge who is nevertheless expected to achieve a balanced and fair trial for all parties.

Clearly, we have come a long way, but there is a distance to travel yet before it can **16.32** be said that the criminal justice system facilitates the fair and equal participation of all vulnerable people—whether complainants, witnesses, or defendants. It is our hope that this book will have assisted on that journey.

INDEX